D0221086

The success of the First Crusade, and its capture of Jerusalem in 1099, has been conventionally explained by its ideological and political motivation. This book looks at the First Crusade primarily as a military campaign and asks why it was so successful. Modern writing about the crusade has tended to emphasise the moral dimension and the development of the idea of the crusade but its fate was ultimately decided on the field of battle. This book looks at the nature of war at the end of the eleventh century and the military experience of all the contending parties in order to explain its extraordinary success. It is the first such examination, taking into account all other factors but emphasising the military.

VICTORY IN THE EAST

VICTORY IN THE EAST

A military history of the First Crusade

JOHN FRANCE

University College, Swansea

CAMBRIDGE
UNIVERSITY PRESS

Published by the Press Syndicate of the University of Cambridge
The Pitt Building, Trumpington Street, Cambridge CB2 1RP
40 West 20th Street, New York, NY 10011-4211, USA
10 Stamford Road, Oakleigh, Melbourne 3166, Australia

First published 1994
Reprinted 1996

Printed in Great Britain at the University Press, Cambridge

A catalogue record for this book is available from the British Library

Library of Congress cataloguing in publication data

France, John.
Victory in the East: a military history of the First Crusade/John France.
p.   cm.
Includes bibliographical references and index.
ISBN 0 521 41969 7
1. Crusades – First, 1096–1099.
2. Military art and science – History – Medieval, 500–1500.
3. Military history, Medieval.
I. Title.
D161.2.F73 1994
940.1′8 – dc20   93-28329   CIP

ISBNO 521 41969 7 hardback

CE

To my wife, Angela

Contents

Figures

Acknowledgments

I am deeply indebted to an enormous number of people who have helped me in the writing of this book. In the spring and summer of 1992 I was awarded grants by the British Academy and the Leverhulme Trust which enabled me to follow the path of the First Crusade from Istanbul to Jerusalem. This book would have been infinitely poorer without the observations which I was able to make, and I would like to thank both organisations for their generous support. We are fortunate that in the United Kingdom there are now two Chairs of crusading studies. Professor Bernard Hamilton of the University of Nottingham has advised me over many years and I am grateful to him for taking the trouble to read part of the present work. Professor J. Riley-Smith of Royal Holloway and Bedford New College and Dixie Professor of Ecclesiastical History-elect at the University of Cambridge has been kind enough to offer me much help and I was privileged to attend his seminar at the Institute of Historical Research in London. Dr David French, Director of the British Institute of Archaeology at Ankara, very generously provided me with invaluable information about the ancient and medieval road system of Asia Minor. I should also like to thank him and his colleagues, particularly Shirley and Stuart Blaylock, for their kind hospitality and advice on travelling in Turkey. Dr Stephen Mitchell of the Classics Department, University College Swansea, was also good enough to help me on the history of Asia Minor and gave assistance with maps. Tim Severin was also helpful in this respect. John Gillingham of the London School of Economics read two vital chapters and made many valuable suggestions. My colleague Mr I. W. Rowlands was also kind enough to look at parts of the typescript. Peter Edbury of University College, Cardiff has been an invaluable source of help and advice and his colleague David Bates has advised on the Normans. I should like to thank Dr Susan Edgington of the Huntingdonshire College for letting me see the text of her forthcoming edition of Albert

xi

of Aachen for so helpfully responding to my requests for information – may her new edition appear soon! I have been pleased to test out my ideas on war in discussion with Matthew Bennett of the Royal Military Academy Sandhurst, while my understanding of middle eastern history, no matter how limited, has been immeasurably improved by discussion with Professor A. K. S. Lambton. Dr A. V. Murray of the University of Leeds was kind enough to let me see some of his work in advance and to offer helpful suggestions. I should like to thank Professor Israel Roll of Tel Aviv University and Mrs Dorit Cohen of the Israeli National Maritime Museum, Haifa, for their specialist advice, and Denys Pringle for his helpful response to my questions. My knowledge of the Crusade of 1101 has been much improved by discussion with Mr Alec Mulinder. Professor D. T. Herbert and his colleague Dr A. H. Perry of the Geography Department, University College Swansea provided much help on matters geographic and meteorological. Mr G. B. Lewis drew the maps used in this book and any errors come from the material I supplied to him. I would like to thank Francis Herbert and David McNeill of the Royal Geographical Society for their patient assist- ance. All the above have contributed ideas and advice, but of course responsibility for the material is mine alone.

All scholars rely heavily on learned institutions and libraries and I have been immensely helped by the Director, Professor P. K. O'Brien, and the staff of the Institute of Historical Research. The library staff of University College Swansea, the British Museum Reading Room, London University Library, the National Library of Wales and the School of African and Oriental Studies bore with me with patience and courtesy. Mr Geoffrey Fisher of the Conway Library at the Courtauld Institute was very helpful in discussing illustrations.

The staff of Cambridge University Press have been extremely helpful and I would like to thank Katherine Boyle the copy editor and always and ever William Davies.

Finally I would like to thank all those who gave me so much assistance on my journey along the route of the First Crusade from Istanbul to Jerusalem.

John France
History Department, University College, Swansea SA2 8PP

The author wishes to thank Dr S. B. Edgington and Mr W. G. Zajac for their kind assistance in offering corrections for this edition.

Abbreviations

AA — Albert of Aix, *Historia Hierosolymitana*, RHC Oc. 4

AASS Boll — *Acta Sanctorum* ed. J. Bollandus, G. Henschenius *et al.* (Antwerp, 1643–   )

AASSOSB — *Acta Sancorum Ordinis Sancti Benedicti* ed. J. Mabillon, 9 vols. (Paris, 1688–1702)

Aleppo Chronicle — Kemal ad-Din, 'Chronicle of Aleppo', RHC Or. 3

Alexiad — Anna Comnena, *Alexiad* tr. E. R. A. Sewter (London, 1969)

Amatus — *Amato di Monte Cassino* ed. V. Bartholomaeis (Rome, 1935)

ASC — *The Anglo-Saxon Chronicle* ed. D. Whitelock (London, 1961)

BD — Bauldry of Dol, *Historia Jerosolimitana*, RHC Oc. 4

BT — *The Bayeux tapestry* ed. D. M. Wilson (London, 1985)

Damascus chronicle of the Crusades — Ibn al-Qalanisi, *Damascus chronicle of the Crusades*, extracts ed. and tr. H. A. R. Gibb (London, 1967)

Ekkehard — Ekkehard of Aura, *Hierosolymita*, RHC Oc. 5

FC — Fulcher of Chartres, *Historia Hierosolymitana*, ed. H. Hagenmeyer (Heidelberg, 1913)

GCA — *Gesta Comitum Andegavorum*, in *Chroniques des comtes d'Anjou et des seigneurs d'Amboise* ed. L. Halphen and R. Poupardin (Paris, 1913) 34–157

GF — *Gesta Francoum et aliorum Hierosolimitanorum*, ed. R. Hill (London, 1962)

xiii

Glaber	*Rodulfus Glaber Opera*, ed. J. France (Oxford, 1989)
GN	Guibert of Nogent, *Gesta Die per Francos*, RHC Oc. 4
GR	William of Malmesbury, *Gesta Regum Anglorum*, ed. T. D. Hardy, 2 vols. (London, 1840)
HBS	*Historia Belli Sacri* RHC Oc. 3
HGM	*Histoire de Guillaume le Maréchal*, ed. P. Meyer, 3 vols. (Paris, 1891–1901)
HH	Henry of Huntingdon, *Historia Anglorum*, ed. T. Arnold (London, 1879)
Ibn Khaldun	Ibn Khaldun, *The Muqaddima: an introduction to history* ed. and tr. R. Rosenthal, abridged N. J. Dawood (Princeton, 1967)
Matthew	Matthew of Edessa, 'Chronique', RHC Arm. 1
MGH	*Monumenta Germaniae Historica*
	MGH Auct. Ant.: Auctores antiquissimi
	MGH SRG: Scriptores rerum Germanicarum ad usum scholarum
	MGH SS: Scriptores
	SS rer. Langob.: Scriptores rerum Langobardorum
Michael	Michael the Syrian, *Chronique de Michel le Syrien, Patriarch Jacobite d'Antioche 1166–99* ed. and tr. J. B. Chabot, 4 vols. (Brussels, 1963, reprint of 1899–1910 edition)
al-Mulk	Nizam al-Mulk, *Traité de gouvernment composé pour le Sultan Malik Shah* ed. C. Schefer, 2 vols. (Paris, 1892–3). There is also an English translation, *The Book of government or rules for kings* ed. and tr. H. Darke (New York, 1960)
OV	Ordericus Vitalis, *Historia aecclesiastica*, ed. M. Chibnall, 6 vols. (Oxford, 1969–79)
PL	*Patrologiae cursus completus, series latina* ed. J.-P. Migne, 221 vols. (Paris, 1844–64)
PT	Peter Tudebode, *Historia de Hierosolymitano itinere*, ed. J. H. Hill and L. L. Hill (Philadelphia, 1974)

RA	Raymond of Aguilers, *Liber*, ed. J. H. Hill and L. L. Hill (Paris, 1969)
Ravandi	Ravandi, Muhammad b. Ali b. Sulaiman, *Rabat al-sudur wa ayatal surur* ed. M. Iqtal (Leiden and London, 1921)
RC	Ralph of Caen, *Gesta Tancredi*, RHC Oc. 5
RH	Roger of Hovenden, *Chronica Magistri Rogeris de Hovenden* ed. W. Stubbs, 4 vols. (London, Rolls Series, 1871)
RHC	*Recueil des Historiens des Croisades* *RHC Ar.: Historiens Arméniennes* *RHC Oc.: Historiens Occidentaux* *RHC Or.: Historiens Orientales*
RM	Robert the Monk, *Historia Iherosolimitana*, RHC Oc. 3
Runciman	S. Runciman, *A History of the Crusades* 3 vols. (Cambridge, 1951–4)
Setton, *Crusades*	K. Setton and M. W. Baldwin (ed.), *A history of the crusades* (Pennsylvania, 1959–89)
Tarsusi	Tarsusi, Murda ben Ali, *Tabsira Arbub al-albad* extracts ed. and tr. C. Cahen, 'Un traité d'armurie composé pour Saladin', *Bulletin d'études orientales*, 12 (1948), 103–63
Vic et Vaisette	C. de Vic et J. J. Vaisette, *Histoire Générale de Languedoc*, 5 vols. (Paris, 1743–5)
Wace	*Wace's Roman de Rou et des Ducs de Normandie* ed. H. Andresen, 2 vols. (Bonn, 1877–9)
WJ	William of Jumièges, *Gesta Normannorum Ducum*, ed. J. Marx (Paris, 1914)
WP	William of Poitiers, *Gesta Guillelmi ducis Normannorum et regis Anglorum*, ed. R. Foreville (Paris, 1952)
WT	William of Tyre, *Historia rerum in partibus transmarinis gestarum*, RHC Oc. 1

CHAPTER I

The roots of victory

The capture of Jerusalem on 15 July 1099 was of enormous importance in the history of the Christian West and the Orthodox and
Islamic East. It was the culmination of five years of incredible effort
which began in November 1095 when Pope Urban II launched the
great expedition at Clermont in the Auvergne. For those who
laboured on it and survived, the seizure of Jerusalem represented a
triumphant consummation. Little wonder that amongst the appalling carnage and slaughter of the sack, in which men 'rode in blood
up to their knees and bridle reins', they believed 'it was a just and
splendid judgment of God that this place should be filled with the
blood of the unbelievers, since it had suffered so long from their
blasphemies' and rejoiced. 'A new day, new joy, new and perpetual
gladness, the consummation of our labour and devotion, drew forth
from all new words and new songs'.[1] For the papacy, which conceived the idea of the expedition, its victory was a vindication of the
pope's claims to be the leader of the Christian world. In the ideological conflict between empire and papacy, which we call the
'Investiture Contest', the victory of the crusade tipped the balance
sharply towards the papacy. The capture of Jerusalem and its port
of Jaffa began the establishment of a western colony in the east. It
was not the first – the crusade had already seized Antioch and
Edessa – but Jerusalem was an ideological imperative for the whole
of Latin Christendom, a spur which for two centuries would drive
men and women on bitter journeys by land and sea to savage war in
the distant Levant. That the pope alone could declare such a war
established his position as something akin to the Caliph's as 'Commander of the Faithful'. For the Christian and Orthodox empire at

---

[1] Raymond of Aguilers, *Liber*, ed. J. H. Hill and L. L. Hill (Paris, 1969) (hereafter cited as
RA), p. 151, tr. by A. C. Krey, *The First Crusade* (Princeton, 1921, Gloucester, 1958), p. 261.

Constantinople with its long tradition of diplomacy, the arrival of the westerners introduced a new and unpredictable factor into the politics of the Mediterranean. The newcomers were at once Christians and strangers whose attitude to Byzantium was ambiguous to say the least.[2] For Islam, the crusader victory marked the arrival of an alien force whose beliefs and attitudes were deeply threatening, though this was only slowly recognised. For western traders the victory opened the way for the growth of new enclaves controlled by friendly forces through which to tap the riches of the east, rivals to established centres like Constantinople and Alexandria.[3] The victory of the First Crusade precipitated great changes, in the ideological and political conflicts of Europe, in the politics of the Levant, and in the trading habits of the Mediterranean basin. It is not difficult to understand why modern historians have enthusiastically addressed the question of explaining the success of an undertaking which had such momentous consequences.

The story of the crusade is fascinating. Urban created a mass movement; an army of about 50,000–60,000, plus non-combatants, was set in motion in 1095.[4] Such numbers were unknown in the west. The army with which William, duke of Normandy, conquered England in 1066 probably numbered 14,000 men, including sailors, delivering effectives of about 8,000–9,000 onto the battlefield, of whom perhaps as many as 3,000 were mounted. Twenty years later the Anglo-Saxon chronicler recorded that William mustered 'a larger force of mounted men and footsoldiers than had ever come into this country' against an invasion threat. In 1081 Robert Guiscard attempted to conquer the Byzantine empire with an army of about 15,000 fighting men.[5] Comparisons must take into account

---

[2] The emperor, Alexius I, had a daughter Anna whose life of her father, *The Alexiad*, reveals Byzantine attitudes to the crusaders. Her angry belief that the Westerners had broken their promises, made to Alexius in 1096, when they seized Antioch in 1098 is a revelation of the importance attached by the Greeks to that city: J. France, 'Anna Comnena, the Alexiad and the First Crusade', *Reading Medieval Studies*, 10 (1983), 21–8. Anna was at pains to conceal that her father had asked for western help at the Council of Piacenza in March 1095, on which see S. Runciman, *History of the Crusades*, 3 vols. (Cambridge, 1951–4), 1. 103–5.

[3] Nor is this hindsight. Genoa responded to Pope Urban's appeal by sending a fleet and as early as July 14 1098 had concluded a treaty with Bohemond establishing their trading privileges in Antioch: H. Hagenmeyer, *Die Kreuzzugsbriefe aus den Jahren 1088–1100* (Innsbruck, 1902), pp. 155–6.

[4] For a discussion of numbers see below pp. 122–142.

[5] B. S. Bachrach, 'Some observations on the military administration of the Norman Conquest', *Battle*, 8 (1985), 2–4 speaks of a 'scholarly consensus' on the figure of 14,000; *The*

the presence, in the crusader army of 1095, of many non-combatants, the elderly, women and children. However, it is evident that the army of the First Crusade was something quite unprecedented in size and, indeed, undertaking. Such a mass movement could not but fascinate later generations, especially since it also appears as David in a contest with the forces of Islam. For the crusade challenged three great enemies, the Turks of Asia Minor, the Sultanate of Baghdad and the Egyptian Caliphate, and to do this travelled great distances. From Cologne to Constantinople via Ratisbon, Belgrade and Sofia is 2,300 kilometres and from Paris via Brindisi and Thessalonika 2,380. On the route followed by the main army Jerusalem is 1,970 kilometres from Constantinople. So the people who set out in 1095 were prepared to walk and ride some 4,300 kilometres.[6] Conditions on the march were appalling; the arid heat of central Asia Minor and the steep passage of the Taurus mountains took their toll.[7] To such natural horrors were added the supply problems attendant on feeding an army of such a size. This was most acute during the nine-month siege of Antioch, while there was a tremendous shortage of water during the bitter siege of Jerusalem.[8] It should be remembered that before the age of modern hygiene and medicine any army reckoned to lose more from disease than from battle. In what appears to be a reliable estimate, the eye-witness chronicler, Raymond of Aguilers, suggested that the army which besieged Jerusalem had only 1,200–1,300 knights and 12,000 foot with an unspecified number of non-combatants and sick. As they marched to Ascalon only a month after the fall of the city, he tells us that the army had shrunk to 9,000 foot and barely 1,200 knights; the siege cost the crusade almost a quarter of its fighting strength. The real casualties may have been worse, for the army mustered for Ascalon included marines and sailors from a Genoese fleet which

---

Anglo-Saxon Chronicle, ed. D. Whitelock (London, 1961), 'E' 1085, 1086. For the campaign of 1081, F. Chalandon, *Histoire de la domination normande en Italie et en Sicile*, 2 vols. (Paris, 1907), 1. 265–84, accepts the figure of 15,000 suggested by the *Little Norman Chronicle*, an. 1080, in *Amalfi im Frühen Mittelalter*, ed. U. Schwarz, but Ordericus Vitalis, *Historia aecclesiastica*, ed. M. Chibnall, 6 vols. (Oxford, 1969–79) (hereafter cited as OV), 4. 17 suggests only 10,000.

[6] I am indebted for these figures and for much other geographical information to members of the Geography Department of University College Swansea, Professor D. T. Herbert, Dr A. Parry and G. B. Lewis. Of course we cannot know exactly how far they travelled, but these and other figures represent approximations based on what we know of their route.

[7] *Gesta Francorum et aliorum Hierosolimitanorum*, ed. R. Hill (London, 1962), pp. 23, 27 (hereafter cited as *GF*).

[8] *GF*, pp. 28–71, 87–92.

had not arrived at the start of the siege. The siege of Antioch lasted
nine months across a winter, and in that time many battles were
fought; the losses must have been horrendous. In the eleventh
century long-distance travel was, in itself, a hazardous business.
Pilgrims anticipated death on their devotions, while in England a
merchant who made three journeys overseas was entitled to the
status of thegn. In the light of this appalling attrition it is little
wonder that historians have seen the crusade as truly a triumph of
the will and have emphasised this as an explanation of its success.
What drove men and women through heat, privation and death to
the liberation of the Sepulchre of the Lord at Jerusalem? The issue of
motivation, seen as the foundation of the morale of the army, has
been explored by modern writers and dominated explanations of the
success of the crusade.

The impact of the preaching of the great expedition by Urban in
1095, which inspired so many to leave their homes for the east,
probably owed something to new and dynamic ideas about war in
Christian society which had been formulated in the course of the
eleventh century. Urban's idea of an expedition to the east was a
novelty but one whose component elements were already known to
his audience. The difficulty of knowing precisely what Urban said at
Clermont in 1095 has, of course, complicated discussion, but he
probably called for an expedition to Jerusalem which would aid the
Byzantine emperor and liberate the churches of the east from the
yoke of Islam. He presented the task as a pilgrimage. Fulcher of
Chartres' important account of Clermont does not mention Jerusalem as the objective of the expedition, but the balance of scholarly
opinion sees this as an aberration on Fulcher's part.[9] To contemporaries, the most astonishing thing about his speech was his offer of
'the remission of sin' to all who took the cross. This was not a new
idea as it had been offered to those undertaking expeditions to
Spain, but it was now widely publicised and clearly linked to the

[9] Fulcher of Chartres, *Historia Hierosolimitana*, ed. H. Hagenmeyer (Heidelberg, 1913) [her-
eafter cited as FC], pp. 65–67; C. Erdmann, *The Origin of the Idea of the Crusade*, tr. M. W.
Baldwin and W. Goffart (Princeton, 1977), pp. 355–71 tried to reconcile Fulcher's omission
by suggesting that Jerusalem was merely the goal of the expedition's march and not the
object of its endeavour; H. E. Mayer, *The Crusades*, tr. J. Gillingham (Oxford, 1972), p. 9 n.
6, gives the idea support, but the arguments of H. E. J. Cowdrey, 'Pope Urban's preaching
of the First Crusade', *History*, 55 (1970), 177–88 supported by J. Riley-Smith, *The First
Crusade and the Idea of Crusading* (London, 1986), pp. 22–23 in favour of Jerusalem having
always been Urban's goal seem to me decisive.

powerful notion of the liberation of the Holy Sepulchre.[10] But why did this idea appeal? Gregory VII had wanted to liberate the Holy Sepulchre and help the Christians of the east in response to a request for aid from the Byzantine emperor, and had written a series of letters to that effect in 1074, evoking little success. Appeals for the Holy War in Spain had even been supported by an offer of indulgence without great responses.[11] In 1095 Urban II was very organised in his approach. Before Clermont he consulted with at least one major secular leader who was later to join the crusade, Raymond IV of Toulouse, and acquired the support of a great ecclesiastical magnate, Adhémar of Le Puy. To the Council he called bishops from a considerable area of France.[12] Afterwards he set out on what appears to have been a well-prepared tour of southern and western France, arousing enthusiasm and commissioning preachers to spread the word. He wrote to areas he had not visited in person soliciting their support. But something much more powerful than mere organisation was at work, for, by the time of his letter to Bologna, Urban II's tone was changing and he was evidently seeking to restrict an enthusiasm which was getting out of hand, and the same feeling comes across in other source material.[13] Urban probably did not expect Germans to join his movement because of the Investiture Contest, so the participation of Godfrey de Bouillon, duke of Lorraine and an important supporter of Henry IV, must have caused special pleasure. The appeal of Clermont spread like wildfire in the west and such was its moral authority that even the Capetian king, at odds with the pope over his marriage, sent his brother, Hugh of Vermandois to show the Capetian family

---

[10] The foundation of almost all modern thinking on Urban's indulgence is Erdmann, *Origins*, but see also P. Alphandéry and A. Dupront, *La Chrétienité et l'idée de croisade*, 2 vols. (Paris, 1954–9) I. 9–80; Riley-Smith, *Idea of Crusading*, pp. 17–25; Mayer, *Crusades*, pp. 8–37.

[11] E. Caspar (ed.), *Das Register Gregors VII*, 2 vols. (Berlin, 1920–3), 1.69–71, 75–6, 172–3; on northern crusaders in the Spanish wars of the eleventh century see M. Defourneaux, *Les Français en Espagne au xi⁰ et xii⁰ siècles* (Paris, 1949).

[12] R. Somerville, *The Councils of Urban II. vol. 1, Decreta Claramontensia* (London, 1972), pp. 9–41; J. H. Hill and L. L. Hill, *Raymond IV Count of Toulouse*, (Syracuse, 1962), pp. 31–2; on Adhémar see J. G. d'Adhémar-Laubaume, *Adhémar de Monteil, légat du pape sur la première croisade* (Le Puy, 1910), and L. Bréhier, *Adhémar de Monteil, un évêque à la première croisade* (Le Puy, 1923).

[13] R. Crozet, 'Le voyage d'Urbain II et ses arrangements avec le clergé de France (1095–96)', *Revue Historique*, 179 (1937), 270–310; R. Somerville, 'The French Councils of Urban II; some basic considerations', *Annuarium Historiae Conciliorum*, 2 (1970), 56–65; Hagenmeyer, *Kreuzzugsbriefe*, pp. 137–8; A. Becker, *Papst Urban II (1088–99)* (Stuttgart, 1964), pp. 232–80.

flag. Clearly at the heart of this spontaneous reaction lay a powerful religious conviction.

It is not difficult to find evidence for a new and deeper religious belief in eleventh-century society. The cult of relics, a devotion which involved all sections of society, reached extraordinary heights. The mass pilgrimages to Jerusalem at the millennia of the Nativity and Passion of Christ, and the contemporaneous wave of church building were clear evidence of a new tenor in Christian society.[14] The spread of reform in the church and the bitterness of the war of ideas, which was an element of the 'Investiture Contest', attest to the continuing force of this new spirit whose temper was puritan. A plethora of religious houses endowed by laymen, the popularity of eremeticism and the foundation of Cîteaux all suggest a widespread piety which touched poor as well as rich.[15] In the great crowds of pilgrims along the roads to the shrines of saints, and above all on the road to Jerusalem, we see the forerunners of the crusaders. In the Peace Movement, and the tumults of the Investiture Contest, the church was mobilising the masses in her chosen cause. But the masses were not the primary target of Pope Urban's appeal for he wanted soldiers, and that meant knights and lords. The kings of the West were preoccupied, but some very important magnates were persuaded to join the expedition. Raymond of Toulouse, Robert of Normandy, Robert of Flanders, Stephen of Blois, Hugh of Vermandois, Godfrey of Bouillon and Bohemond were 'Princes', men of the very highest standing, truly quasi-monarchs, and they were followed by significant numbers of their own vassals and others of equivalent rank.[16] It was once fashionable to see them simply as ruthless seekers after land and loot, covering their greed with the cloak of the cross. Recent research has inclined to the view that as participation was

[14] On the growth of religious sentiment and pilgrimage in the early eleventh century see *Rodulfus Glaber Opera*, ed. J. France (Oxford, 1989) [Hereafter cited as *Glaber*], pp. lxix–lxx, 96–7, 132–3, 198–203; on the cult of saints there is a huge literature but for an interesting local study see T. Head, *Hagiography and the Cult of Saints: the Diocese of Orléans 800–1200* (Cambridge, 1990). See also B. Ward, *Miracles and the Medieval Mind* (Philadelphia, 1982).

[15] I. S. Robinson, *Authority and Resistance in the Investiture Contest* (London, 1978). The life of Robert of Arbrissel illustrates the wide social appeal of the new piety, *Vita beati Roberti de Arbrisello, PL* 162. 1043–1078; on the context of his preaching V. W. Turner, *The Forest of Symbols*, (Cornell, 1967). See also H. Leyser, *Hermits and the New Monasticism* (London, 1984). Glaber, pp. 115–16 noted the rebuilding of village churches as well as those of great institutions.

[16] Of the eleventh century it has been said: 'Le temps du roi semble passé. Le temps des princes commence.' J. Flori, *L'idéologie du glaive; préhistoire de la chevalerie* (Geneva, 1983), p. 168.

costly, the possibility of gain in the East was 'a stupid gamble', leading to the conclusion that 'it is hard to believe that most crusaders were motivated by crude materialism'. . . It makes much more sense to suppose, in so far as one can generalise about them, that they were moved by an idealism'.[17] It is not difficult to trace the development of a powerful piety amongst the European upper class in the eleventh century. Count Fulk Nerra of Anjou who slew a rival for the royal favour before King Robert's very eyes, made three pilgrimages to Jerusalem and founded Beaulieu-lès-Loches.[18] Some lay lords were renowned for their piety, while under Cluniac influence a steady trickle, most famously the duke of Burgundy in 1078, joined religious orders.[19]

But mere piety has not been regarded as enough to explain mass support. The make-up, the identity of that idealism seen as the driving force of the crusading movement, has been the subject of ever closer examination, in which the ideas of the great German historian Erdmann played a formative role. In essence, historians have come to believe that the crusade was the culmination of a series of impulses by which the church sought to reconcile the heroic and militant ideas of knighthood – chivalry in its crudest sense – with Christian ideology[20]. The Peace and Truce of God began in France as an effort to control the savagery of the knights and lords who had long usurped the power of a monarch who was confined to the Ile de France. But this was not a merely negative attitude, for in recognising the role of the knights as the bearers of arms in society, the church was giving them a special role – recognising them as an *ordo* in Christian society, and seeking to direct their brutality to positive ends – to protect the poor and succour the church.[21] The church had

---

[17] Riley-Smith, *Idea of Crusading*, p. 47.

[18] *Glaber*, pp. 106–9, 60 n. 2, 61–5. Fulk has been the subject of much study. For insight into the world of the princes see B. S. Bachrach, 'A study in feudal politics; relations between Fulk Nerra and William the Great, 995–1030', *Viator*, 7 (1976), 111–22.

[19] Caspar, *Gregors VII*, 1. 423–4; Riley-Smith cites two participants in the First Crusade, Anselm of Ribemont and Arnold of Ardres who were famous for their piety and patrons of monastic houses: *Idea of Crusading*, p. 10.

[20] Erdmann, *Origins*; Riley-Smith, *Idea of Crusading*, pp. 1–12.

[21] G. Duby, *La Société aux xie et xiie siècles dans la région mâconaise* (Paris, 1971), pp. 196–204, *The Chivalrous Society* (London, 1977) pp. 123–33, 150–77, *The Three Orders: Feudal Society Imagined*, tr. A. Goldhammer (Chicago, 1980), pp. 296–98; H. E. J. Cowdrey, 'The Peace and Truce of God in the eleventh century', *Past and Present*, 46 (1970), 42–67; 'Genesis of the Crusades: springs of western ideas of Holy War', in T. P. Murphy, ed., *The Holy War*, (Ohio, 1976), pp. 9–32; C. Morris, 'Equestris Ordo: chivalry as a vocation in the twelfth

always imposed penances for murder on those who killed in battle, but it had long been felt that soldiers who fought against the enemies of God, pagans and Muslims, were fighting in a cause so self-evidently just that such a punishment could not be appropriate. As the long external onslaught on Europe ended by the year 1000, so this spontaneous notion of righteous war was transferred to reconquest, in Spain and later in Sicily. In the early eleventh century, the Spanish kings began the *Reconquista* and established close links with the French church. In 1032 Sancho III of Navarre (1000–35) sent the monk Paternus to Cluny and the interest of that great order in Spanish reform must have brought the peninsula more closely into the European consciousness, though Cluny was never a recruiting sergeant for the Spanish wars.[22] The papacy strengthened popular notions of the positive value of violence: in 1053 Leo IX led a military expedition against the Normans of South Italy. His successors supported the Spanish and Sicilian reconquests and approved the Norman conquest of England. In the Investiture Contest an entire theology of war was called into being by the papacy – assisted by such thinkers as Anselm of Lucca and Bonizo of Sutri – as Gregory VII tried to create his *militia sancti Petri* to wage righteous war against Henry IV. In a famous letter to Henry IV before the outbreak of the contest, Gregory sketched a plan for an armed expedition, led by himself, to aid the Greeks after the disaster of Manzikert, in return for recognition of the power of the Holy See, and he even suggested that they should go on to recover Jerusalem, though his proposal lacked the elements of the pilgrim vow and the indulgence added by Urban II.[23] Gregory VII attempted to take the initiative by launching the expedition of Ebles de Roucy to Spain. His claim that lands reconquered there were papal fiefs led to a close alliance between the papacy and the kingdom of Léon which would long endure, giving the Holy See great influence in Spanish

century', in R. Baker, ed., *Religious Motivation: Biographical and Sociological Problems for the Church Historian, Studies in Church History*, 15 (Oxford, 1978) pp. 87–96.

[22] H. E. J. Cowdrey, 'Bishop Ermenfrod of Sion and the penitential ordinance following the battle of Hastings', *Journal of Ecclesiastical History*, 20 (1969), 225–42; *Glaber*, pp. 114–15, n. 206–7; H. E. J. Cowdrey, 'Cluny and the First Crusade', *Revue Bénédictine*, 83 (1973), 285–311.

[23] I. S. Robinson, 'Gregory VII and the soldiers of Christ', *History*, 58 (1973), 169–92; *Authority and resistance*, pp. 99–102; H. E. J. Cowdrey, 'Pope Gregory VII's "Crusading" plans of 1074', in B. Z. Kedar, H. E. Mayer and R. C. Smail, eds. *Outremer: Studies in the History of the Crusading Kingdom of Jerusalem Presented to Joshua Prawer*, (Jerusalem, 1982), pp. 27–40 (hereafter cited as *Outremer*); Riley-Smith, *Idea of Crusading*, pp. 1–12.

affairs.[24] Such interventions show the papacy placing a positive value on violence and asserting its claim to direct it. It is significant that it was in the context of the Spanish reconquest that Urban II would first formulate an indulgence based upon the Jerusalem pilgrimage, for the restoration of Tarragona.[25]

Although there is plenty of evidence to show that the church was changing its attitude to war, and seeking to influence the military classes, it enjoyed little success. The expeditions to Spain were occasional: to Barbastro in 1064–5 and Tudela in 1086. Spiritual benefits were offered by the papacy to those who fought in Spain, though it now seems unlikely that an indulgence was offered by Alexander II.[26] Few took seriously the restrictions of war proposed by the church. Ravaging was, and continued to be, an essential element in war. It was an expedient method of destroying the economic base of an enemy and undermining the loyalty of his vassals, a military tactic in an age when war was dominated by castles and an absolute necessity to support armies which had no logistic train. Yet this was war of a military upper class upon the poor and defenceless, and upon the church whose property suffered badly, the very thing against which the church inveighed. If ravaging was not exactly a path to glory for the chivalrous knight, it was no shame to perform this normal part of the business of war. Only those who engaged in horrific torture and gratuitous mass-murder, like Robert of Bellême, attracted the censure of their contemporaries and even horrors like the massacre of Vitry, did not necessarily damage reputations.[27] At the end of his life William the Marshal, that very embodiment of medieval chivalry, defended his conduct as a soldier against the reproaches of the church which could hardly be

---

[24] Defourneaux, *Les Français en Espagne*, pp. 138–9; D. W. Lomax, *The Reconquest of Spain* (London, 1978), p. 60.

[25] Robinson, 'Soldiers of Christ', 169–92; J. Riley-Smith, *Idea of Crusading*, pp. 18–19.

[26] Defourneaux, *Les Français en Espagne*, pp. 135–7, 143–4. On the supposed indulgence of Alexander II see P. Boissonade, 'Cluny, la papauté et la première croisade internationale contre les Sarracins d'Espagne: Barbastro 1064–65', *Revue des Questions Historiques*, 117 (1932), 237–301, 'Les premières croisades françaises en Espagne: Normands, Gascons, Aquitains et Bourguignons (1018–32), *Bulletin hispanique*, 36 (1934), 5–28, and for the evidence against, A. Ferreiro, 'The siege of Barbastro 1064–5: a reassessment', *Journal of Medieval History*, 9 (1983), 129–47, in which, however, the consistent papal support for war in Spain is made very clear.

[27] See for example a through examination of chivalric society's attitudes to war in the Anglo-Norman world: M. J. Strickland, *The Conduct and Perception of War under the Anglo-Norman and Angevin Kings 1075–1217*, unpublished Ph.D. thesis, University of Cambridge, 1989, especially pp. 177–213, 237–80.

obeyed 'or else no-one would be saved'. Even the crusading movement had only a fitful effect. Only enormous efforts after the fall of
Edessa in 1144 stirred Europe into the Second Crusade, while it took
the collapse of the kingdom of Jerusalem after Hattin in 1187 to
provoke another effort on behalf of the east. Whole areas, like
England, were, for long periods of time, little effected by the crusading movement. Despite this, the appeal of 1095 made an enormous
impact which was sustained, though at varying levels of intensity,
for centuries. Why was this?

Urban cast his appeal for holy war in 1095 in the form of a
pilgrimage whose reward was remission of sin. This may not have
been very different from what was promised by Alexander II in
about 1063, but it came thirty-two years later, during which time
the Investiture Contest and the struggle for reform may well have
heightened that fundamental desire around which almost all
eleventh century piety had been built – deliverance from the burden
of sin. The church had had little luck in influencing lay behaviour
by its theology of war for 'knights stood to gain little temporal profit
... from adherence to the moral dictates of the church'.[28] They had
religious preoccupations – the risks of hell-fire were all too plain –
but with a few individual exceptions the political and military
pressures upon them counted for far more. That dichotomy between
their religious preoccupations and their military direction continued, as the story about William the Marshal would reveal a
century later. Chivalry in its essence was already a reality by the
time Pope Urban launched his great expedition, but within the
notion of the ideal knight as it emerged, there were appalling
tensions and contradictions. The warrior ethic was fundamentally
opposed to the church's ideas about the behaviour of the knightly
class. In an age when monarchy was weak, the church turned its
attention to the 'conversion' of the knights and lords, seeking to give
a Christian gloss to such vital ceremonies of the military class as the
creation of a knight. The 'sanctification' of the knightly class, their
conversion into a parallel order to the monks, was the goal of the
church's endeavours. The success of the process was uneven to say
the least, but this religious ideology of knighthood, devoted to the
the support of the church and the defense of the helpless, formed a
vital base upon which Urban could build, giving it a new and

[28] *Ibid*, p. 347.

dynamic dimension.[29] Such ideas were having an increasing impact upon the life of the upper classes and must have created an enormous tension by their contrast with the reality with which they had to live.[30] It must have been made worse by the growing religious intensity of the age. Urban offered the religious sensibilities of the military class neither a solution nor a synthesis, but an escape route. In 1095 Urban created a window of opportunity – for it must be remembered that contemporaries did not know, as we know, that the crusade would have a great and continuing future – an offer to escape from the burden of sin made in the clearest possible terms by exercising that love of war and all its joys which was the central characteristic of a warrior aristocracy.[31] This was proclaimed in the loudest and most public, possible way. Organisation and publicity cannot make a message popular, but they can make sure that a popular message is broadcast, and that is precisely what Urban II did in 1095. The Investiture Conflict had been a war of ideas, and the church had learned much about propaganda. Urban prepared the way for his appeal carefully, launched it in an appropriate setting 'a gathering of influential churchmen' and aimed it at a market he knew well – the French aristocracy to which he belonged. He then prosecuted a vigorous campaign in person and by letter. A message was forged in the simplest terms – 'Jerusalem, Salvation – Deus Vult' – and like so many simple messages it came across, it spread, with a momentum of its own creating a more complex phenomenon than that suggested by the description 'religious enthusiasm'.

Discussion of crusader motivation has too long revolved around a perceived dichotomy between material and spiritual factors, booty and the love of God. This was a crudely (though not a merely)

---

[29] J. Nelson, 'Ninth century knighthood: the evidence of Nithard', in C. Harper-Bill, C. J. Holdsworth and J. Nelson, eds., *Studies in Medieval History Presented to R. Allen-Brown*, (Woodbridge, 1989), pp. 255–66 has argued for the early existence of ideas of knighthood; J. Flori, 'Les origines de l'adoubement chevaleresque', *Traditio*, 35 (1979), 209–272; *L'idéologie du glaive*, pp. 135–57; *L'essor de la chevalerie, X–XIII siècles*, (Geneva, 1986), pp. 9–42, 223–67; M. Bull, *Knightly Piety and the Lay Response to the First Crusade: the Limousin and Gascony, c. 970–1130* (Oxford, 1992), pp. 155–204; Professor J. Riley-Smith is also preparing a book on early crusaders and I am equally indebted to him for information and discussion.

[30] On contradictions between the elements of developed chivalry, the warrior ethic, ecclesiastical ethics and courtliness see S. Painter, *French Chivalry* (Cornell, 1964).

[31] Here I agree with Riley-Smith, *Idea of Crusading*, pp. 27–9, that what was on offer was literally 'remission of sin'.

materialistic age whose spiritual perceptions were often seen in very concrete forms – not least the flames of hell. It was in the eleventh century that the person of the devil took shape, while the painful literalness of saints lives and their repeated miracles is proverbial.[32] But more to the point is that war and booty were inseparable, for in medieval conditions a leader had to provide opportunities for his followers to plunder. In a modern context we see booty as an extra which the soldier seizes and enjoys on top of his pay. But then it was necessary for subsistence. And the perquisites of war – the 'extras' so to speak, were what war was about. The delight in Girart de Roussillon about war and plunder might be dismissed as poetic rhetoric, except that it tells us something of what contemporary knights liked to hear about themselves. Ordericus twice tells us that the prospects of rich ransom extended war and attracted others to join in – in the valley of Beugy in 1083–5 and in the Vexin in 1097. Even in the context of Holy War such considerations were extremely important. The Spanish conflict had drawn northerners since the start of the eleventh century – Adhémar de Chabannes relates how the Norman Roger de Toeni terrorised the Muslims by pretended cannibalism about 1020.[33] In 1064–5 a large number of northerners led by William VIII of Aquitaine (1058–87), and the Normans William of Montreuil and Robert Crispin attacked Barbastro. There seems to have been no overall commander, and when the city was captured the foreigners killed the population, gathering an enormous booty. In 1065 the Muslims recaptured it and massacred its Christian inhabitants. In 1069 the city's Muslim ruler and Sancho of Pamplona concluded an agreement not to ally with the French or any other foreigners.[34] In 1087 another great military expedition led by Odo of Burgundy and Hugh of Lusignan came to the aid of the Spanish kingdoms after the defeat of Alfonso VI (1065–1109) by the Almoravids at the battle of Sagrajas in 1086. It achieved nothing, for the northerners declined to march deep into

---

[32] See especially the description of the devil in *Glaber*, pp. 219–20. On the emergence of the devil see J. B. Russell, *Lucifer: the Devil in the Middle Ages*, (Cornell, 1984), especially pp. 92–128 and R. Colliot, 'Rencontres du moine Raoul Glaber avec le diable d'après ses histoires', *Le Diable au Moyen Age* (Paris, Aix-en-Provence, 1979), pp. 117–32. On the problem of salvation and its solutions see J. Le Goff, *The Birth of Purgatory*, tr. A. Goldhammer (London, 1984). As an example of eleventh-century hagiography see Bernardus Scholasticus, *Liber de miraculis sanctae Fidis, PL* 141. 127–64.

[33] OV, 4. 49, 5. 217. On 'Girart' see below p. 13, n. 38; Adhémar de Chabannes, *Chronique*, ed. J. Chavanon (Paris, 1897), pp. 178.

[34] Ferreiro, 'Barbastro', 140–1.

Spain and preferred to attack Tudela in the Ebro valley, in the hope of booty. Its siege of Tudela may have been betrayed for money by William the Carpenter, viscount of Melun, whose misdeeds were remembered later on the First Crusade.[35] Love of booty drove knights far and wide. Robert Crispin, one of the leaders of the Barbastro affair, went to Constantinople and took service with the emperor who eventually poisoned him.[36] He commanded a corps of Norman mercenaries which was later led by his fellow-countryman Roussel of Bailleul, who attempted to set up a Norman state in Asia Minor. Anglo-Saxons also sought their fortunes across the sea, even as far away as the Black Sea.[37] It would be difficult to overestimate the lust for booty of the military classes of the later eleventh century. The importance of booty to monarchs and followers alike, in early medieval conditions underlines the point made in Girart de Roussillon.[38] For those who contemplated Urban II's appeal in 1095 righteous war offered its rightful reward. The indulgence decree of the Council of Clermont implicitly recognises the magnetism of gain: 'If any man sets out from pure devotion not for reputation or monetary gain, to liberate the church of God at Jerusalem, his journey shall be reckoned in place of all penance'. It is a statement that can be compared with Glaber's comment, half a century earlier, on the good pilgrim Lethbaud: 'Truly he was free from that vanity which inspires so many to undertake the journey simply to gain the prestige of having been to Jerusalem'.[39]

Loot and glory, such are the lures of war, and in the official decree Urban II was at pains to demand pure and righteous intention for those who would gain a heavenly reward. If, as Robert the Monk suggests, Urban recalled Carolingian glories, the evocation of past

---

[35] Defourneaux, *Les Français en Espagne*, pp. 143–5; *GF*, pp. 33–4. William has been identified as one of the sources for the character of the treacherous Ganelon in the *Song of Roland*, Defourneaux, p. 269, n. 2.

[36] *De nobili genere Crispinorum PL* 150, 735–44.

[37] S. Runciman, I. 62–3, 66–7. On the Normans in Byzantium see also below pp. 87–8, 98–102, 152–3; J. Godfrey, 'The defeated Anglo-Saxons take service with the eastern empire', *Battle*, I (1978), 63–74; J. Shepherd, 'The English in Byzantium', *Traditio*, 29 (1973), 53–92.

[38] 'He does not leave a good knight alive as far as Baiol, nor treasure nor monastery, nor church nor shrine nor censer nor cross nor sacred vase: anything that he seizes he gives to his companions. He makes so cruel a war that he does not lay hands on a man without killing, hanging and mutilating him': Girart de Roussillon, *Chanson de Geste*, ed. W. M. Hackett, 3 vols. (Paris, 1953/55) and OV, 4. 48–9, 5. 216–17, quoted by M. J. Strickland, *Conduct and Perception of War*, pp. 1, 104–5; T. Reuter, 'Plunder and Tribute in the Carolingian Empire', *Transactions of the Royal Historical Society*, 35 (1985), 75–94.

[39] Somerville, *Councils of Urban II*, p. 74, author's own translation; *Glaber*, pp. 200–201.

conquest would have been as evident to his audience as to him, while there is some evidence that he anticipated the formation of principalities in the East.[40] As far as the military classes were concerned, Urban II's endorsement of war against the infidel was also an endorsement of the normal means of war – destruction, death and plunder, and its pleasures. These were inseparable: the church might be concerned about proper intention but for the lay mind such distinctions were too fine: the fate of the Jews in Western Germany, plundered and massacred by departing crusaders who seem to have seen their destruction as an integral part of Urban's appeal, is evidence of that.[41] Crude materialism and pride were integral to the appeal of the crusade, at least as far as the military classes were concerned. We also need to allow for the considerable social mobility of the age. For the young knight seeking to rise, the expedition to the east offered prospects. Baldwin of Boulogne, Godfrey de Bouillon's younger brother, was the very type of a young man, albeit of very high birth, on the make. He had entered the church, but left, probably because the new reform temper limited his opportunities for profit, and made a good marriage. He seems to have felt the allure of the east only well after his brothers had taken the cross and subsequently appears as a skillful politician, who rose to be prince of Edessa and later king of Jerusalem.[42] Perhaps equally important to some, it was an affirmation of the value of war, their chosen means of social mobility.[43] Nor should we dismiss the hope of land as a factor in motivating military men to join the crusade. After the victory at Ascalon most crusaders did return to the West, leaving Godfrey with a total military force of not more than 3,000 men, though this fell somewhat, by the spring of the following year to perhaps as low as 300 knights and 2,000 foot or even fewer. Our accounts are, as usual, not very precise, but on this reckoning between 200 and 300 knights of the army which triumphed at

---

[40] Riley-Smith, *Idea of Crusading*, p. 40 n. 37 quoting Pflugk-Harttung, *Acta Pontificum Romanorum indeita* 2. 205.

[41] H. Liebeschütz, 'The crusading movement and its bearing on the Christian attitude to Jewry', *Journal of Jewish Studies*, 10 (1959), 97–9; R. Chazan, 'The initial crisis for northern European Jewry', *Proceedings of the American Academy for Jewish Research*, 38–39 (1970–71), 101–17 points to earlier persecutions in northern France; Riley-Smith, *Idea of Crusading*, pp. 54–7.

[42] H. E. Mayer, *Mélanges sur l'histoire du royaume latin de Jérusalem*, *Mémoires de l'Académie des Inscriptions et Belles Lettres*, 5 (Paris, 1984), 10–48.

[43] On social mobility amongst the knights see A. Murray, *Reason and Society in the Middle Ages*, (Oxford, 1990), pp. 90–4.

Ascalon stayed behind – between a quarter and a sixth of the 1,200 who went to battle at Ascalon (where they suffered some casualties).[44] This was not an insignificant proportion. They may have been moved to stay by many considerations – amongst which kinship, loyalty and close association with Godfrey were important for many.[45] But it is remarkable that of those who survived to the end, such a large proportion were ready to stay: perhaps as many as 3,000 settled at Antioch with a substantial number remaining at Edessa, so the settlement of Franks in the east was, in terms of the overall effort, not negligible, and we are entitled to consider this in discussing their motives. According to Ekkehard of Aura, many of the poor in the West Frankish lands may have been excited by false prophets and driven on by famine and plague, presumably in the hope of finding better things in the fabled East.[46] However, general statements about famine and want spurring people on need to be handled carefully, for they were often local phenomena. The lesser crusaders probably had much the same mixed motives as their betters. We may suspect that some groups had very specific motives of a gross material kind. For Italian city states like Genoa the crusade must have seemed to be an extension of their long-standing drive to expel Muslims from the trade routes. As soon as Antioch was in Christian hands, the Genoese sought and obtained from Bohemond a quarter in the city with extraterritorial jurisdiction.[47] This is not to say that people from the Italian trading cities did not share the enthusiasm for the crusade; the letter of Pope Urban to Bologna reveals its strength there, while the letter of the people of Lucca shows great pride in one of their citizens who participated in the great expedition. It is merely and self-evidently the case that their motives were mixed and that brute material ends clearly loomed

---

[44] FC, p. 150; William of Tyre, *Historia rerum in partibus transmarinis gestarum, RHC Oc.* 1 (hereafter cited as WT), p. 392; Albert of Aachen, *Historia Iherosolimitana, RHC Oc.* 4 [hereafter cited as AA], pp. 503, 507, 517. For discussion of numbers in the armies see above pp. 2–3 and below pp. 122–42.

[45] J. Riley-Smith, 'The motives of the earliest crusaders and the settlement of Latin Palestine, 1095–1100', *English Historical Review*, 98 (1983), 721–36; A. V. Murray, 'The origins of the Frankish nobility of the kingdom of Jerusalem, 1100–1118', *Mediterranean Historical Review*, 4 (1989), 290–2.

[46] Ekkehard of Aura, *Chronicon Universale, MGH SS* 6. 17.

[47] Hagenmeyer, *Kreuzzugsbriefe*, pp. 155–56. The decision to send a fleet to the aid of the First Crusade was virtually the foundation of the greatness of Genoa: E. H. Byrne, 'The Genoese colonies in Syria' in L. J. Paetow, ed., *The Crusades and other Historical Essays presented to D. C. Munro* (New York, 1928), pp. 139–40.

large. In the case of Bohemond we see an individual whose first act on the crusade was to negotiate a position for himself. Anna tells us that at Constantinople in 1097 he sought the position of Grand Domestic of the East.[48] In a crude old world the niceties of proper intention about which the canon of the Council of Clermont was so concerned, and which lay at the heart of Augustine's theory of Just War and the superstructure which the church had built upon it, went by the board. The appeal to righteous war was a grant of righteous plunder or whatever other advantage was available – Tancred was later to treat the Church of the Nativity at Bethlehem as a mere prize of war. The lure of booty, the hope perhaps of land or position in the exotic east, personal or institutional advantage, a whole spectrum of motives drove men to the east.[49] Without a profound belief in God and a deep-seated fear of His judgment they would never have gone, but the very sanctity of their undertaking also sanctioned gain, and between these impulses they had no sense of dichotomy. Hence when Bohemond's army was pressed hard at Dorylaeum, the rallying cry went round: 'Stand fast all together, trusting in Christ and in the victory of the Holy Cross. Today, please God, you will all gain much booty'.[50]

So religious enthusiasm should be recognised as a simplification, a shorthand, for the sense of drive and purpose unleashed by Urban's appeal, and it should be remembered that large numbers probably had little choice but to go. This explains the fragility of the crusade and the scale of desertion.[51] It was in the end the motivation of many of the upper class who took the cross, but we have tended to see an explanation of motivation as an explanation of why the crusade succeeded. In fact religious enthusiasm had to be controlled and exploited, and buttressed by other solidarities which compounded and interacted with it.

This interaction transformed enthusiasm, itself a thing of fits and starts, into the morale of a fighting army. The crusaders came as the army of God to do His will, but men and women do not live constantly at that level of awareness. The day-to-day business of keeping alive and comfortable, not least perhaps keeping horses

---

[48] Hagenmeyer, *Kreuzzugsbriefe*, pp. 137–8, 165–7; Anna Comnena, *Alexiad*, tr. E. R. A. Sewter (London, 1969), (hereafter cited as *Alexiad*), p. 329; *GF*, p. 12 says that he was promised a principality around Antioch, though the passage is suspect on which see A. C. Krey, 'A neglected passage in the *Gesta* and its bearing on the literature of the First Crusade', Paetow, *Munro*, pp. 57–79.

[49] RA, p. 143.   [50] *GF*, pp. 19–20.   [51] See below p. 126–7.

alive, tends to erode high purpose as do want, hardship and fear, all factors which gravely effected the army. Many who went were following their masters, and could have had little choice in the matter. Urban, however, had disciplined the enthusiasm he tapped by insisting that those who joined the expedition should take a vow. This was not yet the subject of canonistic refinement, but it was nevertheless viewed by contemporaries as binding, an obligation to which the individual crusader could be recalled.[52] Moreover, there also existed an authority to recall him. Urban established Bishop Adhémar of Le Puy as his legate on the crusade. There has been much debate as to what exactly his role was, much of it wide of the mark, for it is evident that after his death on 1 August 1098 there was a vacuum in the ecclesiastical leadership of the crusade, as Raymond of Aguilers clearly discerned.[53] In January 1098, when the army was struggling in the siege of Antioch and famine stalked the camp, Adhémar proclaimed a fast with masses, processions and prayers, and we find precisely the same measures taken at the second siege of Antioch to prepare the army for the attack on Kerbogha. Similar measures were resorted to later – the barefoot procession out of Ma'arra, and the march around Jerusalem in clear imitation of Joshua's at Jericho, though by that time the strong will of Adhémar was gone. There was a conscious adoption of the pilgrim custom of walking barefoot the last few miles to the sacred shrine as the army approached Jerusalem. This liturgical aspect of the crusade is very marked – Raymond of Aguilers twice compared the army prepared for battle to a church procession, and such language is a commonplace.[54] We think of such activities as having a morale-raising effect. Contemporaries conceived their purpose as being to win God's favour and their effect as objective. Stephen of Valence transmitted the words of Christ to the army in Antioch: 'they shall return to me and I will return unto them, and within five days I will send them a mighty help'. It was the conviction of Divine favour, stimulated by penance and obedience to His will, which formed the bedrock of crusader conviction.[55]

---

[52] On those who probably had little choice see below pp. 126–7. On the nature of the vow see J. A. Brundage, 'The army of the First Crusade and the crusade vow: some reflections on a recent book', *Medieval Studies*, 33 (1971), 334–43 and especially 337–9 and more generally his *Medieval Canon Law and the Crusader* (Wisconsin, 1969).

[53] Hagenmeyer, *Kreuzzugsbriefe*, pp. 130–6; RA, p. 152.

[54] RA, p. 54, 137, 145, 81, 125; GF, p. 67.

[55] GF, p. 58. On their view of divine intervention see E. O. Blake, 'The formation of the "Crusade Idea"', *Journal of Ecclesiastical History*, 21 (1970), 11–31.

The importance of Adhémar of Le Puy as the moral arbiter of the crusade is revealed by events after his death. The army fell to quarrelling and many of the leaders seem to have developed ambitions of their own in North Syria. Unless there was a person to mobilise religious enthusiasm, which we are accustomed to seeing as the driving force of the crusade, it was too diffuse and too flaccid to stamp itself on events. But a new and different kind of leadership emerged. A group of Provençal clerics, amongst them the chronicler Raymond of Aguilers, emerged. They were the associates of Peter Bartholemew and the guardians of the Holy Lance which had become the token of the great victory over Kerbogha at Antioch. The visions of Peter Bartholemew are an articulation of the needs of the lesser people, many knights amongst them, who had been left out of the distribution of land and spoils after the fall of Antioch. For them plunder was a necessity impossible in what was now friendly territory in North Syria. Perhaps to their disgust some of the leaders had even taken to making friendly arrangements with nearby Muslim powers.[56] The economic and religious imperatives of these people were one, and they were mobilised by Peter Bartholemew and the Provençal clergy as a pressure upon the count of Toulouse and the other leaders. In the end, this coalition of forces, of the poor and the ambitions of Raymond of Toulouse, succeeded precisely because its ultimate demand, the liberation of Jerusalem, was shared by everyone and could not be argued against.[57] The role of Peter Bartholemew and the chaplains of the count of Toulouse indicates how the basic religious enthusiasm – and that term is itself a simplification for a compound of factors – had to be focussed and provided with leadership if there were to be success.

But the religious drive of the crusaders was buttressed by other solidarities. The people who went on the crusade came from all over Western Europe, and they seem to have fallen quite naturally into nations which grouped round their leading members. Raymond of Aguilers carefully explains which people were called Provençals, to distinguish them from the Franks, then in his account of the battle

---

[56] Albert of Aix records an early example, though Baldwin of Edessa had already paved the way in his treaty with Balduk; AA, pp. 436, 386.

[57] J. France, 'The crisis of the First Crusade: from the defeat of Kerbogah to the departure from Arqa', *Byzantion*, 40 (1970), 276–308. See also C. Morris, 'Policy and Visions. The case of the Holy Lance at Antioch', in J. Gillingham and J. C. Holt eds., *War and Government in the Middle Ages: Essays in Honour of J. O. Prestwich* (Woodbridge, 1984), pp. 33–45.

against Kerbogha indicates that everyone fought with his own leader and in his own *cognatio*, and similar expressions and ideas can be found in every account.[58] This was not invariable and the course of events changed allegiances. The Bretons certainly seem to have set off with the forces of Robert of Normandy – quite a natural alliance in terms of the Breton contribution to the army of 1066.[59] Many northerners seem to have entered the army of Toulouse in late 1098 when it was the only force confronting the enemy and preparing the way to Jerusalem, while at Jerusalem Gaston of Béarn, whose lands lay in the central Pyrenees, supervised the construction of the North French tower.[60] In general, however, people travelled with groups from their own nations. This is one of the bonds which held them together and attached them to strong leaders, for quite naturally such groups tended to gather round major figures. And here, perhaps, we come to one of the key reasons for the success of the First Crusade.

The pages of the chronicles are dominated by the 'Princes' who went on the crusade. Even for men at the time it was a vague term; William of Poitiers, struggling to explain the position of William of Normandy, expressed both the reality and the difficulties of definition when he commented that 'Normandy, long subject to the king of France was now almost erected into a kingdom'.[61]

Urban appealed for support to the rising military class of Europe as a whole – not to the kings and princes alone but to the whole gamut of lords, barons and knights. At the core of every army were the sworn vassals and household knights of the prince who led it. Probably the key factor which precipitated their decision to go was his. Although they were free agents as far as the matter of decision went – in theory no man could be bound to go on crusade by the decision of his lord – once the decision was made the vassal relationship usually continued. Such men, gathered round their great prince, formed the nucleus of each army. Albert of Aachen makes clear references to *sodales*, the household knights accompanying Godfrey, while Raymond of Aguilers speaks of the *familiares* of the

---

[58] RA, pp. 52, 79.

[59] Bauldry of Dol, *Historia Jerosolimitana*, *RHC OC.* 4 [hereafter cited as BD], 28, 33; R. A. Brown, 'Battle of Hastings' *Battle*, 3 (1980), 1–21.

[60] *GF*, pp. 12–13; RA, p. 145.

[61] William of Poitiers, *Gesta Guillelmi ducis Normannorum et regis Anglorum*, ed. R. Foreville (Paris, 1952) [hereafter cited as WP], p. 67. On the 'Princes' see J. Dunbabin, *France in the Making 843–1180*, (Oxford, 1985), pp. 162–222.

count of Toulouse. Bohemond also seems to have had his core following.[62] The riches and status of this group enabled them to dominate affairs. Urban may have revealed something of his intentions to the count of Toulouse. It was he and others who dominated the discussions with Alexius at Constantinople. The chroniclers tell us time after time that it was the council of princes which made the decisions. But beyond their sworn household followers there were many others only loosely bound, if at all, to them. French society below the level of the princes was dominated by lesser men, counts, viscounts, castellans and of course knights. Such people came as individuals to the crusade, many of them with their own followings. Farald, viscount of Thouars, was evidently in the Provençal contingent for he went with the count of Toulouse to witness Peter Bartholemew's revelation of the Holy Lance, yet he was a Poitevin whose ancestor had followed William the Conqueror in the Hastings campaign.[63] Some of these lesser figures appear briefly in the pages of Anna Comnena who describes how her father took oaths from many of them as well as the Princes. Evidently Alexius appreciated that they were free agents who would not feel bound by the promises of others. He was particularly concerned about Tancred who had slipped across the Bosphorous without taking the oath at Constantinople, and staged another oath-taking at Pelekanum to ensnare him.[64] There are hints that some of these people may have had influence on events. In the council held on 1 November 1098 to discuss the resumption of the crusade the *Gesta* reports the dispute between the count of Toulouse and Bohemond, then says that:'The bishops, with Duke Godfrey, the counts of Flanders and Normandy and the other leaders (*aliique seniores*)' considered their judgment. Who were these 'other leaders'? Stephen and Hugh of Vermandois, clearly princes, were long gone and there were no others of this rank. Raymond of Aguilers' account strongly implies that there were

[62] AA, 331; RA, p. 126. Riley-Smith, *Motives*, pp. 721–36, discusses these groups interestingly but A. V. Murray, 'The origins of the Frankish nobility', 281–99, can find only three people who may have been vassals of Godfrey before he went to the east and his kinsman Warner de Grez.

[63] RA, p. 75; C. de Vic et J. J. Vaissette, *Histoire Générale de Languedoc*, 5 vols. (Paris, 1743–5), 2. 309; Riley-Smith, *Idea of Crusading*, p. 76: Dunbabin, *France*, p. 202.

[64] Anna Comnena, *Alexiad*, on the unknown Count Raoul, pp. 323–4, on unnamed Franks, pp. 324–6 and on Tancred who received rich gifts at Pelekanum, p. 340; *GF*, p. 13 says that Tancred and Richard of the Principate deliberately evaded the oath at Constantinople.

many parties to the debate at this point.[65] This may have been an exceptional occasion, but it warns us against being hypnotised by the princes. Such substantial people maintained their own followings, their own nuclei, to which knights attached themselves from time to time as they did to those of the princes. An obvious example is Raymond Pilet who led a raid into Syria in the summer of 1098.[66] Generally the ties of nation and propinquity prevailed in such choices but there were anomalies. Some French knights, amongst them Boel of Chartres whose brother Fulcher played a notable role in the capture of Antioch, were in Bohemond's contingent. They may have come with the unnamed Franks who filtered into South Italy as the crusade got underway, or perhaps they had gone there to make their fortune and decided to press on.[67] Knights involved in the people's crusade attached themselves to others after its break-up, while the crisis provoked by the dispute over Antioch produced a lot of realignments, most notably that of Tancred and the author of the *Gesta* who joined the army of Toulouse. Below the knights there were the lesser crusaders and the non-combatants who in the first place, seem to have followed the main armies simply on the basis of propinquity and nation. Amongst them were the servants and armed followers of the great, but a substantial number of non-combatants were never anybody's responsibility, and they seem to have suffered appallingly. It is in the context of these extremely fluid relationships that the key role of the princes and perhaps some of the other great lords needs to be understood.

If the basic driving force of the crusade was a compound of greed, pride and religious zeal, cemented by personal, feudal and national bonds, the disaster of the so-called 'People's Crusade' enables us to understand the role of the princes and the great. The same motives influenced those who went on the People's Crusade, but there was no princely leadership. The army of Peter and the others was divided into nations which proved to be mutually hostile, and the enterprise fell apart. The powerful leaders were the capstone of the whole structure of the First Crusade. They had wealth, position and social prestige, and control of the common fund established amongst them for the general good.[68] The crusade was made up of free agents

---

[65] *GF*, p. 76; RA, pp. 93-4.   [66] *GF*, p. 73.   [67] *GF*, pp. 8, 7; RA, p. 64.

[68] AA, pp. 325-7 alludes to common funds being used to finance an armoured roof during the siege of Nicaea, and Riley-Smith, *Idea of Crusading*, pp. 68-9 draws attention to Raymond

who looked after themselves, providing their own food, horses and shelter, relating in different ways to the princes, for whom, however, this was not an entirely novel situation. Medieval armies were gatherings of groups who often stood in an uncertain relationship with their commander who could be surest of his household followers, intimates and mercenaries; quite often these last were the most reliable.[69] The crusade was certainly an event on a larger scale and overall it was a very fluid body. However, traditional loyalty, prestige, habit, all bound men to a prince. Above all we must remember the strength of fear which was especially strong on such an uncertain enterprise. The crusade was an experience of terrible hardship and we hear constantly of dearth and destitution. The famine at New Year 1098 was so bad that Adhémar tried to raise morale by religious celebrations, Bohemond threatened to leave because he was too poor to finance a long siege and Tatikios, the imperial representative on the expedition, revived the idea of a distant blockade, though this was prevented by the count of Toulouse.[70] Early in the siege of Antioch Anselm of Ribemont wrote to the archbishop of Rheims asking his prayers for thirteen who had died on the expedition, of whom seven had perished in battle and six by illness. Bishop Adhémar himself would die of plague on 1 August 1098. Stories of illness were commonplace, while at Ma'arra there was actual cannibalism amongst the poor.[71] Knights as well as others suffered from these miseries. Under these pressures, lesser men turned to the princes to sustain them.

The fortunes of individual princes fluctuated. Before the final battle against Kerbogha, Godfrey and Robert of Flanders had to beg horses from the count of Toulouse for themselves, but this should not be taken to indicate simple poverty. For at the same time Godfrey could provide Henry of Esch with commons. Rather, confined as they were in Antioch they could not get horses. Princes were rich and had presumably brought much money with them. They had been given rich presents by Alexius and would have taken the bulk of the loot on all occasions. After the capture of Antioch when

---

of Aguilers' references to something of the sort being used to pay for the Mahommeries Tower at Antioch and siege engines at Jerusalem; RA, pp. 62, 146.

[69] Strickland, *Conduct and Perception of War*, p. 381.

[70] He offered to compensate knights for loss of horses; J. France, 'The departure of Tatikios from the army of the First Crusade', *Bulletin of the Institute of Historical Research*, 44 (1971), 144–47, and see below pp. 242–5.

[71] Hagenmeyer, *Kreuzzusbriefe*, p. 145; RA, p. 84, 101.

the plunder had made them rich they took the poor into their service. During and after the siege of Antioch they obtained bases for themselves, such as that of Count Raymond at Rugia which he had seized at the beginning of the siege.[72] In an interesting aside Raymond of Aguilers tells us what was expected of a prince: Raymond of Toulouse, he says, had been ill and took custody of the Mahommeries tower to avoid charges of sloth, for it was being said in the army that he was prepared 'neither to fight nor to pay'.[73] The nominally independent elements in the army were drawn into the orbits of the Princes by want and the threat of want, as well as by considerations of propinquity, nation, political preference and military necessity. In the end they had little choice, for the situation in which they found themselves was always threatening and often desperate. It was to the princes that they turned to lead them into battle and to succour them in distress – 'to fight, to pay' neatly summarises the role of the princes which bound the army together and made it a dynamic fighting force. When it broke into Antioch but failed to win the citadel, and then was besieged by Kerbogah the army fell into despair. Some refused to fight and had to be burned out of their hiding places, while many fled. In this dark moment of despair Adhémar seized an opportunity to assert the unity of the army. On the night of 10–11 June a priest, Stephen of Valence, had a vision of Christ promising divine aid. Adhémar made the man take a public oath affirming its truth, then obliged the princes to swear that they would not desert.[74] In this moment of peril the crusaders were assured of God's aid, and of the presence and leadership of the princes. This affirmation of the solidarities which bound the expedition together was the basis for its recovery from despair.

The princes riveted the elements of the crusade together. By and large they managed to agree amongst themselves until the issue of the future of Antioch, and with it the whole expedition, became acute. Bohemond had been responsible for securing the betrayal of the city and he was promised control of it if the emperor did not come to their aid. Less than three weeks after the defeat of Kerbogah he was acting as ruler of the city, granting a charter to the Genoese on 14 July. When all met to discuss the future of the crusade in

---

[72] *GF*, p. 72–3, 26; AA, 472–8; Riley-Smith, *Idea of Crusading*, p. 75 shows that Bohemond held land towards Cilicia, Godfrey and Robert of Flanders towards Edessa, while Robert of Normandy held Laodicea.
[73] RA, p. 62.   [74] *GF*, pp. 57–9; RA, pp. 72–4.

November, it was in the knowledge that Alexius had broken off his attempt to relieve Antioch. A letter from the leaders to Urban II, dated 11 September 1098, clearly reflected bitter hostility to the Byzantines, and in these circumstances only Raymond of Toulouse was prepared to stand for the Byzantine alliance.[75] This quarrel over Antioch, the death of Adhémar of Le Puy on 1 August 1098, and many other doubts and worries led the leaders to hesitate, and it was their uncertainty which stalled the crusade and precipitated the alternative leadership of a visionary, Peter Bartholemew and his clerical associates who, playing upon the driving force of the crusade, supplemented the power of the princes. It was an unstable situation which could not continue, but it reveals how powerful was the basic religious motivation of the crusaders and the influence of the princes. When they diverged the crusade stalled.

There can be no doubt that religious enthusiasm was fundamental to the success of the First Crusade. Participation offered an escape from the certainty of hell-fire, and death in such a glorious cause the consolations of martyrdom.[76] This was not an unalloyed and pure idealism. The formulations of the church might separate out 'devotion' from 'honour and money' but for the laity, righteous war invoked rightful reward. Fine distinctions were submerged in a blast of enthusiasm for a skilfully publicised idea which seemed, for a moment, to offer a bridge between the military and religious preoccupations of the European upper classes. But motivation in itself goes only part of the way to explaining the success of the crusade. That enthusiasm was structured by the form of the vow which gave the clergy some influence and, buttressed by national and feudal solidarity, centred on the great princes. The binding role of the princes can easily be underestimated for by modern standards this was a ramshackle army. But contemporary armies were not monolithic and it was of these that the leaders had experience. When they fell to arguing at the very moment that the Papal Legate died, the

---

[75] Hagenmeyer, *Kreuzzugsbriefe*, pp. 161–5; *GF*, p. 75; RA, p. 93.

[76] J. Riley-Smith, 'Death on the First Crusade', in D. M. Loades, ed., *The End of Strife*, (Oxford, 1984) pp. 14–31 has advanced the idea that the concept of martyrdom was developed during the First Crusade, but J. Flori, 'Mort et martyre des guerriers vers 1100. L'example de la première croisade', *Cahiers de Civilisation Médiévales*, 34 (1991), 121–39, establishes clearly that this was already an accepted idea. Flori has also suggested that the ecclesiastical notion of the crusader ideal was met with some reserve in aristocratic circles in France: 'Pur eshalcier sainte crestiënte. Croisade, guerre sainte et guerre juste dans les anciennes chansons de geste françaises', *Le Moyen Age*, 5 (1991), 171–87.

solidarities which had driven on the crusade almost collapsed. The politics of the crusade after the capture of Antioch are fascinating, but they are important because of what they reveal about the forces which drove the expedition on. The basic morale upon which the fighting qualities of the crusade depended had a complex make-up, but it was sufficiently fierce to lay the foundations of victory in the east. That victory, of course, owed something to other factors, most notably the divisions of the Islamic world, the military consequences of which will be considered below. But in this examination of the history of the First Crusade the emphasis will be upon the military experience of its participants and the way they drew upon and adapted this in the novel experience which brought victory in the east.

CHAPTER 2

War in the West

In 1077 Robert Curthose broke with his father, William the Conqueror, after a spectacular quarrel with his brothers William and Henry. He immediately tried to seize the castle of Rouen but was foiled by the vigilance of his father's butler, Roger of Ivry. When Godfrey de Bouillon's enemy Albert of Namur wanted to challenge his control of the family holding at Bouillon in 1082, he tried to build a castle at Mirwart in order to menace the lands which depended on the castle at Bouillon upon which were enfeoffed the knights who formed the core of Godfrey's *mouvance*.[1] In both cases the first step in the campaign was to secure a fortification. Here we come face to face with a most important facet of warfare in the eleventh century – the key importance of strongpoints. The castle at Rouen would have enabled Curthose to control his father's capital, giving a certain reality to his earlier claim to hold the duchy in his own right, and it would have provided a rallying point at which to gather all the malcontents of the duchy who, in the event, proved ready enough to rally elsewhere. Albert would probably have built a wooden castle at Mirwart and from there would have ravaged the lands of Godfrey's vassals around Bouillon in a campaign which could have shaken their loyalty by undermining their economic base and that of Godfrey himself. Both cases illustrate another facet of contemporary warfare – exploitation of the equivocal loyalties of the feudal world. When Prince Louis of France went to war with William II of England, his biographer, Suger, complained that whilst English prisoners were quickly ransomed, French ones, being poorer, had to swear to support the English king.[2] War turned on the possession of

---

[1] OV, 2. 359; C. W. David, *Robert Curthose*, Duke of Normany (Cambridge Mass., 1920), pp. 17–22; F. Barlow, *William Rufus* (London, 1983), pp. 33–34; J. C. Andressohn, *The Ancestry and Life of Godfrey de Bouillon* (Bloomington, 1947), p. 38; H. E. Mayer, *Mélanges*, pp. 24–5.

[2] Suger of St-Denis, *Vita Ludovici grossi Regis*, ed. H. Waquet (Paris, 1929), pp. 8–11.

fortifications, and most military activity was related to possession of them; it was a warfare of position. Fighting in the open field was not uncommon, but it was rarely sought and large-scale battle was especially rare. It was, after all, a very risky business. In 992, a century before the crusade, Conan of Brittany had defeated his enemy, Fulk of Anjou, at Conquereuil, but in the pursuit he paused to strip off his armour because of the heat of the day – alas he had chosen to do so close to the hiding place of some Angevins who promptly killed him and so reversed the apparent decision of battle. Godfrey was almost certainly present in support of Henry IV at the battle of Elster in 1085, when the forces of the anti-king Rudolf triumphed on the field only to see their victory nullified because Rudolf was killed.[3] But it was not merely because it was chancy and uncertain that battle was avoided. All military activity depends on luck and phrases like the 'fog of war' or the 'smoke of battle' express the proverbial uncertainty which surrounds it in all ages. Nor was it merely that in battle the commander's own life was at risk, though that might sometimes have been a factor. Far more important was that seizure or neutralisation of an enemy strong-point, perhaps by subverting a leader's vassals, offered the best and surest, in so far as anything in war could be sure, method of achieving the purpose of war – the destruction of the enemy, or more commonly, his enfeeblement to the point where he could no longer resist your will.

Our perspective upon war is, of course, affected by recent experience in which battle has been central in war. In two terrible world wars the commanders on either side strove to bring their enemies to battle, to smash their armies in the field, to bring them, even, to 'unconditional surrender'. Such strategies were made possible by the advance of technology which by the late nineteenth century was capable of creating, feeding, supplying and controlling a nation in arms. Without the steam engine, without tinned food and all the related technology, there could have been no Verdun, no Somme, none of the astonishing allied victories of 1918 when the great German army, 'the motor of the war' was smashed.[4] Without the

---

[3] *Glaber*, pp. 56–61; H. Delbrück, *History of the Art of War in the Middle Ages in the Framework of Political History*, tr. J. Renfroe (Berlin, 1923, London, 1982), 3. 140–1; H. Glaesener, 'Godefroi de Bouillon et la bataille de l'Elster', *Revue des Études Historiques*, 105 (1938), 253–64.

[4] The phrase is that of J. Terraine, *The White Heat: the New Warfare 1914–18* (London, 1982) pp. 44, 91, 279.

internal combustion engine there could have been no Stalingrad, no Battle of Berlin, no D-Day 6 June 1944. Allied to this technological development was conceptual development. The nation state is the product of changing ideas interacting with technical possibilities. When advanced nations go to war they provide their own vocabulary of totality – 'the Home Front', 'attrition', 'guerre de matériele', unknown to earlier ages. 'Total War', in which all the efforts of an extensive and highly organised society are geared to total victory is the creation of modern industrial society and its apogee is battle: battle on land, on the sea, in the air, or in any combination of these. The aim is to smash the enemy. Of course the second half of the twentieth century has seen more limited wars, but the major conflicts, Korea, Vietnam, the Gulf, have involved the destruction and creation of whole societies. And looming over all has been the fear of the ultimate conflict between the Superpowers, in which not merely nations, but even mankind itself might be annihilated by weapons of mass-destruction. The First World War, the Second and the Cold War have accustomed all the generations of the twentieth century to see the purpose of war as violent and sudden destruction on a total scale in which battle is the necessary way by which our will can be imposed upon the enemy. It takes an enormous effort to look beyond those assumptions to a different kind of war in a different kind of society. Of course the historian's problem always is to step out of his age and look with a clear mind at a different environment. But in the study of war this is peculiarly difficult, for the very image of war today is the image of battle. An entire experience of great complexity and length can be fused on our retinas by a single image – the Second World War by a Lancaster Bomber, for example. A military helicopter instantly recalls Vietnam for a whole generation which lived through it. Television and the media have created not merely pictures of particular moments of conflict, but symbols of combat which instantly spring to mind whenever war is discussed, clouding our minds by their sheer power. And our experience of war is reinforced to an astonishing degree by much modern writing about it. Military history has always been rather a special study in that many of its devotees hope to learn by it and implement its lessons in a direct way. Vegetius remains popular amongst military men not because of its historical value but because he provides practical advice which is still relevant.[5] But the involvement of practitioners of war carries certain risks, most obviously that they will be thinking of their own world whose assumptions they will project upon the past. It is this which has particularly distorted the study of medieval military history.

Clausewitz's *Vom Kriege*, which appeared shortly after his death in 1831 is not a study of medieval history, but no modern writer on war has had more widespread impact on thinkers.[6] His dictum that war is 'a continuation of political relations, a carrying out of the same by other means' is now a cliché. His work appeared and made its greatest impact at the very time when modern scientific historical method was being developed, primarily in Germany. Hans Delbrück (1848–1929) belonged to a generation profoundly marked by such ideas and his monumental work, *A history of the art of war within the framework of political history*, the very title of which reflects Clausewitz's most famous dictum, was extraordinarily influential. His approach to the subject was influenced by Clausewitz's notion of the need to destroy the enemy's forces in battle. The book tends to read as a series of battle descriptions, especially in Book II of the third volume which covers the period under consideration here.[7] From Clausewitz has sprung a whole genre of writing on the theme of 'great battles' and it has coloured our view of war. In the English-speaking world this was greatly reinforced by Sir Charles Oman in his *History of the art of war in the middle ages* which analysed the subject in the light of the nineteenth-century theory of 'decisive battle'. His account of war in the eleventh century turns on two battles, Hastings and Dyrrachium, in a chapter entitled 'Last struggles of infantry'. In the true spirit of Clausewitz whose analysis of his experiences in the Napoleonic wars led him to emphasise mobility ('It is better to act quickly and to err than to hesitate'; 'A

---

[5] Flavius Vegetius Renatus, *De Re Militari* ed. C. Lang (Leipzig, 1885). His was the most popular treatise on war in the Middle Ages and it remains in use to this day. There is an English translation by T. R. Phillips, *Roots of Strategy* (London, 1943), pp. 35–94 based on Clarke's of 1767. On indications of its popularity in the Middle Ages see C. R. Schrader, 'A handlist of extant manuscripts containing the De Re Militari of Flavius Vegetius Renatus', *Scriptorium*, 33 (1979), 280–305 and B. S. Bachrach, 'The practical use of Vegetius's De Re Militari during the early Middle Ages', *The Historian*, 21–7 (1985), 239–55.

[6] K. P. G. von Clausewitz, *Vom Kriege* (Berlin, 1832–4), vols 1–3 of his collected writings. English tr. J. J. Graham, 3 vols (London, 1873), revised F. N. Maude, 3 vols (London, 1908).

[7] See above n. 3.

fundamental principle is never to remain completely passive'),
Oman speaks disparagingly of the Anglo-Saxons, 'The stationary
tactic of the phalanx of axemen had failed', and concludes that 'The
supremacy of the feudal horseman was finally established.' Oman's
history of medieval warfare is truly battle history and his impact
upon English-speaking writers has been enormous.[8] This view of
medieval warfare as dominated by battle has been reinforced by
another trend in nineteenth-century historiography.

The figure of Charles the Great loomed large in the writings of
French and German nationalists of the nineteenth century who
made strenuous effort to claim him as one of their own. Discovering
an explanation for the rise of the Carolingian empire was, for them,
a matter of deep concern. For Delbrück there was a military explanation. Faced with attack by Muslim cavalry from Spain, Charles
Martel invented the knight, the heavily armoured cavalryman, for
whose support he developed the fief, the foundation of feudalism. It
was this unique weapon at its most effective in the massive cavalry
charge with its enormous 'shock effect', which enabled the Carol-
ingians to build their empire. This view was for long repeated by
orthodox text-books and its tenacious hold on historian's minds can
be explained by its extraordinary scope as an explanation. The
invention of heavy cavalry explained not only the rise of the knight
and the growth of the Carolingian empire, but also the development
of feudalism. The depth of explanation was even further improved
by the suggestion that it was the invention and dissemination of the
stirrup which gave the horseman stability and made possible the
armoured knight. Thus technology served as a buttress to an already
impressive and symmetrical structure.[9] Unfortunately there is
almost no evidence to sustain this theory. We know very little about
the battle of Poitiers in 732 when Charles Martel defeated an
Islamic army from Spain, and the whole argument that his immediate successors used a new kind of cavalry whose shock effect shattered their enemies is a nonsense.[10] The truth of the matter would

---

[8] C. Oman, *History of the Art of War in the Middle Ages*, 2 vols (London, 1924), 252, 1. 149–68, 165, 167.

[9] Delbrück, *History of the Art of War* 3. 13–92; L. White, *Medieval Technology and Social Change* (Oxford, 1962), but see the review by R. H. Hilton and P. H. Sawyer, 'Technical determi-nism: the stirrup and the plough', *Past and Present* 24 (1963), 90–100.

[10] B. S. Bachrach, 'Charles Martel, shock combat, the stirrup and feudalism', *Studies in Medieval and Renaissance History*, 7 (1970), 45–75 and 'Was the Marchfield part of the Frankish constitution?' *Medieval Studies*, 36 (1974), 178–86.

seem to be that no-one invented the mailed cavalryman, whom we later in English call the knight and in French *chevalier*. Rather, cavalry had always been an element in armies. The better off preferred to ride rather than walk, and tried to protect themselves with the most effective kinds of armour. By the early tenth century, when we first hear reports of heavily armoured men being used in the mass amongst both the east and west Franks, the stirrup and the high saddle, both of which were necessary to provide security for the horseman, seem to have evolved and spread, and chain-mail appears to have been improving. More decisively the pressure of external attack and internecine conflict within the Carolingian lands led the kings and princes to disseminate land to their followers as a means of providing themselves with well-armed men. Even so, the classic mass charge with couched lance generating shock at the point of impact was not yet any kind of norm, as a glance at the Bayeux tapestry will show.[11] But the real trouble with the Oman/ Delbrück theory was that in focussing upon the knight it provided us all not merely with an idea but also with an image of war as an affair of battle in the open field. If warfare in the eleventh century was an affair of knights, were these surely not romantic figures whose very function was the charge in open battle? This is, after all, the image provided by the *Song of Roland* and much later literature such as the Arthurian cycle, which in one way or another has filtered through into the consciousness of almost all who have dealings with the medieval world. The reality of eleventh-century warfare, to which the leaders and their followers on the First Crusade were accustomed, was altogether less glamorous. The knight as a soldier was adapted to his economic and social context, to the technical possibilities available and their limitations and to the ideas of that day of what war was about.

It is clear that by the end of the tenth century the great cleavage in West Frankish society was that between men who could arm themselves properly for war and those who could not, who formed the mass of the population. But this superior group was not homogenous and the term noble was quite distinct from that of knight. The knights were, in most of Europe, an inferior group often closer to the peasantry than to the aristocracy they served. In Spain, portions of

---

[11] J. France, 'La guerre dans la France féodale à la fin du IX et au X siècles', *Revue Belge d'Histoire Militaire*, 23 (1979), 177–98 and see the discussion below p. 73–4.

land were created for the support of both cavalrymen (*caballerías*)
and infantry (*peonías*) to defend the newly-won plains and *caballeros
villanos* subsisted with *caballeros hidalgos*.[12] In recent years the status
of the Anglo-Norman knight has been highly controversial, but the
balance of discussion suggests that there were enormous differences
in wealth and status in a section of society largely removed from that
nobility.[13] In Southern Europe, knights remained associated with
the peasantry from whom they seem to have emerged, while in the
Germanic lands they arose from the *ministeriales*. Even in the north of
France knights were a very mixed class. Only in the Mâconnais had
their fusion with the nobility seriously begun by the time of the
crusade. Duby found that most of the knights in one area of the
Mâconnais were of noble descent, but he was surveying only
endowed knights.[14] William of Jumièges tells the tale of a smith of
Beauvais who brought a small present for Duke William who
responded munificently with money and two horses; a year later the
smith returned offering his two sons in service, unmistakably military, to the Conqueror.[15] Such men were in the service of the
castellans, counts and princes who dominated contemporary society
and what they offered was council and advice, as all followers ought,
but above all military service. For this they might be rewarded with
cash, with maintenance in a lordly household, or with land, or
indeed with all three either at once or at various times. They were
soldiers as their title proclaimed, and primarily horsemen. In the
south, terms such as *caballarius* remained important. But although
they were a military class many of them were also involved in other

[12] E. Lourie, 'A society organised for war – medieval Spain', *Past and Present*, 35 (1966), 55–6,
60; J. Power, 'Origins and development of municipal military service in the Genoese and
Castillian reconquest', *Traditio*, 26 (1970), 91–112.

[13] For the controversy on the status of the Norman knight compare S. Harvey, 'The knight
and the knight's fee in England', *Past and Present*, 49 (1970), 3–43, with R. A. Brown, 'The
status of the Norman knight', in Gillingham and Holt, eds., *War and Government*, pp. 18–32.
See also J. Gillingham, 'The introduction of knight service into England', *Battle*, 4 (1981),
53–64 and the survey of literature by T. Hunt, 'Emergence of the knight in England', in W.
H. Jackson, *Knighthood in Medieval Literature (Woodbridge, 1981)*.

[14] Duby, *Mâconnaise*, pp. 411–26; for a survey of recent work on the status of the knight in
eleventh century Europe see J. P. Poly and P. Bournazel, *The Feudal Transformation,
800–1200*, tr. C. Higgitt (New York, 1991), pp. 98–102, and pp. 102–107 for a tentative
explanation of the precocity of the Mâconnaise. From a rather different point of view
Murray, *Reason and Society*, pp. 90–4, points to the division at this time between noble and
knight.

[15] William of Jumièges, *Gesta Normannorum Ducum*, ed. J. Marx (Paris, 1914), pp. 106–8,
quoted by R. H. C. Davis, 'The Warhorses of the Normans', *Battle*, 10 (1987), 67; Flori,
L'essor de la chevalerie, p. 119–41.

matters – primarily farming. Thus they were not, in the simple sense, professional soldiers and any sizeable gathering would have had something of the character of a militia.

However, their military function was very demanding for the technology of the age demanded leadership by a military élite. In a relatively poor agricultural society only a few could afford to clothe themselves in iron, with the pointed helmet, the hauberk or chain mail shirt (with or without coif) and the heavy wooden kite-shaped shield which covered the horseman on his left side from thigh to shoulder. The weapons of attack remained largely what they had always been: the sword, the bow, the axe, the club in its various forms and the spear, though perhaps they were better made and more often of iron than ever before. To handle all these successfully, the soldier needed not merely muscles, but an athletic musculature. Only the well-to-do had both the leisure to train their sons from an early age and the wealth to equip them. In the Mâconnais in the eleventh century a horse cost between twenty and fifty sous, five times the price of an ox which was probably the most valuable possession of a peasant, while a hauberk cost 100 sous, the price of a good manse.[16] Godfrey de Bouillon was only sixteen when his uncle Godfrey the Hunchback designated him as heir, but Lambert of Hersfeld describes him as being already active in military matters.[17] Ordericus gives us an interesting insight into the risks of knightly status in his account of the seven sons of Giroie, one of the benefactors of his abbey of St Evroul. Arnold, the eldest, was in a 'friendly wrestling match', when he was thrown against the edge of a step, and with three ribs broken, died within three days. Hugh, the sixth son, was killed by a carelessly thrown lance while he, his brothers and friends were practising. Giroie, the youngest, died of madness returning from a raid, while Fulk, the third son, was killed fighting in the retinue of Gilbert of Brionne. The exercises for war, it seems, were as lethal as the thing itself.[18] The use of weapons was itself demanding, but so was the learning of horsemanship. War-horses were specially bred and trained animals, but even so the rider must have had to master his beast ruthlessly to make it face the horrors of battle. The war for which these young men trained was primarily a

[16] On weaponry in general see C. Blair, *European Arms and Armour* (London, 1958); Duby, *Mâconnaise*, p. 239.
[17] Lambert of Hersfeld, ed. E. Holder-Egger (Hamburg, 1981), *MGH SS* 3. 136.
[18] OV, 2. 23–31.

war of close combat – the killing ground was literally the length of a
man's arm. The Frankish sword of this age was primarily a hacking
weapon with a relatively blunt point. It tended to be about 76–83
centimetres long and to have a shallow valley running down its
length. Such weapons were expensive and individually crafted, and
in surviving cases balance remarkably well so their 1.5-kilogram
weight could be easily swung.[19] The spear might be thrown, as is
seen in the Bayeux tapestry, but in the hands of both footmen and
cavalry it was a weapon for the thrust. The knight's hauberk
probably could not turn a solid thrust from a spear or a cut of the
sword which landed squarely, but it seems to have been worn over a
padded garment and so may have been fairly effective against
glancing blows which must have been common at close quarters in
the flailing scrum of battle when the shield would be relied on for
protection. Its split skirt fell over the thighs giving them some
protection. The conical steel helmet looks a precarious affair, but it
was probably provided with a lining for security. Commonly it had
a nasal to protect the face, and sometimes a metal bar at the rear.
Again it was probably little protection against a direct blow such as
that which fell upon Robert Fitzhamon at the siege of Falaise in
1106 leaving him lingering as an idiot for a while before he died. But
it was evidently well secured and especially when worn over the mail
hood or coif could be effective against the glancing blow; such a
combination saved Henry I from a heavy blow at Brémule in 1119.[20]
Medieval fighting must have looked like a cross between a primitive
football mêlée, Afghan polo and a butcher's yard, as men, mounted
and on foot, hacked and jabbed at one another.[21] The very close
nature of the conflict explains much about the warrior ethic which
underlies chivalry – the emphasis upon personal combat, personal
bravery and comradeship. It was a very intimate affair. At the battle

[19] In the Church of the Holy Sepulchre at Jerusalem the Franciscans hold the 'Sword of
Godfrey de Bouillon'; its blade is approximately eighty-eight centimetres long and about
four centimetres wide at the hilt which is very fine. There is no channel down the middle,
only a markedly raised ridge. I was unable to handle it so the measurements taken through
glass are approximate.
[20] William of Malmesbury, *Gesta regum Anglorum*, ed. T. D. Hardy, 2 vols. (London, 1840)
(hereafter cited as *GR*) 2. 479; OV, 6. 238–9.
[21] On arms and armour in the late eleventh century see I. Pierce, 'Arms, armour and warfare'
237–58; 'The knight, his arms and armour' pp. 152–64. On the special significance of the
sword R. E. Oakeshott, *The Sword in the Age of Chivalry* (London, 1981). For a revealing
discussion of the wounds inflicted by medieval weapons B. Thordeman, *Armour from the
Battle of Wisby 1361* (Uppsala, 1939).

of Elster in 1080 where Godfrey de Bouillon probably fought, the soldiers of Henry IV jeered at the troops of the anti-king Rudolf who were unable to cross marshy land to attack.[22] The young knight who could afford all the panoply of war was well equipped, well protected and mobile – but the limitations of his equipment are all too evident. He needed spare horses, for to ride his *destrier* all the time was an obvious folly. To feed and arm him he needed servants, squires as they would later be called, who would have to have horses to be mobile. His mobility was thus hampered by his supports. To ride alone was of course folly – knights worked with others in the business of war. In close woodland or broken ground his advantages of height and weight were largely nullified. A century after the First Crusade Gerald of Wales would comment: 'When one is fighting only in the hills, woods or marshes ... with a complicated armour and high curved saddles, it is difficult to dismount from a horse, even more difficult to mount and yet more difficult to get around on foot when necessary'.[23] The Welsh about whom Gerald was talking were, of course, pre-eminent as archers who appear to have been an element in almost all forces at this time.

Archers formed a very important part of the 'other ranks' of an eleventh-century army. Our sources tend to focus on the armoured knights, whose clerical relatives were after all the authors of the history of the age. The Bayeux Tapestry, an invaluable source for the military history of the period, shows the battle as essentially one between heavily armoured men, on the Norman side mounted. It was almost certainly commissioned by Odo of Bayeux and such an expensive undertaking must have been directed to the influential – the upper class. Their taste in literature – *Chanson de Roland* – gives us some idea of how they liked to see themselves, and to some extent the tapestry is an epic strip cartoon.[24] But the executors knew that archers played an important part, and they portrayed no fewer than twenty-nine. But of these only six are in the main strip. They appear to be better equipped than those in the lower margin, but this may be simply a function of scale; a lot of the marginal figures are mere sketches. Of the six major representations one is English, a pigmy beside the armoured men, whose small size probably is an indication

[22] Delbrück, *History of the Art of War* 3. 136–9.
[23] Gerald of Wales, *Opera*, ed. J. S. Brewer and J. Dimock, 8 vols. (London, 1867–91), 6. 395–7.
[24] France, 'La guerre dans la France féodale', 195–8.

of low social status. Only one Norman archer is shown mounted and it has been suggested that he had probably seized a horse for the pursuit.[25] But one of the archers is well equipped with the same helmet and hauberk as the knights, and this introduces the possibility that he was of that status. The bow was the weapon of the poor man because it was cheap, a simple stave which at this time was probably not much shorter than the classic six-foot English longbow of the later middle ages.[26] But we know that the Conqueror was a formidable bowman, as was Robert Curthose.[27] These references may be to the bow's use for hunting, but at the siege of Jerusalem Godfrey himself did not hesitate to seize a bow and use it accurately. In 1103 his brother, Baldwin king of Jerusalem, had a *magister sagittariorum*, one Reinoldus who is explicitly referred to as a *miles Regis*, and who was himself a notable archer.[28] The knight was not yet a member of an exclusive social caste with characteristic weaponry. Wace speaks of the archers at the battle of Varaville in 1057, and later during the campaign of 1066, as specialists, but this may reflect the conditions of the time in which he was writing, a century later.[29] The bow was a fearsome weapon, deadly even to the best equipped knights. Henry I was saved from an arrow strike by his mail, but perhaps his armour was of unusually high quality.[30] In the Bayeux Tapestry we have ample testimony to its effectiveness – mailed bodies stuck with arrows. Interestingly, bodies with arrows in them occur in the margin only in those sections where the action in the main part shows arrows in shields, though there are no marginal bodies in the pasage where Harold falls. This appears to be an effort to convey the episodic use of archers between attacks by others.[31] All these figures are armed with the simple stave-bow, perhaps a little shorter than the classic six-foot longbow. It is puzzling that the tapestry never depicts a crossbow, for both William of Poitiers and the *Carmen de Hastingae proelio* say they were used at Hastings. This mechanical bow with its short four-sided heavy-tipped quarrels must have been a very expensive weapon and seems to have been much less common than the ordinary stave-

[25] J. Bradbury, *The Medieval Archer*, (Woodbridge, 1985), pp. 17–38.   [26] *ibid*, pp. 36–7.
[27] *GR*, 2. 335; OV, 2. 357.   [28] Bradbury, *Medieval Archer*, p. 25; AA, 475, 602.
[29] *Wace's Roman de Rou et des Ducs de Normandie*, ed. H. Andresen, 2 vols. (Bonn, 1877–79), 3. 5, 206–208, 3. 7, 685–96, 3. 488–98 (hereafter cited as *Wace*).
[30] *GR*, 2. 477.
[31] *The Bayeux Tapestry*, ed. D. M. Wilson (London, 1985) [hereafter cited as *BT*], Pls. 62, 63, 70, 71.

bow.[32] But contemporaries commented upon its effectiveness, notably Anna Comnena, who, however, was writing long after the First Crusade.[33] Its use is mentioned frequently in the sources for the First Crusade. The crossbow had many distinguished victims. In 1106 at Candé Count Geoffrey of Anjou was killed by a crossbow, and in the same year Roger of Gloucester fell victim at the siege of Falaise while Theobald of Blois was wounded by one at Alençon in 1118. But Richard I of England who was struck by a bolt at Chalus in 1199 is the best known of all.[34] Bows of all kinds could be used with considerable accuracy. At Bourgthéroulde in 1124 Henry I's archers successfully executed orders to cut down horses rather than knights, and William Crispin's charge at Brémule in 1119 seems to have been destroyed by archery which killed his horse and those of eighty-six others. Such events explain Ordericus's comment 'the unarmed horse was a surer target than the armoured knight'. They also explain the savagery with which victorious knights often treated defeated archers, massacring them indiscriminately.[35] The church's ban on the use of such weapons against Christians at the Second Lateran Council in 1139 is a testimony both to the effectiveness of archery, and the ineffectiveness of such ecclesiastical legislation. But the effectiveness of the archer was also circumscribed. In attack archers needed to be protected against sallies for they were lightly protected and vulnerable in the open. They were at their best in defence, and most particularly in defence of fortifications.

The bow was very valuable but it was usually necessary to close with a determined enemy to destroy him. It is this which explains the dominant role of fortifications in war on the eve of the First Crusade, for the attacker was exposed to missiles on his approach and then had to fight at a disadvantage. In 892 a major Danish army landed in Kent and stormed a half-completed *burh* even though it was manned only by a few peasants.[36] Clearly this *burh* was not very formidable – heaped earth, perhaps with a walkway and

---

[32] For the crossbow at Hastings see WP, p. 184, *Carmen de Hastingae proelio*, ed. C. Morton and H. Munz (Oxford, 1972), Appendix C, pp. 112–15; Bradbury, *Medieval Archer*, pp. 26–7, 8–11. For its history R. Payne-Gallwey, *The Crossbow*, (London, 1903).

[33] *Alexiad*, pp. 316–17; J. France, 'Anna Comnena'; 'Loud, 'Anna Komnena' and her sources for the Normans of South Italy', in G. Loud and I. N. Wood, eds., *Church and Chronicle in the Middle Ages: Essays presented to J. Taylor* (London, 1991), pp. 41–57.

[34] AA, pp. 324, 411; OV 6. 76; Bradbury, *Medieval Archer*, pp. 45, 3; *GR*, 2. 475.

[35] Strickland, *Conduct and Perception of War*, pp. 95–7, 140.

[36] *The Anglo-Saxon Chronicle*, ed. D. Whitelock (London, 1961) [hereafter cited as *ASC*], p. 892.

palisade, like so many of the similar structures which Alfred began to build across southern England. Yet the Danes thought it worthy of attack, for it could form a base for operations against them, inhibiting them from spreading across the countryside in raids searching for food. When we think of fortifications we think of walled cities or castles whose crumbling remains are such a feature of the European landscape. But fortifications were often much humbler things. A study of a small part of Normandy covering an area of 12 kilometres by twenty kilometres, has revealed three or four stone castles and no fewer than twenty-eight earthwork strongholds. This multiplicity of defences in the feudal age explains the wide vocabulary, so puzzling to historians, used to describe strongpoints.[37] What is important to realise here is how difficult it was for troops to take even a modest fortification. Any castle could be blockaded, but this exposed the attackers to starvation especially if the garrison had had enough warning to devastate the countryside. On the other hand if it came to assault the attackers had other problems. The medieval soldier, even equipped with full armour, was not massively weighed down by it. The hauberk probably weighed about eleven kilograms and the sword about one and a half kilograms. If we add to that a few kilograms (say two) for the helmet, padded undergarment etc., weight was not excessive. But the shield must have been much heavier: it was made of wood and metal with leather straps and, with its long kite shape, was difficult to manipulate. No examples have survived, but a fair guess about weight would be fourteen kilograms. A total of twenty-seven to thirty-two kilograms for equipment would seem very modest, especially when we consider that a modern infantryman will carry into battle fifty-five to sixty-five kilograms including his rifle.[38] However, negotiating any sharp slope in this rather clumsy clothing must have been a difficult business, especially in wet weather, so that even a modest earthwork, especially if crowned with a palisade and a level platform for the defenders, would find the attacker at a disadvantage. A ditch at the foot of the slope would enhance the

---

[37] M. Fixot, *Les Fortifications de Terre et les Origines Féodales dans le Cinglais* (Caen, 1968), cited in P. Contamine, *War in the Middle Ages*, tr. M. Jones (London, 1984), p. 46; J. F. Verbruggen, 'Note sur le sens des mots castrum, castellum et quelques autres expressions qui désignent des fortifications', *Revue Belge de Philologie et d'Histoire*, 27 (1950), 147–55.

[38] The estimates of the weight of eleventh-century armour are by Pierce, *Battle*, 240, 253–7. My information about the modern infantry comes from the army depot in Pembroke, for which I offer thanks.

defender's position enormously. Of course those assaulting could throw missiles and deploy archers, but so could the defenders and they could hide behind their palisade while the attacker had to expose himself. All this may seem a little elementary, but this kind of reality does not often figure in books about war. A simple earthwork protected by a ditch is an insurmountable obstacle to a horseman, who must descend for an attack on foot in which he is at a disadvantage. Of course a strong and determined attacker could always take a minor fort, as the Danes proved in 892, but at what cost, and how often had it to be repeated? The *burhs* of Alfred were, for the most part, quite minor, but there were a lot of them and the same system may have been used by Henry the Fowler in Germany in the early tenth century.[39] A precisely similar situation arose in Normandy out of quite different circumstances almost on the eve of the First Crusade. After the death of the Conqueror in 1087 William Rufus, king of England, disputed his brother Robert Curthose's possession of Normandy in a war which exacerbated the already poor situation of the duchy caused by the weakness of Robert's rule. In 1091 the two brothers reached an uneasy *modus vivendi* and set about restoring ducal rights in a Council at Caen which insisted that 'No-one in Normandy may dig a ditch in open country unless from the bottom of this ditch the earth can be thrown out of it without the aid of a ladder, nor may he set up more than a palisade which must have neither redan nor rampart-walk'. Clearly it is the problem of the well-built earthwork circle which could be erected easily by anyone with access to labour which the two rulers had in mind. When the Conqueror landed at Hastings in 1066 almost his first act, as shown in the Bayeux tapestry, was to throw up an earthwork crowned by a wooden palisade. Such constructions needed no skilled architect, no masons, and evidently could be built quickly provided there was labour and a modicum of supervision available.[40] A stone-built castle was much more formidable than such simple structures. In the document already quoted William and Robert went on to deal with these. 'Nor may anyone build a

---

[39] On Alfred's establishment of a network of *burhs* see H. R. Loyn, *Anglo-Saxon England and the Norman Conquest* (Oxford, 1962), pp. 132–6; K. Leyser, 'Henry I and the beginnings of the Saxon Empire', *English Historical Review*, 83 (1968), 1–32, but see the caveats of T. Reuter, *Germany in the Early Middle Ages 800–1056* (London, 1991), pp. 142–4.

[40] F. Barlow, *William Rufus*, pp. 286–7. *BT*, Pl. 51; M. W. Thompson, *The Rise of the Castle* (Cambridge, 1991), pp. 48–62, emphasises the care needed to build a good *motte* but many were only used for a short time and they could be erected quickly.

fortification on a rock or on an island, nor raise a castle in
Normandy, nor may anyone in Normandy refuse to deliver his castle
to the lord of Normandy should he wish to take it into his own
hands.'[41]

The first stone castles date from the later tenth century but, for
long, wooden structures remained the norm, like that at Dinan
portrayed in the Bayeux tapestry.[42] He who controlled a castle
controlled the land about it, and in the course of the tenth century in
much of France and Lorraine many strongpoints, formerly in the
hands of the public authority, the duke or count, were increasingly
falling into the private hands of the *Domini* – Lords who used them
for their own ends. Others were being built by these same people
and it was the right of the public authority to control the process
which Robert and William were reasserting in 1091. In a violent
and competitive society the castle-holder could defy even a powerful
overlord and could enjoy the profits of lordship over the countryside. For a castellan to lose his castle was a disaster. Robert Giroie
was out raiding when Robert of Bellême appeared outside his castle
of St Céneri panicking the troops within. Robert of Bellême then
burned the castle causing Robert Giroie to despair, 'So at one blow
the noble knight was utterly disinherited and forced to live in exile
in the houses of strangers'.[43] Even a king had to worry about the
power of the castle. Late in life Phillip I of France (1060–1108)
confessed to his son that the struggle to grasp Montlhéry had made
him old before his time, a consequence of the disloyalty of its
holders.[44] The castellan dominated the landscape and drew the
middling groups into his *mouvance*, above all the knights who served
him and provided castleguard. The community of the castle served
to draw such men together in a common military discipline which
would serve them well in the field. For it seems that the vassals
grouped around their lord were a basic unit of war at this time.
Ordericus comments on Gilbert of Auffay that he was 'kinsman of
the duke, fighting at his side surrounded by his companions in all the

[41] C. H. Haskins, *Norman Institutions* (Cambridge Mass., 1925), p. 282 cited and tr. Contamine, *War*, p. 46.

[42] On castles and their evolution see J. F. Fino, *Fortesses de la France médiévale* (Paris, 1977);
G. Fournier, *Le Château dans la France médiévale* (Paris, 1978); *BT*, Pl. 23.

[43] OV, 3. 294–5; M. Chibnall, 'Castles in Ordericus Vitalis', in C. Harper-Bill, C. J.
Holdsworth and J. Nelson, eds., *Studies in Medieval History Presented to R. Allen-Brown*
(Woodbridge, 1989), 43–56.

[44] Suger, pp. 36–9.

principal battles of the English war'.[45] But the existence of castles
conditioned war in a number of ways. The castle was the key to the
land and warfare in the feudal age was largely about landholding.
Since an attack upon a well-held strongpoint was hazardous, the
constant experience of contemporary warfare, so often private quarrels over possession of lands and rights, was ravaging, perhaps
accompanied by attacks on unsuspecting, unprepared or demoralised garrisons. On the death of the Conqueror in 1087 Robert of
Bellême seized Alençon and other ducal castles and imposed himself
upon his neighbours as well. In the conflicts which characterised
Normandy during the feeble and disputed reign of Curthose the
pursuit of private feuds was a norm manipulated by the competing
brothers, William Rufus, Robert and Henry, in their struggle for the
inheritance from their father. In November 1090 William of Evreux
and Ralph of Conches fell to feuding and William Rufus supported
Ralph, thereby weakening Robert Curthose as overlord. Although
the duke of Normandy and the king of England became involved,
this was essentially a private war caused by the quarrels of the two
men's wives.[46] All over the face of France, except in places and at
times when overlords were exceptionally strong, such squabbles
were the small change of war and the common experience of those
who participated in the First Crusade.

One such conflict pitted Ascelin Goël against William of Breteuil.
It began, says Ordericus, when Ascelin's brother William offended
against a lady and was adjudged guilty by William as overlord.
Ascelin took his vengeance in 1089 by betraying the important castle
of Ivry, which he held for William, to Robert Curthose, who
extracted a large sum for its return. Both families prepared for war,
the Goëls in 1091 enlisting Richard of Montfort and some of the
household troops of Phillip I of France, with whose aid they defeated
William in a skirmish and captured him. This phase of the affair
ended with a peace by which William of Breteuil restored the
castellancy of Ivry to Ascelin, gave him his daughter in marriage
and made various payments. The peace, says Ordericus, was a relief
to all, but it was short lived. William of Breteuil seized the abbey of
St Mary as a fortress against the Goëls, but was ejected when they
attacked and burnt it. However, the considerable resources of the
house of Breteuil were greatly increased 'with the help of ransoms of

---

[45] Duby, *Mâconnaise*, pp. 161–71; OV, 3. 255.   [46] OV, 4. 272.

captives and plunder taken from the country people'. Thus enriched, William persuaded Curthose and Phillip I of France to help him, and in 1092 together they attacked Brévol castle. It was strong, but Robert of Bellême also joined them for he hated the Goëls. His expertise in siege equipment forced Ascelin to a peace which restored Ivry to the Breteuil. However, Robert of Bellême evidently was left out of the peace negotiations and as the siege force broke up he attacked and nearly captured, the castle at St Céneri held by another ally of Curthose, Robert Giroie. The Conqueror's youngest son Henry who had taken Domfront from Robert of Bellême now decided to join the struggle against him, during which St Céneri fell to Bellême.[47]

This convoluted affair, involving some of the greatest men of Normandy and even the king of France, was merely one of many such episodes in the years of Curthose which were unusual in a duchy hitherto strongly ruled. The war was fought for a limited objective – really it was about possession of Ivry. There was no wish to destroy the enemy *à la Clausewitz*, though poor Robert Giroie suffered badly enough, and so it was punctuated by peaces. There was one major skirmish and the fact that at the taking of St Mary's abbey Ordericus mentions the death of a single knight suggests its trivial scale. It was not a war of sieges, although there was one major siege at Brévol, rather it was a war which turned on possession of strongpoints, a war of position. The most significant fact about it we learn only in passing as Ordericus comments on the sufferings of 'the country people', for in such a war the knights deliberately attacked and ravaged the lands of their enemies. In an age of poor logistics and major problems over the preservation of food, ravaging was a military necessity to keep an army in the field. This had always been true. Vegetius commented that 'The main and principal point in war is to secure plenty of provisions and to destroy the enemy by famine'.[48] William of Poitiers described the manner in which his hero, William the Conqueror, made war: 'He sowed terror in the land by his frequent and lengthy invasions; he devastated vineyards, fields and estates; he seized neighbouring strongpoints and where advisable put garrisons in them; in short he incessantly inflicted innumerable calamities upon the land'.[49] Ravaging was inevitable in a world where all

---

[47] OV, 4. 287–96.   [48] Vegetius, *Roots of Strategy*, p. 67.
[49] Quoted and tr. by J. Gillingham, 'William the Bastard at War', in C. Harper-Bill, C. J. Holdsworth and J. Nelson, eds., *Studies in Medieval History Presented to R. Allen-Brown* (Woodbridge, 1989), p. 148.

activities were so directly linked to the peasant surplus. War, though restricted in its extent and usually in its ambitions, often involved destroying an opponent's economic base and this meant appalling suffering for the people who lived on his land. The savagery of the crusade must be seen in this context. But of course it was also the consequence of castles. Assault was expensive and difficult. It took the combined efforts of the king of France, the duke of Normandy and the Breteuil family to take Brévol. Ravaging undermined the economic base and the morale of the enemy. When Bouchard of Montmorency defied a judgement by King Philip in favour of the abbey of St-Denis, Prince Louis initially ravaged his lands and strongpoints, and only later attacked his castle. In the end, losses forced Bouchard to come to a settlement.[50] The same process, of course, shook the allegiance of one's enemy's vassals. In 1055 the Conqueror began the construction of a castle at Ambrières in the lordship of Geoffrey of Mayenne who recognised this as a prelude to the devastation of his lands and appealed to his overlord, the count of Anjou. When this latter was unable to prevent the construction, Geoffrey did homage to William.[51]

It was a much cheaper strategy, indeed one which paid for itself. It is worth noting too that important men, including even the king himself, were quite ready to profit from such affairs which enabled them to pay their retinues and give them an opportunity to plunder, for this remained an important attribute of leadership.[52] In the affair of Brévol this was probably at least as important to Philip I as any notion of weakening the duke of Normandy. This kind of war, so common across the face of France, so brutal to the mass of the population, explains the anxiety of the church to divert or control the energies of the military caste. But, although there was little glory in it, warriors continued to practise what was 'the normal business of war', which, it should be remembered, in the context of a brutal age was not so very different from the coercive practices of civilian government. In 1051 Edward the Confessor ordered Godwin to harass Dover as a judicial punishment.[53] In the early tenth century

---

[50] Suger, pp. 16–17.

[51] The story is told by William of Poitiers and derived here from Gillingham, 'William the Bastard at War', in Harper-Bill, Holdsworth and Nelson, *Allen Brown* p. 151.

[52] On this theme see T. Reuter, 'Plunder and tribute', 75–94.

[53] J. Gillingham, 'Richard I and the science of war', in Gillingham and Holt, *War and Government*, pp. 84–5. See the comments of Strickland, *Conduct and Perception of War*, pp. 238, 344–5 on even the ecclesiastical acceptance of ravaging.

St Odo of Cluny had written his celebrated *Life of St Gerald* in which he praised Gerald for forbidding followers to take peasant goods casually – this was evidently common behaviour then and things had not much changed on the eve of the First Crusade when the first knightly act of Ralph, son of Albert of Cravent, was to despoil a monk.[54] It is important to see the knight in this context – of a war of position where ravaging and skirmishes turned on possession of strongpoints. To attack them by siege was always possible, but could be expensive. Ravaging could undermine both the economic base of the castle and its psychological underpinning, the loyalty of the vassals who manned it, though it could be a protracted affair. Nor should the castle simply be seen as a passive defence point, for its building, as we can see by the example of Ambrières, could be an offensive act, a first stage in bringing fire and sword to an area with a view to its subjugation. It was a style of war which necessitated the mobility of the knight and at the same time demanded that he turn his hand to many tasks, especially when it came to a siege. Even Robert of Bellême turned out to have engineering skills. Nor is the knight the only figure in such skirmishes – footsoldiers figure, usually suffering heavier losses, and archers as well. It was a paradox, but a form of war which turned on possession of strongpoints also placed a heavy emphasis on mobility. And in the set pieces of this conflict, the sieges, the knightly cavalry had their role. After Robert Curthose had rebelled against his father, Duke William raised a great force and cornered the rebels at the castle of Gerberoi where they had received help from the king of France and his allies. After some skirmishing Robert suddenly led out his forces and defeated the royal army. William was engaged and wounded by his son and his horse was shot from under him. One source suggests that an Englishman, Toki son of Wigod, tried to bring him a fresh one but was shot by a crossbow, while another says that Curthose recognised his father's voice and sent him away on his own horse.[55] The incident nicely illustrates the value of cavalry even at a formal siege and explains why horsemen are so often seen besieging cities in manuscript illuminations. The garrison could use mobility to strike

---

[54] Odo of Cluny, *Life of St Gerald of Aurillac*, tr. G. Sitwell (New York, 1958), pp. 115–123; OV, 3. 243.

[55] *ASC* 'D' p. 159; Florence of Worcester, *Chronicon*, ed. B. Thorpe, 2 vols. (London, 1848–49) [hereafter cited as Florence], 2. 13. Ordericus does not mention the king's defeat, simply saying the siege lasted for three weeks.

unexpectedly at their besiegers and the attackers needed to patrol and guard against this and be ready to take advantage of any weakness which might appear in the defence. At Gerberoi, Robert was cornered and probably desperate when he launched his charge which evidently involved horse and foot, but the royal army was caught in disarray and defeated. This was a very successful sally but a lesser objective such as the burning of siege equipment would equally make such mobility desirable.

This warfare of position with its concomitant of brutal ravaging was not confined to the Anglo-Norman world. About 1086 Godfrey's possession of the castle of Bouillon was challenged by Albert of Namur, count of Verdun, who had earlier shown his hostility, as we have noted. He allied with Theoderic bishop of Verdun to besiege Bouillon. Godfrey was able to raise the siege after a costly battle outside and he countered by releasing one of his prisoners, Henry of Grandpré, on condition that he devastate the county of Verdun. The count and the bishop then attacked Stenay, where Godfrey erected a castle, with such persistence that despite much fighting Godfrey was forced to seek help from his elder brother, Eustace of Boulogne, who was accompanied by the younger, Baldwin. The affair was brought to an end by the arbitration of Henry of Liège which was probably a device to save the faces of the count and the bishop, for Godfrey seems to have lost no lands by the peace which followed. Shortly after, in 1087, Godfrey was invested by Henry IV with the duchy of Lower Lorraine.[56] Raymond of St Gilles, who would later lead the largest army on the First Crusade, had to wage a struggle for at least thirteen years against Robert count of Auvergne to assert his claim to the Rouergue which by the time of his success in 1079 was a devastated zone.[57] Even the Papal Legate on the crusade, Adhémar bishop of Le Puy, seems to have been a man of military experience. He was probably of the house of the counts of Valentinois and is spoken of as an exceptional horseman. His election in the late 1070s was imposed by Gregory VII's legate, Hugh of Die, and bitterly contested by the important local house of Fay-Chapteuil, lords of Polignac, who were only defeated by a fine use of military force and diplomacy. He was not secure in his see

---

[56] Andressohn, *Godfrey de Bouillon*, pp. 39–41 and see above p. 26; Mayer, *Mélanges*, pp. 25–30.

[57] J. H. Hill and L. L. Hill, *Raymond IV of St Gilles 1041 (or 1042)–1105* (Syracuse, 1962), pp. 8–9.

until the mid-1080s when he may have gone on pilgrimage to Jerusalem.[58]

The Normans established themselves in South Italy in the early eleventh century by serving as mercenaries of the Byzantines and the Lombard princes. William of Apulia is frank about the methods which enabled them to dominate the area. They lived as brigands serving any who would pay them and preying on anyone, even admitting known criminals into their ranks. Malaterra tells us that Roger of Sicily told him to report his early life as a brigand.[59] Robert Guiscard arrived in South Italy as an impoverished younger son whose older brother Drogo was already established in the area and who finally conferred on him the job of guarding the valley of Crati in Calabria close to Cosenza, from whence he later moved his position to San Marco. Here he lived as a brigand paying his men by ravishing the land and building up a reputation as a ruthless leader. The pattern of conquest is made clear by the story of Peter, the Byzantine governor of Bisignano. Guiscard had concluded a truce with him, presumably the fruit of extortion. He asked to meet Peter who came with an escort only to be ambushed and ransomed for 20,000 ounces of gold.[60] Devastation and brigandage were the foundations of the conquest of Calabria and, therefore, of the greatness of the house of Guiscard. His son, Bohemond, who would be one of the leading figures on the First Crusade, had a great military reputation and was adept in this kind of war. After the death of his father, Robert Guiscard, in 1085, and the subsequent collapse of their effort to conquer the Byzantine empire, Bohemond found himself landless, for the lands of his father had passed to his half-brother Roger Borsa. But Bohemond was able to enlist the help of his family's rival, Jordan of Capua, and to attract young men into his service by his military reputation. He ravaged Otranto and

---

[58] *Chronicon monasterii sancti Petri Aniciensis* ed. C. V. I. Chevalier in *Cartulaire de l'abbaye de Saint-Chaffre du Monastier* (Paris, 1884), pp. 161–2; Adhémar-Laubaume, *Adhémar de Monteil*, pp. 13–17; Bréhier, *Adhémar de Monteil*, p. 13. Heraclius viscount of Polignac was Adhémar's standard bearer at the battle against Kerbogah; one of his nephews was killed and another wounded during the passage across the Balkans: RA, pp. 38, 82.

[59] William of Apulia, *La Geste de Robert Guiscard*, ed. M. Matthieu (Palermo, 1961), p. 109; Geoffrey Malaterra, *De rebus gestis Rogerii Calabriae et Siciliae comitis*, ed. E. Pontieri in *L. A. Muratori, Rerum italicarum scriptores*, 5 (1) (Bologna, 1928), 25.

[60] F. Chalandon, *Domination normande*, 1. 118–121; Amato di Monte Cassino, ed. Bartholomaeis, p. 14. On the origins of the Norman incursion into this area see J. France, 'The occasion of the coming of the Normans to Southern Italy', *Journal of Medieval History*, 17 (1991), 185–205.

Taranto which submitted to him by 1086, together with a number of lands and counties in Apulia; eventually he agreed to hold them of his brother. In 1087 he profited by an alliance with one of Roger's rebellious vassals to gain a foothold in Calabria, from which he attacked and seized the important city of Cosenza which he later exchanged, with the weak duke Roger, for Bari. By the summer of 1089 this able soldier was confident enough to act as host at Bari to the visiting pope, Urban II.[61] Southern Italy presented a different landscape from northern Europe, principally because it was dominated by cities, but the same techniques of ravaging and siege served the same purposes. It is worth noting how self-sustaining war could be. A successful captain could attract knights from far and wide, as Curthose did in Normandy, and Guiscard and Bohemond in the south. Even the king of France saw this as a means of offsetting the costs of his military entourage. The pattern of war imposed by the strength of fortresses and cities did not necessarily result in set-piece sieges; more often than not the technique of destroying food supplies and isolating strongpoints produced some kind of result. But, as we have noted, they were frequent enough and even at the level of localised war the need for the siege caused the development of poliorcetics.

At the siege of Brévol in Lent 1092 the allied forces of the duke of Normandy, the king of France and William of Breteuil needed the assistance of Robert of Bellême who was an expert in siege machinery. Ordericus's description of the machines he built is not very clear. The mention of a machine which was rolled right up against the wall suggests an armoured roof or penthouse which would normally be used to protect troops undermining the wall. However, Ordericus says that it was used to 'hurl great stones at the castle and its garrison' which implies some sort of catapult. It is possible that more than one machine is being described, and certainly the assault was effective for the outer defenses of the castle, its wall and palissades, were driven in and many roofs collapsed on the defenders. It is notable that the local clergy were made to impress their flocks for the purposes of constructing these machines.[62] But at the siege of Paris (885/6) the Danes had built a three tiered siege tower, the construction of which was halted by the killing of its

[61] R. B. Yewdale, *Bohemond I, Prince of Antioch* (Princeton, 1924, Amsterdam, 1970), pp. 26–31.
[62] OV, 4. 288–89.

builders in a raid. At the siege of Laon in 938 Louis IV employed a similar device and covered its forward movement by fire of archers. In 985 King Lothar assaulted Verdun with a siege-tower higher than the ramparts, which was propelled forward by ropes which were turned around stakes planted close to the walls and pulled by oxen out of arrow range. To counter this sophisticated device the garrison built a wooden tower at the point on the wall to which it was to be applied. In 988 Hugh Capet attacked Laon with a similar, through less elaborate, weapon.[63] In 1087 the Pisans and Genoese mounted an expedition, which took upon itself much of the character of a crusade, against Mahdia under its Zirid ruler Tamin (1062–1108) who had encouraged attacks on Christian commerce. In the successful attack on the Islamic fortress of Pantelleria tall wooden towers were built *'de lignis nimis altis facti sunt turrifices'* to dominate the walls.[64] This kind of wheeled wooden tower seems to have been the most effective siege engine of the eleventh century. The vagueness of the sources sometimes makes it difficult to distinguish the siege tower proper from the mobile armoured roof or penthouse which could be wheeled up to the wall to provide shelter for attackers who could then ram or undermine it. Such engines were very important during the First Crusade.[65] The siege tower was a complex machine which seems to have been difficult to build and deploy. Its purpose was to cover the mounting of ladders by fire-power, as well as to deliver troops onto the wall itself. Attackers brought ladders forward and sheltered themselves, and archers, behind mantlets of woven twigs or sheets of leather which provided cover and perhaps protection. But the other kind of machine found frequently in our sources, and mentioned at Brévol by Ordericus, were projectile throwers which are given various names: *mangana, mangonella, petraria, ballista* and all their variants. These are the names used in Roman texts and inherited by medieval writers. Unfortunately there is no uniformity of nomenclature between

---

[63] Abbo, *Siège de Paris par les Normands*, ed. and tr. H. Waquet (Paris, 1942), pp. 33, 42; Richer de Rheims, *Histoire de France*, ed. and tr. R. Latouche, 2 vols. (Paris, 1930), 1. 142; 2. 178.

[64] H. E. J. Cowdrey, 'The Mahdia Campaign of 1087', *English Historical Review*, 92 (1977), 1–29 gives the full text of the *Carmen de victoria Pisanorum*. This expedition is also discussed by R. Rogers, *Latin Siege Warfare in the Twelfth Century*, unpublished D.Phil. thesis, University of Oxford, 1984, pp. 347–72. On the Norman expeditions see D. Abulafia, 'The Norman kingdom of Africa and the Norman expeditions to Majorca and the Moslem Mediterranean', *Battle*, 7 (1984), 26–49.

[65] See below, pp. 163–5; it is also possible that the machines used by Louis IV against Laon in 938 was of this type.

writers and as their descriptions are often very vague it is exceedingly difficult to understand quite what kind of machine is being referred to and how it worked. In the Roman world such weapons were driven by torsion, the effect of huge windings of hair and sinew. However, by the thirteenth century when our sources become much clearer and more precise this principle of propulsion had been completely superceded in favour of lever action often combined with counterbalances. For the period in question here there is much doubt. The *ballista* was a Roman weapon in which the two arms forming the bow were pulled back against torsion coils. In medieval usage it often means simply a crossbow, and sometimes this is made very clear by a reference like *arcu baleari*.[66] But in the context of siege it can mean a machine which was a very large crossbow mounted on a frame used as a flat-trajectory, anti-personnel weapon. In his account of the siege of Paris, Abbo tells us that on one occasion a single ballista bolt killed two skilled workman, while on another Abbot Ebles of St-Germain killed seven Danes with a single shot, causing him to jest that his victims should be sent, like skewered meat, to the kitchen![67] But the other weapons, which we can generically call catapults, were very different. They seem to have thrown stones and other heavy objects, occasionally even bodies or heads, at the walls and defenders. A tentative conclusion based on a survey of our sources suggests that *petraria* and *mangana* refer to heavy weapons, while *mangonella* means lighter machines capable of throwing a projectile of only some five kilograms. In all cases the effective range was very limited – 50 to 75 metres being a maximum. The likelihood is that by the time of the First Crusade torsion had almost totally disappeared in favour of lever action. Certainly the huge windings of rope and sinew used by the Romans are no longer in evidence.[68] The construction of such weapons was a difficult

---

[66] AA. 324. For an illustration of the Roman weapon see O. F. G. Hogg, *Clubs to Canon* (London, 1968) p. 81.

[67] Abbo, 32–33, 22–25. It is, however, a sign of the confusion on this subject that J. F. Niermeyer, *Mediae Latinitatis Lexicon Minus* (Leiden, 1976), p. 637, equates *Manganellus* with *ballista*.

[68] I have relied heavily on Rogers, *Latin Siege Warfare*, for his enlightening discussion of this subject, pp. 5–49. However, I have gone further in dismissing torsion instruments by the time of the First Crusade. this is simply a matter of judgment, but it seems to me that given their relative complexity they would have vanished generations before the sources (in the thirteenth century) make this clear; see also E. W. Marsden, *Greek and Roman Artillery*, 2 vols. (Oxford, 1969–71); R. Schneider, *Die Artillerie des Mittelalters* (Berlin, 1910); K. Huuri, 'Zur Geschichte des Mittelalterichen Geschutzwesens aus Orientalischen Quellen',

business. Ordericus regarded Robert of Bellême as unusual, and the reference by Abbo to very skilled men building the Danish machines used against Paris makes the same point. The siege of Pantellaria was conducted by sailors whose engineering skills were those needed to build machines. But the decision to use siege machinery of any complexity did not simply depend on finding skilled artisans. The commander had to have knowledge of the possibilities and to appreciate what was needed. The raw material, especially tall trees, had to be available. Above all, people had to be organised for the business of siege. This was not simply a matter of ordering soldiers about. Trenches and palisades as well as machines had to be made, and food had to be brought up. At Brévol, Ordericus mentions the impressing and organising of the local populace, and we can see the same phenomenon on the Bayeux tapestry as the Normans built their castle at Hastings.[69] These were the skills of a commander, a vital part of the business of war. The larger the scale of action the more important such skills became. The common experience of those who went on the First Crusade was of a kind of war which turned on possession of strongpoints, which might be assaulted by siege or undermined by ravaging. At all times the castle and the walled city were dominating factors but there was a high premium on mobility and flexibility. The needs of siege also imposed a premium on capacity for organisation and the need to combine all the various arts of war. We have seen these factors at work in smallscale conflict, but it was not so very different in the major military undertakings of the age. However, this distinction is made purely for analysis. Louis VI's biographer catalogues some major expeditions, but for the most part shows him besieging the castles of robber barons. In this he enjoyed the support of the future crusader, Stephen of Blois, who seems to have worked closely with the French monarchy in the years before the First Crusade. At some stage between 1081 and 1084 Stephen killed the notorious robber baron Count Bouchard of Corbeil, with a blow from his lance.[70] Out of this

Studia Orientalia, 9 (1941); J. F. Fino, 'Machines de jet médiévales', *Gladius*, 11 (1972), 25–43. For the later period D. Hill, 'Trebuchets', *Viator*, 4 (1973), 106–16. C. Marshall, *Warfare in the Latin East 1198–1291*, (London, 1992), p. 113 briefly asserts the conventional view in a crusader context.

[69] OV, 4. 288–9; *BT*, Pl. 49–50.

[70] Suger, p. 150–1; Stephen is more properly called Stephen Henry and he succeeded his father Theobald I (1037–1089/90) count of Blois and Champagne in the Blois portion of his inheritance: M. Bur, *La Formation du Comté de Champagne v.950–v.1150* (Nancy, 1977), p. 230.

grinding process emerged royal strength and prestige as exemplified by Louis's appeal to the chivalry of France when Henry V invaded in 1124.[71]

[71] Suger, 219–31. On Louis's struggle with the robber barons and its importance see R. Fawtier, *Capetian Kings of France* tr. L. Butler and R. J. Adam (London, 1960), pp. 19–22; Dunbabin, *Origins*, p. 296.

CHAPTER 3

Campaigns, generals and leadership

William the Conqueror is probably the best known soldier and
general of the eleventh century. The conquest of England in 1066
was not only a major historical event, it was also one which has stuck
in the minds of at least the English-speaking world. William was a
minor when his father died in 1035, and the struggle to impose
himself upon Normandy was long and bitter. It was only with the
help of his overlord, Henry I of France (1031–60) that the greatest
rebellion against him was defeated at the battle of Val-ès-Dunes in
1047 of which we know almost nothing. However, the rebel leader,
Guy of Burgundy, took refuge in the castle of Brionne where he held
out for three years.[1] Thereafter, although William's position
improved, the propensity for rebellion remained. In the wake of his
capture of Tours in 1044 Geoffrey Martel, count of Anjou
(1040–60), turned his attention to Maine, where the major city of Le
Mans was captured in 1051. After the count of Maine's widow, her
son Herbert and daughter Margaret had fled to the Norman court,
Geoffrey seized both Domfront, a fief held of the count of Maine by
the Bellême family, and the Norman town of Alençon, offering as an
inducement to their soldiers a licence to ravage in the Norman
lands.[2] William failed to take Domfront by *coup de main* and built
four castles, probably earthwork and wood structures, to blockade it
while maintaining an active posture which enabled him to rally his

---

[1] The accounts of William of Jumièges p. 123 and WP, pp. 16–18 say almost nothing about
Val-ès-Dunes. Wace's account has very graphic incidents, some of which may reflect actual
events, but tells us nothing of the course of the battle. Guy of Burgundy was the younger son
of the marriage between Raynald count of Burgundy and Adelaide, daughter of Richard II
of Normandy (996–1026), who therefore had a claim to Normandy against the illegitimate
William: *Glaber*, p. 106 n. 2; for the history of the duchy in these years see D. C. Douglas,
William the Conqueror (London, 1964).

[2] Douglas, *William the Conqueror*, pp. 55–9. William's son Robert later was betrothed to
Margaret and, even though she died, assumed the title count of Maine: David, *Robert
Curthose*, pp. 7–10; WP, p. 38.

troops against an effort to relieve it by Geoffrey, whose forces retired intact and watchful. William now faced a difficult situation for their presence prevented him from ravaging. However, William had apparently kept a close eye on Alençon in the meantime, and, when he realised that its defences were weak, suddenly seized it, dealing so harshly with its garrison that Domfront decided to come to terms.[3] The campaign certainly illustrates William's generalship, with its tight control over events. It indicates how the castle and its supply dominated war yet not at the expense of mobility which was the key factor in William's victory. It should also be added that Geoffrey was a good general, but here he was at the very edge of his authority, so his power was attenuated and his ability to bring it to bear without enormous effort limited. William's own stabs against Maine failed for much the same reasons, until after Geoffrey's death in 1063 when, taking advantage of the internal conflict then rending the house of Anjou, he advanced against Le Mans with fire and sword as described by William of Poitiers.[4]

In the years 1051–2 there occurred a major shift in alliances in northern France. The Norman dukes had long been close allies of the Capetian royal house. William's father, Robert I, had sustained Henry against the revolt of 1031 and in return the king had supported his son as we have seen.[5] But the Capetians had also long been friendly with the house of Anjou, who had been their allies against the grave threat posed by the counts of Blois-Champagne, most recently accepting their conquest of Tours in 1044 from the Blésois.[6] When these two allies quarrelled over Maine, King Henry supported the Angevins, posing a grave threat to William whose régime was still far from secure after his recent minority. In 1053 William of Arques, a great lord of upper Normandy with many

---

[3] This account of events is drawn from Gillingham, 'William the Bastard', pp. 149–51 whose careful study establishes the generalship of William, on which see also J. Beeler, 'Towards a re-evaluation of medieval English generalship', *Journal of British Studies*, 3 (1963), 1–10.

[4] See above p. 42. On the succession dispute in Anjou on the death of Geoffrey Martel in 1060 see O. Guillot, *Le Comte d'Anjou et son entourage au xie siècle (Paris, 1972)*, 2 vols., i. 102–116; L. Halphen, *Le Comté d'Anjou au xie siècle* (Paris, 1906, Geneva, 1974), pp. 133–51.

[5] *Glaber*, pp. 138–9, testifies frequently to the good relations between the Capetian kings and the Norman dukes, for example in the matter of the Orléans heresy. It was precisely because of these good relations that he tells us so little about the duchy and its politics: J. France, 'Rodulfus Glaber and French politics in the early eleventh century', *Francia*, 16 (1989), 111. Duke Robert of Normandy gave Henry I (1031–60) support when his vassals rose against him: J. Dhondt, 'Une crise du pouvoir capétien', in D. P. Blok *et al.* eds., *Miscellanea Medievalia in Memoriam J. F. Niermeyer* 137–48.

[6] France, 'Glaber and French politics', 109.

allies, rebelled and his castle of Arques, newly built and well fortified, was the focus of events. William's men at Rouen, his *principes
militiae*, tried unsuccessfully to interfere with the preparation of
Arques, but when William arrived he built a counter-castle and
settled down to a siege. King Henry led an army into Normandy,
ravaging as he went, but was ambushed and, although he got
supplies into Arques, his force was so weakened that the castle fell
soon after his withdrawal. In the following year Henry tried again
with two armies, one under Odo, his brother, striking into Eastern
Normandy and the other under his own command, supported by the
Angevins, advancing via Evreux. The duke adopted the classic
tactic of shadowing his enemy, and one of his detachments fell upon
French ravagers at Mortemer causing such loss that both French
armies withdrew. The same tactics of shadowing the French, preventing them from spreading out to forage, were employed in 1057
and this time William fell upon the French and Angevin army as the
tide cut it in two crossing the Dives at Varaville, causing very heavy
losses. It was at this battle that, according to Wace, archers played a
notable role.[7] There is much to admire in William's generalship in
all these campaigns. He was a master of the contemporary techniques of war and succeeded in impressing his vassals and preserving
their loyalty. Perhaps even more important is to notice the scale of
effort which he managed to sustain despite his internal difficulties.
He, and indeed his opponents, mounted major campaigns intersper-
sed with sieges and lesser affairs over a period of very nearly ten
years. This obviously says a great deal about the economic efficiency
of the manorial economy, but it also says a great deal about the
ability to organise, recruit and sustain armies. It is a theme not
much discussed by modern historians of the period, but it was of
course a vital skill in the circumstances of the crusade.

Even William's admiring biographer, William of Poitiers, admits
that he evaded battle whenever possible. Indeed, Varaville was the
only occasion before Hastings when he engaged on any scale in the
open field and it was then only in the most favourable circumstances. The qualification 'on any scale' is important, for there were
many occasions during these years when there were fights, but they
were of a limited kind which could only have limited results. In 1053

---

[7] J. Gillingham, 'William the Bastard', pp. 151–53 describes these events very clearly; for
Wace, see above p. 36, n. 29.

and 1054 King Henry simply absorbed minor defeats. William's was not a technique without battles – rather he committed himself to a style of war which avoided heavy losses and conserved his forces, preferring the tactics we have noted above. In this he showed wisdom, for battle on any scale could be very expensive and was terribly hazardous. The battle of Cassel on 22 February 1071 was fairly widely noted by contemporaries.[8] In 1070 Baldwin VI of Flanders died and the succession of his fifteen year old son, Arnulf III, who was supported by his mother Richilde, was contested by the dead count's brother Robert I the Frisian, father of Robert II of Flanders who went on the First Crusade. Robert rallied support especially in northern Flanders and struck suddenly at Cassel where Arnulf's army was concentrated; in its ranks was Eustace II count of Boulogne, a major vassal in Flanders and in England and father of three participants in the First Crusade, Eustace III of Boulogne, Godfrey de Bouillon and Baldwin. Arnulf was supported by his overlord Philip of France, whose aunt Adela had married Baldwin V of Flanders (1035–67), amongst whose forces was a contingent of ten knights from Normandy led by William FitzOsborn, a small force whose size indicates that the Conqueror, who had married Baldwin V's daughter Mathilda, was very much more concerned with affairs in England.[9] Robert seems to have advanced quickly toward Cassel, evidently seeing battle as offering a quick decision and needing to force it before the superior strength of his enemies could gather. We do not know for certain who held Cassel at the start of the battle, the details of which are largely lost to us. One source suggests that Robert lured the allies into an ambush by a feint, but beyond this there is confusion.[10] What interests us is the extraordinary outcome of this battle. Arnulf III was killed and so was William FitzOsborn; Richilde was captured by Robert's men, and Robert the Frisian was captured by Eustace II of Boulogne. Within a month the king of France had concentrated a much larger force at Montreuil and was ready to resume the war, but he was

---

[8] OV, 2. 282–3; William of Jumièges, p. 25; Gislebert of Mons, *Chronique*, ed. L. Vanderkina-dere (Brussels, 1904), p. 7; *Annales Egmundani MGH SS* 16. 447; *Flandria Generosa, MGH SS* 9. 322; Lambert of Hersfeld, p. 124.

[9] C. Verlinden, *Robert I Le Frison, Comte de Flandre* (Antwerp/Paris/'S Gravenhage, 1935) pp. 46–70.

[10] It is not certain who held the castle of Cassel. Verlinden, *Robert le Frison*, p. 66, suggests Arnulf, though its castellan Boniface was in Robert's force. A. Fliche, *Le règne de Phillippe I roi de France 1060–1108* (Paris, 1912), pp. 258–9 thinks, therefore, that Robert held it.

forced to recognise Robert who was freed in exchange for Richilde and was elevated to the county through the support of Eustace II. Baldwin of Hainault, the other surviving son of Baldwin VI, later unsuccessfully contested the county of Flanders, but was to die on crusade with Robert's son, Robert II, in 1098.[11] Robert the Frisian had had little option but to seek battle, for most of his support was in the poorer part of Flanders and his rival had powerful allies. The immediate outcome of his strategy was poor reward for his bravery, although in the long run the death of Arnulf opened the way for a favourable political solution. Over a century later the risks were just as great. In September 1198 Richard I of England (1189–99) fell upon the army of King Philip of France (1180–1223) as it tried to relieve Courcelles, inflicting a severe defeat during which the bridge at Gisors broke throwing the French king into the water where he 'had to drink of the river'. Richard reported these events in a letter to the bishop of Durham which has a confessional, almost apologetic note, reflecting the hazards of resorting to battle: 'In doing this we risked not only our own life but the kingdom itself, against the advice of all our councillors'.[12] Such sober reflection from one of the greatest of all medieval generals explains why major battle was only to be undertaken in the most favourable circumstances, as William showed at Varaville, or for the highest stakes, as in the Hastings campaign.

Because of its spectacular and decisive results, Hastings is perhaps the most celebrated of all medieval battles.[13] Certain aspects of the Hastings campaign need to be emphasised, however, because they illuminate the nature of war in the late eleventh century. In the first

---

[11] Verlinden, *Robert le Frison*, pp. 70–71, 80–6; on family relationships see Bur, *Comté de Champagne*, pp. 128–9, 286–7. For Baldwin of Hainault's death see AA. pp. 434–5; Guibert of Nogent, *Gesta Dei per Francos*, *RHC Oc.* 4. [hereafter cited as GN], p. 208.

[12] Roger of Hovenden, *Chronica Magistri Rogeris de Hovenden*, ed. W. Stubbs, 4 vols. (London, Rolls Series, 1871) (hereafter cited as RH), 4. 59. I must thank my colleague in the Swansea History department, I. W. Rowlands, for this reference: on Richard as a general see Gillingham, 'Richard I', pp. 78–91.

[13] There is a vast literature on Hastings amongst which the classic accounts of Delbrück, *History of the Art of War*, 3. 146–61 and Oman, *Art of War*, 1. 151–66 have had enormous influence. For more recent accounts see Douglas, *William the Conqueror*, pp. 194–204; C. N. Barclay, *Battle 1066* (London, 1966); C. H. Lemmon, 'The Campaign of 1066', in eds. D. Whitelock *et al. The Norman Conquest, its Setting and Impact*, (London, 1966); J. Beeler, *Warfare in England 1066–1189* (Cornell, 1966), pp. 11–33; France, 'La guerre dans la France féodale,' 23–6; R. A. Brown, *The Normans and the Norman Conquest* (London, 1969), pp. 158–76, 'The Battle of Hastings', 1–21, *The Battle of Hastings and the Norman Conquest* (London, 1982). This is not a definitive list.

place the scale of the undertaking, requiring the collection and construction of a fleet, was enormous. The devoted biographer of William tells us that when his hero announced his intention of conquering England as news came through of the death of Edward and the usurpation of Harold, many advised him that such an undertaking was beyond the strength of the Normans and some seem to have refused to take part or promised, then reneged.[14] Indeed it was a huge undertaking. William was obliged to consult with his magnates in a series of conferences at Lillebonne, Bonneville-sur-Touques and Caen at which they agreed to unprecedentedly heavy contributions to the army and, also apparently, to the provision of ships such as the sixty raised by William FitzOsborn. It seems likely that William established the number of troops which each lord owed him according to the extent of his lands, and then concluded agreements over and above such figures for the special circumstances of the great expedition. According to Wace, William FitzOsborn exhorted them to provide at least double their obligations and this caused anxiety amongst the magnates lest the increased contribution be seen as a precedent, leading the duke to assure them individually that this would not be so.[15] Indeed, in one sense the critics of the expedition were proved correct, for William had to seek resources outside Normandy. The presence of Flemish, French and Breton troops in the host at Hastings, and afterwards amongst the new aristocracy of England, is too well known to need discussion here. The importance of Eustace II of Boulogne in the Bayeux tapestry testifies to this, and we know of the presence of soldiers from Poitiers. The *Carmen de Hastingae Proelio* suggests the presence of South Italian Normans. This indicates the range of his recruiting effort.[16] Wace gives some hint of the diversity of the Conqueror's arrangements when he speaks of soldiers coming to him in groups and singly. 'Many wished for the duke's lands should he conquer England. Some requested pay and allowances and gifts. Often it was necessary to distribute these, to those who could not

---

[14] WP, pp. 148–9, 156–7, 160–1.

[15] I follow here the conclusions of E. M. C. van Houts, 'The ship list of William the Conqueror', *Battle*, 10 (1987), 159–84, which contains an edition of the ship-list; *Wace* 2. 112–14 quoted and tr. by van Houts, p. 162.

[16] J. Martindale, 'Aimeri of Thouars and the Poitevin connection', *Battle*, 7 (1984), 224–5; G. Beech, 'Participation of Aquitainians in the conquest of England 1066–1100', *Battle* 9 (1986), 1–24.

afford to wait.'[17] Overall some 14,000 men including sailors were mobilised, of whom something like 8,000 were effectives, including 3,000 cavalry. Amongst the 5,000 foot were a lot of archers who appear, from the Tapestry, to have been lightly armed, and a sizable corps of what William of Poitiers calls *pedites loricati*, heavily armed footsoldiers. In the battle the duke would find it convenient to divide his force into divisions of Normans, Bretons and French. This vast assemblage must have stripped Normandy of troops, but such exposure was possible because two inveterate enemies had died in 1060, Henry I of France and Geoffrey Martel of Anjou. The regency of France was in the hands of William's father-in-law Baldwin V of Flanders.[18] This huge force had to be concentrated near Dives-sur-Mer where the fleet gathered in the summer of 1066, and it had to be supplied, for William of Poitiers tells us that William would not allow the troops to plunder and so arose what he describes as an extraordinary situation: despite the presence of squadrons of knights, farmers could get on with their business and travellers come and go without fear, an interesting comment on contemporary chivalry![19]

This concentration of forces at Dives of some 14,000 men and 2,000–3,000 warhorses presented a formidable problem of supply. The task of feeding and watering them, it has been suggested, demanded 9,000 cartloads of grain, straw, wine and firewood along with eight tons of iron for horseshoes alone. They generated 700,000 gallons of urine and five million pounds of horse-shit during their stay and this had to be removed. In addition there must have been many draught animals and indeed the Bayeux tapestry shows us military supplies being moved on specialised vehicles.[20] Warhorses were very valuable and supporting sizable numbers of them was a grave problem. Recent research indicates that the breeding of specialised strains of horses was a great burden, requiring enclosed parks to isolate mares and suitable stallions in well-found stud-farms.[21] In addition, it must be recognised that in western Europe

---

[17] *Wace* 3, 6, 411–16, quoted by M. Bennett, 'Wace and Warfare', *Battle*, 11 (1988), 37–58.

[18] B. S. Bachrach, 'Some observations on the military administration of the Norman Conquest', *Battle*, 8 (1985), 12 suggests that there is a 'scholarly consensus' on these numbers; Douglas, *William the Conqueror*, p. 188.

[19] WP, pp. 152–3.

[20] Bachrach, 'Observations on the Norman Conquest', 12–15; these are only estimates, but they effectively indicate the scale of the problem as Gillingham, 'William the Bastard', p. 56, points out; *BT*, Pl.38.

[21] R. H. C. Davies, *The Medieval Warhorse: Origins, Development and Redevelopment* (London, 1989); 'Warhorses of the Normans', 67–82.

there were few ranges where horses could graze and that these animals were stall-fed with grain and hay. They thus competed with men for grain while for the provision of hay, meadows needed to be developed. This explains the contrast between the west where the development of bigger and heavier animals was a necessary consequence of this costly regime, and the east where the availability of ranges in Asia Minor and the Euphrates plain, as in North Africa, fostered the development of a lighter breed, though the progress of this distinction was limited in the eleventh century.[22] Supporting such animals was a major drain on the peasant surplus at the best of times. In conditions of war, feeding horses presented terrible problems. In August and September of 1914 von Kluck's First Army, which marched on the right of the German attack under the famous 'Schlieffen Plan', had 84,000 horses consuming two million pounds of fodder per day, or twenty-four pounds of grain and hay each. Although they were advancing in a most favourable season the cavalry were tired by the time they crossed the French frontier and in poor condition by the start of the Battle of the Marne on 6 September. The lot of the draught animals was worse and the guns were badly delayed.[23] Difficult as the conditions of 1914 must have been, they were infinitely better for the survival of animals than in the eleventh century. William's concentration at Dives took place at a most favourable time of year and his subsequent deployment enjoyed good fortune. However, the crusaders faced much more difficult conditions and the state of the horses rapidly became a major preoccupation for the army, as we shall see. Once into the Anatolian steppe, animals were very vulnerable, and it seems unlikely that any western Europeans animals survived the journey.

Contemporaries were deeply impressed by the fleet which William gathered, and which is so graphically illustrated in the Tapestry. Its actual size was not definitely known to contemporaries. *The ship list of William the Conqueror* suggests that the Norman lords should have produced some 776 ships, and Wace recollects being told that the fleet which sailed numbered 700 less four, though he had also found the figure of 3,000 written down.[24] It is not necessarily the case that the Norman lords produced their quotas

---

[22] R. P. Lindner, 'Nomadism, Horses and Huns', *Past and Present*, 92 (1981), 3–19 points to the problems of supporting large numbers of horses beyond the great plains without substantial infrastructure.

[23] Terraine, *The White Heat*, p. 97.   [24] van Houts, 'Ship-list', pp. 179, 163.

and figures as low as 400–500 have been suggested, but most writers
believe that a total of between 700 and 1,000 concentrated at Dives
where the army was gathering. William of Poitiers tells us that the
duke ordered that ships be constructed, but it is unlikely that a huge
fleet could have been built in the period between the death of the
Confessor and the landing at Pevensey on 28 September. The
evidence suggests that the duke acquired existing ships, in particular
hiring them along with mercenaries from Flanders. The greater
number of them were merchantmen suitable for the transport of
horses and supplies as well as men, though a number of longships
and skiffs were undoubtedly included. The emphasis on shipbuilding in William of Poitiers and the Tapestry probably owes much to
the excitement generated by this activity. But evidently William was
pressed to find enough ships, for the Tapestry appears to show
unseasoned wood being cut for shipbuilding. It seems unlikely that
William had special transports made for his horses, such as those
used by the Byzantines, for the Tapestry does not show anything
resembling them and the written sources do not give any indication
of such exotic vessels.[25] By early September the concentration of
forces at Dives seems to have been complete and the fleet sailed on a
westerly wind for St Valéry where it waited fifteen days until a
gentle southerly took it to England.[26] By any standards this was a
remarkable logistical and organisational achievement. It is important to recognise that while exceptional, it was not unique.

King Harold of England knew of the intentions and preparations
of the duke of Normandy; indeed William of Poitiers records the
reception given to an English spy.[27] By May Harold set in train his
own preparations, hastened by the raids of his dissident brother

[25] *BT*, pl. 40–44. On the nature of the fleet and its gathering see the very learned article by C.
M. Gillmor, 'Naval logistics of the cross-channel operation 1066', *Battle*, 7 (1984), 105–31.
D. Waley, 'Combined operations in Sicily 1060–78', *Proceedings of the British School at Rome*,
22 (1954), 124–35 suggested that William could have gained knowledge of the specialised
Byzantine horse-transports from South Italy, but this is not usually accepted and the
evidence of the BT is against; J. H. Pryor, 'Transportation of horses by sea during the era of
the crusades', *Mariners Mirror*, 68.1 (1982), 9–27, 68.2 (1982), 103–25; B. S. Bachrach, 'On
the origins of William the Conqueror's horse transports', *Technology and Culture*, 26 (1985),
505–31. On the navigational and related problems see; J. Neumann, 'Hydrographic and
ship-hydrodynamic aspects of the Norman invasion, AD 1066', *Battle*, 11 (1988), 221–243.
[26] And very gentle it must have been. Neumann, p. 234, suggests about 3.5 knots over a very
flat sea, rare conditions in the Channel as the allies discovered in 1944. More severe
conditions would surely have led to losses such as occurred in the passage from Dives to St
Valéry according to William of Poitiers, p. 161.
[27] WP, pp. 154–7.

Tosti on southern England. His fleet was apparently slow to mobilise, but he may well have attempted a spoiling attack on William's forces across the Channel, while on land his troops stood 'everywhere along by the sea' for the English had an efficient military system. This Anglo-Saxon fyrd was centred on the retainers of the king and the great thegns and perhaps some mercenaries, supplemented by shire levies whose localities provided them with support.[28] The peculiarity of the Anglo-Saxon military tradition was the failure to develop any effective cavalry. Although the élite of the army rode to battle there is every evidence that they fought on foot. Thus, although they could move quickly across country, they lacked battlefield mobility, the key factor in the coming war.[29] Then on 8 September the Anglo-Saxon fleet and army broke up, the former going to London with losses, because, as the Chronicle tells us:'the provisions of the people were gone'.[30] It is easy to contrast this logistic disaster unfavourably with the triumph across the Channel. However, to maintain an army and a fleet as long as this was a major achievement, especially as considerable forces stayed in the north to guard against the threat of attack from Tosti and Harald Hardrada.[31] Moreover, when Harold heard of the Norse attack on York, he was able to gather his army and strike very quickly, which suggests that not all had dispersed. Probably the extent of his demobilisation has been exaggerated and the best troops remained with him. Furthermore, the English fleet took to the sea quickly to cut off the Normans after they landed on 28 September. On 12 September the Norman fleet left its concentration area in and around Dives and

[28] On the Anglo-Saxon army see C. W. Hollister, *Anglo-Saxon Military Institutions on the Eve of the Norman Conquest* (Oxford, 1962). The notion that a special corps of housecarls formed an élite amongst the retainers is rejected convincingly by N. Hooper, 'Housecarls in England in the eleventh century', *Battle*, 7 (1984), 161–76. The poorly armed troops in the Tapestry are evidence that peasants continued to serve in the host.

[29] Only R. Glover, 'English warfare in 1066', *English Historical Review*, 67 (1952), 1–18 has maintained that the English had cavalry and this has been decisively rebutted by Brown, *Normans and the Norman Conquest*, p. 94. However, it is interesting that J. Kiff, 'Images of war – illuminations of warfare in early eleventh century England', *Battle*, 7 (1984), 177–94, finds that the designers of the BT drew on an earlier tradition of representations of fighting horses. The scorn of the Normans for this style of war is well known: 'A race ignorant of war, the English scorn the solace of horses and, trusting in their strength they stand fast on foot', *Carmen*, 369–70, pp. 24–5.

[30] *ASC*, C. D 141–2, 140 E.

[31] Brown, *Normans and the Norman Conquest*, pp. 143–4 contrasts the failure of Harold and the success of William in this respect. *ASC*, C, p. 143 says that the coming of the Norwegians surprised Harold but this perhaps refers to the timing. Both invasion armies were very late in the season.

sailed east to St Valéry, just as Harold heard of the landing of Harald Hardrada at York with a fleet of 300–500 ships reinforced by Tosti; they defeated earls Edwin and Morcar at Fulford Bridge on 20 September with a great slaughter on both sides and took possession of York. By 24 September Harold, after a whirlwind march, was at Tadcaster. On 25 September he marched his troops through York and surprised and slaughtered the Danish army at Stamford Bridge. Hearing of the Norman landing at Pevensey of 28 September, he turned his army south and after spending 5–11 October raising more troops in London, marched out to confront William whose spies warned him of the coming of the Anglo-Saxon army on 13 October. The next day the battle took place and Harold was killed.[32] The organisational effort made by both sides in this summer of 1066 was remarkable and it points to the abilities of commanders. It was paralleled elsewhere in Europe at this time. The Norman conquest of South Italy and Sicily reached its climax in the years 1071 and 1072 when the major cities of Bari and Palermo fell. Bari was the last major bastion of Byzantine power in Italy and its powerful fortifications were deservedly feared. When Robert Guiscard began the siege on 5 August 1068 he knew he was starting a major undertaking and that blockade by sea was vital. In 1060–1 the Normans had demonstrated their willingness to take to ships with a series of raids on Messina which culminated in its seizure by a force which included 700–1,000 cavalry whose mounts had to be ferried across to Sicily. This successful lodgement opened the way for a conquest made easier by divisions amongst the three major Muslim Emirates.[33] Bari was a much greater operation in the course of which a land blockade was established and complemented with a sea blockade, during which the Norman ships were linked together to form a barrier to penetration into the port. A Byzantine relief force did break in, however, in 1069, and a sea and land diversion against Brindisi was heavily defeated. However, the Normans enjoyed aid from Pisa whose fleet brought troops and crossbowmen for land as well as sea operations. The defeat of a major Byzantine fleet in 1070 opened the way for negotiations which culminated in a negotiated surrender of the city in April 1071.[34] This long operation was then followed by the

---

[32] For the claims of Harald Hardrada and the disloyalty of Harold's brother Tosti see Brown, *Normans and the Norman Conquest*, upon whose chronology I have relied in this account.

[33] D. Waley, 'Combined operations in Sicily 1060–78', 118–25; Chalandon, 1. 191–3.

[34] Chalandon 1. 186–90; Amatus of Monte-Cassino, *Amato di Monte Cassino*, ed. V. Bartholomaeis (Rome, 1935) 5, xxviii p. 164, [hereafter cited as *Amatus*].

siege of Palermo begun in August 1071, to which the Hauteville brothers, Robert and Roger, brought a force of fifty-eight vessels. On land they built siege machines and on sea a blockade was established which was not totally successful for a North African fleet broke through to provision the city. However, in the end hunger brought the city to a negotiated surrender on 10 January 1072.[35]

These remarkable operations in the south were paralleled as feats of organisation by the German expeditions to Italy. Documentation on the military organisation of the German kings is sparse, but the *Indiculus Loricatorum* is a list of the reinforcements called for by Otto II (973–83) after his defeat in 982 at Cortone. A total of 2,090 mounted men were called to service on the basis of what appears to have been established *servitia debita* which formed the recruiting base of the imperial army. On the marches of Germany a regular levy, the *census*, was imposed upon the Slavs in order to maintain the garrisons and military forces of their conquerors.[36] In 1026 Conrad II (1024–39) undertook the expedition to Italy which led to his imperial coronation. It is not generally seen as a major military action but Italy was unfriendly. After the crowning in Milan, Conrad ravaged the lands of hostile Pavia, though he was unable to take the city. He had to put down a revolt in Ravenna before proceeding to Rome. The imperial coronation was brilliant, but afterwards a German and a Roman quarrelled over a hide and severe fighting broke out involving the entire German army. The 'Investiture Conflict' was a German civil war involving bloody battles in a land where the castle was emerging as an important factor. During its course Henry IV led several major expeditions to Italy including the siege of Rome in 1083 in which Godfrey participated when siege machinery, including rams, was constructed.[37] The regularity and scale of the Italian expeditions of the German emperors made a profound impact on the emergence of the German knightly class, the *ministeriales*. In the twelfth century the codes which governed their conduct were elaborated, particularly with regard to their duties on the 'complicated and onerous imperial

[35] Chalandon 1. 205–208.

[36] K. J. Leyser, *Medieval Germany and its Neighbours* (London, 1982) pp. 76, 89–90.

[37] AA, 440; *Vita Heinrici IV Imperatoris*, ed. W. Eberhard (Hanover, 1899), p. 23. *La Chronique de Zimmern*, ed. H. Hagenmyer, *Archives de l'Orient Latin*, 2 (1884) p. 24 suggests that Godfrey played a major role in the siege of Rome in 1081 and was later ill, but this work has been criticised, on which see below p. 92, no. 36.

ventures into Italy', with both heavy fines for failure to comply and
fitting out allowances payable from their lord. In 1154 the archbishop of Cologne required that all holding land worth five marks
should go, and they were given ten marks for equipment together
with supplies, horses and pay of one mark per month once over the
Alps. In 1161 the archbishop sent 500 men at a cost of 10,000
marks.[38]

The organisation of war was the primary concern of government,
but even at its best it remained, by our standards, simple. In essence
those who held land of the king owed service in one way or another
and this obligation co-existed with an older Germanic tradition that
all free men had a duty to serve the king in moments of emergency.
We have noted the establishment of quotas in Germany and the
same process was at work in Normandy, although it should be
stressed that 'feudalism' was emergent in the late eleventh century
and that as yet there was only 'a tangle of incipient feudal customs,
partly built up from below'.[39] In any case, powerful rulers had
sources other than nascent feudal obligation for the raising of great
armies. It is now clear that paid troops had always played a major
role, as they did, for example, under William Rufus. The distinctions between mercenary, endowed knight and household knight are
not clear – those serving from obligation beyond some fixed period
might well be paid, and there was a strong tendency to argue about
how far obligations went. The aristocracy and the knightly class
certainly provided a large pool of skilled manpower trained in war
from which soldiers could be recruited.[40] Moreover, it was upon the
royal household, their wealth and their leading followers, that the

---

[38] B. H. Hill, *Medieval Monarchy in Action* (New York, 1972), pp. 73–5; for Godfrey's participation see above pp. 63; B. Arnold, *German Knighthood 1050–1300* (Oxford, 1985), pp. 50, 81,
86, 97; R. P. Grossman, *The Financing of the Crusades*, unpublished Ph.D. thesis, University
of Chicago, 1965, pp. 6–7.

[39] On the German *Indiculus* see the comments above p. 63; J. H. Round, 'Introduction of
knight service into England', *Feudal England* (London, 1895) was the great proponent of the
notion of a veritable revolution in which William imported feudalism: modern thinking has
tended to suggest that it came into existence over a period of time becuase there was no
such coherent body of feudal ideas as Round supposed – on which see M. Chibnall,
'Military service in Normandy before 1066', *Battle*, 5 (1982), 65–77; on the likelihood of a
continuation of a preconquest form of quotas and obligation based on negotiations between
the English king and his followers see Gillingham, 'Introduction of knight service', 53–64;
D. R. Cook, 'The Norman military revolution in England', *Battle*, 1 (1978), 94–102.

[40] On mercenaries and the king see the seminal article of J. O. Prestwich, 'War and finance in
the Anglo-Norman state', *TRHS* 4 (1954), 19–43; J. Schlight, *Monarchs and Mercenaries*
(Bridgeport, 1968); S. D. B. Brown, 'The mercenary and his master: military service and
monetary reward in the eleventh and twelfth century', *History*, 74 (1989), 20–38.

Norman kings relied to raise armies. These professional groupings of household followers around the king – paid and aspirant, or endowed and paid and hoping for better – were what the king relied on for the core of his army and its command. In time of war such a body could expand and serve as the command force of a great army. Through them the sinews of war were channelled, for in the end it was money which made victory.[41] Although such bodies, such military households, can only be documented from the early twelfth century, it is unlikely that they were invented – rather they must have evolved over a period of time. In 1101 Henry I negotiated an arrangement with Robert II of Flanders whereby the latter swore to be his man and to provide 1,000 knights in return for a fee. William Rufus almost certainly made the same arrangement when he met Robert in 1093. It is interesting that the treaty specified that each knight was to be provided with three horses.[42] It seems likely that this kind of organisation was the secret of Rufus's reputation for raising and paying armies.[43] A medieval army was a composite of forces around a core of loyal leaders whom we can regard as generals. They were not merely military men; they also formed an administrative corps for the vital task of handling and paying out money. Clearly both William Rufus and Henry I needed such a body if they were prepared to take on large Flemish forces. Of course we cannot describe such organisation with any certainty outside the Anglo-Norman sphere, and clearly for Suger such capacity was a matter of wonder. What is of interest is that such capacity had already come into being amongst the Normans on the eve of the First Crusade; they were a major element in the army of conquest which Urban II called into being in 1095. This organisational development indicates the degree to which war in the late eleventh century was not a matter of instinct, of 'kick and rush', but of guile and organisation, in short of generalship. This explains the rarity not of battle but of battle on a large scale. They understood the context in which they were making war. To attack your enemy's economic base, isolate his castles, starve his population, these were

---

[41] M. Prestwich, 'Military household of the Norman kings', *English Historical Review*, 96 (1981), 1–37; M. Chibnall, 'Mercenaries and the "Familia Regis" under Henry I', *History*, 62 (1977), 15–23.

[42] For the text of the treaty of 1101 *Diplomatic Documents preserved in the Public Record Office* 1. (1101–1272) ed. P. Chaplais (London, 1964) no. 1; on Rufus's treaty Barlow, *William Rufus*, p. 325.

[43] Suger, pp. 8–9.

surer methods and more applicable to the usually limited objectives for which men fought. However, there were occasions when the stakes were so high that all had to be risked on the throw of battle, and on these occasions the men who directed things sought to ensure that their chances of victory were as great as possible in what was the most risky of all undertakings.

Fulk le Réchin, count of Anjou (1067–1109) described how he fought his brother for the county over a period of eight years:

But still he attacked me yet again, laying siege to my fortress of Brissac. There I rode against him with those princes whom God in His clemency, permitted to join me, and I fought with him a pitched battle in which, by God's grace, I overcame him; and he was captured and handed over to me, and a thousand of his men with him.[44]

The repeated invocation of God's name shows how few illusions Fulk had about the chances of battle. Duke William of Normandy shared his wariness, but in the expedition against England battle was unavoidable. Its risks probably underlay the unwillingness already noted of some of the Norman lords to join in the enterprise. William's attack on England enjoyed great good fortune. His preparations had taken a very long time, yet he found exceptionally good weather very late in the year for the crossing on 27 September 1066.[45] In the passage from Dives to St Valéry his fleet had suffered losses, but none are recorded for the main crossing on 27 September and this suggests that the favourable breeze that day did not exceed Force 3.5, about 10 mph. In any greater wind his precious horses would probably have suffered losses for they were housed in ordinary transports, not ships specially designed for the purpose.[46] It seems likely that he had sent out light ships to watch the English fleet and coasts and so would have known of the partial collapse of the enemy defences on 8 September and probably also of Harold's

---

[44] Dunbabin, *France in the Making*, pp. 188–90; Fulk le Réchin, *Fragmentum Historiae Andegavensis*, ed. L. Halphen and R. Poupardin in *Chroniques des comtes d'Anjou et des seigneurs d'Amboise* (Paris, 1913) p. 237 quoted and tr. J. Gillingham, 'William the Bastard', p. 147.

[45] I very much doubt that William had purposely delayed his crossing waiting for the enemy army to break up as suggested by M. Chibnall in Brown, 'Battle of Hastings', n. 20. One has only to think of the deep preoccupation of the allies with weather in the uncertain conditions of the Channel even in 1944 to grasp that William must have awaited the weather, not hoped that it would await his greater convenience.

[46] For the suggestion that William had such ships see above p. 60, n. 25; J. Neumann, 'Hydrographic and ship-hydrodynamic aspects of the Norman invasion', 232–4.

march north.[47] Since William seems to have been well aware of Norse interest in England and had encouraged Tosti, Harold's estranged brother, in his attacks on England, this was not mere good luck. William's diplomacy to isolate Harold had been intensive and he was able to unfurl a papal banner before his army.[48] After landing at Pevensey William soon realised that Hastings was a better site, and moved there a day later. Immediately he began to fortify his bases, building castles at both to protect themselves and provide safe harbour for the fleet.[49] At the same time he raided the countryside, a process shown vividly in the Tapestry. It is possible that this ravaging, in Harold's own earldom, was intended to provoke the enemy into an overhasty attack, but the feeding of such a large host would have compelled it anyway.[50] With a secure base William could dominate the Sussex coast, but in the longer run his situation was not very favourable, for the English fleet would soon threaten his communications which in any case were at risk as the weather deteriorated and the autumn storms blew up. William wanted a quick solution, as he had probably known all along; he needed to seek battle and to capitalise quickly on his strength and the high morale of his army buoyed up by promises of English land.[51] On the other hand, he hardly dared risk deep penetration of an enemy hinterland where he would find difficulties enough later, even unopposed.[52] But he was ready for battle. According to William of Poitiers, a Breton servant of the Confessor, Robert Fitz-Wimarch, sent a message warning him of the coming of the Saxon army and urging him to take refuge in his fortifications, but William rejected this advice eagerly stating his desire for battle.[53] It was William's great good fortune that Harold played into his hands, but this was a miscalculation brilliantly exploited by the Norman duke.

Harold's victory over the Danes at York on 25 September was, by all accounts, a bloody affair which, coming on top of the losses at Fulford on 20 September, must seriously have reduced the available effectives in the Anglo-Saxon army. Traditionally, he is supposed to

---

[47] Gillmor, 'Naval Logistics', p. 124.   [48] Douglas, *William the Conqueror*, pp. 191–2.
[49] WP, pp. 168–9.
[50] Gillingham, 'William the Bastard', p. 158, follows William of Poitier's suggestion, p. 180–1, that the devastation caused Harold to hasten his march.
[51] WP, p. 158, tr. Gillingham, 'William the Bastard', p. 157.
[52] In Kent, on the way to London, his army would later run short of supplies: WP, p. 212.
[53] WP, pp. 170–1.

have heard of William's landing on or shortly after 1 October and then to have been obliged to retrace his thirteen-day 190 mile march to London, arriving at Hastings on 13 October. If this chronology is in any way correct, then we can suppose that not all of his army came with him, for Ordericus says he spent five days in London raising forces. This may or may not be precisely true, but Harold would have needed some time to concentrate troops and surely no considerable army could have moved so far so fast.[54] Harold then set off and reached Battle on the evening of 13 October. We do not know what his intentions were. It is possible that he hoped to take the Normans by surprise as he had the Norse and this was certainly what the Normans later thought, even fearing a night attack which caused the army to spend an uncomfortable and sleepless night.[55] It is equally possible that he wanted to force William's army to concentrate by its fortifications, cutting it off from food – a tactic we have noted used by William himself. In either case his error was to march as close to his enemy as Battle, a mere seven miles from the main enemy encampment. This was the edge of the wooded lands and he could go no further for, like all Anglo-Saxon forces, his army was used to fighting on foot – although its leading members travelled on horseback. On the open Downs such an infantry force could be cut to pieces by the Norman cavalry. The error was compounded because William pounced on it. For William had been at pains to keep a close watch for enemy movements – his emphasis on good reconnaissance was a life-long characteristic.[56] Early on the morning of 14 October he marched quickly to Battle and deployed his army catching Harold unawares, as the Chronicle E has it: 'before all the army had come' and D more interestingly: 'And William came against him by surprise before his army was drawn up in battle array. But the king nevertheless fought hard against him with the men who were willing to support him'. Florence of Worcester says that only half Harold's army had assembled and only a third deployed when the Normans struck.[57] Harold managed to seize a strong position at the mouth of a funnel through the woods on the

---

[54] OV, 2. 172-3.
[55] Brown, 'Battle of Hastings', 8; on the battle see the accounts of Barclay and Lemmon mentioned above p. 56, n. 13 and the comments of Gillingham, 'William the Bastard', 156-8.
[56] as Gillingham, 'William the Bastard', quite rightly insists.
[57] ASC, pp. 141-3; Florence 1. 226.

main road by the present village of Battle.[58] He had a strong position for defence and his men were determined. But they had no way of attacking the enemy who could retreat easily and attack once more, unless they obligingly panicked. Nor could Harold's forces retreat for the enemy were upon them. Harold's impetuous rush forward meant that his army was immobilised, unable to go forward or back, and though it barred William's route inland the initiative in the forthcoming battle would lie with the Normans. This is the force of William of Poitiers's famous comment: 'What a strange contest then began, in which one of the protagonists attacked freely and at will, the other enduring the assault as though rooted to the ground'.[59] Moreover, there was an additional problem springing from Harold's haste; his army appears to have had very few archers.[60] This does not mean that they were without missile throwers – javelins, axes and clubs fly through the air in the Tapestry. But the bow outranged all these: it was a striking vulnerability, and William's deployment was organised to exploit it. His army advanced in three lines with archers thrown forward, followed by armoured foot and then the cavalry. In addition his line was divided into three divisions, with the Bretons on the left, the Normans in the centre and the French on the right.[61] In effect William was assaulting a fortress – the close-packed Anglo-Saxon and Danish infantry settled in a strong position on top of the hill.[62] Of these many were professionals as well armed as their enemies, but as the Tapestry shows there were many lesser folk, lacking anything except a spear.

William clearly intended that his archers should weaken the enemy by their fire, probably from about fifty yards, protected from enemy sally by the presence of heavily armed infantry who would then charge in to the assault making breaches which the cavalry could exploit. The strength of the Saxon position and the

---

[58] Perhaps the point of the *Carmen*'s story, p. 25, of the Saxons dashing forth from the forests is that Harold unexpectedly managed to rally his surprised force.

[59] WP, p. 195.   [60] As noted above p. 35 the *BT* shows a single English archer, Pl. 61.

[61] The source for this division of the Norman army is the *Carmen*, vv. 413–14 upon whose account much doubt has been cast: R. H. C. Davis, 'Carmen de Hastingae Proelio', *English Historical Review*, 93 (1978), 241–61; 'The Carmen de Hstingae Proelio: a discussion', *Battle*, 2 (1979) 1–20. However, its value as a contemporary, though very literary, source has been effectively restated by E. M. C. van Houts, 'Latin poetry and the Anglo-Norman court 1066–1135: the *Carmen de Hastingae Proelio*', *Journal of Medieval History*, 15 (1989), 38–62.

[62] WP, p. 186 says that the Danes had sent much help.

effectiveness of their weapons balked the Normans.[63] The cavalry then joined in the melée until, on the left, the Bretons were repulsed and pursued by the English: William rallied his men by showing them that the rumour of his death was untrue and they fell upon the exposed English with great slaughter. It was perhaps a result of this near disaster that William resorted to feigned flight, twice drawing out substantial forces of his enemy who were then cut to pieces.[64] This attrition was reinforced by direct assault on the English position, supported by volleys of arrows. In his description of this final stage of the battle, William of Poitiers makes it clear that the English continued to fight hard but were gradually surrounded, losses forcing the contraction of their line. However, it was probably the death of Harold and his brothers which led to the eventual flight.

The battle illustrates the skills of a late eleventh-century commander. The marshalling of resources speaks volumes for the duke's ability to exploit the peasant surplus. Many of the soldiers in the Norman army were paid professionals from all over France, and there were similar people, English and Danish, in Harold's force. William sought battle, but he had obviously planned to fortify his bases and to live off the country. He kept a close watch on his enemy who failed to surprise him. Unable to advance or retreat, Harold was himself caught, on the morning of the 14 October, by the speed with which the Normans advanced and deployed, but he managed to seize a strong position. The Norman order of battle was well designed, for the assault and the mobility which had given them the initiative was used with skill to erode the English strength. A feature of the battle was William's control of his army. He led by example, an essential quality of a medieval commander, having three horses killed under him, while at the same time supervising his forces and encouraging them even at the very end when some English made a stand at the Malfosse.[65] Harold's failure to await reinforcements meant that he lacked archers and so exposed his men cruelly.

The decisive arm in the battle was, however, the Norman cavalry. It was not that they could charge home sweeping all before them, for

---

[63] WP, pp. 186–9 testifies to the effectiveness of the English as soldiers. Perhaps the two-handed axe was particularly effective (see *BT*, Pl. 62): Pierce, 'Arms and armour', 245–6.

[64] WP, pp. 190–3, 194–5; the use of the feigned retreat at Hastings has often been doubted but it seems to have been a well-established tactic of cavalry in the eleventh century, on which see B. S. Bachrach, 'The feigned retreat at Hastings', *Medieval Studies*, 33 (1971), 344–7.

[65] WP, pp. 198–9, 202–5.

clearly they could not. The Tapestry shows them not so much charging into the enemy as jabbing and hacking at them. The mass charge with the lances couched, which would be the feature of cavalry warfare later in the twelfth century, was not a feature of Hastings: in the Tapestry some figures carry their lances couched, but for the most part those with spears jab at their enemies overarm or underarm, or even throw them, while others hack with their swords. The question of when this style of 'shock tactics' was developed, with riders *en masse* in close order clamping their long and heavy lances under their arms, has been much debated. It is now generally accepted that the technique was only in its infancy in 1066, but views of when it became a widely accepted method vary from about 1100 to the 1140s. Inevitably much of the discussion has been based on medieval illustrations and their interpretation, a factor which has also complicated discussion of the size of horses. However, the illustrations used too often show individual warriors and discussions have focussed on these portrayals. In fact mounted soldiers must quite often have tucked their lances under their arms; it was a natural and useful way of using the weapon, though others could be just as useful as the Bayeux Tapestry shows. What was novel was the employment of this technique by large numbers in disciplined units, a matter on which the illustrative material is not very helpful. It would appear to the present writer that the First Crusade represents a critical stage in the evolution of this technique, as will be indicated later.[66] The Normans who fought at Hastings probably owed their cohesion and discipline, which enabled them to manoeuvre as in the feigned flights, to long practice in fighting alongside their neighbours grouped around the local lord.[67] This

---

[66] On the use of the lance see: D. J. A. Ross, 'L'originalité de 'Turoldus': le maniement de lance', *Cahiers de Civilisation Médiévale*, 6 (1963), 127–38; V. Cirlot, 'Techniques guerrières en Catalogne féodale; le maniement de la lance', *Cahiers de Civilisation Médiévale*, 28 (1985), 36–43 who argues for a date later in the twelfth century; J. Flori, 'Encore l'usage de la lance: la technique du combat vers l'an 1100', *Cahiers de Civilisation Médiévale*, 31 (1988), 213–40 who argues for an earlier date; on the development suggested here see below p. 73. On the size of horses see below pp. 372–3.

[67] Brown, 'Battle of Hastings', 16, suggests that the discipline of the Norman army and its coherence were based on the groupings of five or ten knights called *conroi*, which are known to have existed in the twelfth century: J. F. Verbruggen, 'La tactique militaire des armées de chevaliers', *Revue du Nord*, 29 (1947), 161–80. I think it is likely that such units emerged on the model of vassal-groupings which formed an important element of armies in the eleventh century, and perhaps largely as a result of the need to order mercenaries being used on an ever greater scale. Men were used to fighting alongside their neighbours. Much

was not the triumph of cavalry over infantry as portrayed by Oman, rather it was the triumph of a good commander who used all the means at his disposal to break down a courageous enemy. His campaign was methodical and his battle formation well adapted for its purpose. The archers weakened the enemy and were guarded by heavy foot who then moved to the assault followed up by cavalry. The resilience of Harold's force blunted this plan but William was able to extemporise the feigned flights which weakened his enemy for the final bloody assault in which, amongst the English, it seemed as though the dead as they fell moved more than the living.[68] It was not the shock value of the cavalry which triumphed, but their disciplined mobility and courage. Unbroken infantry was always highly dangerous to cavalry. At Bourgethéroulde in 1124 some of the rebels rejoiced when the English king's household troops dismounted, but the experienced Amaury de Montfort took a more realistic view. 'A mounted soldier who has dismounted with his men will not fly from the field – he will either die or conquer'.[69] At Tinchebrai in 1106 Henry I of England (1099–1135) dismounted much of his force and it was these that halted Robert Curthose's last charge.[70] Indeed, the value of infantry in anchoring a line of defence was always recognised – Leo VI 'the Wise' (886–912) had suggested that infantry be posted behind cavalry in the line of battle so that the latter could withdraw behind them if things went badly, and King Baldwin of Jerusalem (1118–32) would use just this formation at Hab in 1119.[71] An eleventh-century Spanish Muslim writer, Abu Bakr at-Turtusi suggested a rather more complex though not dissimilar tactical formation:

The tactics we use and which seem the most efficacious against our enemy are these. The infantry with their antelope [hide] shields, lances and iron-tipped javelins are placed, kneeling in ranks. Their lances rest obliquely on their shoulders, the shaft touching the ground behind them, the point directed towards the enemy. Each one kneels on his left knee with his shield in the air. Behind the infantry are the picked archers who, with their arrows, can pierce coats of mail. Behind the archers are the cavalry.

of the army of 1066 was, effectively, mercenary and large groups of such men would have needed a parallel organisation, but we do not known precisely how they were used.
[68] WP, pp. 194–5.   [69] OV, 6. 350–1.
[70] Henry of Huntingdon, *Historia Anglorum*, ed. T. Arnold (London, 1879) [hereafter cited as HH], p. 235 and see below pp. 372–3.
[71] J. F. Verbruggen, *The Art of Warfare in the Middle Ages*, tr. S. Willard and S. C. M. Southern (Amsterdam, 1977), pp. 192–3.

When the Christians charge, the infantry remains in position, kneeling as before. As soon as the enemy comes into range, the archers let loose a hail of arrows while the infantry throw their javelins and receive the charge on the points of their lances. Then infantry and archers open their ranks to right and left and through the gaps they create, the cavalry rushes the enemy and inflicts upon him what Allah wills.[72]

In recognising the limitations of cavalry and the value of infantry we need to bear in mind that the horses used at Hastings were comparatively small animals. Recent research suggests that in the late eleventh century a horse of twelve hands was quite large, and one of fourteen or more exceptional. To put this into perspective, a Shetland is ten hands, a twelve hand horse would now be classified as a pony, and fourteen a small hunter. These estimates are based on examining the representations of horses in the Bayeux Tapestry, particularly in relation to their riders.[73] In the Tapestry all the horsemen are riding 'long', that is with their legs at almost full-stretch and feet in stirrups fully extended, a configuration which gives stability. In all cases the rider's legs project well below the body of the horse, suggesting a small animal. It is possible that this is an artistic convention but the story of Richard, son of Ascletin of Aversa, who liked to ride horses so small that his feet almost touched the ground is well-known. Moreover, similar representations are known in quite different contexts; an eleventh-century Spanish marble relief and the early twelfth-century *Commentaries* of Beatus (BM Add 11695) are examples and many more could be cited. It is interesting that in the Aquileia mural of a crusader with spear couched pursuing and killing a Saracen, no difference in the size of horses is suggested, and this seems to be generally true of early twelfth-century pictures.[74] William's knights charging uphill against steady infantry must have needed good nerves and it is doubtful if they were aware of the 'shock' effect which later writers would ascribe to them. What happened along the crest of that hill where Battle Abbey now stands must have resembled the sixteenth-century 'push at pike', not the charge of some Hollywood Light

[72] Quoted by Lourie, 'A society organised for war', 70.
[73] R. H. C. Davis, 'Warhorses of the Normans', 69, 80 81 and see also his book *The Medieval Warhorse*. In these two works the difficulties of breeding really good strains of horse in medieval conditions are carefully explored.
[74] G. Jackson, *Medieval Spain* (London, 1972), Pl. 36; D. Nicolle, *Early Medieval Islamic Arms and Armour* (Madrid, 1976), Pl. 41; Flori, 'Encore l'usage de la lance', 220 1; V. Cirlot, 'Techniques guerrières an Catalogne féodale', 36 43.

Brigade. William exploited his good luck and, decisively, used the mobility of his cavalry with great skill. But the fact that cavalry was decisive does not mean that it was totally dominant, as later experience mentioned here shows. William was certainly careful to bring plenty of foot-soldiers with him.[75] Battle was always chancy – William was able to rally his men against one early moment of panic which could have destroyed him. Once this crisis was over he held the initiative and could plan his attacks and he did so to great effect. Hastings was a decisive battle largely because the killing of Harold and his brothers, together with a large number of thegns whose deaths came on top of the butchery at Fulford and Stamford, deprived the Anglo-Saxon realm of much of its leadership. Harold himself paid the price for his folly in engaging too soon. Even so, the battle did not deliver the whole realm to William. He would soon be crowned, but it was only by terrible devastation in the north and covering the land with a network of castles that he was able to secure his hold. This process of conquest was greatly facilitated by the lack of castles in England. The English learned – Hereward built a castle at Ely in 1071 – but by then it was too late and William's long war of attrition, which followed Hastings, was on the brink of success.[76]

The conquest of England is not isolated as an example of large scale and complex military effort in late eleventh century Europe. Only a few years later Robert Guiscard, the Norman conqueror of South Italy, launched a great expedition to capture the Eastern Roman Empire. This involved the raising of a fleet and a great army which was kept in the field for some four years from 1081–5. Guiscard had been seeking a Byzantine marriage for his family and when his efforts collapsed he took advantage of the internal weakness of the empire in the early years of Alexius I Comnenus (1081–1118). It was an extraordinarily bold act, for Robert's brother, Roger, would not complete the conquest of Sicily until 1091, while he himself had promised to aid Pope Gregory VII (1073–85) against

[75] France, 'La Guerre dans la Fance féodale', 197–8.
[76] Gillingham, 'Knight service', 55; he also cites OV, 2. 218: 'For in the lands of the English there were very few of those fortifications which the French call castles; in consequence the English, for all their martial qualities and valour, were at a disadvantage when it came to resisting their enemies'; however there were fortifications in Anglo-Saxon England: G. Beresford, 'Goltho Manor Lincolnshire; the building and the surrounding defences c. 850–1150', Battle, 4 (1981), 13–36, and note also E. Roesdahl, 'Danish geometrical fortresses and their context', Battle, 9 (1986), 209–26. On the later stages of the Conquest see OV, 2. 221–37 and for its horrors 231–33; W. E. Kapelle, The Norman Conquest of the North (London, 1979).

Henry IV of Germany. In these circumstances the Byzantines were able to create diplomatic difficulties by subsidising Henry IV, inflaming hostility amongst the many Norman leaders who had resented the Hauteville domination, some of whom were actually employed as mercenaries by Alexius, and by playing upon Venetian concern about a Norman dominion on both sides of the Adriatic. This diplomatic background severely hampered the Norman campaign.[77] War opened late in 1080 when Bohemond landed at Avlona with the vanguard of an army 15,000 strong whose core was a purely Norman force of 1,300 knights.[78] By 17 June 1081, after seizing Corfu, Robert and Bohemond were before Dyrrachium, the western terminus of the Via Egnetia, the great road to Constantinople, held for Alexius by George Paleologus. A close siege was established around Dyrrachium with the construction of a great leather-covered siege-tower. Against it, Paleologus built a tower on the wall equipped with wooden beams to hold off the Norman attack, and as the two towers engaged, his troops sallied out and burned the siege-tower.[79] In July 1081 the Venetians largely destroyed the Norman fleet, and Guiscard was now faced with a strong Greek army under Alexius which by 15 October was close to Dyrrachium. Guiscard's situation was now extremely difficult, his communications were cut and an enemy force was in the field. Alexius debated whether to attack, or to establish a counter-blockade which would starve the Normans. There was much to commend either course of action. The problem with blockade was that it would take time and Alexius had problems elsewhere, and it was probably because of this that he advanced to battle on 18 October 1081. Guiscard burned the remnant of his fleet, forcing his troops to fight. He seems to have surprised Alexius by leaving his camp early in the morning, so that it was captured by the garrison of Dyrrachium and other forces sent by Alexius. As the Greek army deployed, the Varangian guard, numbering in its ranks many Anglo-Saxons, prepared for action.[80] Then they charged, contrary to Alexius's orders and though they pushed back the horse and infantry under the count of Bari, they

---

[77] F. Chalandon, *Essai sur le règne d'Alexis I Comnène (1081–1118)* (Paris, 1900, New York, 1971), pp. 51–94; *Domination Normande* 1. 258–84.

[78] See above p. 62. for the 1300 see Malaterra, p. 71.   [79] *Alexiad*, pp. 142–3.

[80] On the Anglo-Saxon participation in the Varangian guard see Godfrey, 'The defeated Anglo-Saxons', 63–74; S. Blondal, *The Varangians of Byzantium*, tr. and revised B. Benedikz (Cambridge, 1978).

were overextended and defeated by an infantry charge in the flank. Many of Alexius's compound force, including the Turks and the large Slav force under their ruler Bodin, then fled making no effort to intervene as the Normans fell upon Alexius in the centre.[81] Guiscard's victory opened the way for the fall of Dyrrachium in February 1082 enabling the Normans to advance via Deabolis to Kastoria in the spring of 1082. At this point Guiscard was forced to return to Italy by revolt in his own lands, fanned by Byzantine money and by Henry IV's assault on Rome which Alexius had encouraged, leaving Bohemond to conduct a campaign whose immediate purpose was probably to secure a firm base for further advance. Although a number of cities fell and Bohemond twice defeated Alexius's efforts to relieve Joannina the Norman expedition was now in difficulties. Bohemond failed to seize Ochrida and Berroea, while the fort at Moglena fell to a Byzantine counterattack. Skopia, Pelagonia and Trikala, amongst others, fell, but the siege of Larissa was undertaken late in 1082 at a time when there had been desertions and treachery in the Norman force.[82] These symptoms of exhaustion prepared the way for Alexius to challenge Bohemond in the open field. His earlier experience had not been good. Anna tells us that after the defeat at Dyrrachium Alexius had decided that: 'the first charge of the Keltic cavalry was irresistible'. In his attempts to relieve the siege of Joannina he used strategies to counter this. In his first effort he strengthened his centre with wagons mounted with poles, whose presence was intended to break up enemy cavalry assault. However, Bohemond was forewarned and attacked on the flanks. It was not a decisive defeat and the emperor returned, this time protecting his centre with coltrops, iron barbs scattered on the ground – but Bohemond again attacked on the flank. At Larissa in the spring of 1083, however, Alexius lured much of Bohemond's force away from his camp which the Byzantines captured, thus forcing the Normans to raise the siege, although the victory left the Norman army intact.[83] Bohemond was now faced with retreat and a discontented army which had not been paid and this forced him to return to Italy, while Alexius mopped up his garrisons. In the summer of 1083 a Venetian fleet took Dyrrachium and with the fall of Kastoria to Greek forces in November it seemed

[81] *Alexiad*, pp. 145–53; Oman, *Art of war*, 1. 166–7; Chalandon, *Alexis I Comnène*, p. 79.
[82] Chalandon, *Alexis Comnène*, pp. 87–8.
[83] Chalandon, *Alexis Comnène*, pp. 86–7, 90; *Alexiad*, pp. 163–73; Yewdale, *Bohemond*, pp. 20–1.

that the campaign was over. In the autumn of 1084 Robert Guiscard raised another army and a fleet of 150 ships. He defeated the Venetian fleet before Corfu, which he again seized, but his army was decimated by illness on the mainland and it dissolved totally when he died in July 1085.[84]

The Norman war against Byzantium was a long affair. It was almost certainly prompted by the weakness of the empire at this juncture, but Guiscard had underestimated his own problems and the range of his enemies, whose various attacks sapped his army. It became a war of attrition in which both sides were desperately short of resources. After his defeat at Dyrrachium Alexius had to resort to seizure of church wealth to raise another army. Bohemond, left in charge by his father, prosecuted a skilful campaign. The Normans continued to be a strong fighting force, but their two victories over Alexius were inconclusive, as was his sole victory over them. In the end, shortages of money and men were more acute on the Norman side than on the Greek, but it was a close-run affair. It is remarkable that the Normans of South Italy could sustain such an effort at all in the circumstances. Certainly the campaign made Bohemond's name as a soldier.

The campaigns of William the Conqueror and Robert Guiscard were, however, somewhat unusual for the ferocity with which they were fought and the readiness of both sides to resort to battle. When the Conqueror died in 1087 he divided his land between his sons. Robert Curthose held Normandy and William II 'Rufus' became king of England. The third son, Henry, was given money which he used to found a lordship in the Cotentin. These dispositions were soon challenged by the brothers, each of whom hoped to gain the whole inheritance of his father. When Rufus died in a hunting accident in 1099 the youngest brother, Henry, took up the challenge with ultimate success, for he seized the English throne and then Normandy with the victory of Tinchebrai in 1106. In nearly twenty years of war Tinchebrai was the only major battle. In the first stage of the conflict, Odo of Bayeux conspired with many of the nobility of England against the king, and Robert Curthose sent Robert of Bellême and Eustace of Boulogne who seized Pevensey and Rochester. However, he failed to raise an expedition to support them and the plot fizzled out. In the next phase, William, with his

[84] Chalandon, *Alexis Comnène*, pp. 92-3.

far greater resources, set about seducing the duke's vassals and thereby securing castles as bases. It was in eastern Normandy north of the Seine that William concentrated his efforts from 1089 onwards, building a strong position. Robert's counter-offensive was supported by King Philip of France who, however, allowed himself to be bought off by William. In November 1090, the English king was able to take advantage of factional struggles in Rouen and all but seized the city. It was not until 1091 that William came in person to the scene of this desultory fighting and raiding, which were brought to an end in February 1091 by a peace between the warring brothers. This gave William a strong position in Normandy, in part at the expense of Henry's lands in the Cotentin and inaugurated a period of rapprochement during which the two brothers tried to impose order in Normandy.[85] By 1093, however, the two brothers were again at war and the following year William led a strong army into Normandy. This time Robert waged quite a successful campaign against William and his allies, seizing important castles and threatening his long-established hold on eastern Normandy, until Philip of France was once again bought off with English bribes. It was probably in anticipation of this campaign that in 1093 William met Robert II of Flanders and concluded a treaty under which the count of Flanders undertook to supply mercenaries to the English king. In the end, the English campaign came to a halt when Robert Curthose took the cross. Abbot Jarento of St Bénigne, the papal legate, then negotiated an arrangement whereby Robert pawned the duchy to William for three years for the sum of 10,000 marks. This freed Robert Curthose to join the crusade and provided finances for him.

The men who went on the First Crusade were clearly familiar with the eternal verities of war – above all the need to seize food and deprive your enemies of it. In the context of eleventh-century society, that meant a war of position against castles which guarded lands and lordships, in which battle was to be avoided in favour of attrition. The strength of castles could be challenged by siege, and specialised equipment for this purpose was devised, but more often it was circumvented by raiding which brought the knight, whose mobility and heavy equipment prepared him for every eventuality to the fore. The manorial system, which underpinned this warring

[85] David, *Robert Curthose*, pp. 46–51, 53–69; Barlow, *William Rufus*, pp. 70–98, 273–96.

world, enabled its masters to sustain and organise warfare over long periods of time. Even at the most trivial levels we have noted, fighting often went on for years. Kings and great lords had the economic capacity to make very considerable military efforts, like the conquest of England or the German expeditions to Italy, which must excite our admiration. They could draw on large reserves of trained manpower from within and without their borders – a wide and rather ill-defined range of people were able to raise their sons in the skills of war and for them almost any war could exert enormous attractions. It was as lances for sale that Normans had emigrated to South Italy at the very beginning of the eleventh century; knights were attracted to war for the pay and the profits and, one is tempted to add, the pleasure. For plunder and ravaging were not merely a way of war, they were a way of life against which the church's injunctions made little headway. The expedition to the east proclaimed by Pope Urban in 1095 offered an outlet for this drive, reinforced by a sense of righteousness. Some of its leaders were experienced in command. Robert Curthose had fought a long and bitter war, while Godfrey had participated in major expeditions and battles. By contrast Stephen of Blois, Hugh of Vermandois and Robert of Flanders were relatively untried while the count of Toulouse had risen to power in different circumstances. Bohemond alone had commanded a large army and had knowledge of eastern methods of fighting. The real challenge for all of them, however, was working together, for of that none of them had any real experience. Urban II provided an able Legate, Adhémar of Le Puy, who had military experience, but he never appointed a single commander. That was the problem which the leaders had to resolve.

CHAPTER 4

Preparations and prelude

Urban II launched his appeal for an expedition to the east at Clermont in November 1095 and in a calculated campaign aimed primarily at the nobility and knighthood undertook a great journey through western and southern France. In other areas he relied on bishops and enthusiastic preachers to spread the word. We know very little about the mechanics of this process, and only rarely do we have insight into the reasons why and how individuals took the cross. Raymond of Toulouse, the first major layman to take the cross, seems to have conferred with Urban before Clermont. Indeed, William of Malmesbury was later to write erroneously, that he persuaded Urban to launch the expedition.[1] The general reasons which we have already noted as underlying crusading enthusiasm applied to the leaders as much as to anyone else, but we know enough about them as individuals to be able to speculate intelligently. Robert Curthose faced a difficult political situation in 1095, for his brother William Rufus wanted the whole inheritance of the Conqueror and could bring great resources to bear to this end. Robert was an able soldier – he had once captured Brionne, a castle which occupied the Conqueror for three years, 'between the ninth hour [3pm] and sunset', but he lacked self-discipline and liked the pleasures of life – 'to sleep under a roof'. According to the hostile Ordericus it was because of the weakness of his position that: 'fearing still worse to come since everyone had abandoned him, he resolved on the advice of certain men of religion to hand over the administration of his duchy to his brother and, himself taking the cross, to go on pilgrimage to Jerusalem to make amends to God for his sins'.[2] Robert lacked the grasping drive of his father and brothers, but his

---

[1] Crozet, 'Le voyage d'Urbain' 274–7; Hills, *Raymond IV*, pp. 105–8; *GR*, p. 456.
[2] OV, 4. 85, 211, 115; 5. 27.

valour and personal geniality made him the most attractive of the
Conqueror's sons. Stephen of Blois and Robert of Flanders chose to
accompany him on the march south from Normandy while his own
large army included a number of erstwhile enemies like Stephen,
count of Aumale.[3] But Robert was seeking refuge from his political
troubles and although he would show great valour, would display
also his notorious laziness on the crusade.

Godfrey de Bouillon may well have felt that his future lay behind
him. His family lands were not vast and his hold on them was
challenged by Albert of Namur and Mathilda, countess of Tuscany,
the widow of Geoffrey the Hunchback. The duchy of Lorraine
which had been conferred on him by Henry IV in 1087 was 'an
empty dignity'. The Investiture Contest placed him in an unenvia-
ble position – he was the enemy of the papal ally, Mathilda, but in
Lorraine had failed to support Henry IV's champion Otbert bishop
of Liège, for local reasons.[4] He may well have felt that the crusade
offered him a possible escape from the frustrations of his position in
Germany, though it is unlikely that he swore an oath never to
return, as later tradition asserts. His decision to support an initiative
by Henry IV's enemy, Pope Urban, was a great triumph for the
reform papacy. His near-neighbour, Robert of Flanders, held a truly
great and rich fief. His father Robert the Frisian (1071–93) had gone
on pilgrimage to the Holy Land in the years 1086–9. It was probably
while returning from Jerusalem in 1089 that he arrived at Constantinople and there was asked by Alexius I for military assistance
in the form of 500 cavalry, which probably arrived in the spring of
1091. Alexius wrote a letter to Robert, probably in 1090, reminding
him of his promise, and this was later transformed into crusading
propaganda.[5] This family connection goes some way towards
explaining his decision to go.

It was probably a family conference which decided the only
crusader with royal blood, Hugh of Vermandois, often referred to in

---

[3] David, *Robert Curthose*, p. 228.
[4] Andressohn, *Godfrey de Bouillon*, pp. 34–5, 39–40, 41, 43–5; Mayer, *Mélanges*, pp. 20–1.
[5] It is not certain whether Robert called at Constantinople on his outbound or return
journey. Verlinden, *Robert le Frison*, p. 158–9, suggests that Robert met Alexius whilst
returning in 1089. *Alexiad*, pp. 229–30, 232–3 reports the meeting and the request for aid
without giving any dates. On the letter of Alexius and its use as a basis for forgery, Verlinden
pp. 162–4; on Robert II, see M. M. Knappen, 'Robert of Flanders on the First Crusade', in
L. J. Paetow, ed., *The Crusades and other Historical Essays presented to D. C. Munro* (New York,
1928), pp. 79–100; he gained great prestige from crusading, Dunbabin, *France in the Making*,
p. 291.

the crusading sources as Hugh Magnus, to take the cross. The house of Capet was embarrassed by the success of Urban's appeal, for King Philip was excommunicate because of his marriage to Bertrada of Montfort. A meeting of the Capetians and their leading nobles was held in February 1096 and in July the king wrote a letter to Urban at Nîmes, announcing the participation of his younger brother, Hugh of Vermandois, and his own submission to the pope's judgement on his marriage.[6]

According to the anonymous author of the *Gesta Francorum*, Bohemond heard of the crusade only in September 1096 when Frankish forces (which are not identified) began to move through Italy and he was at the siege of Amalfi with his uncle Roger of Sicily and his half-brother Roger Borsa. Thus inspired, he cut his most valuable cloak into crosses which he gave to those who would follow him with the result that the besieging army melted away. It is unlikely that Bohemond had remained so long in ignorance of a major papal initiative. He was a rear-vassal of Pope Urban, whom he had received at Bari in 1089 and again at Taranto in 1092. They had met at Anglona in 1092 and again at Monte Cassino in 1093.[7] The scene at Amalfi was a *coup de theâtre* staged by Bohemond in a setting, an important siege, which would enable him to find recruits. There can be little doubt that the great expedition offered Bohemond an outlet for his adventurous temperament and military talents. He outshone his half-brother Roger Borsa easily, but Roger of Sicily's formidable power meant that further expansion at Borsa's expense was out of the question. The Normans of the south must have had a very different perspective on Urban's expedition. The Byzantine east was a close and familiar neighbour. Unsuccessful Norman rebels commonly fled to the Byzantine lands – amongst them William of Grantmesnil, a brother-in-law of Roger, who fled there in 1094. Norman-Italians, as we have seen, often took service in the East: Bohemond's own half-brother Guy was in imperial service at the time of the First Crusade.[8] So for Bohemond here was an opportunity and if things did not turn out well he could return as

---

[6] Fawtier, *Capetian Kings*, p. 18; GN, p. 149; P. Jaffé, *Regesta Pontificum Romanorum*, 2nd edition, 2 vols. (Leipzig, 1885–6), 1. 688.

[7] GF, p. 7; Malaterra, p. 102, says that because of Bohemond's recruiting activities, the armies of the two Rogers so melted away that the siege had to be abandoned; Yewdale, *Bohemond*, pp. 31–2.

[8] Yewdale, *Bohemond*, p. 33; GF, p. 63; see above p. 13.

many others had done before. It was a different perspective from
that of the northerners for whom the east was less familiar.

Of Stephen of Blois's reasons for going on crusade we know very
little. His family were very important princes on a par with the
dukes of Normandy and the counts of Anjou. Reputedly one of the
richest lords in France, Stephen was evidently fairly experienced in
contemporary war and politics but he lived much of his life under
the shadow of his great father. One of the few things we know about
him is that he married Adela, the daughter of the Conqueror, and a
letter he sent to her while on crusade suggests that he was frightened
of her, hence the idea that it was she who made him join the crusade
from which he would defect.[9] Eustace of Boulogne was the elder
brother of Godfrey, yet his role on the crusade was so subdued that
we are not even sure with whom he travelled to the east.[10] It is
worth noting that Robert of Flanders and Stephen had only just
emerged as rulers in their own right and so they may have seen the
crusade as a chance to assert themselves.[11] The leaders of this
northern group of crusaders were closely interrelated. Stephen of
Blois married Adela, Robert Curthose's sister whose mother was
Mathilda, the aunt of Robert of Flanders. Robert's grandmother
was Adela, aunt of Hugh of Vermandois. The house of Boulogne,
Eustace III, Godfrey and their brother Baldwin stood outside this
immediate kin-group, but Eustace was a vassal of the English king
and the count of Flanders, while Baldwin had married Godehilda of
the great Norman house of Tosny.[12] Only two major lay crusaders
came from outside this tight-knit group from the north of France
– Raymond of Toulouse, and Bohemond. As his second wife,
Raymond had taken Mathilda, daughter of Count Roger of Sicily, a

---

[9] *Chronique de Saint-Pierre-le-Vif de Sens, dite de Clarius*, ed. R. H. Bautier and M. Gilles (Paris,
1979), p. 381; Hagenmeyer, *Kreuzzugsbriefe*, pp. 138–40; Runciman I. 165; *GF*, pp. 63–5.

[10] AA, 314 says Eustace travelled with the North French forces but he is never mentioned by
their chronicler, Fulcher of Chartres: Runciman, I. 147 n. I. It is possible, as Runciman
suggests, that his may have been one of the many smaller independent contingents which
arrived at Constantinople in the spring of 1097.

[11] Robert II of Flanders (1093–1111) had succeeded his father only in 1093; above p. 56;
Stephen Henry, count of Meaux and Blois, was quite experienced but had long lived under
the shadow of his father Theobald (1037–1089/90): Bur, *Comté de Champagne*, p. 230;
Eustace III of Boulogne was the successor of the famous Eustace II whose death is usually
dated between 1082 and 1088: Andressohn, *Godfrey de Boullion*, p. 25, but there is room to
think it may have occurred as early as 1076: Mayer, *Mélanges*, pp. 20–1.

[12] Bur, *Comté de Champagne*, pp. 286–7; on the house of Boulogne see above p. 45; Mayer,
Mélanges, pp. 32–6.

cousin of Bohemond, but she seems to have been replaced by 1094.[13] On the face of it Bohemond was the most far removed of the leaders, but he was a Norman. His half-brother, Roger Borsa, married Robert of Flander's sister and widow of Cnut II of Denmark (1080–86), Adela.[14] Raymond of Toulouse was the most isolated, though he appears to have had a big army. He worked in close alliance with Adhémar of Le Puy, the Papal Legate, until his death in 1098, but he appears to have been unloved by the other leaders. These two men, Raymond and Bohemond, were to exercise great influence on the crusade. It is a reflection of this and the very different perceptions of their motives that the gossipy monk, William of Malmesbury, tells us that Bohemond persuaded Urban to call the crusade as a cloak for his ambitions on Byzantium, while Raymond and his ally the bishop of Querci persuaded Urban to the same end to provide them with a worthy spiritual exercise.[15] This group of major leaders – the 'Princes' as the sources call them – were experienced men, almost all of whom had participated in war and knew its demands. Of them all only Bohemond, and to a lesser extent Robert Curthose, had experience of commanding large military forces, though Godfrey had served in great expeditions as a subordinate. Bohemond alone had experience of eastern affairs and had commanded a big army in a major campaign and in open battle. Once they had agreed to go on crusade the princes, like the other participants, needed to find money.

A peace was arranged between Robert Curthose and his brother William Rufus by the papal legate, abbot Jarento of St Bénigne. Robert agreed to pawn the duchy of Normandy to his brother for 10,000 marks, which would have to be repaid over three or five years. The collection of such a sum necessitated a levy of four shillings on the hide in England where the barons and bishops resorted to extreme measures to collect it.[16] Godfrey's preparations were complex and on a smaller scale. To bishop Richer of Verdun Godfrey sold his claims to the county of Verdun together with Mosay, Stenay and castle Falkenstein, all for silver and gold, while

[13] Hills, *Raymond IV*, pp. 15–19.
[14] Verlinden, *Robert le Frison*, p. 165; Dunbabin, *Origins of France*, pp. 291–2; on the question of the 'Norman world' and its sense of identity see G. Loud, 'Gens Normannorum – myth or reality?', *Battle*, 4 (1981) 104–16.
[15] *GR*, 2. 523, 603–4.
[16] Grossman, *Financing of the Crusades*, pp. 36–7; David, *Robert Curthose*, pp. 91–6.

properties at Genappe and Baisy went to a nunnery at Nivelles. Some minor holdings near Maastricht were sold or given to the church, but he was forced to retract his dissolution of the priory of St Peter at Bouillon which belonged to the abbey of St Hubert through the intervention of his mother. He extorted 500 pieces of silver each from the Jewish communities of Cologne and Mainz. Against his county of Bouillon he borrowed from Bishop Otbert of Liège the sum of 1,300 silver marks and three marks of gold; the debt was redeemable by him if he returned or by his brother if he did not. The collection of such a sum caused Otbert considerable difficulties.[17] It has often been suggested that Godfrey swore to stay in the east, but this is later legend. He retained the option of redeeming the mortgage on Bouillon and was careful to ask his overlord, the Emperor Henry IV, for permission to leave the realm. He kept his title of duke of Lower Lorraine and was not replaced until after his death.[18] Stephen of Blois, in a letter to his wife written at Antioch, speaks of the 'gold silver and other riches' with which he left the west though nothing is known of how he raised the money and Hugh of Vermandois's preparations are similarly obscure.[19] Bohemond gave considerable financial support to his nephew Tancred and it is likely that his army was well-disciplined precisely because it relied on his great resources, but there is no record of sales or gifts except for a charter empowering Guidelmus Flammengus, his captain at Bari, to sell or dispose of his property in the area.[20] Robert of Flanders was rich enough to decline financial help from Roger Borsa.[21] Throughout the crusade Raymond of Toulouse would show clear evidence of financial resources on a scale quite different from the other leaders, and the source of this wealth has generated much interest and controversy amongst historians. A number of gifts to churches made on the eve of his departure for the East may represent disguised sales. He probably passed the county of Rouergue to Richard of Millau in return for cash but the evidence for this is not

---

[17] Andressohn, *Godfrey de Bouillon*, pp. 51–2; Grossman, *Financing of the Crusades*, pp. 31–2; A.V.Murray, 'The army of Godfrey de Bouillon 1096–99: structure and dynamics of a contingent on the First Crusade', *Revue Belge de Philologie et d'Histoire* 70 (1992), 301–29. I am very grateful to Dr Murray for allowing me to see an advanced copy of this article; (Soloman) Bar Simson, *Chronicle*, *The Jews and the Crusaders*, tr. S. Eidelberg (Wisconsin, 1977) p. 25.

[18] Mayer, *Mélanges*, pp. 43–4.   [19] Grossman, *Financing of the Crusades*, p. 35.

[20] *Ibid*, p. 34 who notes that Bohemond seems to have kept control of much of his property in Italy

[21] Grossman, *Financing of the Crusades*, p. 36 citing Hagenmeyer, *Kreuzzugsbriefe*, p. 143.

totally clear. Southern French society was enjoying a great prosperity at this time as cities and a money economy grew. Mints can be traced in many of the cities of the south: indeed the visionary, Peter Bartholemew, was to direct that a church should be built near Arles to house the Holy Lance, and that a mint should be established there for its support. It is worth noting that Raymond of Aguilers lists seven coinages used in the army. Of these, four came from Southern France (Poitou, Valence, Melgueil and Le Puy), two from France north of the Loire (Le Mans and Chartres), one from Italy (Lucca). This suggests that the count of Toulouse ruled over a rich society and was perhaps able to finance his crusade from revenue without pledging major assets.[22] We really have no evidence upon which to base a decision on the matter. It is possible that Count Raymond was just vastly richer than any other leader, but it is more likely that his wealth was generated by political arrangements in the east.[23]

The activities of the great as they raised money were mirrored by lesser crusaders who equally sold claims and rights, lands and dues, to finance their long journey. Evidence of only a fraction of this activity has survived but a substantial number of cases have been unearthed and here one may stand for all, Achard of Montmerle, a Burgundian who mortgaged his properties to Cluny:

because I wish fully armed to join in the magnificent expedition of the Christian people seeking for God to fight their way to Jerusalem ... I give in mortgage to these eminent men one of the properties which came to me by right of inheritance from my father, receiving from them the sum of 2,000 solidi of Lyons and four mules ... no person ... can redeem it except myself. Thus if I die in the pilgrimage to Jerusalem, or if I should decide to stay in those parts, that which is the subject of this mortgage ... shall become a rightful and hereditary possession of the monastery of Cluny in perpetuity.[24]

---

[22] On southern French society and economy at this time see A. R. Lewis, *The Development of Southern French and Catalan Society 718–1050* (Austin, 1965) pp. 395–400; RA, p. 88, 111–12; for the importance of the fair at St Gilles, R. H. Bautier, *The Economic Development of Medieval Europe*, by H. Karolji (London, 1971), p. 104; Grossman, p. 33, argues for the sale of the Rouerge, but this is contested by Hill and Hill, *Raymond IV*, p. 37 who believe that Raymond could easily have financed his crusade from income. On the coinage used, see D. M. Metcalf, *Coinage of the Crusaders and the Latin East* (London, 1983), pp. 2–6.

[23] On which see below pp. 311.

[24] *Recueil des Chartes de l'Abbaye de Cluny*, ed. A. Bernard and A. Bruel, 6 vols. (Paris, 1876–1903), 5. 51. Cluny got the land, for Achard died in a skirmish between Jerusalem and Jaffa on 18 June 1099: RA p. 141. For other grants see Grossman, *Financing of the Crusades*, pp. 44–56; Cowdrey, 'Pope Urban's preaching of the First Crusade', 177–88; Riley–Smith, *Idea of Crusading*, pp. 45–7.

This sale, or some variant, seems to have been common and we hear also of lords taxing their dependents. Many means of raising money had been used by pilgrims. In 1088 Aimeric II, count of Fézensac, sold some windmills to the canons of Auch to finance his pilgrimage but with the rider 'if I come back alive from Jerusalem I can have them back until my death'. Such methods of finance, along with levies on tenants which became customary feudal dues in some parts of France, are frequent in the sources for the eleventh century and later.

A modern estimate suggests that a pilgrim to Jerusalem needed to consecrate at least a year's income to this purpose.[25] It is more difficult to estimate the cost of crusading. Money was needed not merely for subsistence, travel, servants and equipment, but also for political purposes. The princes and the lords were masters of men and wealth was necessary to maintain this status on the journey. The princes knew that they would be surrounded by multilayered entourages, ranging from their personal retinues to any poor pilgrims they might choose to maintain or who became their hangers-on. This was not unlike the general nature of the armies of the age, as we have noted, and it was also the natural consequence of pilgrimage. In 1064 a group of important German clerics, the archbishop of Mainz and the bishops of Utrecht, Ratisbon and Bamberg, set off on pilgrimage to Jerusalem. A band estimated to have been some 7,000 strong gathered around them including people from all walks of life. When they were ambushed by brigands close to Jerusalem their sheer numbers enabled them to give a good account of themselves.[26] There was a well-established tradition of mass pilgrimage, dating back at least to the vast crowds inspired to travel by the millennia of the Nativity and Passion of the Lord.[27] Indeed, the preparations which were being made took place amongst people who must have been fairly knowledgeable about the route and its difficulties. Robert Curthose's grandfather had died returning from the Holy Land in 1035, while the pilgrimage of Robert of Flanders' father

---

[25] J. Sumption, *Pilgrimage* (London, 1975), pp. 169, 205–6.
[26] The sources for the great German pilgrimage are: *Annales Altahenses Maiores, MGH SS* 20. 782–824; Lambert the Monk, *Annales Hersfeldenses*, MGH SS 3. 18–116; Marianus Scotus, *Chronicon, MGH SS* 5. 558–59. For commentary see E. Joranson, 'The Great German Pilgrimage of 1064–65', in L. J. Paetow, ed., *The Crusades and other Historical Essays presented to D. C. Munro* (New York, 1928), pp. 3–43.
[27] Glaber, pp. 96–7, 132–7, 198–205. On the abortive French pilgrimage of 1054 see L. Bréhier, *L'Eglise et l'Orient au Moyen Âge* (Paris, 1921), pp. 44–5.

took place only a few years before Urban launched his crusade. The leaders knew about the difficulties of the journey and made their preparations accordingly. This was even true of that remarkable phenomenon which we call the 'People's Crusade'.

The title 'People's Crusade' is something of a simplification. It was a remarkable phenomenon, for Urban clearly had in mind an expedition of nobles and knights. But the religious fervour of the eleventh century had infected a wide social range. The church had enlisted the people of the countryside into the 'Peace Movement' as a moral pressure upon the mighty. Peasants were amongst those who had responded to the ideas of hermits and popular preachers like Robert of Arbrissel who attempted to create for them a new religious order. We know little of Peter the Hermit but he seems to have been much the same kind of charismatic figure as Robert who, significantly, was commissioned by Urban to preach the crusade. So great was his skill that he touched off wild enthusiasm for the crusade, beginning in his own area of Berry and extending across all of France. So profound was his impact that later generations credited him with inventing the whole idea of liberating Jerusalem.[28] This was not just a crusade of the lesser people which collapsed through lack of skill in arms and military leadership, for there were a considerable number of people of rank amongst them.[29] We know of five major groups of people, all of whom left the west long before the date fixed by Urban II, 15 August 1096, for the gathering of the armies at Constantinople. Peter the Hermit quickly whipped up enormous excitement with his preaching in northern France and by early March 1096 he had dispatched a large force of foot-soldiers with only eight knights under Walter Sans Avoir. Their arrival in the Rhineland seems to have set off a savage wave of persecution and

[28] The tradition that Peter went to Jerusalem and was inspired to preach its liberation by his sufferings has been thoroughly examined by E. O. Blake and C. Morris, 'A hermit goes to war; Peter and the origins of the First Crusade', W. J. Shiels, ed. *Monks, Hermits and the Ascetic Tradition* (Oxford, 1985), 79–107, who suggest that the notion that he may have influenced Urban II cannot be totally dismissed. The present writer sees the roots of the Crusade in papal policy and Urban's own thinking, though their idea that Peter might have been an official preacher appointed by Urban, p. 83, cannot be dismissed. On popular religious movements and the 'Peace of God' in the eleventh century see above pp. 6–7 n. 21.

[29] For a general survey see H. Hagenmeyer, *Peter der Eremite* (Leipzig, 1879). The original work exploding the idea that this was simply a peasant rabble was that of F. Duncalf, 'The Peasants' Crusade', *American Historical Review*, 26 (1921), 440–453. This has been given considerable precision by Riley-Smith's research on individuals in *Idea of Crusading*, pp. 49–57.

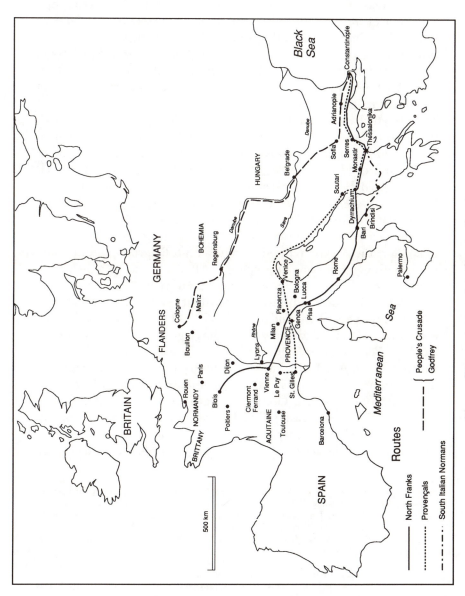

Fig. 1   The armies march to Constantinople

massacre of Jews driven by religious hatred and the desire to raise money. This phenomenon had its more genteel side in Godfrey's extortion of money from his local Jews. Peter seems to have mistreated Jews in France, for they sent a letter warning their co-religionists of the danger; he would arrive at Trier in early April 1096, bearing letters from French Jews suggesting that support be provided for the crusaders. This is not the place to explore the roots of this bitter religious hatred. It does reveal, however, the underlying hatreds which drove on the crusaders, and their preoccupation with the sinews of war.[30] The groups inspired by Peter the Hermit seem to have intended to use the classic pilgrim route across Hungary and so Walter marched to Cologne which he left on 15 April (see fig. 1). They crossed Hungary peacefully, entering on 21 May, but at the border with the Byzantine empire, on or about 11 June, they left sixteen men behind to buy arms in Semlin and these were set upon and mistreated. Once across into imperial territory problems multiplied, for they were refused a market at Belgrade, presumably because the empire was unprepared. After a fracas in which sixty pilgrims were killed, Walter and his army were well received by the imperial authorities and hastened on their way to Constantinople, where they arrived in mid-July 1096.[31] Only a reasonably well organised and supplied army could have gone so far with so little trouble. Peter's army, after menacing Jewish communities, left Cologne by 20 April and was at Semlin by 12 June.[32] His force was much larger, and within it military command seems to have been vested in four captains; Godfrey Burel in charge of the infantry, Raynald of Broyes, Walter FitzWaleran and Fulcher of Chartres who joined Godfrey's army later and would end as a major vassal in the county of Edessa. To these were joined some Germans.[33] The

---

[30] H. Hagenmeyer, *Chronologie de la Première Croisade* (Paris, 1902) pp. 13, 18; on the persecution at this time see Riley-Smith, *Idea of Crusading*, pp. 52–7. This was not the first great persecution, the 'First Holocaust' as he calls it. Jewry had already suffered one major persecution amongst the West Franks, on which see R. Chazan, '1007–1012: the initial crisis for northern European Jewry', *Proceedings of the American Academy for Jewish Research*, 38–39 (1970–71), 101–17.

[31] AA, 274–6.

[32] For the chronology of Peter's march and that of Godfrey through Eastern Europe I have followed J. W. Nesbitt, 'The rate of march of crusading armies in Europe: a study and computation', *Traditio*, 19 (1963), 181 in his revision of Hagenmeyer.

[33] AA, 286–7; Riley-Smith, *Idea of Crusading*, pp. 50–2 identifies Hugh of Tübingen and Walter of Tegk as amongst the Germans, but doubt has been cast on the source of this information, on which see below p. 92, n. 36.

presence of men of such status argues also for that of armed retinues and servants, who would have formed a strong core for the force. We know of no troubles in Hungary until the army reached Semlin where news of the beating of Walter's sixteen men and rumours about Hungarian and imperial intentions led to an attack on the city between 5 and 12 June. This was evidently an organised affair, for Albert of Aachen speaks of knights in full armour leading the attack and the division of two hundred foot commanded by Burel breaking in first.[34] After a further skirmish with imperial troops at a river crossing Peter's army arrived at Nish on 27 June where the Byzantine governor, Nicetas, had withdrawn, abandoning Belgrade because of events at Semlin. He agreed to provide a market in return for guarantees and hostages and all went well until a dispute between a Bulgar merchant and some Germans led to the burning of some mills and Nicetas ordered an attack which captured many of the crusaders' supplies and inflicted losses on the rearguard. Peter was a mile away at the head of the column of march, which suggests that his army was very large. He led them back to Nish to patch up a peace, but some 2,000 of his men got out of hand and attacked the city and though the rest remained in good order the massacre of their hot-headed colleagues drew them into a conflict at the end of which the army as a whole was scattered. Peter and his four captains rallied some 500 men, then gathered together 7,000 more, but Albert says they had originally had 40,000 and 2,000 wagons. He soon received messages from Alexius, his men gathered again and came on peacefully via Sofia (7 July), Philipopolis (modern Plovdiv) (13 July), Adrianople (modern Edirne) (22 July) to arrive at Constantinople on 1 August.[35] Both these forces seem to have been well organised for they had crossed Hungary with little trouble and it was the inability of the Byzantines to procure supplies which caused the real trouble. Under pressure, however, the military organisation of Peter's force had broken up – it was a bad omen for the future.

In early August a formidable army under the command of a Count Emicho arrived at the Hungarian border. He was a south German noble who was followed by Count Hartmann of Dillingen-Kybourg and a contingent of French, English and Lorrainers including William the Carpenter, viscount of Melun, Thomas of Marle lord of Coucy, and Drogo of Nesle. In May they massacred

[34] AA, 277.   [35] AA, 277–84.

Jews at Spires and Mainz, but this was not a sign of their disorganisation, for when the Hungarian king forbade them passage through his lands they settled down to capture the border fortress of the Wieselburg with an army which Albert of Aachen says was 200,000 strong including 3,000 knights. This can only be an exaggeration, but Ekkehard agrees that it was formidable and the fact that the siege continued for three weeks before the Hungarian king eventually defeated them suggests good organisation. In the course of the siege the crusaders built a bridge which enabled them to attack the walls with a machine and were close to victory when a sudden panic enabled the Hungarians to win. The French leaders returned to France and joined Hugh of Vermandois in his journey to the east.[36] The prohibition on crossing into Hungary by King Coloman I (1095–1114) was probably a result of the troubles caused by other crusading bands. Folkmar and his Saxons were probably involved in attacks on Jews at Prague on 30 May, but in late June they were broken up by the Hungarians because 'sedition was incited'. Another group, led by a Rhineland priest Gottschalk, was 15,000 strong, according to Albert, and numbered as many knights as foot, but they took to pillaging and cruelty and the Hungarians massacred them in late July. Apparently they were quite well organised; after initial fighting, Coloman proposed a truce under which the crusaders gave up their arms. This enabled the Hungarians to massacre them, but presumably only a cohesive group would have actually surrendered in this way.[37] These were probably not the only such groups which made up the People's Crusade, for we hear of attacks on Jews at various times and places in the Rhineland which are hard to match with the suggested journey times of these known groups. As late as June and July 1095 there were a number of massacres of Jews north of the main departure areas at Neuss, Werelinghoven, Altenahr, Xanten and Moers. We do not know who

---

[36] Emicho is usually identified as the Count Emicho of Leiningen listed along with other crusaders in the *Chronicle of Zimmern*, ed. H. Hagenmeyer, pp. 17–88. In a devastating critique of the value of this source A. V. Murray, 'The army of Godfrey Bouillon', 315–22 has shown this to be almost valueless and cites a recent study, Ingo Toussaint, *Die Grafen von Leiningen: Studien zur leiningischen Genealogie und Territorialgeschichte bis zur Teilung von 1317/18* (Sigmaringen, 1982), pp. 25–8 which suggests that Emicho may have come from Flonheim on the middle Rhine. Bar Simson, pp. 28–9; Ekkehard of Aura, *Hierosolymita*, *RHC Oc.* 5 [hereafter cited as Ekkehard], p. 20; AA, 292–5; Riley-Smith, *Idea of Crusading*, pp. 50–1.

[37] AA, 289–91; Ekkehard, pp. 20–1.

was responsible for these any more than we know who the people were who were led on their journey by a goose and a goat.[38] The departure of the People's Crusade was a deeply confused affair and we may suspect that there were forces heading for the east of which we know nothing. The Hungarian king must have been thoroughly exasperated by their passage. This spontaneous gathering of forces also affected Italy, for Peter's forces met with a large Italian contingent at Constantinople, but we know nothing of them or their journey.

Peter arrived at Constantinople on or about 1 August 1095 and was well received by Alexius. He advised that the crusaders should await the main armies now equipping in Western Europe, and shipped them all over into Asia Minor to a camp at Civitos (on the coast north of modern Altinova) on the southern shore of the Gulf of Nicomedia some fifty kilometres west of that city (now Izmit), where Albert makes it clear that ample supplies were provided (see fig. 2).[39] Peter had charge of a significant military force, elements of which quickly began to tire of camp life and despite his prohibitions, to pillage. Nicaea, the capital of the Seljuk Turks, only lay some forty kilometres to the south down a steep road up the valley of the river Dracon (now Yalaç) and this acted as a magnet to would-be ravagers. A force of 7,000 foot and 300 knights was particularly successful in raiding this vicinity. A group of Germans and Italians of 3,000 foot and 200 knights, provoked by this example of Frankish daring, then attacked and seized Xerigordo, close to Nicaea, in late September and were massacred there by the Seljuks.[40] Peter was at Constantinople asking for a reduction in food prices; presumably their level must have been a factor in these outbreaks. Walter Sans Avoir was now faced with demands for vengeance but he refused and most of the other captains of the army, Raynald de Broyes, Gautier de Breteuil and Fulcher of Orléans, supported him. However, Godfrey Burel, the leader of the infantry, disagreed and this crack in the front of authority enabled the popular clamour to succeed. An army of 25,000 foot and 500 knights sallied out to seek vengeance leaving behind only the women, children and the infirm. The Sultan Kilij Arslan's forces were now well prepared and seeking

---

[38] Hagenmeyer, *Chronologie*, pp. 26–8; (Eliezer) Bar Nathan, *Chronicle*, in Mainz Anonymous, *The Jews and the Crusaders*, tr. S. Eidelberg (Wisconsin, 1977), pp. 85–91; AA 295.

[39] *GF*, pp. 2–3; *Alexiad*, p. 311; AA, 283, 284.

[40] AA, 284–5; *GF*, pp. 3–4. The location of Xerigordo is unknown.

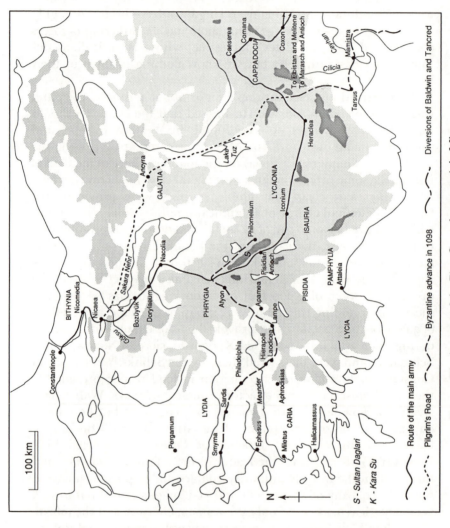

Fig. 2   The journey of the First Crusade across Asia Minor

the crusaders, who left camp on 21 October. They were organised in six groups, each formed around a banner. When they entered woodlands the Turks retired before them into the open plain at the edge of which they stood ready for battle. The westerners paused and sent forward the two groups of knights who were quickly encircled by Turks, who sent up a barrage of arrows and noise. The knights attacked, then recoiled towards the foot at the edge of the forest, and with their aid attacked again, but their horses were cut down by arrows so they were forced to fight on foot and were overwhelmed. Amongst the dead were Walter Sans Avoir and Raynald de Broyes, and when the survivors of the attack rejoined the main body its people took flight and were massacred.[41] Peter's camp soon fell and some 3,000 pilgrims sought refuge in an old fort which the enemy attacked, only to be driven off by imperial forces. Amongst the survivors it would seem that a large proportion were knights.[42] The People's Crusade had ended in tragedy, but not, it is worth saying, in farce. Albert of Aachen provides the only detailed account of events, but it shows an organised force which fought coherently until its élite, the 500 knights, were defeated. Obviously we cannot be certain of the numbers, but the Sultan was sufficiently alarmed to take the field himself at a time when he had other preoccupations. But if Peter's army was much more than a mere rabble of poor men, it also lacked leadership. His charismatic figure sufficed to hold them together until there was trouble – in the Balkans accidental skirmishing, in Asia Minor rising prices. Even without him his captains knew military common sense when they saw it, but they were unable to present a united front. The failure of the People's Crusade was a failure of authority – that was the contribution of the princes, who were assembling their forces in the West.

We have seen the princes gathering money, and we can guess that they were also providing themselves with supplies, like those carried in Peter the Hermit's wagon-train which was captured by the Byzantines in the fighting near to Nish.[43] But how did they conceive

[41] It is now impossible to fix the location of this battle, for Albert is alone in describing it and the only clue is that it took place at the edge of the woods and vegetation patterns have changed. Probably it was fought on the upper Yalac near the present route 595, along which there are several possibilities, from the Gulf of Izmit (Nicomedia) to Iznik (Nicaea) via Yalakdere.

[42] AA, 287–9.   [43] AA, 287–92.

their military task – what had Urban communicated to them and suggested or commanded, and what did they know of the lands for which they were setting out, and what of their new enemies? Those who set off on the People's Crusade obviously saw their task as the annihilation of the enemies of Christ – they began with the Jews, may have extended it to the Hungarians in some cases, and were certainly hell-bent on it in the east. For them the crusade was the realisation of the command of God, 'vengeance is mine' and they His instruments. That this attitude was shared by all on the crusade is self-evident – the great massacres, such as that at Jerusalem, are clear evidence, but not everyone extended the idea to Jews. The notion of vengeance was an integral part of Urban's appeal and in a certain sense was the chief objective of the crusade.[44] But in the minds of the princes, with their great responsibilities, means and methods must have loomed as large as goals. What could they have learned from Urban II? For Urban the new expedition was part of the wider struggle against Islam, and he would actively prevent Spanish Christians from joining the expedition. He most certainly announced that the goal of the whole expedition was the liberation of Jerusalem, as we have noted.[45] He appointed Adhémar, bishop of Le Puy as Legate and leader 'in our stead' and he fixed a date for their departure, 15 August 1096.[46] He established a political objective which conditioned the conduct of the crusade – assistance for the Christians of the east. In practical terms this meant, above all, assistance for the Byzantine emperor. One of the most striking facts about the early twelfth-century histories of the crusades is the persistence in their accounts of Urban's speech, of references to the need to help the Greeks. This is remarkable precisely because the contact between Latin and Greek, generated by the crusade, led to bitter hostility to Byzantium in the West. Despite this, Christian fraternity, upon which Urban's appeal was based, remained a powerful influence upon crusader behaviour towards the Greek empire.[47] It must, therefore, have been a powerful element in Urban's original impulse to the crusade and we may presume that behind it lay the objective, so explicitly stated by Gregory VII in

[44] See above p. 4 and the very clear discussion in Riley-Smith, *Idea of Crusading*, pp. 50–7.
[45] Riley-Smith, *Idea of Crusading*, pp. 19–20; see above p. 4
[46] Hagenmeyer, *Kreuzzugesbriefe*, pp. 136–37.
[47] W. M. Daly, 'Christian fraternity, the crusaders and the security of Constantinople', *Medieval Studies*, 22 (1960), 43–91.

1074, of uniting the churches of east and west under the authority of the Holy See, in other words 'that the union of the Latin and Greek churches was one of the impelling motives in the call for the First Crusade'. Adhémar's carefully conciliatory attitude to the Orthodox patriarch of Antioch who was restored to authority in his city after the crusader conquest, appears to confirm this.[48] Certainly the crusade came at the end of a long series of negotiations between Urban and Alexius on unity.[49] However, although Urban had laid down what was effectively a political condition which the crusaders had to meet, he appears not to have suggested how this might be done. Urban left military preparation to the leaders under the guidance of Adhémar who, however, does not seem to have been given the authority of an overall military commander, despite his military experience.[50]

He went, perhaps, a little further than this. We may assume that it was Urban who informed the Byzantine emperor that he could expect important armies led by major leaders. He suggested that they gather at Constantinople. Conceivably he suggested that they should write to Alexius anouncing their coming, as some did.[51] He certainly consulted with one of the leaders, Raymond of St Gilles, count of Toulouse, who had been the first to take the cross. The pope was in Raymond's lands before Clermont and later was in his company in June and July of 1096 at a series of Councils in the Languedoc and Provence.[52] It has been suggested that Raymond knew the mind of Urban, who had given him command of the entire expedition. Later he pursued a firm policy of friendship towards the Byzantine empire which we can presume was dear to Urban's heart, but this is explicable in other terms for Raymond may have followed this line because he found it in his interests so to do. There is no firm

---

[48] A. C. Krey, 'Urban's crusade; success or failure?', *American Historical Review*, 53 (1948), 235–50; Cowdrey, 'Pope Gregory VII's "Crusading" plans' 27–40.

[49] On which see P. Charanis, 'Aims of the medieval crusaders and how they were viewed by Byzantium', *Church History*, 21 (1952), 123–134, and the same author's brief note in *American Historical Review*, 53 (1948), 941–4.

[50] J. Richard, 'La Papauté et la direction de la première croisade', *Journal des Savants*, (1960), 49–58.

[51] It is very evident that Alexius knew that major armies were on the way and was making preparations to provide for them, although the 'People's Crusade' arrived early; see above pp. 88–95. *Alexiad*, p. 308, is mendacious in suggesting that Alexius had no foreknowledge.

[52] Hill and Hill, *Raymond IV*, pp. 30–2, 'Justification historique du titre de Raymond de Saint-Gilles; "Christiane milicie excellentissimus princeps"', *Annales du Midi*, 66 (1954), 101–12.

indication of Raymond of St Gilles having been given any special
position by Urban, and judging by the later efforts of the princes to
resolve the question of leadership it is safe to conclude that he
enjoyed no such eminence though it is important that he may have
known Urban's mind.[53]

In leaving the planning up to the crusader leaders, Urban was
conforming to the dictates of common sense. He was not a soldier
and the conditions of the day, and in particular the tight timetable
which he had laid down, precluded any meeting with them to seek
their advice or to hammer out a plan. Moreover, he must have
known that he could count on a considerable knowledge of eastern
affairs amongst the leaders and their advisers. One striking feature of
the First Crusade, which will be explored later, was the participation of fleets whose naval aid was essential for the success of the
expedition. Most notable were the fleets of Genoa, Pisa and the
'English', which seem to have attacked the coastline of North Syria
even before the crusaders arrived. We do not have any evidence that
any of the military leaders of the crusade, nor the pope, made
specific plans with those in charge of these expeditions.[54] It is
remarkable that they should have materialised in the waters off
Antioch at such a propitious moment. The Genoese expedition of
thirteen ships perhaps tried to co-ordinate its departure with the
movements of the crusaders, for Urban had dispatched a legation to
Genoa led by Hugh, bishop of Grenoble, and the later crusader,
William bishop of Orange. Raymond of Toulouse may have suggested this for he was later closely associated with the Genoese. It
sailed in July 1097 by which time the main armies were deep into
Asia Minor.[55] The fact that it took until mid-November to arrive at
Antioch suggests that it sought information about the armies en
route, for this was a long sailing time: by comparison the French
fleet on the Third Crusade left Messina on 30 March 1191 and
arrived at Acre on 8 June, while in 1183, Ibn Djobair travelled from
Ceuta to Alexandria in twenty days.[56] The English fleet must have
set off much earlier to have reached the coast near Antioch well

[53] See below especially pp. 297-324.
[54] On the role of the fleets and their actions see below pp. 209-220.
[55] P. F. Kehr, *Regesta Pontificum Romanonum. Italia Pontificia*, 10 vols. (Rome, 1906-75), 6. 2.
    323: Hills, *Raymond IV*, p. 34; Caffaro, *De liberatione civitatum orienti, RHC Oc.* 5, 49-50.
[56] M. Mollat, 'Problèmes navales de l'histoire des croisades', *Cahiers de Civilisation Médiévale*,
    10 (1967), 351.

before the arrival of the crusaders in October 1097. It is, however, difficult to see how all these groups could have co-ordinated their movements. After the seizure of Laodicea, the English seem to have had close relations with Robert of Normandy, but the sources make no mention of any discussions in the West and the term *Angli*, used of this fleet group, may refer to the peoples generally of the North Sea area. Another English fleet called at Lucca where it picked up a local citizen, Bruno, whose adventures were later described in a letter sent out by the people of Lucca.[57] In fact, the Italians must have been very well informed about the eastern Mediterranean. The merchants of Venice, Amalfi and Bari traded with Constantinople and Antioch. Indeed, in 1087, sailors from Bari stole the relics of St Nicholas from Myra. Shipping in this age tended to cling to coasts, and the northern route to the east via the Cyclades and Asia Minor was far safer than that along the North African coast onto which the fragile ships of the age could be easily driven by prevailing norther-lies.[58] The merchants of Amalfi had close relations with the Fati-mids who had been based in their familiar trading area of Tunis before their conquest of Egypt in 969, which may have been assisted by Amalfitan sea-power. In 996 more than a hundred merchants of Amalfi were killed and property belonging to the city valued at 90,000 dinars was destroyed in a riot in Cairo but contact continued. At the end of the eleventh century, Palermo was a thriving trading city with numerous contacts with the Islamic lands.[59] Pisa and Genoa, which both interested themselves in the crusade, were out-siders in this trade for their power was concentrated in the western basin of the Mediterranean, but they would also have known about the east into whose trade they were anxious to break – it is notable that Amalfitans joined the Genoese expedition against Mahdia of 1087.[60] Amalfi and Bari were of course within the Norman domin-ion in South Italy. The trading cities of Italy would have had a

[57] Hagenmeyer, *Kreuzzugsbriefe*, p. 145.
[58] Bautier, *Economic Development*, p. 99; J. H. Pryor, *Geography, Technology and War: Studies in the Maritime History of the Mediterranean 649–1571* (Cambridge, 1988), pp. 87–101 and see map, p. 14.
[59] A. O. Citarella, 'The relations of Amalfi with the Arab world before the crusades', *Speculum*, 42 (1967), 300, 310; C. Cohen, 'Un texte peu connu relatif au commerce oriental d'Amalfi au X siècle', *Archivio Storico Napoletano*, 34 (1955), 61–67; D. Abulafia, *The Two Italies* (Cambridge, 1977), pp. 42–49.
[60] Cowdrey, 'Mahdia Campaign', 15–16, though Citarella, pp. 311–12 believes that Panta-leone took part in this as an individual and that Amalfi, because of its good relations with Arab powers, held aloof. On the Mahdia campaign see above p. 48.

considerable knowledge of the east, and it was probably upon their knowledge that the 'English' fleet drew when making for Cyprus and the North Syrian littoral.

Knowledge of the east was not, however, confined to the Italian trading cities. The pilgrimage to Jerusalem had become a mass movement in the eleventh century. Glaber's famous passage about the mass of pilgrims going to the east in and around 1033, provoking some thinkers to speculate that it presaged the end of the world, is well known. In a nearby passage, however, he mentions the death of Robert the Magnificent, duke of Normandy (1027–35) at Nicaea while returning: his son, William the Conqueror, would later have his remains removed to Apulia. Fulk Nerra, count of Anjou, went to Jerusalem no fewer than three times.[61] Further, a pattern of mass pilgrimage had developed which would have been familiar to the leaders of 1095. Richard of St Vannes was accompanied on his pilgrimage of 1026–7 by William II Tallifer, count of Angoulême, along with many Aquitanians, Normans and Germans (a total of about 700), and his costs were defrayed by the duke of Normandy. In 1054–5 3,000 followed Lietbert of Cambrai on a journey to Jerusalem which was frustrated by war in the area. The decision of some West German bishops to go to Jerusalem in 1064 had also attracted great crowds of followers, perhaps as many as 7,000, and their ostentatious show of wealth attracted attack from brigands who had also troubled Richard of St Vannes, perhaps for the same reason.[62] Pilgrimage to Jerusalem went on right up to the First Crusade; a knight from Jumièges appears to have travelled back from Jerusalem at the very time that the crusaders were fighting their way across Asia Minor.[63] There was the obvious experience of Robert the Frisian, father of the Robert of Flanders, who joined the crusade. It is likely that he took different routes going to and from Jerusalem. From Anna Comnena we hear of him fighting with Alexius against the Patzinacks and promising to send him military support at Berrhoia (modern Stara Zagora), which is close to the route from the Danube down to Adrianople and thence to Con-

---

[61] *Glaber*, pp. 204–5, 202–5, 60–1. On Robert's remains see K. Ciggaar, 'England and Byzantium', 83.

[62] H. Dauphin, *Le Bienheureux Richard, abbé de St-Vanne-de-Verdun* (Louvain, 1946), pp. 281–94; E. Joranson, 'Great German Pilgrimage', in L. J. Paetow, ed., *The Crusades and other Historical Essays presented to D. C. Munro*, (New York, 1928), pp. 3–43.

[63] Riley-Smith, *Idea of Crusading*, pp. 20–1.

stantinople. He also arranged the marriage of his daughter Adela, widow of Cnut II of Denmark, to Roger Borsa duke of Apulia, which would suggest that he took the route down through South Italy and across the Adriatic to the Via Egnatia and Constantinople. We have no certain knowledge, however, nor do we even know how long Robert spent in the east on a journey which took place between July 1086 and October 1089, but a period of over two years appears likely.[64] The 500 knights whom he sent to Alexius served in the Balkans and in Asia Minor and presumably many of them returned to spread their knowledge widely. It is likely, therefore, that very recent and direct knowledge of the roads to the east and the distances to be travelled would have been common knowledge in the circle of the count of Flanders and his close associates, the house of Boulogne. More generally, any of the leaders would have known about the east from vassals and churchmen who had been on pilgrimage. Nor were pilgrims and merchants the sole sources of knowledge of the east. Many Normans took service with the Byzantine emperor, as we have noted. So did many Anglo-Saxons, whose service in the Varangian guard after 1066 is well known. Others settled under imperial auspices in the Crimea on the Black Sea.[65] It seems very likely that the Anglo-Saxon monarchy had relations with the imperial court at Constantinople, and a seal of the Confessor bore the curious title *Anglorum basileus*. Robert II (996–1031) of France sent Ulric bishop of Orléans, as his ambassador to Constantinople in the reign of Constantine VIII (1025–8) with gifts of a precious sword and a reliquary; probably he was seeking a Byzantine bride whose glory would raise the prestige of the house of Capet. In the event his son Henry married Anna of Kiev, a lady with Byzantine relatives.[66] A whole host of connections existed between the leaders of the First Crusade and the Byzantine east. They were not launching themselves into an unknown land, and their preparations presumably reflected knowledge of what was ahead of them. When Stephen of Blois, in a letter home to his wife Adela, estimated that, after the fall of Nicaea, Jerusalem was only five weeks away, he was probably drawing upon pilgrim experience which may have been

---

[64] C. Verlinden, *Robert le Frison*, pp. 152–7, 168; *Alexiad*, pp. 229–30, 232–3.

[65] Godfrey, 'The defeated Anglo-Saxons', 68–74.

[66] Cigaar, 'England and Byzantium', 86; *Glaber*, p. 202–3; Dunbabin, *France in the Making*, p. 136.

widely shared.[67] In summary, the leaders (and indeed many of those they led) would have known about the journey to Constantinople down the pilgrim way, and they would certainly have known something of the Greeks and their dealings. Even beyond Constantinople, the leaders would have had some notion of roads and distances. The South Italian Normans, whose relatives had fought for the emperors, should have known much more and so should the merchants of the Italian trading cities. So the men who would lead the crusade were not rushing headlong into the unknown. The pope had given them objectives and they could draw on a substantial body of knowledge. It was against this background that they prepared their armies and decided on their routes to Constantinople.

Hugh of Vermandois was to be the first of the major leaders to depart. Significantly, he wrote to inform Alexius of his imminent arrival; Anna Comnena has preserved a memory of the letter, but gives it in a bombastic form intended to mock the westerners. Alexius's immediate reaction to the letter was to alert the Governor of Dyrrachium (modern Durrës or Durazzo), which suggests that, in its original form, the letter mentioned Hugh's proposed route. He travelled through Italy and, in October, crossed from Bari to Dyrrachium in company with Bohemond's nephew, William son of the Marquis (see fig. 1). After their small fleet was shipwrecked, Hugh was rescued by the Governor and treated honourably 'but he was not granted complete freedom' as he was sent on to Constantinople where he arrived in November.[68] The biggest group of north French nobles, led by Robert of Normandy, Robert of Flanders and Stephen of Blois, took the same route, meeting Urban II at Lucca in late October, the occasion when two of their clergy were given legatine powers. Thence they proceeded to Rome, where the disorders attendant on the division of the city between pope and anti-pope scandalised them. After that they journeyed via Monte Cassino to Bari where they were advised that it was too late in the season to make the crossing. Robert of Flanders crossed anyway; his was only a section of the combined force and perhaps he was more strongly motivated.[69] We know nothing about his journey nor his relations with Alexius, for he had no chronicler with him. Anna makes no mention of him which is curious, for he was the son of

---

[67] Hagenmeyer, *Kreuzuggesbriefe*, p. 140.   [68] *Alexiad*, pp. 313–15; *GF*, pp. 5–6.
[69] FC, pp. 75–6; on the chaplains see below p. 303 n. 17.

Alexius's friend and supporter Robert the Frisian. As for Curthose and Stephen, they stayed comfortably in Norman South Italy where they and their nobles could be sure of hospitality, presumably a factor which influenced the comfort-loving Robert to take this route in the first place. Significantly, Fulcher records that during this stay many poor pilgrims deserted – presumably because they were unable to maintain themselves in friendly territory which they could not pillage. It was during this sojourn in Italy that Odo of Bayeux died and was buried in Palermo, where Count Roger created a splendid monument to him. Attendant at his burial was Gilbert bishop of Evreux, though it is not certain that he had taken the cross for we hear nothing of him on the journey.[70] It was not until early April of 1097 that Robert and Stephen prepared to cross the Adriatic. After this they enjoyed a peaceful march to arrive at Constantinople on 14 May 1097 by which time the other crusaders were besieging Nicaea. But their journey was not without interest. A ship capsized in Bari harbour drowning four hundred and causing many others to turn back. At the crossing of the river of the Demon (Skumbi) many of the poor were drowned and the foot-soldiers were saved only by the prompt action of the knights with their horses. This kind of attrition, coming on top of the ravages of disease and malnutrition must have appreciably reduced the crusader forces before they reached hostile territory.[71]

For Bohemond and his south Italian Normans the journey to Constantinople across the Adriatic was a familiar one. In late October his force landed in a number of places, then concentrated near Avlona well to the south of Dyrrachium, and did not join the Via Egnetia until Vodena (see fig. 1). This curious choice of route took Bohemond into an area where he had campaigned against the Byzantines little more than ten years before and where the Normans had been well-received. He probably avoided Dyrrachium, the scene of such heavy fighting in Guiscard's expedition, because of its concentration of Byzantine forces which were escorting crusaders.[72] Bohemond's particular problem was to transform himself from a much-feared enemy of the Byzantines, whom Anna treats with the gravest of suspicion, into an ally.[73] However, only one serious

[70] FC, p. 76; David, *Robert Curthose*, pp. 223–4.   [71] FC, pp. 76–8.

[72] *GF*, pp. 7–8; On Guiscard's expedition see above pp. 74–7.

[73] On Byzantine attitudes to the Normans see J. Hermans, 'The Byzantine view of the Normans', *Battle*, 2 (1979) 78–92.

incident occurred: at the Vardar crossing, on the Via Egnetia, when imperial escorts harassed the Normans and were put to flight. Bohemond began the march by ordering his army not to pillage, and certainly sent an embassy on to Constantinople to assure Alexius of his good intentions. When it returned with a senior Byzantine official his guidance was accepted and animals, stolen at Kastoria when the inhabitants refused to grant a market, were returned. After that, presumably as a sign of goodwill, Bohemond agreed to leave his army in the charge of Tancred and go on to Constantinople where he arrived on 1 April. However, Bohemond's march took a very long time to reach Constantinople, a fact of considerable importance.[74]

The peaceful passage of such substantial armies was a triumph for Alexius's organisation. He had alerted his governors at frontier points like Dyrrachium and moved his fleet into the Adriatic to control the Franks. Along the routes were disposed Patzinack and other troops, who formed a policing force, while food was stockpiled.[75] However, to have a friendly army march through your territory was, as the king of Hungary had discovered earlier, almost as bad as to be attacked by a hostile one. In either case food was demanded, and linguistic and cultural differences made the prospects of trouble very great indeed. The count of Toulouse left the west in mid-December 1096 with what historians believe was the largest of all the armies, accompanied by substantial numbers of poor pilgrims. We assume that they crossed the plain of the Po and moved through Istria before we are quite definitely informed by their chronicler, Raymond of Aguilers, that they entered *Sclavonia*, and followed the old Roman road south parallel to the Dalmatian and Montenegrin coast via Scodra (modern Shkodër) to Dyrrachium. The wild inhabitants of this obscure region caused them much trouble. Even a treaty with Constantine Bodin king of Zeta (by 1070 – after 1101), had very little effect in curbing their attacks.[76] Probably Raymond did not travel through Italy to Bari because it was December, when it was not easy to cross the sea. A sea passage for such a large army would have been costly and ships might not have been available. From Aquileia he could have taken the old Via Gemina into the Save valley and down to Belgrade on

---

[74] *GF*, pp. 8–11; see below pp. 106–7.   [75] *Alexiad*, pp. 315, 324.
[76] RA, pp. 36–8.

the main pilgrim route and we do not know why he turned south. As it was, the army, which arrived at Dyrrachium in February 1097 after much skirmishing with the natives, was hungry and tired, and relieved, as its chronicler tells us, to be in what was assumed to be friendly territory.[77] They were travelling along the Via Egnetia at the very worst time of the year, late winter and early spring, when food stocks were at their lowest, and efforts to forage were frustrated by attacks from imperial troops who killed, amongst others, Peter and Pons of Fay-Chapteuil, while, in mid-February, the bishop of Le Puy was wounded by Patzinacks and was later left at Thessalonica to recover. Exchanges with the imperial escorts came to a climax at Roussa which the Provencals sacked on 12 April 1097.[78] However, at Dyrrachium Count Raymond seems to have received letters of safe-conduct from the Byzantines and he had apparently sent on envoys to Constantinople for about 18 May these met the army at Rodosto. They brought with them assurances of safe-conduct from the Emperor and asked that Raymond should hasten on to Constantinople to discuss matters with Alexius and the crusader leaders who had already arrived. A few days after this, to the great annoyance of Count Raymond, his army was scattered by imperial forces, probably as a result of ravaging the countryside.[79] The problems of the Provençals were the result of travelling through the winter when food was short. They were compounded because, for part of their journey, they were following behind Bohemond's troops.

For Godfrey it was natural to take the route via Ratisbon and then down the Danube into the Byzantine empire but this route had been closed by the king of Hungary because of the disorders of the People's Crusade. As he approached Hungary in early September, Godfrey met survivors of the earlier debâcles who were returning home. He camped at Tulina and sent his relative, Godfrey of Esch-sur-Sûre, who had gone on crusade with his brother Henry, to investigate the situation and to ask King Coloman for passage.[80] Godfrey of Esch had apparently been used by the duke on an earlier embassy to Coloman, and this was perhaps why Godfrey was soon able to meet Coloman and to arrange terms. By the treaty which

---

[77] RA, p. 38; A. C. Krey, *The First Crusade* (Princeton, 1921, Gloucester, 1958), p. 65: 'We believed we were in our own country, thinking that the Emperor and his satellites were our brothers and helpmates'.
[78] RA, pp. 38-9.   [79] RA, pp. 40-1.   [80] AA, 299-302.

Godfrey had proclaimed, in the army there was to be no ravaging or attacks and all goods were to be paid for. Coloman agreed to provide a market at fair prices. To guarantee the peace, Godfrey gave his brother Baldwin (who was unwilling), his wife and members of his household as hostages. In the event, Godfrey got on well with the king, his army entered Hungary at the end of September and its journey passed off well. It was a good time of the year to be on the march, and food was no problem. At the Save crossing into imperial territory in early November the presence of imperial troops caused such anxiety that Godfrey sent on many of his knights, Albert says 1,000, to secure passage, which they did without meeting any resistance. Alexius had evidently prepared for the coming of the Franks, for shortly afterwards, his envoys met Godfrey and offered a market for food-providing that the newcomers agreed not to ravage. Albert reports ample supplies at Nish, where they arrived on 4 November and rested for four days, and a positive plenitude at Phillipopolis, where they rested for eight in late November and early December.[81]

The trouble which erupted in the last stages of the journey was not about food, but about politics. Godfrey was informed that Alexius was keeping Hugh of Vermandois together with Drogo of Nesle and Clarembold of Vendeuil in prison. He sent envoys to demand their release and, when this was refused and food was denied at Adrianople, he allowed the army to ravage the area of Salabria until Franks, sent as imperial envoys, came bearing promises that the prisoners would be released; perhaps what this really means is that they convinced Godfrey that the distinguished Franks were not prisoners and that all was well. It was in this affronted mood that Godfrey left Adrianople on 8 December and arrived at Constantinople on 23 December 1097, the first of the great princes. He had travelled at a good time of year, and the closing of Hungary meant that there was no army immediately ahead of him to eat up supplies. Byzantine organisation worked well to feed one of the biggest of the western armies.[82]

The army of the North French must also have been large, but it had presumably resupplied in Italy, and it was able to make very good time, landing at Dyrrachium on 9 April and arriving at Constantinople on 14 May. This was a very quick march: 920

---

[81] AA, 303–5.   [82] AA, 304–5; on the size of his army see below pp. 129–30.

kilometres in thirty-six days, averaging twenty-five per day. By contrast, Bohemond left Avlona on 1 November 1096 and his army arrived at Constantinople on 26 April, a journey of 178 days at a daily average of just over five kilometres. The count of Toulouse arrived at Dyrrachium in early February 1097 and was at Constantinople at virtually the same time as the Italian Normans, 27 April; almost the same distance in half the time with a much bigger army averaging over 11 kilometres per day.[83] It is tempting to think that the chronologists have made an error about the dating of Bohemond's march, but this does not appear to be the case. The author of the *Historia Belli Sacri* states quite baldly that Bohemond crossed the Adriatic on the Feast of All Saints, 1 November 1096, and agrees with the Anonymous who was certainly with Bohemond's army, that Christmas was spent at Kastoria.[84] To make the point even more forcefully the Anonymous is unusually clear about the date of the skirmish at the Vardar crossing on 18 February which means an average march of only four kilometres per day up to this point; by this time the count of Toulouse's army had only just left Dyrrachium. The Provençals were the largest army and might have been expected to move slowly, yet by Roussa they were only four days behind the Normans who averaged only 7.3 kilometres per day for this part of the journey, and as Tancred, in the absence of Bohemond, rested the army, they were only a day behind by the time they got to Constantinople. It took Bohemond three months to reach the Via Egnetia, and then another three to get to Constantinople. Such delay must have been deliberate; Bohemond was travelling through an area in which he had fought in 1082, and he knew the roads. He remained in the general area of his earlier victories from November 1096 to mid-February of the following year, apparently free from Byzantine military supervision. Even when he reached the Via Egnetia, at which point imperial forces appeared, he dawdled. This was purposeful procrastination.

As the leaders approached Constantinople they were probably

---

[83] Compare the figures suggested for the march through the Balkans of between 29 and 17.6 kilometres per day, on which see above p. 90, n. 32. The average daily mileage figures used here are not to be taken literally. Speed of march must have varied enormously according to the nature of the country, tiredness of army etc: the Provençals were tired by the time they reached Dyrrachium and had troubles with the Byzantines, while the North French were rested and local arrangements went smoothly. The figures are used here to indicate comparative rates of progress and they can be very revealing.

[84] *Historia Belli Sacri, RHC Oc.* 3 [hereafter cited as *HBS*], 177; *GF*, p. 8.

pondering two closely related problems: how the crusade was to be led and how they were to regularise their relationship with the emperor. Equally, each would have been wondering how any settlement would effect his individual power and prestige. Raymond of Aguilers says that Count Raymond was led to believe that Alexius was about to take command of the crusade to Jerusalem by messengers from Alexius and the crusader leaders at Constantinople urging him to leave his army and hasten on to see the emperor. This may, however, only be a version of camp rumour for the chronicler was always bitterly anti-Byzantine. Raymond of Toulouse's later offer to Alexius to give him homage if he would come to Jerusalem may have been a bargaining step. The Anonymous alone suggests that the emperor was intending to come on the journey in person, but this should be seen in the context of his reporting.[85] The princes most certainly knew of Urban II's political directive. There is a tendency to see this as the determinant factor in the minds of the Franks as they approached Constantinople, but in fact it is likely that more prosaic military and political considerations were in their minds. Their difficulty was that they were approaching Constantinople as individuals who had not spoken to one another and had no clear view of what to do. Urban had not developed a plan for the crusade, but an idea, and had left the participants to work out the details. The leaders probably appreciated the simple truth which Fulcher of Chartres would later point out so clearly to posterity. 'For it was essential that all establish friendship with the emperor since without his aid and counsel we could not easily make the journey, nor could those who were to follow us by the same route.' They must also have wanted help on supplies, guidance on routes, knowledge of enemy dispositions and methods, the presence of allies and all the myriad things that an army needs to know if it is to fight well. The mention of reinforcements was a deep preoccupation of the crusaders, and would appear frequently in their letters to the west.[86] However, because they lacked any plan and were each on his own, the initiative lay with the emperor. He probably had a good idea of Urban II's wishes, but he too had military and political priorities

---

[85] RA, pp. 40–2; *HBS*, 179 also relates that Count Raymond received letters urging him to press on to Constantinople ahead of his army and stating that the emperor would lead them to Jerusalem, but this interesting source, which has been insufficiently explored, depends on Raymond of Aguilers at this point; *GF*, p. 12 and see below p. 113–14.

[86] FC, p. 80; *Kreuzzugsbriefe*, pp. 141–2, 146–9, 154–5, 165.

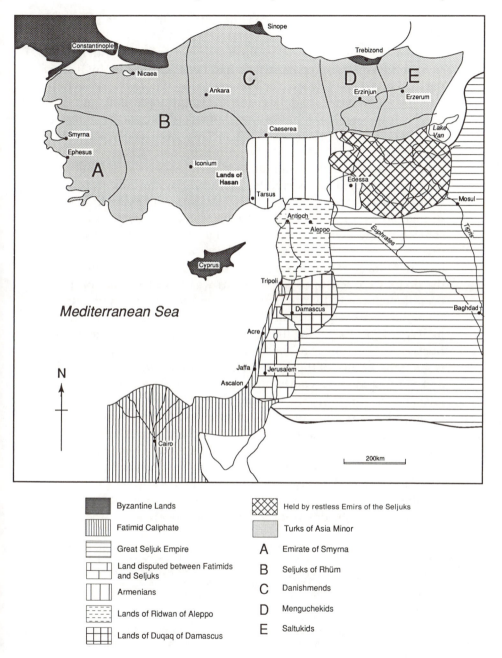

Fig. 3 Friends and enemies in the Middle East, 1095

which would strongly influence the settlement between the two sides.

When Alexius appealed to Urban II for military aid he was seeking mercenaries like those who had been sent to him by Robert the Frisian. As late as 1090, the Patzinacks, in alliance with the Emir Tzachas of Smyrna, had besieged Constantinople and had only been defeated with the aid of the Cumans at Mount Levunion in 1091. The Cumans then became a menace until 1094, when their siege of Adrianople collapsed. Byzantine diplomacy had neutralised the ambitious Tzachas by an alliance with the Seljuks of Rhum but their huge dominion virtually excluded Byzantium from Asia Minor. Nicaea was their capital while Antioch, Byzantium's last stronghold in the east, had fallen in 1085 and come under the control of the Syrian Seljuks (see figs. 2 and 3).[87] During the desperate 1080s Alexius had often been very short of money, and indeed Anna says that at one stage the treasury was so empty that the doors were left open and Alexius was forced to take property from the church.[88] By the time of the crusade such complaints are becoming rarer, and, presumably as Alexius's régime stabilised, the underlying prosperity of the empire enabled him to replenish his reserves.[89] His appeal to the west for aid was carefully timed. He would have known of the divisions amongst the Turks in Asia Minor and Syria, and there can be little doubt that he wanted to use his unexpected allies, just as he had wanted to use the mercenaries before, for the restoration of his empire.[90] However, grave difficulties arise for understanding the relationship between Alexius and the crusaders because of the sources available. Anna Comnena's life of her father, *The Alexiad*, is at first sight a godsend to the historians; it is an account of Alexius's attitudes and policies from an intimate member of the family. However, Anna was writing some forty years after the events she describes which happened when she was a child

[87] G. Ostrogorsky, *History of the Byzantine State*, tr. J. Hussey (Oxford, 1956), pp. 317–20 summarises the position of Byzantium on the eve of the crusade. See also R. J. H. Jenkins, 'The Byzantine Empire on the eve of the Crusades', *Historical Association Pamphlet* (1953); P. Charanis, 'The Byzantine Empire in the eleventh century', in K. Setton and M. W. Baldwin, eds., *A History of the Crusades*, 6 vols. (Pennsylvania, 1959–) (hereafter cited as Setton, *Crusades1*), 1. 177–219.

[88] *Alexiad*, pp. 156–8.

[89] A. Harvey, *Economic Expansion of the Byzantine Empire 900–1200* (Cambridge, 1989), p. 244: 'However, the eleventh century is most notable for a steady expansion which extended into the twelfth century and affected all aspects of economic activity.'

[90] On the situation in Syria see below pp. 197–205.

of thirteen, so she is unlikely to have had any real recollection of events. Her access to official sources was very uneven, and for much of the work she probably relied on the recollections of elderly people.[91] In these circumstances it is entirely natural that her account of the form of the relationship is often vague. She speaks of Hugh of Vermandois swearing to Alexius 'the customary oath of the Latins' and of Bohemond taking the 'customary Latin oath', while some unnamed Franks, like Tancred, simply swear an oath to the emperor; no oath is mentioned as having been demanded from the count of Toulouse.[92] Some confusion has been caused by translators rendering Anna's rather general language into specifically feudal terms; Hugh of Vermandois's oath is translated wrongly, as necessarily implying that he became the 'man' of the emperor, but the Greek was not a translation of a Latin term and simply means retainer or supporter, while the phrase 'liege-man', applied to the nameless Franks, may be quite wrong in its connotations.[93] But sometimes Anna is very specific. She gives us an account of the conflict between Godfrey de Bouillon and Alexius over the Frankish leader's refusal to come to any arrangement with the emperor which is broadly comparable to that of Albert of Aachen and concludes that:

Godfrey was soon obliged to submit to the will of the emperor. He then went to find him and took the required oath to him; its tenor was that all towns districts and fortresses which he might in the future subdue and which had previously belonged to the empire of the Romans would be handed over to the senior officer sent by the emperor for this purpose.[94]

This a good basis for a treaty between the crusaders and the emperor; Alexius could hope to regain lost land, and we know that he did so hope because he sent Tatikios with the crusaders to be that 'senior officer'. The crusaders would be relieved of the responsibility of holding cities whose garrisons would erode the strength of their army on its way to Jerusalem.[95] But what was the import of that vague phrase 'customary oath of the Latins' with its 'feudal' overtones? Moreover, the prominence of return of land in her

---

[91] France, 'Anna Comnena', 20–1; G. Loud, 'Anna Komnena', 41–57 shows how good Byzantine intelligence about the Normans of South Italy may have been; J. H. Pryor, 'The oath of the leaders of the First Crusade to the Emperor Alexius; fealty, homage', *Parergon*, 2 (1984)', 112.

[92] *Alexiad*, pp. 315, 325, 327, 329, 341.

[93] *Alexiad*, pp. 315, 325; Pryor, 'Oaths of the leaders', 117, 122–4

[94] *Alexiad*, p. 323, tr. Pryor, p. 122.   [95] *Alexiad*, p. 341.

account, and her vilification of Bohemond, need to be seen in the context of the hindsight which informs her writing. In 1098 Bohemond seized Antioch with the connivance of most of the crusader leaders and its possession then became a matter of dispute between Byzantium and the Franks of the east for all of Anna's lifetime. In Anna's view this was a breach of their promise; the crusaders held that Alexius had failed to deliver on his side of this bargain made at Constantinople in 1097. The desire to justify her father in this respect is a very powerful element in Anna's account of the crusade.[96] On the other hand, some of the western sources written by eye-witnesses were not very interested in detailing events which led to one of the most squalid and divisive incidents of the crusade, the quarrel over Antioch which almost broke up the crusade. Fulcher of Chartres speaks of friendship being concluded at Constantinople; in later passages he never mentions the quarrel over Antioch and although he refers to the departure of Stephen of Blois from Antioch he does not tell us that on his flight westward he met Alexius, at Philomelium, who concluded from his report that the crusaders were doomed and turned with his army back to Constantinople.[97] The three western eyewitness accounts of the crusade, the Anonymous author of the *Gesta*, Raymond of Aguilers and Albert of Aachen, never mention the issue of returning land to Alexius in their account of events at Constantinople in 1097. However, all three admit that after the final capture of Antioch the issue of the promise they had made to Alexius to return the city to him became a divisive issue in the army, primarily between Bohemond and Count Raymond.[98] Clearly this was an element in the agreements made at Constantinople, but all these and other eyewitness or near eyewitness sources use language of the agreement which suggest another element which clarifies Anna's 'customary oaths of the Latins'.

According to the *Gesta* Alexius demanded that Hugh Magnus, the first of the leaders to arrive at Constantinople in November 1096, should swear fealty to him, 'ei fidelitatem faceret'; this was certainly a customary oath in the west. Bohemond, the same source tells us, took a precisely similar oath. However, the Anonymous gives a long account of Godfrey's dealing with Alexius and concludes simply that he made a pact, 'pactum iniit cum imperatore', with no mention of

[96] France, 'Anna Comnena', 22–31.
[97] France, 'Crisis of the First Crusade', 289–90; Runciman, 1. 320.
[98] *GF*, pp. 75–6; RA, pp. 83, 93–4; AA, 434.

an oath of any kind. However, in describing negotiations between Alexius and the count of Toulouse, the Anonymous says that Raymond refused to become his vassal, 'hominum et fiduciam', and Raymond of Aguilers agrees, but his passage is largely based on that in the *Gesta*.[99] The implication is that others had taken such an oath. This inconsistency is a matter of some importance, for the oath of vassalage represented a much closer tie between one man and another than that established by mere fealty, and it is usually a consequence of the giving of a fief, of which there is no question here. The caveat has to be taken seriously, for vassalage did not always imply a landed relationship. In the famous oath of Bonneville, Harold first swore fealty to William, 'ei fidelitatem ... juravit', and promised to safeguard his succession to the throne of England. This act made Harold a vassal of William, for it was accompanied by the placing of Harold's hands between those of the duke 'satelliti suo accepto per manus', and only then did he proceed to confirm Harold's possession of lands – fealty, homage and investiture are all separate elements.[100] Moreover, there is another element in the Anonymous's account of events. Just as Anna stresses one-sidedly the obligations of the Franks, so he stresses those of the emperor who:

guaranteed good faith and security to all our men, and swore also to come with us, bringing an army and a navy, and faithfully to supply us with provisions both by land and sea, and to take care to restore all those things which we had lost. Moreover he promised that he would not cause or permit anyone to trouble or vex our pilgrims on the way to the Holy Sepulchre.[101]

The Anonymous gives a particular picture of events at Constantinople; the oath is a 'crafty plan' of 'the wretched emperor' and he claims that all the leaders refused to swear it, and only consented 'driven by desperate need'. The implication is clear; the oath is devalued by the circumstances in which it is taken. Further, there was no occasion when the leaders conferred on the matter to reject it, as stated here in a passage which includes one obvious interpolation. There then follows the careful enumeration of the Byzantine

---

[99] *GF*, pp. 5–7, 11; RA, p. 41, who explains that the count's anger was a result of hearing of his army being attacked on the road to Constantinople by imperial troops.

[100] WP, pp. 104–5; Pryor, 'Oaths of the Leaders', 115–22 takes the view that it was unthinkable for men of the status of the leaders to become vassals when they already had lords at home and were not receiving lands.

[101] *GF*, p. 12.

obligations.[102] Overall the account in the *Gesta* is highly convenient in view of the later dispute over Antioch when Bohemond would make the case that the Byzantines had broken their oath. It is as if the later comment about the princes having become vassals of Alexius slipped through in the drama of the passage about the count of Toulouse's refusal to take the oath. Moreover, Albert of Aachen quite consistently says that the leaders became the men of Alexius, and his account is peculiarly interesting.

Godfrey is Albert's hero and his reputation is carefully safe-guarded. His was the first major army to approach Constantinople, where it arrived on 23 December 1096. Even before he reached Constantinople, Godfrey heard of the supposed 'captivity' of Hugh of Vermandois and had raided the countryside in vengeance. At Constantinople Hugh was sent to invite Godfrey to a meeting with Alexius, but Godfrey refused to go on the advice of some mysterious strangers, originally Franks but now inhabitants of the city. The emperor withheld supply, then restored it and a Christmas peace was arranged. In late December Godfrey, still under the influence of the mysterious strangers, refused again to meet Alexius. The issue was distrust and fear of treachery, and Godfrey sent envoys to explain this to Alexius who responded with assurances which the Lorrainer spurned. Food supplies were again withdrawn by Alexius and this led to friction and an open attack on Constantinople by the Franks on 13 January 1097 and, after this had been repulsed, six days of ravaging. Anna Comnena's account is broadly comparable, except that the attack on Constantinople is wrongly dated to Easter 1097, but she makes it clear that Alexius feared that Godfrey might intrigue with Bohemond. It is interesting, therefore, that Albert of Aachen tells us that Godfrey received ambassadors from Bohemond, on or about 20 January, who suggested that he should fall back on Adrianople for the winter and await Bohemond's forces with a view to a joint attack on Constantinople. Albert says that disgust at this suggestion of Bohemond's was Godfrey's prime motive for arriving at a peace with Alexius. However, Godfrey was also subject to harrassment by imperial forces and threats of withdrawal of food supplies. Moreover Alexius complimented this pressure by diplo-

---

[102] *GF*, pp. 11–12; A. C. Krey, 'A neglected passage in the *Gesta* and its bearing on the literature of the First Crusade', in L. J. Paetow, ed., *The Crusades and other Historical Essays presented to D. C. Munro* (New York, 1928), pp. 57–79, shows clearly that Alexius's promise of Antioch to Bohemond recorded here is an interpolation.

matic overtures and offers to exchange hostages.[103] Once hostages had been exchanged, the emperor's own son John amongst them, Godfrey went for an audience with Alexius in a scene in which Albert notes the etiquette of the imperial court in which Alexius remained seated. Godfrey then took what was unmistakably an oath of vassalage: '[Godfrey] gave him [Alexius] his hand and declared that he was his vassal, and all the leading men who were present at the ceremony or came later did the same.'[104] In the course of his account, Albert reveals that all the leaders became the 'men' of the emperor. This, however, includes Raymond of Toulouse who we know took a modified oath of a type customary in Provence under which he promised not to harm the emperor or his lands.[105] The overall impression that the leaders swore an oath of vassalage is enhanced by Ralph of Caen whose *Gesta Tancredi* is unrelievedly hostile to the Byzantines. He says that Bohemond gave *hominagium* to Alexius, but that Tancred slipped across the Hellespont to avoid it and later at Pelekanum refused any oath. The *Gesta* confirms Tancred's evasion as do Albert and Anna who, however, say that he swore eventually at Pelekanum.[106] The overwhelming impression is that the leaders of the crusade were asked to take a very serious oath. Godfrey's resistance owed much to a general sense of distrust fanned by misinformation, and the count of Toulouse was angry because his army had been attacked. All the leaders found themselves exposed as individuals in a strange land to the diplomatic wiles of the emperor, of whose determination there can be no doubt. Alexius wanted to control the army while it was in his dominions and to make sure that it restored any lost imperial land. He wanted something much more than a simple agreement to this effect – he knew something of western society and was determined to cast the arrangement in the most solemn form possible. He had wanted mercenaries; by making the independent leaders who came his sworn men, his vassals, he very nearly achieved this end. Alexius was able to approach each leader separately, and use the oath of one as a pressure to achieve that of the next, and we must not forget that he

---

[103] AA, 305–11; *Alexiad*, pp. 319–23.   [104] AA, 311.

[105] AA, 312–13; RA, pp. 41–2; J. H. Hill and L. L. Hill, 'The convention of Alexius Comnenus and Raymond of St-Gilles', *American Historical Review*, 58 (1953), 322–7, *Raymond IV*, pp. 48–52.

[106] Ralph of Caen, *Gesta Tancredi*, RHC Oc. 5 [hereafter cited as RC], 612–13, 619–21; *GF*, p. 13; AA, 313; *Alexiad*, p. 341.

extracted it not only from the princes, but also lesser lords like Tancred whom he pursued so mercilessly. Bohemond was in a different position; under the will of his father Byzantium was his inheritance. His own army was much too small to attack, but he deliberately travelled very slowly watching events. He sent envoys to Godfrey proposing an alliance against Alexius, and Anna says that her father took steps to intercept any further communications of this sort. When he failed to attract support for his designs on Byzantium, Bohemond changed tack. He adopted a policy of friendship, swore the oath of homage, then asked to be made Grand Domestic of the East, commander of the imperial forces in Asia. Bohemond understood that Alexius was seeking to place the crusaders in much the same position as the mercenaries he had hired before who had also sworn 'customary oaths', and so shrewdly asked for an office which would make him commander of the whole crusader force – it was refused, but in temporising terms.[107] Alexius had wanted mercenaries – he tried to reduce the crusaders to as near to that status as was possible. Fulcher is extremely evasive about the whole vexed question – he wrote as a servant of the house of Boulogne and was aware of the controversy over Antioch. But in a revealing passage he tells us that after the capture of Nicaea 'our barons received permission from the emperor to depart'.[108]

The form of the agreement between the leaders and Alexius was therefore that of an oath of vassalage. This was a very solemn undertaking, but it reflects the flexibility of such undertakings which were sometimes used by major princes as forms of peace between them.[109] All the princes already had lords in the West, but multiple homage was commonplace. Robert of Flanders was the vassal both of King Philip of France and Henry IV of Germany. The new vassalic tie, into which he and others entered, was clearly for a specific set of circumstances and would have made little difference to their lords in the west. The notion of liege-homage was only slowly establishing itself: in the treaty between Henry I of England and Robert of Flanders, Henry was effectively allying with Robert against their overlord the king of France, and the solution to the

---

[107] *Alexiad*, p. 329; Pryor, 'Oaths of the Leaders', 115 draws attention to the oaths of earlier Frankish mercenaries.

[108] FC, p. 83.

[109] J. F. Lemarignier, *Recherches sur l'Hommage en Marche et les Frontières Féodales* (Lille, 1945), pp. 113, 161.

problem was for Robert to promise to advise King Philip against war with England and, if pressed, to send as few troops as was compatible with his vassal status. By such devices would liege-homage emerge, but not yet.[110] However, the demand seems to have shocked Godfrey, but in the end he was isolated and vulnerable to the threat of withdrawal of supply. His oath was a tremendous pressure upon all who came after, particularly as it was preceded by that of Hugh of Vermandois and his companions and followed by those of many in his own force. The count of Toulouse took a different kind of oath but one customary in the south where fealty rather than acts of homage was central in relationships between nobles.[111] And it may be that in the course of the discussions he came to see the value of the friendship with Alexius which Urban had advocated. But whatever the form of the oath, in substance Alexius and the leaders were creating a treaty, or at least an understanding. What was its nature?

Anna Comnena insists that return of conquered imperial territory was a vital part of the agreement. Although her insistence on the one-sided nature of the agreement which placed obligations upon the crusaders almost certainly reflects the Byzantine view that the crusaders were, virtually, mercenaries at the command of Alexius at least within the old Byzantine lands, there is no doubt that Alexius had to enter into obligations as well. Such obligations are detailed only in the *Gesta* and its derivatives in a form which probably represents a maximal interpretation, to say the least. That Alexius gave military assistance to the crusade at Nicaea is self-evident from all accounts, and we know that Tatikios accompanied them on the march to Antioch, while Byzantine ships were active in their support and in bringing supply.[112] However, it is extremely unlikely that Alexius swore to come with them at any stage as the Anonymous would have us believe. Raymond of Aguilers says that Alexius explicitly ruled out personal participation. He certainly did not

---

[110] *Diplomatic documents preserved in the Public Record Office* (London, 1964), pp. 1–4. A recent study of Byzantine-Crusader relations, not used by Pryor, 'Oaths of the Leaders', concludes that the leaders took oaths of vassalage, but is sceptical of the notion of liege-homage being applied to the relationship; R. J. Lilie, *Byzanz und die Kreuzfahrerstaaten* (Munich, 1981), pp. 22–3. The notion has been applied, however, to the relationship between Bohemond and Alexius: J. Ferluga, 'La ligesse dans l'empire byzantin', *Sbornik Radova*, 7 (1961), 97–123.

[111] Poly and Bournazel, *Feudal Transformation*, p. 75 and see the article by Hill and Hill above p. 115, n. 105.

[112] On the siege of Nicaea see below pp. 162–5 and on Byzantine naval aid pp. 210–20.

participate in the siege of Nicaea and Anna tells us quite plainly that this was because he did not trust the crusaders and, indeed, she shows that he later deceived them in the 'drama of betrayal' by which Nicaea surrendered.[113] If Alexius really had promised to go, all the sources would have said so – it was not the kind of statement that could be kept secret. The *Gesta*'s statement should be read in the context of its presentation of the betrayal at Philomelium – it is a deliberate exaggeration of Alexius's promise to give military aid to the crusaders. There were good reasons why Alexius could not join the western army for, as he said to Raymond of Toulouse, he had many enemies on many frontiers. What he did not say was that Jerusalem was strategically irrelevant to the empire and that any emperor who went off on such irrelevancy would be endangering his throne.[114] Of course this does not mean that Alexius could not decide to join them at some future date when conditions might be very favourable, merely that he had no intention of binding himself to such a dangerous course of action, and did not. From the emperor's point of view the treaty with the leaders was very satisfactory. The leaders were his vassals. He recognised that this was a fragile bond, hence his insistence on some renewing their oaths at Pelekanum after the siege of Nicaea and on making a wide range of senior crusaders take the oath. In this capacity they were sworn to return to him all former imperial territories. There must have been some geographical limitation on this, for, if one goes back far enough in time, all of the Middle East had been ruled from Constantinople. In September 1098, Raymond of Toulouse seized Albara and installed a Latin bishop there. Since at this time he was the champion of imperial rights, and was resisting Bohemond's seizure of Antioch, he would hardly have offended his ally Alexius by holding the city himself and appointing an alien bishop. Furthermore, Count Raymond was later to hold Laodicea of the emperor (see fig. 4).[115] Antioch and its immediate area probably formed the boundary of the old imperial posessions which were to be restored. Of course, the Greeks were very sceptical of the ability of the westerners to conquer any of this, as Anna indicates, but should they succeed Alexius was in a position to profit with a minimum commitment of his own.[116]

[113] *Alexiad*, pp. 336–7.   [114] RA, p. 41.
[115] RA, p. 91–2. On Laodicea see David, *Robert Curthose*, pp. 230–44.
[116] Tatikios's instructions were to take over any cities which the crusaders conquered 'if indeed God granted them that favour': *Alexiad*, p. 341.

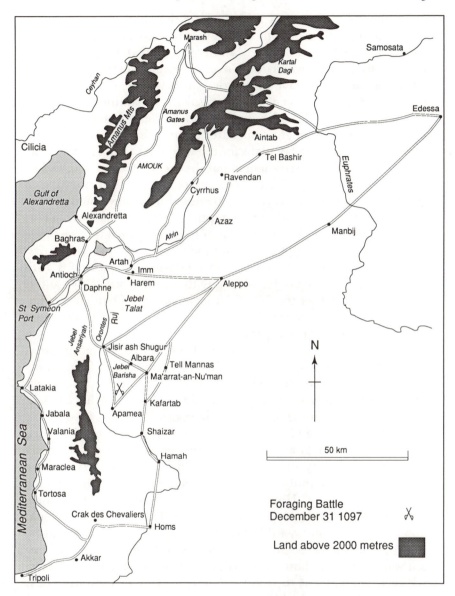

Fig. 4   Syria and the First Crusade

From the point of view of the crusaders they had obeyed Urban's directive and profited from the addition of imperial forces which would be substantial at Nicaea, rather less thereafter. In the longer run the Byzantines would take over cities and fortresses which it would be unwise to leave unguarded in their rear, but which were irrelevant to the achievement of Jerusalem. In addition, they were promised naval aid and supplies and a clear passage for any reinforcements that might come after them. It is very probable that they were also able to lay plans for the war in Asia Minor, for Anna says that Alexius advised them about the tactics of the Turks and he must surely have explained something of the political situation in the Middle East for he certainly suggested how they could exploit this by negotiating with the Egyptians.[117] Adhémar was ill at Thessalonica at the time that most of the arrangements were made and we know nothing of his dealings with the imperial authorities. However, he was later at pains to establish close relations with Simeon, the Patriarch of Jerusalem, with whom he wrote two letters to the west, and after the fall of Antioch John the Oxite, its Ortho- dox Patriarch, was restored.[118] This suggests that after the initial difficulties, good relations prevailed.

In addition, the negotiations at Constantinople produced a special relationship between Alexius and Raymond of Toulouse. Quite how this was achieved is not clear; they had begun on very bad terms indeed, according to the Latin sources, as we have noted, with Raymond refusing any oath of homage. However, by the time the army was setting off to Nicaea Raymond was at Alexius's court, hence his late arrival at Nicaea.[119] Anna never mentions the early hostility; in her story all is sweetness and light from the first, and she suggests that it was mutual mistrust of Bohemond which brought the two men together.[120] However, this may well reflect later events – hindsight is highly developed in the *Alexiad*. Later, Raymond would appear as by far the wealthiest of the crusaders and when the army was frustrated at Antioch by the quarrels of the princes the suggest- ion was made that those who favoured the imperial party, amongst whom Raymond was the most prominent, were in Byzantine pay, but this may merely have been camp rumour. Raymond appears as

---

[117] See below pp. 165, 166.
[118] Hagenmeyer, *Kreuzzugsbriefe*, pp. 141–2, 146–9; on the restoration of John the Oxite, see AA, 433.
[119] *Alexiad*, p. 330; AA, 314.   [120] *Alexiad*, pp. 329–31.

far wealthier than any of the other leaders – in the spring of 1098 he took over the Mahomeries tower at Antioch when his followers were murmuring about his meanness, paid Tancred to man the fort by the St Paul Gate and produced money to compensate knights for loss of horses. In early 1099 he offered huge sums to the other leaders to enter his service.[121] After the crusade was over Raymond would hold Laodicea for Alexius and act with him in dealing with the crusade of 1101.[122] There is no clear evidence, but it is possible that Alexius gave Raymond of St Gilles significant military subsidies. What is certain is that under the pressure of events at Antioch in the summer of 1098 Raymond became a close ally of the emperor. Between the conversations at Constantinople and this time there is little direct evidence of his attitudes, though Albert of Aix says he received rich presents from the emperor.[123]

The arrangements at Constantinople laid the basis for co-operation between Byzantium and the crusading army. Militarily the crusaders were strengthened by the deal with Alexius. But one matter never seems to have been discussed at Constantinople – leadership of the crusade in the absence of the emperor. The princes had made their arrangements with Alexius as individuals. None of them had overlords with any real power and even men of the second rank were used to a high degree of independence. The device of a council of leaders seems to have emerged quite naturally in this situation and Adhémar would seem to have been its mentor and political guide – as a priest would later say.[124] But this was a dangerous omission for a military expedition, and one for which they would later pay dearly. However, after the arrangements made at Constantinople the leaders could turn their attention to the clash of arms which was now imminent.

[121] RA, pp. 62–3, 94, 100.
[122] *Alexiad*, p. 353; J. L. Cate, 'The Crusade of 1101', in Setton, *Crusades*, 1. 354.
[123] France, 'Tatikios', 143–5; AA, 314.   [124] RA, p. 73.

CHAPTER 5

The size of the crusader army

After the conclusion of the agreements between Alexius and the leaders, the crusader forces gathered in Asia Minor. Godfrey's army had crossed in Lent of 1097 and doubtless they were joined by other contingents such as that of Robert of Flanders. Bohemond's force crossed under the command of Tancred in late April though he stayed with the emperor, while the army led by Godfrey, Robert of Flanders and Tancred, including the 'feeble debris' of the 'People's Crusade', marched along the Gulf of Nicomedia to that city via Rufinel to begin their approach to Nicaea. The Anonymous says that they were too numerous to take the road used by the 'People's Crusade' and opened up their own route direct to Nicaea using 300 men to clear and mark the way. This probably means that the old Roman road from Nicomedia to Nicaea was badly overgrown and had to be cleared for the army. This road crosses the Naldökan Daglari, mountains which rise to over 1,400 metres, and the crusaders marked it with crosses for those who would follow them (see figs. 2 and 5). They arrived at Nicaea on 6 May 1097 and even at this early stage food was short and the army was relieved when Bohemond arrived with supplies.[1] The count of Toulouse had also stayed behind, according to Anna Comnena establishing very cordial relations with Alexius, and did not arrive before Nicaea until 14 May, while the north French under Robert of Normandy and Stephen of Blois only arrived at Constantinople on that day and did not reach Nicaea until 3 June. The crusader force was augmented by a Byzantine contingent of some 2,000 under Tatikios, to which was later added a smaller force under the command of Boutoumites with boats to cover the Ascanian Lake which lay along the city's western perimeter. Both these men were trusted confidants of

[1] AA, 311–12, 314; GF, p. 13–14.

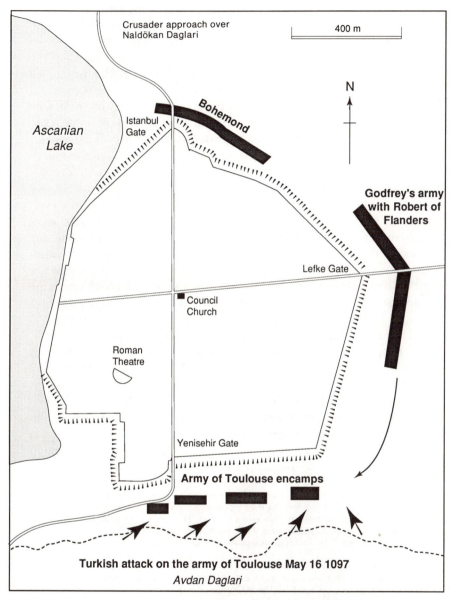

Fig. 5   The Siege of Nicaea and the Turkish attack of 16 May 1097

Alexius and had considerable experience in dealing with westerners. Alexius himself settled at Pelekanum (on the north coast of the Gulf of Izmit, opposite Civitos) and from there manipulated the activities of his commanders.[2] It was only slowly that the full strength of the western army gathered and it seems likely that it did not reach maximum until after the siege of Nicaea, for at that time Alexius (at Pelekanum) was at pains to demand the oath be taken by those who had not done so, which suggests the late arrival of some contingents.[3] But as more than one crusader source produces a figure for the strength of the army at this time, when they were about to march into enemy territory, it is an appropriate juncture to consider the matter of numbers.

It is often said that medieval people were not good at numbers. It was an essentially local world in which large gatherings were uncommon and therefore impressed themselves unduly upon the imaginations of participants. Literacy was relatively rare and numeracy even rarer.[4] But the fact is that most people in most eras are pretty bad at estimating large numbers of people. I recall one large demonstration in which I participated in Hyde Park in the summer of 1982 for which the organisers claimed an attendance of 300,000 and the police suggested 60,000 – a discrepancy of positively medieval proportions. Of course politics has something to do with such estimates; the police, as the guardians of law and order, try to play down such events while the organisers have the opposite tendency. Just such political considerations entered into the crusade's own estimates. Simeon, Patriarch of Jerusalem and Adhémar wrote to the west asking for reinforcements and stating: 'We have 100,000 mounted knights and armoured men, but what of it? We are few in comparison with the pagans, but verily God is fighting in our

---

[2] *Alexiad*, pp. 336–7; Boutoumites had much naval experience but he was also a diplomat who dealt with Hugh of Vermandois. Tatikios was an experienced soldier who had commanded western mercenaries against the Patzinacks in 1090. The two had campaigned together in Bithynia in 1086: B. Skoulatos, *Les Personnages Byzantins de l'Alexiade* (Louvain, 1980), pp. 181–5, 287–92. On the reasons for Alexius not joining the crusaders, see below pp. 156–7.

[3] *Alexiad*, p. 340.

[4] On numeracy see Murray, *Reason and Society*, especially pp 141–212. There is a remarkable passage on numbers by Ibn-Khaldûn, *Muqaddima; an Introduction to History* ed. and tr. F. Rosenthal, abridged N. J. Dawood (Princeton, 1967) (hereafter cited as Ibn-Khaldûn), pp. 11–13, when Ibn-Khaldûn attacks uncritical use of sources which produces gross exaggerations: 'An army of this size (600, 000) cannot march or fight as a unit. The whole available territory would be too small for it. If it were in battle formation, it would extend two, three, or more times beyond the field of vision'. Such common sense is rare in any age!

behalf'.[5] The rhetoric warns us that though this may be a serious estimate, the writer must have been anxious not to pitch the figure too high or too low lest he discourage people from coming, hence also the stress on the magnitude of the task. We must recognise that large numbers in round figures need to be treated with caution, but that smaller figures may be quite accurate if there is reason to believe that the source is in any way authoritative. Furthermore, the leadership must have felt the need to know what troops were at their disposal and this must have become very acute in the later stages of the crusade when numbers seem to have been heavily reduced by the attrition of battle, starvation and illness. The Papal Legate Daimbert who arrived in the East at the very end of the crusade wrote to the West announcing its success and stated that an army 300,000 strong at Nicaea had been reduced to 20,000 by the battle of Ascalon on 12 August 1099. We need not accept these numbers, or even the proportion of losses implied, only that the crusaders themselves recognised that they had suffered terrible attrition.[6] Since nobody actually tried to conduct a count of participants we can only hope to arrive at a general estimate, but a view of numbers is vital if we are to understand why the crusade was successful.

However, before numbers can be calculated we need some definition. The contemporary chroniclers refer to the leaders, whom they often call 'Princes', knights, foot and the poor. Setting aside the Princes and lords of high rank of whom we often have some individual knowledge, men like Anselm of Ribemont, two of whose letters to the West have survived, or Raymond Pilet who played a notable semi-independent role, it is important to realise that knights, foot and poor are not watertight categories. Knights were social superiors well equipped for war – yet on the road across the Anti-Taurus many abandoned that equipment and many more lost horses in the course of the campaign. Raymond of Aguilers distinguishes between knights and *milites plebei*, poor knights who seem only to have been mounted at times when horses were plentiful.[7] Such poor knights must have slipped easily into the great mass of the army – but who were they? The term 'poor' is a difficult one. Contemporary sources were clearly aware of armed men other than knights – the letter of Simeon and Adhémar to the West written in

[5] Hagenmeyer, *Kreuzzugsbriefe*, p. 142, Krey, *The First Crusade*, p. 132.
[6] Hagenmeyer, *Kreuzzugsbriefe*, pp. 168, 172.
[7] *GF*, p. 27; RA, p. 106.

October speaks of mounted knights and armoured men who were presumably the professional retinues of the lords and the greater knights.[8] As horses became scarcer knights reinforced this group which became a very important element of the crusader army by the end of the siege of Antioch. But in addition to this group there were the servants, who must have formed the largest single group in the army. Many of these would have had a military function – to look after horses and arms as well as to perform menial tasks. Horses need a great deal of looking after and for this purpose alone knights must have taken large numbers of followers. In the West we have noted that a whole infrastructure was needed to support the warhorses of the upper classes, but humbler riding and draught animals also needed much care. Every knight must have started with at least three animals: a warhorse, a palfrey and a pack-horse. The mercenaries which William Rufus and Henry I arranged to employ from Robert of Flanders were each to be provided with three warhorses, but I am assuming that this represents the equipment of a really professional soldier. Many of the knights would have had as many warhorses plus numbers of palfreys and pack animals and undoubtedly the richer knights and great nobles had many more.[9] Thus, in association with the knights (whose numbers are below estimated to have been about 6,000–7,000) a minimum of 20,000 horses would have begun the journey, and in addition there were pack and draught animals including oxen for the carts. The servants needed in order to look after these 20,000 alone would have constituted a substantial army. In the following of important men, servants and retainers of all kinds must have been numerous; almost any knight would have had at least one. If those with a quasi-military function could arm themselves they could be pressed into service easily, but on the other hand if his master died a man of this type could easily find himself in the wider mass of general domestic servants and non-combatants. For the army attracted large numbers of poor pilgrims, some infirm, with women and children. This last group of genuine non-combatants must have dwindled quickly

[8] See above, p. 125, n. 5.

[9] On the treaty see above pp. 116–18; M. Bennett, 'La règle du Temple as a military manual, or how to deliver a cavalry charge', in C. Harper-Bill, C. J. Holdworth and J. Nelson, eds., *Studies in Medieval History presented to R. Allen-Brown*, p. 7 says that the *Rule of the Temple* limited each knight to one or two warhorses, one riding animal and one packhorse with a squire for each warhorse. This reflects the military conditions of the later twelfth and thirteenth centuries.

under the impact of deprivation and disease, for they must have been the poorest and therefore most vulnerable to disease. By 1099, however, anyone fit enough to bear arms, except for clergy, was probably in the infantry. They were disciplined and trained by sheer force of circumstance. Many of them were dismounted knights who might from time to time find horses. Thus an army with a huge civilian tail became progressively smaller and more militarised as time went on, under the pressure of enemy attack.

Fulcher of Chartres' statement that the army gathered at Nicaea was 600,000 strong including 100,000 'protected by mail hauberks' is clearly sheer fantasy, as is Ekkehard's figure of 300,000. Albert of Aachen says the army was 300,000 strong at Nicaea (manuscript variants say 600,000) with women and children in addition, and he also indicates that the Turks believed that 400,000 were attacking Nicaea. Anna Comnena says that Godfrey's army alone numbered 10,000 cavalry and 70,000 infantry, which is surely as wild as the statement by Albert that Godfrey led 60,000 knights to the rescue of Bohemond at the battle of Dorylaeum.[10] On the other hand, Albert reports Godfrey attacking the enemy leader with fifty *sodalibus* during this battle and adds that the enemy suffered losses of 3,000, a surprisingly modest figure in the light of the implied size of the Turkish army – which Anselm of Ribemont placed at 260,000 and Tudebode at 360,000.[11] Indeed, when it comes to specific battles the total numbers suggested by the sources reduce dramatically. On 31 December 1097 a force under Bohemond and Robert of Flanders sent out to forage ran into the army of Damascus attempting to relieve Antioch. Albert of Aachen says that the westerners had 15,000 foot and 2,000 knights and the Anonymous gives an overall figure of 20,000 – though Raymond of Aguilers suggests that there were only 400 Frankish knights present.[12] There is a much greater consensus on the second battle fought against the relieving force of Ridwan of Aleppo on 9 February 1098. On this occasion the approach of an enemy army came at a moment when suffering in the bitter winter was at its height and losses in horses had been heavy. The council of leaders decided to send all their knights under the command of Bohemond to ambush the enemy at a narrow passage

[10] FC, p. 81; Ekkehard, p. 21; *Alexiad*, p. 318; AA, 329–30, 365.

[11] AA, 330, 331; Hagenmeyer, *Kreuzzugsbriefe*, p. 145; Peter Tudebode, *Historia de Hierosolymi-tano Itinere*, ed. J. H. Hill and L. L. Hill (Philadelphia, 1974) [hereafter cited as Tudebode], p. 36.

[12] AA, 373–5; *GF*, p. 30; RA, pp. 52.

between the river Orontes and the lake of Antioch, leaving the foot to defend the camp. Albert says that only 700 could find horses and this figure is confirmed by Raymond of Aguilers and by Stephen of Blois in his second letter to his wife Adela.[13] Of course this is a measure of horses rather than men as we have already noted. The figure 700 occurs again for Albert says that when the crusaders were preparing for the betrayal of Antioch at a time when Kerbogah's relief army was approaching, they pretended to repeat the tactics of the Lake battle and allowed the garrison to see 700 cavalry march away – suggesting that even then this was the size of the cavalry component.[14] In the later stages of the crusade Albert's estimates of the total size of the army grow much more modest. In February 1099 Godfrey de Bouillon and Robert of Flanders were forced by public opinion to leave Antioch with an army 20,000 strong which when joined to that of Raymond of Toulouse, Robert of Normandy and Tancred at 'Akkār made a total of 50,000, of which only 20,000 were fit to fight. The total figure had risen at Jerusalem to 60,000 'including both sexes', which I take to mean including non-combatants. By the end of the siege the Christians could muster only 20,000 fighting men against the Egyptians at Ascalon on 6 August 1099.[15] These figures suggest that in the later stages of the crusade there was a core fighting force of 20,000 men which could be augmented in emergency by a number of less well-armed people drawn from amongst the poor. There is nothing impossible about these figures in themselves, but the suggestion that in the army at Ascalon Godfrey alone could lead 2,000 cavalry (and 3,000 foot) does not sit well with the attrition of horses which we have observed, and generally 50,000 seems a lot after three years of fighting and marching. In many ways the evidence of Raymond of Aguilers is far more impressive.

Raymond of Aguilers says that at the start of the siege of Antioch the army had 100,000 armed men (*armatorum*), a figure which reappears in the two letters sent by Simeon Patriarch of Jerusalem to the west, although in the second, that of January 1098, it is specifically stated that this figure includes losses so far incurred.[16] As both these letters were inspired by Adhémar, and Raymond was in his *mouvance*, we can assume that this was some sort of quasi-official

---

[13] AA, 400–1; RA, pp. 380; Hagenmeyer, *Kreuzzugsbriefe*, p. 151.   [14] AA, 400–1.
[15] AA, 454, 461, 463, 496.
[16] RA, p. 48; Hagenmeyer, *Kreuzzugsbriefe*, p. 147 and see above p. 125, n. 5.

estimate of numbers at the start of the crusade. As such it is likely to be an overestimate, and we must note that it does not include non-combatants. But it is for the later stages of the crusade that Raymond of Aguilers furnishes us with very consistent and convincing indications of numbers. Historians have noted some of his figures but have not noticed how full a picture he offers of the manpower situation of the crusade in the period after the fall of Antioch.[17]

As we have noted, after the capture of Antioch the army fell to quarrelling over its fate and the advance to Jerusalem was stalled in North Syria for over 5 months (July 1098–January 1099). By this time Raymond of Aguilers was a chaplain to the count of Toulouse and thus close to an important leader. At Rugia on 4 January 1099, Raymond of Toulouse offered money to the other leaders, and we know that amongst them was Tancred who accepted it: 'on the agreement that he would be in his service until they gained Jerusalem'.[18] We can assume that similar terms were offered to the other leaders. Such a deal would have restored momentum and had the effect of making Count Raymond leader. The offer made was as follows: 10,000 *solidi* to Godfrey de Bouillon and Robert of Normandy; 6,000 to Robert of Flanders; 5,000 to Tancred. This must reflect the strength of the forces disposed of by each leader at that time, and as the quality and constitution of the foot element was uncertain probably reflects their strength in knights. Now Tancred accepted and followed Count Raymond with forty knights and a number of foot-soldiers.[19] On this basis we can guess that Robert of Flanders had fifty knights, while Robert Curthose and Godfrey each had 100. In addition, Raymond says that money was given to other leaders proportionately (*prout*). This presumably refers to secondary figures whose stature has been discussed above, but we know no details of the offers made to them. The sources give the impression that Raymond of Toulouse had by far the biggest of the armies, and at this very juncture, as the army was contemplating the march south, Raymond tells us that the count had 300 knights in his army.[20] When he was joined, therefore, by Tancred and Robert of Normandy Raymond of Toulouse had only some 450–500 knights, allowing for any independents who may have joined him, while

---

[17] Riley-Smith, *Idea of Crusading*, p. 63 and Runciman 1. 363, for example, both quote Raymond of Aguilers' figure for the army at Jerusalem.
[18] RA, pp. 100, 112.   [19] RA, p. 102.   [20] RA, p. 102.

150–200 remained in the service of Godfrey and the count of Flanders at Antioch and its environs, together with those in any independent groups who refused the offer. Raymond of Aguilers makes clear that all this must be read in the context of a shortage of men. At Ma'arra where they were starving some Provençals deserted, despairing of proceeding 'without the help of the Frankish people', and when the count decided to conduct a *razzia* to revictual his army they complained that he could not do that and hold Ma'arra with a mere 300 knights. Furthermore, the count was so anxious about the manpower situation that when he marched south he made the bishop of Albara leave only a tiny garrison of seven knights and thirty foot to hold the city.[21] The *razzia* improved the food situation and at Homs a friendly reception from its ruler enabled the pilgrims to buy precious horses, increasing their cavalry strength to about 1,000. When an attack on Jabala was proposed Tancred opposed it, pointing to the weakness of an army which had started with 100,000 knights and 200,000 foot and now had barely 1,000 of the one and 5,000 of the other.[22] This shortage of manpower must explain the many doubts and hesitations of the leaders in the summer of 1098 and their desperate hope for reinforcements expressed in their letter to Urban II of 11 September 1098.[23]

The count of Toulouse must have had the question of numbers very much in his mind when, after a prosperous march with much good foraging and looting, he halted the army before 'Akkār which was conveniently close to the coast where sea power facilitated communications with the other forces in and around Antioch. Godfrey and Robert of Flanders eventually left Antioch and besieged Jabala, then came to the aid of Count Raymond when he announced that an enemy army was in the field. This proved to be a chimera and the joining of the two forces was marred by bitter divisions over whether to continue the siege of 'Akkār which was eventually abandoned in early May 1099. Raymond gives no figures for the combined force at this stage. In his account of the discussions at Ramla when a suggestion was made that the army should attack Egypt, those who were against it pointed to the weakness of an army which had barely 1,500 knights and few foot-soldiers.[24] He gives an estimate of their strength on the eve of their assault on Jerusalem on 13/14 July 1099. There were, he says, 1,200–1,300 mounted men

[21] RA, pp. 101–2, 105.   [22] RA, p. 104.   [23] Hagenmeyer, *Kreuzzugsbriefe*, p. 165.
[24] RA, p. 136.

and 12,000 foot, with in addition the disabled and the poor: the reduction in the number of knights from 1,500 probably reflects the deaths of horses and men during the siege. These figures are broadly in line with those we have already noted: a force of around a thousand knights and 5,000 or more infantry under Count Raymond was joined at 'Akkār by one of 200 knights and, we may guess, roughly 4,000–5,000 infantry. These would have been augmented by stragglers, and by men from the English and Genoese fleets.[25] In August the crusaders marched out of Jerusalem against an Egyptian relief force gathering at Ascalon and destroyed it in battle on the twelfth of that month. On the eve of the battle Raymond estimates the crusader army at 1,200 knights and 9,000 foot.[26] These figures suggest that the capture of Jerusalem had cost the army almost a quarter of its fighting strength. It may seem odd that the complement of knights recorded is not much smaller, but fluctuations in their number were related to supply of horses and while they must have suffered losses, the garrison's horses were captured during the sack.[27] These figures have the ring of truth, as many commentators have remarked, but what is impressive is the consistency with which we can trace numbers in Raymond's account since the time of the fall of Ma'arra and the Rugia meeting. In January 1099 a force of some 14,000 fighting men, including at the most 1,500 mounted troops, was available to march to Jerusalem. This allows for losses due to sickness and disease, the fighting around 'Akkār and, in addition, some coming and going of which we hear no trace. These figures relate to numbers of fighting men – there is simply no way of estimating the non-combatants. By the time Ascalon had been fought this number had dwindled to not many more than 10,000, of whom something like 3,000 stayed at Jerusalem.

The figure seems strikingly small only because we have become hypnotised by the huge numbers mentioned in other sources, but it should not surprise us. The army must have suffered appalling losses since it set out. As we have noted, even before it left Europe pilgrims were dying. Nicaea was a major siege with intense and large-scale

---

[25] RA, pp. 134, 142, tells us that the English burned their worn-out boats as the army left 'Akkār, while six Genoese ships put into Jaffa during the siege of Jerusalem only to be trapped by the Egyptian fleet, whereupon, on 19 June, they were burned and the sailors joined the siege.

[26] RA, p. 156.   [27] AA, 477.

military activity which must have been costly. During the siege the Christians fought off an enemy relief army and then engaged the Turks of Asia Minor in a major battle at Dorylaeum. The siege of Antioch lasted for nine months and during it the army fought off three major relief expeditions, while we hear of numerous minor clashes which we can be sure represent only a fraction of the totality. There followed the savage second siege of Antioch, the attack on Ma'arra and the fighting around 'Akkār. This attrition of battle must have been costly in lives, but there was also starvation, disease and accident. The army had barely started the siege of Nicaea when it was asking for food, while Albert records the deaths of 500 poor due to thirst only a few days after Dorylaeum when even the falcons and hunting-dogs of the rich were dying. By December 1097 the army at Antioch was starving, a state which must have been semi-permanent during the winter which followed.[28] The count of Toulouse was desperately ill during the crossing of Asia Minor, during much of the siege and even at the moment of the great battle with Kerbogah in which he was unable to participate. Baldwin of Boulogne's English wife died at Marasch and a knight of the house of Boulogne, Adelrard of Guizan, in mid-October 1097. Godfrey de Bouillon was mauled by a bear while hunting and suffered a long illness.[29] Matthew of Edessa actually says that during the siege of Antioch the Franks lost one in seven of their men to plague.[30] But in addition to these obvious attritions of strength there were other factors at work to reduce the size of the army by January 1099. In the autumn of 1098 Baldwin had begun operations in conjunction with native Armenians, in the area of their settlement east of Antioch, capturing many places including Tell-Bashir and Ravendan. In early February Thoros, prince of Edessa, asked for his support and Baldwin gathered 500 mounted troops, only to be repulsed by a Turkish attack. Eventually he got through to Edessa with 200 *sociis* and by March he had overthrown Thoros and was in complete control of the city.[31] It is, of course, difficult to be certain how many of Baldwin's troops were native Armenians – a group with a strong military tradition – and how many Frankish. Matthew of Edessa says that he had 100 with him at Tell-Bashir and took only sixty to Edessa. Fulcher says that he had only eighty knights with him when

---

[28] *GF*, pp. 14, 30; AA, 339–40; RA, p. 50.   [29] RA, pp. 46, 62, 79; AA, 358.
[30] Matthew of Edessa, *Chronicle*, RHC arm. 1 (Hereafter cited as Matthew), 33.
[31] AA, 351–5.

he went to Edessa.[32] Possession of Edessa was militarily extremely useful to the crusade, but it had to be garrisoned, as had its dependencies, and Frankish troops used for this purpose could not go on to Jerusalem. When Baldwin wanted to complete his pilgrimage at Christmas 1099 he took only a small force and joined Bohemond and Daimbert of Pisa's bigger force in marching to Jerusalem, but when his brother died on 18 July 1100 he could afford what Fulcher describes as 'a little army' of 200 knights and 700 foot, without stripping Edessa.[33] At the start of the siege of Antioch Raymond of Aguilers remarks on the number of cities and forts held by the crusaders which had to be garrisoned, with the result that many knights were leaving the army.[34] Anselm of Ribemont, writing in November 1097, said that the army held 200 fortresses and cities, while Stephen of Blois, writing late in the first siege of Antioch gave a figure of 165.[35] Some of these must surely have been garrisoned by Tatikios's troops on behalf of Alexius, but even so the Franks seem to have been left with many on their hands and would not have been willing to abandon all. Moreover, there was the question of Antioch and its area which by the winter of 1098 was firmly in the hands of Bohemond.[36] The quarrels between the leaders in the summer and autumn of 1098 and the creation of a Frankish dominion in North Syria created a fluid and confusing situation and considerable opportunities for wealth. The leaders took many of the poor into their service.[37] We have noted that Raymond of Toulouse stripped Albara of its garrison so that only seven knights and thirty foot were left to hold it, but this very rapidly grew to sixty knights and seventy foot, presumably from stay-behinds. Albert says that immediately after the crusade Godfrey had a force of 3,000 troops in Jerusalem, which fell to 200 knights and 1,000 foot by the following spring.[38] It

[32] FC, p. 90; Matthew, 35.   [33] FC, pp. 129–30, 137.   [34] RA, pp. 46–8.

[35] Hagenmeyer, *Kreuzzugsbriefe*, pp. 145, 151.

[36] Runciman 1. 338 gives Bohemond's army a strength of 500 knights when it left Italy, on the basis of unverified evidence, but Yewdale, *Bohemond*, p. 37, found the same figure in Lupus Protospatarius. The 10, 000 knights plus many foot mentioned by Albert in Bohemond's army at Constantinople is clearly a nonsense: AA, 312. However, the general impression is that Bohemond had a small and well-disciplined army and a figure approaching 500 plus servants would not seem unreasonable. By the time he reached Antioch that would have been reduced substantially, and some may have left him in order to go to Jerusalem, as did the author of the *Gesta Francorum*.

[37] *GF*, pp. 72–3.

[38] RA, p. 105; AA, 507, 517; on conditions in the early kingdom see J. Prawer, 'The Settlement of the Latins in Jerusalem', *Speculum*, 27 (1952), 491–5; Riley-Smith, 'The settlement of Latin Palestine', 721–36; Murray, 'The origins of the Frankish nobility of the

is unlikely that Edessa could have been held by many fewer, though its total forces included good quality native troops and we can assume that Antioch required something like the same numbers to hold it. Quite possibly a lot of these men subsequently made their way to Jerusalem and then returned to the west – accounting for the disparity between the figures which Albert gives for 1099 and 1100. We can reasonably assume that some 300–500 knights and a commensurate number of foot, say about 3,000–5,000, were tied up in the nascent principalities of North Syria and places like Albara, Maraclea and Tortosa, but this may be an underestimate.

The army also suffered from desertion. Early in 1098 Louis, archdeacon of Toul, left the siege of Antioch for a safer place forty-eight kilometres away, though perhaps he returned. In the second siege of Antioch desertions grew numerous – William of Grandmesnil, Bohemond's brother-in-law, fled with a group of North French, while most notorious of all was the flight of Stephen of Blois who was ill just before the betrayal of Antioch and seems to have believed that the arrival of Kerbogah had doomed the army. After the capture of the city the leaders sent Hugh of Vermandois to Alexius to see if he would take control of the city; an ambush en route killed his companion, Baldwin of Hainault, and Hugh never returned.[39] All these men would have had escorts and companions and their departure was, therefore, a considerable blow to the army. To counter this attrition the crusaders did receive some reinforcements. Fleets put into Port St Symeon, notably the English who took with them Bruno, a citizen of Lucca. He returned to his city in the summer of 1098, but the stream of western ships arriving in North Syria brought others, like the 1,500 Germans from Ratisbon who came to Antioch in the summer of 1098 and died of the plague.[40] But it is unlikely that such reinforcements were in any way commensurate with the losses the crusader army suffered, for we hear too little of them.

It is hardly surprising that the army which captured Jerusalem should have been so small; it was of much the same order as that with which William conquered England in 1066 and Guiscard attacked Byzantium in 1081. Clearly it had started out very much

kingdom of Jerusalem', 281–300, and 'The army of Godfrey de Bouillon 1096–99, 328–9.

[39] Yewdale, *Bohemond*, p. 68; AA, 375, 434–5; *GF*, pp. 56, 63–5, 72.
[40] Hagenmeyer, *Kreuzzugsbriefe*, pp. 165–7; AA, 446.

larger: we have Daimbert's figures suggesting losses of 93.4 per cent which means that only one in fourteen of those who gathered at Nicaea in June 1097 assembled for departure in September 1099.[41] Of course, we must remember that many stayed, either permanently or for more or less short periods, in Syria, but that is still a quite staggering loss. Losses in pre-industrial armies could be appalling. In the Seven Years War (1756–63) 135,000 of the 185,000 recruited for the Royal Navy died of disease.[42] It has been calculated that 70 per cent of the class of twenty-year-olds called to the colours in France in 1812 became casualties.[43] Amongst such losses battle casualties were not the greatest single element. Napoleon's huge invasion army of 1812 lost 30 per cent of its effectives to desertion and sickness before it fought its first battle at Smolensk on 17 August 1812. Of a total force of 611,000 which crossed the Russian frontier at various times after 24 June 1812, only 107,000 returned; of the rest 400,000 were casualties and 100,000 prisoners but only 74,000 died in open battle.[44] It needs to be stressed that most of these losses were not the result of the legendary Russian winter. In the Crimean War 4,285 British soldiers died in battle or of wounds, while 16,422 died of disease. The Union army in the American Civil War lost 96,000 in battle to 183,287 to disease. Even in the First World War the ratio of battle to non-battle casualties was 1:1.3.[45] As Daimbert's letter shows, contemporaries believed that the crusade's losses had been huge, and our knowledge of the general conditions of war, and the specific hardships of their theatre of battle, tends to confirm this. Is it possible to estimate the number in the army at the start of the campaign – when they prepared to leave Nicaea?

Raymond of Aguilers suggests that 60,000 died in Asia Minor in the destruction of the People's Crusade, but he was not well informed about this event and refers to it only in a context of attacking the emperor Alexius whom he blamed for its failure.[46] This is a political figure if ever there was one. Albert tells us that

[41] See above p. 125, n. 6.

[42] J. Keegan and R. Holmes, *Soldiers: a History of Men in Battle* (London, 1985), p. 144.

[43] J. Houdaille, 'Le problème des pertes de guerre', *Revue d'Histoire Moderne et Contemporaine*, 17 (1970), 423.

[44] G. F. Rothenberg, *The Art of Warfare in the Age of Napoleon* (Indiana, 1978), pp. 54–5, 251; G. Lefebvre, *Napoleon from Tilsit to Waterloo, 1807–1815*, tr. J. E. Anderson (Paris, 1936, London, 1969), pp. 311, 317.

[45] Keegan, *Soldiers*, pp. 143–4.   [46] RA, p. 44.

3,000 foot and 200 knights were lost in the German raid on Nicaea, and that the army, which was shortly afterwards destroyed by the Turks, numbered 25,000 foot and 500 knights. He states specifically that the non-combatants were left behind in the camp. So the final strength of the People's Crusade was 28,000 foot and 700 knights plus non-combatants; of these, 3,000, including a disproportionate number of knights, survived to join the main army.[47] These figures do not sound unreasonable for this People's Crusade was obviously a large-scale and striking affair. It is impossible to suggest how many there were in contingents which never got to the east or to estimate Peter the Hermit's losses in the Balkans, but if we assume Albert's figures are somewhat optimistic and should be read to include non-combatants, we can estimate the People's Crusade at somewhat above 20,000. It is much more difficult to suggest an overall figure for the main armies. We have noted that a figure of 100,000 may well have represented some kind of official guess. The largest ever crusading army was probably that of Frederick Barbarossa which set out from Ratisbon in May 1189 and is generally reckoned to have been 100,000 strong including perhaps 20,000 mounted troops.[48] Therefore the figure of 100,000 is not impossible. It should be noted, however, that Barbarossa had immense authority and went to considerable lengths to prepare his way diplomatically and to organise his army. Even so when he died it fell apart. The business of holding together and above all feeding a host of 100,000 would have been enormously difficult and indeed until the era of modern industrialisation, such considerations continued to be a major brake on the size of armies. During the period 1700–1763 only some two million men served in the armies of France, the greatest European power of the day, and there were never more than 200,000 in its forces at any one time. Napoleon's army in Russia in 1812 collapsed through indiscipline, largely brought about by a scorched earth policy which deprived it of food.[49] There are some indications of just such problems on the march across Asia Minor. A day or two after leaving Nicaea the army divided into two with Bohemond, Robert of Normandy, Stephen of Blois and Tancred in the vanguard and the

[47] AA, 284–7.
[48] E. N. Johnson, 'The Crusades of Frederick Barbarossa and Henry VI', in Setton, *Crusades*, 2. 87–122; Runciman 3. 11; Barbarossa's army took three days to pass a single point; Nesbitt, 'Rate of march', 178–9.
[49] Houdaille 'Le problème des pertes', 54; Rothenberg, *Art of Warfare*, pp. 316–17.

larger part of the army following on.[50] Fulcher confesses he did not understand why this was and Raymond of Aguilers blames the rashness of Bohemond, but Albert says clearly that it was the need for foraging which enforced this division. On 1 July 1097 the vanguard was ambushed by the Turks of Anatolia near Dorylaeum, and after their victory the crusader leaders resolved to keep the army together, but not long after, Albert says, they again had to divide for foraging purposes and this time Tancred and Baldwin formed a smaller vanguard.[51] Even so the army was in for a fairly grim passage through Anatolia. After Dorylaeum, the army experienced the heat of the Anatolian plateau where in July a daily maximum of 28° centigrade and a minimum of 15° centigrade can be expected. Albert reports that in this arid zone 'water was in shorter supply than usual' and 500 died. So terrible were the sufferings that women abandoned newly-born babies and when water was reached some died from excessive drinking. The Anonymous and Fulcher both confirm these problems though without mentioning numbers.[52] However, it is difficult to get any sense of the scale of the army's loss beyond the general feeling that it was very large. What the evidence does permit, however, is a sense of very deep suffering.

The road across the Taurus Mountains was so steep that knights and others threw away their equipment rather than carry it. At Caeserea-in-Cappadocia in September mean temperatures of 12–15° centigrade can be expected. By Christmas, as we have noted, food was short but the siege of Antioch began with plentiful food supplies in a pleasant climate. However, the weather gradually became more severe. The temperatures and precipitation during the siege of Antioch were as follows:

	Oct.	Nov.	Dec.	Jan.	Feb.	Mar.	April	May	June
Temp (°C)	20	15	11	9	10	12	16	20	25
Rain (mm)	109	96.5	168	259	178	127	78.7	53.3	35.6

Little wonder that Stephen of Blois commented on the excessive cold and immoderate rain so like winter in his homeland which was so hard on the poor. He had been led to expect heat in an exotic clime.[53] By Christmas, as we have noted, food was short and the

---

[50] AA, 328–9; RA, p. 45; *GF*, p. 18; FC, p. 85; Hagenmeyer, *Kreuzzugsbriefe*, p. 145.
[51] AA, 332–3, 340–1.
[52] AA, 339–40; *GF*, p. 23; FC, pp. 87–8.   [53] Hagenmeyer, *Kreuzzugsbriefe*, p. 150.

military expedition of Bohemond and Robert of Flanders, although it fought off a relief force, was unable to improve the situation, and starvation led to a wave of desertions which Adhémar tried to counter with a period of religious celebration intended to improve morale.[54] For the main army at Antioch this was a bitter winter and to find food they were obliged to form into groups of 200–300 because of marauding Turks. So frequent were their attacks, however, that the knights were reluctant to protect such groups until the count of Toulouse offered to replace horses lost in such skirmishing.[55] On the other hand, the crusaders did receive supplies from Armenian princes and the monks of the Black Mountain and later from Baldwin of Edessa and ships which put into St Symeon Port.[56] Further, although the crusaders had decided at the very start of their siege that they would invest Antioch closely, the fact that they had acquired so many cities and fortresses, such as the base established by Raymond of Toulouse at Rugia even before they got to Antioch, meant that the army had bases for foraging and supply. Godfrey and Robert of Flanders seem to have got help from Baldwin at Edessa and to have had forts on the roads leading there. Tancred later had land near 'Imm and Harem and Bohemond gained Cilicia.[57] Indeed, in the summer of 1098, after the defeat of Kerbogah, the Anonymous reports that all the princes retired to their own lands. Ralph of Caen alleges that Robert of Normandy, whom Raymond of Aguilers notes as absent from Antioch by Christmas 1097, spent most of his time at Laodicea and had to be dragged back in the final crisis of the siege.[58] The visionary, Peter Bartholemew, seems to have spent most of the winter of 1098 travelling about looking for food. He saw his first vision at Antioch in January 1098, and his second while foraging near Rugia on 10 February, while a third occurred at St Symeon port and a fourth at Mamistra from whence he was seeking to sail to Cyprus with his lord. Ralph of Caen gives us a diatribe on the sufferings of the army during the winter.[59] In the spring of 1098 as conditions improved the crusader leaders made it a priority to blockade the Bridge Gate from which the Turks

---

[54] GF, pp. 27, 33–4; RA, pp. 53–4.   [55] AA, 375; RA, p. 55.

[56] AA, 203–4; Matthew, p. 33; on fleets see below, pp. 209.

[57] RC, 649–50. I have followed Riley-Smith, Idea of Crusading, p. 75 in identifying these areas.

[58] GF, pp. 26, 72; RC, 649; RA, p. 50; on Robert's relations with Laodicea see David, Robert Curthose, pp. 230–44 and below pp. 215.

[59] RA, pp. 68–72; RC, 650–1.

were sallying forth and interrupting their communications with St Symeon which was the handiest port for contact with Byzantine Cyprus. So important was it that they were prepared to defeat heavy enemy resistance and later to invest in a big garrison for the new strong-point.[60] Thereafter, we hear less of starvation until the second siege of Antioch, when the crusaders found themselves trapped in a city which they had besieged for nine months and then sacked. All our sources are agreed on the horrors of starvation which now overcame the army; Albert, who stresses that the leaders tried to get food into the city before Kerbogah arrived, tells us about the awful camel meat for which Godfrey had to pay so much.[61] These appalling conditions were repeated during and after the siege of Ma'arra when the army was desperate for food and there were accusations of cannibalism.[62] Thereafter, shortages of food seem to have occurred only momentarily during the siege of Jerusalem where thirst was the major problem for they were attacking the city in June and July when the average minimum temperature is 17° centigrade and the average maximum 29° centigrade.[63] In general we can probably assume that disease became more of a problem in the heat of Syria and Palestine. Overall the record is one of suffering and much death. In a letter written early in the siege of Antioch, probably at the end of November 1097, Anselm of Ribemont asked those at home to pray for his dead companions and gave a list of thirteen, seven of whom had died in battle and six through illness.[64] We can assume that this was a list of those whom he knew and would be likely to be known to the recipients of his letter; of course, these are men of some substance, knights and in one case an abbot. Given that this list comes at a time before the worst horrors of the siege of Antioch, at a time when Anselm says that food was plentiful, we can see that losses were mounting very steeply indeed. Overall, there seems to have been no sudden holocaust, simply a steady attrition due to disease and hardship which increased at moments of crisis – Albert's 500 dying at once from thirst appears to be exceptional. But to this attrition must be added that of fighting and here again the evidence is very limited.

The sources are very coy about crusader losses in battle. A letter of

[60] *GF*, pp. 39–42; RA, pp. 59–62; AA, 383–6.
[61] RA, p. 59; *GF*, pp. 62–3; AA, 407, 412.
[62] *GF*, p. 80; RA, pp. 100–1; RC, 675; AA, 450.   [63] *GF*, p. 89; RA, pp. 139–40.
[64] Hagenmeyer, *Kreuzzugsbriefe*, p. 145.

the leaders to the West refers to 10,000 being lost in the fighting around Nicaea; this is a nice round number but it suggests heavy losses.[65] The Anonymous says that during the fighting around this city 'many of our men suffered martyrdom', though it must be admitted that he rarely mentions numbers anyway.[66] Albert of Aachen says that at Dorylaeum the vanguard suffered 4,000 casualties, including some knights, and he records the massacre of 300 of Bohemond's men outside Tarsus.[67] There was, however, one occasion when numerous sources took notice of crusader losses – in the fighting on the St Symeon road which followed the decision to build the Mahommeries Tower and so prevent enemy sallies from the Bridge Gate. About 4 March 1098 an English fleet put in to St Symeon and the crusader leaders decided to use the material and reinforcements to fortify a small hill with a mosque which stood outside the Bridge Gate from which the garrison had hitherto been able to interrupt their communications with the sea. On 6 March Bohemond and Raymond returned to Antioch with a great convoy bearing the equipment, food and reinforcements brought by the fleet. They were ambushed and their forces scattered. However, the crusaders rallied and drove the Turks back into the city with heavy losses.[68] This was a comparatively small engagement, not on the scale of Dorylaeum or the two battles against the relief forces from Damascus and Aleppo, but it was fought out in the presence of the whole army. For this reason it stood out in the minds of those who witnessed it and they gave figures. Albert says that 500 Christians died, with many wounded and taken prisoner in the initial ambush, but gives no figures for Christian losses in the subsequent fighting. Raymond of Aguilers suggests losses of 300 Christians in the initial battle, but gives no further figures except for enemy losses of 1,500. The Anonymous reports crusader losses of 1,000 and enemy losses of 1,500 and he is followed by many others like Tudebode. In his second letter written in July 1098, Anselm of Ribemont says the army lost 1,000 and the enemy 1,400, while Stephen of Blois suggests 500 foot and two horsemen on the Christian side and 1,230 of the

[65] Hagenmeyer, *Kreuzzugsbriefe*, p. 154.

[66] *GF*, p. 17. *GF* gives the numbers on the foraging expedition as 20,000 knights and foot. In February 1098 he says that there were barely 1,000 horses in good condition, reports the death of 1,000 Christians and 1,500 of the enemy in the battle on the St Symeon road and says that the Egyptian army at Ascalon numbered 200,000: pp. 34, 40–1, 96. It is unfortunate that so many medieval writers who used the *Gesta* copied this reticence.

[67] AA, 329–30, 346–7.   [68] *GF*, pp. 39–42; RA, pp. 59–62.

enemy. In the letter of the people of Lucca 2,055 Christian losses are reported and only 800 enemy.[69] This was a sharply fought battle but on a limited scale; crusader losses, however, seem to have been well over 500 in all, and perhaps very much higher. This was partly because there were a lot of foot-soldiers in the convoy which was overrun, while the knights could flee to fight again. But there was much fighting of just this kind around Antioch with small forces, 200–300 with mounted escorts setting out to forage; Albert describes one which got into trouble and had to be rescued. Raymond of Aguilers, as we have noted, tells us that these expeditions were so costly in horses that at one stage knights refused to go. Albert and Tudebode describe siege activity which must have been costly in manpower. From time to time there was larger-scale action such as that on 29 December 1097 when the Turks killed twenty knights and thirty foot and captured the standard of Adhémar of Le Puy.[70] When we add to this heavy attrition the major battles and the savage and continuous combat which characterised the second siege of Antioch (for none of which, unfortunately, are figures given) the impression grows of very heavy crusader losses. In the end we can only get an impression of battle losses for the evidence is not satisfactory. Taken together with our knowledge of numbers at the end of the crusade which is reasonably certain, we can at least make an educated guess at the size of the army which left Nicaea.

In September 1099 when Daimbert of Pisa, Raymond count of Toulouse, Robert of Normandy and Robert of Flanders wrote to the West anouncing the crusader victory they stated that the army at Ascalon was 20,000 strong. If this figure was based on the numbers arriving at Laodicea for transport home it may have represented a pardonable exaggeration. The force which came up from Jerusalem under Raymond and the two Roberts, including non-combatants, was of the order of 10,000. Many of the 4,000–5,000 troops, here estimated as being in North Syria, would also have made for the city and the opportunity to go home.[71] A milling mass of 12,000 or more arriving and going off at various times would have been difficult to count. In addition, 3,000 remained at Jerusalem and probably something of that order at Edessa and Antioch. A round figure of the order of 20,000 survivors seems likely of whom fewer than 2,000

---

[69] AA, 383, 386; RA, p. 59; *GF*, pp. 40–41; Tudebode, pp. 54–5; Hagenmeyer, *Kreuzzugsbriefe*, pp. 151, 158, 166.

[70] AA, 367–8; Tudebode, p. 57; RA, p. 51.   [71] See above pp. 133–4.

would have been knights. In the light of all they had gone through and all the attritions they had faced an overall loss rate of 3:1 would appear reasonable. That would have fallen rather more heavily on the followers than on the knights and lords; they might have been more at risk in battle but battle losses were only a fraction of total losses and their superior wealth must have meant they were less exposed, though never immune, to malnutrition and its attendant risks. So a likely figure for the army at its greatest would be around the 50,000–60,000 mark including non-combatants. Losses at Nicaea probably were quite heavy for, as we shall see, they attacked the city vigorously, so there were probably about 50,000 in the army as they left Nicaea, of which 7,000 were knights or lords. They and an unknown number of trained soldiers formed the core of an army which could call up as many as it could arm in an emergency. In time, the proportion which fought must have been very high, for the old, the sick, the children and the weak must have died like flies, the need for men was acute and there must have been plenty of captured weapons available. It has already been noted that the main force of the People's Crusade was of the order of 20,000, of whom about 3,000 survived to march on, so a total of 70,000–80,000 reached Asia Minor at one time or another. Thousands more must have died on the road to Constantinople, or turned back before they got there and yet others may never have left. By any standards it was a very large force indeed which left Nicaea in late June 1097; its main enemies were those of every army, starvation, malnutrition, disease but they were familiar ghosts which haunted medieval men. They are commented on in our sources when they strike the important, or reached unusual heights, but the daily attrition was so much to be expected, so commonplace, that it has left little record. However it was the best ally of the Turks.

CHAPTER 6

The first enemy: the Turks of Asia Minor

On 6 May 1097 elements of the crusader army appeared before the city of Nicaea held by Kilij I Arslan, the Seljuk Sultan of Rhüm (1092–1107). The city lies in a fertile basin bounded to the west by the Ascanian Lake (Iznik Gölü). From the south gate (Yenişchir Gate) the land rises sharply into the 800-metre-high Avdan Daglari. From the north gate (Istanbul Gate) the rise into the much higher Naldökan range which the crusaders had crossed is much gentler and only becomes appreciable after three kilometres. To the east (Lefke Gate), a wide and gently sloping valley rises to a watershed then slopes mildly down to the valley of the Sangarius (Sakarya Nehri) and the military roads to Ankara and the Anatolian plateau (see fig. 5). Raymond of Aguilers and Albert of Aachen were much impressed by Nicaea's fortifications which the leaders examined carefully. Fulcher remarked on the determination and cruelty of its garrison.[1] Its fortifications were Roman, dating from the fourth century, but they had been modified and kept in repair under the Byzantine empire. A great wall, pierced at the points of the compass by four main gates, surrounded the city. It was probably about ten metres high and studded with 114 round or square towers rising to seventeen metres, and its circuit measured 4,970 metres. There was a double ditch around the outside.[2] These fortifications were made the more formidable because the garrison needed to defend only half their circuit. From the north to south gates the western wall of the city followed the Ascanian Lake whose huge size, forty kilometres long, made it impossible to blockade unless the attacker had boats. It is very important to recognise that until the crusaders brought up

---

[1] RA, pp. 42–3; AA, 314; FC, pp. 81–2.
[2] A. M. Scheider and W. Karnapp, *Die Stadtmauer von Iznik-Nicea* (Berlin, 1938); S. Eyice, *Iznik-Nicaea: the History and the Monuments* (Istanbul, 1991). Stephen of Blois was exaggerating when he said that the city had 300 towers: Hagenmeyer, *Kreuzzugsbriefe*, p. 149.

boats they faced an enemy who had only to defend half the circuit, and this is the key to understanding the course of military events at Nicaea.[3]

Amongst the crusader contingents arriving for the siege was, as we have noticed, a force of Byzantine troops under the command of Tatikios. They were later reinforced by more soldiers and some small boats under Boutoumites who blockaded the Ascanian lake on the western perimeter of the city. This was a comparatively small force for Alexius to send in support of what he regarded as his men, almost his hirelings. This is especially true because, as Anna Comnena says, he had twice before attacked the city which seems to have fallen into Turkish hands in 1078, in 1081 and 1086.[4] Here was an ancient city whose loss to the empire was deeply felt. The Seljuks were converting it from an outpost into a real capital, thus threatening to stabilise their régime, yet the emperor would hazard only a small force, and, above all, would not come himself. Anna stresses that her father was anxious to regain Nicaea, but offers only the feeblest of excuses for his refusal to join the siege – that he feared the enormous numbers of the Franks.[5] Anna's insistence on the bad faith and untrustworthiness of all Latins is intimately connected with her case that they had broken their oath to Alexius in the matter of Antioch and owes much to hindsight.[6] It is, in fact, a revelation of the extent to which much modern writing about the crusades has been from a pro-Byzantine standpoint that her statement has passed unchallenged.[7] Alexius had reasons to distrust Latins – the expedition of Guiscard is clear evidence – but he distrusted almost everybody else as well and he had actively sought them as mercenaries.

[3] At present the north gate is 250 metres from the lake, but the extensive marshes at this point are very much closer and point to the advance of the shoreline since the eleventh century. The same phenomenom is remarked by the south gate which at present is 350 metres from the shore, but there modern filling has taken place on a large scale. The re-entrant of the walls on this south-west corner of the city is probably to be explained by the shoreline and marsh in ancient times. The three landward gates of the city and almost all the enceinte still surround the small town of Iznik, although the walls are ruinous in places by the lake, where the watergate has long perished. There is an outer wall which terminates north and south on the shore, protecting the littoral of the city, but this is a late construction and its crudity is particularly evident at the gates in comparison with the fine work of the inner Roman gates. It is a construction of the thirteenth century.

[4] *Alexiad*, pp. 335–6, 130, 206; on the last occasion Alexius's commander was Tatikios.

[5] *Alexiad*, p. 330–1.

[6] France, 'Anna Comnena', 22–3.

[7] See in particular Runciman's declaration of faith, 1. 171: 'he [Alexius] believed that the welfare of Christendom depended on the welfare of the historic Christian Empire. His belief was correct.'

His caution on this occasion probably owed much to his attitude to the Seljuks of Rhüm and the curious process by which they conquered Anatolia.

The Turks are part of a vast family of steppe peoples who include the Mongols. They first appear in western history in the guise of the Huns and later as the Hungarians of the middle Danube. The Patzinacks and Uzes, who were such a scourge of the Byzantine Balkans, are also of the same people. It is, however, with the people of Turkestan – the nomadic tribes occupying a vast area from the Black Sea to Central Asia – that we are concerned, and in particular with the Oghuz who pressed on the frontiers of Islamicised Asia and Persia. Amongst them a pre-eminent family were the descendants of the legendary Seljuk.[8] The expansion of Islam into Transoxania brought these Turks into intimate conflict with Islam along the frontiers where *ghazis*, Islamic volunteers, and nomads waged war. But the Shamanist Turks began to be converted in large numbers to Islam, and in the tenth century we see the creation of Turkish Islamic powers like the Karakhanids of Bukhara and the Ghaznavids who ruled on the borders of India.[9] Thus the border between Islam and the Turks became porous to Islamicised Turks, some of whom were already established in the Islamic heartlands by a different process. The Arabs who destroyed the Roman and Persian empires in the seventh century were a warrior aristocracy ruling over diverse peoples and sheer military need forced them to incorporate those peoples into their armies.[10] This diversification facilitated the recruitment of peoples with special skills – the Daylamis of the Caspian area provided good infantry until the crusader period. Kurds provided light cavalry and infantry. For a long time Khorasanian horse archers and cavalrymen were important but they tended to be replaced by Turks. At the same time, rulers favoured such processes which lessened their dependence on the tribal elements to which they owed their power.[11] The destruction of the Umaiyad Caliphate of Damascus in 750 and the rise of the Abbasids

---

[8] C. Cahen, *Pre–Ottoman Turkey* (London, 1968) pp. 19–20.

[9] C. Cahen, 'The Turkish invasion: the Selchukids', in Setton, *Crusades* 1. 139–40.

[10] B. Lewis, *The Arabs in History* (London, 1958), pp. 49–63.

[11] C. E. Bosworth, 'Recruitment, muster and review in medieval Islamic armies', in V. J. Parry and M. E. Yapp, eds., *War, Technology and Society in the Middle East* (London, 1975), p. 60; J. D. Latham and W. F. Paterson, *Saracen Archery* (London, 1970), p. xxiii; this cycle of rulers throwing off tribal dependence is a major theme of Ibn-Khaldûn, especially pp. 123–263.

of Baghdad marked a political transformation which favoured Iranian groups, especially a military élite associated with Khorasan, and Mesopotamian groups at the expense of Arabs.[12] The Caliphate developed a complex military organisation and placed more and more emphasis on *mamlūk* troops, slave-soldiers who were often recruited from the Iranian and the Eurasian steppe. Under the Caliph Al Mu'tasim (892–902) Turkish troops became well established in the Islamic armies and he created the great palace complex of Samarra near Bagdad to house these élite forces.[13] By the eleventh century Turks were a powerful element in almost all Islamic forces, even as far afield as Egypt, and at this very time political developments on the frontier made them more important. In 1025 a group of Oghuz, having been settled in Khorasan, rebelled and were ejected by the Ghaznavids, but they were followed by another in 1035, pre-eminent amongst whom were Tughril and Chagri who by 1040 dominated all of Khorasan including Merv and Nishapur and drove out the Ghaznavids. While Chagri consolidated their position in the east Tughril turned west. He and his people had imbibed a fierce Islamic orthodoxy and the domination of the Caliph at Baghdad by Shi'ite Buwaihids and others was a scandal upon which he capitalised. His entry into Baghdad in 1055 was a peaceful one facilitated by contacts with Turkish elements around the Caliph, and though he had to fight later, by 1059 Tughril was master of the Caliphate and enjoyed the title of Shah.[14] In the process of constructing his power in the heart of Islam Tughril and his successor, Alp Arslan, were happy to adopt the composite armies of their predecessors in which the tribal element of the Turks was only a part, though Turkish enlistment as slave-soldiers, *mamlūks*, continued to be important. This was a vital element in the stabilisation of their dynasty and as a corollary they encouraged the nomadic Turks to attack the Fatimids of Palestine and the Byzantine frontier. Patronage of such a holy war would give the Shah prestige and allow the tribes to plunder, while providing a reservoir for recruitment. The

---

[12] H. A. R. Gibb, 'The Caliphate in the Arab States', in Setton, *Crusades* 1. 81–2.

[13] D. Ayalon, 'Preliminary remarks on the Mamluk military institution in Islam', in V. G. Parry and M. E. Yapp, eds., *War, Technology and Society in the Middle East* (London, 1975), pp. 51–4, Bosworth, 'Recruitment, muster and review', pp. 62–3; O. S. A. Ismail, 'Mu'tasum and the Turks', *Bulletin of the School of African and Oriental Studies*, 29 (1966), 12–24.

[14] Cahen, 'The Turkish invasion', 143–6.

scale of their success was remarkable. In 1057 they sacked Melitene (modern Malatya), in 1059 Sebasteia (modern Sivas) and in 1064 Ani and by the late 1060s they were virtually raiding at will in eastern Asia Minor, even devastating the land behind the advance of imperial armies under Romanus IV Diogenes (1067–71) when he campaigned against them in 1069.[15]

Such success owed something to their tactics. Traditionally steppe people ride light ponies, perhaps ten to twelve hands on average, and depend on strings of them to provide speed and endurance in battle. We have very little information about Turkish horses, though in contrast to the Mongol armies we do not hear of large strings of spare horses. When Alp Arslan fought at Manzikert in 1071 he took with him 15,000 picked cavalry, and the fact that all had a spare horse is remarked upon by the sources suggesting that it was unusual and a mark of their élite status.[16] In fact, for nomads the difficulties implicit in the raising of heavier breeds with the need for stall-feeding, stud farms and the isolation of dams were overwhelming.[17] Their special forté was mounted archery and they provided extraordinary fire-power and accuracy combined with speed of manoeuvre. A ninth-century Arab writer remarked of the Turkish troops then becoming common: 'The Turk can shoot at beasts, birds, hoops, men, sitting quarry, dummies and birds on the wing, and do so at full gallop to fore or to rear, to left or to right, upwards or downwards, loosing ten arrows before the Kharijite [Arab tribesman hostile to the Abassids] can nock one.[18]

This combination of speed of manoeuvre with the range of the bow was extremely difficult to combat. They used the composite bow – wood with horn which reacts to compression bound on the belly side, and sinew on the back to increase elasticity. Thus, despite its shortness, the nomad's bow had great strength and considerable range. Albert of Aachen salts his chronicle with poetic clichés; his Franks seize helms and armour as they fly to battle, but the Turks seize bows, often described as being of horn and sinew. Such vivid

[15] S. Vryonis, *The Decline of Medieval Hellenism in Asia Minor* (London, 1971), pp. 87, 94–5.
[16] C. Cahen, 'Les changements techniques militaires dans le Proche Orient médiéval et leur importance historique', in V. G. Parry and M. E. Yapp, eds., *War, Technology and Society in the Middle East* (London, 1975), 115 comments on the need for research on Turkish horses. Lindner, 'Nomadism, horses and Huns', 3–19; Bundari, *Dawolat al-Saljuq* (Cairo, 1900), p. 37 – I owe this reference to Professor A. K. S. Lambton.
[17] A matter which Davis stresses. See above p. 73.
[18] al-Jahiz quoted in Latham and Paterson, *Saracen Archery*, p. xxiii.

word pictures convey sharply the difference in style of warfare.[19] In a famous passage after his account of the battle of Dorylaeum, the Anonymous praises the skill of the Turks as soldiers, but Albert gives a very much more specific example of their archery. During the pursuit after Dorylaeum, he says, the enemy remained dangerous and often turned at bay. Gerard of Quiersy, spotting a Turk on the brow of a hill, drew his shield across him and attacked with his lance; his intended victim, however, fired an arrow which went through the shield and struck him between the liver and lungs, and while he lay dying the Turk made off with his horse. As the Franks forced the crossing of the Iron Bridge he again mentions Turkish arrows piercing a hauberk.[20] If we think of a Turkish horseman drawing a bow with a pull of between twenty-seven and thirty-six kilograms, he might have an effective range of well over sixty metres so the Anonymous's comment on their 'astonishing range' makes sense. Consider the effect of many such individuals firing together and it is possible to understand the frequency with which the western accounts mention the sleets of arrows which the Turks produced in battle. Fulcher speaks of the clouds of arrows which overcame the army at Dorylaeum, and Albert describes hails of arrows as the Turks fought back in the pursuit after the battle and which destroyed Swein of Denmark's reinforcements and Renaud of Toul's force in the final battle at Antioch.[21] Such language is too frequent to be mere extravagance, as are references to the fast horses of the Turks. Raymond of Aguilers describes their hit-and-run tactics in which speed was essential to avoid crusader retribution. Ralph shows them manoeuvring outside 'Artāh to lure Franks into ambush, while according to Albert warriors on speedy mounts opposed the crossing of the fords near the Iron Bridge and later lured Roger of Barneville to his death.[22] It is possible that they had developed light tubular crossbows, throwing darts to augment their firepower.[23] It was by throwing a hail of arrows that the Turks demoralised their enemies, isolated and broke up their formations

---

[19] AA, 344, 359, 369, 400.

[20] AA, 331–2, 362: *La Chanson d'Antioche*, ed. S. Duparc-Quioc, 2 vols. (Paris, 1977–8), 2. 1606, 8979 mentions Gerard at Nicaea and later at the battle against Kerbogah.

[21] Latham and Paterson, *Saracen Archery*, pp. xxv, 30; AA, 334, 377, 424; FC, p. 85.

[22] RA, pp. 50–1; RC, pp. 639–41; AA, 362, 408; see below pp. 192–3, 206, 271–2.

[23] Latham and Paterson, *Saracen Archery*, pp. xxiv–xxxi; C. Cahen, 'Un traité d'armurerie composé pour Saladin', *Bulletin d'Etudes Orientales de l'Institut Français de Damas*, 12 (1947/48), 132–3 and 'Les changements techniques militaires' pp. 116–17, points to the development of this light crossbow which threw large numbers of darts, hence its nickname 'hailstone', which is described in some detail by Latham and Paterson, pp. 145–51.

before charging in for the kill at close quarters with sword and spear. This was how they had destroyed the forces of the People's Crusade. Once at close quarters their primary weapon was the sword, at this time a straight edged weapon rather narrower and more sharply pointed than the Frankish weapon, but otherwise little different.[24]

It is difficult to comment on the armour of the nomads. As early as 1037/8, Bayhaqi says that when Tughril Bey entered Nishapur his 3,000 cavalry were mostly armoured. Much of our evidence about the Seljuks comes from Byzantine sources of the twelfth century which show mail shirts and poncho-like garments of mail. By this time Greek influence upon their protective equipment and style of war was becoming very strong.[25] However, there is ample evidence for the use of armour, scale, chain-mail and lamellar armour throughout the Middle East. Strips or scales fastened to cloth or leather seem to have been outmoded in the West, but such lighter equipment would have suited the warfare of the area very well and so have remained in use. There is no reason to think that the nomads of Asia Minor were ignorant of armour. Ralph of Caen gives a very vivid description of the fighting at Dorylaeum and tells us that in the press of battle the Turks 'trusted in their numbers, we in our armour' which implies that they did not have armour. However, he does not explicitly say that they had none and it would be very surprising if they were prepared to close with the Franks with no protection at all. In much of the Middle East armour was worn under the cover of other materials, most often in the form of a *Hazagand*, a leather jerkin with mail or lamellar within and there were variations on this like the later western brigandine. Felt or fur caps were often worn by Turks at this time.[26] We can think, therefore, of the Turkish horsemen wearing rather lighter armour than the western knights, and, above all, carrying a much smaller and lighter shield. However, their skilful horsemanship and tactics were not in themselves a sufficient advantage to account for the victories of the Turks in Asia Minor – they owed far more to Byzantine weakness.[27]

[24] There are some fine eleventh-century examples in the armoury of the Topkapi Palace in Istanbul.

[25] D. Nicolle, 'Early medieval Islamic arms and armour', *Gladius*, special volume (1976), 53.

[26] Nicolle, 'Early medieval Islamic arms', 26, 53–82; M. V. Gorelik, 'Oriental armour of the Near and Middle East from the eight to the fifteenth centuries as shown in works of art', in R. Elgood, ed. *Islamic Arms and Armour* (London, 1979), pp. 30–63; RC, 621.

[27] On the destruction of the People's Crusade see above p. 93–5; W. E. Kaegi, 'The contribution of archery to the Turkish conquest of Anatolia', *Speculum*, 39 (1964), 96–108 rather exaggerates the influence of archery. After all, many Turks fought for the Byzantines with the same tactics.

The death of Basil II (976–1025) saw the Byzantine empire in a position of strength, extending from Mesopotamia to Bulgaria.[28] But Basil's success, and the manner in which it was achieved, left considerable problems for the Byzantine state. He significantly changed Byzantine military organisation. In the seventh century the Byzantine army had been reorganised with the division of the empire into Themes, each of which was defended by its own military-force locally recruited, housed and financed. When an imperial expedition was mounted, the army of the *themata* combined with the central army based at Constantinople, the *tagmata*, at selected *aplèkta*, camps on the military highways such as that at Dorylaeum which was the gateway to the Anatolian plateau.[29] However, the settlements of peasant soldiers, which were the basis of this army, were being absorbed into the estates of the aristocracy of Asia Minor who thus were able to control the armies of the Themes. In 987 a group of these families revolted against Basil and were only defeated in 989 with the aid of a corps of 6,000 Russians, the basis of the later Varangian guard. From this time onwards Basil found it prudent to rely more and more on mercenaries for the regular army which was the basis of his successful expansion of the empire in the Balkans. The increasing wealth of the empire, evidenced by the growth of cities, facilitated the replacement of territorial forces by mercenaries.[30] As a result, the old armies of the Themes were somewhat neglected, except on exposed frontiers where they continued to serve a useful purpose. At the same time, he revived old legislation to prevent the great families of Asia Minor from absorbing peasant holdings into their estates in order to protect the tax base which was even more necessary to pay his professional armies. On the basis of his victory of 989, Basil established a harsh government which dominated the great noble houses and at the same time demanded a

---

[28] The general explanation of Byzantine decline here relies on: M. Angold, *The Byzantine Empire 1025–1204, a Political History* (London, 1984), pp. 1–113 and Vryonis, *Hellenism*, pp. 70–142. See also Charanis, in Setton, *Crusades* 1. 177–219; Jenkins, *Byzantine Empire*; Ostrogorsky, *Byzantine State*, pp. 280–315.

[29] On the Byzantine army see J. D. Howard-Johnstone, *Studies in the Organisation of the Byzantine Army in the Tenth and Eleventh Centuries*, unpublished D.Phil. thesis, University of Oxford, 1971; H. Ahrweiler, 'L'organisation des campagnes militaires à Byzance', in V. J. Parry and M. E. Yapp, eds., *War, Technology and Society in the Middle East* (London, 1975), pp. 89–96 is particularly useful on its subject. See also Ostrogorsky, *Byzantine State*, pp. 87–90; on Dorylaeum which had baths for 1,000 troops see Vryonis, *Hellenism*, pp. 31–2.

[30] Angold, *Byzantine Empire*, pp. 63–5; C. Mango, *Byzantium* (London, 1988), p. 57.

crushing taxation to support a professional army and a policy of expansion. The strains that this imposed on the empire meant that when Basil died there was bound to be change, and this was complicated by the lack of a clear line of succession on the death of his brother Constantine VIII (1025–8) whose daughters' marriages determined the succession for the next twenty years without ever producing heirs to prolong the Macedonian house. This failure inevitably produced uncertainty and promoted the emergence of aristocratic factions who competed for power; there were thirty rebellions in the period 1028–57, such as that of Tornikios in 1047–8 which was only defeated by stripping the frontiers of troops.

Competition for power amongst aristocratic houses was a feature of Byzantine history, and this period produced able, as well as feeble, emperors, but this came at a time when the empire had severe problems. The rise of a mercenary army imposed massive financial burdens and it is hardly surprising that, with the less expansionist stance after 1025, efforts were made to cut back on military expenditure. Constantine IX Monomachus dismantled the army of the theme of Iberia. The policy was logical for the local army duplicated the mercenary one, but, to its great discontent, this area now had to pay taxes and it was exposed to hostile attack. In the East, the Turks began to press on the frontier, while in the Balkans the Patzinacks were a potential menace and in Italy the Normans became a major force in the 1040s. Thus, economy in military matters came at a time of increasing external threat. Moreover, in the east, there were a number of populations whose religious affiliations made them suspect to the Byzantine authorities (most notably the Jacobite Syrians and the Armenians), and the efforts of Constantine X Doukas (1059–67) to settle problems with these churches, intended to strengthen the frontiers, simply aroused hatred. Thus, every effort of the imperial government worsened the security situation in the eastern provinces and, by the 1060s, the Turks were raiding deep into Asia Minor with Iconium and Chonae falling victim towards the end of the decade. Even more importantly, the vacuum of power at the centre continued to be filled only intermittently and the autocracy was the subject of bitter factional conflict which prevented consistent policies from emerging. The factional struggle allowed other forces to emerge within the state – the church especially under the Patriarch Michael Keroularios (1043–58) became a major factor in the state and not a mere arm of the autocracy, while the mob of Constantinople had also to be considered. This was the background to the reign of Romanus IV Diogenes (1067–71).

When Constantine Doukas died he had invested imperial power in his wife Eudocia, to exercise on behalf of his young sons, but there was widely felt to be a need for a strong ruler and as a result, she married Romanus IV Diogenes, a successful soldier who had defeated the Patzinacks in the Balkans. He consolidated his power and produced two sons, but inevitably this aroused the hostility of the Doukas.

Romanus was determined to end the Turkish attacks on the eastern provinces, but there was considerable uncertainty about how best to do this. A considerable body of thought suggested that he should make the border provinces, with their disloyal populations, a desert and crush the Turks in central Asia Minor. He preferred to try and oust the Turks by a strategy of large-scale expeditions to the eastern frontier which would put pressure upon the Sultan Alp Arslan. But the Turks were steppe horsemen to whom the Anatolian plateau presented a congenial and familiar habitat across which they could move quickly and they melted before the lumbering Byzantine army, returning to isolate the fortresses once they had gone.[31] In 1068 Romanus attacked Aleppo, and the campaign of 1069 was directed against the upper Euphrates although the rebellion of the Norman mercenary Crispin was a considerable diversion. These expensive forays produced no results and it is likely that the emperor's enemies, led by the Caesar John Doukas were becoming a threat. In 1071, Romanus led a huge Byzantine army with the intention of bringing the Sultan Alp Arslan, who was preparing for an attack on Fatimid Egypt, to battle: Romanus needed a victory. The army was overwhelmingly mercenary with contingents of Greeks, Russians, Khazars, Alans, Georgians, Armenians, Turks and Franks; it was the Germans, amongst these latter, who attacked the emperor at Cryapege when he tried to curb their excesses. Some of the units were very good but there was enormous variation in quality and they were not used to working together. As they moved eastwards there was friction with the Armenians. It was a huge army, though the 300,000 suggested by some Arab sources is a gross exaggeration: it was probably of the order of 40,000–60,000. Alp Arslan was surprised by their coming –

---

[31] W. C. Brice, 'The Turkish colonisation of Anatolia', *Bulletin of John Ryland's Library*, 38 (1955), 18–44.

he had negotiated a truce with Romanus in the previous year, but the Byzantines saw continued Turkish raiding, over which the Sultan had no control, as a breach. Manzikert (east of modern Erzerum (see fig. 3)), a fortress recently captured by the Turks, was quickly recaptured, but a large section of the imperial army was dispatched to take Chliat. When Alp Arslan arrived, the Norman mercenary leader, Roussel of Bailleul, and Tarchaniotes who commanded many of the Turks, simply fled. In the crisis of the battle Andronicus Doukas seems deliberately to have betrayed Romanus who was captured in the ensuing rout.[32]

Manzikert was not quite the overwhelming victory that has been supposed, for much of the army was never engaged and many units escaped intact, but the emperor's guard was slaughtered.[33] Alp Arslan concluded a very merciful treaty with Romanus, for he was preoccupied elsewhere and had no wish to see a major Turkish power in Anatolia. It was the Byzantine reaction which turned the situation into a disaster. Romanus's enemies, led by Michael VII Doukas (1071–8), denounced the treaty and blinded Romanus. The Byzantine state now dissolved in a series of civil wars, in which the numerous contenders were all prepared to call in the Turks. This was why the cities of Asia Minor which could have resisted a nomadic people with no experience of siege warfare did not do so. Instead, the keys of their gates were handed over to the Turks by the contending magnates. In the chaos, the Norman mercenary leader Roussel of Bailleul attempted to create a new state in Asia Minor and his success brought 3,000 Franks into his following. In an effort to divide his enemies he championed the imperial pretensions of John Doukas. He was only defeated in Bithynia when the imperial authorities brought in the Turkish Emir, Artuk, whose activities so far to the west are a revelation of Byzantine weakness. Even then, he escaped and in the end was betrayed to Alexius Comnenus.[34] In Cappadocia and

---

[32] On Manzikert see C. Cahen, 'La campagne de Mantzikert d'après les sources musulmanes', *Byzantion*, 9 (1934), 613–42, and for corrections based on the Greek sources Vryonis, *Hellenism*, pp. 96–103; A. Friendly, *The Dreadful Day. The battle of Mantzikert, 1071* (London, 1981), pp. 163–92; J. C. Cheynet, 'Mantzikert. Un désastre militaire?', *Byzantion*, 50 (1980) 410–38.

[33] Cheynet, 'Mantzikert', p. 431 suggests losses of five to ten per cent in total much less than those of Alexius Comnenus's, reputedly 5,000 at Dyrrachium ten years later, on which see above pp. 75–6.

[34] J. Schlumberger, 'Deux chefs normands des armées byzantines au XI siècle: sceaux de Hervé et de Raoul de Bailleul', *Revue Historique*, 16 (1881), 289–303; L. Bréhier, 'Les aventures d'un chef normand en Orient au XI siècle', *Revue des Cours et Conferences*, 20 (1911–12), 99–112; see also Marquis de la Force, 'Les conseillers latins d'Alexis Comnène', *Byzantion*, 11 (1936), 153–65.

Cilicia, independent Armenian princes were happy to see the back of Byzantine rule and to take over the cities of the area. Amongst them was a former Curopalate and Domestic of Romanus IV who had fought with him at Manzikert, Philaretus Brachamius, who refused to recognise Michael VII and created a principality based on Marasch, Ahlistha and Melitene (see figs. 2 and 4). In 1074 he defeated Isaac Comnenus, duke of Antioch, and by 1078 he had acquired this major city. Nicephorous Botaneiates, who rebelled against Michael in 1078, was a former comrade in arms of Philaretus and recognised his independent principality to which he added Edessa in 1083–4. When Sulayman, leader of the Anatolian Turks, was peacefully admitted to Antioch in 1085, it is not impossible that local factionalism within the city was encouraged to this end by Alexius I Comnenus – in order to get rid of an adherent of the overthrown Botaneiates.[35] When Nicephorous Botaneiates began his rebellion in 1077 he was able to gather very few troops but the government, beset by the rebellion of Nicephorous Bryennius in the west which allowed the Patzinacks in once again, called upon Sulayman, leader of the Anatolian Turks. He changed sides, however, and Botaneiates used his forces to hold down many of the cities of western Asia Minor, including Nicaea which appears to have fallen into Turkish hands at this time. Much of the army which Botaneiates used against Bryennius in the west under Alexius Comnenus was Turkish, and it was turned against Botaneiates whom Alexius succeeded in 1081, only to face the rebellion of his brother-in-law, Melissenus, who turned over more of the cities of western Anatolia to Sulayman. There can be no doubt that for the Byzantine magnates and generals, civil war in their own interests was far more important than defence of Anatolia. It seems almost as if these great nobles were quite happy to loan a vast and rich province to barbarians for whom they had the greatest disdain and whom they never seem to have regarded as rivals, like the Arabs against whom Nicephorous Phocas (963–9) and John Tzimiskes (969–76) had waged a holy war.[36] It was the Emperor, Alexius Comnenus

---

[35] On Philaretus see J. Laurent, 'Byzance et Antioche sous le curopalate Philarète', *Revue des Etudes Arméniennes*, 9 (1929), 61–72; T. S. R. Boase, *The Cilician Kingdom of Armenia* (Edinburgh and London, 1978), pp. 3–4; Skoulatos, *Anna Comnena*, pp. 263–5; Cahen, *Turkey*, pp. 76–7; Vryonis, *Hellenism*, pp. 109–10. E. Sivan, *L'Islam et la Croisade; Idéologie et Propagande dans les Réactions Musulmanes aux Croisades* (Paris, 1968), p. 19 suggests that Sulayman was acting for the emperor in his capture of Antioch.

[36] Cahen, *Turkey*, p. 76; Ostrogorsky, *Byzantine State*, p. 257.

(1081–95), who finally brought to an end the chaos in the Byzantine state and established himself as the head of a group of aristocratic families who dominated the machinery of state. He was not a great soldier: he would suffer heavy defeats, such as that at Dyrrachium, and win few real victories. He was as prepared as any of his rivals to make arrangements with the Turks. He was, in the end, a skilful and cautious politician anxious to nurse his deeply wounded empire. The spirit of the crusade was deeply alien to this cautious politician. He 'came to power as the head of a powerful aristocratic network', so it is hardly surprising that he offered no revival of that spirit of holy war which a century before had enabled the warrior emperors, Nicephorous Phocas and John Tzimiskes, to drive the Byzantine frontier deep into Syria.[37] But the Comneni and the families allied to him were all from Asia Minor which they regarded as the heartland of the empire, hence the importance which he attached to regaining it, and hence the appeal of 1095.

Anna Comnena clearly understood the importance her father attached to Asia Minor. She portrays him as a Byzantine hero, but his relations with the Turks were complex. There was never any question of holy war, on either side. It was during his reign that Byzantine sources began to refer to Sulayman of the Seljuk house and leader of the Turks of Anatolia as Shah – a title not conferred by either the Sultan or the Caliph at Bagdad.[38] Sulayman was killed in 1085, and it was not until his son Kilij Arslan escaped from the Sultan's custody in 1092 that the Sultanate of Rhüm, as it came to be called, could rise again. The Turks remained a largely nomadic people and their dominion consisted of garrisons in the cities and control of the key routes. Kilij Arslan held the important cities of Nicaea and Iconium, but on the Aegean coast were emirs like Chaka at Smyrna, and Tangripermes at Ephesus, who were at best his allies and at worst his rivals. Cyzicus, on the Propontis, was held by another emir, as were some of the ports along the Black Sea coast. At

[37] A. R. Gadolin, 'Alexius I Comnenus and the Venetian trade privileges. A new interpretation', *Byzantion*, 50 (1980), 439–46, suggests that the great trading concessions, extended to the Venetians in the Golden Bull of 1082, were intended as much to stimulate the damaged Byzantine economy as to persuade them to give support against the Normans; M. Angold, 'The Byzantine State on the eve of the Battle of Manzikert', in A. Bryer and M. Ursinus, eds., *Manzikert to Lepanto: the Byzantine World and the Turks, 1071–1571*, Byzantinische Forschungen 16 (Amsterdam, 1991), 33.

[38] Sivan, *L'Islam et la Croisade*, p. 19 stresses the lack of any spirit of *jihad* amongst the Seljuk leaders. In taking over Antioch, Sulayman was at pains to safeguard the Christian population; Cahen, *Turkey*, p. 75.

Erzerum the Saltukid Turks had established a dominion as had the Menguchekids at Erzinjan . Further south, the Danishmends had carved out a great principality based on Sivas, Kayseri and Ankara. Then there were lesser powers like Baldaji or Hasan, who ruled an enclave including much Armenian territory in Cappadocia.[39] Underlining the precarious nature of these conquests were the independent Armenian princes in the Taurus range, prominent amongst whom were Constantine son of Roupen, Pazouni and Oschin, Gabriel a former associate of Philaretus who held Melitene and Thoros of Edessa.[40] The Turkish powers enjoyed a very uncertain relationship with the centre of power at Baghdad where Malik Shah (1072–92) ruled. When Sulayman had threatened to become a power in Syria after his conquest of Antioch, he was defeated and killed by the Sultan's brother Tutush in 1085 and Antioch was absorbed into the lands of the Sultan Malik Shah. Faced with this complex situation, Alexius proceeded carefully. He sent forces against Nicaea in 1081 but the attack of Guiscard in the west forced withdrawal, and he was unable to take real advantage of the weakness of the Sultanate of Rhüm on Sulayman's death because of threats in the Balkans from the Patzinacks and others. In 1086 Malik Shah had been prepared to consider an alliance against the Turks of Asia Minor, which would have cleared the western part of the peninsula, and at the time of his death, was negotiating with Alexius for an imperial marriage which might have opened the way for an alliance against Rhüm.[41] In the rivalries of the rulers of Asia Minor and the tensions between them and the Sultan at Baghdad Alexius could see opportunity which was, if anything, increased by the deaths of Malik Shah in 1092 and his brother Tutush in 1095, leaving Syria divided between the latter's bickering sons, Duqaq of Damascus and Ridwan of Aleppo.[42] It was presumably in an effort to exploit this complex situation that Alexius had asked Urban II for aid. He was presented with an independent force, the crusade, which, despite his best efforts, was not entirely within his control. His refusal to join the army as it marched against Nicaea, and indeed his whole policy towards the Franks, has to be seen in the

[39] Vryonis, *Hellenism*, pp. 114–16; Cahen, *Turkey*, pp. 76–82.
[40] Matthew, 30–33; Michael the Syrian, *Chronique de Michel le Syrien, Patriarch jacobite d'Antioche 1166–99*, ed. and tr. J. B. Chabot, 4 vols. (Brussels, 1963, reprint of 1899–1910 edition) [hereafter cited as Michael], vol. 3. 179; see below pp. 168–9, 304–7.
[41] Cahen, *Turkey*, pp. 77–80.   [42] Cahen, 'The Turkish invasion', 161–3.

light of this situation. To back the Franks so unequivocally as to join them in person would make relations with Rhüm difficult, should they fail. And failure might trigger internal unrest. Better by far to leave them to fight, so that, if they failed, other means could be pursued and his relations with Kilij Arslan could remain. Alexius had not attacked Nicaea in person before – he had used his generals and now he continued this policy. Alexius would support the Franks as long as they succeeded. With this equivocal ally a comfortable distance behind them, the crusader army prepared for battle against the first of its enemies – the Seljuk Sultanate of Rhüm and its principal city of Nicaea.

It is very difficult to estimate the military capacity of the Sultanate of Rhüm in this period. The Turks had never been numerous – Cahen suggests that only about 20,000–30,000 warriors entered the Caliphate at the time of its conquest.[43] As steppe people like the Huns, Avars and Magyars before them, they relied on mobility and a training in horsemanship from birth. It has been suggested of earlier nomad peoples who entered Europe that to maintain their speed of assault each rider needed a string of ten horses. Therefore, nomad forces needed huge open ranges to graze their ponies. The Hungarian plain, where the Huns, Avars and Magyars settled, could only support 150,000 horses, an army of 15,000 men.[44] We simply do not know if the Turks used such vast strings of spare horses but is likely that they did not. Much of the once rich agriculture of Asia Minor had been destroyed by the Turkish invasions, but there was still a large native population with settled cultivation, while a lot of the land was wild and mountainous. It certainly could not support horses on anything like the scale of the Syrian and Mesopotamian plains where later the Mongols had difficulty in maintaining their huge horse trains.[45] It is only possible to guess, but it seems unlikely that Kilij Arslan could find as many as 10,000 Turks, even with the allies he brought to the field of Dorylaeum. It was not the vast numbers of the Turks that made them dangerous, but their sheer courage, ruthlessness and daring tactics which the crusaders themselves recognised. At the siege of Nicaea, Fulcher testifies to their savagery while the Anonymous author of the *Gesta* is lavish in

[43] Cahen, 'The Turkish invasion', 157.
[44] Lindner, 'Nomadism, Horses and Huns', 8, 15.
[45] A. V. S. Lambton, *Continuity and Change in Medieval Persia* (London, 1988), pp. 21–4 and especially 21, n. 60.

his praise of their valour[46]. Their battle tactics are very well attested as we have noted – their reliance on mobility, seeking to surround their enemies and bombard them with arrows, to draw them into ambush by feigned retreat, breaking up their cohesion before venturing to take them on at close range. A passage from Nicephorous Bryennius describing what he believed happened at Manzikert nicely illustrates Turkish methods:

Taranges divided the Turkish army into many groups and devised ambushes and traps and ordered his men to surround the Byzantines and to discharge a rain of arrows against them from all sides. The Byzantines, seeing their horses struck by arrows, were forced to pursue the Turks. They followed the Turks who pretended to flee. But they suffered heavily when they fell into ambushes and traps. The emperor, having resolved to accept a general engagement, slowly advanced hoping to find an army of Turks, attack it and decide the battle, but the Turks scattered. But wheeling, with great strength and shouting, they attacked the Byzantines and routed their right wing. Immediately the rear guard withdrew. The Turks encircled the emperor and shot from all directions. They prevented the left wing from coming to the rescue for they got in its rear and forced it to flee. The emperor, completely deserted and cut off from aid, drew his sword against the enemy and killed many and compelled them to flee. But encircled by the mass of the enemy, he was struck in the hand and recognised and surrounded on all sides. His horse was hit by an arrow, slipped and fell, and threw down his rider. And in this manner the Byzantine emperor was made prisoner.[47]

This is a description that the crusaders would soon come to recognise. The Anonymous describes their surprise and dismay as the Turks, making an enormous and frightening noise, surrounded the army of Bohemond and poured arrows into it. Raymond of Aguilers commented of a later conflict: 'The Turks have this custom in fighting, even though they are few in number, they always strive to encircle their enemy.' Albert of Aachen emphasises, in an attack at Nicaea, that 10,000 mounted bowmen appeared and that just such men surrounded and broke into Bohemond's camp at Dorylaeum.[48] Turks formed an important element in all the armies which the crusaders faced, and indeed in the Byzantine army, but in Anatolia the crusaders were confronted by forces which were entirely

---

[46] FC, pp. 82–83; GF, p. 21.
[47] Nicephorous Bryennius, *Commentarii*, ed. A. Meineke (Bonn, 1836), pp. 41–2 cited and tr. Kaegi, 'Archery' p. 106.
[48] GF, p. 19; RA, p. 52 Krey, *First Crusade*, p. 135; AA, 320, 328–31.

Turkish, and they showed themselves keenly aware of the difference between them and other armies. Raymond of Aguilers speaks of Turks and Arabs, and Albert refers to Turks and Saracens, present in the army of Duqaq of Damascus, but both writers speak only of Turks in Asia Minor.[49] The composite armies of the Sultan and his emirs were quite different from the forces of the Anatolian Turks who were the crusaders first enemy. In Anatolia, the Turks remained largely nomadic and their Seljuk Sultanate had not yet developed, as far as we can tell from inadequate sources, the kind of central administration which could control a composite army.[50] This was the wild frontier of Islam and what confronted the crusaders was a brave, dangerous but not very numerous enemy. However, there must have been some diversity in the Turkish army, for Nicaea was strongly garrisoned and resisted bitterly. It is unlikely that these were simple mounted nomads – presumably some more specialised forces had been recruited to defend this important but exposed city, which the Byzantines had attacked more than once. In this connection it is perhaps important that Nicaea was the only city of Asia Minor to hold out. Iconium was not defended; at Hereclea the Turks tried to ambush the crusaders as they approached, then fled.[51] Defence of the cities of Asia Minor was no easy matter for the Turks because these were still populated by Christians: the Turks had not captured them, they had been admitted, as garrisons, by feuding Byzantine lords or after a long period of isolation before a Turkish dominion outside their walls.[52] The countryside was in the hands of the nomads but the cities were different. As soon as the crusaders began to win victories, the peoples of the cities along their route began to eject their Turkish garrisons. The Anonymous says that after his defeat at Dorylaeum Kilij Arslan had to pretend to have been victorious in order to gain admission.[53] The attitude of the native population was to have an important influence on the crusade, as we shall see. It was certainly to have a great influence on the siege of Nicaea for, at the very moment that the army attacked it, Kilij Arslan was preoccupied with far-off Melitene.

In late October 1096 Kilij Arslan had totally destroyed the armies of the People's Crusade. Leaving his family at Nicaea he set out to

---

[49] *GF*, p. 30; RA, p. 52; AA, 375.   [50] On which see below pp. 200-6.
[51] *GF*, pp. 23-4.
[52] Vryonis, *Hellenism*, pp. 112-13; Cahen *Turkey*, pp. 76-7, 83-4.   [53] *GF*, p. 22.

intervene in Melitene. This city was a vital communications centre
on the roads from Anatolia to Mesopotamia and Iran. It was held by
Gabriel, a former officer of Philaretus, who claimed the Byzantine
title of Curopalate yet nominally held it of the Caliph.[54] It was
important for Kilij Arslan that Melitene should not be in the power
of the Sultan. In 1097 the divisions of Syria and the rivalries with
Baghdad, where the Seljuk Sultan Berkyaruk (1094–1105) was
preoccupied with events in the East, offered a splendid opportunity
to intervene, but he almost immediately found himself in competition with the Danishmends who also wished to control Melitene.
Conflict was avoided for the moment because news reached the
Sultan of the new threat to Nicaea, and he hastened westwards. It
was perhaps easier for these nomads to move quickly than a conventional army, but this journey of not much less than 1,000 kilometres
must have been very tiring. The crusaders reached Nicaea on 6 May
1097 but with only a part of their army. Bohemond and the
Normans took up a position along the north wall of the city, with
Robert of Flanders and Godfrey to the east. The south gate was left
open for Raymond of Toulouse, whose delay at Constantinople we
have noted: the North French had not yet arrived at Constantinople. The piecemeal nature of the siege underlines the lack of unity
in the crusader force; it was a huge host made up of a number of
major armies grouped around important leaders, but there was no
overall command. In fact, they approached Nicaea from the north
and simply fanned out in order of arrival, probably arranging
details by consultations amongst the princes. Kilij Arslan arrived in
the general area of his capital shortly before 16 May when his attack
precipitated a major battle.

We have two versions of the nature of this attack. According to
Raymond of Aguilers it was two-pronged: one force fell upon the
Germans on the east side of the city, while the other attempted to
enter the city through the vacant south gate, with the intention of
sallying out against Godfrey while he was distracted. According to
this version, the Provençals happened to come before the south gate
and were pitching camp when the enemy arrived; they fought off the
southern attack, thereby enabling the Germans to fight off the other
force. This account gives the South French a *beau rôle* indeed, and
one wonders just how Raymond could have known of the intentions

[54] Matthew, 28; Cahen, *Turkey*, pp. 81–2; Michael 3. 179.

of the enemy. The Anonymous makes little of the affair, saying that Count Raymond fought off an initial attack which was renewed but defeated 'by our men'. Albert says that, alerted by the capture of an enemy messenger trying to reach the garrison, the leaders asked Count Raymond to hasten his march, but agrees with Raymond of Aguilers that the Provençals were attacked just as they were making camp. He says that 10,000 enemy archers fell upon the southerners and that the Germans, supported by the Normans of Bohemond, then attacked the enemy who were put to flight.[55] This version is much the more convincing. The enemy attack clearly came from the south; the Anonymous explicitly states that the enemy came down from the hills, and Albert confirms this.[56] From this location the Turks would have had a magnificent view of Nicaea and the basin which surrounds it and so could not have missed the slow progress of the Provençal forces round the city to the south gate. Clearly the Turks chose to attack when they were most vulnerable, as they prepared their camp after the forced march to the city. Kilij Arslan hoped to brush them aside, and at the least reinforce Nicaea, at the most inflict a discouraging defeat on the westerners (see fig. 5). The attempt failed because the Provençals put up a stiff resistance (and to Raymond of Aguilers they must have seemed to have been at the very centre of the affair), drawing the Turks into a close quarter battle and so giving time for Godfrey's attack from the east on Kilij Arslan's right flank. The sheer numbers of the crusader army were decisive in the narrow area between the wooded hills and the city wall because the Turks had little room for manoeuvre. The Anonymous, who gives the impression of a skirmish, was probably with the Normans to the north of the city. Albert makes it clear that it was a savage and close-fought battle with heavy losses on both sides. There was no overall command on the crusader side but, nonetheless, we can see generalship of a very high order at work. The count of Toulouse held his troops together at a difficult moment as they were making camp, while Godfrey seems to have rallied his forces to their relief quickly. These are not small achievements, especially when

[55] RA, p. 43; *GF*, pp. 14–15; AA, 320–1. It must be admitted, however, that some aspects of Albert's account of the early siege are confused. A long list of those present, 315, includes Robert of Normandy who, however, is not amongst the leaders who urged Raymond of Toulouse to hurry, 319, yet is recorded as taking part in the battle, 320. In fact he did not arrive until 3 June. I would guess that Albert was trying to reconcile confused and contradictory information from his sources.

[56] *GF*, p. 15; AA, 320.

one considers the looseness of command and the uneven quality of the western forces. For many this must have been the first experience of battle, and for others their first of anything on a large scale. It was essentially the mass of the crusader army operating in a confined space which frustrated Turkish tactics and drove off Kilij Arslan, but in the circumstances, the cohesion of what must have been pretty green troops in the individual armies within the host was remarkable. Anna Comnena is quite right to speak of the Franks winning a 'glorious victory'.[57] Afterwards, the crusaders stuck the heads of the enemy dead on lances, and sent others to Alexius as tokens of victory. They were now free to besiege the city as Kilij Arslan fell back to rally more troops.

Most of the accounts we have of the siege of Nicaea are quite brief. The Anonymous says that when the crusaders first arrived, and even before the coming of the Provençals, they built siege machinery including towers and undermined the wall, but this was interrupted by the Turkish attack. After the defeat of Kilij Arslan he tells us that the count of Toulouse and Adhémar of Le Puy set troops protected by crossbowmen and archers to undermine a tower, which duly fell, but so late in the evening that the enemy were able to refortify the gap. Thereafter, it was the boats sent by the emperor to blockade the Ascanian lake at the west end of the city which forced a surrender. Raymond of Aguilers mentions fruitless efforts to storm the walls and the building of unspecified machines. He reports the same story of the undermining of a tower by the Provençals which came to nothing and stresses the importance of the boats which brought the siege to an end. This is very much the story told by Anna Comnena who says that the Count of Toulouse built a wooden tower on whose upper stories men engaged the enemy, while others below undermined what she calls the Gonatas tower, but in her account this simply has no outcome. She praises her father for providing the Franks with designs for machines and the boats on the lake, adding much detail on the negotiations for the surrender of the city.[58]

---

[57] *Alexiad*, p. 334.

[58] *GF*, pp. 14–17; *RA*, pp. 43–4; *Alexiad*, pp. 335–6. The famous 'Greek Fire' was not included in the aid which Alexius offered to the crusaders. Much has been written on the nature of this mysterious substance: J. Bradbury, 'Greek Fire in the West', *History Today*, 29 (1979), 326–31; H. R. E. Davidson, 'The secret weapon of Byzantium', *Byzantinische Zeitschrift*, 66 (1973), 66–74; J. Harvey and M. Byrne, 'A possible solution to the problem of Greek Fire', *Byzantinische Zeitschrift*, 70 (1977), 91–9; J. R. Partington, *A History of Greek Fire and Gunpowder* (Cambridge, 1960); C. Zenghetin, 'Le feu grégois et les armes à feu

Because so many latin sources based themselves on Raymond and the Anonymous they tend to add little. Baudry of Dol gives a few names of participants and stresses losses in the army. The *Historia Belli Sacri* says, after the story of the Provençal tower, that all the leaders made machines and Robert the Monk mentions the building of wooden towers. Fulcher of Chartres gives a generally vague account but includes a list of the many siege machines used.[59] The reasons for this brevity are clear; Raymond highlights the doings of his Count, while the Anonymous's master Bohemond does not seem to have had a lot to do. But there are hints of a much more intensive siege and the account of Albert of Aachen makes it clear that the Franks went to great lengths to assault Nicaea with elaborate machinery.

Albert does not mention the early assaults on the city before Kilij Arslan's attack and his dating is obscure. He says that it was only after seven weeks of siege that the leaders set in train the construction of catapults and assault equipment. The primary element in the assaults seems to have been the penthouse, a wooden structure with an armoured sloping roof within which attackers could undermine the wall in relative safety.[60] Albert mentions an assault in which Baldwin Calderin and Baldwin of Ghent were killed, and another in which the count of Forez and a knight called Guy died. Then, on a day during which the walls were under attack by crusader machines, two men in the force of Godfrey, Henry of Esch and Count Herman, built a penthouse which they called 'the Fox', which was brought up against the wall with enormous labour, but it collapsed killing all twenty knights within it, though not the originators of the project who refrained from trusting their lives to the device. Such machinery required careful design and construction skills which were evidently rare, as we have noted from Ordericus's story about Robert of Bellême.[61] The next major assault which Albert mentions was launched by the count of Toulouse whose forces, covered by the fire of mangonels, crossed the ditch protected

byzantines', *Byzantion*, 7 (1932) 265–86; the crusaders claimed it was used against them at Jerusalem: see below p. 350.

[59] BD, 27–9; *HBS*, 181; Robert the Monk, *Historia Iherosolimitana*, RHC Oc. 3. (hereafter cited as RM), 756; FC, p. 82.

[60] Rogers, *Siege Warfare*, studied this and other sieges and has helped to clarify my thinking considerably. Rogers prefers 'armoured roof' to my term 'penthouse'.

[61] Murray, 'Army of Godfrey de Bouillon', says that Henry was related to Godfrey de Bouillon (his brother Godfrey was also on the crusade) and came of a family which held the castle of Esch-sur-Sûre in the Ardennes; AA, 321–2; see above p. 105.

by a *testudo*, the same word as used by Raymond of Aguilers, and assaulted a tower. However, the enemy built a wall of stone within the tower, frustrating the attack which had to be broken off. Albert goes on to tell how boats were brought up to blockade the Ascanian lake and says that Raymond then renewed the attack. This time the Turks burned the equipment which brought the wooden penthouse and other instruments forward, and then repaired the wall which had been breached during the night. When the attack was resumed the next day only a single Norman knight could be found to press it; he was killed and his body dragged up the walls by the defenders and left hanging there. This account broadly corroborates that of Raymond of Aguilers and makes it clear that Raymond's *testudo* was a penthouse.[62] All these assaults were causing heavy losses which worried the leaders, especially as the catapults were having no effect on the walls. Then a Lombard engineer offered to build a machine if the leaders would finance him; they agreed to pay him fifteen pounds in the money of Chartres (where in the twelfth century thirty would buy a fine house) from their common fund.[63] This first mention of the common fund points to the development of rudimentary organisation to sustain the siege. In fact, a properly built penthouse was constructed and pushed across the ditch up to the wall which was undermined and propped with wood. These props were fired and in the middle of the night the upper part of the tower fell. This frightened Kilij Arslan's wife who attempted to flee across the lake but was captured, while the garrison of Nicaea decided to surrender.[64] Albert's account of the siege fills out considerably the rather schematic view given by the other sources, though it is chronologically confused and it is likely that he was attempting to conflate the stories of several individuals. What it does not make clear is the importance of the boats provided by Alexius, which is very evident in the other schematic accounts. This new attack from the lake, coming shortly after the arrival of the North French on 14 June, effectively doubled the length of the walls which needed to be defended as well as completely isolating the garrison, and was probably the decisive factor in precipitating their surrender on 19 June after another Frankish assault, under cover of which the Byzantines implemented the secretly-agreed surrender arrangements.[65]

---

[62] AA, 322–5; RA, p. 44.   [63] AA, 325 and n.a.   [64] AA, 325–8.
[65] *Alexiad*, pp. 337–8.

The army had a considerable knowledge of siegecraft and we can discount Anna's view that Alexius invented machines for them. They prosecuted the siege vigorously and suffered heavy casualties which worried the leaders; of the thirteen dead named by Anselm of Ribemont, two died in battle and three of disease during the siege of Nicaea. Albert's mention of a common fund indicates that, although the armies in the host were grouped round several leaders, the need to cooperate was forcing organisation.[66] The army must have relied on the Byzantines for supplies – wood, clamps, nails etc. and certainly it was Alexius who provided the boats which closed the Ascanian lake.[67] The major problem of a besieging army, especially one this size, was food, and both Albert and Fulcher stress that Alexius sent this in good quantities, although the Anonymous remarks that some of the poor died of starvation.[68] By and large the alliance had worked well in a military sense. The surrender of the city came as a surprise to the crusaders who must have sensed the intrigue from which they were excluded, but the emperor seems to have been reasonably generous in distributing the spoils of war to the westerners. Stephen of Blois tells us that Alexius sent food for the poor during the siege and agrees with Anselm of Ribemont and the Anonymous that he was subsequently very generous to the knights and princes. Only Raymond of Aguilers complains about this and his general attitude is deeply hostile to Alexius. The freeing of the Turkish garrison, however, deeply disturbed the Anonymous who feared they would later attack the Franks.[69] The military value of the Byzantine alliance had been clearly demonstrated, and they prepared to march into Anatolia with an imperial contingent commanded by the Turk Tatikios.

However, this was not the only military assistance which they received. Anna reports that Alexius warned them of Turkish tactics, but he seems to have provided them with other information and ideas.[70] During the siege Alexius had observed events from nearby Pelekanum and after the fall of the city he met most of the leaders, presumably to discuss strategy. It may well be that this followed up earlier discussions, of which we hear nothing. According to the

---

[66] AA, 325; Hagenmeyer, *Kreuzzugsbriefe*, p. 145.

[67] Rogers, *Siege Warfare*, p. 81: *Alexiad*, p. 336; *GF*, p. 16; RA, p. 44; FC, p. 82.

[68] FC, p. 82; AA, 320; *GF*, p. 17.

[69] RA, p. 44; FC, p. 83; Hagenmeyer, *Kreuzzugsbriefe*, pp. 140, 144–5; *GF*, p. 17–18.

[70] *Alexiad*, p. 336.

Historia Belli Sacri he suggested that they send an embassy to Egypt seeking the friendship of the 'Emir of Babylon'. It was as a consequence of this that an Egyptian embassy came to the siege of Antioch, happily at the very moment when they inflicted a heavy defeat upon the Turks at the Lake Battle in early February 1098.[71] The encouraging noises made by these envoys probably exercised a considerable influence over the leaders in the summer and autumn of 1098. It was a skillful piece of diplomacy, reflecting Alexius's intimate knowledge of the politics of the Middle East. The decay of the Abassid Caliphate in the later ninth century and the ensuing disorders enabled the dissident Shi'ites to establish a Caliphate of their own in Tunisia in 909, and from there they grasped Cairo in 969 where they set up the Fatimid Caliphate. The Fatimids sought to expand their control over Syria, but the restoration of Abassid power under the implacably Sunnite Seljuks after 1055 threatened these new conquests. In 1060 serious internal conflict broke out in Egypt amongst the diverse elements of the army which, on the pattern of the other Islamic powers, was a composite of peoples, in this case Berbers, Sudanese, Africans and Turks. By 1077 an Armenian general, Badr al-Jamali, was able to restore order but revolt and Seljuk intervention meant that Egyptian power in Syria and Palestine was confined to the cities of the coast, and by 1079 Malik Shah's brother Tutush held Damascus and was overlord of Jerusalem, held of him by Artuk. The fragmentation of the Seljuk Sultanate after the death of Malik Shah in 1095, offered the Egyptians an opportunity to recover their lost dominion in Syria and Palestine (see fig. 3).[72] Badr al-Jamali's son al-Afdal saw the crusade as offering golden opportunities. The proliferation of tribes and powers in the Middle East meant that the precise nature of the crusaders' interests were not perceived by the Islamic powers – they were simply another factor in a complex game, to be used, allied with as self-interest dictated. Alexius shared this mentality, and the crusader leaders were eager to capitalise.

In their discussions with Alexius at Pelekanum and before, the

[71] *HBS*, 181, 189–90, 212; *GF*, p. 37; RA, pp. 58, 109–10. On this embassy and the whole issue of diplomatic relations between the crusaders and Islamic powers on the First Crusade see M. A. Köhler, *Allianzen und Verträge zwischen frankischen und islamischen Herrschern im Vorderren Orient* (Berlin, 1991), pp. 1–72.

[72] Gibb, 'The Caliphate', 85–95; P. M. Holt, *The Age of the Crusades* (London, 1986) pp. 9–15; Y. Lev, *State and Society in Fatimid Egypt* (Leiden, 1991); on the fragmentation of the Seljuk power and its impact on the crusade see below pp. 357–8.

princes must have discussed the coming journey. Stephen of Blois did not join the other leaders at Pelekanum but he must have known of their discussions and in a letter to his wife written from Nicaea he refers to Antioch as their next target. The crusaders must have been aware from pilgrim days of the importance of this city which lay firmly across the road to Jerusalem. But they did not intend to conquer all the cities between Nicaea and Jerusalem, and Stephen's letter holds out the possibility that Antioch might not resist.[73] This surely reflects knowledge of the situation in Syria. The death of Malik Shah in 1092 precipitated a bitter succession conflict between his brother Tutush, who held Syria, and his son Berkyaruk. When Tutush was killed in 1095 Syria was divided between his sons, Ridwan of Aleppo and Duqaq of Damascus. Malik Shah's governor of Antioch, Yaghisiyan, was able to achieve much independence (see fig. 3). For Alexius the reconquest of Antioch was an alluring possibility. Sulayman of Nicaea had attempted to seize the lands of Philaretus in 1086 and had died at the hands of Malik Shah for his pains. The old duchy of Antioch stood between Anatolia and Syria and within striking distance of the great route centre at Melitene. It offered considerable opportunities to any power of Asia Minor. To the crusaders it was important to have it in friendly hands as they entered Syria and Palestine, the real object of their quest. Between the Byzantines and the crusaders there was a considerable community of interest.

But the crusaders appear to have been aware of other factors in the political situation of the lands they were entering. In the Taurus area there were a number of independent Armenian princes amongst whom Thoros of Edessa was very important. Oschin, who claimed to be descended from the Arsacids, held the castle of Lampron and was loyal to Alexius whom he served as governor. He seized part of Adana as the crusaders approached.[74] Constantine, son of Roupen, claimed to be a descendant of the old Armenian ruling family of the Bagratids and held the fortress of Partzapert near Sis. Tatoul was at Marasch, Kogh Vasil at Raban and Gabriel at Melitene.[75] These princelings throve in the complex politics of the area, playing off the Turkish emirs of neighbouring cities. It is clear that the crusader leaders had heard about them, for Matthew of

[73] Hagenmeyer, *Kreuzzugsbriefe*, p. 140.   [74] *Alexiad*, pp. 372–4; Boase, *Armenia*, pp. 3–4.
[75] Runciman, *Crusades*, 1. 299; Boase, *Armenia*, p. 4.

Edessa says that they wrote letters to Thoros and to Constantine son of Roupen.[76] It is probable that such matters were discussed with Alexius who perhaps suggested a course of action to take advantage of the situation. The Armenians had a tradition of hostility to Byzantium, as we have noted. Constantine, son of Roupen, was particularly hostile but on the other hand Oschin was friendly. Furthermore, both Gabriel of Melitene and Thoros of Edessa claimed to be imperial officials – *Curopalatoi*; the latter, we are told, was 'expecting to hand it [Edessa] over to the emperor'.[77] It is possible that the Armenians themselves made contact with the Franks but were this the case Alexius would surely have wanted to control subsequent events. When Tancred entered Cilicia and appeared before Tarsus in late September 1097 he was met by an Armenian, who was already known to him and had resided with him, who offered to attempt to negotiate the surrender of the city. At Nicaea Baldwin of Boulogne, Godfrey de Bouillon's younger brother, had made the acquaintance of Bagrat, brother of Kogh Vasil of Raban. Baldwin also entered Cilicia, but on Bagrat's urging left for Ravendan and the great adventure which eventually made him lord of Edessa.[78] The hope of support from such eastern Christians was probably fed by the uprisings in the cities of Anatolia after the crusader victory at Dorylaeum, and it seems likely that it had a profound effect on crusader policy. What we have to see at this stage is that the crusaders probably knew a great deal about the lands into which they were venturing. Norman and Frankish mercenaries had long served in the Byzantine armies. Roussel of Bailleul, Crispin and, before them, Hervey had held land in the Armenian theme. William of Apulia wrote his *Gesta Roberti Wiscardi* as the crusaders left for the East and could give a good account of the battle of Manzikert, presumably from Norman veterans of the Byzantine service.[79] So Alexius had no monopoly of information, but for the moment he and the Frankish leaders enjoyed a community of interest, but it was not one to which he was willing to contribute more than a few troops under Tatikios, charged with guiding the

---

[76] Matthew, 30.

[77] Michael, pp. 173–4; Matthew, 35; 'Anonymous Syriac Chronicle', ed. and tr. A. S. Tritton and H. A. R. Gibb, *Journal of the Royal Asiatic Society* (1933), 69.

[78] AA, 342–3, 350–1.

[79] William of Apulia, ll. 1–110. See also M. Mathieu, 'Une source négligée de la bataille de Mantzikert: Les "Gesta Roberti Wiscardi" de Guillaume d'Apulie', *Byzantion*, 20 (1950), 89–103. On the Normans in Byzantium see above p. 153, n. 34.

crusaders and taking over any cities they might capture. Anna's caveat, 'if indeed God granted them that favour', probably reflected Alexius's thinking. He would take what profit he could without heavy commitment, for there was much danger ahead for the expedition. They were not venturing into the unknown, merely into a dangerous hinterland that had been Turkish now for a generation.

The crusader leaders acted quickly. Nicaea fell on 19 June. On 26 June the first contingents left Nicaea, amongst them the Normans of South Italy. Various groups left subsequently, the last being the Provençals on 28 June and the army gathered at a place where there was a bridge, which Anna Comnena identifies as Lefke, about twenty-five kilometres east of Nicaea. A number of crusaders had stayed behind at Nicaea and took service with the emperor, while Anselm of Ribemont was sent to the imperial court by the leaders in order to settle outstanding business.[80] They had already decided to go to Antioch, so necessarily they had to direct their path towards the old Byzantine fortress at Dorylaeum (Eskişehir) which was the gateway to the Anatolian plateau. The sources are quite clear that in the two days of march after the concentration of the army they broke into two groups, a vanguard and a main force. Raymond of Aguilers says that this happened after one day's march, which suggests that the Provençals had left Nicaea a day later than the first contingents. We know how they divided; the vanguard was led by Bohemond, Tancred, Robert of Normandy and Stephen of Blois, probably fewer than 20,000 in all. The second, larger force, comprising the rest of the army was under Robert of Flanders, Hugh of Vermandois, Godfrey de Bouillon and Raymond of Toulouse, – rather more than 30,000 strong.[81] It is more difficult to suggest why this happened. Fulcher, who was in the vanguard, simply confesses that he does not know; the Anonymous says there was confusion in the dark as the army left its place of concentration, while Raymond of Aguilers says that it was the fault of Bohemond and his companions who rushed on rashly (*temere*). Albert of Aix says that it was the result of a deliberate decision of the princes who after two days of marching the army together, now felt the need to divide it for foraging. Ralph of Caen tells us that some thought the division deliberate, and specifically denies this, which suggests that even

---

[80] *Alexiad*, p. 341; Hagenmeyer, *Kreuzzugsbriefe*, p. 145.
[81] AA, 328–9; *GF*, p. 18 does not mention Stephen of Blois; Hagenmeyer, *Kreuzzugsbriefe*, p. 145.

after the crusade the matter was still being debated. It is likely that
sheer size and the lack of any overall commander were the real
reasons. The army of Frederick Barbarossa on the Third Crusade
was 100,000 strong and seems to have taken three days to pass any
single point. The sources for the battle of Dorylaeum make clear
that most of the casualties were suffered by stragglers between the
two forces, which would suggest that the host became strung out
simply as a result of the natural frictions of the march.[82] The
disagreements and uncertainty of the three eyewitnesses – Raymond
with the main force, Fulcher and the Anonymous with the vanguard, support this view. It also reflects the incoherence of the
crusade's command arrangements. It is worth remembering that the
baggage train of Peter the Hermit's much smaller force straggled a
mile along the road and that the crusader army at its maximum
strength was well over twice that size. But perhaps the leaders
conferred at some point and gave their blessing to a division already
becoming apparent. At the time of the battle Raymond of Aguilers
says quite clearly that the two parts of the army were two miles apart
– over five kilometres.[83]

The crusaders had now begun a march which would result in
what is conventionally called the battle of Dorylaeum, for Anna
Comnena says that it took place when Kilij Arslan ambushed
Bohemond and the vanguard 'on the plain of Dorylaeum'. In a
letter of the leaders to the West on 11 September 1098, they referred
to the battle at 'Dorotilla' which sounds very like the same place.
One manuscript of the chronicle of Raymond of Aguilers refers to
the battle 'in campo florido'. Albert says that the battle took place
'in vallem Degorganhi', now called the Orellis, but later has Bohemond's messenger to the other leaders say that the enemy attacked
down the Orellis into the Degorganhi: neither of these place names
can be identified and Albert does later use the name Orellis to mean
somewhere quite different.[84] However, there are grave difficulties

---

[82] FC, p. 85; *GF*, p. 18; RA, p. 45; AA, 328–9; RC, 620–1; on losses amongst the stragglers see
below p. 181, n. 104; Nesbitt, 'Rate of march', 178–80.

[83] RA, p. 45; he later, p. 49, tells us that St Symeon Port was ten miles from Antioch – it is
actually twenty-seven kilometres.

[84] Bibliothèque Nationale 5131A, in which Raymond's account is conflated with that of
Fulcher, also represents a conflation of traditions of his own work. The life of Adhémar in
the *Chronicon monasterii sancti Petri Aniciensis*, which is known separately as *Gesta Adhemari
Episcopi Podiensis Hierosolymitana*, RHC Oc. 5. 354–5, refers to this battle as taking place 'in
campo florido'. This work is most certainly based on Raymond's, but I think it was written
close to the time with other recollections added, and the story that the battle was fought 'in

about the idea that the battle was fought at or near Dorylaeum. The Anonymous says that the army marched one day from Nicaea and encamped for two days by a bridge while all the contingents gathered, then marched for two days until the battle on the third day. Raymond of Aguilers says that on the third day after the concentration of the army they met the enemy. Anselm says that after a two day march they encountered the enemy on the morning of the third day which was 'kal. Iulii', 1 July; Fulcher confirms the date and confirms that the battle began in the morning.[85] Thus the crusade began to leave Nicaea on 26 June and concentrated at a river crossing, from which it departed on 29 June. It then marched for two days and fought the enemy in the morning of 1 July. When we examine the distances and the likely rates of march of the crusader army it is evident that they could not have reached the close vicinity of Dorylaeum in this time. Anna Comnena says that the army concentrated at the bridge of Lefke, which probably means the bridge over the Göksu, a western tributary of the Sakarya Nehri. Nicaea to Lefke on the Roman road is twenty-five kilometres, and Dorylaeum another ninety kilometres. If, as has been suggested, the army marched south to the Göksu and crossed it in the vicinity of Yenişhehir (a distance of thirty kilometres) they still had to cover roughly the same distance to Dorylaeum. A study of the rates of march of the individual armies across Europe to Constantinople suggests that, in the most favourable circumstances, the forces of Godfrey and Peter the Hermit never did more than twenty-nine kilometres per day. The army which left Nicaea was much larger and lacked a clear overall command and is likely to have progressed much more slowly. Barbarossa's army probably managed about twenty-nine kilometres per day in Europe.[86] Even at these rates the army would have been about thirty kilometres short of Dorylaeum after two days of marching, but they were probably moving much more slowly for they were in the presence of the enemy and encumbered with a heavy baggage-train. We can reasonably accurately date the departure of the army from Dorylaeum and its arrival at Antioch as being 4 July to 20 October. In 105 days of marching

a flowered field' may be one of them. It is unfortunate that the editors of Raymond of Aguilers in *RHC Oc.* 3. 240 capitalised the name without making clear its derivation. The latest edition by Hill and Hill, p. 45 n. 4 gives only a cryptic note; AA, 329–30.

[85] *GF*, p. 18; RA, p. 45; Hagenmeyer, *Kreuzzugsbriefe*, p. 161.

[86] Nesbitt, 'Rate of march', pp. 173–4, 178–80.

(with fifteen days of rest) they travelled 1180 kilometres, an average of thirteen kilometres per day which the *Chronologie* of Hagenmeyer suggests varied between eight and eighteen kilometres. There is no point in seeking comparison with events after Antioch when the army was much smaller. Furthermore, the crusaders knew the enemy were about and this would have restricted their speed, even if the vanguard did push on somewhat. All this suggests that the battle could not have taken place more than forty kilometres, or just conceivably fifty kilometres, south of Lefke or the Göksu crossing. Hagenmeyer recognised the problem and suggested Bozüyük just over fifty kilometres south of Lefke and about the same from Yenişhehir. This is probably as far as the army could conceivably have reached and it certainly could be regarded as being in the valley of Dorylaeum, as suggested by the letter of the leaders. Runciman points out that a Byzantine road runs further north through Sögüt and enters the plain ten kilometres short of Dorylaeum, where he thinks the battle took place. However, as Runciman admits, although this road does cross rivers, the countryside was very steep indeed and this probably rules out any of these crossings. But more simply, this was most certainly further than the army could have reached.[87] What is clear is that the battle took place in a wide valley, for Albert says that Bohemond's force was well to the right of the main force as well as ahead of it. Moreover, there was a river, for Albert mentions streams and Ralph of Caen, whose description is detailed, says that it was fought after a river crossing. William of Tyre follows Albert for the most part but with some variations. He says that the army followed a river in the valley of *Gorgoni*, and that the main force was to the right of Bohemond's, reversing Albert's statement.[88] Albert's account of a battle fought where two valleys join, taken together with Raymond's mention of the 'flowered field' and the general description of the battle, suggests that it was fought in open land on the road towards Dorylaeum, and the comments of Albert and Ralph indicate not far from a river crossing or crossings, although these played no role in the major action. In fact to understand the battle we need to understand fully the circumstances in which the army found itself, the country and its road system.

---

[87] Hagenmeyer, *Chronologie* 169, p. 85; Runciman 1. 186, n. 1.
[88] AA, 328–9; RC, 621; WT, p. 129; Runciman, 1. 186, n. 1 has an ingenious reconstruction of the battle.

After the capture of Nicaea it is clear from Stephen's letter that the leaders had decided to march to Antioch, and evidently they had decided not to take the coastal route. They also rejected the 'Pilgrim Road' due east from Nicaea via Iuliopolis (near the modern village of Çayirbano) and Ancyra (Ankara) down through the heart of Asia Minor and across the Cilician Gates to Tarsus.[89] Instead they decided to mount the Anatolian plateau towards the Byzantine military station at Dorylaeum (modern Eskişehir) which, at 800 metres commands the obvious point of entry to the plateau via a broad valley the sides of which rise to 1,200 metres and beyond (see fig. 2). Because Anna Comnena mentions the bridge at Lefke it has been assumed that the host marched east from Nicaea up the gently sloping plain, over the watershed and into the valley of the Sakarya and then up that of its southern tributary, the Kara Su, to its upper reaches just north of Bozüyük, where the land opens out into the wide valley which leads to Dorylaeum. But it is difficult to believe that the army would have taken this route, for the valley of the Kara Su, even in its lower reaches, is very steep and difficult and at Bilecik enters a spectacular gorge before narrowing even further into a grim steep defile which would have formed a perfect ambush site. The Byzantine road forked at Bilecik providing a road via modern Söğüt to Dorylaeum, but this road too is dangerously scenic and offers no open sites until it is very close to Dorylaeum. It is far more likely that the crusaders marched south from Nicaea. The first stage of this journey over the Avdan Dagi, whose peaks rise to 835 metres would have been quite difficult but thereafter they could cross the Göksu in the vicinity of modern Yenişehehir. From there a Roman road crossed the Ahl Dag, which rise to 1000 metres and emerged into the broad valley above Bozüyük, roughly where the modern E90 road from Bursa meets route 650 from Bilecik, just south of the narrow gorges of the Kara Su and some three to five kilometres north of Bozüyük. While by no means easy this route is no longer and offered a much more open approach to the high plateau.[90] It is very likely that it was at this junction of roads in the plain that the

---

[89] On which see D. French, *Roman Roads and Milestones of Asia Minor: Fasc. 1. The Pilgrims' Road*, British Institute of Archaeology at Ankara Monograph No. 3, British Archaeological Reports, International Series 105 (Oxford, 1981).

[90] I would like to thank Dr David French, Director of the British Institute of Archaeology at Ankara, who told me of the existence of this road. He is currently writing an article on the routes of the crusades and very generously explained his ideas to me.

battle of Dorylaeum took place (see figs. 2 and 6). Albert clearly indicates that the site was where two valleys meet, and the open ground here is about the right distance from the crossing of the Göksu. Moreover, the Anonymous says that when the crusader force came it formed up to the right of Bohemond's trapped vanguard – it was, therefore, from the right that the attack came. This is also the force of Albert's insistence on telling us that the vanguard moved to the right of the main force and William of Tyre's careful correction that they were to the left, which fits with the Anonymous's account. Both are explaining the subsequent alignment of the battle.[91] This would fit with the suggestion made here that the crusaders approached along the gentle valley from the west and were ambushed by the Turkish army lying in the southern valley to their right. The logic of the battle is clear. Kilij Arslan and his Turks were returning to the fray. This time he had concluded an alliance with the Danishmend Emir and together they were ready to attack the Franks. They chose to do so on the approaches to the high plateau and at a point of maximum advantage where they could lay an ambush and destroy an isolated part of the crusader force before its main weight could be brought to bear. It was the strategy of the Nicaea attack, but this time in less confined ground where Turkish speed of manoeuvre could be maximised.[92] The Turkish army was probably much smaller than the total force of the crusaders and so had to avoid direct conflict with the main force and defeat their enemy in detail. Fulcher's 360,000, though supported by the Anonymous, is sheer fantasy. In the accounts of the Crusade of 1101 we hear of the 700 knights in the rearguard of the main Lombard army being savaged by 500 Turks, while the army which destroyed the Bavarian and Aquitainian army was only 4,000 in all.[93] The Turkish force was entirely mounted and was probably roughly equal to the knights in the whole crusader host. Therefore, a battle of movement involving the cavalry element would nullify the huge

[91] WT, 129; GF, p. 20.

[92] Ibn al-Qalanisi, *Damascus Chronicle of the Crusades*, extracts ed. and tr. H. A. R. Gibb (London, 1967) [hereafter cited as *Damacus Chronicle of the Crusades*], pp. 41–2.

[93] FC, p. 84; GF, p. 20; AA, 565; Ekkehard, p. 31; These forces may have been detached elements of a much larger allied force formed by Ridwan of Aleppo, the Danishmend Malik Ghazi and Karajan of Harran. The full size of their army which finally defeated the Franks, whose army probably started 50,000 strong, at Mersivan is unknown but the long harassment which preceded the final attack suggests that it was even smaller than the Western force.

numeric advantage of the western forces and, in the attack on the crusader vanguard, Kilij Arslan would actually outnumber the western knights. If the Franks had marched up the gorge of the Kara Su they would surely have attacked them there, just as they would later destroy the Byzantine army at Myriokephalon in 1176.[94]

On the evening of 30 June Fulcher and Ralph of Caen both say that the vanguard saw Turkish forces, substantiating intelligence which had already suggested that they were in the vicinity; this last comment suggests that Tatikios was with the vanguard, although no chronicler mentions him. Clearly at least, the vanguard, more than five kilometres ahead of the main force, were aware of the enemy presence.[95] Albert of Aachen places the battle in the evening – starting as the army camped at the ninth hour, late afternoon. However, Albert here seems to be trying to make sense of his sources, hence perhaps his error on which side of the valley the vanguard was following, for his suggestion of an evening battle is connected with the act of making camp. But the Anonymous says that the battle raged from the third to ninth hour, and Fulcher suggests that the vanguard was on its own from the first to sixth hour (6–7am–noon). As these writers were actually with the front force they should be preferred, particularly as Ralph of Caen confirms their story that contact was made with the enemy on the evening before the battle and that the march was resumed the next morning when the crusaders were forced to pitch camp when it became apparent that a large enemy army was present. It was probably making sense of this sequence of events which confused Albert whose account, however, contains much valuable information.[96] Fulcher's account is peculiarly vivid for he was in the camp where: 'We were all indeed huddled together like sheep in a fold, trembling and frightened, surrounded on all sides by enemies so that we could not turn in any direction', while the Anonymous was with the knights of the vanguard who were outside the camp from which the women brought water.[97] Ralph says that after an anxious night the army moved on and forced the passage of a river after which the appearance of the enemy compelled them to pitch their camp; Fulcher says they camped by a marsh which gave them some protection from the enemy and that later the enemy broke across the marsh. His account

[94] Vryonis, *Hellenism*, pp. 123–5; on numbers see above pp. 157–8.
[95] FC, pp. 83–4; RC, 621.
[96] *GF*, p. 21; FC, p. 86.   [97] FC, p. 85; *GF*, p. 19.

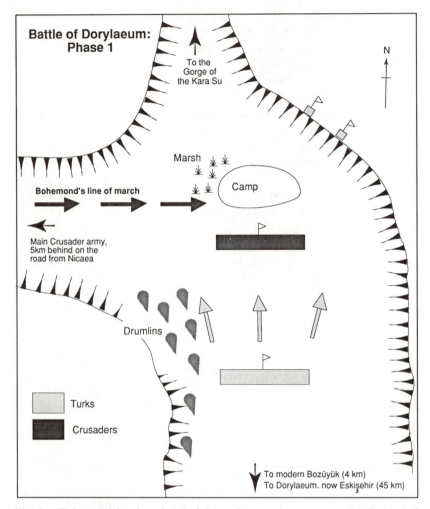

Fig. 6a Bohemond is 5 km ahead of the main army in company with Robert of Normandy and the Counts of Blois and Flanders together with the Byzantines; having descended from Nicaea to the northwest they enter the main valley leading to Dorylaeum and see the Turks. Bohemond orders his foot to make camp quickly and throws forward his cavalry to protect them.

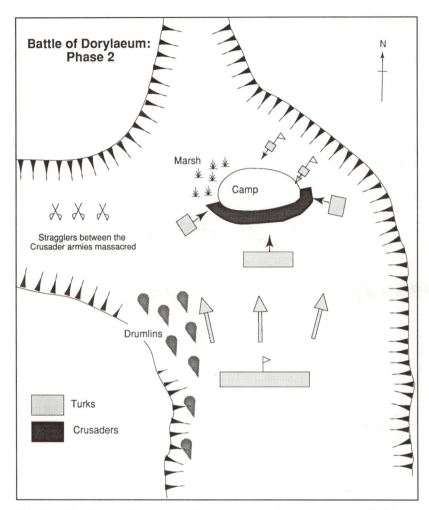

Fig. 6b   The Franco-Norman cavalry is driven back on the camp, rallied by its leaders, and forms the outer shell of resistance in a 'wearing-out fight'. The crusader army is surrounded, though partially protected by a marsh (location conjectural). They cling on, relying on their compact mass hoping for help from the main force.

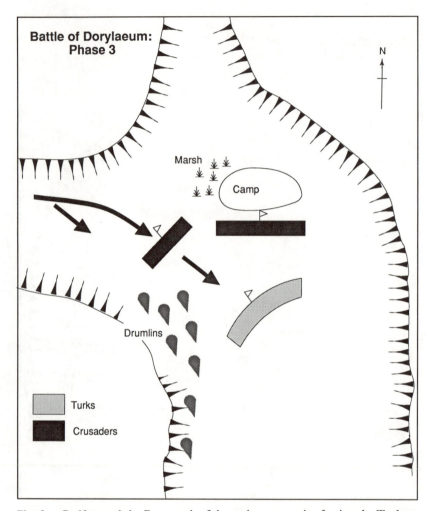

**Battle of Dorylaeum:
Phase 3**

N

Marsh

Camp

Drumlins

Turks

Crusaders

Fig. 6c   Godfrey and the Provençals of the main army arrive forcing the Turks to break off their attack and turn to meet the new threat to their left. The new arrivals form up to the RIGHT of Bohemond's beleaguered force

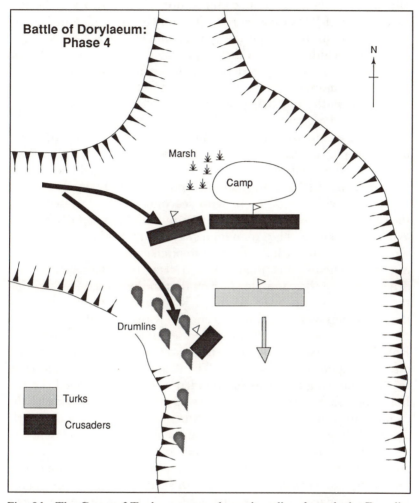

Fig. 6d   The Count of Toulouse enters the main valley through the Drumlins which mark its western shoulder, and his attack on their rear and left forces the Turks to flee leaving victory to the Crusaders.

of murderous fighting in the camp is supported by Albert, who says that Robert of Paris died there trying to help the rank and file and adds the picturesque detail that young women tried to make themselves look beautiful so that they would be spared the sword. Ralph of Caen shows the knights depressed by their inability to save the others.[98] Crusader sources therefore suggest two distinct actions within the battle. Fulcher speaks of the leaders fighting while those like him in the camp desperately resisted. Albert says that at the sight of the enemy Bohemond and the knights rode forward but were unable to prevent the Turks getting into the camp. Ralph tells us that when the camp was pitched the knights attacked the enemy, but were driven back in disorder and saved only by Robert of Normandy who rallied them with scornful words – subsequently they were involved in heavy fighting in which Tancred's brother William was killed. The Anonymous says that when the enemy were sighted Bohemond ordered the foot to pitch camp and the knights to attack the enemy, and then makes it clear that the cavalry were driven back on the camp, for he says that in the subsequent fighting the women brought water to them. Raymond of Aguilers suggests that the camp was sacked by the enemy. Ralph says that thereafter the knights fought hard, commanded separately by Bohemond and Robert of Normandy, and appears to show these men imposing solid discipline upon their followers.[99] The Anonymous tells us that from the first the vanguard was surrounded – 'we are encircled' he has Bohemond say – yet Fulcher speaks of a marsh on one side of the camp protecting them and the subsequent development of the battle was to the vanguard's right. This can be explained by reference to the lie of the land. The convergence of the two valleys forms a natural basin against the northern rim of which Bohemond was pinned by the Turkish main force, but smaller troops of the enemy probably menaced from the surrounding hills, for the Anonymous mentions the enemy presence there.

Throughout the morning there was heavy and unpleasant fighting at close quarters. The western knights seem to have been pinned against the southern side of their camp holding off the Turks who, however, were able to penetrate from other sides despite the difficulties presented by a marsh on one side and the considerable

[98] FC, pp. 85–6; AA, 329–30; RC, 622–3.
[99] FC, p. 86; AA, 329–30; RC, 622–23; RA, p. 45.

resistance of the crusader footmen. About noon, after five to six hours of this bitter fighting, the knights of the main force came up to relieve their comrades. The Anonymous describes the formation of a battle line, but this is the tidiness of hindsight (see fig. 6c).[100] The main force was probably well out of sight of the battle in the western valley and, although messages seem to have been sent back early, it was not until about noon that they appeared. This is not surprising, for the main army's knights had to prepare themselves for battle and then to ride five kilometres along a road which was probably choked with transport and stragglers. It is unlikely that they had much time to form into line. Far to the right, the bishop of Le Puy seems to have charged behind a small hill and come upon the enemy now turning to face the new threat on their left, from the rear. At the convergence of the two valleys there are a number of glacial drumlins and one of these was probably the hill to which reference is made.[101] There is no reason to believe that this was planned; rather a pell-mell battle developed in which skirmishes such as that in which Godfrey with 50 *sodales* attacked what they believed to be Kilij Arslan and his household on a low hill were the rule.[102] A running fight ensued in which the enemy often turned to fight causing casualties like Gerard of Quiersy. The enemy's camp was sacked and the nomads were pursued along the road so that, for two or three days after, the army passed enemy soldiers and horses fallen by the wayside.[103] Casualties appear to have been heavy although how far we can regard Albert's 4,000 Christians and 3,000 Turks as precise figures is a different matter. They do, however, sound small enough to be credible and large enough to suggest heavy fighting. Large numbers of the main force, the foot, the non-combatants generally and presumably some knights, were never engaged at all. It is interesting that Fulcher says that most of the casualties were those caught straggling between the two crusader armies, a comment substantiated by Raymond of Aguilers.[104]

Dorylaeum was a nasty experience for the crusaders. They were not caught totally by surprise in that they knew the enemy were near, but it is odd that the leaders in the vanguard did not warn the main force behind them. Presumably, they simply took it for granted that the enemy was around but could not guess that his main force

---

[100] *GF*, p. 20.   [101] *GF*, p. 19.   [102] AA, 331.   [103] RA, p. 46; AA, 331.
[104] AA, 330, 323; FC, p. 86; RA, p. 45.

was so close. It is unlikely that Kilij Arslan was ignorant of the whereabouts of the crusader main force. He attempted to destroy their smaller element in favourable circumstances, counting on numeric superiority to bring victory in a mobile battle over the knights in the vanguard. The crusaders were alert and their foot prepared to pitch camp while an element of the knights confronted the enemy and were put to flight, falling back on the camp where their solid formation, and the fact that the site was confined by the edge of the plain and a marsh, enabled them to resist the Turks. The Turks were drawn into close quarter fighting both against the knights and in amongst the tents and baggage. 'The enemy were helped by numbers', says Ralph, referring to the knights, 'we by our armour', which suggests that the knights adopted a solid formation and refused to be broken up by the enemy's attacks with arrows and missiles. The stall-fed horses of the western knights may have been larger than the ponies of the Turks, and this weight advantage may have helped to solidify their resistance but, in general it was of no more use to them than it had been to the Byzantines. The western knights in the vanguard must have been quite helpless and the progress of the Turks in the camp would have destroyed their entire position, but relief came. Both sides seem to have been surprised by the enemy. The crusaders were appalled by the enemy tactics which struck the Anonymous as menacing and daring and Fulcher as totally new: 'to all of us such warfare was unknown'. He was also struck by the fact that the enemy were entirely mounted: 'All were mounted. On the other hand we had both footmen and bowmen.' Albert of Aix remarks time after time in his account on Turkish use of the bow which clearly struck the crusaders as novel.[105] But the leaders had been warned by Alexius and Frankish contact with the east, and even those in the vanguard managed to keep control of their forces – though luck played its part in this. Furthermore, they seem to have made sure that all were alert, for although the timing of the attack was a surprise, as probably was its direction, when it came, camp of a sort was made quickly. From the viewpoint of the crusaders, what is striking is that the battle evolved and was never directed. Although only a fraction of the crusader army was engaged, their advantage in numbers had much to do with their victory – just as it had at Nicaea. For Kilij Arslan seems to have

[105] *GF*, 19, 21; FC, p. 85; AA, 328–9.

repeated the error made at Nicaea; he counted on the enemy panicking under a surprise attack. When they resisted he was drawn into a bloody close-quarter battle in which the crusader footsoldiers in the camp made stiff resistance, partly because of their very numbers. As at Nicaea the appearance of a relief force, in this case one part of which under Adhémar came from an unexpected direction, drove his men from the field. That this was a pell-mell affair with no evidence of overall command (which led to the division in the crusader ranks in the first place) should not be allowed to detract from the quality of the crusader leadership.[106] The army was alert and when the surprise attack came managed to establish a camp which subsequently formed a fortress. Robert of Normandy rallied knights alarmed by the novel methods of the enemy and subsequently he and Bohemond imposed a discipline upon them. The enemy broke into the camp and did much destruction, but the foot evidently fought hard, otherwise the camp which anchored the cavalry in their struggle would have been swept away. All of this suggests a formidable coherence in the crusader army and a considerable will to fight. It must be remembered that the terror which they inspired had served the Turks well in their fights with the Byzantines and others who found their missile tactics difficult to counter. Above all, the sense of isolation created by encirclement panicked large forces time after time. At Dorylaeum some of the knights did panic – those under Bohemond – but they were rallied by Robert of Normandy. Once discipline and solidity of formation was reimposed, partly because they simply couldn't do anything else pinned against their own tents, the knights found that they could resist – though fairly passively. It was a lesson Nicephorous Botaneiates had learned as a general under Constantine IX during a retreat in the presence of the Patzinacks:

[Botaneiates] ordered his men not to spread out as the rest of the men were seen to be doing and not to turn their backs to the enemy making themselves into a target for Pecheneg arrows. ... The Pechenegs on seeing a small group which advanced in formation and in battle order, made a violent sortie against them. ... retired when they saw it was impossible to disperse the Byzantines. ... They were unable to engage the Byzantines in hand-to-hand combat for having made a trial of close fighting, they had many times lost a great number of men.[107]

[106] AA, 330 implies that Godfrey was in command of the main force but this reflects his general prejudice in favour of his hero.

[107] Attaliates quoted by Kaegi, 'Archery' p. 103.

In any case, there was a limit to the losses the Turks were prepared to take. The loss of Nicaea was a blow to the Seljuk Kilij Arslan for like his father he aspired to be something more than a ruler of nomads – hence the acquisition of Nicaea as a capital and the effort to seize Antioch under Sulayman. But he was a lord of nomads and for them murderous casualties were simply not worthwhile before an enemy who could be evaded and whose departure would allow them to return to their pasture-lands. If Albert's figure of 3,000 is in any way to be believed they had suffered badly enough for their leader's ambitions. Only once again would they stand and fight – at Heraclea where an ambush was attempted and failed but it seems to have been so feeble that most of the sources do not mention it.[108] But if the Turks were now in no position to check the crusaders, they did not know that and Fulcher says that from this time the army proceeded very carefully, while Albert says they resolved not to break up again.[109] The Turks of Anatolia had been defeated, in so far as that means anything when speaking of a nomadic people who had clearly not been driven out of Asia Minor. Their ruling house had suffered a severe blow. They had lost a capital which gave them prestige, access and control over the emirates of western Asia Minor who were now at the mercy of the Byzantines. It opened the way, as we shall see, for a Byzantine reconquest in western Asia Minor. It was a stunning triumph for the crusaders for hitherto the onward march of the Turks had been unstoppable, as they themselves recognised for, as the Anonymous says, 'the Turks . . . thought that they would strike terror into the Franks, as they had done the Arabs and Saracens, Armenians, Syrians and Greeks by the menace of their arrows'.[110]

In part they had been defeated by luck. Kilij Arslan had mistaken the People's Crusade for the totality of the western effort and had to return from Melitene when they besieged Nicaea. His attack on the Provençals at Nicaea was mistimed, as was that against the vanguard near Bozüyük. But the victors made their own luck. It was their solid resistance that Kilij Arslan underestimated, hence their victory and his defeat. This rested on their manner of war in the west, which called for disciplined close-quarter fighting in which heavily armoured men played a key role. Ultimately, however, they differed from earlier enemies of the Turks by their motivation, their religious

---

[108] *GF*, p. 23; for the rest it is authors who follow him who mention it: Tudebode, p. 30; *HBS*, 184; RM, 767.
[109] FC, p. 87; AA, 333.   [110] *GF*, p. 21.

fanaticism which underpinned their fighting style. In the crisis of the battle at Dorylaeum that zeal showed in their password, 'Stand fast altogether, trusting in Christ and in the victory of the Holy Cross. Today, please God, you will all gain much booty'.[111] And so of course they did, and their spoils were much more than merely the pickings of the nomad camp. For the defeat at Dorylaeum seems to have sparked off revolts in some of the cities along the crusader line of march. The Anonymous says that as the Sultan fled he had to trick his way into the cities which his forces then looted. By contrast, the Christian army was welcomed in the vicinity of Iconium and this reception would become even warmer in the Armenian lands to the east. These were truly the fruits of victory, for as a later eastern source commented, 'The land was shaken before them.'[112]

Dorylaeum was a great Roman way-station and the key to the route system of the Anatolian plateau.[113] From there they had a choice of routes to Antioch (see fig. 2). From Dorylaeum ran the great military road through Ancyra to Sebasteia and the far frontiers, towards Lake Van and the Caucasus. At Ancyra the traveller could turn south to the 'Pilgrims' Road' to Tyana, the Cilician Gates and on to Antioch. This road forked east for Caeserea-in-Cappadocia, whence it led down to Comana, Germanicea Caeserea (Marasch) and thence to Antioch. It was along this road network that the Byzantine emperors had gathered the forces of the provinces on their way to the frontiers. They could have taken this route, which they would have known from earlier pilgrimage, direct from Nicaea; that they did not reflects serious political considerations. The Byzantines were, above all, interested in the south and west of Anatolia, and it can hardly be a coincidence that the route chosen facilitated the campaign by Alexius and his generals which would carry them to Philomelium by June of 1098.[114] However, there was a choice of routes south from Dorylaeum: the quickest lay via Pessinus (near modern Ballihisar), Archelais (modern Aksaray), Tyana (Kemerhisar, south-west of modern Nigde) and the Cilician Gates, but this would have taken the army across the arid heart of Anatolia with all the problems of watering

---

[111] *GF*, pp. 19–20.   [112] *GF*, pp. 23–4; Tritton, 'Anonymous Syriac Chronicler', p. 70.

[113] W. M. Ramsay, *The Historical Geography of Asia Minor*, Royal Geographical Society Supplementary Papers, 4 (London, 1890), pp. 212–13; K. Belke *et al.*, eds., *Tabula Imperii Byzantini*, 5 vols. (Vienna, 1977–84), 4. 94.

[114] On Alexius's campaign of 1098 see below pp. 299–302.

and the extremes of temperatures which we have noted. It was possible to fork south and east at Pessinus and descend via Philomelium (modern Akşehir) towards Iconium (modern Konya), or south and west via Amorium to the vicinity of modern Afyon. Another road ran due south via Nacolia (modern Seyitgazi) to join the route to Iconium just north of Afyon, while further west was another route via Cotiaeum (Kütahaya) to Afyon.[115] The sources are very vague about this early part of the journey: they all wrote long afterwards when the memory of hard marching had been eclipsed by much later doses of the same thing, and many more spectacular events. There is, however, some indication that they took the route via Nacolia. Albert of Aachen says that on the fourth day of their march, having suffered terrible thirst, they rested in the *Malabranias* valley, which cannot be certainly identified, where many died of drinking too much. Nacolia (Seyitgazi), on the river Seydi, is eighty kilometres from the battlefield of Dorylaeum, very roughly four days march, and could thus be *Malabranias* – though there could be no certainty. This tale of hardship and suffering is confirmed by Fulcher and the Anonymous who was very worried by the heavy loss of horses.[116] Here in high summer with temperatures around the 30° centigrade mark, the crusaders were crossing the Anatolian plateau; this is not flat land, but highly scenic, scarred by deep scarps and dry valleys, and almost waterless. It is a majestic, rather frightening landscape, and a harsh environment for a large force to traverse. Albert tells us that the army divided after a while, with Godfrey's brother, Baldwin, and Bohemond's nephew, Tancred, setting off on a different route from the main army. Baldwin took a difficult road into the valley of the *Orellis*, while Tancred went to Philomelium and thence to Iconium and Heraclea (modern Erégli), and the main

[115] Ramsay, *Historical Geography*, pp. 199–221. For an outline of the ancient and Roman roads of the area see W. M. Calder and G. E. Bean, *A Classical Map of Asia Minor* (London, 1959) and the useful map with Gazeteer in Vryonis, *Hellenism*, pp. 14–15 and the comments pp. 30–3; D. French, 'A study of Roman roads in Anatolia', *Anatolian Studies*, 24 (1974), 143–9, 'Roman road system in Asia Minor', *Aufstieg und Niedergang der Romischen Welt* 2. 7. 2 (1980), 698–729; *Roman Roads and Milestones of Asia Minor, Fasc. 2: An Interim Collection of Milestones, Pts. 1–2*, British Institute of Archaeology at Ankara, Monograph 9, British Archaeological Reports International Series 392 (i) and (ii) (Oxford, 1988), p. 540 and map, *The Pilgrims' Road*, especially p. 130 and map; Belke, *Tabula Imperii Byzantini*, 2. 32.

[116] FC, p. 87; GF, p. 23. It is possible that the valley of *Malabranias* is that of the Porsuk near Kütahya (ancient Cotiaeum) which is about four days march south of Eskişehir (Dorylaeum) for this, I am fairly certain, is the route they took.

army proceeded to Antioch-in-Pisidia (Antiochetta, now modern Yalvaç) which lies to the south of the Sultan Daglari. At this point, however, Albert's account is at its worst. Antiochetta is described as being next to Heraclea, which is listed on Tancred's journey as coming before Iconium. Moreover, there is no further mention of the journey of the main army until it reaches Marasch, presumably because Albert's informants were with Baldwin on his diversions to Cilicia and Edessa. Fulcher confirms that the army went to Antiochetta, but offers no information on the route taken.[117] In fact the army could have taken any of the routes from Dorylaeum. However, no source describes anything remotely resembling the crossing of the Sultan Daglari mountain range which rises suddenly and sharply out of the steppe to over 2,600 metres; the accounts of suffering reflect the passage across the dry steppe, not that over a formidable mountain barrier. Therefore, the likelihood is that they took a western route, probably via Nacolia approaching Antioch-in-Pisidia roughly via the modern Afyon and passing to the south of the Sultan Daglari via their western foothills, which are relatively gentle (see fig. 2). Tancred and Baldwin probably left the main army in the vicinity of Afyon and pushed along the more direct route to Iconium north of the Sultan Daglari via Philomelium, presumably watching for enemy attack; perhaps one took the road via the ancient Hadrianopolis (south-east of Akşehir) and the other that through Laodicea (modern village of Halici, east of Akşehir).

The really interesting question is why the army went to Antioch-in-Pisidia at all, for the road from Dorylaeum via Polybotus (modern Bolvadin) and Philomelium (modern Akşehir) to Iconium is shorter (by at least three days march) and more direct. Albert attributes the splitting of the army to the needs for supply. He and Fulcher stress that Pisidia was a fertile and pleasant land, where the army enjoyed a brief rest and Godfrey was injured by a bear while out hunting. After his account of the hardships and want on the dry steppe the Anonymous mentions a 'fertile country, full of good and delicious things to eat' which may well be Pisidia.[118] Indeed, Pisidia is a fertile rolling country, a great contrast with the steppe to the north of the Sultan Daglari, and this must have been a real consideration in planning the route of the army. At the same time, the Anonymous indicates that the populations of the cities of Asia Minor

[117] AA, 341–2; FC, pp. 87–8; *GF*, p. 23.   [118] FC, p. 87; AA, 341–2.

rose against the Turks and that, for the Byzantines, Antioch, the chief city of Pisidia, was a desirable prize. The foraging needs of the army, together with the cooperation with Byzantium, probably combined to draw the army along this route. Hagenmeyer suggests that they left Antioch about 5 August, arriving at Iconium on 15 August, a rate of march of about twelve to thirteen kilometres per day through this relatively flat country, though the last forty kilometres into Iconium pass through harsh and waterless hills.

Tancred and Baldwin seem to have rejoined the main army at Iconium which the Turks made no effort to defend, although its Byzantine defences were probably still intact. The local population welcomed the crusader army and advised them to carry much water because the land to the east was dry. The road to Heraclea passes over a featureless plain, probably then something of a salt desert, but now brought back to life by irrigation. We do not know which of three possible routes they took from Iconium to Heraclea, which vary in distance between 140 and 170 kilometres for the only clue is that they spent two days resting at a river after two days march eastwards. This must refer to the Çarasamba which, however, cuts all the routes, but there is no reason to believe that they did not take the shortest route.[119] At Heraclea the Turkish garrison attempted to

[119] Even if they took the longest route, however, and allowing for delay as they heard of the enemy forces, Hagenmeyer's chronology of this part of the journey is surely wrong. He suggests that after a two day march they arrived at the Çarasamba on the 20 August where they rested for two days, then arrived at Heraclea about 10 September. This means a march of between 140 and 170 kilometres over a period of twenty-one days. A daily march rate of seven or eight kilometres per day over these flat lands seems unduly slow. By contrast, Hagenmeyer suggests that the army left Heraclea about 14 September and reached Caeserea-in-Cappadocia (modern Kayseri) on 27 September, a daily rate of seventeen kilometres up into the mountains. We can never be precisely certain of any dates other than 4 July for the departure from the field of Doylaeum and 20 October for the arrival at the Iron Bridge outside Antioch. I would suggest, however, that they must surely have reached Heraclea by the end of August but that we must allow for a slower rate of march in the mountains. All such dates must be approximate but I suggest:

(C) = Hagenmeyer's dates

Heraclea 31 August. (10 Sept)

Heraclea–Caeserea: 240 km
4–21 September, eighteen days march at 13/14 km per day
(14–27 September, 14 days march at 17 km per day)

Caeserea–Comana: 86 km
24–30 September, seven days march at 12 km per day
(end September–3 October, four days march at 21 km per day)

ambush them but their scouts had warned them and the enemy were brushed aside easily and the city captured.[120] The army rested there for four days. They now faced a very important choice of route, for east of Heraclea lay the Taurus mountains, in a great arc from south-west to north-east, dividing Anatolia from Syria. They could either journey south-east on the 'Pilgrim Road' via the Cilician Gates, Tarsus, Adana and Alexandretta (Iskenderun) to Antioch which was the more direct route, or they could take the road to Caeserea-in-Cappadocia (Kayseri) across the Taurus and down via Coxon (Göksun) and Marasch (Kahramanmaraş). The difference between these two routes was considerable: Heraclea to Antioch via the Cilician Gates is a journey of some 350 kilometres, but via Caeserea over 630 kilometres. It was extraordinary that they chose the latter route for the main army, while dispatching Tancred and Baldwin into Cilicia. Why was this strange choice made?

It needs to be stressed how difficult travelling overland was in this period. Although the road system of Asia Minor was basically that of the Romans, it is unlikely that the roads were in good condition after thirty years of political chaos and then Turkish domination.[121] Though sometimes the journey was relatively easy there were other occasions, as in the pass south of Göksun, when every step was a calvary. For most of the time it must have been simply very unpleasant and dangerous, even without considering the possibility of enemy attack. The death of horses and pack animals must have been appalling and militarily disastrous; just after Dorylaeum, we hear of knights mounted on oxen, their horses

Comana–Göksun: 55 km
1–4 October, four days march at 12/13 km per day
(4–6 October, three days march at 17 km per day)

Göksun–Marasch: 80 km
7–14 October, eight days march at 10 km per day
(8–13 October, six days march at 13 km per day)

Marasch–Iron Bridge: 150 km
15–20 October, six days march at 25 km per day
(14–20 October, seven days march at 20 + km per day)

This dating tries to take account of geographical differences. It is acknowledged that distances and dates can only be approximate.

[120] *GF*, p. 23.
[121] French, 'Roman road system', 713, points to the lack of evidence about maintenance in the Byzantine period.

having perished on the dry steppe.[122] Only the strongest of motives could have led the army to march northwards to Caeserea, deliberately ignoring a much shorter route. Historians have been strangely slow to grasp the scale and importance of the diversion via Caeserea. It has been suggested that the narrowness of the famous Cilician Gates – only twenty-five metres at one point, and the hostile climate of Cilicia explain the decision. However, although the road to Caeserea is less abrupt than that over the Cilician Gates, the long sustained climb (Caeserea is at 1,254 metres) would have been sapping, while the road down to Marasch offers going every bit as difficult and narrow as either the Cilician Gates or the Belen pass from Cilicia to Antioch over the Ammanus Mountains, often called the 'Syrian Gates'. Further the road rises to a maximum of over 1,700 metres, while the Cilician Gates never rise above 1,000 metres. The real military risk of the direct route was that the garrison of Antioch might challenge their crossing of the Belen Pass but from their perspective at Heraclea there were unknown risks of a similar kind facing them in the mountains. Moreover, the season was quite advanced and, while the army was now hardened, the loss of animals must have slowed it down. This opened the risk of being caught by the snows which can come as early as October in the high passes, for the road to which they were committed rises to 1,700 metres.

It is likely that what we see is the development of an Armenian strategy which had been discussed with Alexius, either at Constantinople or at Pelekanum after the fall of Nicaea.[123] As the Crusade advanced many of the cities in their path ejected their Turkish garrison and welcomed the crusaders. In addition, they had contact with Armenians as we have noted and, at Iconium, Christians gave them intelligence about local conditions. The Christian population of Asia Minor had suffered badly at the hands of the nomadic Turks, whose violent and arbitrary dominion was resented. Raymond of Aguilers knew that Antioch had only fallen to the Turks some fourteen years before, and he catalogues the sufferings of

[122] FC, p. 88.
[123] C. Cahen, La Syrie du nord à l'époque des croisades (Paris, 1940) pp. 209–10 was much struck by the 'vaste détour' which the army took to reach Caeserea-in-Cappadocia and thought it was the result of an 'intérêt essentiellement byzantin' to seize this area which controlled routes to north and east. The point made here is that at this stage Byzantine and Crusader interests were very close and, perhaps for different reasons, favoured this course of action. See above p. 187; GF, p. 23.

its Christian people.[124] When the Emperor Alexius retreated from Philomelium, about 20 June 1098, most of the local population chose to leave with him rather than again face their Turkish masters.[125] In a passage which has received surprisingly little attention, Stephen of Blois says that in Cappadocia the army directed its march against a powerful local emir, Hasan, who is probably more correctly called Baldajii. His brother, Abu'l-Qasim, had ruled at Nicaea after the death of Sulayman, whose son Kilij Arslan was held captive by Malik Shah (1086–92). Hasan himself briefly held power at Nicaea after his brother, but Kilij Arslan escaped from prison on the death of Malik Shah in 1092 and resumed power at Nicaea.[126] The crusaders, therefore, were prepared to confront real opposition in pursuit of what we may call their Armenian strategy, and they drove into his lands as they advanced towards Caeserea and then turned south to Antioch.

The long uphill march took the army past the area of modern Nigde over a series of dramatic scarps into wide upland plains, often watered by great lakes. Towards Caeserea they captured a strong place which was given to Simeon, a local man whose presence in the army points to forethought. Beyond Caeserea, which they reached about 21 and left about 24 September, they travelled through steep and broken country for some eighty-six kilometres to a city which had held out for three weeks against Turkish siege; there Peter d'Aups, a westerner in the service of Alexius, was given control (see fig. 2 and 4). This place has been identified as 'Plastencia', on the authority of Bauldry of Dol, and recent research identifies the Greek place of that name with Elbistan, a city well off the crusaders' path to the east on the road to Melitene. The likelihood is that this was Comana where the army seems to have arrived about 30 September.[127] The army left Bohemond to pursue the besiegers of Comana and went on to Coxon (Göksun) on 4 October, which the local Christians promptly surrendered to them. There a false rumour that

---

[124] RA, p. 64.   [125] Vryonis, *Hellenism*, pp. 194–223; *Alexiad*, pp. 349–50.

[126] Hagenmeyer, *Kreuzzugsbriefe*, p. 150; Cahen, *Turkey*, pp. 78–80.

[127] Hagenmeyer, *Chronologie*, 188, pp. 97–8 suggested Comana but the most recent edition of the *Gesta*, p. 25 follows BD, 39; for Elbistan see Belke, *Tabula Imperii Byzantini*, 2. 109–10. Dr David French thinks that 'Plastencia' may be somebody's recollection of, quite literally, 'a pleasant place' whose name he had forgotten, transformed by Bauldry into a proper name. The case for Comana is that there was certainly a city there on the route and it is difficult to see where else could be intended. For the probable line of the road to Comana see French, *Roman Roads and Milestones of Asia Minor*, Fasc. 2. Pt. 2, p. 550 and map.

the enemy were deserting Antioch led Raymond of Toulouse to send a force of 500 knights, under Peter of Castillon, to seize the city; at a settlement of heretic Christians near to Antioch they were informed that the rumour was false whereupon some of them under the command of Peter de Roaix, went on to establish a Provençal base in the valley of Ruj, parallel to the Orontes valley on the eastern side of that river. Rugia was about seven kilometres from Rusa to the south of Antioch.[128] The main army followed along down the bitter and painful pass near what is now called the Püren Geçidi, which rises to 1,630 metres, the downward slope of which is a penance even in modern transport. The Anonymous records that horses and animals died in falls and knights sold off their arms at any price rather than carry them across this 'damnable mountain'.

At Marasch the Turkish garrison had fled and the army was welcomed by its Armenian ruler, Tatoul, who, as a supporter of Alexius, continued to hold the place.[129] The army had now emerged from the mountain passes and stood at the head of a great flat valley, the Amouk, which stretches down to Antioch and the coast beyond, between the Ammanus range to the west and the Kartal Daglari range to the east on the edge of Syria. The success of their Armenian strategy had delivered the mountain cities over to them, and now the army was able to set out on the last leg of the journey down the Amouk. But before they set out, local inhabitants told the leaders that 'Artāh, which the crusader sources call Artasia, would welcome them but had a strong Turkish garrison. The leaders sent Robert of Flanders ahead with 1,000 knights, on whose arrival the Armenian population butchered the Turkish garrison and opened the gates. Ralph of Caen suggests that Baldwin and Tancred commanded this expedition and never mentions Robert, but his account confirms that of Albert in its main outlines. Once the Franks were installed they were besieged by a force which Albert numbers at 20,000. They provided a lesson in tactics for the crusaders. A small number of lightly armed Turkish horsemen trailed their coats outside the walls and when a lot of Franks, foot and horse, rushed out they fled

---

[128] *GF*, pp. 25–7; R. Dussaud, *Topographie Historique de la Syrie Antique et Médiévale* (Paris, 1927), pp. 163–7 identifies this area, and points out that as the Antiochenes held the Iron Bridge over the Orontes (on which see below pp. 206–8) that it must have been to the east of that river. As RA, p. 99, makes it clear that Rugia was relatively close to Albara and Ma'arra which can be identified, this is almost certainly correct. On the importance of this acquisition see below p. 224.

[129] AA, 136–7; Boase, *Armenia*, p. 4.

drawing their enemies into an ambush which cut them off from the city. Robert of Flanders rescued them by a charge from the city, but Christian losses in men and horses were heavy. Ralph of Caen also tells us that many Franks were lured out of the city and suffered heavy losses in close-quarter combat with the Turks. The survivors retreated into the city where the depleted garrison now had to face a close siege. The siege was lifted with the arrival of 1,500 reinforcements and the city was given a Frankish garrison, which Ralph says was in the control of Baldwin. The bitter fight underlines the importance of 'Artāh to the crusaders and the fact that it later changed hands, for it was captured by Kerbogah, strengthens the point.[130] From this it would appear that the main army had marched down the Amouk until it was just north of the great lake to the north of Antioch. There the road forked; to the west it passed the Belen Pass and arrived before the Bridge Gate on the west side of Antioch. The eastern fork led the army to 'Artāh, which Ralph of Caen would later describe as the 'shield of Antioch'.[131] It stood close to the modern Reyhanli across the road to 'Azāz, and just north of its junction with the Antioch-Aleppo road to the east of the Iron Bridge, which controlled the crossing of the Orontes to the north of Antioch. The capture of 'Artāh helped to secure the eastern approaches to Antioch as a prelude to a siege, thus isolating the city from its obvious source of support. The Armenian strategy provided a friendly hinterland and a springboard for this isolation of Antioch, which was increased by the expedition of Tancred and Baldwin to Cilicia. Albert emphasises that all this was done with the agreement and consent of the leaders of the army and this must include the Byzantine representative, Tatikios, whose man took over Comana and, presumably, at least some of the other cities. This was much more than mere individual opportunism, the reason usually given for the expedition to Cilicia.

Tancred and Baldwin of Boulogne's expedition to Cilicia is very well known and has generally been treated as a private enterprise affair (see fig. 2).[132] The sources are often not very informative on how it came about. Raymond of Aguilers never discusses this event, perhaps because the Provençals were not involved; Fulcher was

---

[130] AA, 358–61; RC, 639–41.   [131] RC, 712.
[132] This is the clear implication of Runciman 1. 197. Mayer, *The Crusades*, p. 48 remarks: 'The two of them were almost certainly seeking their own personal gain', while Riley-Smith, *Idea of Crusading*, p. 58, speaks of the two men breaking away from the main force.

much more concerned about the expedition to Edessa, in which he participated, and says that Baldwin took his own men into Cilicia, while the Anonymous, as so often, simply reports the events without explanation. Ralph of Caen, who likes to present Tancred as an emerging leader, tells us that Tancred chose to undertake this expedition.[133] Albert of Aix reports that, probably in the region of Afyon, Tancred and Baldwin were sent along the northern road to Iconium, but that Tancred was ahead after Heraclea and went down to the coast through Cilicia, leaving Baldwin who got somewhat lost following behind.[134] This presents events in a different light and it should be noted that each of these young men seems to have had substantial forces at his disposal. When they came to blows at Mamistra Tancred attacked with 500 men but was defeated by the larger force of Baldwin. Earlier, at Tarsus, Tancred had been reinforced by 300 men from Bohemond, and in the quarrel over this city both young men claimed that they were acting in the name of their superiors, Bohemond or Godfrey, in passages which smack of the 'my big brother is bigger than yours' syndrome.[135] The impression is of an expedition in which the ardour and greed of two young men got out of hand. It is interesting that friendly locals once more appear in a notable role. Tancred had with him an Armenian whom he had known earlier and it was perhaps this influence, and their fear of Bohemond, that led the Armenian population of Tarsus to prefer his rule – though they eventually submitted to Baldwin.[136] At Adana Tancred found a city already half-liberated by the local Armenian prince Oschin and partly occupied by a Burgundian, Welf; given Oschin's good relations with Alexius it would seem likely that Welf was another westerner in imperial service.[137] At the end of the Cilician adventure Baldwin was persuaded by Bagrat, an Armenian whom he had got to know at Nicaea and who was the lord of Ravendan, to strike east into the Armenian territories towards Edessa to Tell-Bashir, but we know from Fulcher that he first returned to the main army.[138] Baldwin then became embroiled in the complex politics of the Armenian princes and in February of

---

[133] FC, p. 89; *GF*, pp. 24–5; RC, p. 629.   [134] AA, 340–2.

[135] AA, 349–50, 347, 343–5.

[136] AA, 342; E. A. Hanawalt, 'Norman views of eastern Christendom: from the First Crusade to the Principality of Antioch', in V. Goss and C. C. Bornstein, *The Meeting of Two Worlds* (Michigan, 1986), pp. 115–21, stresses Tancred's pragmatic attitude to Eastern Christians.

[137] RC, 634; AA, 345.   [138] FC, p. 89.

1098 received a request from Thoros, the Armenian ruler of Edessa, to go to that city which after many adventures he reached on 20 February.[139] By 8 March 1098 Baldwin had intrigued with disaffected citizens to overthrow Thoros and was in effective control of the city.[140] Local Christians, as we have already noted, delivered over many key cities as far south as Ruj to the Franks and this is corroborated by the *Damascus Chronicle* which specifically mentions the fighting at 'Artāh.[141] It was no wonder that Anselm of Ribemont would boast in a letter to the west that the army held 200 forts and cities, while Stephen put the figure at 160.[142] This should be seen as the fruits of a deliberate policy of which the Cilician expedition was a part.

At Heraclea, or shortly thereafter, the princes must have decided to implement their Armenian strategy which probably aimed to reproduce the principality which Philaretus had ruled in the years before 1085, elements of which (such as Edessa) remained independent and in some sense attached to the empire. Gabriel of Melitene seems to have held aloof from the crusade. The idea of creating such a liberated zone was probably developed in discussions with Alexius – Tatikios was his man on the crusade and he seems to have aided and abetted the process – but it was made possible by the success at Dorylaeum and the reaction of the native population to it. After Heraclea the leaders decided to capitalise on their success and launched the main army into a long diversion over very difficult territory, driving back the forces of Hasan. Into the more sheltered area of Cilicia a small force led by Tancred and Baldwin was dispatched. It was a risk, but one which succeeded handsomely. The establishment of a great bastion of Byzantine power on the Syrian border was welcome to both Alexius and the crusader leaders. It would enable the Byzantines to conquer southern Asia Minor. For the crusaders liberation of the persecuted Christians of the east was one of the objectives of their journey. Furthermore, such a Byzantine bulwark would provide a secure base for the real objective of their

---

[139] FC, pp. 90–1; AA, 352–3; on Edessa see M. Amouroux-Mourad, *Le Comté d'Edesse 1098–1150* (Paris, 1988) Chap. 1, 'Fondation et Evolution du comté d'Edesse 1098–1150', pp. 57–91; J. Laurent, 'Des Grecs aux croisés; étude sur l'histoire d'Edesse 1071–98', *Byzantion*, 1 (1924), 347–449. Tritton, 'Anonymous Syriac Chronicle', p. 70, says that Baldwin was sent by Godfrey who had been asked for help by Thoros.

[140] Matthew, 37; Fulcher alone of the contemporary sources tries to pretend that Baldwin was not a party to the plot, pp. 91–2, and WT, 158–9 follows him; AA, 354–5.

[141] *Damascus Chronicle of the Crusades*, pp. 42–3.   [142] See above p. 133 n. 35.

endeavour – Jerusalem. We have to remember that they had come for Jerusalem, for Palestine, not Antioch or some North Syrian domination. It is a point which the mass of the army would make forcibly to its leaders in the later months of 1098.[143] As things turned out this plan was never properly realised. Its central assumption was a common interest between the Byzantine empire and the crusaders; the stress of events undermined this. Even so, despite a heavy price in garrison troops detached from their force the conquests paid off handsomely for the First Crusade. Food, useful intelligence and supplies reached the crusade from the Armenians whose merchants frequently visited the city and Armenians helped in the routing of Turkish forces and the slaying of Yaghisiyan.[144] The possession of so many bases in the general area of Antioch, the old dominion of Philaretus, gave the crusade a much needed platform for their assault on Antioch. Baldwin's possession of Edessa enabled him to send aid and supplies to the army at Antioch. It was also a powerful distraction for local Islamic leaders. In May 1098 this factor caused Kerbogah to divert his huge relief army for a three-week siege, which was fatal for his chances of success against Antioch.[145] Militarily, the policy was a striking success and the choice made on the road from Heraclea proved to be a correct one, dangerous though it must have appeared. It enabled the crusaders to confront their second enemy, the Turks of Syria, with a considerable territorial base and much assistance which was extremely valuable.

[143] See above, pp. 1–25 and below, pp. 310–11.
[144] Matthew, 33; GF, 33, 37, 70, 48.
[145] See below, pp. 261–2.

CHAPTER 7

The second enemy: the siege of Antioch

At Antioch the army of the First Crusade had arrived in the fractured borderlands of Islam – an area of acute political fragmentation where small political units proliferated. It is tempting to consider the victory an inevitable triumph of the unified and zealous crusaders over a disunited and poorly prepared Islam. It is true that some of the Islamic powers took little notice of the crusade and continued with their internecine conflicts. To later generations of Muslim writers, raised on the spirit of Holy War, this was shameful, but at the time it was to be expected because of political circumstances. However, too much scorn should not be poured on the Islamic powers of North Syria.[1] The major cities of the area were a firm underpinning for its defence; the siege of Antioch would last nine months. Three major battles would be fought in efforts to lift the crusader siege and there were innumerable minor ones. For the crusaders it was a terrible struggle, a military epic indeed, the success of which was a more than adequate demonstration that their journey was the work of God.[2] Political fragmentation in this area was real, but even so military resistance was considerable (see fig. 3).

North Syria lay far from Constantinople and it was not until the crusade was approaching Antioch that its ruler, Yaghisiyan, began to realise that his position was at stake. He has been appointed by Malik Shah to rule Antioch and a substantial part of the former lands of Philaretus in 1086–7 in what amounted to a check to the Shah's brother, Tutush, who held Damascus and Jerusalem. With

---

[1] 'Thus the princelings of Syria, when the crusaders arrived, had for making war only the handful of slaves which the revenues from their meager provinces enabled them to buy.': Cahen, 'The Turkish invasion', 165.

[2] On this theme of God's delivery of the army see especially Blake, 'The formation of the Crusade Idea', 11–31, and the further discussion in Riley-Smith, *Idea of Crusading*, pp. 91–119.

the death of Tutush in the war for the Sultanate against his nephew Berkyaruk (1094–1105), in 1095 his sons became rivals for power; Ridwan at Aleppo, where Tutush's vizir Ibn-Badi held much power but was soon replaced by Janah-al-Dawlah, and Duqaq at Damascus, where the emir Sawitakin was at first influential. Ridwan of Aleppo (1095–1113) and Duqaq of Damascus (1095–1104) met in the battle of Qinnisrin on 22 March 1097 when victory for the former brought his restless governor of Antioch to heel, but Ridwan's restless atabeg Janah-ad-Daulah was able to hold Homs against him. In this context Ridwan made an alliance of convenience with Fatimid Egypt which initiated his pro-Shi'ite policies.[3] This process of fragmentation was greatly facilitated because Berkyaruk was deeply preoccupied with events in the east, and he relied on Kerbogah, atabeg of Mosul to watch events in the west.[4] It was the preoccupation of the Seljuk Sultan, and his failure to dominate Syria, that gave free rein to the divisions which were endemic there. Kurds, Turks, Circassians, Arabs, Bedouin, all were very different peoples who were in no sense united by Islam, and they ruled over or alongside Armenian and Syrian Christians who were very numerous. And the land itself, with stretches of desert between fertile zones around major cities, favoured these divisions. The Great Seljuks had never succeeded in attaching Anatolia to their dominion despite the relative weakness of its divided Turkish clans, but they had imposed a precarious stability in Syria until the death of Tutush. The position of Ridwan of Aleppo, a Sunnite in a zone with a large Shi'ite population who negotiated with the Fatimids against his brother Duqaq and later allied with the Assassins, is indicative of the political complexities of the area.[5] At the time of the arrival of the crusaders, he and Yaghisiyan were in alliance with Sokman of Diyār-Bakr, who, with his brother Il-Ghazi (the Artukids, the sons of Artuk who died in 1091) also, ruled Jerusalem as vassals of Duqaq of Damascus, against Abou'n Nedjim of Homs. Yaghisiyan promptly returned to Antioch, alienating both his allies, and set about expelling many Christians from Antioch and prepar-

[3] R. W. Crawford, 'Ridwan the maligned', in J. Kritzeck and R. Bagley-Winder, eds. *Studies in Honour of P.K., Hitti* (London, 1959), pp. 135–9.
[4] Cahen, 'The Turkish invasion', 152, 165–7.
[5] B. Lewis, 'The Isma'ilites and the Assassins', in K. Setton and M. W. Baldwin, eds., *A History of the Crusades*, I. 111; Crawford, 'Ridwan the maligned', 135–44 sees his policy purely in political terms. On his relations with the Fatimids see Köhler, *Allianzen und Verträge*, p. 58.

ing its defence. The Orthodox Patriarch of the city was imprisoned, though not all his flock were driven out.[6] He was too weak on his own to take action against the approaching Franks and soon found it prudent to send one son, Shams-ad-Daulah, to appeal for help to Duqaq and another, Muhammed, to the Turks of Anatolia and to Kerbogah of Mosul. It is interesting to note that at the time the crusaders were aware of this, for in a letter written just after Easter 1098 Stephen of Blois comments on Shams-ad-Daulah's diplomatic efforts.[7] This was a fairly comprehensive diplomatic effort, for the other powers of Syria were not much interested. Shams-ad-Daulah would abandon Damascus for Ridwan only when Duqaq had been defeated by the crusaders in December 1097, but he seems to have ignored the other powers of the area. The Banū-Munqidh of Shaizar were an Arab dynasty with no affection for Turks and no leaning towards Jihad. The founder of their greatness, Abu el-Hasan 'Ali ben Munqidh, claimed that he persuaded rather than coerced the Byzantine population of Shaizar into accepting his rule, even 'permitting their pigs to graze with my flocks.'[8] The Banū-'Ammār ruled an independent principality based on Tripoli which was Shi'ite. Duqaq ruled at Damascus with the support of his great minister, Tughtigin, while Janah ad-Daulah, atabeg of Homs, was no friend of his former master Ridwan and much concerned to pursue his vendetta with Yousuf ben-Abiks, lord of Marbij. In the north, Balduk of Samosata was deeply concerned with Baldwin and his encroachments in Edessa.[9] Undoubtedly, in the normal course of events a dominant force would have emerged in the area, but at the very moment when the crusade appeared there was nobody, and the result was a critical delay which allowed the crusaders to establish their siege at Antioch and to strengthen their hold on the surrounding countryside, which rebelled against Yaghisiyan's tyranny as soon as the Franks appeared.[10] It was, however, only a delay, for relief was attempted and for the moment Antioch was strongly defended by its geographic situation and its formidable walls. Although most modern writers stress that the crusade was unexpec-

---

[6] *HBS*, 186.

[7] Kemal ad-Din, *Chronicle of Aleppo, RHC Or.* 3. [herafter cited as *Aleppo Chronicle*], 577–8; Hagenmeyer, *Kreuzzugsbriefe*, pp. 150–2.

[8] Sivan, *L'Islam et la Croisade*, p. 18.

[9] Cahen, Setton, *Crusades*, pp. 165, 322; *Aleppo Chronicle*, 579; Holt, *Age of the Crusades*, p. 26.

[10] *Aleppo Chronicle*, 577.

ted and that its nature was misunderstood, the nearby Islamic powers did mobilise substantial forces and showed considerable determination to resist this new enemy.

At the start of his account of the siege of Antioch Raymond of Aguilers tells us about the garrison of the city, 'There were, further-more, in the city two thousand of the best knights, and four or five thousand common knights and ten thousand and more footmen'.[11] There is no need to suppose that these figures are accurate but, though his terminology is vague, Raymond here confirms what we have already noted, that the crusaders understood the composite nature of the forces they were now facing. The model of state organisation in the Islamic world was the Caliphate, although the Caliphs themselves since the ninth century had been excluded from effective power at Baghdad by the rise of major groups and factions at the court, of which the Seljuks, after 1055, were only the latest. The Islamic world was literate and sophisticated, and the régimes at Baghdad under the Abbassids controlled a number of specialist offices which amounted to ministries, Diwans, whose efforts were controlled and co-ordinated by a Vizir. Under the Seljuks the Vizir Nizam-al-Mulk (died 1092) and his family, who were of Iranian origin, dominated the machinery of government.[12] But the vital importance of the army meant that the office of the army, the Diwan al-Jaysh headed by the Arid al-Jaysh, was a central force which spawned subordinate offices such as those which looked after mer-cenaries and māmluks. The connection between war and finance was patent and much commented upon.[13] The importance of this office was enhanced by its control of the 'Iqta. These were originally quite small grants of the right to gather state incomes with modest tax-exemptions, made for the maintenance of soldiers and used for that of tribal elements associated with the holders of power at Baghdad. However, the need to maintain groups of Turkish soldiers and the tendency of all régimes, culminating in that of the Seljuks, to unify military and civil authority, meant that governorships of important provinces and cities, like Antioch, were held as 'Iqta, the holder in his turn letting out 'Iqta to the troops of his command, who thus became tied to him. In the more fluid society of the Near East, with a flourishing money economy, the 'Iqta never became terri-

---

[11] RA, p. 48; Krey, *The First Crusade*, p. 127.   [12] Cahen, 'The Turkish invasion', 153-4.
[13] Ibn Khaldun, pp. 198–201 expounds upon this.

torial, as did the fief or honour in Europe, and political instability and changes of régime tended to prevent 'Iqta becoming hereditary.[14] Cash payment to professional troops continued to be an important element in their pay, and the complex diversity of the machinery controlled by the Vizirs under the power of the Shah administered a relatively complex army. Nizam al-Mulk (*c.*1018–92) had been in the administration of the Ghaznavids before he served Alp Arslan and Malik Shah, until his assassination in 1092. In his *Book of government* he demanded that the wise king should pay careful attention to the regular payment of proper wages to soldiers, and he relates an occasion when a ruler needed to conciliate the local population and executed a soldier for pillaging, justifying the act by reference to his regular pay, *bistgani*.[15] The Seljuk Sultans were as anxious as any of their predecessors to reduce their dependence upon their tribal supporters, the Turks whose courage and skill had raised them up, a general point noted by Ibn-Khaldûn.[16] The machinery which they found in Baghdad from 1055 enabled them to do this, and Nizam al-Mulk emphasises the need for a composite army selected from appropriate races in the tradition of the Caliphate, though it is interesting that he appears to acknowledge the supremacy of cavalry. The heart of the military system were slave-soldiers who were often Turks, the *māmluks*, who formed the guard of the Sultan (and indeed of the Caliph). Since the ninth century these Turkish troops had been replacing Iranians as the élite force and many of their commanders had come to hold important offices of state.[17] The Seljuks preferred to recruit from their own people into such formations, which were far more disciplined and loyal under the eye of the ruler, and it was clearly politic to give large numbers of them honorific and highly visible positions at court, such as the 1,000 of their sons enrolled as pages. They received careful military and other training, intended to inculcate loyalty and a spirit of service. The Seljuk Sultans brought leading families from the Turkish tribes into their service; we have noted the example of Artuk who was employed by Malik Shah in Bahrain and

---

[14] On the iqtâ' see C. Cahen, 'Contribution à l'histoire de l'iqtâ', *Annales: économies, sociétés, civilisations,* 8 (1953), 25–52 and 'The Turkish invasion', 153–60; Bosworth, 'Recruitment, muster and review', pp. 59–77; R. C. Smail, *Crusading Warfare (1097–1193)* (Cambridge, 1956), pp. 65–6.

[15] Nizam al-Mulk, *Traité de gouvernement composé pour le Sultan Malik Shah,* ed. C. Schefer, 2 vols (Paris, 1892–3) [hereafter cited as al-Mulk], vol. 1. 99, 113–14.

[16] ibn-Khaldun, pp. 146–7.   [17] al-Mulk, 1. 100–1; On the Turks see above pp. 145, 149.

Mesopotamia and, finally, by Tutush in Jerusalem. Such notables could play a major role as special troops in Islamic armies.[18] By such methods, the Turkish tribes were either domesticated or encouraged to move out of the settled heart of Islam – especially to the Byzantine frontier where they could expend their warlike energies and form a reservoir of military talent. However, substantial Turkish tribal forces were maintained by the Caliphs and by their quasi-feudal governors like Yaghisiyan on 'Iqta and represented the élite element in their forces. It was these māmluks who formed the core of the personal followings, the 'Askars, of the princelings and emirs of Syria. Overall, the military potential of the Sultan, ruling over all of Syria, Mesopotamia, Iran and the eastern realms and able to call on allies elsewhere, was enormous when the Seljuks were at their greatest. This was made possible by the administration in Baghdad and there is some evidence of a systematic infrastructure. Local government was required to keep stocks of fodder, as Nizam al-Mulk indicates, and it is probable that under Malik Shah central government tried to retain parcels of land in the provinces for its provision. Huge numbers of troops are sometimes mentioned – 46,000, even 70,000 horsemen alone, though Nizam al-Mulk suggests smaller numbers between 10,000 and 25,000.[19] In 1086 Anna Comnena says that Bursuk advanced into Asia Minor on the orders of Malik Shah with 50,000 men, which must surely be an exaggeration. In 1071, Romanus IV's army at Manzikert was numbered at 300,000 by the Moslem sources which show that he reduced his effectives by dispersing effort and engaged in battle with only 100,000, but even this figure is excessive, while the mere 14,000 attributed to Alp Arslan seems rather small.[20] At the time of the First Crusade a maximum all-out effort by the Fatimid Caliphate could raise only an army of 15,000, and that seems to have been the case for some time.[21] It is almost certain that the Seljuks under Malik Shah were much stronger than their Egyptian enemies, but the princelings of Syria were individually weaker. However, Kemal ad-Din, although he gives a figure of 320,000 for the whole crusader army and implies

[18] al–Mulk, 1. 102, 103–4, 111; see above p. 198 and Cahen, 'The Turkish invasion', 158.

[19] al–Mulk 1. 98; Muhammad ben Ali ben Sulaiman Ravandi, *Rabat al-sudur wa ayatal surur*, ed. M. Iqtal (Leiden and London, 1921) [hereafter cited as Ravandi], p. 131 – I owe this reference to Professor A. K. S. Lambton.

[20] *Alexiad*, p. 206; Cahen, *Turkey*, pp. 79–80, 'The Turkish invasion', p. 168, 'La campagne de Mantzikert', 629–31. On the numbers at this battle see above pp. 152–3.

[21] See below pp. 359–60.

that their force of 30,000 was defeated by an inferior number of the army of Damascus on 30 December 1097 (the Foraging Battle), tells us that the army of Ridwan of Aleppo defeated in February at the Lake Battle was larger than the crusader force. His emphasis on division in the army of Kerbogah as a cause for its defeat implies its numerical superiority over the Franks as does Ibn al-Qalanisi's remark that, at the time of Kerbogah's relief force, the armies of Islam 'were at the height of their strength and numbers'.[22] We need not think of the powers of Syria as being helpless before the crusaders. The 'Askar of Yaghisiyan, Ridwan or Duqaq might be limited, but in the face of a perceived threat it could be augmented by recruiting a composite force and making allies. This process involved a policy of conciliation and co-operation which would naturally be complex and, above all, slow. No effort was made to strike at the Franks as they approached Antioch, although Kemal ed-Din says that 'Artāh sought reinforcements, presumably from Aleppo.[23] Of all the local powers Sokman of the Artukids had by far the most consistent record, for he fought with Ridwan and Kerbogah, but his family's hold on Jerusalem was directly threatened by their coming.[24] For other rulers, the Franks were just a novel force, like the great Byzantine expeditions of earlier days, which would pass away, and for now simply had to be endured. Hence Balduk's alliance with Baldwin and the indifference of the rulers of Tripoli who actually allowed the Franks to buy food and supplies in their city.[25] The divisions in Syria certainly played into the hands of the crusaders, and the divorce from the centre of Seljuk power in Baghdad was probably even more serious. In that sense, divisions within Islam of course cleared the way for the crusade's victory, but this in itself will not do as an explanation. For the powers of Syria, though divided and slow to act, were not febrile and could field considerable forces from secure bases against an army whose strength was sapped by the long and bitter siege of Antioch. There was nothing inevitable about the Christian victory and they could easily have been overwhelmed by the local Syrian powers whose equipment and fighting methods proved formidable.

[22] *Aleppo Chronicle*, 578, 579, 583–4; *Damascus Chronicle of the Crusades*, p. 46.
[23] *Aleppo Chronicle*, 578; AA, 358–60; RC, 669.
[24] *Aleppo Chronicle*, 579–80.
[25] The Provençal priest Ebrard was at Tripoli seeking food just before the capture of Antioch: RA, p. 117.

In the armies which the crusaders now faced the speed, mobility and fire-power of the élite Turkish cavalry remained an important element. Such tactics were not usually in themselves enough to win against determined enemies; for that, battle at close quarters was essential. The Turks were fully prepared to fight at close quarters, and indeed it was precipitate haste to do so which caused their defeats at Nicaea and Dorylaeum. As we have noted they probably wore rather lighter armour than the Franks but at Dorylaeum were fully prepared to fight at close quarters.[26] As the crusaders moved into the more settled lands of Islam they understood that the armies facing them were rather different, as has been noted already. Infantry was clearly a feature of these armies, in contrast to the entirely mounted nomads. They were bowmen or spearmen, and in general were not armoured.[27] The western chroniclers do not often describe their enemies but the Anonymous reports that in the army of Kerbogah there was a heavily armoured element, even more comprehensively protected than the crusaders because their horses wore a special kind of armour: 'The Agulani numbered three thousand; they fear neither spears nor arrows nor any other weapon for they and their horses are covered all over with plates of iron.'

The description inevitably reminds one of the heavily armoured Persian cavalryman so feared by the late Roman army, the 'cataphract' or in colloquial Latin *clibanarius*, 'boiler boy'. There was a marked tradition of heavy cavalry in Persia which may well be where these people originated, although it should be noted that rather similar troops appear in Egyptian armies.[28] Cahen thinks it is possible to see a general development in Islamic armies towards a heavier type of horseman. This probably arose from settlement, for the skills of the Nomad, particular for his kind of fighting, vanish with the open ranges which dictate his way of life, hence the emphasis in Islamic thinking on recruiting Turks directly from the steppe. Almost certainly any such tendency to heavier horses was accelerated by the experience of the crusades.[29] Certainly from

---

[26] See above p. 180.   [27] Nicolle, 'Early medieval Islamic arms', 60.

[28] *GF*, p. 49. Oddly the Anonymous had twice mentioned these unidentifiable people, pp. 20, 45, without commenting on them in any way; There is a famous second–third century graffito of a *clibanarius* reproduced in P. Brown, *The World of Late Antiquity* (London, 1971), p. 162; Nicolle, 'Early medieval Islamic arms', 34; on Egyptian armies see below pp. 359–60.

[29] 'Djaysh', *Encyclopaedia of Islam*, 2. 506; Ibn-Khaldun, pp. 95, 109, 114, 228 but he is pursuing a general idea that primitive men decay from the luxury of civilisation.

about the time the army approached Antioch references grow to well-armoured Turks with hauberks. Albert mentions them at the crossing of the Iron Bridge and comments on them again in the battle on the St Symeon road in March 1098, while it is difficult to see how the desperate closequarter fighting within Antioch during the second siege could have been possible if the Moslems lacked armour. In the battle against Kerbogah Engelrand of St Pol was clad, according to the *Chanson d'Antioche*, in a splendid eastern 'hauberc jaseran'. Raymond of Aguilers was presumably registering the differences between well-equipped and less well-equipped Turks when he spoke of the garrison of Antioch having 'two thousand of the best knights, and four or five thousand common knights'.[30] The garrison must have had ordinary infantrymen who also formed an element in the relief forces, and specialist troops equipped with siege machinery. Albert mentions a mangonel used against the crusaders in the early fighting near to the Dog Gate, while Fulcher records *petrariae* and *fundibula*. It was, Albert tells us, with such a machine that the garrison of Antioch tossed the heads of two of their more notable victims, Adalbero of Metz and his lady back to the crusaders.[31] The sources also speak of Armenian archers fighting in the garrison at Antioch. In the fighting on the St Symeon road the Anonymous says that the Armenians and Syrians, under the command of the Turks, were made to fire arrows at the crusaders – he had earlier commented that the Turks held their wives and made them spy on the army. Armenians had a high reputation as archers, both on foot and on horseback; Albert says that Baldwin attacked Kerbogah's army as it approached Edessa 'with the bows of the Armenians and the lances of the Franks'. There were Armenian archers in the service of all the Islamic armies at this time. In Egypt the ruling Vizirs, Badr al-Jamali (1074–94) and his son al-Afdal Shahanshah (1094–1121), were Armenian Moslems and so numerous was the Armenian community at Cairo, which provided nearly half the regular army stationed in the capital, that they had their own church and Patriarch.[32] The Islamic armies in no way lagged behind the crusaders in the range of military skills and capacities.

[30] AA, 363, 385; *Chanson d'Antioche*, 8133; RA, p. 48.
[31] AA, 367–71 for the fighting at the Dog Gate see below p. 228; FC, p. 94.
[32] *GF*, pp. 41, 29; AA, 397; Holt, *Age of the Crusades*, pp. 12, 14, 75; J. Hamblin, *The Fatimid Army during the Early Crusades*, unpublished Ph.D. thesis, University of Michigan 1985, pp. 18–23.

Their military technology was clearly the equal of that of their new enemies and their officers enjoyed a tradition of training and writing about the theory and practice of war unequalled in the West. If Ibn-Khaldûn is accurate Moslems had long recognised the need for fighting in close formation, though he acknowledges the speciality of the Franks in this art. The novelty of Turkish mounted bowmen in Latin sources should not disguise from us the fact that Islamic armies understood the need for all arms and formations to work together in disciplined formation.[33]

The Armenian strategy followed by the crusader army since it left Heraclea created a large friendly area to the north and west of Antioch, acting as a shield for their siege. The march down the Amouk and the capture of 'Artāh provided a strong grasp over a rich agricultural area. The road now brought them to the 'Iron Bridge' which the Antiochenes held in force.

This was a fortified bridge across the Orontes with a tower at either end, probably built shortly after the time of Justinian (527–65) (see fig. 7).[34] The Anonymous mentions the fight at the Iron Bridge briefly and Raymond of Aguilers not at all, but Albert provides a vivid description. The army had concentrated at the approaches to the bridge and received a sermon from Adhémar alerting them to the dangers which they faced, so on the morning of 20 October they approached the Iron Bridge in battle order – Robert of Normandy and his knights going ahead as a vanguard, supported by a corps of foot-soldiers 2,000 strong. The garrison of the bridge, a hundred strong, offered fierce resistance. Then another 700 Turks from Antioch (the figure is probably exaggerated) arrived at the river bank to prevent the army using the fords across the river. They were well equipped with mail shirts, and a duel of archery ensued in which the Turks had the upper hand. In the end Adhémar exhorted the soldiers and they formed a tortoise (testudo), a wall of interlocked shields held over their heads against the enemy missiles, and by this means seized the bridge. Once this had

---

[33] Ibn-Khaldun, pp. 223–30. See also the manual of war studied by G. Tantum, 'Muslim warfare: a study of a medieval Muslim treatise on the art of war', in R. Elgood, ed. *Islamic Arms and Armour* (London, 1979), pp. 187–202. There were evidently many earlier models for this late medieval example.

[34] E. S. Bouchier, *A Short History of Antioch* (Oxford, 1921), p. 195 who suggests it owed its name to the fact that iron was used in the structure of the towers, a point mentioned by AA, 362. However, the Orontes was called the 'Far' – GF calls the Bridge the *Pontem Farreum* – but this may have been corrupted to Fer – 'Iron': GF, p. 28, n. 1.

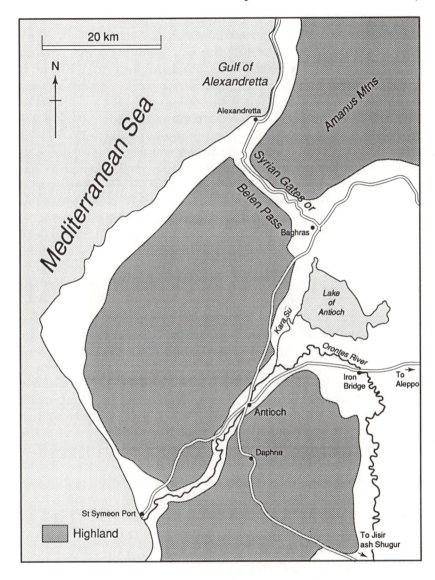

Fig. 7   Antioch and vicinity

happened, others charged across the river by the fords and drove the enemy back in an engagement in which Guy, the French king's *Dapifer*, distinguished himself.[35] But the enemy were not pursued for the army was determined to approach Antioch carefully and it rested on the battlefield.[36] It might almost seem perverse for the crusaders to have taken this route obliging them to challenge a well-defended crossing, but its seizure meant that they commanded the road from Aleppo and the extensive agricultural resources of the Orontes valley. It was not that the bridge was all that formidable an obstacle – Kerbogah would seize it in June 1098 although it was defended. Probably the fords close by, which Albert mentions as a feature of the battle, made it vulnerable.[37] Rather, possession of this crossing made it impossible for any large enemy force to surprise the crusaders encamped around Antioch and it provided a bridgehead for raids out into Syria. Possession of the valley of Ruj held by the Provençals also facilitated such raids. The other major fortress commanding the approaches to the Iron Bridge, Harem, was not attacked and was causing the crusaders grave difficulties by November 1098. Harem stands on the northern spur of the Jebel Talat, which forms the east bank of the Orontes with superb views of the Iron Bridge and the Antioch-Aleppo road.[38] Its garrison was well placed to harass the Franks around Antioch and make communications with Ruj difficult (see fig. 4). It fell to the Armenians only after the defeat of Ridwan's relief army in February 1098, improving control over the approaches to the Iron Bridge; later Kerbogah captured it.[39] But the crusader army had put Antioch in a vice; the only possible approach for a relief army lay along the Aleppo road across the Iron Bridge which was thus an outwork of defence for the besiegers. Of course small parties could always attack, and as we shall see they did. But Antioch had been largely cut off by the Armenian strategy of the crusader army and it was further isolated by sea-power which made a vital contribution to the success of the First Crusade.

[35] He was perhaps the same as Walo the Constable whom Anselm reports was killed towards the end of the siege of Antioch: Hagenmeyer, *Kreuzzugsbriefe*, pp. 157–60

[36] AA, 362–4.   [37] *GF*, p. 50.

[38] On Harem see Dussaud, *Topographie*, p. 172; G. Lestrange, *Palestine under the Moslems* (London, 1890), p. 449; The modern village is dominated by the huge citadel from which one can see the Iron Bridge, the modern Jisr al-Haleb, and to far beyond the modern Syria/Turkey frontier post at Bab al-Hawa beyond which, alongside the Aleppo road, are 1.2 kilometres of the Roman road.

[39] See below p. 272; *Aleppo Chronicle*, p. 579.

We hear a good deal about naval activity in support of the crusade. Ships from Genoa, Pisa, Venice, Greece and England are all mentioned as being active during the crusade.[40] Of their value to the crusaders there can be no doubt at all. By Christmas 1097 the army had eaten up everything in the immediate vicinity of Antioch and, despite its ability to draw upon a friendly hinterland across which much of the army had dispersed, was forced to mount major military expeditions to fend off starvation. In these circumstances food brought in by sea was probably a vital element in sustaining the army. Raymond of Aguilers speaks of western ships plying to Cyprus and protecting Greek shipping engaged in the same task and the visionary Peter Bartholemew sought food in Cyprus, while Bauldry mentions the sailors and merchants living by the coast who were killed during the second siege of Antioch.[41] Ralph of Caen says that goods were imported into Laodicea from Cyprus and sent on to Antioch.[42] Indeed, Cyprus seems to have played a key role as a source of food and supply for the army; when the leaders discussed their strategy with Alexius at Constantinople and Pelekanum, Cyprus must have been seen as a very important supply base. The crusaders arrived at Antioch about 20 October 1097; by the end of the month Adhémar, the Papal Legate, was sending a letter back to the West in conjunction with Symeon, Patriarch of Jerusalem, who is known to have been a refugee in Cyprus at this time, during which he sent lavish presents to the crusaders at Antioch.[43] When Alexius promised to send supplies to the crusaders he was presumably thinking of Cyprus, the convenience of which, for the projected siege of Antioch, would have been known not only to the emperor but to all concerned. Most trading ships making for the Levant would have used Cyprus as a port of call and it was certainly known to pilgrims. Ordericus tells us that Abbot Thierry of St Evroul (1050–7) rested at St Symeon, the port of Antioch, before taking ship for Cyprus where he died.[44] Ralph of Caen says that during the siege of Antioch, Robert of Normandy resided at Laodicea but sent food, brought from Cyprus, to the main camp at Antioch. As the army of Raymond of Toulouse, Robert of Normandy and Tancred marched south, it was the prospect of contact with Cyprus which was one of

---

[40] BD, 18; OV, 5. 31 (using BD), 271; RA, p. 134–5.
[41] RA, pp. 134–5 and see above p. 138; BD, 65.
[42] RC, 649.   [43] Hagenmeyer, *Kreuzzugsbriefe*, pp. 141–2; AA, 489.
[44] OV, 3. 68–75.

the factors which decided them to turn towards the coast instead of inland along the Damascus road.[45] It is remarkable that chroniclers, as hostile to the Byzantines as Ralph of Caen and Raymond of Aguilers, mention Cyprus as a source of food for the army. This underlines the importance of the Byzantine alliance, and it was probably the Cyprus connection that made the other leaders reluctant to support Bohemond's bid for Antioch at the conference of November 1098. The food and supplies they had received made it difficult to argue that Alexius had never supported them, and there was the prospect of more yet to come. This logistical and naval support was essential for the crusaders – it is hardly possible to believe that without such Byzantine help they could have survived the siege of Antioch.[46]

Sea power was important to the crusaders' communications. According to a manuscript of Bauldry of Dol, a Greek living on the coast near to Antioch was able to take ship for Constantinople three days after the victory over Kerbogah on 28 June 1098 and bring news of it to Alexius in eleven days. At almost exactly the same time Hugh of Vermandois was sent to Constantinople overland, but did not arrive until 25 July.[47] The relative speed of sea travel explains why the crusaders could write letters home. The risks of the slow overland journey to Constantinople were revealed when Hugh of Vermandois and Baldwin of Hainault were ambushed on their diplomatic mission to Constantinople and the latter killed, and by Albert's story of the Danish reinforcements who were killed near Philomelium during the siege of Antioch.[48] Adhémar of Le Puy was in contact with Symeon Patriarch of Jerusalem in exile on Cyprus within a fortnight of the arrival of the army before Antioch. He was probably in Cyprus again early in 1098; for he almost certainly inspired Symeon's letter to the West of late January 1098 and it is likely that he was not present for the Lake Battle on 9 February. We are told that arrangements for the battle were finalised 'in the house of the bishop' which implies his absence. The bishops of Orange and

---

[45] RC, 649; RA, p. 105.

[46] A. Lewis, *Naval Power and Trade in the Mediterranean 500–1100* (Princeton, 1951), pp. 225–49 suggests that Byzantine mercantile and naval power was in decline at this time especially relative to that of the Italian cities, and this may well be true but the Greeks made a major effort from Cyprus. On Byzantine naval power see H. Ahrweiler, *Byzance et la Mer*, Bibliothèque byzantine, Etudes 5. (Paris, 1966).

[47] BD, 80; Hagenmeyer, *Chronologie*, pp. 180, 304, 305.   [48] *GF*, p. 72; AA, 435.

Grenoble were brought to the East on a Genoese fleet.[49] According to Ralph of Caen, when the crusaders at 'Akkār thought an enemy was threatening, they dispatched Arnulf of Choques to Antioch on a little boat which travelled via the ports of Maraclea, Valania, Jabala and Laodicea to Antioch, while Stephen of Blois fled by sea, probably to Attalia, before striking inland to meet Alexius at Philomelium. One manuscript of the work of Bauldry of Dol reports that two *clientes* of Bohemond, who were present at Philomelium were determined to give their lord a Christian burial and so went to St Symeon by ship from Cyprus and there found 500 reinforcements newly arrived, presumably by boat. Reinforcements were brought by sea – Albert of Aachen mentions 1,500 arriving at St Symeon in August 1098 from Ratisbon, only to die of plague.[50] Bruno of Lucca boarded an English ship in late 1097 and was at Antioch by early March 1098. Sea travel in winter was very hazardous and this journey demonstrates the determination of the sailors. He returned by the autumn of 1098 when his proud fellow-citizens wrote to inform the world of all that had happened.[51] His journey shows just how far the crusaders could remain in touch with the distant West. Their envoys to the Egyptian Caliphate were told to go by sea and the Egyptian envoys, who came to Antioch in February 1098, certainly also travelled by boat. After the defeat of Kerbogah's army, Bohemond sent the defeated prince's tent to Bari as a trophy of victory.[52] The naval power of the Greeks and the West which was concentrated in the Levant was absolutely essential to the success of the crusade, for although the reinforcements they brought were probably few their skills were of very great importance to the land army.

On 15 July 1097 a Genoese fleet of thirteen ships, twelve galleys and one hybrid oared ship, a *sandanum*, filled with armed men and equipment left for the East. It put into St Symeon, the port of Antioch, on 17 November 1097. A few days later, on 23 November,

[49] Hagenmeyer, *Kreuzzugsbriefe*, pp. 141–2, 146–9; RA, p. 56; Caffaro 49.

[50] RC, 681; AA, 417; Hagenmeyer, *Chronologie*, 387, p. 237; BD, 73, n. 17; such large figures need to be treated with caution for ships were quite small carrying of the order of eighty passengers, fifteen crew and forty horses in the twelfth century. Later vessels could carry up to 1,000: S. M. Foster, *Some Aspects of Maritime Activity and the Use of Sea-power in Relation to the Crusading States*, D. Phil. thesis, University of Oxford, 1978, pp. 109–20; AA, 446.

[51] Hagenmeyer, *Kreuzzugsbriefe*, pp. 165–7.

[52] HBS, 181, 206; AA, 383; GF, pp. 37–8, 42 speaks of the Egyptian envoys being at the coast.

the leaders resolved to build a fortress on the mountain called Malregard.[53] On 4 March 1098 an English fleet put into St Symeon, bearing Bruno of Lucca, and the very next day the leaders decided to build the fort outside the Bridge Gate which would be known as the Mahommeries Tower.[54] On 17 June 1099, as the crusaders were besieging Jerusalem, a fleet of six ships put into Jaffa, amongst them two Genoese vessels. Immediately the leaders dispatched a strong armed escort to bring the supplies to Jerusalem, and when an Egyptian fleet threatened, the sailors burned their boats and went to Jerusalem where William Ricau served as the engineer who built the siege tower and other machines of the count of Toulouse.[55] On this last occasion our sources stress the shortage of wood in the area. An early assault on the city had failed because only a single assault ladder could be built. It would seem that the fabric of the dismantled ships, the lumber they were carrying and above all the skills of the sailors must have been absolutely vital for the building of machines. Albert also reports that, because there was a lack of wood during the siege of Antioch an effort was made to build a fort by the St George Gate with stone and earth.[56] This remarkable sequence demonstrates the close connection between supplies coming by sea and siege activity. Sailors were used to spars, masts, lashings and all the paraphernalia which was needed to build siege equipment – their coming meant not just raw material but much needed skills. It is worth remarking that at Nicaea Henry of Esch had built a machine which had collapsed in use, probably because of his lack of know-how.[57] Fleets, therefore, provided a vital element of support for the crusader army and it is difficult to see how they could have succeeded without such naval support. The connection with Cyprus was probably essential during the long siege of Antioch, and this was kept open by a continuous Greek and western naval presence. They were fortunate that the Turks had no fleet, though corsairs and the like could easily have cut their communications with Cyprus if there had been no naval forces to protect them. Once they attacked the Fatimid lands the Egyptian fleet made itself felt, which underlines

[53] Caffaro, 49–50; RA, 49; GF, p. 30.
[54] Hagenmeyer, Kreuzzugsbriefe, pp. 165–7; RA, p. 59; GF, pp. 39–40 mentions the decision but not the fleet; AA, 383 refers to ships without specifically mentioning any new arrival.
[55] Caffaro, 56–7; RA, pp. 141, 147; GF, p. 88.
[56] AA, 467, 377; RC, 688–9; RA, p. 139; GF, p. 88.
[57] Rogers, Siege Warfare, p. 126, suggests that the coming of the ships transformed the crusaders' engineering capacity; see above p. 163.

the importance of the crusader negotiations in neutralising it.[58] Sea power was a vital element in the success of the crusade, but unfortunately it is very poorly chronicled and the particulars of its exercise are hidden from us. We know that a Genoese fleet of thirteen ships came into Levantine waters in November 1097, but we do not know how long it stayed or whether the two ships which appeared at Jaffa during the siege of Jerusalem were part of it or had come later. Pisan and Venetian ships are mentioned only in passing and we are given some highly confusing information about the English.[59] We are very poorly informed on the question of ports.

During the siege of Antioch three major channels of supply are mentioned: the ports of Cilicia, Mamistra (Misis), Alexandretta (Iskenderun) and Tarsus, Laodicea (Latakia) on the Syrian coast, and St Symeon which was the port of Antioch some twenty-seven kilometres away at the mouth of the Orontes (see figs 2, 4 and 7). St Symeon port was by far the most convenient of these, for it was very close to Antioch, but the road passed in front of the Bridge Gate and so the Turks could easily attack people travelling down to the sea. Caffaro of Genoa has a vivid description of the fighting on the road to Antioch in November 1097, when a Genoese fleet of thirteen ships put into St Symeon.[60] Alexandretta was more than sixty kilometres away, and to reach it involved a march over the Ammanus range via a road which Ralph of Caen described as very difficult; it also lead from the Bridge Gate so the early stages of any journey would be difficult. Laodicea was over eighty kilometres distant, and was not materially nearer to Cyprus than St Symeon.[61] We know that the cities of Cilicia were captured by the forces of Baldwin and Tancred, but the question of how and when St Symeon and Laodicea fell to the crusaders is much more difficult. There is no mention of them being captured by any element of the army. Raymond of Aguilers

---

[58] On Cyprus see P. Edbury, *The Kingdom of Cyprus and the Crusades 1191–1374* (Cambridge, 1991), pp. 1–5. On the strength of Egyptian naval power on the Palestinian littoral see below p. 327, n. 7.

[59] See above p. 98 and below p. 336; Foster, *Maritime activity*, p. 56, points out that the only firm figures we have of Western naval strength are thirteen Genoese ships which put into St Symeon in October 1097, the thirty English ships mentioned by RA and six ships which entered Jaffa of which two were Genoese: see above p. 98, below pp. 214, 336.

[60] Caffaro, 50; this reads very like other descriptions of the fighting on 6 March 1098, but only Bohemond is mentioned as escorting the sailors. Caffaro mentions some of the Genoese knights as fighting on horseback, which could mean that they had transported horses from the west – but not necessarily.

[61] RC, 639.

tells us that when the army left 'Akkār in May 1099 they were joined
by a number of English sailors who burned their nine or ten vessels,
all that remained of the thirty with which they had come originally.
According to Raymond they had responded to the appeal for the
crusade and 'captured' the ports of Laodicea and St Symeon even
before the crusader army arrived at Antioch. His word *obtinuerunt*
has recently been translated simply as 'arrived at', for which there is
warrant though the sense of acquisition would be more frequent and
more natural.[62] However, we can be quite sure that Laodicea was
captured by the time that the crusaders arrived at Antioch because
Kemal ad-Din tell us that twenty-two ships came from Cyprus on 19
August 1097 and seized it, though he does not say to whom these
ships belonged. In a letter written early in the siege, Anselm of
Ribemont says it was captured at the same time as Tarsus, which
tends to confirm Kemal ad-Din and Raymond of Aguilers that it
had fallen before the army arrived at Antioch. The *Florinensis Brevis
Narratio Belli Sacri* suggests that Laodicea fell after Nicaea.[63] The
sources are less precise on St Symeon, but they all seem to assume
that it was in crusader hands from the moment of their arrival at
Antioch without ever mentioning its capture. Moreover, within a
fortnight of the start of the siege on 20 October 1097 Adhémar was
in Cyprus with Patriarch Symeon of Jerusalem, and within a month
a Genoese fleet could put into this harbour.[64] There seems, therefore, good reason to believe that both St Symeon and Laodicea were
captured from the sea before the crusaders reached Antioch, and
every reason to accept Raymond of Aguilers's statement that this
was the work of an English fleet originally some thirty ships strong.
This was clearly quite different from the English fleet which brought
Bruno of Lucca to the East seven months later in March 1098.[65] The
existence, therefore, of an English fleet which arrived in the east
before the crusade and continued through to the bitter end is
established, though how it related to the English who brought Bruno
of Lucca is unknown – and what did they do in the meantime? Some

---

[62] RA, p. 134, Hills' own translation, *The History of the Frankish Conquerors of Jerusalem*
(Philadelphia, 1968), p. 113; Niermeyer, *Mediae latinitatis lexicon minus* (Leiden, 1976),
p. 733.

[63] On Laodicea see David, *Robert Curthose*, pp. 230–44; *Aleppo Chronicle*, 578; *Florinensis
Brevis Narratio Belli Sacri, RHC Oc.* 5. 371.

[64] See above pp. 98–9.   [65] See above p. 134.

light is cast on this matter by Ralph of Caen who says that during the siege of Antioch Laodicea was held by the English who were sent by the Emperor Alexius. After the Norman Conquest of England many Anglo-Saxons took service with Alexius, perhaps with the consent of William, and formed a permanent element in the Byzantine forces. Amongst them was a fleet which probably helped to save Constantinople in 1091 under Sigurd or Siward Barn. It is entirely possible that it was just such a force which took Laodicea. Finding themselves threatened from landward attack, these English appealed to Robert of Normandy as in some senses their natural lord and he came to the city where he found life so easy that it was only much later, and after three appeals for help, that he was persuaded to abandon it, for it was well supplied from Cyprus. However, he did send generous supplies to Antioch. Ralph gives no dates, but his suggestion that Robert was absent from the siege is supported by the fact that the sources do not often mention any activity of his during much of the siege, and Raymond of Aguilers says that by December 1097 Robert was absent.[66] The implication of Ralph's statement is that the capture of Laodicea, and perhaps St Symeon also, was the result of co-operation from the emperor, presumably based on Cyprus. It does not precisely contradict Raymond's statement that the English had come from their own lands for we know of another English fleet which came in March 1098 and Raymond may have muddled the two. It would be remarkable if the departure of an English fleet to the East had not attracted some attention from native chroniclers, and Ordericus Vitalis records that during the second siege of Antioch (June 1098) Edgar Aetheling led a fleet with 20,000 men from England and the other islands and seized Laodicea, which he afterwards gave to Robert Curthose who left a garrison there during his march to Jerusalem. However, the Greek protospatharius Ravendinos drove out the Franks.[67] Now much of this story was clearly confused. Laodicea was conquered long before the second siege of Antioch. In late 1097 Edgar the Aetheling was engaged in imposing his nephew on the Scottish throne so it is unlikely that he joined the crusade. Moreover his actual pilgrimage to Jerusalem is very

[66] RC, 649; RA, p. 50; AA, 380–2 lists him as being at the Lake Battle in February 1098, but Albert's lists of names are often erratic. Tudebode, p. 43, says he was told to defend the camp; Shepherd, 'The English in Byzantium', 52–93.
[67] OV, 5. 271.

precisely dated to 1102 by William of Malmesbury.[68] In any case, it is hard to believe that if Edgar had come to the East the fact would have escaped the attention of crusading chroniclers, simply because he was of royal blood. Ordericus's evidence strengthens the suggestion that Robert of Normandy held Laodicea at some time, as does Guibert's remark that the citizens of Laodicea revolted against Robert and abjured the use of the money of Rouen.[69] But Ordericus does add something more – that after Robert Laodicea passed to the Greeks. Ordericus's story was told in order to explain Bohemond's siege of the port which was definitely held by the Greeks in September 1099 at the time when the main army was returning from Jerusalem.[70] Caffaro of Genoa, who had been in Syria early in the twelfth century, records that at the time of the final capture of Antioch the city was held by Eumathios Philokales, duke of Cyprus.[71] As Robert Curthose quite definitely fought against Kerbogah in June 1098 this suggests that he relinquished the city to the Greeks – who, after all, are portrayed as the masters of the English – either because of revolt in the city or because of repeated calls from the other leaders, as reported by Ralph of Caen, to come to Antioch or indeed possibly because of both factors. It is very likely that the Greeks were in control of Laodicea by the autumn of 1098 at the latest, because Raymond of Aguilers reports that at the end of the siege of 'Akkār after a vision, Raymond of Toulouse sent Adhémar's brother to recover the dead bishop's cross and mantle which had been left at Laodicea.[72] Raymond would surely only have left such valuable things at Laodicea in the care of friends – and after the fall of Antioch he was in close alliance with the Byzantines. However, the story of Laodicea and the English fleet is immensely complicated by the very different stories told by Albert of Aix.

According to Albert, when Baldwin was at Tarsus during the Cilician expedition he suddenly saw a fleet 'whose masts of won-

[68] GR, 2. 366, 310; Barlow, William Rufus, p. 371; N. Hooper, 'Edgar the Aetheling: Anglo-Saxon prince, rebel and crusader', Anglo-Saxon England 14 (1985), 208–210, emphasises that Edgar left England with an army to support the claim of his nephew Edgar to the Scottish throne in 1097 and thinks it unlikely that he could have reached the east as Ordericus suggests, but accepts William of Malmesbury's account of the pilgrimage of 1102 when he fought at Ramla.

[69] Edgar was the son of Edward the Exile and grandson of Edmund Ironside (died 1016): Hooper, 'Edgar the Aetheling', 197–214; GN, p. 254.

[70] Bohemond persuaded Daimbert of Pisa to lend his fleet for this enterprise: AA, 500–1; Yewdale, Bohemond, pp. 87–9.

[71] Caffaro, 66.   [72] RA, p. 128.

drous height were covered in the purest gold and shimmered in the rays of the sun'. The sailors were commanded by Guinemer of Boulogne, their *caput et magister* who had been a man *de domo comitis Eustachii* a close associate, therefore, of the house of Boulogne. They explained that they were men of Flanders, Antwerp and Frisia who had been living for eight years as pirates and had landed in order to divide their loot, and they asked Baldwin and his friends what they were doing. On hearing of the crusade they agreed to join it. Three hundred of them joined with two hundred of Baldwin's men to garrison Tarsus, while the rest reappear in the suite of Tancred as he seized fortresses in Cilicia and the port of Alexandretta.[73] Subsequently, just as he is about to tell us of the Lake Battle in February 1098 Albert says that Guinemer, after he had left Baldwin and Tancred at Mamistra, took once more to the sea and captured Laodicea, but got no support because he contributed nothing to the army. His guard was lax and the Greeks managed to take the citadel of Laodicea and threw him into prison, from whence he was later liberated after the victory at Antioch at the special request of Godfrey of Bouillon.[74] This is all very odd and is further complicated by a quite separate story which Albert tells later. At the end of the crusade the returning armies found Bohemond and Daimbert of Pisa besieging Laodicea, which, Albert says, had been captured from the Saracens by Guinemer with a fleet manned by the same people as before, but this time including Danes, and allied with the men of the lands of Raymond of Toulouse. After the fall of Antioch, Guinemer handed the city over to Raymond of Toulouse; after this he was captured and imprisoned by the Greeks and freed at the request of Godfrey. When Count Raymond marched south, faithful to his oath to Alexius, he turned the city over to the Greeks.[75] The contradictions in these stories are evident. In one story Guinemer seems to have been thrown into gaol during the siege of Antioch, while in the other he appears as holding the city until the summer of 1098 when he turned it over to Raymond, and was then put in gaol. In the earlier story he is clearly stated to have been freed at the request of Godfrey shortly after the victory over Kerbogah when Yaghisiyan's wife was being ransomed – but this date was not possible in the later story. In the second story the Danes are added to the list of people in the fleet and the Provençals suddenly appear as allies, apparently as

[73] AA, 348–9, 357.   [74] AA, 380, 447.   [75] AA, 500–1.

a result of early contact with them. Furthermore, the passage about the masts of the fleet has a very poetic ring and Albert is known to have used poetic source material including that which underlay the *Chanson d'Antioch*.[76] However, we need not dismiss Guinemer altogether, for such wanderers were not so very unlikely. Robert the Frisian, a younger son, was given money and a fully equipped boat by his father, Baldwin V of Flanders, in order to make his fortune and, although the stories which accrued later about him were fantastical, the simple core of the story indicates how adventurous people could travel afar.[77] It seems likely that some of the Anglo-Saxons who fled England after the conquest were accommodated in the distant Crimea and there was probably an important English presence at Constantinople.[78] When we consider the range of western mercenaries serving the Byzantine emperor and the Zirids of North Africa at this time, we ought perhaps to see Guinemer as a real person, and it should be noted that his story does not appear to derive from the *Chanson d'Antioch* and that Albert does break into lyrical passages from time to time, as in his description of Godfrey's army rushing to the relief of Bohemond at Dorylaeum.[79] Albert was not generally interested in fleets at all – his sources were apparently men of the army, generally incurious about maritime matters. It is remarkable that, although he gives us a very detailed account of the capture of Jerusalem, he never mentions the arrival of ships in Jaffa whose importance we have noted; it was the Provençals who provided their escort from the coast and the men of Godfrey were not involved.[80] The great exception to his disinterest, and probably that of his informants, was Guinemer and the reason for that is obvious – he was a close connection of the house of Boulogne. Guinemer probably did help in Cilicia as indicated, but Albert attributes the capture of Laodicea, by a northern fleet, to him. Albert was then faced with different accounts of his activities, probably given to him

[76] David, *Robert Curthose*, pp. 237-8 handles Albert's account very roughly and makes some of these points.

[77] Lambert of Hersfeld pp. 121-5 is the chief source for the stories which are analysed by C. Verlinden, 'Le chroniqueur Lambert de Hersfeld et les voyages de Robert le Frison', *Comte de Flandres*', *Annales de la Société d'Emulation de Bruges* 76 (1933), 83-94.

[78] See above p. 101.

[79] M. Brett, 'The military interest of the battle of Haydaran', in V. J. Parry and M. E. Yapp, eds., *War, Technology and Society in the Middle East* (London, 1975), pp. 60-77; *Chanson d'Antioche*, 1. 143-70 and see also S. Duparc-Quioc's 'La composition de la Chanson d'Antioche', *Romania*, 83 (1962), 11-12; AA, 331.

[80] RA, pp. 140-2.

at different times, which he could not reconcile. The essential difference between the two stories as they concern Laodicea is the influence of the count of Toulouse in the later version and the different dating which, by implication, this imposed. Guinemer, after helping in Cilicia, was captured by the Greeks, perhaps held at Laodicea, and released at the request of Godfrey. Laodicea was captured on 19 August 1097 by an English fleet either acting on Alexius's orders or in conjunction with Byzantine forces in Cyprus, which then based itself in the city to which it invited Robert of Normandy. His departure, almost certainly at the time of Kerbogah's march to Antioch, saw the city fall to the power of the Byzantine Governor of Cyprus, who may well have co-operated with Raymond of Toulouse before the latter's departure south. After the siege of 'Akkār the English sailors abandoned their now useless ships and joined Raymond who, after the crusade, took possession of the citadel of Laodicea with 500 men in the name of the emperor.[81] At some time after the main army had gone home, Alexius ordered Raymond to hand over Laodicea to Andronicus Tzintziloukes.[82] The matter of Laodicea is important, for it shows us the degree of co-operation between Byzantium and the crusaders. The early arrival of the English fleet in Byzantine service in August 1097 prepared the way for the crusader army, for whom its activities protecting the route to Cyprus were very important. Of the other English fleet which arrived in March 1098 we hear no more, but it is possible that elements of it joined the English already in the East and based at Laodicea. The Genoese fleet which arrived in November 1097 also seems to have left ships behind, or perhaps was followed by others, and they too plied to the islands as we know from Raymond of Aguilers. Bauldry of Dol mentions Venetian ships, as does Raymond of Aguilers, and also Pisans – which probably refers to Daimbert's fleet.[83] Of the Venetians' activities we know nothing, but then there seems to have been quite a settlement of sailors and

---

[81] AA, 503-4.

[82] *Alexiad*, pp. 353-4; David, *Robert Curthose*, p. 238 rightly criticises P. Riant, 'Inventaire critique des lettres historiques des croisades', *Archives de l'Orient Latin*, 1 (Paris, 1881), 189-91 and Chalandon, *Alexis I Comnène*, pp. 212-17 for assigning this letter to the first half of 1099. In fact Anna's account of the later stages of the First Crusade is a mess – she confuses their victory at Ascalon on 12 August 1099 with the near disaster of Baldwin I at second Ramla on 17 May 1102; the letter makes much more sense if read as part of the Provençal-Greek alliance as it developed after the crusade.

[83] BD, 18; RA, pp. 134-35. Ordericus's references to fleets are based on those of Bauldry 5. 31 – BD, 18, 5. 99 – BD, 65, 5. 161 – BD, 98, except for the story of Edgar Aetheling p. 271.

traders at port St Symeon, and small contingents like that of Guinemer must have arrived from time to time to play a role.[84] This great maritime endeavour, led and supported by the Byzantines, was one of the key factors which enabled the crusader army to survive the bitter nine-month siege of Antioch and to triumph over their enemies.

The arrival of the army before Antioch on 21 October triggered a debate on strategy. The suggestion was made in the council of leaders on 21 October that the army should mount a distant blockade of Antioch. Those who favoured the idea pointed out that the army was tired – they had after all been marching for some four months – and much of it was dispersed amongst captured strongpoints. Better to sit out the winter in comfort, they urged, and wait for the arrival of reinforcements from the emperor and the West. It was an intelligent idea and evidently was supported, and perhaps even conceived of, by Tatikios who may well have known that this was the method by which the Byzantines had recaptured Antioch in 969 when Baghras was an important base (see fig. 7).[85] Tatikios revived the idea when the army was starving in January and February 1098. The count of Toulouse, however, urged his comrades to trust in God and pressed successfully for an immediate and close siege, and this was the course of action taken.[86] The great virtue of the close siege was that it kept the army together under the control of its leaders; a distant blockade could have had a very adverse effect on the sense of purpose of the Christian army. However, many crusaders were on garrison duties away from Antioch and Raymond of Aguilers says that knights were all too eager for such work.[87] These captured fortresses and cities were the fruits of the Armenian strategy which the crusaders had followed, and despite Raymond's fulminations it now served them well. As already noted, the Armenian population sent aid and their merchants sold food, albeit at a high price, but the availability of these lands as a source of food was very valuable. The presence of many knights in fortresses facilitated this and reduced the food problem to

---

[84] AA, 414; BD, 80.
[85] As Rogers, *Siege Warfare*, p. 83 points out; on the siege of 969 see Bouchier, *Antioch*, pp. 216–19.
[86] RA, pp. 46–7, 54; the matter is discussed by France, 'The departure of Tatikios from the Crusader army', 138.
[87] RA, p. 48.

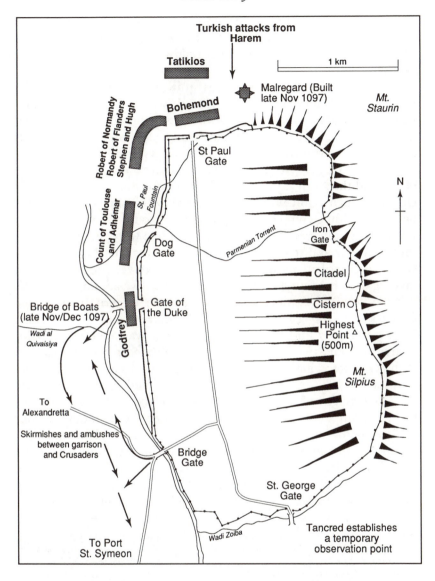

Fig. 8   Siege of Antioch, October 1097 – February 1098

a degree. In effect, the crusaders imposed a close siege upon Antioch and enjoyed some of the benefits of a distant blockade and their situation was later improved when Baldwin of Boulogne took over Edessa.

The reason for this debate was quite simply the scale of the problem which they now faced. Antioch was no longer the magnificent city of late Roman times, when its population had reached 300,000 and it rejoiced in its position as capital of the East. Its prosperity was ruined by a series of disasters – the fire of 525, the earthquakes of 526, 528 and 588, the Persian sack of 540, the plague of 542 and the Arab capture of 638. However, though the inhabited city was much reduced, it still sheltered within the walls of Justinian's rebuilding completed by 560 and as modified by earthquake, war and the ravages of time.[88] The crusaders were much struck by the splendour and strength of the place, as was Ibn Butlân in 1051 when he described its walls as having 360 towers: archaeological investigation has found evidence of over sixty (we are not sure of the original total).[89] Antioch was built on the eastern bank of the Orontes river, though its walls touched the stream only at the Bridge Gate (see figs. 7 and 8). The fortified area was about three kilometres long and two kilometres deep extending up the eastern wall of the Orontes valley formed by the northern extension of the Jebel al-Ansariye. The mass of Mount Silpius included in the enceinte rises to a height of 512 metres and about 700 metres north of its highest point stood the citadel, rebuilt after the Byzantine reconquest of 969 and dominating the whole enclosure. The wall then dropped into the deep gully of the Parmenian torrent where the Iron Gate restrained this dangerous stream before climbing onto the southern flank of Mount Staurin and then descending sharply to the plain by the Orontes at the northern edge of the city.[90] The cru-

---

[88] G. Downey, *A History of Antioch in Syria* (Princeton, 1961) pp. 528–9, 545–552.

[89] RA, pp. 47–8; *GF*, pp. 76–7; Ibn Butlân cited and tr. G. Lestrange, *Palestine under the Moslems*, p. 370; G. Rey, *Étude sur les monuments de l'architecture militaire des croisés en Syrie et dans l'île de Chypre* (Paris, 1871), Pl. 17.

[90] AA, 365 describes the city as two miles long and 1½ wide. On Antioch see: Rey, *Étude sur les Monuments*, pp. 183–204 and Pl. 17; Lestrange, *Palestine under the Moslems*, pp. 367–77; the massive account of the excavations done in the 1930s, G. W. Elderkin et al., eds. *Antioch-on-the-Orontes: the Excavations of 1932* (Princeton, 1934–48), is skilfully distilled in Bouchier, *Antioch*, and for the walls see especially p. 220. Antioch has expanded enormously since these books were written. The old city (to the east of the Orontes) has grown far beyond the line of the walls on the plain and the lower slopes and their remains have vanished. It is only on the ridge high above the city (Mounts Staurin and Silpius) that there are

saders approached the city from the north, and here in the valley bottom the wall was pierced by three gates which the crusaders called the St Paul Gate at the very foot of the mountain, the Dog Gate further along and then the Gate of the Duke nearer the river. This northern wall of the city was a double wall, for Albert of Aix mentions an outer wall in connection with operations outside the Dog Gate and tells us that Tancred lurked in the space between the main wall and the barbican before launching a surprise attack on the besiegers during the second siege.[91] Beyond the Dog Gate the wall angled towards the river bank, though it is not clear that the outer wall continued at this point, which it met at the Bridge Gate giving access to the plain on the west bank of the Orontes and the roads to St Symeon Port, Alexandretta and Marasch. After that the wall followed the river fairly closely then turned away from it to the St George Gate, from which a road ran to the ancient suburb of Daphne and beyond down to Laodicea and inland to Syria via the Jisr ash-Shogur. The wall then followed the line of a gorge, the Wadi Zoiba, rising up onto Mount Silpius. The inhabited part of the city nestled down on the lower slopes of Mounts Staurin and Silpius and the narrow strip of plain by the Orontes. In ancient times the city's dominating feature had been the great colonnaded Street of Herod and Tiberias, running from north to south. It must have existed in some form in crusader times, for its line has now survived in the modern Kurtulus Caddessi. But there was a huge and barely inhabited area within the circuit of some twelve kilometres, amply studded with towers. In Byzantine times the city was held by a garrison of 4,000, such was the passive strength of the defences and their inaccessibility. Yaghisiyan seems to have had forces of about the same size. Raymond of Aguilers, as we have noted, suggests a

substantial remains, most notably of the citadel, as modified by the crusaders. On the southern side these extend down into the edge of the town by the Hastahane, the city hospital, where the remains of the aqueduct remain a notable feature. The west bank of the Orontes forms the new city and here all evidence of the past has been buried under a carpet of concrete flats and shops. The various water courses have all been culverted and therefore we are reliant on the observations of the pre-war and earlier scholars, though the Parmenian torrent remains evident above the city. In 1972 the ancient bridge over the Orontes was demolished and replaced. At present the citadel and the walls high on Mount Silpius are approached by what I have called the 'back road' which goes via Altinözü to the Syrian plain through the mountains. It may give readers some sense of the scale of the ancient enceinte to know that from the Bridge Gate to the wall above the city on this road is a drive of fourteen kilometres.

[91] AA, 367-8; 407-8.

garrison of 2,000 first-rate knights,4,000–5,000 other mounted men
and more than 10,000 foot. Stephen of Blois gives a total number of
5,000 enemy troops in the city which was probably much nearer the
mark for the evidence of events suggests that the garrison was no
more than adequate for its task. At the end of December 1097 the
crusaders sent a major foraging expedition out into Syria at a time
when Duqaq of Damascus was approaching with a relief army; on 9
February 1098 the crusaders fought against another relief force
under Ridwan of Aleppo. On both occasions Yaghisiyan's garrison
mounted major sorties in support of the expected relief but although
these punished the crusaders they were not strong enough to inflict a
major defeat upon them nor to burn the Bridge of Boats which
enabled the crusaders to cross the Orontes and threaten the Bridge
Gate or travel to St Symeon. When the crusaders threatened to
build a counterfort outside the Bridge Gate, Yaghisiyan made a
desperate effort to prevent it by ambushing the supply column
coming up from the coast, but despite initial success he was unable
to prevent the construction.[92]

Once they had resolved upon a close siege the crusader leaders
were forced into a cautious strategy. Because Antioch was so large
the risk to the attacker was dispersal of his strength. There could be
no question of surrounding this huge area; the crusader army was
not big enough and any effort to invest a considerable section or
sections would open the way for the enemy to sally out and defeat
the crusaders in detail. Nor was there much chance of a sudden
assault being successful. In the flatter areas the defences were formidable and the enemy could move their forces about quickly. In
the mountains it would be very difficult to move large bodies of
troops across the jumble of rocks, ravines and harsh slopes and to
sustain them while they tackled the walls which rise to twelve metres
and are sited to take advantage of the very rough terrain. Of course
this cut both ways – the enemy could not seriously assault them from
this direction, but with their knowledge of the pathways of the area
the Turks could and did mount raids which sapped crusader
strength. There is a back road to the high eastern defences of the
city; today it leaves the Aleppo road some two kilometres north of
what was the St Paul Gate and winds around the city passing via the

---

[92] Ibn Butlân writing in 1050 cited and tr. Lestrange, *Palestine under the Moslems*, p. 370; RA,
pp. 48, 51–2, 58, 60–1; Hagenmeyer, *Kreuzzugsbriefe*, pp. 149–52; *GF*, pp. 32, 39–41; on the
Bridge of Boats see below p. 230 and on the fighting on the St Symeon road p. 254.

modern Altinözü into the upper Orontes valley near the Roman bridges at Jisr ash-Shugur which give access to the Syrian plain. There was certainly at least a path here, for its use was vital in the final crusader assault on the city and it probably led to the Roman road from Antioch via Delphi to the Jisr ash-Shugur (see figs. 4 and 7).[93] It was presumably used by both sides for raiding. But the dominating factor which shaped the actions of the army, once they had decided on a close siege, was the need to avoid dispersal of effort. This explains the very slow and very systematic extension of the siege, so that as late as March 1098 Bruno of Lucca could tell his fellow citizens that the army 'had surrounded the city in siege, though not very well'.[94] The crusader army had approached from the north and it was from here that they systematically extended their grasp over Antioch. It was not perhaps the ideal position but they were well placed to fend off enemy attack coming down the Orontes valley onto their rear and to have attempted to establish major forces on the west bank of the Orontes opposite the Bridge Gate immediately would have strained the army's resources (see fig. 8). The sheer size of Antioch enjoined upon the crusaders a cautious strategy of building up the blockade; Kerbogah's failure to appreciate this problem was later a major factor in his defeat. In the first phase of the siege, which would last until Christmas 1097, the crusader army steadily extended its grip on the city, though at a great cost in lives.

Albert of Aachen's account of the order of battle of the besieging army is largely supported by that of Ralph of Caen. Neither the Anonymous nor Raymond of Aguilers gives an order of siege such as that which they provide for Nicaea.[95] Albert says that Adhémar of Le Puy commanded the army for the approach to Antioch but does not make clear that Bohemond had already gone before and arrived at Antioch on 20 October.[96] He gives a poetic description of the army in all its glory and numbers – 300,000 – as it took lunch on 21 October 1097 close to the city at a place called *Altalon*. He then records its deployment for the siege (see fig. 8). Albert seems to have been given an order of siege related to the point at which the army came up to the city on its north wall by the St Paul Gate. He says that a group of lesser figures, Tancred together with Roger of

[93] See below pp. 263–4.   [94] Hagenmeyer, *Kreuzzugsbriefe*, p. 166.
[95] *GF*, 14–15 provides some information but RA, p. 43 is much fuller for Nicaea.
[96] AA, 364–5; *GF*, p. 28.

Barneville and Adam FitzMichael established themselves close to 'Altalon' and kept the Turks blockaded there which suggests that this group was close to Bohemond who took 'the gate towards Persia, at the point where the mountain meets the plain' – a good description of the location of the St Paul Gate, the natural point of entry for any force coming down the valley of the Orontes. Ralph confirms that Tancred was close to Bohemond but suggests that he was encamped with the next contingent along, the North French. Albert says that Tatikios, whom Ralph never mentions, took up station somewhat back from the city wall, but forward of him were Baldwin of Hainault, Robert of Normandy and Robert of Flanders. Beyond these were the forces of Stephen of Blois and Hugh of Vermandois. This is confirmed by Ralph, with the exception of the names of lesser leaders. Somewhat later, after a brief description of the city, Albert makes it clear that Adhémar and Raymond of Toulouse were attacking the Dog Gate, and that beyond them was the gate besieged by Godfrey opposite which a pontoon bridge was later constructed across the Orontes. Ralph's more schematic description also appears to confirm this. This left the army with major problems which are rather well summarised by Ralph of Caen.[97] St Symeon was their obvious port of supply, but via the Bridge Gate the garrison was in a position to cut the road and to raise havoc with small groups or individuals foraging in the plain to the west and south of the city. They could also attack traffic going to Laodicea and, to a lesser extent, Cilicia. Their access made it difficult to establish a force along the southern part of the wall; south of the Bridge Gate the western wall was so close to the river that an attacking force could have done nothing, while the southern wall was built on a deep gully, the Wadi Zoiba, which made it almost unapproachable. On this side the St George Gate, giving access onto the road to Laodicea, was the only point on the southern circuit worth attacking but as long as the enemy had free access over the Bridge Gate this was hazardous. In addition, the garrison could sally forth from the western side of the river and fire on the Frankish camps close to the walls, and this, as Raymond of Aguilers reports, they did.[98] Control of the bridge over the Orontes in front of the Bridge Gate was therefore the vital point in the attack on the city. As long as that gate was open the garrison could take the initiative and

[97] AA, 366;RC, 641-2, 643.   [98] RA, pp. 48-9.

could easily bring in supplies via the unguarded St George Gate which it covered. There was, however, a limit on what a garrison of not more than 5,000 could achieve. Yaghisiyan could only harass the crusaders in the hope that they would tire of the siege or that they would be defeated by the allies he was actively seeking. For the crusaders, it was vital that they close the Bridge Gate because of the damage the garrison could inflict upon them. This was not achieved until March of 1098, by which time the siege was six months old. In that period there were other priorities pressing upon the crusader army.

The crusaders seem to have recognised that there was little chance of taking Antioch by assault, and nothing of the sort seems ever to have been suggested. Stephen of Blois, who would later be chosen to command the crusade, remarked to his wife that Antioch was 'a city great beyond belief, very strong and unassailable' and this opinion was supported by Raymond of Aguilers while Fulcher suggests that the leaders adopted a Micawberish policy of sticking out a siege and seeing if something would turn up.[99] All these are writing with hindsight but Fulcher was probably right in a sense. All they could do was to conserve their own forces and squeeze Antioch, disrupting the normal life of the city in the hope that something would give. They were probably aware that the Greeks had seized it in 969 after a blockade, by corrupting one of the commanders, and that treachery had opened its gates to Sulayman in 1086.[100] This strategy of blockading Antioch meant that there were very few siege operations such as those we have noted at Nicaea. Early in the siege Adhémar and Raymond were faced by constant sallies from the Dog Gate. Outside it, just below the confluence of the Parmenian torrent and the stream from St Peter's fountain, was a marshy area with a small bridge (see fig. 8). The Provençals first tried to demolish the bridge with hammers and other tools but it was too strong. Then they built a wooden penthouse covered with osier which they pushed onto the bridge; this would not only have prevented sallies but would have also acted as a base for operations against the gate. The enemy showered the machine with arrows – probably the real reason the bridge could not be demolished – and the Christians replied with bows and crossbows, but the defenders sallied forth and

[99] Hagenmeyer, *Kreuzzugsbriefe*, pp. 149–52 Krey, *First Crusade*, p. 155; RA, pp. 48–9; FC, p. 93.
[100] Bouchier, *Antioch*, p. 218; Cahen, *Turkey*, pp. 76–7.

drove off the attackers and set the penthouse on fire. Then three mangonels were built in the hope of destroying the outer wall which defended the city at this point, but they failed. In the end the Provençals organised masses of men (Albert says 1,000) to block the bridge with huge stones and tree-trunks.[101] Albert never dates this fight but it seems to have occurred early on, before the Bridge of Boats, which was certainly in place by December 1098, was built.[102] Another machine was used in late March or April 1098. After the building of a fort outside the Bridge Gate, the leaders decided to built another penthouse, a *talpa* which they pushed onto the bridge with a view to breaking it down, thereby preventing any further enemy sallies. Although it got onto the bridge and began its work, the enemy caught its crew asleep and burned it, much to the irritation of the army as a whole.[103] In neither case was the machinery used in an all-out assault – merely as a means of tightening the screw on Antioch.

The very early part of the siege was remembered by the chroniclers as a happy time when food was plentiful and the enemy quiescent; with the resources of the Orontes valley and the Amouk at their disposal, and fairly free access out into the Syrian plain foraging was easy. But this did not last for long as enemy forces from Antioch and Harem began to harass the army. The main effort of the garrison seems to have been devoted to attacking along the west bank of the Orontes from both the Bridge Gate and the St George Gate, near which there was a ford, cutting communications with St Symeon (see fig. 8). Their activities figure large in the accounts of Raymond of Aguilers and Albert, for the forces about which they are best informed were close to this area. The Anonymous does not mention this fighting – he was preoccupied with enemy raiding down the valley of the Orontes and the mountains above Bohemond's camp.[104] The crusaders identified Harem as the main base of these raiders and sent Bohemond and Robert of Flanders to attack it (see fig. 4). Their scouts found it but were driven back to where Bohemond's main force lay in ambush. In the subsequent fighting, Alberadus of Cagnano was killed and Herman of Cannae lost a horse, but the enemy suffered numerous casualties. Harem was not taken and remained such a grave threat that when materials and

[101] AA, 367–8.   [102] RA, p. 51.   [103] Tudebode, pp. 50–1.
[104] RA, pp. 49–51; AA, 367–73, 419; *GF*, pp. 29–30.

skilled men arrived with the Genoese fleet on 17 November the leaders resolved to build a fort, which later rejoiced in the name *Malregard*, on the hill above the camp of Bohemond.[105] It was well placed to check enemy raids coming down the Orontes valley or around the back of the city's defences.

Much greater pressure was exerted upon the garrison of Antioch by the construction of the Bridge of Boats (see fig. 8). Albert of Aachen is very clear about its purpose – to check enemy raids and open the road to St Symeon, and he is quite clear that it was situated near to the Duke's Gate which the Germans besieged.[106] It enjoyed a limited protection because attackers had to cross the Wadi al Quivaisiya which flowed into the west side of the Orontes a little way to the south. Unfortunately, nobody says when it was built, but it was certainly in place by the time of the foraging expedition of December 1097.[107] Ralph mentions the new bridge but his account of the siege is schematic and the author of the *Gesta Francorum* never mentions it. Albert's dating at this point is very poor and he is ignorant of the expedition to Harem, the building of Bohemond's tower and the arrival of the Genoese fleet, but the context of his account suggests that the Bridge of Boats was built in November 1097. Christmas can certainly be taken as the absolute outside date for the building of this bridge and the probability is that it was built much earlier, drawing on the materials and expertise brought by the Genoese. The pace of siege warfare was, by modern standards, intolerably slow but we can see just how active and organised the crusaders must have been. It was no small achievement to construct Malregard and the Bridge of Boats, which must have been fortified to withstand enemy attack, in a period of less than six weeks, at a time when the army was depleted by knights who were keen to serve outlying forts and when there was a good deal of continued small-scale fighting.[108] This is a tribute to the smooth functioning of the collective leadership which was probably well suited to the conduct of a siege with its deliberate pace. The crusaders must have been painfully aware of how open Antioch was on its southern flank, and Albert says they awarded Tancred forty silver marks per month and

[105] *GF*, pp. 29–30; RA, p. 49 tells us that Robert of Flanders went on this expedition; Tudebode, p. 36; *HBS*, 187.

[106] AA, 368, 366.   [107] See above p. 224.

[108] RA, p. 48 comments on this, though it should be noted that AA, 366 says that some had returned to Godfrey's army from Mamistra.

sent him into the mountains to establish a camp to blockade two gates on that side of the city and observe enemy movements. It is not clear which two gates are intended but one is described as being in the mountains and the other near the Orontes, which suggests that Tancred was between the St George Gate and the posterns above it.[109] Raymond of Aguilers and the Anonymous both say that Tancred was paid to establish a fortress outside the St George Gate in April 1098. It is possible that Albert has misdated the event but he appears to be telling us about some earlier initiative so perhaps the episodes of gallantry and success related by Ralph of Caen occurred at this time. Moreover, in the New Year of 1098 the Anonymous describes this area as 'Tancred's mountain' and Albert says specifically that Tancred abandoned this position at the end of 1097. Indeed, the emphasis in Albert's account of Tancred's doings is on surveillance and fighting in the mountains, rather than the counter-fort at the St George Gate of which we hear later.[110] If Tancred did establish himself here for a time it must have been a blow to the city. Their garrison was aggressive in its efforts to attack the crusaders and they enjoyed the great advantage of height, for from Mt Silpius they could observe the whole crusader army and its movements. This was the other side of the coin. The crusaders had begun a war of attrition – Yaghisiyan tried the same thing. By the Gate of the Duke there were woods where some of the Franks relaxed. On one occasion a noble archdeacon of Metz was playing dice with a lady when they were ambushed and on another Arnulf of Tirs was killed going to the rescue of some people who had been ambushed. After this, Godfrey ordered the clearing of the woods.[111] Albert lamented the sufferings of the army: 'Morning, noon and night every day there were these sudden attacks, sallies, scenes of carnage and endlessly you could hear in the Christian camp always new lamentations over further losses'.[112]

Tancred on his eminence could not always check the enemy. In vengeance for such suffering, Hugh of St Pol and his son Engelrand crossed the Orontes by night and the next day sent a foot-soldier out onto the road before the Bridge Gate as a lure. They killed two of the Turks who pursued him and captured the two others, and the rejoicing in the camp at the sight of these prisoners indicates the

[109] See the map p. 221.   [110] AA, 370, 374; RC, 64–45; RA, p. 63; GF, pp. 32, 43.
[111] AA, 370–1.
[112] AA, 372.

strain of the siege.[113] On another occasion the Turks were shooting across the river at the Christians; they hoped to inflict losses and to draw any force sent against them into an ambush. Engelrand of St Pol led a force across the Bridge of Boats and killed a Turkish horseman, but he had to be careful not to pursue the Turks into their ambush. The strategy to which the crusaders were committed meant a long drawn-out war around Antioch in which encounters such as this, and the business of blocking roads, raiding and bearing enemy raids, would be the day-to-day experience of the army. Sometimes there were greater deeds. The Anonymous records the attack on Harem. Albert tells us that after the building of the Bridge of Boats, which was about a kilometre upstream of the Bridge Gate, there was a major fracas. A group of 300 knights and foot crossed the bridge to forage when the enemy sallied forth, causing heavy casualties and driving the survivors back to the new bridge. The leaders then launched 5,000 mounted men (the figure is surely a gross exaggeration), mostly in mail shirts, against the enemy, Henry of Esch swam across, though fully armoured, rather than endure the delay to get on the bridge. The Turks retreated, then called up reinforcements who pushed the Franks back to their bridge causing heavy losses, especially amongst the foot-soldiers.[114] This kind of warfare must have been nerve-wracking and exhausting to both sides. However, the effect upon the crusaders must have been brutal for they were out in the open while the Turks at least had a secure base.

Against this background, the advance of the siege by the building of Malregard and the Bridge of Boats indicates a pattern of considerable effort and organisation in the period up to Christmas 1097. As we have already noted, there was a common fund and presumably it was from this that Tancred was paid. The committee of leaders seems to have had real authority. It was their collective decision, as we have seen, to impose a close siege on Antioch, to attack Harem, to build Malregard and to launch the expedition which resulted in the foraging battle of 30 December 1097. In the absence of Adhémar and perhaps Robert of Normandy, the leaders met to decide on dispositions for the Lake Battle on the night of 8 February 1098 and decided on the building of the Mahommeries tower in March and

---

[113] AA, 372; Hugh and Engelrand figure in the *Chanson d'Antioche*, 11. 1354, 1377, 1380, 2638, 2673, 2729, 2890, 3651, 4704, 4724, 6135 which develops the theme of the rivalry between the father and son enormously.
[114] AA, 368–70.

Tancred's fort outside the St George Gate in early April. The matter of how to deal with the proposed betrayal of the city was debated by them, probably in two meetings at the end of May or early June 1098.[115] It is no wonder that, speaking of the decision to launch the foraging expedition of late December 1097, Albert speaks highly of the authority of the Council: 'For it had been decided from the first that no person, great or small had the right to oppose that which was ordered in the name of the whole army.'[116] This committee was probably rather wider than the important princes and it is possible that yet wider assemblies were held for special purposes on occasion. At the start of the siege, all the leaders swore an oath to see the matter through and there was a similar oath taken in the emergency of the second siege of Antioch. The Anonymous's account of the decision to build the Mahommeries Tower can be read as having been taken in a wider assembly in which all applauded the proposal of the leaders.[117] They certainly seem to have run the siege competently. The construction of counterforts like Malregard and Tancred's more temporary structure by the St George Gate was a familiar part of the repertoire of war as we have seen, but considerable authority, organisation and, above all, harmony would have been needed to achieve it in the difficult circumstances at Antioch.[118]

In a general sense they were very experienced in this war of attrition which they were now embarked upon, for it resembled the campaigns so many of them had waged or participated in throughout the west; raiding, destroying, foraging, small-scale conflict, this was what they were used to. But the hit-and-run methods of the Turks, evolved out of the circumstances of steppe warfare, were peculiarly well suited to the circumstances of the siege of Antioch where small-scale skirmishes were the norm, as we have observed and rapid fire very effective. These tactics had been grafted onto Moslem armies generally.[119] Albert describes the sallies which killed Adalbero of Metz and Arnulf of Tirs, but stresses that the Turks were always pouncing on pilgrims in the plain, opposite the city, going to St Symeon or looking for food. Raymond of Aguilers, speaking of the fighting outside the city when the Turks

---

[115] *GF*, pp. 29–30, 35, 39, 43–46; RA, pp. 46–7, 49, 56, 58, 59, 64.   [116] AA, 374.
[117] On the make-up of the Council which governed the crusade see above pp. 20–1; FC, p. 93; RA, p. 74; *GF*, pp. 39, 58–9.
[118] For example see above pp. 41–3.   [119] al–Mulk, pp. 111–13.

had heard of the absence of much of the army on the foraging expedition at the end of December 1097, makes it clear that this kind of thing had become a way of life:

'They repeated their customary assaults. The Count, moreover, was compelled to attack them in his usual manner'.[120]

The use of language in this passage is a revelation of military reality.[121] But the crusaders did learn from the march across Asia Minor and the dangerous small-scale fighting outside Antioch. Albert reports how Hugh of St-Pol was moved by the losses of the foragers and mounted a revenge attack with his son Engelrand and their following. The garrison then sent out twenty mounted men who turned in their saddles and fired arrows backwards across the river into the camp, hoping to provoke the Franks into a pursuit which could then be ambushed from inside the Bridge Gate.[122] This was certainly what happened, according to Raymond of Aguilers, during the absence of the foraging party in December 1097, when Turks sallied out from Antioch and drew the Provençals up to the Bridge Gate where reserves fell upon them. Although it was recognised that the Turks were trying to provoke the crusaders on this occasion, Engelrand of St Pol was again sent out to prevent them from being seen to have gained a victory of sorts by enjoying immunity, but he took care not to pursue the enemy too far, and a general and highly confused mêlée then developed on the plain before the city, with knights and Turks criss-crossing like Spitfires and Messerschmits in a dogfight, and indeed the comparison is apt for in both cases there was a huge audience watching their champions. Albert records evident delight and applause when Engelrand unseated and killed a Turk with his lance, but stresses that he was very careful not to get trapped.[123] The crusader instinct, indeed the only sensible tactic in view of Turkish fire-power, was to close with their enemies. When attacked by the army of Damascus during the foraging battle of December 1097, Raymond of Aguilers says that Robert of Flanders charged at them, forcing them to retreat. The dangers of this instinct were all too obvious – they led to heavy losses

---

[120] See above p. 231; RA, pp. 54–5.

[121] See above pp. 229–32 and AA, 372; RA, p. 50, Krey, *The First Crusade*, p. 134.

[122] See above pp. 147–8; Latham and Paterson, discuss this technique of firing backwards in *Saracen Archery*, p. 74 and illustrate it in their 'Archery in the lands of Eastern Islam', in R. Elgood, ed. *Islamic Arms and Armour* (London, 1974), 82–4.

[123] RA, p. 51; AA, 371–3.

at 'Artāh and to the loss of Roger of Barneville at the start of the
second siege of Antioch as small crusader forces were drawn into
ambushes.[124] To prevent charging too far, there needed to be clear
command in any particular action – supplied by Hugh of St-Pol in
Albert's story, but this was a very difficult problem on a larger scale
in an army run by a committee. Another natural response of the
crusaders was to close ranks for mutual protection, a tactic we have
described used by the Byzantines and the crusaders themselves at
Dorylaeum. During the fighting on the plain outside Antioch, at the
time of the foraging battle, Raymond of Toulouse organised his
footmen into close order and it was with a tortoise of interlocking
shields that the Iron Gate was carried. In the spring of 1098, when
the Mahommeries Tower had been built, some Provençal knights
were ambushed nearby; they formed a circle abutting an old house
and so prevented the enemy from outflanking them. A manageable
solidity was organised in the cavalry in the Lake Battle by dividing
them into squadrons.[125] There is every sign that the mass close-order
charge of knights with lances couched was being used increasingly.
In the disastrous charge at 'Artāh, Ralph says that after initial
disorder the Franks organised themselves and charged. 'At the first
shock the lance goes forward, pierces and throws [the enemy]
down.' Describing the relieving charge led by the count of Flanders
in the same fight Albert says that the Franks 'attacked the enemy
with their lances held before them'. We have noted that Engelrand
of St Pol unhorsed his victim with his lance before killing him, the
classic pattern of knightly encounter and in his skirmish the Turks
are described as fighting with bows, the crusaders with lances.
Baldwin of Edessa fell upon the advance guard of Kerbogah's attack
on his city 'with the lance of the Franks and the bow of the
Armenians'.[126] The examples of Hugh of St Pol in the plain outside
the Bridge Gate and Bohemond during the attack on Harem show
the Franks learning to set ambushes themselves. It was a difficult
business, but the disciplines of war were forcing the Franks into
methods of countering Turkish tactics, and above all the fire-power
upon which they were based.

We tend to make a sharp distinction between a siege and field
warfare, but in reality this is false. A siege was a kind of battle

---

[124] RA, pp. 51–2; see above pp. 192–3.
[125] RA, pp. 51, 56, 57, 63; AA, 363; *GF*, p. 36.
[126] RC, pp. 639–41; AA, 331, 373, 397.

involving most of the general techniques of war in addition to some specialised ones. In the case of Antioch the nature of the crusader strategy – a close blockade without assault – makes the point very clearly. The opening phase of the conflict had seen the crusaders gradually tightening their grip on the city, though at a terrible price. In the next phase they were to be seized by a crisis of supply. One vital aspect of all war – and we have noted Vegetius on the point – was to deny the enemy food. For the crusaders this was easier said than done, for Antioch appears to have been well-stocked. Had it not been, then the siege simply could not have endured. But also food could find its way into the city through the St George Gate and the Iron Gate, even perhaps the Bridge Gate, and, in addition, all the posterns along the mountains. In the end such supply was not satisfactory for a major city, especially one with large disaffected elements – Syrian and Armenian Christians of which the crusaders were well aware. The Anonymous claims that many of them were forced to fight for the Turks because their womenfolk were hostages.[127] But it must be repeated that attrition cuts both ways. In any siege the attackers are at least as likely to starve as the defenders – and by Christmas 1097 this situation was hurting the army badly.

[127] *GF*, pp. 29, 41.

CHAPTER 8

The siege of Antioch; crisis and delivery

The siege was significantly tighter by December 1097 but by that time operations were running into a new phase for the sources are unanimous – food was desperately short. This crisis of supply saw the crusade come desperately close to failure. Albert of Aachen says they had simply eaten up the resources of the countryside and the surrounding cities round about. Ralph of Caen speaks of shortage, stressing how food had to come from afar: Syria, Cilicia, Rhodes, Cyprus, Chios, Samos, Crete and Mytilene. It was a bitter winter, quite unexpectedly like home as Stephen of Blois would remark, and Ralph speaks of its harshness rotting the weapons of the army. Even Stephen of Blois, who was an incorrigible optimist, speaks of the suffering and starvation amongst the North French from which many were rescued only through God's aid and the wealth of the leaders. Anselm recalled that bitter winter: 'Why recount the trials of many kinds, which, even if passed over in silence, are sufficiently evident in themselves – hunger, intemperate weather and the desertion of faint-hearted soldiers.'[1] Such hardship must have had a devastating effect on the army encamped in the plain outside Antioch and exposed to the worst of the weather. In December 1099 Baldwin of Edessa and Bohemond met at Baniyas south of Laodicea and marched south to Jerusalem where they arrived in fulfilment of their crusading vows on 21 December. During this march of only some three weeks in winter weather Fulcher records deaths due to exposure. The attrition in the crusader camp must have been appalling. The nature of casualties has already been discussed but it is worth remembering that in the American Civil War 200,000 men died in battle, and twice that number from disease.[2] Moreover, the enemy were pressing hard, especially from their bases beyond the

---

[1] Hagenmeyer, *Kreuzzugsbriefe*, 150, 157–60.   [2] FC, p. 131; Terraine, *White Heat*, p. 17.

Iron Bridge, so that the Anonymous confesses: 'No-one dared to go into the land of the Saracens except with a strong force.'[3]

A strong force led by Bohemond and Robert of Flanders was accordingly assembled and sent off to ravage for food towards the lands of Aleppo only to encounter a powerful enemy army led by Duqaq of Damascus. The Anonymous says that Bohemond volunteered, but both Raymond of Aguilers and Albert report that he and Robert of Flanders were sent by the leaders, Raymond noting that Godfrey was ill and Robert of Normandy absent. It is not clear who was in command, and probably neither leader was. It was a substantial force but surely not as large as the Anonymous's 20,000 infantry and knights nor Albert's reported 2000 knights and 15,000 foot; Raymond of Aguilers says there were 400 knights, which sounds reasonable in view of what we know of loss of horses, and mentions the infantry, whose numbers we cannot estimate, only in passing when he says that Bohemond was alerted to the presence of the enemy by some of his peasants. His figure of 60,000 for the enemy must be regarded as a gross exaggeration.[4] The expedition entered the valley of the Orontes, for according to the Arab sources it met the army of Damascus near Albara and later fell back on Ruj, the base which Raymond of Toulouse had captured on the eve of the siege of Antioch. This suggests that they aimed to ravage the rich area of the Jebel Barisha where they would later establish a strong lodgment.[5] It is likely that the expedition reached Ruj by taking the road via Daphne to the Orontes crossing at the Jisir ash-Shogur, for Bohemond came back over 'Tancred's mountain', which is crossed by the Antioch – Daphne road and so-called because Tancred later blockaded the St George Gate there.[6] This route must have been the normal line of communication with Ruj and explains how they managed to keep such an exposed area in their control through the bitter winter of 1097. Harem effectively cut them off from the plain of North Syria (see fig. 4). The force which they encountered was that of Duqaq who had left Damascus about the middle of the month and was accompanied by his great atabeg, Tughtigin, and Janah-ad-Daulah of Homs. He was responding to the supplications

[3] AA, 374; RA, p. 50; *GF*, p. 30; FC, p. 94; Hagenmeyer, *Kreuzzugsbriefe*, pp. 149–52; RC, 647.

[4] *GF*, p. 30; RA, p. 51; AA, 373; on horses see below pp. 281–2.

[5] See below pp. 309–10.

[6] *GF*, p. 32.

of Shams-ad-Daulah who, as we have noted, had been sent by his father to seek aid for Antioch.[7]

The Franks were completely unaware of the presence of an enemy force in the vicinity of Albara; according to Raymond of Aguilers the crusaders were attacking a village when some of their footmen cried out that the enemy was at hand and Robert of Flanders and a small group which included some Provençals rode out to chase them off. They were successful, then suddenly saw the enemy main force, notably many foot, on a nearby hill. Albert says they awoke one morning to find the enemy all about them. The Damascus army was making its way north and had reached Shaizar when news came of the Frankish incursion and it moved to the attack.[8] The Arab accounts tell us little else about the battle. Amongst the Western sources Ralph of Caen makes no mention of it at all, perhaps because Tancred was not present, and neither does the second letter of Stephen of Blois, written in April 1098. Anselm of Ribemont, writing in July 1098, gives it only a brief mention. The Anonymous was not present and was obviously reporting second hand. He does not mention surprise and simply says that as the enemy approached they divided into two forces with the intention of surrounding the Franks, but that Robert of Flanders and Bohemond charged shoulder-to-shoulder in a single line into the enemy who took to flight, and so 'we came back in great triumph' and 'our men took their horses and other plunder'. It all sounds very straightforward – a brief hard fight and to the victor the spoils. But it is precisely on this point that equivocation sets in, for having told us that they were victorious and seized spoil, the Anonymous goes on to say that when they returned to Antioch very few of Bohemond's men had any plunder.[9] Raymond of Aguilers was not an eyewitness either and presumably got his information from the Provençals who accompanied Robert of Flanders. He says that enemy scouts caught Bohemond unawares when he was plundering; they were driven off by Robert of Flanders who then confronted the enemy main force. Robert was reinforced and sent against the enemy as a vanguard while Bohemond trailed behind to prevent the enemy surrounding them: 'For the Turks have this custom in fighting: even though they

---

[7] *Damascus Chronicle of the Crusades*, p. 43; *Aleppo Chronicle*, p. 579; on the capture of Rugia see *GF*, p. 26.
[8] RA, pp. 51–52; AA, 373; *Damascus Chronicle of the Crusades*, p. 43.
[9] *GF*, pp. 30–3; Hagenmeyer, *Kreuzzugsbriefe*, pp. 150, 158.

are few in number, they always strive to encircle their enemy. This they attempted to do in this battle also, but by the foresight of Bohemond the wiles of the enemy were prevented'. According to him when the enemy saw that the Franks were determined to close they fled and were pursued for 3.2 km, while Bohemond joined in the execution. However, this account suffers from the same strange inconsistency as that of the Anonymous – the admission that there was no plunder, and Raymond's explanation strains credulity – it was he said: 'A strange result of this achievement . . . after the enemy had been put to flight the courage of our men decreased, so that they did not dare to pursue those whom they saw headlong in flight'.[10] Surely, if there had been any pursuit at all the enemy camp would have been looted? These two accounts are fairly compatible if we take the Anonymous's reference to Bohemond and Robert riding to battle side-by-side figuratively rather than literally, but it is a strange battle in which the victor gains no spoils. This can be explained in part; the crusaders had fought a hard battle and avoided encirclement but, unable to destroy the enemy, they feared to press and fell back on Ruj. This theory of a drawn battle is perfectly plausible and the Moslem sources which simply say that the Franks fell back to Ruj and Duqaq to Homs can be read as substantiating it. In this view the Anonymous and Raymond were claiming victory when the reality was rather different for almost any victory would have yielded the plunder of the enemy camp.[11]

There is another weakness in these two accounts; they both report a battle of knights – whatever happened to all the infantry whom Raymond mentions and the Anonymous says were present in large numbers? Albert of Aachen tells us about them. He was dependent upon Lorrainer knights for information and as far as we know none were present, but the Lorrainers were later to enjoy close relations with the Flemings, so we cannot just dismiss his account. According to Albert, on the morning of 31 December the crusaders found themselves surrounded. Bohemond called the knights together and formed them into a phalanx, 'a tightly-packed front, a tortoise of shields', and broke out of the enemy encirclement abandoning their booty and leaving the foot to be massacred – presumably the heavy

---

[10] RA, pp. 51–2.
[11] Runciman, 1. 221 offers this explanation; Smail, *Crusading Warfare*, p. 171 offers no general comment, simply observing that, on the basis of these two sources, the crusaders had learned not to allow themselves to be surrounded.

casualties mentioned in the Arab sources. The following day Robert of Flanders, who had become separated from Bohemond, gathered 200 knights and attacked the enemy who were by now thoroughly dispersed, and recovered some of the plunder but was forced to abandon it. The main difficulty of the account is Bohemond's role – he is said to have returned to Antioch crestfallen and what little glory there was thereby went to Robert of Flanders, but Raymond of Aguilers, otherwise no friend of Bohemond, says that he gained a great reputation at this time. However, Albert generally minimises Bohemond's deeds, perhaps consciously in order to exalt Godfrey – this shows most clearly in the battle against Kerbogah.[12] If we allow for this bias Albert's account explains the salient facts rather better than any other, especially the lack of plunder and the fate of the infantry. Moreover, his explanation of the fate of the infantry receives a kind of endorsement from Raymond of Aguilers who says that when six weeks later the leaders were planning the Lake Battle, they decided not to send infantry out against Ridwan's approaching army for fear that some in their ranks would panic.[13] This is rather puzzling, because by this time a large number of horseless knights could have provided high-quality infantry but it becomes much more understandable if there were clear experience that infantry could not stand in the open, and anyway they were likely to remember, by recent example, that knights could abandon them all too easily. Moreover, in a more general way the accounts of this conflict are sketchy, which suggests that it was something less than a glorious victory. Since we do not even know where the battle took place and are faced with contradictory and vague accounts, it cannot be reconstructed with any certainty.[14] The foraging battle was a drawn battle; the crusaders were surprised but their cavalry broke out of an enemy trap and fought well, in close order and perhaps with a rearguard. They even returned to the fray again the next day, but they were unable to gather food and their victory was gained at the expense of a massacre of infantry. The enemy, for their part, were either unable or unwilling to follow up their advantage

---

[12] AA, 373–4, 425; RA, p. 53.   [13] RA, p. 56.

[14] The tendency of later writers to present tidy and logical accounts of battles which are essentially chaotic affairs is thoroughly criticised by J. Keegan, *The Face of Battle* (London, 1976). It is worth noting that in 'Operation Battleaxe' in the Western desert in 1941 twenty tanks of Seventh Armoured Brigade, one fifth of their strength, simply went missing and were not accounted for until two years later, and even that story was unconfirmed: B. Pitt, *The Crucible of War: Western Desert 1941* (London, 1980) pp. 300–1.

and contented themselves with having repulsed an attack. From the crusader viewpoint the result of the battle was in a sense victory, for survival was victory and it may well have been from this perspective that a rather inglorious episode was later written up by those chroniclers who mentioned it, albeit with inconsistencies. It was ignored by others or dismissed briefly. Albert was not personally involved and simply recorded what he had learned, with all its limitations and confusions, some years later. But the episode shows that the crusaders were learning to deal with Turkish attacks. They knew the need for close order at Dorylaeum. The use of a rearguard was in a sense developed during the attack on Harem in November 1097 when knights attacking the castle fell back upon Bohemond's main force which then crushed the enemy.[15] That such a sensible adaptation to the needs of war against the Turks could be employed in an army taken by surprise points to a high degree of discipline and order at least amongst the knights. A factor in instilling this was undoubtedly the sense that they had to win together or die separately, and this was probably an even more powerful incentive on the next occasion when they met an enemy army, at the Lake Battle some six weeks later. The Foraging Battle was a near-disaster for the crusader army, perhaps because of the lack of a single command. They suffered heavy losses and returned *victore et vacuo*, victorious but empty-handed, as Raymond of Aguilers puts it, with little food for the army.[16]

The check administered to the army deepened the crisis. Starvation continued with appalling losses, we have already observed. There was unrest and the crusader leaders established judges to impose order and peace. Associated with this were the ecclesiastical celebrations in early January 1098, called for by Adhémar, whose most notorious measure was the expulsion of women. This was a desperate effort to revive morale which had plummeted in the wake of the failure of the foraging expedition. To reassure their followers the princes promised to see out the siege. Even so there were deserters, most notably William the Carpenter, Lord of Melun and Peter the Hermit who fled 'because of this great wretchedness and misery'. Bohemond caught both of them but William later sloped off any-

[15] *GF*, pp. 29–30.
[16] *GF*, p. 33; RA, p. 53; AA, 375; on the battle see below pp. 246–52.

way.[17] Others secretly considered leaving and even Bohemond wavered, announcing that he could not bear to watch his men and horses dying of starvation. Louis, archdeacon of Toul fled with 300 followers to a place about 4.8 km from Antioch which was well-supplied, only to be slaughtered by the Turks.[18] The fact that food was to be found reminds us that this was the period of the wanderings of Peter Bartholemew in search of food.[19] Food was available – the Anonymous says that after the failure of the foraging expedition Syrian and Armenian merchants bought up supplies and sold them at high prices.[20] The problem was not just lack of food, although that was to a degree inevitable in winter, but getting it to the camp. For in the winter sea travel was difficult and the Turks were stepping up their attacks on the crusader army. Albert says that it was at this time of great misery that the crusaders got into the habit of foraging in well-protected groups of 200–300, but even so there was terrible carnage.[21] The Provençal knights refused to cover such foraging expeditions in January 1098 because of the loss of horses, and Count Raymond was obliged to offer them compensation. The military significance of this event has escaped notice somewhat. It was a profoundly ominous sign for the crusader army – that knights were fearful of escorting foraging expeditions. In the war of attrition this was a clear sign that the strain was telling, the balance tilting away from the crusader army in favour of the enemy. If this continued then the army would starve to death. It was not something confined to the Provençal army – all the leaders were obliged to offer compensation for lost horses in the same way as the Count.[22] It cannot be too heavily emphasised that the first object of war is to get food and to deny it to your enemy; if the crusaders were becoming unwilling to fight for it they faced starvation and collapse. This is a tribute to the skill of the Turks in Antioch and their allies in Harem and along the Aleppo road. The absence of Robert of

---

[17] *GF*, pp. 33–4; AA, 378–9 FC, p. 95; *Gesta Francorum Iherusalem expugnantium, RHC Oc.* 3. 499; RA, pp. 54–5; on the attempted disciplinary action see J. A. Brundage, 'Prostitution, miscegenation and sexual purity in the First Crusade', in P. Edbury, ed., *Crusade and Settlement in the Latin East*, (Cardiff, 1985), pp. 58–9.

[18] FC, p. 94; RA, pp. 53–4, who suggests that Bohemond was even then trying to gain Antioch; AA, 375.

[19] See above pp. 209–10.   [20] *GF*, p. 33.   [21] AA, 375.

[22] RA, pp. 54–5; on this see France, 'Departure of Tatikios', 145; J. Richard, 'La confrérie de la première croisade: à propos d'un épisode de la première croisade', in B. Jeannau, ed., *Etudes de civilisation médiévale: mélanges offerts à E. R. Labande*, (Poitiers, 1974), pp. 617–22.

Normandy, who remained at Laodicea, and the illness of Godfrey and Raymond of Toulouse could not have helped matters while the departure of Tatikios, the imperial representative, in early February 1098 must have depressed morale even further.[23]

The Anonymous says Tatikios departed promising to fetch supplies and reinforcements and, according to Raymond of Aguilers, to bring imperial aid. Their comments are, however, deeply informed by hindsight; the general tenor of their remarks is a charge of cowardice but it appears that Tatikios left before news of the approach of a major enemy relief force reached the army. Albert lists Tatikios amongst those present at the start of the siege, remarks that he took up a position behind the others because he was 'ever ready for flight', and draws attention to his presence later at Philomelium as one who had deserted the army; however he gives no account of his actual departure, a subject on which Ralph of Caen is also silent. The letters of Stephen of Blois and Anselm of Ribemont, which are contemporary documents, do not mention his departure at all. Perhaps, in the circumstances, it seemed quite a good idea for him to seek imperial aid and this story was accepted at the time. In retrospect the event assumed a quite different importance and indeed it was to have disastrous implications for the Byzantine alliance.[24] It is likely that Tatikios had resurrected his idea of a distant blockade of Antioch, precipitating a quarrel with the count of Toulouse who was obliged to develop a scheme whereby he compensated knights who lost horses on foraging expeditions, thus depriving Tatikios's policy of its chief rationale. Tatikios thus found himself isolated, suspicious of Bohemond and at odds with the count of Toulouse, and so he decided to leave the army to seek help. In the circumstances of isolation and starvation in which the army found itself this must have appeared pretty reasonable at the time.[25] Albert of Aachen mentions further efforts to mount foraging expeditions by Godfrey de Bouillon and Raymond of Toulouse, both of which failed. So severe was the crisis of morale that in the face of disorders in the army severe measures had to be taken to enforce discipline and morality; one of the victims was an adulterous couple who were whipped and paraded naked round the army as per the arrange-

[23] RA, 50, 55–6; 62, *GF*, pp. 34–5.   [24] *GF*, pp. 34–5; RA, pp. 54–5; AA, 366, 417.
[25] RA, p. 55; France, 'Depature of Tatikios', 144–6; see also Richard, 'La confrérie de la première croisade', 617–22.

ments made in the New Year.[26] This appalling winter of 1098 with its severe losses was a terrible test of the will of the crusader army and in these dark hours efforts to tighten the siege all but came to a halt.

Albert of Aachen records what may have been one effort to close a major gate of the city early in 1098. He is vivid in his descriptions of the savagery of the enemy raids coming out of Antioch. He believed that the main source for these raids was in the mountains and far away from the St Paul Gate which was besieged by Bohemond, this suggests the St George Gate, but his topography is always weak and it is possible that the Bridge Gate was intended. Here, he tells us, Count Raymond made an effort to establish a redoubt and one day ambushed an enemy attack, capturing a young man of noble family. The princes tried to use him to get his family to betray the city but Yaghisiyan heard of the matter and stopped negotiations. The unfortunate young man, accused by native Christians of having persecuted them, was tortured and decapitated. This may be the same person whom the *Historia Belli Sacri* describes as an Emir who had put to death twelve pilgrims by throwing them off the city wall; he was captured by Peter Raymond of Hautpoul and an effort was made to use him to gain a lodgment in the city. When this failed he was killed.[27] Albert's dating is very confused and it is possible that the story relates to Raymond of Toulouse's tower, the Mahommeries, built in March 1098 outside the Bridge Gate, especially as Raymond of Aguilers says that until this tower was built the Count had done little due to illness and was accused of laziness.[28] It is probable, however, that this was an earlier effort to tighten the siege for Albert later refers to the construction of the Mahommeries in the clearest terms.[29] However, there can be no doubt that the starving army was quite clearly on the defensive in January and February 1098 and indeed perilously close to defeat. The Anonymous's comment on the situation of the army at this time is eloquent and apposite:

We were thus left in the direst need, for the Turks were harrying us on every side, so that none of our men dared to go outside the encampment. The Turks were menacing us on the one hand, and hunger tormented us on the other, and there was no-one to help us or bring us aid. The rank and file, with those who were very poor, fled to Cyprus or Rum or into the

---

[26] AA, 378-9.　　[27] AA, 378-9; *HBS*, p. 189.　　[28] RA, p. 62.　　[29] AA, 386.

mountains. We dared not go down to the sea for fear of those brutes of Turks, and there was no road open to us anywhere.[30]

It was at this point that the crusaders heard of the approach of a strong enemy relief army under Ridwan of Aleppo. Yaghisiyan had sent his son Shams-ad-Daulah to seek assistance and after Duqaq's failure to relieve the city in December 1097 he proceeded to Aleppo.[31] The increased enemy pressure which the Franks seem to have been feeling by the end of January, was probably the result of this diplomacy for from Harem Ridwan was in a good position to mount attacks on the crusaders. Matthew of Edessa suggests that the crusader leaders tried to counter Antiochene diplomacy by telling Duqaq after the foraging battle that they had no designs outside the old Byzantine lands. *The Historia Belli Sacri* suggests that the battle took place because a converted Turk, who had taken the Christian name Hilary, defected and told the Aleppans of the plight of the crusader army though this seems unlikely.[32] The besiegers were now, as the Anonymous makes clear, in some sense besieged. In early February Ridwan's army was approaching and on 8 February the leaders held a meeting to discuss what to do about the approaching enemy army which was by now very close. Aleppo is only one hundred kilometres from Antioch – Raymond of Aguilers says a mere two days journey and he is supported by Ibn Butlân, who says it was a 'day and a night's march'.[33] Ridwan achieved a high degree of surprise for the leaders met in the house of the bishop (who presumably was absent) on 8 February, by which time they knew the enemy were encamped at Harem only thirty-five kilometres away (see fig. 4). The central fact about this battle on the crusader side was that they had very few mounted knights at their disposal – only 700 in all and many of them mounted on pack animals and even oxen.[34] The leaders then took a highly significant step: for the first time they appointed a single commander for the whole force. They chose Bohemond. Even before the crusade he had enjoyed a great military reputation, as Albert tells us, and Raymond of Aguilers testifies to the glory he had won fighting against Harem

[30] *GF*, p. 35.   [31] *Aleppo Chronicle*, p. 579.   [32] Matthew, 33; *HBS*, 190.

[33] RA, p. 49; Ibn Butlân, tr. and cited in Lestrange, *Palestine under the Moslems*, p. 370.

[34] On the shortage of horses see below pp. 281–2; there is virtual unanimity on the figure of 700; RA, p. 56, AA, 380, Stephen of Blois and Anselm in Hagenmeyer, *Kreuzzugsbriefe*, pp. 151, 157. The only dissenter is RC, 647 who gives a figure of 200.

and on the foraging expedition.[35] The dangers of the situation had forced the leaders to accept one commander against all their instincts for independence. It was almost certainly Bohemond's plan which they now followed; it was agreed to divide the army taking almost all the knights available (700) out by night under the command of Bohemond so as to avoid warning the garrison, leaving the foot to defend the camp.[36] Even the Islamic sources agree with the western accounts that their army was very small as compared to that of Ridwan. Kemal ad-Din reports that the Aleppan army was defeated by a smaller Frankish force.[37] We do not know how long it took Ridwan to raise his force nor are there any indications of its size from the Islamic sources. Albert of Aix suggests 30,000 but more impressive is the testimony of two near-contemporary crusader letters, those of Stephen of Blois and Anselm of Ribemont, which suggest that it numbered 12,000.[38] That might appear quite modest, and indeed the only major allies supporting him were Sokman the Artukid emir of Amida and the emir of Hamah, but it must be judged in relation to the military strength of the crusader army which had dwindled markedly.

According to the Anonymous the engagement took place 'between the river and the lake' and Raymond of Aguilers agrees, adding that the army used these obstacles on its flanks to prevent the enemy encircling them. They formed, he says, into six squadrons each in a little valley. Raymond's account of the fighting is very schematic – at first the crusaders pushed forward against an enemy firing arrows and it was pretty hard going with heavy losses, but then the enemy front line became entangled with the main force and the enemy fled to Harem, which was promptly burned. The Anonymous corroborates this account with rather more detail. According to him, Bohemond was placed in command by the council of leaders and at dawn sent forward a reconnaissance force which reported the enemy marching with two squadrons thrown forward of a main force. Bohemond then organised his army into five squadrons thrown ahead with his own held in reserve. The description of the fighting is very vivid – the Anonymous was evidently there and gives dramatic detail from which it would appear that the crusaders charged and hand-to-hand fighting ensued. The enemy main force

[35] AA, 344 and see above pp. 75–7, 239–41; RA, pp. 53–54.
[36] RA, p. 56; *GF* p. 35.
[37] *Aleppo Chronicle*, p. 579.   [38] AA, 380; Hagenmeyer, *Kreuzzugsbriefe*, 149–52, 157–60.

then came up and at the climax of the battle, at the very moment when the crusader line seemed about to break, Bohemond committed the reserve and the enemy fled, setting fire to Harem in their precipitate retreat.[39] This virtual unanimity is impressive, but Raymond did employ the *Gesta Francorum* as a source, particularly for the period February–March 1098 using no fewer than three passages concerned with the Lake Battle itself, and others with events in this period, which seems to indicate that Raymond was relying on it.[40] Moreover, neither of these accounts makes the location of the battle clear, while Raymond's remark that the army chose to rest its flanks on the river and the lake appears to be an elaboration based on the Anonymous's statement that the battle was fought between the lake and the river and should be seen in the light of Raymond's earlier comments about the enemy technique of surrounding. Furthermore, his notion of a defensive battle with the crusaders forming a line backed by a reserve is not quite what appears in the *Gesta Francorum* and is rather vitiated by his statement that the distance between the river and the lake at this point was a mile, for he also tells us that St Symeon was ten miles from Antioch (actually twenty-six kilometres) which appears to mean that a small force of 700 in six squadrons, of which one was held in reserve, was strung out across two and a half kilometres as a blocking force.[41] Moreover, if the leaders had wished to fight a purely defensive battle, why did they not take their infantry and hold the Iron Bridge? Raymond and the Anonymous give no real idea of the site, although the latter refers to the enemy coming towards the army from the river. Stephen of Blois who was present says that it was fought in a little plain near the Iron Bridge but does not say which side of it. Ralph of Caen was writing rather later at Antioch and says that the crusaders crossed the Iron Bridge into a little plain where a small hill concealed them. Further, he tells us that Conan of Brittany died in the battle and reports that he had seen his grave on the site in question.[42] This is convincing evidence of the location and Ralph's account of the battle is interesting. According to him the crusaders deployed, hidden from the enemy by a small hill, and

[39] RA, pp. 56–8; *GF*, pp. 35–8.
[40] *Anonymi Gesta Francorum*, ed. H. Hagenmeyer (Heidelberg, 1890), pp. 50–8 passages number 7 and 8 (2), and see also 6, 9, 10. My own work confirms this dependence.
[41] RA, pp. 49, 52; Smail, *Crusading Warfare*, p. 171 follows this interpretation.
[42] Hagenmeyer, *Kreuzzugsbriefe*, pp. 149–52; RC, 647–8.

charged at them; this disconcerted the enemy who feared that more were concealed behind the hill. The suggestion is that it was an ambush which succeeded because the attack with lances forward (*erectis hastis*) was fully co-ordinated and the enemy were apprehensive that the little hill might conceal more troops. Albert's account is suspect because he tells us that Adhémar, who probably was away, played a major role, that Raymond of Toulouse, whom no other account mentions, was present, and that Robert of Normandy, who was probably away at Laodicea, fought. However, we have no very definite evidence of where they all were and Raymond does not mention the count of Toulouse in his account of the infantry fighting back at Antioch. Moreover, Tudebode says that Adhémar, Eustace of Boulogne and Robert of Normandy were left behind to defend the camp.[43] Albert agrees with the Anonymous that the 700 knights set out by night. This is an important point for any force crossing the Iron Bridge in daylight would have been observed either by scouts or from Harem. At day-break, Albert says, they sent forward scouts led by Walter of St-Valéri-sur-Somme and Bohemond the Turk on the basis of whose information Adhémar and the other leaders led a charge into the massed ranks of the enemy who fled. Albert's account tends to exalt the role of Godfrey and ignore Bohemond, but he does add the interesting detail that the enemy's resistance was somewhat lessened because heavy rain had made their bows useless.[44]

We have, therefore, two views of the battle – that of Raymond of Aguilers who portrays it as a defensive struggle in which the crusaders stood between the river and the lake, and that of Albert and Ralph who portray it as an ambush. The account of the Anonymous is very much that of one caught up in the event and, while undoubtedly true as far as it goes, lacks context and could be read as corroborating either view. In fact, the crucial factor is location. What is certain from the information of Ralph is that the battle was fought beyond the Iron Bridge and that a hill featured in it. To this we can add that the army was between the river and the lake,

---

[43] RA, pp. 56, says that the leaders met on 8 February: 'in the house of the bishop' which strongly suggests that he was away, and later tells us that Count Raymond had been ill for much of the winter, p. 63; on Robert of Normandy see above pp. 215–19; RC, 647 lists Godfrey, Stephen of Blois and Bohemond as present, and to this list common sense would suggest we add Tancred and Hugh of Vermandois who seem to have spent much time with Stephen, but this list is a guess; PT, p. 43

[44] AA, 380–2.

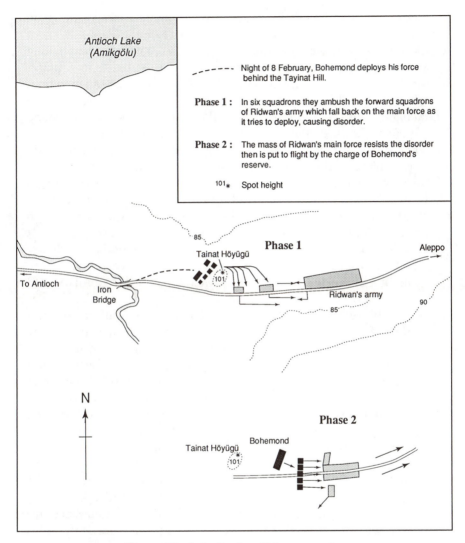

Fig. 9   The Lake Battle: 9 February 1098

according to the Anonymous and others. The land beyond the
Orontes is a rolling plain with elevations between 86 metres and 90
metres crossed west–east by the Antioch–Aleppo road which climbs
very gently away from the Iron Bridge. To the north and below the
81 metres contour line was the great Antioch Lake (Amikgölu) whose
southern shore was then quite close to the road, probably on the 86

metres contour line. A little over two kilometres east of the Iron Bridge, and on the north side of the road is a hill, the Tainat Höyügü (Arabic, Tell Tayinat), rising to 101 metres, and 622 metres long and 503 metres wide. It was surely here that the battle took place, for this site agrees perfectly with what Ralph and the other sources tell us – a small hill between the river and the lake (see fig. 9).[45] By taking up this position just north of the road Bohemond was placing the enemy towards the river, as the Anonymous suggests. It was a terrible risk, for behind and to his left lay a marsh, and the only retreat back to the Iron Bridge would be cut if the enemy broke through along the road. But if the crusaders had wanted to block Ridwan's path and fight a grinding battle they would surely have chosen to do so at the Iron Bridge where geography gave them advantages and where their infantry would have been very useful. It is evident that the crusaders, and specifically Bohemond, decided to attack Ridwan before he was prepared, hence the secret departure by night and the decision to take only cavalry whose mobility would enable them to prepare an ambush. In any case the battle was extremely well conceived. The crusaders could not afford to stand on the defensive and they outmanoeuvred Ridwan by marching by night and ambushing him. Their troops were marshalled in squadrons which made control easier. They obviously kept together and because of surprise and the wet weather which inhibited the use of bows, they were able to close with the enemy in what seems to have been a tight compact formation. Ridwan's main force was preceded by two squadrons, according to the Anonymous, and it would have been these that the initial charge of Bohemond's five forward units took in the flank. These two squadrons fell back and became enmeshed with the main body. At this point the sheer mass of the enemy army threatened to break through the crusader army, but Bohemond recognised the crisis of the battle and unleashed his reserve whose charge finally crushed the disordered enemy. This

---

[45] The Lake of Antioch has now all but vanished due to drainage schemes. Pre-war maps show it to have been three to four kilometres north of the Aleppo road, but, by then, drainage efforts had made an impact on its size. Moreover, Raymond of Aguiler's statement that it was only two kilometres above the river refers to mid-winter when it would have been at its greatest. There are other mounds along this road (indeed, the Amouk is dotted with them) but the Tell Tayinat is the only one which can be described as being between the river and the lake. Set north of the Aleppo road it is aligned NE to SW. On its southern end, close to the road, is a Moslem cemetry, but the top of the hill is disfigured by an abandoned factory of 1950s vintage.

was generalship of a very high order and shows the crusaders maximising their resources and learning from the enemy. The use of a reserve quite clearly held back to engage the enemy main force once committed is the salient feature of Bohemond's dispositions. The Anonymous and Albert speak of a sharp charge in squadrons, and Ralph of Caen adds that this occurred, *erectis hastis* – the suggestion is of a classic charge of knights with couched spears falling upon an exposed enemy. The coherence and discipline of the crusader army enabled it to destroy a much larger force which may well have expected them to fight defensively on the Iron Bridge. It was the aggressive tactics of Bohemond which won the battle. But there was here a further point of some importance for the future. This was the first time the crusaders had fought a major engagement under single command: at Dorylaeum nobody was in command, while there was a similar problem in December 1097. This raised the question of an overall leader. It was perhaps no coincidence that shortly after this Stephen of Blois seems to have been chosen as overall commander.[46]

The success at the Lake Battle ushered in the third and decisive phase of the siege, during which the crusaders were able to tighten the screw on Antioch (see fig. 10). It must have been a great relief that Harem, commanding the approaches to the Iron Bridge now passed to the Armenians.[47] The defeat of Ridwan happened at a happy moment, for in the crusader camp were envoys from Egypt who had come in response to the embassy they had sent by sea earlier. This delegation was given the heads of slain enemies as tokens of victory. They seem to have stayed for some time according to the Anonymous who mentions their presence in the camp on 9 February and at St Symeon in the wake of the victory over the garrison on the St Symeon road on 6 March. Stephen of Blois actually says that some kind of understanding was reached with them: 'the Emperor of Babylon ... established peace and concord with us', while Albert of Aix describes this as a friendly meeting and in the context of the siege of Jerusalem accuses the Fatimids of having broken the agreement then made. Islamic tradition strongly asserts that at this time the Egyptian Vizir, al-Afdal, pursued a policy of friendship towards the Franks and that indeed he later regretted this.[48] From the Fatimid point of view the westerners could offer

[46] See below p. 256.   [47] *Aleppo Chronicle*, p. 579.
[48] On the sending of the embassy see above p. 211; *GF*, pp. 37, 43; RA, p. 58; AA, 379, 383, 463, 484–5; Hagenmeyer, *Kreuzzugsbriefe*, pp. 149–52; Köhler, *Allianzen und Verträge*, pp. 64–5.

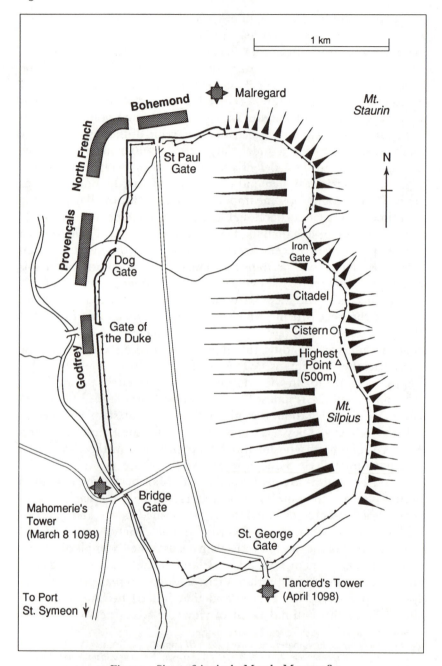

Fig. 10   Siege of Antioch, March–May 1098

important aid against the Turks and indeed in July 1098 in the wake of Kerbogah's defeat they were able to seize Jerusalem. The question of Jerusalem was of course an important stumbling block for only twenty years before it had been in Egyptian hands. Raymond of Aguilers, who gives the only clear account of the terms of discussion, reports that the army was willing to agree to ally with al-Afdal and restore to him all that he had lost to the Turks, provided that he would give them Jerusalem and the lands around it. However, if al-Afdal saw the crusade as primarily a Byzantine expedition it was possible to see this demand for an arrangement there in the light of the past Byzantine protectorate over the city.[49] It is clear that some kind of *modus uiuendi* was reached with the Egyptians which perhaps anticipated, rather than agreed, the formation of a protectorate over Jerusalem on earlier Byzantine models. A crusader delegation returned to Cairo with the Egyptian emissaries and was to spend a year there.[50] This may well have contributed to the inactivity of the leaders in the summer and autumn of 1098 and increased their reluctance to attack the Fatimid sphere of influence, something which was undertaken only reluctantly.

It was the arrival of an English fleet at St Symeon on 4 March 1098 which enabled the crusaders to take the next step in tightening the siege. The following day a meeting of the leaders resolved to build a counterfort outside the Bridge Gate, and Bohemond and Raymond of St Gilles were dispatched to escort the sailors and reinforcements bringing up material from the coast. It is hardly surprising that this evoked a very sharp response from the garrison who ambushed the convoy and dispersed it, only to be defeated

---

[49] RA, pp. 109–10; Köhler, *Allianzen und Verträge*, p. 64. Köhler pp. 56–69, thinks that the Egyptians saw the crusade as a Byzantine force but their ambassadors were at Antioch for a month and had the chance to examine the crusader legates who returned with them for a year; even if there were also Byzantine emissaries there, they could hardly have failed to understand the differences. However, this does not alter the possibility that they were prepared to consider making arrangements reflecting earlier Byzantine dealings with the new force.

[50] Köhler, *Allianzen und Verträgen*, p. 60, suggests that they were accompanied by a Greek embassy, but there is no evidence for this. Indeed, given that Tatikios had left the crusader camp by the time of their arrival, it is difficult to think who would have had the authority to create a Byzantine delegation. Lilie, *Byzanz*, pp. 51–2, thinks it is unlikely that the Byzantines would have wished to see contact between their allies and Egypt and is sceptical of Raymond of Aguilers' report of the contacts between Egypt and the crusade, which he sees in the light of this writer's known hostility to Byzantium. Köhler, *Allianzen und Verträgen*, pp. 66–8 argues strongly that Raymond was reliable in this context. Essentially, it seems unlikely that Raymond would have invented such controversial material.

when reinforcements were called up. This action received considerable and detailed attention, as we have noted, because it took place
close to the crusader camp. Albert of Aachen says that it was
Godfrey, acting on the orders of Adhémar, who organised the
counter-attack. He sent out ten knights to reconnoitre, and these
were challenged by twenty Turks. When thirty knights were sent the
enemy responded with sixty and, as a result, a general mêlée
developed and the garrison was drawn into a sharp battle in front of
the Bridge Gate and driven back onto it. Godfrey commanded this
and distinguished himself by hacking a Turkish knight in half
despite his hauberk. Raymond of Aguilers says that Godfrey played
a very notable part cutting the enemy in two and adds that early in
the action a Provençal knight, Ysoard of Ganges, led an infantry
charge against the enemy with distinction.[51] Ambushes of this kind
were the staple of Turkish warfare and in particular of the war of
attrition. This kind of action continued even after the establishment
of the Mahommeries Tower which was confided to the care of Count
Raymond. So important was the Bridge Gate that the Turks
attacked the new fort savagely, forcing an action in which the count
distinguished himself. It was presumably in an effort to prevent this
kind of thing that the leaders attempted to destroy the bridge with a
penthouse and all but succeeded.[52] The Mahommeries Tower, as
the crusaders called it, was built on a hill, the site of a Moslem
cemetery, close to the Bridge Gate. The entire west side of the
Orontes is now a built-up area with considerable alterations to its
topography. However, about fifty metres beyond and to the right of
the bridge the land slopes quite sharply northwards: by contrast,
there is only a gentle rise to the left. It is likely that the tower was
erected in this area where, in the nineteenth century, there was still
a Moslem cemetery.[53] With the Bridge Gate blocked, the crusaders
were then able to complete the siege by establishing Tancred at a
monastery outside the St George Gate on 5 April 1098 where shortly

[51] On the sources and the numbers involved see above pp. 140–41; AA, 384–5; RA, p. 60
[52] RA, pp. 62–3; PT, pp. 50–1; above, p. 229.
[53] GF, p. 42; RA, p. 61–2. For the Moslem cemetry see Rey, Monuments, Pl. xvii. About 250
metres to the right of the Bridge the excavations at Antioch revealed the remains of a late
Roman cemetry: J. Lassus, 'Cimitière au bord de l'Oronte', in W. Elderkin, ed., Antioch on
the Orontes: Excavations of 1932 (Princeton, 1934) pp. 85–92. On the west bank at the entry
to the modern bridge there is a roundabout and the slope in question is now covered by a
cinema and, across the road, the main Antioch post-office, both dating from French
colonial days.

before a crusader raid had captured a rich booty of horses (see fig. 10). He would soon capture a rich caravan attempting to enter the city. Because he was a secondary leader Tancred had to be subsidised to the tune of 400 silver marks, of which 100 were provided by Raymond of Toulouse.[54]

The active role of Raymond of Toulouse at this time is very notable. Raymond of Aguilers says that he had been ill earlier in the siege and was seeking to re-establish his reputation, and there may be truth in this. However, he had led a foraging expedition, albeit abortive, into Syria, played a major role in the fighting on the St Symeon road and taken responsibility for the Mahommeries tower which was bound to be a flashpoint, as well as subsidising Tancred. He seems to have been wealthier than the other leaders and to have had the largest army, for Tudebode remarks that he was given the new counterfort 'because he had more knights in his household and also more to give'.[55] Bohemond also had a formidable reputation at this time; he had led the expedition against Harem, accepted custody of Malregard, led the foraging expedition, commanded the army which defeated Ridwan of Aleppo and played a major part in the fighting on the St Symeon road.[56] By any standard these were the two leading princes in the army, so it is very odd that in his second letter to his wife Stephen of Blois announced that he had been made by the other princes 'lord and director and governor of all their acts up to the present time' and this is supported by other sources.[57] Unfortunately, we do not know when this election was held, though the natural sense of the passage in Raymond of Aguilers suggests fairly shortly before the capture of the city in June 1098. Certainly Stephen did not command any major military action of which we know. The suggestion that he was a kind of quartermaster is seductive, but hardly in accord with the terms used by the sources, the Anonymous's *ductor* and Raymond's *dictator*.[58] It can only be a guess but perhaps he was chosen to chair the meetings of the leaders, possibly at Easter 1098. He seems to have been ill shortly after that and so never exercised any real authority. Certainly such an appointment would have been logical by the spring of 1098, for the blockade of the city was now very tight and needed a high degree of co-ordination for its maintenance. The council of leaders was prob-

[54] *GF*, p. 43; RA, pp. 63–4.   [55] PT, p. 50   [56] *GF*, pp. 29–32, 35–41.
[57] Hagenmeyer, *Kreuzzugsbriefe*, p. 149; *GF*, p. 63; RA, p. 77.
[58] Runciman, I. 232, n. 1.

ably the only way in which final authority could be exercised, but the near-disaster of the foraging battle and the success in the Lake Battle exposed its limitations. The army needed a single commander, even though such a dominance was alien to the leaders, and this was a step towards giving it one. They agreed on Stephen of Blois who never seems to have been a masterful personality.

The blockade was not, of course, perfect. It could not be because access to the city via the mountains was always possible. However, the key importance of the steps which they had taken, and especially of the blocking of the Bridge Gate, was clearly recognised. Albert has a long imaginary passage in which Sulayman advises Yaghisiyan to seek aid from Kerbogah, and messengers are sent all over the Moslem world to such exotic places as Samarkand and Khorasan. It is a piece of high drama, signally poetic and interesting because it refers to many real people, amongst them Balduk of Samosata. The drama of the piece underlines the point made at the start – the building of the new counterforts meant that the fate of Antioch now lay in the hands of its allies.[59] Even so, there was still much hard fighting for the crusaders. Albert describes the sufferings of the army and in particular the dearth of horses. Baldwin sent help from Edessa, including horses and arms. It was at this time that Nichossus of Tell-Bashir sent a tent to Godfrey, but this was seized by his rival Bagrat of Cyrrhus who diverted it to Bohemond. This caused dissension in the crusader camp as Godfrey and his ally Robert of Flanders confronted the Norman; probably the story reflects Frankish involvement in the rivalries of the Armenian princes.[60] The supply situation must have been considerably eased by the establishment of outposts around Antioch by some of the leaders: Raymond of Toulouse continued to hold Ruj in Syria, while Godfrey and Robert of Flanders dominated the 'Afrin valley, and Tancred may have been charged with Harem and perhaps 'Imm (both of which he held in the summer of 1098) on the Aleppo road. But there was also much fighting. After the attempt to destroy the bridge with a penthouse, Peter Tudebode tells us that Raynald Porchet, a knight who had been captured, was led onto the wall of the city and, in the sight of the Christian army required to renounce his religion. When he refused he was beheaded at the order of Yaghisiyan who also burned to death other prisoners held in the

[59] AA, 389–95.   [60] AA, 395–6 and see above p. 167.

city.[61] Of course such savagery served a political purpose – to make it difficult for any of the garrison to betray the city by exacerbating hostility and, in this case, playing on religious hatred. A little later, Anselm tells us that some of the enemy pretended to be willing to surrender the city, then trapped and killed the crusaders, including Guy the Constable, who tried to receive their surrender.[62]

The story of the capture of Antioch is a familiar and dramatic tale of betrayal. Perhaps the crusaders knew that Antioch had fallen to a similar act of treachery in 969 and that the Turkish capture of 1086 also owed much to treachery.[63] The story as told by the Anonymous has been generally accepted by historians. He reports that one Pirus (translated as Firuz), the commander of three towers, 'struck up a great friendship with Bohemond' who approached the other leaders and suggested that a single commander should be appointed who should be given control of the city. Anna Comnena says that Bohemond, confident in his arrangements with Firuz, proposed a competitive siege with the winner being given the city, and Kemal ad-Din says much the same.[64] This idea was rejected on the grounds that all had shared in the labour and all should share in the rewards. Shortly after news came of an enemy relief army, in fact that of Kerbogah Atabeg of Mosul, and an assembly of the leaders agreed that if Bohemond could seize the city he should have it, providing that the emperor did not come to their aid. Bohemond then got in touch with Firuz who sent him his son as a hostage, and suggested that on the next day the army should pretend to prepare to go out into the Saracen lands. Then, in council with Godfrey, Robert of Flanders, Raymond of Toulouse and the Legate, it was arranged that the forces of knights and foot in this expedition should separately approach Firuz's towers, the former by the plain, the latter by the mountains. There followed an exciting episode, in which the Anonymous clearly participated, as the crusaders got into the city. In all this the only date mentioned is the fall of the city on the night of 2–3 June 1098.[65]

The identity of Firuz and his reasons for betrayal are naturally interesting. The Anonymous tells us nothing about him except his

---

[61] RC, pp. 649–50; PT, pp. 79–81.   [62] Hagenmeyer, *Kreuzzugsbriefe*, pp. 157–60.

[63] Bouchier, *Antioch*, pp. 217–19, 226–7; Cahen, *Turkey*, p. 77.

[64] AA, 400, says that Bohemond had made contact with Firuz seven months before; *Alexiad*, p. 344; *Aleppo Chronicle*, 581.

[65] GF, pp. 44–8.

name. Raymond of Aguilers says that he was an unnamed Turk, on which point Fulcher agrees but tells a fanciful story of him being commanded to betray the city in a vision. Albert tells us nothing about the betrayer but says that a converted Turk called Bohemond was active in the negotiations, and he appears to be repeating camp gossip when he says that it was believed that Bohemond had captured the betrayer's son in a skirmish. Bar-Hebraeus says that a Persian betrayed the city.[66] Ralph of Caen gives no name but says that the betrayer was a rich Armenian whose wealth had been confiscated by Yaghisiyan, and that he sent word to Bohemond because of his high reputation, although the towers held by himself and his family were some distance away. Anna Comnena agrees that the traitor was an Armenian renegade and this is supported by Michael the Syrian who simply says that Armenians betrayed the city. This identification receives support of a kind from Matthew of Edessa who describes the traitor as one of the chief men of the city but gives no nationality.[67] The *Damascus Chronicle* describes the betrayer as an armourer in the service of Yaghisiyan called Firuz, information also adduced by Ibn al-Athir. Kemal ad-Din names the armourer as Zarrad and says that he was punished by Yaghisiyan for hoarding.[68] In a city with a polyglot population such confusion is not unnatural and it is tempting to see attrition working upon a man of uncertain loyalty, perhaps Armenian, straining his relations with his master – hoarding is a classic crime of shortage. However, we cannot be certain of the truth of such an elegant and symmetrical explanation, although we can be reasonably sure that Ralph's remark that Bohemond had promised him great wealth and honour is a better explanation for his behaviour than are the friendship proposed by the Anonymous and the miracle reported by Fulcher.[69]

But the question of the dating of events is rather difficult and a matter of some importance. The date of the fall of Antioch on the

---

[66] This Turk Bohemond was presumably identical with Bohemond the converted Turk, whom Raymond of Aguilers mentions in connection with the negotiations at Ascalon as having been the godchild of the Bohemond himself: RA, p. 159; RA, p. 64; FC, pp. 98–9; AA, 399–400; Bar-Hebraeus, p. 234.

[67] RC, 651–2; Anna's dating at this point is very erratic, for she evidently confuses the relief expeditions of Ridwan and Kerbogah, on which see France, 'Departure of Tatikios', 138–9; *Alexiad*, p. 342; Michael, p. 184; Matthew, 39.

[68] *Damascus Chronicle of the Crusades*, p. 45; *Aleppo Chronicle*, 580; Ibn al-Athir, p. 192.

[69] RC, 653.

night of 2–3 June 1098 is not in doubt.[70] What the chronology of the Anonymous would suggest is that Bohemond opened the question of Antioch at an unspecified date before its fall, then reopened the question when news had come of the approach of Kerbogah's army. At this council he was promised the city. A few days of exchanges ensued, then Firuz suggested that 'on the morrow', i.e. 2 June, the army set off on its feigned march. As it happens, the date of this council of leaders can be fixed, because Albert of Aachen says that rumours of the approach of Kerbogah's army had caused the leaders to send out reconnaissance forces in all directions. These reported the presence of the enemy to an assembly of leaders which met and promised Bohemond the city, seven days before Kerbogah's arrival – 29 May 1098.[71] According to Fulcher of Chartres, Kerbogah's army besieged Edessa for three weeks before moving on to Antioch where we know its first elements arrived the day after the crusader capture of the city on 4 June. Matthew of Edessa confirms that there was such a siege but gives no dates other than to say that the siege lasted until the harvest time. Albert says that the attack on Edessa lasted a mere three days, but Fulcher was most certainly present at Edessa at this time. If we allow a week for the army to reach Antioch from Edessa, this suggests that the siege lasted from 4–25 May 1098.[72] The problem is that as we have noted, the crusaders were in close touch with Edessa and its outlying fortresses were only a day or two's march away, yet they appear to have been entirely ignorant of the enemy attack until late May; if we allow four days for the reconnaissance force to go out and return, then their ignorance still lasted until 21 May, by which time, Albert says, rumours were causing consternation in the crusader camp. The approach to Edessa of such a huge army as that credited to Kerbogah could hardly have been a secret affair, and indeed Albert says that Baldwin knew enough of it to arrange to attack its advance guard 'with the bows of the Armenians and the lances of the Franks' very successfully.[73] It is quite extra-

---

[70] As Hagenmeyer, *Chronologie* no. 265, comments, citing *GF*, p. 48 (and many derivatives); RA, p. 66; letters of Anselm of Ribemont, People of Lucca, and Princes to Urban II, Hagenmeyer, *Kreuzzugsbriefe*, pp. 157–60, 165–70.

[71] AA, 398–400.

[72] FC, p. 101; it must be said that the major Arab chronicles, of Aleppo and Damascus and Ibn al-Athir, do not mention the siege of Edessa, though the *Aleppo Chronicle*, 580, says that they attacked Tell-Mannas which was restored to Duqaq who took tribute and hostages.

[73] AA, 397.

ordinary that the crusaders should have been unaware of the pres-
ence of an enormous and hostile army only a few days march away.
It is true that they seem to have bumped into the relief force of
Duqaq in December 1097 but that was coming up from deep in
hostile Syria. They certainly had to plan hastily for the approach of
Ridwan in February 1098 but Aleppo was fairly close – Raymond of
Aguilers says only a two day march away – and they did not control
the approaches along the road.[74] Baldwin of Edessa was aware of
Kerbogah's approach – he was clearly not taken by surprise.

Perhaps the inaction was due to a mistaken appreciation of the
purpose of the attack. Kerbogah has been much blamed for spending time attacking Edessa, giving the crusaders the opportunity to
seize Antioch. It is worth noting, however, that he did not know
Antioch was going to fall and that his arguments with Yaghisiyan's
son over terms seem to have gone on very late in the day. More
importantly, we need to recognise that the army which he raised was
an alliance and that this had implications. Kerbogah was acting on
the authority of Bagdad but he had to deal with independent rulers
and at some stage he had to gather his army. It is possible that he
chose to bring much of it together at Edessa where an attack might
bring results and would in any case please the local Moslem rulers.
His attack there was perhaps not at first perceived as a threat to the
main crusader army at Antioch, especially as his force may have
been gathering strength. Kerbogah could not take the short route
from Mosul to Antioch via Sindjar and Aleppo because of the
hostility of Ridwan. Instead he must have travelled via Nusaybin
(ancient Nisbis) to Edessa. Albert says that Kerbogah concentrated
his forces at Sooch, perhaps Tell ach-Chaikh near Mardin, before
moving on to Edessa.[75] He had to get together a very large number
of allies; Fulcher lists twenty-eight of whom seven are also mentioned by Albert. Of the twenty-eight no fewer than fourteen can be
identified including five of those in common with Albert who,
however, adds another three, Pulagit, Amasa of Niz and Amasa of
Cuzh who are unknown, plus Ridwan who definitely never joined
the army. Of those identified five are confirmed by Kemal ad-Din
and four by Ibn al-Athir who adds the name of Arslan-Tasch of
Sindjar.[76] We can, therefore, identify with some certainty some of

---

[74] RA, p. 49.   [75] AA, 396; Cahen, *La Syrie du Nord*, p. 215 n. 35.

[76] FC, ed. Hagenmeyer, p. 250, n. 12 lists the variants which appear to come from his first
redaction; AA, 394; *Aleppo Chronicle*, 580; Ibn al-Athir 194.

the allies of Kerbogah: Duqaq of Damascus, Arslan-Tasch of Sindjar, Qaradja of Harran, Balduk of Samosata, Janah-ad-Daulah of Homs, Tughtigin atabeg of Damascus, Sokman of Mardin whose Artukid clan also held Jerusalem, the Arab commander Wassab ibn-Mahmud to whom can be added the sons of Yaghisiyan, Shams-ad-Daulah and Muhammed.[77] Fulcher's Emir Bajac may well be Albert's Balas of Amacha and Sororgia, for this town was involved in the politics of Edessa and would have been known to both of them.[78] Overall, it was a huge army; Matthew of Edessa suggests incredible figures of 800,000 cavalry and 300,000 foot attacking a Frankish force of 15,000 knights and 50,000 foot, while Bar-Hebraeus and Michael the Syrian settle for 100,000 mounted men. Such figures are probably fantasy, but the *Damascus Chronicle* says that they were an 'uncountable force'.[79] It was certainly a very large army indeed and its concentration must have taken time both for military and diplomatic reasons. Further, the concentration at Edessa could only have been partial – the chroniclers are surely listing the army as it was at its greatest and we have already noted the comment of Kemal ad-Din that en route Duqaq subjugated Tell-Mannas, a city to the east of Ma'arra (Ma'arrat, an-Nu'mān) which had asked for Frankish aid.[80] This and simple geography suggest that the Damascene force came up to meet Kerbogah at Antioch. Kemal ad-Din also reports the presence in the Moslem army of nomads, probably from Asia Minor, who feared Ridwan, and Bar-Hebraeus reports that Kerbo-gah's army, perhaps meaning elements of it, encamped at Baghras which is at the foot of the Belen pass (see figs. 4 and 7).[81] In his account of the reconnaissance forces sent out by the crusader leaders, Albert stresses that they reported to the leaders that the enemy were coming from all directions.[82] This suggests an army gathering strength as it went along, a process requiring careful military and diplomatic preparation which may well explain both the delay at Edessa and the failure of the Franks to recognise its size and ultimate purpose.

[77] Cahen, *La Syrie du Nord*, p. 215, n. 35 identifies the Boldagis of Fulcher and Buldagiso of AA with Bouldadji of Djahan, but AA 390, 392, 409 makes it clear that he was the son of Yaghisiyan.

[78] AA, 356–7.

[79] Matthew, 39, 42; Bar-Hebraeus, p. 235; Michael, p. 184; *Damascus Chronicle of the Crusades*, p. 45.

[80] See above p. 260.   [81] *Aleppo Chronicle*, 583; Bar-Hebraeus, p. 235.

[82] AA, 398; the leaders, says Albert, tried to keep the news secret for fear of demoralising the army.

Once the nature and scale of the threat which Kerbogah posed was known to the crusader leaders they acted very quickly. Bohemond had demanded a price for entry into the city and something like it was quickly conceded. Albert simply says that all promised the city to Bohemond, but the Anonymous makes the promise conditional and makes the leaders say that 'we will thereafter give it to him gladly, on condition that if the emperor come to our aid and fulfil all his obligations which he promised and vowed, we will return the city to him as it is right to do.'[83] Even this is probably an overstatement. As we have noted the Anonymous tends to exaggerate the obligations of Alexius to the army, and if there had ever been any question of the emperor coming in person, as this passage suggests, then there would have been no grounds for an argument in November 1098. Rather, even under the extreme pressure of this desperate situation, the leaders were mindful of the oaths they had sworn and of all the benefits that they had received in the past and might receive in the future, and promised only that Bohemond could have the city if the emperor did not make arrangements to take and protect it. This promise appears to have been made by a very small coterie of leaders. Albert says that all met to discuss the report of the coming of the enemy army and a debate took place with Godfrey, Robert of Flanders and Raymond of Toulouse urging that the army as a whole march out to attack Kerbogah, while others urged that the camp should be manned and the army divided as before. It was then that Bohemond took aside Godfrey, Robert of Flanders and Raymond of Toulouse to a secret place and told them of the plot with Firuz and his demand to be ruler of the city, to which they then agreed.

Ralph of Caen tells us later that Tancred was kept in ignorance of the plot to seize the city and the arrangements for it.[84] The Anonymous says that it was Firuz's idea to pretend that a section of the army was going out as if to plunder Syria in order to lull the defences. Albert credits Bohemond with the plan and says that Godfrey and Robert of Flanders led out this force of 700 knights on 2 June as though signalling to the garrison of Antioch their intention to repeat the tactic of the Lake Battle by ambushing the enemy's vanguard, but they came back under cover of night by secret paths led by Bohemond the Turk and approached the section of the wall

---

[83] *GF*, p. 45.   [84] AA, 398–400; RC, 657.

held by Firuz. The Anonymous simply says that by night knights returned by the plain and the footsoldiers by the mountain to the appointed spot.[85] On 2 June this expedition set out and under cover of night turned back and returned to what the Anonymous has Firuz call 'the western mountain', the southern side of the defences, for it is clear that Firuz's tower was on that side of the city.[86] The Anonymous has Firuz suggest this feint so that the army 'should pretend to go out and plunder the land of the Saracens', which is rather an odd statement, for at this critical juncture nobody would have been thinking of such a thing. However, it is probably expressed this way because the direction of their march reminded the Anonymous of the expedition which led to the Foraging Battle, for it was surely in that direction that they set out. Once into the mountains by Daphne the army probably rested, then the infantry took the paths into the mountains towards the back road and Firuz's tower, while the cavalry rode back up towards the St George Gate then climbed on foot to the appointed spot (see fig. 11). Once they had gathered under cover of night they prepared to mount a two-pronged attack. Albert's informants were with Godfrey, while the Anonymous was with Bohemond's force, and this conditions their accounts.

The Anonymous participated in the secret entry into the city and describes it as a commando raid by an élite group. A party of knights approached the wall with a ladder just before dawn and sixty of them mounted into the tower of Firuz, who became worried by the absence of Bohemond and the small numbers. Bohemond and his followers, including the Anonymous, then came to the foot of the ladder and showed themselves, calling up. A large number of them ascended when suddenly the ladder broke, but those inside opened a small postern gate and as more and more crusaders poured in cries of horror arose in the city and the main army began its assault and a great slaughter.[87] It is very much the story of a participant, vivid and clear but lacking in context which is to some extent provided by Albert. According to him a Lombard interpreter from Bohemond's household approached the tower and spoke in Greek (mentioned by the Anonymous as the language used between the traitor and the Franks) to its occupants who urged the Franks to come up and get established before the coming of the watchmen who toured the

---

[85] AA, 400–1; *GF*, p. 46.   [86] On the location, see below p. 266.
[87] *GF*, pp. 46–8.

defences every night – a detail mentioned by Raymond of Aguilers who, however, says the Franks waited until they had passed.[88] There was much hesitation amongst the attackers, according to Albert, and this may have been because of the earlier experience when Guy the Constable was killed. However, Godfrey exhorted those who were hesitating, a rope was lowered, a leather ladder hauled up and sixty men entered until the weight of people dragged down the portion of the wall to which the ladder was attached causing losses; this is rather different to the Anonymous's statement that the ladder broke. Raymond of Aguilers adds that Fulcher of Chartres was first up and Ralph gives the name as Gouel. The watch then arrived and was killed and as the fighting spread most of the 700 knights were admitted through a postern gate and hard fighting ensued.[89] The two accounts and that of Ralph are generally compatible, but Albert gives a very prominent role in the commando party to Godfrey and Robert of Flanders. Bohemond, Raymond of Toulouse and Tancred then, he says, rallied the main army which was totally surprised to find Christian forces in Antioch – a detail supported by Raymond of Aguilers.[90]

However, Albert does add some interesting information which provides us with a strong clue as to the location of Firuz's tower. He says that as the assault force got into the city it sounded trumpets as a signal to Godfrey and Robert of Flanders who attacked a gate near the citadel; the purpose was surely to seize the citadel – in which they failed. The next day Bohemond would make a determined but fruitless attempt to seize the citadel in the course of which he would be wounded by an arrow in the leg.[91] So the night attack was two-pronged. Almost certainly Bohemond led the effort to enter Firuz's tower which it appears was quite close to the citadel for Godfrey and Robert of Flanders, who led the attack on it, were in the same general area. The contemporary sources are very vague on the location of Firuz's towers. The Anonymous says cavalry reached it by the plain and infantry by the mountain. Albert confirms that a force of 700 knights was led to it by night over small paths by Bohemond the Turk, while Ralph of Caen describes it as a long way from the tents of Bohemond. William of Tyre is much more specific; he tells us that Firuz held a tower called the Two Sisters in the south

[88] AA, 401; RA, p. 64.   [89] RA, p. 64; RC, 654; AA, 402–3.

[90] AA, 404; RA, p. 65.

[91] AA, 403; RM, 806–7.

wall of Antioch, close to the St George Gate, and this has been presumed to reflect traditions current in the Principality of Antioch in the twelfth century.[92] However, it is evident from Albert's description that the point of entry must have been much closer to the citadel. The implication of the Anonymous's account is that Firuz's three towers were in a lonely place. Raymond of Aguilers speaks of them being 'on the hill of the city' and Ralph says that it was at a point too wild for horses to venture; this argues against the vicinity of the St George Gate which had been invested by Tancred and would have been well manned. Furthermore, the Wadi Zoiba is a formidable barrier along these southern defences. In addition, the Anonymous reports that as day broke and the Franks became established in the city Bohemond set up his banner where all could see it on 'a hill opposite the citadel'. It has been suggested that this must refer to the high point to the south of the citadel where there is a tower still visible across the whole of Antioch, however this is not precisely opposite the citadel. There is another tower further along which is at the top of the south side of the gully facing the citadel and though this could not be seen across the whole city, it could be seen plainly by the main crusader army mainly concentrated outside the northern defences (see fig. 13). William of Tyre says that by this time the Franks had captured ten towers, and by counting we can arrive at Firuz's towers, roughly at the point where the defences turn west to form the south wall of the city, descending Mount Silpius. Moreover, the accounts agree that near Firuz's tower was a postern and there is one in this area. There can be no certainty, but it is very likely that these towers at the south-east corner of the defences were those betrayed by Firuz (see fig. 11).[93]

The failure to seize the citadel was to have considerable consequences for the crusader army. But what followed the break-in to the city was a terrible massacre in which many Christians, as well as Moslems, died – how could it be otherwise, as Albert says, when much of the fighting was in the shades of night; 10,000, he says,

---

[92] *GF*, p. 46; AA, 400; RC, 652; WT, 212–13. In view of the Arab sources on the identity of the betrayer, it is interesting that William says the family were called the Beni Zerra, meaning 'sons of the armourer.

[93] RA, 64; RC, p. 654; Rey, *Monuments*, pp. 196–201. The weakness of the argument is that only WT, 229, refers to ten towers, but the point about the raising of Bohemond's flag is a good one. On the postern Rey was writing at a time when the walls were more intact than they are now but he was a very careful observer. My own exploration of the remaining foritifications confirms his ideas.

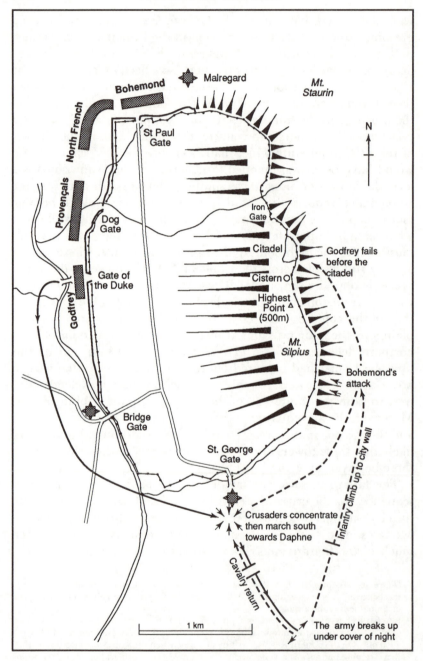

Fig. 11   Crusader capture of Antioch, night of 2/3 June 1098

perished, and the Franks were assisted by an uprising of the native Christians.[94] One of the casualties was Yaghisiyan himself who fled the city and was killed by local Christians.[95] Kemal ad-Din says that he panicked, thinking that the citadel had also fallen, rode off with an escort and later fell off his horse and was killed by Armenians, a story confirmed by Bar-Hebraeus and Ibn al-Athir, who adds that he was decapitated by an Armenian butcher. The *Damascus Chronicle* simply says that he died at Armanaz near Ma'arrat Masrin on the Aleppo road north of Idleb, through constantly falling off his horse.[96]

The capture of Antioch is a great story in the best Bulldog Drummond tradition. Such incidents have so often formed key moments of films about the Second World War that one can almost see the participants in khaki bearing sten-guns, rather than encumbered with swords, shields and armour. And it is a cliff-hanger in another sense – for advancing towards the city was the huge army of Kerbogah. The plot to get into Antioch was a last ditch effort by the crusader army. Had it failed, then disaster would surely have followed, but that, of course, is in the best tradition of all great stories. Naturally this is to look at events in our idiom. For the crusaders, what happened was nothing less than a miraculous delivery by the hand of God. Raymond of Aguilers rejoiced in the slaughter of the enemy – 'the Lord had confounded them!' and bewailed not the massacre of people but the loss of horses when some Turkish riders were driven off a cliff: 'Our joy over the fallen enemy was great, but we grieved over the more than thirty horses who had their necks broken there'.[97] Reports of the spoils after the victory are contradictory. Raymond of Aguilers describes a vast booty, but Albert says there was not much. Above all there was not much food – hardly surprising, for Antioch had been invested for nine months and its stores were badly run down.[98] In any case, there was little time for plundering, although Raymond of Aguilers accuses the army of dallying over pagan dancing women and so failing to take

---

[94] AA, 405–6.   [95] *GF*, pp. 47–8; RA, p. 66; AA, 406.

[96] *Aleppo Chronicle*, 581; Bar-Hebraeus, p. 235; Ibn al-Athir, p. 193; *Damascus Chronicle of the Crusades*, p. 44.

[97] RA, p. 65, tr. Krey, pp. 154–5; AA, 405–6, tells a rather similar tale of numbers of the enemy falling to their death after taking a wrong route in an effort to reach the citadel but he suggests there were 1,000 of them. The road up to the citadel from Antioch proper is so steep and dangerous that it is easy to envisage such an event.

[98] RA, p. 65; AA, 407.

the citadel, because on the day after its fall the vanguard of Kerbo-gah's army arrived at Antioch.[99]

The siege of Antioch had lasted for over eight months and during it the crusader army suffered appalling privations and terrible casualties. It was a close blockade rather than a set-piece siege in the usual sense of the word. The central problem which the army faced was simply staying alive in the face of enemy efforts to deny them food. By early February 1098 the army was in a desperate situation and it was saved by the brilliant victory over Ridwan's army. But the crusader leaders showed themselves well able to organise their huge force and avoided overstretching it. Leaders and led learned a lot about their enemies in the course of the siege during which all the techniques of contemporary war were tested. Raiding, wasting, small-scale combat by horsemen and infantry were the day-to-day experience of an army which was becoming more cohesive and more experienced. In the long agony of the siege the morale of the army, their faith in their destiny was tested to the full and this was what delivered them in the end. But the army was also becoming much smaller and the fall of the city produced no relief, but yet more disasters.

[99] RA, p. 66; *GF*, p. 49; AA, 407; FC, 101.

CHAPTER 9

The siege of Antioch: victory

The second siege of Antioch was to be a desperate affair. From the outset it was clear that it would be very different from the first siege, for both sides must have recognised that it would be fairly short. The crusaders had broken into a city with food supplies depleted after a nine-month siege. Some effort was made to purchase food at St Symeon, but the speed of Kerbogah's arrival meant that there was simply no time. Sitting out the siege was, therefore, not an option for the crusaders.[1] In any case their military situation was quite different from that of the earlier defenders for the enemy controlled the citadel which was commanded by Kerbogah's man Ahmad ibn-Marwan, and far outnumbered the crusaders even if seven to one is an exaggeration.[2] It is unfortunate that there are no good estimates of the size of Kerbogah's army but it was very large. The crusader army must have been very reduced and even before the fall of Antioch there were further desertions when news came of the approach of Kerbogah's army, although they were in part compensated for by troops coming in from outlying places.[3] Their numbers cannot have been as high as 30,000, including non-combatants, and were probably much lower so Kerbogah's army could quite credibly have been twice or three times the size.

In these circumstances it is little wonder that the early reactions of the crusader army were dominated by fear. Fulcher says that Stephen of Blois left the siege on the day before Kerbogah's arrival but gives no clear reason. Raymond of Aguilers says frankly that Stephen was frightened by rumour of the coming of Kerbogah and

---

[1] AA 407–408.
[2] Runciman, I. 319; Cahen, *Syrie du Nord*, p. 217; *GF*, p. 50, has a vignette of Shams-ad-Daulah reluctantly conceding the citadel to Kerbogah: on the size of Kerbogah's army see above p. 203: Matthew, pp. 39, 41.
[3] RA, p. 64.

the Anonymous implies as much by saying that he pretended to be ill. Albert on the other hand actually says that he was ill and went to rest in Alexandretta where he remained in a state of indecision until other deserters joined him about 11 June; their reports impelled him to flee with 4,000 in his train. Fulcher seems to have been closely connected with Stephen, whose career he followed with interest, so his guardedly neutral tone suggests the worst.[4] Stephen was a major leader, elected, as we have seen, to lead the army during the siege of Antioch. His departure had a considerable effect on the morale of the army.[5] He was not alone, for after initial fighting in the city Bohemond's brother-in-law William of Grandmesnil, his brother Aubré, Guy Trousseau Lord of Montlhéry, Lambert the Poor count of Clermont and William the Carpenter joined the ranks of the 'rope-danglers', so named from the method of their escape down the walls of Antioch. So general was the terror in the Christian army that the Anonymous says that Bohemond fired part of the city to drive out deserters.[6] Such desertions weakened the army and sapped its morale. Rumours were rife; Albert says many believed that the princes would desert, perhaps the foundation of Matthew of Edessa's reports that the leaders of the army had decided to surrender on terms when a vision revealing the Holy Lance changed their minds. It was against this background that when the priest Stephen had a vision promising divine aid, Adhémar took the opportunity of making all the leaders swear publicly not to abandon the siege.[7]

The vanguard of Kerbogah's army arrived before Antioch on 4 June and sent thirty men ahead to trail their coats. Such Turkish tactics had not lost effectiveness through repetition for they were obligingly attacked by Roger of Barneville with fifteen knights who were in turn ambushed by a hidden force some 300 strong and Roger was killed in sight of the city walls; a lance was stuck in his back and he was decapitated. According to a variant story his horse stuck in a bog and, after defending himself well on foot, he was

[4] FC pp. 6, 97; RA, p. 77; GF p. 63; AA, 414–15.
[5] J. A. Brundage, 'An errant crusader: Stephen of Blois', Traditio, 16 (1960), 388, suggests that the last part of Stephen's letter to Adela written in late March 1098; Hagenmeyer, Kreuzzugsbriefe, p. 152, in which he says that he will see her soon, means that he had already resolved to leave the crusade, perhaps delaying until Antioch was in Christian hands. Even if the passage could be interpreted in this way it would have been extraordinary for him to persist in such a course of action as Kerbogah closed in on the city. Stephen was a deserter.
[6] GF pp. 56, 61: AA 41; RC, 660–1, says that it was Robert of Flanders who fired the city.
[7] AA, 418; Matthew, 41: GF, p. 59.

struck in the head by an Arab with a long lance and killed. He was North French, but evidently well known in the army for his death was widely noted. Albert reports the jubilation of the enemy and the shame of the Christians for no-one had dared to go out to his assistance, a circumstance which Albert attributes to the shortage of horses.[8] A large element of Kerbogah's force encamped near the Iron Bridge on 5 June; the crusaders had apparently attempted to defend it because its garrison was destroyed and its commander was found in chains after the great battle. On 6 June Kerbogah's main army approached Antioch, apparently around the northern side of the Antioch Lake for they encamped, according to the Anonymous, 'between the two rivers'.[9] This could mean by the Wadi al Quivaisiya which entered the Orontes on the west bank just south of the Bridge of Boats. Much more likely, however, is at or near the junction of the Orontes and the Kara Su which drains from the Lake above the city and meets the Orontes about five kilometres above Antioch (see fig. 12).[10] This is an odd position from which to conduct a siege, but it is confirmed by Raymond of Aguilers who says that Kerbogah camped some two miles (five kilometres in his usage) from Antioch because he believed that the crusaders would fight outside the city – this must be hindsight. Albert says that Kerbogah made camp 'in the plain' and that subsequently he and a section of his army climbed into the mountains near to the citadel while another part of his force established itself outside the St Paul Gate; this implies that the original camp was to the north of the city.[11] Since encampments are mentioned later much closer to the city we can perhaps assume that Kerbogah established his main base at the confluence of the two rivers, probably to prevent a sally from the three northern gates of the city against his forces, and that other encampments were set up according to need.[12]

After their experiences during the siege the crusaders were determined to hold sally-points protecting two of the gates of the city. On 5 and 6 June the Turks attacked the Mahommeries Tower and there was savage fighting as Robert of Flanders held it for the Christian army. On 8 June, however, it was abandoned as untenable.[13] At a date unknown, but presumably about the same time, a similar

---

[8] AA, 407–8; *HBS*, 198; RA, p. 66.   [9] *GF*, pp. 50, 51.

[10] The Wadi has now vanished under the concrete of the new city. By June it was probably dry anyway. The Kara Su is the only waterway which could be described as a river.

[11] RA, p. 66; AA, 411.   [12] See below, p. 275.   [13] RA, pp. 66–7: AA, 411–12.

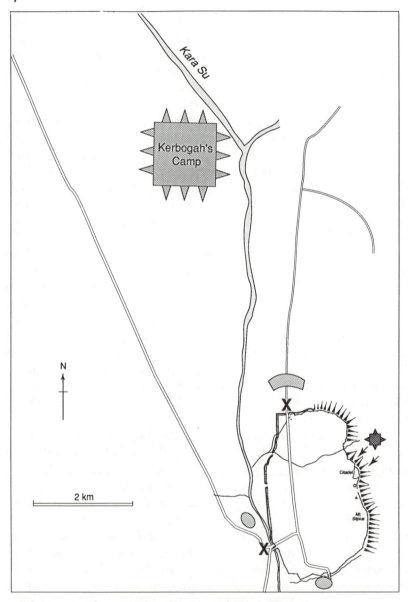

X   5 – 7 June: Kerbogah's army drives in the crusader outposts

    8 – 14 June: Kerbogah establishes a camp and attacks via the citadel

    14 – 28 June: Kerbogah establishes a full blockade of the city

Fig. 12   Kerbogah's siege of Antioch, 4–29 June 1098

redoubt outside the St Paul Gate was held by Godfrey whose troops were driven back into the city after heavy fighting with 200 casualties.[14] But much of the fiercest fighting in the early part of the siege took place close to the citadel on the eastern wall of the city at the top of Mt Silpius.

It is important to recollect that the city of Antioch covered only a small part of the area enclosed by the walls on the lower slopes of the mountain and on the flat area by the Orontes. The walled circuit protected access to this but for the most part the land within was as wild and precipitous as it was outside. When the city fell in 969 the attacking force was isolated for three days on the lonely part of the wall where they had entered through bribery.[15] Both Kemal ad-Din and Ibn al-Athir implicitly blame Yaghisiyan for panicking instead of holding the citadel as his son did[16] and with reason, for the citadel, though not a particularly powerful fortification, was very difficult to approach. At the time of the city's fall Bohemond had placed his banner on a tower which stood on the high ground overlooking the citadel some 300–400 metres to the north. Between this tower and the citadel was a steep gully accommodating an ancient cistern, across the mouth of which ran the only access road to the citadel on a piece of flat land less than thirty metres wide along the edge of a precipitous drop (see fig. 13). Thus the crusaders controlled the only road by which the garrison could get into Antioch, for the land to the west and north is simply almost impossible to cross.[17] Immediately after the fall of the city Bohemond seems to have advanced along the wall to the last tower on the opposite side of the gully below the citadel, but was ejected from it by the Turks and wounded by a Turkish arrow in the process. In the fighting here this tower seems to have been one of the key points in

[14] AA, 409–10 is the only source for this event, which he appears to place early in the siege.

[15] Bouchier, *Antioch* pp. 218–19.   [16] *Aleppo Chronicle*, 581; Ibn al-Athir, p. 193.

[17] RA, p. 67 Krey, *First Crusade*, p. 169, has an extremely accurate, almost photograhic description of this battlefield: 'The Turks who had entered the fortress wanted to go down into the city. For the valley between our mountain and their fortress was not large, and in the middle of it was a certain cistern and a little level place. Nor did the enemy have a path down into the city except through our mountain; wherefore they strove with every intent and all their might to drive us out and remove us from their path.'

The roughness of the land and the steepness of the gulley must be emphasised. It is possible to pick one's way down from the citadel and then up the mountainside to the crusader positions, but it is a slow and difficult business for the walls of the gulley are sown with rocky projections often waist-high, with loose shale below, the whole masked by a covering of low scrub. Effectively an attack against or from the citadel can only proceed either along the line of the wall or on the access road – two very narrow fronts.

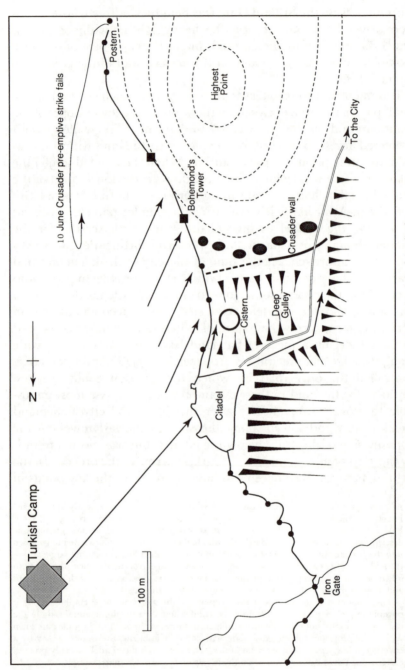

Fig. 13   The fighting around the citadel of Antioch

no-man's-land.[18] The Turks of the citadel could either advance along the line of the wall, from which the land drops sharply away to the cistern, towards Bohemond's tower, assisted by forces on the outside, or attack along the road: two very narrow fronts. This set the scene for the savage fighting which erupted with the arrival of Kerbogah's army on 6 June which the Anonymous emphasises so vividly. He fails to mention attacks on other areas which suggests that he was involved in this part of the city.

According to the Anonymous on the third day after his arrival, by which is meant 8 June, Kerbogah led a major force up the mountain towards the citadel. This began a serious assault, for the Turks established a camp on the mountain outside.[19] Their purpose was obvious: to reinforce the citadel whose forces could then drive down into the city while further assaults on the outside of the wall held by Bohemond distracted the defenders. The crusaders sallied out of the city by a postern gate to attack them. Raymond of Aguilers says that after initial success the crusaders were driven back into the city with terrible losses; the visionary Peter Bartholemew was badly crushed in the scrum to get through the gate. The failure of this pre-emptive strike by the crusaders is confirmed by Anselm of Ribemont.[20] The enemy was now in a position to take the fight to the crusaders and the Anonymous describes ferocious fighting over the next two days, both outside and inside the walls, which ended only with the exhaustion of the combatants, and this is confirmed by Raymond of Aguilers, by Anselm and by the letter sent to the pope by the Princes in September 1098 which says that the enemy were driven back into the citadel. The demoralising effect of all this was making itself felt on the army for on the night of 10 June many deserted the city and fled to St Symeon – amongst them William of Grandmesnil.[21] On 11 June fighting was renewed and Peter Tudebode's brother Arved was killed. Perhaps it was during this stage of the fighting that Bohemond was nearly killed and rescued only by the combined efforts of Robert of Flanders, Godfrey and Robert of Normandy who now reappears at Antioch. The Anonymous reports that the enemy got into a tower trapping three knights, including Hugh the Beserk who fought bravely after the others fled wounded. This is not unlike another episode in which Albert reports that the enemy got into a

[18] RM, 806–7. [19] *GF* p. 56l AA, 411.
[20] *GF* p. 56; RA, pp. 66–8; Hagenmeyer, *Kreuzzugsbriefe*, pp. 157–60.
[21] *GF* pp. 56–7; RA, pp. 66–8; Hagenmeyer *Kreuzzugsbriefe*, pp. 157–65.

tower left unguarded by laxity, and were driven out by Henry of Esch, a relative of Godfrey. It may well be that this is the tower on the slope below the citadel in no-man's-land which Bohemond had already tried to seize.[22] Pressure from the citadel was so severe that the crusaders built a wall to counter attacks. Albert mentions it, as does Ralph of Caen, but Raymond of Aguilers implies that it was built just before the great battle on 28 June.[23] The Anonymous twice refers to the building of this wall; on the first occasion after he tells us how the deserters fled to St Symeon, which would imply a date about 11–12 June 1098; the second was the day on which a meteor fell into the enemy camp, the night of 13–14 June. It seems likely, however, that the wall could be built because Kerbogah changed the emphasis of his attack.

Anselm of Ribemont says 'But they moved their camp and set siege to all the gates of the city', while the letter sent by the Princes in September 1098 states:

when they saw that they could do no harm on that side [by the citadel], they surrounded us all about, so that none of our men could go out or come to us. As a result of this we were all so destitute and afflicted that many of our men, dying of starvation and many other wants, killed and ate our famished horses and asses.

The Anonymous says that after a meteor fell in the enemy camp on the night of 13–14 June 1098 the enemy fled down to the plain 'to my lord Bohemond's gate [the St Paul Gate besieged by Bohemond]' which precisely dates the change of attack.[24] It must surely be the case that the wall against the citadel was built during the lull as the enemy changed the emphasis of the attack from assault through the citadel to investment and blockade, almost certainly on and just after 14 June. It was probably little more than a barricade across the access road to the citadel and along the crest of the gully up to the wall. (see fig. 13) This does not mean that fighting stopped in the city altogether for even at the last, as the army prepared for the great battle, they left a considerable force under Count

---

[22] *GF* pp. 56–7, 60–1: PT, p. 67; RA, pp. 67–8; AA ,410–11, 413. On the tower, see above, p. 266; the suggestion is that of Rey, *Monuments*, pp. 201–2.

[23] AA, 410; RC, 659–60; RA, p. 79.

[24] AA, 411: Hagenmeyer, *Kreuzzugsbriefe*, pp. 157–65; Krey, *First Crusade*, p. 190, 193; *GF*, p. 62. Presumably the St George Gate to the south of the city had remained open and this explains the contact between Antioch and St Symeon noted above, p. 211, and below p. 278, after the coming of Kerbogah.

Raymond of Toulouse to blockade the citadel.[25] Kerbogah probably withdrew because this line of attack was proving unprofitable. The crusader defence was stubborn and able to take advantage of the passive strength of Antioch's defences and the extremely confined space outside the citadel which made it difficult for the Turks to bring their superiority in numbers to bear. The large Turkish force outside provided reinforcements for the citadel and attacked the wall but it must have been difficult to maintain a protracted effort in this wild and waterless terrain: Albert of Aachen says that the camp in the mountains was abandoned because the enemy found it difficult to supply it with food and fodder. Water must have been even more difficult to carry up the mountain side. Perhaps also it was expensive in manpower and Kerbogah was beginning to understand how desperate was the situation of the crusader army. He was also discovering the problems posed to an attacker by the sheer size of Antioch which threatened to disperse even his strong army. Kerbogah's decision to switch the emphasis of his attack was a great relief to the crusaders on whom the fighting in the city had imposed great strains. On the night of 11 June the priest Stephen had his vision in the church of St Mary where he had retired in terror at the news that the enemy might get down into the city. The reduction in this pressure was undoubtedly a grave mistake.

Conditions in the city, however, did not improve, for starvation now set in.[26] The sources are eloquent, particularly the Anonymous with his account of poor food and high prices:

many of us died of hunger, for a small loaf cost a bezant, and I cannot tell you the price of wine . . . men boiled and ate the leaves of figs, vines, thistles and all kinds of tree. Others stewed the dried skins of horses, camels, oxen or buffaloes.[27]

Raymond of Aguilers tells much the same tale but he says that the rich could afford the high prices; even so the knights found things difficult and some were reduced to bleeding their horses for nourishment.[28] Albert of Aachen has much the same story of awful things

---

[25] *GF* p. 68; RA, p. 79; AA, 422.

[26] On the impact of starvation on numbers see above, pp. 132, 133.

[27] The story of the visions of Stephen of Valence and Peter Bartholemew is given in the *GF*, pp. 57–60. The building of the wall against the citadel, and the initial comments on starvation, occur on p. 57 and are repeated, the latter in vastly expanded form, p. 62. The sense is of a work which has been quite violently chopped around, *GF*, p. 62–3.

[28] RA, pp. 76–7 may have based his account here on GF.

which had to be eaten, but adds the curious detail that they were made palatable by the addition of cumin, pepper and other spices; these were normally luxury goods, but presumably had been captured in Antioch. He says that many of the poorer people died and that some were in the habit of sneaking off to St Symeon to buy food until the enemy ambushed a group, burned the port and then drove away the ships. Later he reports that during the famine even substantial men were reduced to poverty. The noble Herman went to war on an ass and he and Henry of Esch were reduced to beggary and rescued by Godfrey.[29]

This was the state of the army in Antioch within less than two weeks of siege – starvation, bitter fighting, panic, desertion, even, according to Raymond of Aguilers, treachery when some crusaders went over to the enemy.[30] It was against this background that there occurred a remarkable series of visions. On the morning of 11 June a priest, Stephen of Valence, revealed that Christ had appeared to him and promised divine aid to the crusaders in a vision which he was commanded to reveal to the Legate Adhémar who accepted the tale and took the opportunity to make the crusader leaders swear not to abandon the army.[31] And well he might, for this visionary was highly respectful of church order and in his account invoked the structure of the divine economy in his icon-like portrayal of the Virgin interceding for her people. Far different was the other revelation by a poor Provençal, Peter Bartholomew, who inveighed against Adhémar for not preaching to the people and promised not merely divine aid in return for penance, but a material token of God's favour to His chosen people, the Holy Lance which was discovered in the church of St Peter on 14 June.[32] It is undoubtedly true that these two visions, and others such as that of St Ambrose reported by Albert, expressed the deepest beliefs of the crusaders that God was on their side, a combatant in the great struggle who would give them aid according to their desserts.[33] Nor is there much doubt of the impact upon the army as a whole. Raymond of Aguilers speaks of joy and exultation in the city when the Lance was discovered. He was a great partisan of the Lance in its later troubles, but the Anonymous was not and yet he is even clearer: 'throughout the city there was boundless rejoicing'.[34] In a letter written very

---

[29] AA, 412–414, 427.   [30] RA, p. 77.   [31] RA, pp. 72–4; *GF*, pp. 57–9.
[32] RA, pp. 68–75; *GF*, pp. 59–60.
[33] AA, 417.   [34] RA, p. 75; *GF*, p. 65.

shortly after the siege was over Anselm of Ribemont says of the Lance 'So when this precious gem was found, all our spirits were revived' and the crusading princes in their letter of September 1098 to Urban II were absolutely explicit: 'We were so comforted and strengthened by finding it, and by many other divine revelations that we, who before had been afflicted and timid, were then most boldly and eagerly urging one another to battle'.[35] The visions are a deeply interesting topic in themselves, but what matters here is their military effect; they profoundly improved the depressed morale of the crusader army.[36] However, the impression given by the Anonymous that spirits revived and the army was ready to proceed to battle once it had received the Lance is a mistaken product of the fractured nature of his narrative at this point.[37] The Lance was discovered on 14 June, but it was not until 28 June that the army ventured out to battle, and Raymond of Aguilers makes it clear that there were another two visions and much suffering before the army was ready to march out.[38] One of the most important events of this period was the selection of Bohemond to command the army on 20 June. Raymond says he was chosen because Count Raymond and Bishop Adhémar were both ill, but he had already admitted his high military reputation. Previously, he and Adhémar had abruptly closed the gates of the city to prevent the army melting away from desertion.[39]

The appointment of a single commander showed that the leaders were now acting to prepare the army for the inevitable, an attempt to break out of the city and destroy Kerbogah's force. It was a dangerous gamble, though not without precedent, for we have noted that when he was cornered by his father at Gerberoi Robert Curthose suddenly sallied forth, knocked his father from his horse and scattered the besiegers. The practical alternative for both Curthose and the crusaders was slow destruction and dissolution. In the end, as Albert says, they had little choice: 'All, great and small, declared that they could no longer endure such suffering, and when they were asked said it would be better to die fighting than to

---

[35] Hagenmeyer, *Kreuzzugsbriefe*, pp. 157–65; Krey, *First Crusade*, pp. 190, 193.

[36] On the visions see Morris, 'Policy and Visions', pp. 33–45 and J. France, 'Prophet, Priest and Chronicler on the First Crusade', (forthcoming).

[37] The words of the finder of the Lance, *GF*, p. 65, clerly refer to the vision as reported on p. 60. This account has been changed a good deal.

[38] RA, pp. 75–8.   [39] RA, pp. 53–4, 74.

succumb to the cruel famine and watch the miserable Christian people perish day by day'.[40] What distinguished the crusader situation and made it especially perilous was that because the citadel of Antioch was in enemy hands, its garrison could see all preparations to sally out; on 28 June Albert reports that they duly raised a black flag as a sign of the coming break-out.[41]

But before then the leaders sent an embassy to Kerbogah. In the version of the Anonymous this is made to appear purely as a morale-raising episode in which the ambassadors, Peter the Hermit and his translator Herluin, defied Kerbogah. Raymond of Aguilers gives much the same impression, and adds that at the time when the army sallied out Kerbogah announced that he was ready to take up their suggestion of five or ten from each side fighting a kind of trial by battle – but it was then too late. Albert presents the matter rather differently. According to him the leaders were still very uncertain because of the weakness of the army, and in particular the loss of horses; Peter first offered the city to Kerbogah if he would become a Christian. When this was refused he suggested a trial by battle with twenty on each side. When this was refused he left and reported back, being told by Godfrey not to talk about what he had seen in the enemy camp lest it demoralise the army.[42] It is very hard to take this embassy as seriously as Albert suggests; perhaps his attitude reflects distrust of the princes amongst ordinary crusaders who were his informants. The embassy of Peter the Hermit was probably also the root of the story in Matthew of Edessa that the leaders were prepared to surrender on terms until the Lance was revealed.[43] Now, strengthened by fasting and the rites and ceremonial of the church, almost certainly decreed by Adhémar, the army prepared to attack Kerbogah in a desperate sally.

This battle was profoundly affected by one simple fact – the army had lost almost all its horses. Speaking of the skirmishing around Antioch, Raymond of Aguilers remarks:

'And so it came about through assaults of this kind that they lost all their horses, because the Turks, not prepared to fight with lances or swords, but with arrows at a distance, were to be feared while they fled, as well as when they pursued.'

[40] AA, 421 and see above, p. 44.   [41] AA, 423.
[42] GF, pp. 65–7; RA, pp. 79, 81; AA, 419–21.
[43] See above, p. 271, n. 7.

The description is vividly endorsed by Ralph of Caen and reminds one of the careful instructions in Islamic manuals on how to fire to the rear.[44] Quite apart from its effect on foraging, loss of horses was disastrous for the crusader army. The scale of the loss has not usually been appreciated by historians.[45] Overall the chronicles give us more specific information about numbers of horses than they do about numbers of people; even allowing for the fact that numbers were much smaller, this shows an interesting perception of priorities. But it was a correct one, for without mobility the army would be gravely weakened. Anselm of Ribemont says that by late November 1097 after the construction of Malregard the army could muster only some 700 horses. Raymond of Aguilers, whose comment that the enemy killed many horses has been noted, remarks that for the expedition against Harem shortly before this Bohemond and Robert of Flanders could raise only 150 knights and that for the major foraging expedition of late December 1097 the army raised only 400. During the famine of early 1098 Raymond reports that horses were dying and that the Provençals were reduced to 100 horses when their count invented the compensation scheme for losses. While Bohemond and Robert of Flanders were foraging there was fighting around the city, in the midst of which the cavalry broke off the battle to pursue a riderless horse – an event which caused panic and heavy losses and indicates the value of a horse by this time. The Anonymous states that by late January or early February 1098 there were only about 1,000 horses in the army and this figure is supported by Albert of Aix. However, we have already noted that for the Lake Battle, for which the knights as a whole were mobilised, the sources agree that only 700 could be found – the only dissenter from this figure is Ralph of Caen who speaks of only 200, but he was surely exaggerating and we can suppose that some mounts were left in the camp, so between 700 and 1000 were available at this time. However, Albert says this figure included many on mules, asses and pack horses. Albert mentions horses dying in May 1098, and explains that nobody went to rescue Roger of Barneville because there were few horses; only 150 were left in the army at the time of the fall of Antioch when a further 400 were found in the city. Many of these must have died during the second siege because the Anony-

[44] RA, p. 50; RC, p. 715; see above, p. 147.
[45] Though useful comments are made by Riley-Smith, *Idea of Crusading*, p. 65.

mous speaks of horse-flesh and hides being eaten during the famine, while Raymond of Aguilers stresses that many knights, expecting battle, lived on the blood of their horses but would not slaughter them. Albert records a sally against the Turks outside the city which broke down because of the exhausted state of the crusaders' horses. By the time the army was ready to face Kerbogah he says that they had lost all the horses they had brought from France and that there were only 200 horses fit for war left in the army. At this time the German Count Hermann was reduced to riding an ass so small his feet dragged, and even Godfrey de Bouillon and Robert of Flanders had to beg horses from the Count of Toulouse.[46] As usual with medieval numbers there is some doubt; could it be that the chroniclers were exaggerating weakness to maximise the sense of achievement? In this case the general impression of the sources all points in much the same direction – a dramatic reduction in numbers. It is hardly surprising. The crusade had endured a bitter journey across the arid Anatolian plateau in the summer of 1097 during which, the Anonymous says:

we lost most of our horses, so that many of our knights had to go as foot-soldiers, and for lack of horses we had to use oxen as mounts, and our great need compelled us to use goats, sheep and dogs as beasts of burden.

A little later the passage of the Taurus range took its toll of men and beasts, according to the same author.[47] Many horses were lost, according to Raymond of Aguilers, in the fighting around Antioch and disease and starvation must have accounted for most. In sum, it would appear that by the time the army reached Antioch it had little more than a 1,000 horses and their numbers had dwindled to 700, including beasts of burden, by February 1098 and to 200 or so by the time they fought Kerbogah on 28 June 1098.

The decision to break out of the city on the morning of 28 June 1098 was undoubtedly taken by all the leaders but we can safely attribute credit for the dispositions of the army to Bohemond. The subsequent battle resulted in a remarkable crusader victory; to those who were eyewitnesses and others who later described it, it was no

---

[46] Hagenmeyer, *Kreuzzugsbriefe*, p. 157; RA, pp. 49, 51, 53, 55, 77; *GF*, pp. 34, 62; PT, p. 44; RC, 646–7; AA, 381, 395, 408, 418–19, 426–8; on the figure of 700 in February 1098, see above, p. 281.

[47] *GF*, pp. 23, 27; in 1984 the author Tim Severin, *Crusader* (London, 1986), followed the path of the first crusade on horseback and had the greatest difficulty looking after his horses, even with modern aids and the support of motorised transport.

less than a miraculous delivery, the very climax of the crusade. So important was it that 'The sources give more exact detail concerning this battle than of any other fought in Latin Syria during the twelfth century'.[48] As a result scholars have felt able to reconstruct the battle in some detail. It is the account given by Raymond of Aguilers, supplemented by that of the Anonymous, which has been most credited by historians, partly because he is known to have been present as standard-bearer in the army of Adhémar of Le Puy, partly because it is a very clear description and partly because it reports a particular tactical formation in which foot-soldiers were thrown forward to protect the cavalry which was later much used in the crusading kingdom.[49]

Raymond of Aguilers tells us that the Provençal army formed up inside the Bridge Gate under the command of Adhémar. Raymond of Toulouse their natural commander, was ill and therefore stayed behind to protect the city against the garrison of the citadel. According to Raymond of Aguilers this army divided into two squadrons each of two lines with the foot thrown forward of the cavalry and this formation was replicated in the other divisions of the army each of which comprised broadly national groups organized around the great leaders. There were four of these when they marched out, the first led by Hugh of Vermandois, Robert of Flanders and Robert of Normandy, the second by Godfrey, the third by Adhémar and the fourth by Bohemond. As they emerged Kerbogah was playing chess with one of his followers, Mirdalin, and their dialogue suggests that he was frightened by the Franks, but nonetheless formed his army although he allowed the Franks to exit from Antioch unopposed. Raymond says that in order to evade encirclement (a theme we have noted in Raymond before) Adhémar's force marched towards the mountains some two miles (five kilometres) away, disregarding Kerbogah's offer to undergo a trial by battle as Peter the Hermit had suggested. Some of the Turks did move to the left of the crusader line to take them in the rear and a crusader infantry detachment fought

[48] Smail, *Crusading Warfare*, p. 173, n. 5.
[49] Smail, *Crusading Warfare*, pp. 173–4, based his reconstruction upon that of O. Heerman, *Die Gefechtsführung abendländischer Heere im Orient in der Epoche des ersten Kreuzzugs* (Marburg, 1888), p. 41, though he had reservations about his methods notably expressed p. 171, n. 8. Heerman depended heavily upon Raymond of Aguilers. In its main lines, this reconstruction has been followed by modern scholars, notably C. Morris in his computer program published by the HIDES Project of Southampton University, 'The battle at Antioch', which provides a sequential representation of the battle.

them off well until the enemy set fire to the grass and drove them back. Adhémar's force, though encircled, fought its way towards the mountain, then the army in eight divisions (augmented by five more, by a miracle and their horses wonderfully refreshed by light rain) charged the enemy who fled. The Anonymous makes it clear that Bohemond's force was in reserve and that the North French led by Godfrey, Robert of Flanders and Hugh were on the Christian right by the river and they engaged the main enemy force.[50] The general outline of the plan and its outcome has been summarised neatly thus:

The Franks were marshalled in four divisions, each of two squadrons, in which were both horse and foot-soldiers. The infantry were arrayed in front of the knights . . . Bohemond was again commander . . . he led the fourth and last division which was to be in reserve . . . As soon as the first division had passed through the gate and crossed the Orontes bridge, it was to turn into line, and to march upstream with its right flank on the bank of the river. The second division marched across the rear of its predecessor and turned to face the enemy in line when it was in a position to advance in line with and on the left of the first division. The third did likewise and came into line on the left of the second. The plan ensured that each division as it left the city changed its formation from column into line at the earliest possible moment, so that it faced the enemy ready to attack, and covered the deployment of the succeeding column. . . The flanks were covered by natural obstacles . . . Some two miles ahead of the Franks as they left the city was high ground. The head of the third division was ordered to reach this before it turned into line; after it had done so the left flank of the Franks was protected just as its right was covered by the river . . . The battle developed almost in accordance with Bohemond's plan. The Turks resisted the attempts of the third division . . . and were able to send a detachment across the head of the Latin column . . . a body of crusaders was detailed to meet its attack and in the resulting encounter the *pedites* showed they were well able to defend themselves . . . the three leading divisions . . . were able to attack in echelon. The Turks . . . fled with little resistance to the Latin charge.[51]

Now something like this must have happened, but the neatness of the event as described must, on *a priori* grounds, raise some suspicions. Deployment from column into line is a notoriously complicated manoeuvre and undertaken after crossing the rear of a force under attack, in the close presence of the enemy, is a military nightmare. Raymond asks us to believe that the crusader force was seeking to block the plain as it executed a right turn, yet the plain in

[50] RA, pp. 79–83; *GF*, p. 70.   [51] Smail, *Crusading Warfare*, pp. 173–4.

question is four to five kilometres wide as he says. Moreover, his account suffers from some internal contradictions. He tells us that the army was divided into four divisions but does not explain whence came the infantry unit which dealt with the enemy to the rear. Adhémar's division was opposed and encircled yet no arrows were shot against it and nobody killed – but Raymond himself tells us that he replaced Heraclius of Polignac who was wounded in the face by an arrow as the standard-bearer of the bishop. Finally he refers to a total victory and pursuit to the setting of the sun, but remarks that few of the enemy's mounted men were killed, though many foot. When we look at other accounts we can see some indication of the difficulties simply from the variant numbers of divisions in the crusader army which they record. The Anonymous, who was certainly present, gives six and Ralph agrees on the number and the make-up but suggests a different order. Anselm, who was a participant and wrote his second letter very shortly after the battle, mentions only five divisions and omits the name of Godfrey de Bouillon who was most certainly present and in charge of a major division. Albert of Aachen says there were no fewer than twelve divisions which he carefully enumerates specifying who the leaders were.[52] Anselm's slip of memory should remind us that this was an exciting and emotional occasion. The importing of camp gossip by Raymond and his concern with enemy encirclement point to his efforts to explain events *post facto*. The Anonymous does much the same – he refers to Kerbogah at the start of the battle ordering that grass-firing be used to signal retreat and records its use against the crusader infantry deployed against the enemy in the rear as signalling the end of the battle – but nobody else does this. Presumably he connected the appearance of a grass-fire with the enemy flight, though there is clear reason to believe that it signified nothing of the sort.[53] There is always a tendency to tidy up a battle in retrospect, to give it a shape which will inevitably reflect the deductions and predilections of the writer as much as events, and that is what we are dealing with here in what was a remarkable event and a

---

[52] *GF*, p. 68; RC, 666; Hagenmeyer, *Kreuzzusbriefe*, pp. 157–60; AA, 422; FC, pp. 105–6 is entirely dependent on RA for his account of the battle.

[53] Using smoke to confuse and choke the enemy was a well-known device of Islamic armies, employed, for example, at Hattin; Ibn al-Athir, 684. More exotic and even poisonous substances were also sometimes used: A. L. S. Muhammad Lutful-Huq, *A critical edition of the Nihayat al-Sul of Muhammad b. Isn b. Isma'il Al-Hanafi*, Ph.D thesis, University of London (1955), p. 15.

deeply felt experience for all who lived through it. If we bear all this in mind it seems to me that the crusaders had a much simpler battle plan than has been suggested and that the reasons for their victory are fairly clear.

The most remarkable thing about the battle against Kerbogah was that it was a victory of a largely infantry army over a much larger force with infantry and cavalry. For the crusaders must have been overwhelmingly dismounted. Albert of Aachen says that there were only 150–200 horses in the army fit for battle. This would suggest that there were barely more than thirty knights on average in each if there were six crusader divisions. It is possible that the Provençal force was stronger in horses than others, for Godfrey and Robert of Flanders had begged horses from Count Raymond, but if that was the case then other divisions would have been weaker in mounted men.[54] Albert makes his comments about the shortage of horses in the context of explaining that its consequence was that there was little pursuit of the enemy after the battle. The other sources seem to point in the same direction. Raymond of Aguilers, who does not comment directly at this point on the number of horses, says that few of the enemy's horsemen were killed, but many of their footmen. Ralph of Caen says exactly the same thing – only Tancred and his small force really pursued the enemy beyond his camp as far as 'Artāh. This is confirmed by Kemal ad-Din who says that there was no pursuit and no prominent men were lost although many volunteers became casualties. Matthew of Edessa stresses that it was the Islamic infantry which bore the weight of the crusader attack.[55] We need not suppose that Albert was exactly right, and he does qualify his number by saying that the 200 were those fit for battle. However Fulcher, without giving figures, says much the same thing: 'They [the enemy] knew that our knights had been reduced to weak and helpless footmen'.[56] The crusader army was overwhelmingly an army on foot and the few horsemen in its divisions must have been precious nuclei round which the others could rally. We can assume that in this desperate situation every fit man was pressed into service, for after the capture of the city they would have had ample supplies of arms for even the poorest. Amongst these were the *Tafurs*, a hard-core of poor men organised under their own

---

[54] See above, pp. 281–2.
[55] AA, 427; RA, p. 83; RC, 669–70; *Aleppo Chronicle*, 583; Matthew, 43.
[56] FC, p. 103.

leaders, whose name may be derived from the big light wooden shield which many of them carried, the *talevart* or *talevas*. Their ferocity and in particular their cannibalism would later repel friend and foe alike, although their supposed 'king' may well have been a later invention grafted on like the nobility of Robin Hood. These desperados seem to have been pre-eminently North French and Fleming in origin and to have represented a quasi-autonomous force within the army.[57] Such troops as these would have been well-stiffened by large numbers of dismounted knights, so that a formidable infantry existed, and would continue to exist for the rest of the crusade. The use of infantry thrown forward of the knights was not so much a skilful tactical invention – rather a necessity, for the shortage of horsemen meant that the foot would have to carry the battle to the enemy. In the event the battle proved their value in spectacular fashion.

Here we come to the whole point of the crusader deployment. They needed to get to close quarters with the enemy as quickly as possible and in the most favourable circumstances. They could not afford to fight at a distance for that would be to the enemy's advantage. This was why they chose to break out of the Bridge Gate. The main enemy camp was situated up the valley of the Orontes some five kilometres above Antioch, as we have noted (see fig. 12). It seems to have remained there for all the sources indicate that after the battle the enemy were pursued up the valley and their camp sacked.[58] To have attacked through the three north-facing gates would have sent the army into the narrow funnel of the Orontes valley, close to where the enemy main force lurked in its camp at the confluence of the Orontes and the Kara Su. It is clear that his main force was there, for the crusader sources speak of Kerbogah being in the camp at the time of their sally and being separated from the main focus of the fighting.[59] To have attacked south through the St George Gate would have been folly, for the enemy would have been massed behind an army which would inevitably have fled to the sea. Rather, a key factor in the defeat of Kerbogah was the decision of the

[57] The origin of the name is suggested by L. A. M. Sumberg, 'The *Tafurs* and the First Crusade', *Medieval Studies*, 21 (1959), 227–8; on the Tafurs see *La Chanson d'Antioche*, 11. 2987, 4042, 4049, 4066, 4087, 4100, 4106, 4115, 4118, 4299, 4318, 6395, 6398, 6417, 8251, 8921; GN, 242 says their lord was a Norman knight who had lost his horse.

[58] See above p. 286; on pursuit up the valley see AA, 426; RA, p. 83; RC, 670; GF, p. 70. Other Turkish camps were made at various times; for example, that on Mount Silpius which was soon abandoned, and then down in the plain to the north of the Bridge Gate.

[59] *GF*, pp. 68–9; RA, p. 80; RC, 667; AA, 426.

crusaders to attack against the force in the plain above the Bridge
Gate and the speed with which this was achieved. It is easy to forget
the sheer size of Antioch. This had troubled the crusaders who for six
months could only sustain outposts on the west bank. Kerbogah made
the fatal mistake of dispersing his forces, something the crusaders had
been at pains to avoid during their siege. He held much of his army to
the north but this separated him from the force by the Bridge Gate,
much of which was mainly on foot to judge by comments in the
sources that the infantry suffered the bulk of the losses. If all the gates
of the city were invested as the crusader sources say we can envisage
much of his huge army rallying to the battle which developed to the
north of the Bridge Gate and being committed to action piecemeal
(see fig. 14). Presumably some of those who attacked the crusaders in
the rear came from the force outside the St George Gate. As the crusaders marched out, all these groups would have had to concentrate
and either await the coming of their commander or rush into a devel-
oping battle without any direction.[60] The formation adopted by the
crusaders was designed to strike at the enemy in the plain and to seize
them in close combat; this was the job of the first divisions to emerge.
The long march of the Provençals across the plain was to protect their
own flanks and this was especially useful as Kerbogah and his main
force approached, while the reserve under Bohemond was there to
give support as needed. Bohemond probably counted on the distance
between Kerbogah and the forces in the plain to aid his plan; Kerbogah was suffering from dispersal of his forces, which the crusader
leaders had been at such pains to avoid. In the event, the crusaders
were able to achieve success because of hesitations in the enemy camp
and the speed of their own action.

When the garrison of the citadel flew the black flag to warn
Kerbogah that a break-out was imminent the news seems to have
triggered not action but a debate in the enemy camp. Some crusader
sources report a dialogue between Mirdalin and his commander
which shows Kerbogah as fearful. This follows the poetic tradition of
imaginary exchanges amongst the enemy, in this case designed to
explain an extraordinary fact, the slowness of the enemy army to
react to the attack.[61] According to Kemal ad-Din, the Arab leader

---

[60] See below, p. 293.

[61] RC, p. 667 repeats exactly the same story, telling it, however, as a rumour. It was probably
current in the crusader camp to explain events, and it is worth noting that Mirdalin passed
into the corpus of crusader legend: Cahen, *Syrie du Nord*, p. 215, n. 35.

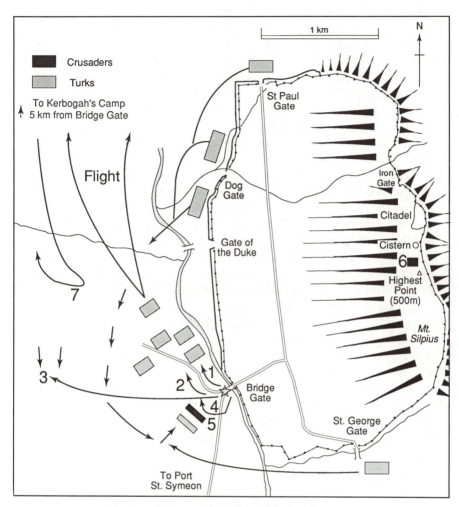

Fig. 14   The defeat of Kerbogah

☆   Turkish bowmen routed by Hugh of Vermandois

1 and 2 : Godfrey and the North French attack the Turks by the Bridge Gate

3 : South French under Adhémar, attempting to outflank the enemy, are engaged by piecemeal attacks

4 : Bohemond's forces act as a reserve and engage only when the enemy wavers

5 : Renaud of Toul's force holds off the enemy in the rear

6 : The Count of Toulouse continues to blockade the Citadel

7 : Kerbogah with his main force advances from the base camp, then turns back as he sees the rest of his army breaking up in defeat

Wassab ibn-Mahmud and some emirs urged Kerbogah to fall on the Franks as they appeared at the gate but the majority of the commanders wanted to let the enemy out to attack them in the plain. Ibn al-Athir says there was in any case considerable friction between many of the emirs and Kerbogah, and that some favoured an immediate attack but Kerbogah favoured letting the enemy out.[62] Kerbogah's view seems to have prevailed, but that is not to say that no effort was made to attack the Franks as they left the Bridge Gate. According to Albert of Aachen a force of 2,000 mounted bowmen rode up to the Bridge Gate as it opened. However, the crusaders had concentrated a force of bowmen with Hugh of Vermandois at the very head of their column and they advanced with shields held up against the enemy arrows and drove back the enemy until they got his horses in range, at which point the Turks took flight; they may well be the Turkomen to whom Kemal ad-Din refers as causing disorder in the ranks of Kerbogah's army. Anselm of Ribemont then led his forces into the retreating enemy, followed by Hugh of Vermandois and the whole group of the North French as they turned right across the Bridge Gate – Robert of Flanders, Robert of Normandy, Baldwin of Hainault and Eustace of Boulogne.[63] It was here on the Christian right by the Orontes that the main engagement was fought largely by the North French and against a largely infantry force (see fig. 14). The Anonymous says they were led by Godfrey, Robert of Flanders and Hugh of Vermandois, and it is these people that Albert mentions in his vivid, though often confusing description of events. As we have noted, the other accounts give much the same list of divisions in the army and Albert identifies some of these major groupings – those of Hugh of Vermandois, Robert of Flanders, Robert of Normandy, Adhémar who he says marched across the plain, Godfrey, Tancred and Bohemond whose force he describes as the biggest of all in knights and foot, committed to supporting the others according to need. Since his description of the main course of the battle accords with that of other sources, we can assume that the long list of divisions given earlier were the units in which men actually fought, and which they recalled being amongst and told Albert about later.[64] Each of these

[62] AA, 423; *Aleppo Chronicle*, p. 583; Ibn al-Athir, p. 195.
[63] AA, 423; *Aleppo Chronicle*, p. 583.
[64] The following are the other groups mentioned by Albert:

groups, as they crossed the Bridge, turned right and attacked the enemy to the left of its predecessor, fanning out like the fingers of a hand. It is unlikely that there was a deployment into tidy formations in line and far more likely that each charged in column pell-mell against the enemy. But the general battle plan was followed. Raymond of Aguilers describes how the army of the bishop struck across the plain, surrounded by the enemy who swarmed about it like flies, but never came to close quarters. It is quite likely that enemy cavalry forces, coming up piecemeal from their siege deployments, were attracted into attacking Adhémar's force, leaving their infantry isolated. An important action was caused by a large group of the enemy led, so Albert says, by Soliman and Rossilion, who moved to the left of the bishop's force with the obvious intention of taking the Christians in the rear. The Anonymous says that to counter this the leaders improvised a force from the armies of Godfrey and Robert of Normandy under Count Renaud of Toul. Albert says that this enemy force of 15,000 fell by chance into conflict with the corps led by Renaud III of Toul and others who are all associated with Godfrey. Raymond of Aguilers remarks that a group of the enemy moved to their rear and were attacked by crusader infantry who fought well, and Ralph of Caen says that an enemy force of 100,000 passed across the Frankish column to take them in the rear precipitating a two-faced battle. Raymond of Aguilers simply records that this infantry force fought well, but the Anonymous says that it had heavy casualties. Albert says that it was wiped out, save for the knights and, like the Anonymous, says that the enemy set fire to the grass in order to defeat them. Ralph never mentions Renaud and his men, but says that Bohemond fought the two-faced battle.[65] It is at least possible that after the infantry was wiped out Bohemond's force lent support. The improvisation of such a force in an emergency suggests that the

a Peter of Astenois* and his brother Renaud III of Toul*, Warner count of Grez*, Henry of Esch-sur Sûre*, all kinsmen of Godfrey, Renaud of Hamersbach and Walter of Domedart.
b Raimbaud d'Orange, Louis count of Mousson*, Lambert son of Cono of Montaigu*.
c Hugh of St Pol and his son Engelrand, Thomas de Fé, Baldwin of Bourcq*, Robert FitzGerald, Raymond Peleth, Galon of Calmon, Everard of Puiset, Dreux of Nesle, Rodolfus son of Godfrey, and Conan and another Rodolfus, both Bretons. Albert says they formed two divisions. Robert FitzGerard is surely the standard-bearer of Bohemond who fought with such distinction at the Lake Battle: *GF*, p. 37–8.
d Gaston of Béarn, Gerard of Roussillon, William of Montpellier.
On those marked * see Murray, 'The army of Godfrey de Bouillon'.
[65] AA, 424; *GF*, p. 69; RA, p. 81; RC, 667.

leaders had established very tight control over their forces which had become disciplined and trained through hard and long contact with the enemy. This was a grim and costly engagement fought out in the rear of the main crusader force, but their sacrifice bought time for the main army. The only writer to give any detail about the fighting near the Bridge Gate is Albert of Aachen whose account is confusing and, in at least one minor respect, demonstrably erroneous. His account tends to exalt the role of Godfrey and very much to play down that of Bohemond who he never suggests to have been in command. According to Albert, while the fight in the rear was going on, Bohemond was attacked by a force led by Qaradja of Harrân, Duqaq of Damascus and Ridwan of Aleppo. It is quite definitely known that Ridwan was not present. Godfrey was, at this time, engaged in attacking a force led by, amongst others, Balduk of Samosata and, as he defeated them, received a call for help from Bohemond. Godfrey rallied to Bohemond's aid with Hugh of Vermandois, and it is interesting that they changed position slowly so that horse and foot could stay together. The enemy then fled, crossing a stream which flowed into the Orontes, probably the Wadi al Quivaisiya, which must mean that they fled north, and dismounted on a hilltop to resist, but were driven off. This could well represent confused memories of what the Anonymous records in tidier form; he says that at the moment that the Saracens to the rear were setting fire to the grass around the beleaguered force led by Renaud of Toul, Godfrey and the North French began to press forwards on the right by the river, Bohemond committed his own force to the charge and the enemy fell into disorder and retreat.[66] Albert is reporting recollections of confused close-quarter fighting which was witnessed from a distance by the Anonymous who was caught up in it just at the moment that the enemy broke. But such fighting was confined to this part of the battlefield and to the gallant stand of Renaud of Toul's men. Raymond reports being attacked with arrows but:'the enemy turned in flight without giving us a chance to engage in battle', by which he probably means they never got to close quarters.[67] In the meantime it would appear that Kerbogah's main body had reached the battlefield on the Christian left where, Albert says, it stood still unable to come to the aid of the retreating Turks by the river. This was not divine intervention as

[66] AA, 425–6; *GF*, p. 70.   [67] RA, p. 83; Krey, *First Crusade*, p. 189.

Albert suggests, but because of the presence of Adhémar's force in the valley which would threaten his right wing should he undertake such a difficult manoeuvre as to gallop to the rescue of an already broken force. Albert says that at this point Kerbogah was informed that the crusaders were in the camp, which presumably means the camp in the plain immediately above the Bridge Gate, and he retreated, barely pursued because of the lack of horses. This general picture of really hard fighting in only a limited area of the battlefield is confirmed by Ibn al-Athir who says that only one division of the Islamic army stood, fought and was wiped out.[68]

The Islamic sources tend to attribute the defeat of this great army to divisions in its own ranks. According to Ibn al-Athir there had been a lot of friction which came to a head in the debate over whether to attack the crusader army as it emerged from Antioch and as a result most of the army took flight out of sheer irritation with Kerbogah. Kemal ad-Din is rather more specific. According to him, Kerbogah opened negotiations with Ridwan of Aleppo during the siege, annoying Duqaq while Janah ad-Daulah of Homs feared vengeance for his part in the murder of a rival, Youssef ben Abiks, and the nomad Turks disliked Ridwan.[69] There is a sense in which this is making excuses. After all, if the fortune of battle had gone the other way doubtless the nascent disputes between Raymond of Toulouse and Bohemond would have been blamed for the defeat. This is not to say that friction within Kerbogah's coalition was not a factor, but it was only a factor. Kerbogah's army was very large, as even the Islamic sources admit, but the dispersal of its forces and its commander's hesitations meant that its power was never brought to bear. It is possible that he had always intended to allow the Franks to exit from Antioch, counting on his 2,000 archers to exact a heavy toll of their numbers, and so was surprised by the speed with which this force was brushed aside. But he also seems to have hesitated over plans and this was fatal. By contrast the Franks knew what they wanted, to engage the enemy rapidly and in this they succeeded by a well-planned and swift exit. Battle was therefore joined on the river bank between only a part of Kerbogah's army and a very large proportion of the Franks, and despite the initiative of a Turkish force which tried to attack from the rear, there seems to have been a piecemeal commitment of the Islamic army which became dis-

[68] AA, 426; Ibn al-Athir, 196.   [69] Ib al-Athir, 194–6; *Aleppo Chronicle*, 582–3.

ordered under Frankish pressure. As Kerbogah's main force appeared on the right, his allies' forces on the left by the river were breaking up while Adhémar's sizable force was uncommitted. This was the situation in which all the distrusts and frictions in the Moslem army came into play and *sauve qui peut* became the rule. The Frankish battle plan, which was surely Bohemond's, was to engage a proportion of Kerbogah's army closely, while, as far as possible, taking precautions against being surrounded and overwhelmed. It worked because of the dispersal of Kerbogah's army, his hesitations and the distrust which this unleashed, and also because of another factor. The Franks were desperate for battle by 28 June. It is certain that their spirits had been revived by the finding of the Holy Lance and other divine messages, and the leaders may have noted with interest Kerbogah's failure to press home his attacks from the citadel in favour of simple attrition. But the army was faced with starvation – they had to fight and win if they were to survive and Albert says that they expressed this view to the leaders.[70] Of course, such an experience could have broken them, but sustained by faith and determination, by that driving religious enthusiasm which was the motor of the crusade, they fought for the chance to live. It was a gambler's throw of all or nothing which their enemies did not fully understand. Some of the Moslems did – the volunteers seem to have fought to the death as the chronicles of Aleppo and Damascus point out.[71] But for most of the emirs of Kerbogah's army this was a war for this or that advantage – that was the tradition in this fractured borderland of Islam. When things went badly distrust flourished, and this vile plant was fed all the more by the military incompetence of Kerbogah. So a combination of factors destroyed this great army, as it has destroyed so many others which were never, as a whole, brought to battle. The great, the rich and the lucky saved themselves – the foot, the women and children and other camp followers were destroyed. Fulcher, speaking of the fate of women in the enemy camp, expresses the true savagery of the crusader spirit: 'In regard to the women found in the tents of the foe the Franks did them no evil but drove lances into their bellies'.[72]

In this great victory we can see the improving military technique of the crusader army. There was no single tactical or technical

[70] See above, p. 279.
[71] *Damascus Chronicle of the Crusades*, p. 46; *Aleppo Chronicle*, 583.
[72] FC, p. 106.

advance. Its leaders were now very experienced soldiers, and Bohemond was an exceptional commander. By the end of the siege of Antioch the army was cohesive and disciplined. This was the result of working together in shared hardship. The leaders knew that solidity in formation was important before they left the west, and any doubts they may have had would have been dispelled by the advice of Alexius and the experience at Dorylaeum where it is evident they knew what was important but were handling a much less skilled and practised army. It took time for this kind of lesson to percolate through the army as it welded itself into an effective fighting unit. For knowing what is needed and bringing troops to the point where they can achieve it are two different things. Luck was a major factor in their early battles in Asia Minor. It continued to be important, but the army was becoming more cohesive and the Lake Battle and the fight against Kerbogah demonstrated this. There are some indications, especially at the Lake Battle, that the army was using the mass charge with couched lances which is so characteristic of warfare later in the twelfth century, but of which there is little evidence before the crusade.[73] The crusaders enjoyed no technical advantage over amongst their enemies though we do not hear of lamellar and scale armour amongst the Franks and it is possible that chain-mail was more widespread amongst them than their enemies and this would reflect their predilection for close-quarter combat. Even the large kite-shaped shield, which is clearly an adaptation to this style of war, was known in the East, though smaller round ones were perhaps commoner. The westerners were adaptable, with the knights, the key element in the army, quite capable of fighting on foot. The real innovation was in command. The near disaster of the Foraging Battle forced them into appointing a single commander and, in the person of Bohemond, they found an able general. The enemy was particularly adept at avoiding close quarter fighting until their opponents were suitably weakened, and used encirclement and ambush to that end. Bohemond turned the tables on the enemy by ambushing them at the Lake Battle, holding his own force as a reserve to reinforce weak points. At Antioch he again sought to bring the enemy to battle at close quarters by a sudden sally against a part of his army, and devised a formation which offered some protection from encirclement to the Frankish force most closely

[73] See above, pp. 71–2, 74.

engaged. The hallmark of his dispositions was aggression – he never stood on the defensive and never allowed the enemy to settle his formation. The crusader army was by this time a seasoned and disciplined force fired by religious fervour and the desperate need to win food. The lessons of war were gradually learned, though at enormous cost in lives. The deadly effectiveness of ambush, which might trap a handful of men, or overwhelm a whole army as at the Foraging Battle, was only slowly brought home to the Franks. This continued to be a weakness, as it was of all armies, in part because of poor communications and in part because of weak discipline. Also it is a simple and unavoidable fact that armies, like all organisations, fall into routine or are obliged to do predictable things. At the Lake Battle they ambushed Ridwan; less than a month later Bohemond, who had commanded them and devised the stratagem, was himself ambushed on the St Symeon road but then it was the only road down to the sea and it seems to have been a well-laid ambush. But two clear-cut victories, in February and June 1098, achieved over larger forces in very adverse circumstances, showed an army whose cohesiveness was growing and whose commanders were adapting to new conditions. Franks and Turks were used to different styles of war, and the Franks worked hard to bring their enemy to battle at close quarters. Theirs were victories of military ability, but also of militant temperament. Their enemies did not, in the main, share that willingness to conquer or die – the very essence of crusading. For the most part they fought for more limited ends without properly understanding the nature of their new adversary. Having said this, we need to recognise that the savagery during the siege of Antioch and the fate of the volunteers outside in the final battle show that a quite different spirit could be engendered in their enemies. It is a fine irony that this supreme triumph of the crusading spirit in the battle over Kerbogah opened the way to a marked change in the way the army conducted itself.

CHAPTER 10

Divisions

Immediately after the flight of Kerbogah's army the citadel of
Antioch surrendered. According to the Anonymous its commander
offered submission to Raymond of Toulouse, but some South Italians suggested that he accept the banner of Bohemond instead, and
so the citadel went to the South Italian leader.[1] It was a sour note of
division after the great triumph, and it set the tone for a prolonged
period of conflict within the crusader army. For Bohemond's
ambition to control Antioch triggered a crisis which was exacerbated by other factors and which had a severe impact upon
practical military necessity. Bohemond had made contact with
Firuz, the betrayer of Antioch, and in the end the other leaders
made him a conditional promise of the city: 'on condition that if the
emperor come to our aid and fulfil all his obligations which he
promised, we will return the city to him as it is right to do'.[2]

Immediately after the defeat of Kerbogah the princes met and
sent Hugh of Vermandois to Constantinople, presumably to explain
the situation to Alexius and ask for his help. It is interesting that
even in the emergency, as Kerbogah's force approached, the majority of the leaders of the crusade stood by their oath to Alexius, but
conditions now conspired to undermine that fidelity. Bohemond
never regarded Antioch as anything other than his personal possession. Raymond of Aguilers, who says nothing of Bohemond's role in
the betrayal of the city, reports that he seized the citadel, confirming
the story of the quarrel told by the Anonymous, and persuaded all
the leaders except Raymond of Toulouse to surrender to him the
gates and towers they held along the city wall, with resultant
internal strife.[3] On 14 July 1098 Bohemond made an agreement
with the Genoese and granted a charter conceding extraterritorial

---

[1] *GF*, p. 71.   [2] *GF*, pp. 44–5 and see above, pp. 260–2.   [3] *RA*, pp. 83–4.

privileges in return for promises of support. There was no mention of the rights of the emperor in these documents. In the pact the Genoese promised military support against any who attacked the city: 'But they will not fight against the count of St Gilles; if he wishes to withdraw we will give him council, if not we will remain neutral'.[4]

It is evident that Bohemond and the count of Toulouse had become rivals in the matter of Antioch even before the final echoes of the great victory had died away and it was probably partly because of this that on 3 July the leaders decided to delay their journey. As the Anonymous says, it was sensible to delay for the army was tired and the summer was not a good season to continue, though Raymond of Aguilers believed that the enemy, terrified by the defeat of Kerbogah, would have offered little resistance. He was probably appalled by the extraordinary decision to put off the journey until 1 November 1098, a delay of four months. Presumably this was to allow plenty of time for an imperial army to arrive – it had, after all, taken the crusaders themselves nearly four months to march to Antioch from Nicaea. For most of the princes a solution to the quarrel was the priority and the coming of the emperor, or at least substantial imperial forces, would provide that. Its failure to materialise swayed them somewhat to Bohemond's view, however, and this may well have been hastened by matters of personality. Raymond of Toulouse, for reasons at which we can only guess, was evidently not popular as a man. He had suffered various illnesses during the long siege of Antioch, yet had shouldered a considerable burden. He never seems to have been a distinguished soldier but was certainly reasonably competent. Yet he was later accused of being in the pay of the emperor and this is perhaps the key to understanding his position. At a time when it was bound to be unpopular he espoused the imperial cause and this isolated a man who was already somewhat isolated in the ranks of the leaders by his origins and by his age.

If the princes were anxious to appear to be fair to the emperor, there were plenty of others in the army who must have regarded this delay as a disaster. For the poor, and even many of the knights, a halt in what had become friendly territory which they could not ravage was a disaster. For the moment many of the leaders used the vast plunder of Antioch to take men into their service, but the delay must have caused tension, not least because it seemed to be contrary to the spirit of their whole undertaking the ultimate object of which was the liberation of Jerusalem. With Provençals and South Italian Normans holding strongholds in the city – Count Raymond held the Governor's Palace and the Bridge Gate – there was a real possibility of violence.[5] The question of who held Antioch was clearly tied to the wider question of the Byzantine alliance, hence the mission of Hugh of Vermandois in early July 1098. But soon after he left the crusaders must have heard of Alexius's encounter with Stephen of Blois on or about 20 June 1098.[6]

Stephen had fled from the siege of Antioch when Kerbogah approached, but he encountered Alexius at Philomelium. Anna Comnena would have us believe that the emperor was there, 'ready to march to the aid of the Kelts in the Antioch region'. This, however, must be read in the context of Anna's work where her account of the crusade and relations with the Franks is dominated by the question of Antioch. She constantly accuses the Franks of being oath-breakers, because of Bohemond's seizure of the city. Her view is that Alexius kept his word to the Franks, while they broke theirs to him and this is the central thesis of the *Alexiad* as far as the crusade is concerned. Anna's version of Alexius's purposes needs to be seen in that light, and it should be remembered that the crusader army had taken well over two months to march from Antioch-in-Pisida, which is just west of Philomelium, to Antioch. Of course, Alexius had a smaller army and need not have taken the long detour of the main crusader army up to Kayseri, but even so when he met Stephen of Blois on or about 20 June 1098 he was at least three to four weeks march from Antioch (see fig. 2).[7] Alexius's movements at this time need to be seen in the light of his general position. According to his daughter, Alexius was at first restrained from rushing to the aid of the Franks at Antioch by the need to defend his western provinces against local emirs, and so sent out a military and naval expedition led by his brother-in-law John Doukas to south-

---

[5] *GF*, p. 72.

[6] *AA*, 417–19, says that the crusaders found out about the matter during Kerbogah's siege, but Hagenmeyer, *Chronologie* no. 287, thinks that it took Stephen eleven days by land and sea to reach Philomelium on or about 20 June, which makes it unlikely that news of the matter could have got back to Antioch by 28 June.

[7] *Alexiad*, p. 348; France, 'Anna Comnena', 22–5; Hagenmeyer, *Chronologie* Nos. 175, 176.

western Asia Minor. Doukas persuaded many enemy outposts to surrender by displaying Tzachas's daughter, who had been captured at Nicaea, negotiated the surrender of Smyrna and defeated the Turks at Ephesus. He appears to have left his fleet to clear islands like Chios and Rhodes. Doukas pursued the retreating Turks up the Maeandros valley, seizing Sardes, Philadelphia, Laodicea, Lampe and reached Polybotus (modern Bolvadin) near Philomelium on the great road across Asia Minor. Alexius took the field and marched down the Royal Road, perhaps via Dorylaeum to Philomelium where he arrived in mid-June of 1098. This junction of Byzantine forces could hardly have been accidental.[8] A glance at the map and the roads shows this to be a sensible plan to profit from the crusade. It was almost certainly with such propects in mind that Alexius and the western princes had made their decisions on the route of the crusade. The loss of Nicaea and the defeat of Kilij Arslan did not destroy Seljuk power in Asia Minor but rolled it back from the western end of the sub-continent. The emirs of western cities like Ephesus and Smyrna were virtually cut off from the support of the Seljuk Sultan, with whom their relations had always been difficult, and Alexius's campaign in the spring of 1098 with its two axes of advance was intended to follow up this success.[9] The Byzantine empire had certainly profited from the victories of the crusader army, just as it had profited from Byzantine support. The question which arises is did Alexius intend to march to their aid as Anna suggests and the crusader chroniclers assumed?

Anna stresses that her father was anxious to provide aid to the Franks in person when at Philomelium he encountered William of Grandmesnil, Stephen of Blois and Peter of Aups, whose presence astonished him. They informed him of the desperate situation in Antioch and this increased his anxiety to proceed despite opposition from his own entourage. However, news came of an impending attack by Ismail, brother of Malik Shah. Alexius was also informed, although Anna does not say by whom, that the Franks were planning to surrender. This story is found also in Matthew of Edessa which perhaps reflects a later distortion of the embassy of Peter the Hermit to Kerbogah on 27 June. Alexius was persuaded to abandon his intentions and to retreat, taking with him large sections of the

[8] *Alexiad*, pp. 345–8; Vryonis, *Hellenism*, pp. 116–17.
[9] Vryonis, *Hellenism*, pp. 115–19 sets this in context.

local population who would otherwise be exposed to the vengeance of the Turks. In the midst of this Anna gives a long diatribe about the impulsiveness and untrustworthiness of the Franks and the account ends with a note that Ismail eventually attacked Paipert in north-eastern Anatolia which was held by Theodore Gabras of Trebizond.[10] Amongst the Latin writers two make no mention of the episode at Philomelium: Fulcher, perhaps because of his earlier connection with Stephen, and Raymond of Aguilers perhaps out of regard for the susceptibilities of his master the count of Toulouse. Raymond, however, does mention the desertion of Stephen and later at 'Akkār comments on the emperor's untrustworthiness and earlier desertion of the army. The Anonymous says that Stephen and his followers fled and met the emperor at Philomelium, but the centrepiece of his account is a speech by Guy, Bohemond's half-brother who was in imperial service, which is scornful of Alexius (and so could never have been given) and tends to justify ignoring the rights of the emperor: 'if the word which we have heard from these scoundrels [Stephen and friends] is true, we and the other Christians will forsake thee and remember thee no more'. He adds that many of the pilgrims with Alexius died in the subsequent retreat.[11] Ralph of Caen confirms the presence of Guy and adds that Alexius had an army of 100,000 together with 10,000 Frankish reinforcements but his account is brief and includes nothing of the great speech by Guy. Both Ralph and the Anonymous had evidently heard some reliable information about Philomelium for they confirm Anna's statement that Alexius devastated the land and evacuated the local population. It is possible that Bauldry's story of some Franks leaving Philomelium for Antioch has some truth in it and that they were the source for this information.[12] Albert of Aachen says that the deserters were Stephen of Blois, William the Carpenter and another William, who must have been William of Grandmesnil, and that they fled by sea and met Alexius at Philomelium where he had 40,000 troops and 40,000 new pilgrims and was accompanied by Tatikios. The emphasis of his account,

[10] *Alexiad*, pp. 348–9; Matthew, 41. On Theodore Gabras and his later martyrdom see Vryonis, *Hellenism*, pp. 360–1.

[11] *GF*, pp. 63–5.

[12] *GF*, p. 65; RC, 658–9; for Bauldry's story see above, p. 211; the other copyists of the Anonymous, PT, pp. 74–6; *HBS*, 203–4; RM, 815, add nothing although GN, 200, has a short diatribe about deserters and mentions Hugh of Vermandois. It should be noted that at first the siege of Antioch was incomplete: see above, p. 270.

however, is on the treachery of Stephen and the deserters who insisted that there was no point in Alexius pressing on.[13] The Latin sources show no insight into Alexius's intentions and we are left only with Anna's observations, written long afterwards and unmistakably self-exculpatory in content. Is it likely that Alexius, who had refused to join the crusaders at Nicaea, would now have been prepared to join them in adversity at distant Antioch, especially as it is quite clear that there was no formal obligation upon him to go? Had he actually promised at any stage to come in person, or had it been a condition of the offer made in the embassy of Hugh of Vermandois to Constantinople as the Anonymous suggests, it would have been mentioned and been conclusive in the arguments at the crusader conference of 1 November 1098. It is far more likely that Alexius was prepared to assist the crusaders if conditions were right – if they were already successful. The march of the imperial forces to Philomelium makes sense in terms of liberating western Anatolia. Philomelium was a long way from Antioch and the likelihood is that Alexius was prepared to proceed eastwards only in the most favourable circumstances and when these were not forthcoming he turned back. It must be said that he had assisted the crusaders enormously during their siege of Antioch with naval aid and supplies. He was prepared to help but not to take serious risks. From his point of view this was sensible for as Anna says, if he ventured to their aid, 'He might lose Constantinople as well as Antioch'. It was sensible, but in its impact upon the alliance with the crusader army, disastrous. It is unlikely that Alexius's decision to retreat on or about 20 June could have become known to the crusaders in Antioch, but news of it seems to have emerged in the summer and caused a violent reaction, as witness the letter of the Princes to the west dated 11 September 1098 with its vitriolic attacks on the Greeks and the emperor.[14]

News of events at Philomelium complicated an already difficult situation for the crusader army. The leaders must have recognised that the Byzantine alliance was now in doubt. They had some hope of an arrangement with the Egyptians, as we have noted. They must have been deeply worried about containing the quarrel between Bohemond and Raymond of Toulouse. There was an evident shortage of manpower which could only be worsened by the attractions of

[13] AA, 414–15.
[14] Hagenmeyer, *Kreuzzusbriefe*, pp. 161–65. As Hagenmeyer points out this may well have been written wholly or in part by Bohemond.

Edessa and the need to garrison Antioch.[15] But there is an additional factor which resentment against the Byzantine alliance must have let loose. We tend to see the crusade as a movement with a single standpoint, as an ideological movement. This is partly the consequence of crusader historiography which, at least since the work of Erdmann, has focussed on an exploration of the origins of the crusading movement, of the crusading idea. That there was such an ideological unity is undoubted, but it is only one side of the story, for ideology co-existed with many other and individual standpoints. This was the importance of the death of Adhémar on 1 August 1098. He was the only churchman with the authority, personality and standing to insist on Urban's intentions being carried out, the only one of the leaders to personify the ideological goal of the expedition – the liberation of Jerusalem. Without him there was no clear leadership for their ultimate intention and purpose – no-one of rank who stood for the pure and unallayed spirit of the crusade.[16] On his deathbed he is said to have commended the care of the army to Arnulf who, along with Stephen of Blois's chaplain Alexander, had also been given legatine powers by Urban II. Raymond of Aguilers later says that the Bishop of Orange took up his mantle but died at Ma'arra.[17] The fact was that none of these men had both the status and personal qualities of Adhémar, hence the moral vacuum left by his death. Into it stepped the visionary Peter Bartholemew who tried to influence the conduct of events through the prestige which he had achieved as the discoverer of the Holy Lance. However, his main influence lay with the Provençals and, from another point of view, he could be seen as acting in the interests of the count of Toulouse.[18]

---

[15] On the Egyptian embassy and the question of numbers see above, pp. 122–42, 253–4 and below, pp. 325–7.

[16] Adhémar's reputation has been attacked by J. H. and L. L. Hill, 'Contemporary accounts and the later reputation of Adhémar, bishop of Le Puy', *Medievalia et Humanistica*, 9 (1955), 30–8 and defended by J. A. Brundage, 'Adhémar of Puy, the bishop and his critics', *Speculum*, 34 (1959), 201–12. It is evident to the present writer that Adhémar was the fulcrum around which all the forces unleashed during the crusade turned and that he was a figure of the highest importance.

[17] RC, p. 673; J. Richard, 'Quelques textes sur les premiers temps de l'église latine de Jérusalem', *Recueil des Travaux Offerts à M. Clovis Brunel*, 2 vols. (Paris, 1955), 2. 420–30 drew attention to the legatine commission of Arnulf and Alexander mentioned by Clarius pp. 184–7; see also B. Hamilton, *The Latin Church in the Crusader States. The Secular Church.* (London, 1980) p. 13; RA, p. 152.

[18] On the general character of the crisis which afflicted the crusade after the defeat of Kerbogah see France, 'The crisis of the First Crusade, 276–308 and on the role of Peter and the visionaries Morris, 'Policy and Visions', and France, 'Prophet, Priest and Chronicler'.

There can be no doubt that a desire to liberate Jerusalem was common to all who went on the crusade: this was sharpened amongst the poor and the lesser knights for whom delay was an economic disaster but their anxiety was influential precisely because it was shared by all. However, as we have already remarked, unalloyed idealism is rare and the tendency of human kind to identify individual interest with the greater good a commonplace. Moreover, the erosion of the Byzantine alliance was both a practical check to the crusade – perhaps further imperial help would not be forthcoming, and an ideological blow, for it was a keystone of Urban's intentions, as we have noted. In such a situation many of the leaders and their more important followers may well have felt justified in exploiting present benefits – the lands they already held around Antioch which we have noted – while awaiting developments. Bohemond's seizure of Antioch and Baldwin's capture of Edessa set precedents for personal gain and represented only particularly successful efforts amongst a group of leaders all of whom could enjoy similar, if smaller holdings. The temptations of North Syria were all the greater when we consider the weakness of the army and the prospect of challenging the power of Egypt, whose rulers were in any case seriously considering some kind of agreement. Now the pressure was off the crusaders could look about them, and they found that they were in a particular political culture – a culture of fragmentation and division, which was particularly congenial to feudal princes who had lived all their lives in not dissimilar political circumstances.[19]

We think of Baldwin as coming to the aid of the Armenians of Edessa against their enemies – this is how the matter is presented by both Fulcher and Albert of Aachen. However, as Albert's account makes very clear, the reality was that Baldwin was called in by one faction of Edessans in order to use him against Thoros their ruler.[20] This is not to say that Baldwin's force was militarily insignificant in the local context – Fulcher says he took eighty knights, with him, Matthew refers to sixty and Albert to 200. Indeed, ultimately his acceptability was determined by his military prowess for Edessa was beset with enemies.[21] Albert tells us that after considerable dispute

---

[19] J. A. Forse, 'The Armenians and the First Crusade', *Journal of Medieval History*, 17 (1991), 13–22, emphasises the cultural affinity between Franks and Armenians.

[20] 'He [Thoros] was much afraid for many of the townsmen [of Edessa] hated him': 'Anonymous Syriac Chronicle', p. 70.

[21] FC, p. 90: Matthew, 36; AA, 352, on whom see A. A. Beaumont, 'Albert of Aachen and the county of Edessa', in L. J. Pactow, ed., *The Crusades and Other Historical Essays presented to D. C. Munro* (New York, 1928), pp. 101–38; Amouroux-Mourad, *Comté d'Edesse*, p. 59.

with Thoros, in which Baldwin demanded recognition as heir to the city and refused to accept merely a position in his service, he took 200 of his own forces, which presumably means Franks, and all the mounted men and foot he could find in the town on an expedition against Balduk of Samosata. They were attacked by Balduk and there were heavy losses amongst the Armenians, though only six westerners were killed. Baldwin then established a garrison in the nearby village of St John in order to harass Samosata. Undoubtedly the military skill of the Franks had impressed the citizens and Baldwin's continued bravery, best shown in his bold attack on Kerbogah's forces, was a vital factor in maintaining his régime as was his conciliatory rule and marriage to an Armenian princess.[22] But if we think of Armenians simply as a group distinct from Syrians or Turks we have a mistaken perspective. The Armenians were divided into shifting factions focussed around various princes – Gabriel of Melitene was a former lieutenant of Philaretus and claimed to be a Byzantine official, though he was a vassal of Malik Shah.[23] This was an area where fragmentation was a norm and had been for more than a century. The decline of Abassid power and the expansion of Byzantium in the late tenth century had moved the Christian/Islamic boundary eastwards, but Antioch was a border outpost after its recapture in 969 and on both sides of the religious divide political structures were fissured. The coming of the Turks did not radically change this situation, for the nomads of Asia Minor did not build a state but were able to defy the Seljuk Sultans. Even Malik Shah at the height of his power was obliged to create a network of competing emirs through whose divisions he could rule. The collapse of the Seljuk domination freed all the particularist forces of the region, and it was into this maelstrom of competing and often tiny entities that the crusaders plunged. Baldwin had confirmed his reputation by the attack on Samosata, but when he gained Edessa its emir, Balduk, handed over the citadel of Samosata and became his *condomesticus et familiaris*, appealing to him for aid in subduing the rebellious city of Sororghia. The terrorised inhabitants turned to Balduk for protection but Baldwin prepared for a full scale siege, with engines and mangonels and this forced them to surrender, abandoning Balduk who hastened to make his peace. Subsequently Balduk joined Kerbogah's army but after its defeat is

[22] AA, 352–4, 397; Matthew, cxiii, where his first wife is named as Arda.
[23] Cahen, *Turkey*, pp. 81–2.

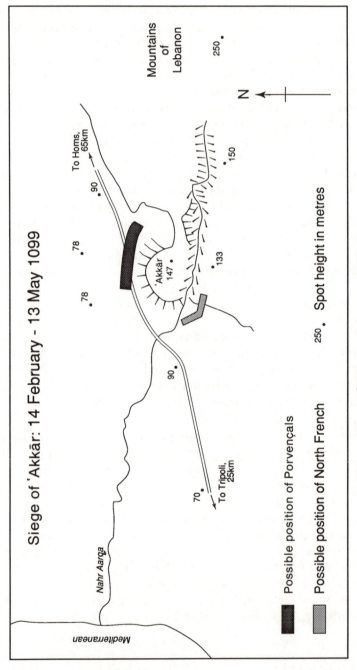

Fig. 15   Siege of 'Akkār: 14 February–13 May 1099

found once more in association with Baldwin.[24] It is hardly strange that Baldwin should have adapted so quickly to this culture of fragmentation, for it was very like the feudal world of the principalities of France. The precedents set by Bohemond and Baldwin, and the proposed treaty with the Fatimids produced a change in mood amongst the crusaders which was intensified by the failure of the summer rest to heal the divisions of the army. Godfrey held Tell Bashir, Ravendan and a dominion in the ʿAfrin valley of Baldwin after he fled the plague in Antioch and was closely associated with Robert of Flanders (see fig. 4). He began to expand this and intervened in the affairs of the Armenians, supporting some monks against Bagrat of Cyrrhus and avenging an earlier insult when this Armenian prince had diverted gifts and notably a tent to Bohemond which had been intended for him. A fort was seized and twenty of its defenders were blinded and shortly afterwards another strong place of Kogh Vasil of Kesoun fell. When Ridwan of Aleppo besieged his troublesome vassal the emir of ʿAzāz, a city on the road to Edessa, its emir appealed to Godfrey who with the help of his brother Baldwin, Raymond of Toulouse and Bohemond raised the siege and established cordial relations with this new ally though only after Ridwan had inflicted losses on their stragglers. Tancred seems to have continued to hold Harem and ʿImm on the Aleppo road.[25] When, in January of 1099, the crusader army began its march south treaties and arrangements with Moslem rulers became common. The rulers of Shaizar and Homs were more than anxious to allow the crusaders supplies, even to purchase badly needed horses, and free passage. The ruler of Tripoli's similar offers were rebuffed as the army attacked his city of ʿAkkār, but ultimately he came to terms, as did Jabala, Acre and other places (see figs. 4 and 16).[26] The pervasive influence of the culture of fragmentation affected the crusaders in that summer and autumn of 1098, adding to the delay and ultimately significantly modifying their methods.

It is very difficult to understand the attitude of the Islamic world to its invaders in the years of the crusade. The attitude of the nomads of Asia Minor is impenetrable, but we ought to know more than we do of those in the civilised heartlands which the army had now reached. Unfortunately, although our sources are often based on

[24] AA, 355-7.
[25] AA, 441, 436-40; RA, pp. 88-9; *Chronicle of Aleppo*, 586; RC, 649-50.
[26] RA, pp. 103, 107, 111-12, 125, 135-36; *GF* pp. 81, 83-6.

contemporary material they are overlaid by later attitudes and knowledge. The Islamic powers may have seen the coming of the army in terms of the great expeditions which the Byzantine emperors had once been wont to send to the east, but it is difficult to believe that this idea persisted beyond their arrival.[27] The spirit of *jihad* was not entirely dead for there were 'volunteers' in the Islamic armies, certainly in that of Kerbogah and later in the Egyptian army which fought at Ascalon.[28] But for the most part the authorities in the cities were untouched by any such spirit. For them the newcomers were another force in the complex middle-east political game and one which was not so different in its nature from others. In this area there were ancient centres of settlement – Antioch, Aleppo, Damascus, Shaizar and the rest which create an appearance of stability. But sweeping around them were much more restless forces – the Bedouin, the Arab tribes, invaders from the steppe, of whom the most recent were the Turks, in the past Byzantine armies. They might be unwelcome, but the risks of confrontation were high – better to pay them off and see what the future has to bring. These cities had a long tradition of neutrality (perhaps opportunism puts it better) in the Seljuk-Fatimid conflict and saw no reason to abandon this.[29] As to the crusade's ultimate objectives, these must have seemed opaque to the Islamic powers. Their attitude is best exemplified by the Kemal ad-Din's brief dismissal of the fall of Jerusalem, a mere one-line notice of an event which took place in a far-away land, not worth, perhaps, the bones of an Aleppan soldier. Once the major powers of Syria had failed in their policy of confrontation with the Franks before Antioch, accommodation, albeit grudging, became the rule.[30]

Military activity in that summer and autumn of 1098 was much

---

[27] A. Maalouf, *The Crusades through Arab Eyes* (London, 1984), relies heavily on this idea, but his work is to crusader historiography as D. Brown, *Bury my Heart at Wounded Knee* (London, 1971), is to that of the western expansion of the United States, chiefly concerned with establishing an alternative viewpoint; Sivan, *L'Islam et la Croisade*, pp. 25–6, points to evidence that, in Syria, the crusaders were at first seen as instruments of the Byzantines. The 'Anonymous Syriac chronicle', p. 69, is quite clear that they were allies of Alexius who 'sent ambassadors to Alexius to prepare to go out with them ... Alexius promised to help them in all they needed', but this was written in the late twelfth century.

[28] *Aleppo Chronicle*, 583. *Damascus Chronicle of the Crusades*, p. 48. But overall there was little sense of *jihad* in the Islamic world as Sivan, *L'Islam et la Crusade*, pp. 21–35 makes clear; on Holy War in the two cultures see M. Canard, 'La guerre sainte dans le monde islamique et le monde chrétien', *Revue Africaine*, 79 (1936), 605–23.

[29] Köhler, *Allianzen un Verträgen*, p. 72.   [30] *Aleppo Chronicle*, 587.

more purposeful than has usually been recognised. Godfrey and Robert of Flanders were strengthening their hold on an area which they had long dominated. Bohemond left to strengthen his hold on Cilicia, a vital buttress of the emerging Principality of Antioch, though we know nothing of his activities. The problems for a medieval army of resting in friendly territory were clearly illustrated by Albert who reports that after the 'Azāz campaign knights and nobles in groups of fifty or a hundred, including quite notable people like Drogo of Nesle, Gaston of Béarn, Renaud of Toul and Fulcher of Chartres trailed along to Edessa driven by want. It may have been Baldwin's generosity to them which provoked an Armenian plot against him. Certainly Balak of Sororghia was concerned by the rising power of Baldwin and tried unsuccessfully to trap him by offering to surrender Amasya. Fulcher of Chartres was given command of Sororghia in order to harass Amasya.[31] Albert's picture of knights in want, trekking out to offer their services in Edessa, supports Raymond of Aguilers' general picture of a disgruntled and rather dispersed army and forms the background to the discontent which would well up in the winter.

In July 1098 the Provençal knight Raymond Pilet, lord of Alais in the Limousin, led a raid which captured Tell Mannas, the Christian population of which surrendered to him and became his allies. His force was later badly mauled by the garrison of Ma'arra (see fig. 4).[32] Such expeditions by lesser figures may have been much more common than we suppose, for they answered the imperative to feed and support idle troops. As the army lingered in the summer of 1098 such men must have found many opportunities opening up for them. Raymond Pilet was probably back in the service of Raymond of Toulouse when he captured Tortosa in mid-February 1099 and he played a notable role in the siege of Jerusalem.[33] It was because of the poor that Raymond of Toulouse joined in the expedition against 'Azāz in mid-September. But Count Raymond probably had other motives for his attack on Albara, not far from his base at Ruj, later in the month. Ruj formed an important base for the Provençals, and it was surely from there that Raymond Pilet was operating when he seized Tell Mannas to the east of Ma'arra. Albara and the neigh-

[31] AA, 441–5.

[32] *Aleppo Chronicle*, 584; *GF*, pp. 73–4; Riley-Smith, *Idea of Crusading*, p. 61 thinks that the Anonymous was in Raymond Pilet's following at this stage.

[33] *GF*, pp. 84, 89; RA, pp. 141–2.

bouring Roman cities of Sirjyla, Deir Sambil and Ba'ouda dominate the Jebel Barisha massif and they are so close to one another that the fate of one must have been the fate of all. The bishop of Albara once held a great dominion in this area, including the important city of Kafartab, and it was probably for this reason that Raymond of Toulouse installed Peter of Narbonne as bishop there. Later, even when he was very short of troops, Raymond would permit a small force to be left to garrison Albara. Most commentary on Peter's appointment concerns the fact that he was the first latin bishop in the east, which suggests that the Count saw this city as being outside the terms of the agreements with Alexius. However, equally interesting,especially in the light of the later expedition to Ma'arra, is the fact that the count of Toulouse was building up a powerful bastion in Syria about 100 kilometres south-east of Antioch, whose eventual conquest of Ma'arra would threaten the roads between Aleppo and the southern cities of Hamah, Homs and Damascus.[34] Thus a whole group of nascent Frankish dominions was emerging – Edessa, Antioch, the 'Afrin valley, Ruj and the Jebel Barisha. With hindsight we know those which would endure, but at the time this was not so evident and the rise of these dominions must have been deeply worrying to many crusaders.

It is against this background that the visions of Peter Bartholomew, acting as spokesman for the rank-and-file and demanding that the crusade press on to Jerusalem, must be seen.[35] This is the context of the conference on 1 November 1098 which the leaders had arranged for the resumption of the march to Jerusalem. The conference revealed an army bitterly divided. Raymond of Toulouse would not accept Bohemond's seizure of Antioch. Raymond of Aguilers says that the other leaders sympathised with Bohemond but were afraid to say so lest they be charged with oath-breaking.[36] Perhaps they were also mindful of the aid which they had received and might hope to go on receiving from Cyprus. In any case, the

---

[34] RA, pp. 91–2, 104–5; Dussaud, *Topographie*, pp. 187–8, who tends to see their conquest as part of a plan of advance against Hama; for the capture of Ma'arra see below, pp. 311–15. The 'deserted cities' of the Jebel Barisha are almost intact Roman cities in gradual decay. They were presumably deserted because of the erosion which has stripped the upper reaches of the massif of its soil, but their very existence points to former wealth. They are within sight of one another. This area was later annexed to the Principality of Antioch until it was lost in 1135: Smail, *Crusading Warfare*, p. 32.

[35] France, 'Prophet, priest and chronicler'.   [36] RA, pp. 93–4.

stubborn stance of Count Raymond was now a barrier to the obvious solution of giving Bohemond the city, because Raymond held the Palace and the Bridge Gate. Judgment between the two risked open offence to the Byzantines and alienating the loser – it seemed that they were trapped in the situation. In military terms the failure of a whole contingent to join the march must have seemed to presage disaster. In the end it was popular pressure which forced the leaders to what Raymond of Aguilers, in a striking phrase, calls a 'discordant peace' (*discordem pacem*). The Anonymous does not use the phrase but describes the reality – Bohemond and Raymond were to promise to press on to Jerusalem, but each was free to fortify his position in Antioch.[37] The demoralisation of the rank and file of the crusader army who had been left to their own devices through a bitter summer comes out in their cynical view of the parties to the quarrel in which each side is merely out for gain; Count Raymond in the pay of Alexius, Bohemond seeking his own benefit: 'Let them who wish to have the emperor's gold have it, and those who wish to have the revenues of Antioch likewise. Let us, however, take up our march with Christ as leader, for whom we have come'.[38] This revival of the spirit of the People's Crusade was generated by the strains of the long summer in Antioch. Albert gives no account of the conference as such, but he tells us that after the count of Toulouse had gone south, the forces of Bohemond, Robert of Flanders and Godfrey lost men who were anxious to press on, and that this eventually forced these leaders, with the exception of Bohemond, to resume the march.[39]

Fortified by the 'discordant peace' the crusader army prepared for its march southwards and the Provençals and the Flemings arrived before Ma'arra on 27 November 1099 (see fig. 4). Its citizens were defiant, for they had defeated Raymond Pilet's force during the summer and the city was prepared for a siege which the crusader forces systematically applied. It was neither a large nor an important place and its defences were not strong. The city wall enclosed only some five square kilometres and there may have been a citadel. As it is situated in a flat plain Ma'arra enjoyed few natural advantages. Only along the south side was there a ditch and since his army is reported as trying to fill it in Raymond of Toulouse evidently

[37] RA, p. 94; *GF*, p. 76. [38] RA, p. 94; Krey, *First Crusade*, pp. 208–9.
[39] AA, 449–50.

attacked from this direction, and the other forces from the north.[40] It seems odd that a city of such little importance should have been assaulted. Much more important places would later be bypassed, sometimes after the conclusion of an agreement affording free passage, but sometimes, as in the case of Sidon, without. Perhaps the leaders felt that for reasons of prestige they needed to destroy a city which had defied them once. Perhaps also it suited them to delay for the peace within the army was fragile and Ma'arra was chosen because it was on the very edge of the Provençal dominion – Albara is only some ten kilometres away. Such a siege would satisfy the opposition within the army and bring them into contact with enemy lands which could be ravaged. This impression is reinforced by the clear evidence that at least one major prince and probably two were not at Ma'arra. Raymond of Aguilers who was present throughout the siege says that Raymond of Toulouse and Robert of Flanders opened the attack with an assault on 28 November, which failed because they had only two ladders and needed four more. The next day Bohemond arrived and another assault was made without success. He mentions no other princes and adds that Godfrey was not at the siege.[41] The Anonymous mentions only Raymond of Toulouse and Bohemond, and as he clearly describes the assault which took place when Bohemond was present it seems likely he was in his army. Robert of Normandy is never mentioned in his account of the siege, but he later states that Robert joined Count Raymond in January 1099 at Kafartab after the meeting at Ruj. Albert of Aachen says that Count Raymond was supported by Robert (but does not tell us which Robert), Tancred and Eustace; his account of events is fairly schematic but it is evident that Godfrey was not present. Ralph of Caen does not mention Bohemond's participation but says the city was captured by Raymond and Robert of Normandy who is not mentioned by anybody else; perhaps this is a confusion with Robert of Flanders. Fulcher says that Bohemond and

---

[40] The location of the city, its topography and the events of the siege have been closely studied by Rogers, *Latin Siege Warfare*, pp. 106–17, who speaks of the ditch on the southern wall. But Ma'arra is now a sizeable place and has long outgrown its medieval walls. In its north-west corner there is a citadel with a ditch on its southern side, but it is not clear whether this was the site of the city in the eleventh century. The Iranian traveller Naser-e Khosraw, *The Book of Travels*, tr. W. M. Thackston (New York, 1986), p. 11, visited Ma'arra in 1047 and described it as a walled and prosoperous place with its own cultural life.

[41] RA, pp. 94–5, 99.

Raymond attacked Ma'arra while the other princes stayed around Antioch.[42] Since it is very clear that Godfrey was not at Ma'arra it is hard to avoid the conclusion that the siege was a stop-gap activity which kept the army occupied but did not represent a serious beginning to the campaign for Jerusalem. Its proximity to Count Raymond's dominions probably explains much of the suspicion which emerged after its capture.

However, the siege was conducted very vigorously. Raymond of Aguilers says that after arriving on 27 November the forces of Count Raymond and Robert of Flanders launched an assault the following day, and that it failed due to lack of scaling ladders. Bohemond's force then arrived and a new assault was launched on 29 November involving, on the count's sector, an effort to fill in a ditch before the wall, and this too failed. The Anonymous evidently arrived with Bohemond's force for he begins by describing this assault which clearly again depended on vigour and was unsupported by machinery: it was a matter of scaling ladders and raw courage.[43] Thereafter Count Raymond began more systematic preparations for an assault on the south wall including the building of a siege tower, but while the Anonymous goes immediately into his account of the final attack, Raymond of Aguilers makes it clear that some time supervened before this was launched on 11 December 1099. According to him Peter Bartholemew had yet another vision – much mocked by Bohemond's men. There was great hunger in the army, a point supported by Ralph of Caen and by Albert of Aachen who says that during the great siege of Antioch this area had been scoured of food causing many of its people to flee. There certainly may be truth in this last point, but it should be remembered that exactly one year before the army outside Antioch had begun to suffer badly from famine. Obviously seasonal factors were at work and the army needed to extend its foraging range.[44] Both accounts make it clear that Bohemond and the count of Toulouse attacked the city from opposite sides and that it was Count Raymond who built and employed a siege-tower, using, according to Albert, wood found in the mountains near *Talamria* which he seized in a raid.[45] This wooden tower was simply pushed up against one of the towers of Ma'arra once the ditch had been filled in. It had no bridge; those

---

[42] *GF*, p. 81; AA, 450–1; RC, 674–75, 679; FC, pp. 112–13.   [43] RA, pp. 94–5; *GF*, p. 38.
[44] RA, pp. 904–7; RC, 675; AA, 450.   [45] *GF*, p. 79; RA, p. 95; AA, 450.

in its top storey, including Evrard the Huntsman and William of Montpellier, cast heavy stones down upon the wall, and so covered undermining operations which were conducted at its base. In the final assault on 11 December the men of Bohemond who used only ladders made no progress on their sector. On the Provencal side the siege tower attracted fire from enemy catapults – the crusaders seem to have built none of these. The defenders also tried unsuccessfully to set fire to it, while Raymond adds that they cast lime and beehives at the crusader force. However, while the enemy defence was preoccupied by the tower, ladders protected with mantlets were brought forward and Geoffrey of Lastours was the first to get onto the wall. Although he and his party were cut off when the ladder broke the enemy were disheartened by progress made on undermining the wall and fell back into the town. The Anonymous says that the breakthrough came as evening fell, and Raymond adds a curious sequel – that the poor in the Provençal army broke in and carried on the fighting by night, so winning much plunder in a ferocious massacre. Bohemond, he says, got a lot of booty thereby arousing jealousy, and the Anonymous says that this was by negotiating a surrender in his sector of the siege.[46] The *Chronicle of Aleppo* confirms that the Franks used a tower and broke through by night when a massacre followed with a very systematic search for loot. However, the *Damascus Chronicle* says that the crusaders had several times offered the city surrender on terms, about which the citizens had been divided, and that when the city fell there was a terrible sack during which the crusaders broke promises of conditional surrender. Ralph of Caen says that the crusaders debated the question of terms, but those in favour of a massacre won.[47] This seems to reflect the confusion on the fall of the city, with Bohemond offering terms at the same time as the Provençal poor broke in and carried out a massacre.

In a military sense the chief interest of the siege of Ma'arra was the construction of the siege tower. Its function was to dominate the city wall and so to cover mining operations and the placing of ladders.[48] The assault was not delivered by troops mounting the tower and passing over a drawbridge onto the walls. The fact that Raymond of Toulouse built it and that his force played the leading role points to his clear emergence as the leading figure in the army.

---

[46] *GF*, pp. 78–80, is much the clearer of the two accounts but it is supported by RA, pp. 97–8.
[47] *Aleppo Chronicle*, 587; *Damascus Chronicle of the Crusades*, p. 47; RC, 679.
[48] Rogers, *Siege warfare*, p. 110 thinks there was no drawbridge.

This was not to the liking of Bohemond, who tried to use his possession of part of the city as a bargaining counter to obtain Raymond's strong-points in Antioch when the latter wanted to give Ma'arra to Peter, bishop of nearby Albara. This broke down the 'discordant peace' which had made the attack on Ma'arra possible and reopened the great quarrel between Bohemond and Count Raymond. According to Raymond of Aguilers, the bishop of Albara and the rank-and-file petitioned Count Raymond to lead them to Jerusalem, while Bohemond tried first to delay the journey, and then to bring it forward. The Anonymous does not mention these quarrels, but tells us that the army stayed a month and four days at Ma'arra although food was so short that desperate elements amongst the poor, the *Tafurs*, resorted to cannibalism.[49] Ralph of Caen and Albert support Raymond of Aguilers's account of starvation and despair in the army after the fall of Ma'arra, but his is much the most detailed. He says that Bohemond left the army and returned to Antioch whereupon Count Raymond tried to assume the leadership of the crusade by calling a meeting at Rugia and offering money-fiefs to the other leaders. This further delay provoked the poor to attempt to demolish the fortifications of Ma'arra and in the end Count Raymond was forced to agree to leave for Jerusalem on 13 January 1099, taking in his train Robert of Normandy and Tancred who had evidently accepted the money. As we have noted, during this time the Provençals felt they had been deserted by the Franks and complained that their force was quite small. In preparation for his departure, Raymond of Toulouse led an aggressive raid into enemy territory which brought in welcome plunder for the poor, and thus prepared the army marched south on 13 January 1099.[50] His decision to do this was probably reinforced by Bohemond's seizure of the Provençal strong points in the city after the failure of the Rugia conference. By this time it must have been clear that Count Raymond intended to march south and this enabled Bohemond to use force in Antioch with little fear of retribution.[51]

---

[49] RA, pp. 98–100; *GF*, p. 80; on the *Tafurs* see above, p. 287, n. 57; M. Rouche, 'Cannibalisme sacré chez les croisés populaires', Y. M. Hilaire ed. in *la Réligion Populaire* (Paris, 1981), pp. 56–69.

[50] RA, pp. 99–102; on the size of the crusader army and the terms of the money-fief and its importance see above, p. 129–30.

[51] RA, pp. 125, says that Bohemond drove out the Provençals when he heard that Count Raymond had left Ma'arra. PT, p. 95 also speaks of a violent expulsion at some stage

The subsequent course of events suggests that the count never intended to march to Jerusalem with his relatively small force. He left Ma'arra on 13 January barefoot as a pilgrim, but in reality the campaign which followed was never intended as anything more than an extended raid whose continuation was provisional on better conditions, and one which might be made to serve self-interest if all else failed.[52] Raymond of Aguilers indicates the small size of the army which travelled with the count. He was accompanied only by Tancred whose force was small, and Robert of Normandy; Robert of Flanders and Godfrey stayed behind at Antioch with Bohemond. They set off inland, marching south via Kafartab to Shaizar, Raphania and Homs, the rulers of which were more than ready to grant them free passage and the right to buy goods, even including vital horses which they were able to obtain in large numbers.[53] The willingness to come to terms with Islamic rulers denotes a conjunction of zeal for Jerusalem and a new pragmatic approach to getting there. For those who were eager to reach the Holy City nowhere else much mattered, while the count must have been anxious to avoid taking on any serious major military commitment. These arrangements greatly facilitated the march, although enemy forces did attack the army's stragglers forcing Raymond of Toulouse to mount a strong rearguard. In late January, as the army turned westwards north of Homs towards the coast, their foragers were attacked by enemy forces based on the Hisn al-Akrad, the later Crac des Chevaliers. The count of Toulouse attacked them forcing them to abandon their flocks and take refuge inside the fortress. Many of his men drove off the animals and the enemy were emboldened by this. Raymond was

during the stay at Ma'arra or shortly thereafter, while AA, 448, reports a violent expulsion, but his dating is uncertain. RC, 675 says that Tancred quarrelled with Count Raymond earlier, during the siege of Ma'arra and, returning to Antioch, tricked the Provençal garrisons into surrender; he then explains why the Normans and the South French were enemies and gives a very hostile view of the Lance before returning to the fall of Ma'arra. It is not impossible that RA, who remarks on the affair only in passing, is imprecise on the date. The greatest objection to Ralph's story is that it was only shortly after the siege of Ma'arra that Tancred took Count Raymond's pay and swore to serve him even to Jerusalem. However, even Bohemond was called to Rugia, so evidently considerable efforts at reconciliation were made. It is not at all impossible that Bohemond seized Antioch late in the siege of Ma'arra; he would have seen that the temper of the army prevented Count Raymond from returning to Antioch.

[52] Though Hill and Hill, *Raymond IV*, pp. 113–15, suggest that Raymond and the North French agreed to march by different routes and rendez-vous at 'Akkar. In view of the sequence of events this seems unlikely.

[53] On numbers see above, pp. 129–30; RA, pp. 102–3; *GF*, pp. 81–2.

now dangerously exposed, but he feigned an attack and then with-drew before the two groups of the enemy, one in the castle, the other on the mountain, could join to attack him. Even so he escaped only narrowly and vented his rage on his knights. It was a nice example of the problems of controlling a medieval army. By the next day the enemy had fled and Crac was taken.[54] However, there are strong hints of uncertainty about where they were going. Shortly after the departure from Ma'arra it was suggested that the army should turn towards the coast to attack Jabala. This was probably made as the army approached Hamah (ancient Epiphanea) from where a road leads across the Jebel Ansariye range to Jabala (see fig. 4). We are not told who made this suggestion, but it was attacked by Tancred who spoke in favour of marching on to Jerusalem. Raymond of Aguilers clearly sympathised with this viewpoint and his failure to indicate the proposer suggests the count of Toulouse. Indeed this would make sense, for it is probable that he controlled Laodicea and the acquisition of a neighbouring port would have strengthened his emerging Syrian dominion. The idea was rejected but this same lack of purpose was soon evident again. To the south of the mountains the army debated whether to take the inland route to Damascus, or to turn towards the coast, eventually taking the latter and much less dangerous alternative which had the benefit of giving access to shipping.[55] Even then, doubts and hesitations were at work, for at first the count of Toulouse seems to have been of a mind to come to an agreement with Tripoli, and was only persuaded to attack his city of 'Akkār (Caeserea Libani) by his envoys in the hope of extorting yet more wealth from him.[56] Such a policy must have seemed militarily wise for his army numbered only some 6,000–7,000 including not more than 1,000 mounted men, hardly a force with which to challenge the might of the Fatimid Caliphate, which in any case might yet offer terms. For the moment the prosperity of the march from Ma'arra seems to have quelled agitation in the army. A siege of 'Akkār might prove highly profitable; it would put pressure on the dissenting leaders, Godfrey de Bouillon and Robert of Flanders whose forces remained aloof at Antioch, while keeping the Provençals reasonably close to friendly Laodicea only about 100 kilometres to the north. Moreover, from the point of view of the

[54] RA, p. 104–6.   [55] On the importance of which see above, p. 209–20.
[56] RA, pp. 103–7.

count of Toulouse, the acquisition of 'Akkār would strengthen his Syrian redoubt. The capture of the port of Tortosa by Raymond Pilet and the surrender of Maraclea on terms must have encouraged the crusader army and helped their communications with the north.[57]

The attitude of Godfrey de Bouillon and Robert of Flanders, whose forces remained with Bohemond at Antioch, is very difficult to understand. They had clearly rejected the leadership of the count of Toulouse and preferred to wait on events. Albert of Aachen, who is usually at pains to present Godfrey as a Christian hero, casts no light on their reasons, but admits that popular pressure built up within their armies in favour of completing the journey to Jerusalem. Their forces and those of Bohemond were eroded by troops leaving them for Count Raymond, and in an assembly on 2 February the two leaders announced their intention of gathering their forces at Laodicea which they reached at the end of February; there Bohemond left them. On 1 March they besieged Jabala – but still held off joining the Provençals. It was only when news came from 'Akkār of the approach of an enemy army threatening the Provençals that Godfrey and Robert took a tribute from Jabala and rallied to their aid on 14 March 1099. The spirit of unity was strong enough to prevent them standing by while Count Raymond's force was attacked by the enemy, but it extended little further for they were greatly annoyed to discover that the rumour was false. Albert of Aachen's story that Count Raymond was bribed by the people of Jabala to draw Godfrey and Robert south probably reflects the bitterness felt amongst the rank and file which enabled Tancred to plant this story. There was great tension between the two contingents: Raymond of Aguilers says that Tancred stirred up discontent, anxious to leave the service of Count Raymond for that of Godfrey and Albert adds that Tancred had quarrelled with Raymond over money. However, Count Raymond was able to reconcile Godfrey by diplomacy and the gift of a horse and so all pursued the siege, although Tancred remained hostile. In fact we later find that Tancred seems to have become the vassal of Godfrey 'whose knight he was' by the time of the capture of Jerusalem, and this statement of Albert's seems to confirm Raymond of Aguilers' assertion that the young Norman had abandoned Raymond for Godfrey.[58] At last a

[57] GF, pp. 83–4; Hill and Hill, Raymond IV, p. 121.
[58] RA, pp. 110–11; GF, p. 84; AA, 454–5, 479.

substantial proportion of the crusaders had been brought together in a single army, but they were far from united, and the difficulties of the siege created problems. The junction of the Provençals and the North French was fortuitous and the crusader host remained fissured. It was lucky for them that they were operating in a military vacuum. Even so the sapping effect of these quarrels made itself felt in the siege of 'Akkār.

The actual siege attracted very little attention in the chronicles. Raymond of Aguilers says that there were many deaths including that of his co-author Pontius of Baladun killed by a stone from an enemy catapult, while Anselm of Ribemont was killed in the same way while repelling an enemy sally. The Anonymous mentions the deaths of Anselm, William the Picard 'and many others' but says nothing of the circumstances. He reports the raids conducted by the crusaders which gave them possession of Tortosa and control of Maraclea, then provided booty from el-Bukcia and terrorised Tripoli itself.[59] Albert of Aachen describes 'Akkār as a strong place against which the crusaders constructed catapults, to which the enemy replied in kind, and there is similar information in Ralph of Caen. It was in a duel between these machines that Anselm of Ribemont was killed. Albert and Guibert of Nogent say that the leaders tried to sap the walls of the city, but were foiled by enemy counter-mines.[60] The impression we have is of an attack which at first was sharp, causing heavy casualties, but then tapered off. Indeed, it has been suggested that after the arrival of Godfrey and Robert of Flanders no serious attack was launched on the city, but this seems to be a result of the way Fulcher, who was not present, reports the siege.[61] In fact too little attention has been paid to the situation of 'Akkār which was formidable (see fig. 15). It stands on a spur on the lower slopes of Mount Lebanon, projecting due west at a height of 147 metres above sea-level. The modern road across the plain at its foot from Homs to Tripoli runs at 90 metres. The top of the spur is a small plain some 600 metres long and 250 metres wide from which stone columns and masonry project at intervals and around which the remains of walls can clearly be discerned. The sloping flanks of the spur have probably been artificially sharpened, strengthening what is in any case a formidable position. The

[59] RA, pp. 107–9; *GF*, pp. 85–6.   [60] AA, 451–2; RC, 680, 682; GN, 218–19.
[61] Hagenmeyer, *Chronologie*, No. 355.

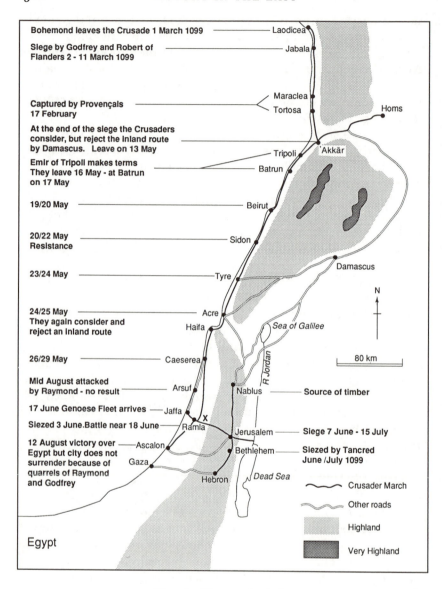

Bohemond leaves the Crusade 1 March 1099 ———— Laodicea

Siege by Godfrey and Robert of ————————— Jabala
Flanders 2 - 11 March 1099

Captured by Provençals ————————————— Maraclea
17 February   Tortosa   Homs

At the end of the siege the Crusaders
consider, but reject the inland route ————————
by Damascus. Leave on 13 May   Tripoli   'Akkār

Emir of Tripoli makes terms
They leave 16 May - at Batrun ——————— Batrun
on 17 May

19/20 May ——————————————————— Beirut

20/22 May ——————————————————— Sidon
Resistance

23/24 May ——————————————————— Tyre

                                                                      Damascus

24/25 May ——————————————————— Acre
They again consider and   Haifa   Sea of Galilee
reject an inland route   N

26/29 May ——————————— Caeserea
                                                              80 km

Mid August attacked
by Raymond - no result ———— Arsuf
                                            Nablus ———— Source of timber

17 June Genoese Fleet arrives —— Jaffa

Siezed 3 June.Battle near 18 June— Ramla   Jerusalem ——— Siege 7 June - 15 July

12 August victory over ———— Ascalon   Bethlehem ——— Siezed by Tancred
Egypt but city does not   June /July 1099
surrender because of   Gaza
quarrels of Raymond   Hebron   Dead Sea
and Godfrey
                                                                    ∿∿∿ Crusader March

                                                                    ∼∼∼ Other roads

Egypt   Highland

                                                                          Very Highland

Fig. 16   The march south

southern flank of the city is very steep, forming the wall of the gorge of the river 'Akkār; in spring this would have been in spate, making an impassable barrier. To the north the slope is less steep, though still very sharp, and an attacker can mount the slope to get access to the neck of the spur. It is this feature which truly makes 'Akkār impregnable. The neck of the spur has been cut into by the river and perhaps by human action as well, so that the eastern approach is almost as high and certainly as steep as any other, and very narrow indeed. Although the neighbouring mountain spurs are actually higher than 'Akkār, they are so far away as to be of no value to an attacker. The natural strength of its position made it difficult to approach and this probably ruled out the use of a siege-tower. Ralph of Caen says that the army was divided by the river which was crossed by an ancient stone bridge; probably the Provençals attacked from the north while Robert of Normandy and Tancred (and perhaps later Godfrey and Robert of Flanders) attempted to assault from the east. That mining formed part of the assault is evident because Albert says that the army became exhausted by it but we do not know anything of the direction of this attack though common sense would suggest that it was concentrated on the north and east of the city. The steep slopes would have made mining difficult from any direction.[62] But the failure before 'Akkār was, above all, a failure of will resulting from divisions within the crusader army. The army was never defeated – a fact which the emir of Tripoli recognised when he payed them generously to pass on their way south. The siege simply languished while internecine politics were dominant.

The Anonymous and the works which derive from his, and also that of Fulcher of Chartres, provide a very bland account of events but Albert of Aachen and Raymond of Aguilers, from their very different viewpoints give a different picture. Albert says that after Raymond had mollified Godfrey the leaders faced popular pressure resisted by Raymond of Toulouse, to abandon the siege of 'Akkār and to move on to Jerusalem. Raymond of Aguilers says that the siege

---

[62] RC, 680, 682; Rogers, *Siege Warfare*, pp. 118–19 describes the city. For Dijebel 'Akkar, its general location and history see Dussaud, *Topographie*, p. 88, and for more detail, 'Voyages en Syrie, Oct–Nov 1896', *Revue archéologique*, (1897) (1), 305–8; M. van Berchem, 'Notes sur les Croisades', *Journal Asiatique*, 1 (1902), 421, 448; Lestrange, *Palestine under the Moslems*, pp. 80, 390. The present writer was able to visit 'Akkar in the spring of 1992 and personal observation is the basis of this description.

was never popular and describes repeated quarrels amongst the leaders after Godfrey came, fanned by Tancred who wished to leave Count Raymond's service; Albert says that he and Raymond had quarrelled over money.[63] In addition, the question of the Holy Lance was raised; Raymond of Aguilers reports a vision of Peter Bartholemew which blatantly supported the case of the count of Toulouse for continuing the siege of 'Akkār and accused the leaders and members of other armies of offending against God in their faint-heartedness. The visionary had prospered by representing the views of ordinary crusaders, but now his support for Count Raymond was at odds with the popular desire to get to Jerusalem, and this enabled his enemies to attack him and to force a trial by fire. This is widely reported in the sources and though Raymond of Aguilers defends Peter Bartholemew its result was at best inconclusive and must have harmed the prestige of the count of Toulouse.[64] The ruler of Tripoli had attempted to buy off the crusaders but the resistance of 'Akkār encouraged him to resist, so in mid-April a strong raid was mounted on Tripoli with heavy fighting along the line of the aqueduct into the city, resulting in a major crusader success. The more generous terms now forthcoming seem to have further sapped the army's resolution, and Raymond of Aguilers suggests that the visions of Stephen of Valence and Peter Desiderius encouraged the people to demand a resumption of the march.[65] According to Albert of Aachen, Godfrey set himself at the head of the popular clamour to press on to Jerusalem, and when Count Raymond resisted he, Robert of Flanders and Tancred burned their camp and marched to Tripoli, and desertion from within his own army forced Raymond to follow. Raymond of Aguilers presents a strikingly similar picture, but he sets the debate in a different context. According to him it was the arrival of an embassy from the Emperor Alexius in early April of 1099, asking the army to delay until he arrived in June, which triggered off the debate.[66] The count

---

[63] RA, pp. 108, 111–12, 124; AA, 454–6.

[64] RA, pp. 112–24; RC, 682; AA, 452; GN, 217–18.

[65] RA, p. 124, 128–9, 131–4; GF, pp. 85–6.

[66] Lilie, *Byzanz*, pp. 42–3, suggests that, in the wake of the dispute over Antioch, Alexius was simply trying at all costs to prevent the formation of Frankish lordships, hence, also, his letter to Al-Afdal revealing crusader weakness (RA, p. 110). However, it seems to the present writer that Alexius's attitudes were somewhat more ambivalent especially in view of his alliance with Raymond of Toulouse, and that his essential purpose was to enlist aid against Bohemond.

wanted to stay and in the meantime press the siege of 'Akkār whose abandonment, he pointed out, would be a great blow to their prestige, and he expressed great concern that the army on its own would not be strong enough or well enough supplied to take Jerusalem. Other princes poured scorn on Alexius' offer which they suspected was intended to embroil them in his dispute with Bohemond, and urged the army on, but the count's influence was strong enough to prevail for a while. Ultimately, Godfrey put himself at the head of the discontent and, on 13 May, marched to Tripoli; he was followed by many in the Provençal army who burned their tents, forcing Count Raymond to follow along to Tripoli where he unsuccessfully pressed for a siege. The leaders then concluded a favourable treaty with Tripoli and the whole army marched south on 16 May 1099. In fact the imperial embassy arrived at 'Akkār in early April, before Easter as Raymond says, so this points to a long running debate in the army from that time onward. The fact was that in military terms there was little point in the siege of 'Akkār for it had no special military value and once Godfrey and Robert of Flanders had joined, the army had reached its maximum strength. A number of factors, including the weakness of his army, led the count to attack 'Akkār in the first place. Once battle was joined, however, and even when Godfrey and Robert of Flanders had come, considerations of 'face' and prestige, and perhaps a not unreasonable caution about attacking the Fatimid Caliphate with what remained quite a small army, moved the Provençal leader. And then there was self-interest – his Syrian bastion. We need not see this as totally opposed to his desire to go on to Jerusalem, but it was certainly a factor in his stubborn resistance to popular agitation.[67] But the whole rationale of the siege of 'Akkār collapsed as anxiety within the ranks to press on to Jerusalem arose.

The departure from 'Akkār marked the end of an era for the First Crusade. They had set out under the rule of a committee of leaders, pre-eminent amongst whom was the Papal Legate, Adhémar of Le Puy. From early 1098 their affairs were increasingly dominated by Bohemond. His desire to hold Antioch precipitated a crisis in their affairs and led to a bitter conflict with the count of Toulouse who stood for the rights of the Emperor Alexius and responded to

---

[67] Hill and Hill, *Raymond IV*, p. 124, think that the siege of 'Akkār helped Count Raymond to establish a claim to Tripoli for the future.

agitation in the army to continue on to Jerusalem. In the vacuum of authority after the death of Adhémar on 1 August 1098 he associated himself uneasily with the visionary Peter Bartholemew and his clerical associates. In the end this forced him to abandon his position in Antioch and to make a bid for leadership of the crusade. However, he was never able to convince all the other leaders that they should accept him, perhaps because he was an abrasive and domineering personality and without them he lacked the military strength to satisfy the popular enthusiasm for the journey to Jerusalem. Both Bohemond and Raymond of Toulouse, for all their abilities and resources, succeeded only in establishing a transient pre-eminence. Bohemond had great military ability, but he settled at Antioch. Raymond commanded the largest army in the crusader force but his dominance was undermined by events at 'Akkār. He insisted too stubbornly on persisting with an unpopular siege on the success of which he felt his prestige depended and he was damaged by the death of Peter Bartholomew. Above all, he had long occupied a paradoxical situation: he was apparently the leader who wanted to press on to Jerusalem, yet he seems to have had considerable doubts about the wisdom of attacking it with the limited resources the crusaders controlled: this was part of his reason for awaiting the emperor and it was probably from him that doubts appeared at Ramla.[68] This enabled Godfrey to undermine his position without in any way attacking him. But Raymond of Toulouse had served the crusade well. At a crucial time when the army was becoming infected by the political culture of North Syria he was responsive to the basic driving force of the crusade and, however reluctantly at times, he helped to keep the whole enterprise together. He remained important, but he was an isolated figure, and increasingly the crusade reverted to what it had been before, an alliance led by a committee. The long and painful course of events from the defeat of Kerbogah showed that there could be no single command of the army – it had been a crisis of authority and it was one which would infect crusader armies in the centuries to come. But the army now had to confront a third enemy, the Fatimid Caliphate of Egypt (see fig. 3).

[68] On Raymond and the imperial embassy see above, pp. 323–3, and for events at Ramla see below, p. 330.

CHAPTER II

Jerusalem: triumphant ending

Just as the crusade was about the leave 'Akkār in considerable disarray on 13 May 1099, there occurred an event of great importance for the coming campaign. Their ambassadors to Cairo finally returned with proposals from the Fatimid Caliphate. The leaders had first dispatched envoys to the Egyptians from Nicaea in late June 1097 at the suggestion of Alexius and we have seen that some kind of understanding was reached, or at least anticipated, after discussions between the leaders and a Fatimid embassy in February–March 1098 which returned home with a crusader delegation.[1] According to Ekkehard these Franks were in al-Afdal's camp before Jerusalem during his siege of the city when he threatened its defenders with his Frankish allies; the *Historia Belli Sacri* simply says that they spent Easter 1099 in the Holy Sepulchre obviously on friendly terms with their hosts.[2] This strongly reinforces the idea that the Egyptians were negotiating seriously. Raymond of Aguilers makes it clear that a partition of land captured from the Seljuks was the basis of discussion, with Jerusalem being allocated to the Franks, and the *Historia Belli Sacri* suggests the same kind of arrangement. It is difficult to know how serious the crusaders were in pursuing these negotiations by this time. Things had changed since the ambassadors had been sent in March 1098. The Byzantine alliance was no longer operative and the crusade had become much more focussed on Jerusalem as its sole objective. At the same time, the success in North Syria had made the princes much more hopeful of tangible gain. In these circumstances an arrangement with the Egyptians would have seemed less than attractive to all elements in the army. For his part, al-Afdal was securely in possession of Jerusalem and was pursuing discussions with the Turks of Syria, as Raymond of

---

[1] See above, pp. 252–3.   [2] Ekkehard, pp. 171–2; *HBS*, pp. 214–15.

Aguilers reveals.[3] He was in a strong position and was probably well aware of the divisions between the westerners and Alexius from letters sent to him by the Emperor which were later found in his camp after the battle of Ascalon. He would also have been well aware of the cautious policy of Raymond of Toulouse who had barely infringed the Fatimid sphere of influence in attacking the independent-minded ruler of Tripoli. In these circumstances al-Afdal made only a minimal offer to the crusaders, but one which presumably he felt was within the ambit of the discussions. According to Raymond of Aguilers, at Tripoli the Egyptian Embassy proposed only that groups of unarmed crusaders should be allowed to enter the Holy City. The crusaders knew that the Fatimids had profited greatly from their attack in the north to seize Jerusalem and some of the coastal cities of Palestine and this may have contributed to the anger with which they rejected the terms offered. Essentially, however, opinion had moved on since the crusader embassy was sent and what had seemed then a real possibility was now unacceptable, especially in the light of the turmoil in the crusader camp.[4] But the negotiations had served the crusaders well. The Egyptians had obviously been expecting an arrangement with the Franks and al-Afdal's offer was perhaps meant either as a preliminary offer or a delaying tactic. It was a terrible miscalculation for the Fatimids appear to have been unprepared for war. Only after the collapse of the negotiations at Tripoli did the Fatimids begin to make military preparations.[5] It was because of this that the crusaders would enjoy a fairly peaceful and easy march south. The Fatimid cities of the coast offered little resistance and, indeed, some concluded arrangements to allow the Franks to pass. What else could they have done in the light of the unpreparedness of their master? For much of the route down what is now the Lebanese coast the army would be confined by the mountains to a narrow and dangerous coastal road. Jaffa's fortifications were slighted and the city abandoned before the

---

[3] It is interesting that RA, p. 110, accuses the Egyptians of negotiating with the Turks as well and shows a real knowledge of the importance of the line of descent from the Prophet in the disputes of Islam.

[4] RA, pp. 109–10; *HBS*, pp. 181, 189–90, 212–215; AA, 379, 463; Köhler, *Allianzen und Verträge*, pp. 67–8 argues that, once al-Afdal knew that Alexius had turned against the crusaders, they lost all credibility in his eyes and hence were made only a very limited offer. However, it seems to the present writer that he would have known, for some time, the kind of people with whom he was dealing and simply overplayed his hand.

[5] See below, p. 358.

crusaders even approached. The road from Ramla to Jerusalem passes through the Judean Hills which are perfect for harassment but none was experienced (see fig. 16). The signs are that the garrison of Jerusalem was no more than adequate for its task and had to be augmented at the last minute and throughout the siege the scale of enemy harassment was limited. All the indications are that the Fatimids had not made any military preparations against the crusader army.[6] The army at Tripoli could never have guessed what a free run lay before it, but what they did know was that time mattered. Once they had rejected the terms offered and resolved to enter Fatimid territory it was only common sense to anticipate an enemy reaction. This explains the extreme haste of the march which contrasts sharply with their earlier pace. The army left Ma'arra on 13 January 1099 and travelled the 160 kilometres to 'Akkār by 14 February, some thirty-two days, giving a crude average daily rate of march of only five kilometres. They rested for five days at Shaizar and passed fifteen at Crac, so that the actual average daily rate of march was 13 kilometres. By contrast they left Tripoli on 16 May and took twenty-three days to cover the 360 kilometres to Jerusalem where they encamped on 7 June, a crude average daily rate of fifteen kilometres. During the march they rested only for eight days, giving an average daily rate of 24 kilometres. Between Tripoli and Beirut they seem to have made 40 kilometres per day for two days. Time was against the crusaders and from their point of view the whole campaign was dominated by the need for haste, hence the speed of march and the early assault on Jerusalem. This gamble against time was all the more risky because of the naval situation. The Egyptian fleet was far from dominant in the Mediterranean but it enjoyed a strong position along the Palestinian coast and so, for the first, time the naval supremacy of the crusaders could not be taken for granted.[7]

---

[6] See below, pp. 329–30, 357–61.

[7] A. S. Ehrenkreutz, 'The place of Saladin in the naval history of the Mediterranean sea in the Middle Ages', *Journal of the American Oriental Society*, 75 (1955), 100, says that, at this time, Egypt was the 'strongest naval power in the Mediterranean' but Y. Lev, 'The Fatimid navy, Byzantium and the Mediterranean sea 909–1036', *Byzantion*, 54 (1984), 220–52, doubts if it was ever so powerful and draws attention to the rise of Byzantine naval power in the early eleventh century. A. R. Lewis, *Naval Power and Trade in the Mediterranean*, pp. 225–49, sees the late eleventh century as a period of decline. In fact, Byzantine naval power could hardly have been on the increase after 1071 and Alexius's hold on Cyprus must have been strengthened by friendship with Egypt. M. Lombard, 'Un problème cartographié, le bois dans la mediterranée musulmane', *Annales Économies, Sociétés, Civilisations*, 14

The leaders had already consulted with native Christians about the routes to Jerusalem; these are called Syrians by Raymond of Aguilers but they were almost certainly Maronite Christians for he says they lived in the mountains of the Lebanon. They had enjoyed much autonomy under Moslem rule and as warriors would soon command the respect of the Franks. They had indicated three possible routes – inland via Damascus, across the mountains of Lebanon into the Jordan valley or down the coast (see fig. 16). It was probably the possibility of naval aid which lead them to choose the latter route, despite the narrow defiles of the road along the littoral. They were accompanied by the crews of an English fleet whose vessels had all but fallen apart from use but, as we have noted, this was not the only friendly fleet operating in Levantine waters.[8] In the treaty with Tripoli its emir promised to facilitate the passage of the crusader army, conversion to Christianity and subordination to the crusader command if they could defeat Egypt, and similar terms were made with Beirut and later Acre which they reached in late May, and probably other cities as well. His attitude was hardly surprising, for he had sought friendship with the crusaders from the very first, and even during the siege of Antioch had allowed them to come to buy food.[9] As part of his agreement with the crusader leaders he released 300 prisoners. Even during the siege of Antioch arrangements to release prisoners had been so common that Roger of Barneville had earned a great reputation as a negotiator in such matters.[10] According to Albert the emir of Tripoli kept his word and provided them with a guide who took them along the dangerously narrow passages of the coast road via Batrun to Djebail and saw to it that those entrusted with various strongpoints along the route allowed the crusaders to pass. It is possible that he provided Count Raymond with a kind of liaison officer who was later of use at the siege of Jerusalem.[11]

(1959), 54, points out that the Egyptian navy suffered from a shortage of timber because of depletion of resources in North Africa and the Middle East, and had long been importing from Europe. It seems likely that, because of this, they were anxious to hold on to Lebanon with its forested mountains.

[8] RA, p. 134; on the Maronites see Hamilton, *The Latin Church in the Crusader States*, pp. 207–8; on fleets see above pp. 209–20.

[9] RA, pp. 107, 117.

[10] GF, p. 86; AA, 407–8; I understand that a new book *The Laws of War on the Crusades and in the Latin East 1095–1193* by W. G. Zajac will discuss prisoner exchange.

[11] GF, p. 86; RA, p. 135; AA, 457–8; J. France, 'The text of the account of the capture of Jerusalem in the Ripoll manuscript, Bibliothèque nationale latin 5132', *English Historical Review*, 103 (1988), 645–6.

The cities along the coast were too strongly fortified for the army to have any chance of capturing them and they could count on help from the Egyptian fleet, but they had only garrison troops which could not block their way in the absence of reinforcements from Egypt (see fig. 16). Beirut (19–20 May) and Acre (24–6 May) concluded treaties with the crusaders very much on the model of Tripoli, while Tyre (23–4 May), Haifa and Caeserea offered no resistance. There was some harassment of the Christian army by the inhabitants of Sidon where they stayed 20–2 May and suffered the attentions of poisonous snakes. During the three day halt here the knight Gautier de la Verne was sent off on a foraging expedition but ran into strong enemy forces guarding flocks and was never seen again. All down what is now the Lebanese coast from Tripoli the army was marching along a corniche between the sea and the mountains; as noted this was particularly steep and narrow north of the Dog River near Beirut, but even after this it was confined. It must have been a relief to find the coastal plain opening up north of Acre, where they rested between 24 and 26 May and then celebrated Pentecost with a four-day rest at Caeserea, 26–9 May. In early June the army reached Arsuf where it turned inland towards Ramla but their bold advance down the coast had brought an enormous dividend. The enemy abandoned and destroyed Jaffa, the nearest port to Jerusalem, presumably because they assumed that the crusaders would take it as their base for resupply.[12] This is a revelation of how weak the military position of the Fatimids was in Palestine and confirms the impression that they had expected to continue an arrangement with the Franks. On 2 June the army encamped at Wadi Djiudas close to Ramla which the enemy deserted during the night, apparently leaving it in good condition with plenty of food and there the crusaders paused until 6 June, presumably preparing themselves for the ordeal of the siege ahead. The city was a major crossroads and so extremely useful to the crusaders who would later concentrate there in preparation for the battle at Ascalon.[13] At

---

[12] AA, 458–60; RA, p. 141; FC, p. 115; AA suggests that when they were at Acre they discussed the three possible routes, via Damascus, the Jordan valley or the coast at Acre. The first of these was geographically impossible as a route to Jerusalem by that time. However, it is possible that at Acre they considered the route into the Jezreel Valley and down to Jerusalem via Nablus, and that AA's informants simply confused this with an earlier discussion in the vicinity of 'Akkār/Tripoli which, RA says, considered the route via Damascus, on which see above p. 317.

[13] I. Roll, 'The Roman road system in Judaea', *The Jerusalem Cathedra*, 3 (1983), 137–61; on the battle of Ascalon see below pp. 360–1.

Lydda near Ramla, was a famous shrine of St George and in celebration of its easy delivery the crusaders appointed their first bishop, Robert of Rouen. His establishment in the city with a garrison of course served to guard crusader communications with the coast. While they were at Ramla they held a council of leaders. Here a suggestion was made that the army should attack Egypt and thus secure not only Jerusalem but all its rich cities. Raymond of Aguilers, who alone reports this discussion, does not indicate who made the suggestion, but whoever it was feared the problems of besieging Jerusalem in arid Judea. In a strategic sense, of course, to conquer Jerusalem through Egypt anticipated the grand strategy of the thirteenth century. It was presumably the count of Toulouse who suggested the idea for he had once before, in the debate over whether to await the coming of the Emperor Alexius at 'Akkār, expressed doubts about the ability of the army to capture Jerusalem unaided. Moreover he was probably the only one of the leaders who had the strategic vision to suggest such a scheme though the long negotiations with Egypt had showed clearly the strategic possibilities. However, those who argued that the army was far too small for such a vast undertaking and would not even be able to hold any captured city, were quite right – the vision was far beyond their means.[14]

The army left Ramla on 6 June and arrived at Qubeiba which was then supposed to be the biblical Emmaus sixteen kilometres west of Jerusalem. That evening Tancred left the army in response to calls for help from the Christians of Bethlehem.[15] The army which approached Jerusalem on 7 June 1099 numbered only some 1,200–

[14] GF, p. 87; RA, pp. 136–7, 125–6; FC, p. 115; AA, 460–1. Köhler, *Allianzen und Verträge*, p. 68 suggests that this idea of an attack on Egypt arose from the long negotiations conducted with al-Afdal. During his persecution of Christians in 1009/10 the Caliph Al-Hakim bi-Amr Allah (996–1021) ordered the destruction of the shrine of St George as Glaber, pp. 132–5, noted at the time.

[15] FC, p. 115; on the approach to Jerusalem see J. Prawer, 'The Jerusalem the crusaders captured: contribution to the medieval topography of the city,' in P. Edbury, ed., *Crusade and Settlement in the Latin East* (Cardiff, 1985), p. 5, who acknowledges his debt to C. Shick, 'Studien über Strassen- und Eisenbahn Anlagen zwischen Jaffa und Jerusalem', *Mitteilungen aus Justus Perthes geographischer Anstalt von A. Petermann* (Gotha, 1867), pp. xiii, 124–32. The ancient road from Ramla passed north-eastwards through the Latrun area on the edge of the Judean hills (where the crusaders later built an important castle) and followed something like the present track between Beit Liqya and Beit I'nan, to approach Jerusalem via Qubeiba and Nabi Samwil. This is well to the north of the dramatic gorges which carry the modern Tel Aviv–Jerusalem road along which the twisted remains of vehicles destroyed in the 1948 war are still to be found. Even so, the hills are pretty forbidding and excellent for ambushes.

1,300 knights and 12,000 other armed men, according to Raymond of Aguilers, a small force indeed to take on the Fatimid empire. They were working against time and the leaders were divided amongst themselves by the events of the preceding months. The count of Toulouse moved his camp early in the siege, against the advice of the other princes and despite much hostility in his own army which he only overcame by paying lavishly.[16] Gaston of Béarn was an important magnate in Raymond of Toulouse's army in the early stages of the crusade. During the siege of Jerusalem he was in charge of the building of the siege engines of the North French. Later he was closely associated with Raymond of Toulouse's enemy Tancred.[17] The fact that two Provençals, Galdemar Carpenel and William of Montpellier, are both later found in the service of Godfrey may indicate tensions within the Provençal army.[18] Count Raymond's quarrel with Tancred, who we have seen left his service at 'Akkār, certainly continued, for we are told that on the eve of the final assault on the city after the procession around it and during the accompanying religious celebrations on 8 July they were reconciled.[19] It was the custom of the army that when a crusader took a castle or town his banner flying over it would be respected by the others. Tancred seized Bethlehem and was arraigned by other leaders for it (see fig. 16). Later, after the fall of Jerusalem, he would plunder the Dome of the Rock to the scandal of the faithful which would involve him in a quarrel with the Patriarch.[20] His attempt to ransom those of the enemy who took shelter there was frustrated by the blood lust of the Franks who massacred them, much to his annoyance.[21] When the leaders censured Tancred in early July for his treatment of Bethlehem another problem arose, for Raymond of Aguilers alleges that its church was so holy that it could not be treated like any temporal possession. Then some of the clergy protested at the idea of choosing a ruler for Jerusalem when that matter was discussed because they regarded it as a special possession of the church. Raymond of Toulouse was clearly associated with this group amongst the clergy. Thus, to the personal rivalries of the

---

[16] RA, p. 138; Hill and Hill, *Raymond IV*, p. 129, doubt the truth of Raymond of Aguilers' statement.

[17] PT, p. 50; RA, pp. 145–6; *GF*, p. 92. [18] Riley-Smith, *Idea of Crusading*, p. 79.

[19] RA, p. 112; AA, 470.

[20] FC, p. 122; AA, 482–83; RC, 699–703.

[21] RA, pp. 107, 137, 143; FC, p. 122; *GF*, pp. 91–2; Nicholson, *Tancred*, pp. 96–8.

leaders was added an ideological quarrel which would have a considerable influence on events after the fall of the city.[22] The question of the government of Jerusalem was not raised again until 22 July 1099 when the leaders met to choose a ruler. The election was bitterly contested. Many of the clergy protested that a Patriarch should be elected first as a symbol of the church's rights. This was rejected, but Count Raymond refused the offer of the kingship and what was offered to Godfrey was something else, the Advocacy of Jerusalem.[23] However, the count clearly intended to keep a strong position in Jerusalem for he refused to hand the citadel which had surrendered to him over to Godfrey, and gave way only to considerable pressure from other leaders and much discontent within his own army. Bitter at this, he sulked in company with his ally Robert of Normandy and was even reluctant to believe the news of the landing of the Egyptian army at Ascalon in early August. After the victory he disputed control of Ascalon and Arsuf with Godfrey, and as a result neither city surrendered to the crusaders.[24]

Throughout the struggle for Jerusalem there would be two Christian armies rather than one, and at no stage was there a single commander. This makes their achievement all the more remarkable. The basic religious motivation of the crusaders reasserted itself and substituted a driving sense of purpose for leadership. It was this spirit which had rallied and triumphed over Kerbogah and then held the crusade together through the second half of 1098 when it had filled a real vacuum in the leadership and direction of events. In Raymond of Aguilers's chronicle the death of Peter Bartholemew, who had played such a major role in articulating the demands of the mass of the army, is clearly followed by the reappearance of Stephen of Valence and then the emergence of Peter Desiderius in the later stages of the siege of 'Akkār. It is possible that Raymond has tidied up events somewhat, but the outburst of enthusiasm for the journey which he says accompanied the arrival of Adhémar's cross in the camp at 'Akkār is consistent with later manifestations. As they approached Jerusalem many marched on to seize forts and settlements, but Raymond says that some at least approached the city

---

[22] J. France, 'The election and title of Godfrey de Bouillon', *Canadian Journal of History*, 18 (1983), 321–30. For a different view of these events see A. V. Murray, 'The title of Godfrey de Bouillon as ruler of Jerusalem', *Collegium Medievale*, 3 (1990), 163–78.

[23] France, 'Election of Godfrey de Bouillon', 321–30.

[24] RA, pp. 152–3, 155; AA, 497–8.

barefoot and penitent as Peter Bartholemew had commanded. Albert describes the joyful emotions and the ceremonial as the army arrived before the city on 7 June 1099 and the Anonymous speaks of their 'rejoicing and exulting' at this time.[25] In this spirit, the leaders consulted a hermit on the Mount of Olives and launched an almost immediate and fruitless attack on the city on 13 June. Peter Desiderius had a vision of Adhémar, as a result of which on 8 July the whole army made a solemn procession around the city in the style of Joshua before Jericho in preparation for the great assault which they were preparing. In the final assault on Jerusalem it is alleged that Adhémar was seen in the thick of the fighting while the ultimate catharsis of this overwhelming spirit of righteousness was the terrible massacre which followed the fall of the city when the Anonymous records that 'our men were wading up to their ankles in enemy blood'.[26] The army which encamped before Jerusalem on 7 June 1099 was sadly divided in leadership, but in spirit it was united at this culmination of their quest. Without this they would undoubtedly have failed, for the task which they faced was immense and had to be achieved quickly.

The Christian army was dangerously isolated for the nearest friendly Christian base was Laodicea, (held by the Byzantines over 500 kilometres to the north), and no reinforcement could be expected from them nor from Bohemond, who was consolidating his position at Antioch another eighty kilometres away. Between these Christian bridgeheads in North Syria and Jerusalem was a string of Moslem cities about the fundamental attitudes of which the westerners could have had no illusions, especially after they shot down a carrier pigeon bearing messages from the governor of Acre to Caeserea.[27] Even sea communication with the friendly north would be difficult as the fortifications of Jaffa, the nearest port to Jerusalem, had been dismantled by the enemy (see fig. 16).[28] Moreover, the crusaders were aware that they were challenging the great power of Egypt, which had seized Jerusalem from the Artukid Turks in August 1098 taking advantage of their defeat of the Turks at Antioch. This had produced doubts about the wisdom of attacking

[25] RA, pp. 130, 136–7; AA, 463.   [26] RA, pp. 139, 143–5, 151; RC, 685; *GF*, p. 91.

[27] RA, pp. 135–6; on carrier pigeons see the extract from Abu-Shama, *Kitab al-Ravdatayn* in Lewis, *Islam from Mohammed to the Capture of Constantinople*, 1. 223–4.

[28] On relations with the cities, see above, p. 329; France, 'The capture of Jerusalem', 640–57; RA, pp. 135–6, 141.

Jerusalem when the army reached Ramla and Albert alleges that the Egyptians were in breach of promises they had made to the crusaders at Antioch.[29] Albert of Aachen interrupts his account of the final attack on Jerusalem to report on the interception of messages from the Vizier, al-Afdal, to the garrison of Jerusalem, assuring them that he would come to their relief in fifteen days. According to Albert, deserters from the garrison told the crusader leaders that messengers were passing into the city on the eastern side which was not invested. An ambush was mounted killing one envoy and capturing the other. He was tortured to report his message and then tossed into the city on a mangonel with fatal results.[30] The placing of Albert's story emphasises the simple and obvious fact that the crusaders were engaged in a race against time and feared an attack from Egypt catching them during the siege of Jerusalem. Ascalon was a major Egyptian base on the coast only about eighty kilometres away, and it seems likely that some of those who attacked the crusader army during the siege were from there. So it was evident to all the parties that the issue would be decided quickly for time was against the Christian army. This imperative explains the early and ill-prepared attack on the city on 13 June, only a few days after their arrival.

Jerusalem was a formidable nut to crack. Its defences seem to have been put in order after the fall of the city in 1098 and the Fatimid governor, Iftikhar-ad-Daulah, had a garrison which included negroes, whom Fulcher describes as Ethiopians, and a *corps d'élite* of 400 cavalry, specially sent from Egypt, which acted as a reserve during the siege. Many of the Christian population had been driven out of the city, for Albert mentions those who had fled to Bethlehem petitioning the crusaders for protection – whereupon Tancred was sent there. The Patriarch of Jerusalem was in Cyprus though the Armenian Catholicus remained in the city for part of the siege. In fact, it is likely that many Christians, and not just women, children and the old as William of Tyre suggests, remained in the city, for there were priests and others to welcome the crusader entry. The Jews stayed and suffered in the crusader sack. Despite these security precautions deserters from within the city informed the leaders of the comings and goings of Egyptian messengers and told

---

[29] *Damascus Chronicle of the Crusades*, p. 45; Ibn al-Athir, 197; RA, pp. 110, 136–7; AA, 380, 463–4.
[30] AA, 473.

Tancred about the plunder in the Dome of the Rock, while it was 'brothers from within the city' who warned the army that the fire cast at their towers could only be put out by vinegar.[31] The garrison tried to drive off animals and destroy food in the vicinity of the city, but Gaston of Béarn and Tancred captured a lot of stock as they raided ahead of the approaching Christian army. Ralph of Caen speaks of the army tormented by hunger and thirst and virtually in a state of siege, cut off from supply by enemy raiders, but this was at a point late in the siege and as Fulcher remarks, there never seems to have been a desperate food problem. The Anonymous says that the army was short of bread until the arrival of a fleet at Jaffa on 17 June and this may have been a crucial factor in the supply of food. What all the sources complain of most bitterly was the shortage of water. The enemy had poisoned or blocked wells, forcing the crusaders to travel at least three kilometres or more. The threat of enemy ambushes obliged them to form convoys. As a result, water was sold at great cost in the camp and this was the cause of quarrels and dispute. Some was sold with leeches in it, which when swallowed caused swelling of the throat and stomach and ultimately death. The water shortage had direct military effects. Count Raymond's camp outside the Zion Gate was very close to the walls and was assailed by an enemy fire machine and shortage of water made it difficult to put out the fires. The same problem aided and abetted enemy efforts to burn the ram during the final assault. Only the pool of Siloa provided water in the immediate vicinity of the city and its supply ebbed and flowed and it was, in any case, within bowshot of the walls. The conveying of water seems to have become a major activity of the army during the siege but supply of other goods seems to have been reasonable. Albert reports that while the poor struggled over water the rich had grapes and wine.[32]

[31] FC, p. 121; AA, 463, 477; on the Patriarch see above, p. 209; Runicman, 1. 280, n. 1; WT, 373; H. Dajani-Shekeel, 'Natives and Franks in Palestine', in M. Gervers and R. J. Bikhazi, eds., *Conversion and Continuity: Indigenous Christian Communities in the Islamic Lands* (Toronto, 1990), p. 166; S. D. Goitein, 'Contemporary letters on the capture of Jerusalem by the Crusaders', *Journal of Jewish Studies*, 3 (1952), 162–77, 'Geniza sources from the crusader period: a survey', in B. Z. Kedar, H. E. Meyer and R. C. Smail, eds., *Outremer: Studies in the History of the Crusading Kingdom of Jerusalem presented to Joshua Prawer* (Jerusalem, 1982), pp. 161–84.

[32] As late as the nineteenth century, Jersualem in summer suffered from a terrible water-shortage and families had to exist on one or two goat-skins per week. The Pool of Siloa and its source, the springs of Gihon, remained important for the water supply of the city and the discoverers of Hezekiah's tunnel noted that the spring sent out only a small continuous flow

As the crusaders approached Jerusalem many of the knights, like Tancred, went ahead seizing properties. Raymond of Aguilers grumbled about this, but it was essential that they dominate the land around Jerusalem, for hostile raiders were present in force. Some of these may have been based in Jerusalem, which was never completely blockaded, but perhaps others came from Ascalon. On 9 June, Raymond Pilet and Raymond of Turenne attacked 200 Arabs. These raiders were a major problem for, as we have seen, they forced the army to convoy water supplies. The failure of the initial assault on Jerusalem on 13 June was partly due to the lack of wood to build ladders and machines, and a meeting of the leaders two days later agreed that machines would have to be constructed. There was no suitable timber in the general area of Jerusalem and Robert of Flanders was told to provide escorts for timber-cutters who found material near Nablus over fifty kilometres away, whose general area was later raided for supplies by Tancred in the period 10–13 July. Finding wood was a major problem for the army. After the conference on 15 July, Albert says that a Christian Syrian showed them where to find it in the mountains towards Arabia, some 'four miles' away. Since Albert's miles are very fluid and the description vague it is impossible to know where this was. Later the young, old and non-combatants were sent to Bethlehem to gather light branches and twigs for the outer coverings of the assault machines. Ralph of Caen says that Tancred found the wood to build the only scaling ladder used in the initial attack on 13 June, and subsequently found some used by the Egyptians in their siege the year before and hidden in a cave where he sought privacy during a bout of dysentery.[33]

However, it was undoubtedly the arrival of the fleet of six ships at Jaffa on 17 June which was the key event in providing wood and the skilled labour and technical knowledge with which to manufacture. A major force was gathered to protect the sailors in the undefended port, but even so it was ambushed on its way to the coast on 18 June (see fig. 16). This was the largest encounter during the siege and all

with a surge at intervals of four to ten hours: M. Gilbert, *Jerusalem, Rebirth of a City (1838–98)* (London, 1985), pp. 4–5, 152. There is a reference to a late twelfth-century refurbishment of the structure under the Latin Kingdom: M. R. Morgan, *La Continuation de Guillaume de Tyr (1184–1197)* (Paris, 1982), pp. 22–3; AA, 462–3, 469–470, 472; RC, 691; RA, pp. 139–2; *GF*, p. 88; FC, pp. 119–20; France, 'Capture of Jerusalem', 644–5.

[33] RA, pp. 137, 139; *GF*, pp. 88–9; RC, 690, 688–90; BD, 100; AA, 467–8.

the crusaders were chosen from Count Raymond's army, a reflection perhaps of his close relations with Genoa which had provided four of the six ships. According to the Anonymous 100 knights including Raymond Pilet, Achard of Montmerle and William of Sabran set out, but thirty became separated from the others and were ambushed by 700 Arabs with heavy loss including Achard and some poor foot-soldiers. Raymond Pilet's forces were sent for and the enemy fled with heavy casualties, leaving 103 horses to be captured. Raymond of Aguilers describes three parties, the first of which led by Galdemar Carpinel, consisted of twenty knights and fifty foot. They fell in with 200 Arabs whom they attacked boldly with knights and archers to the fore, but they were encircled and all but overcome by the enemy whose archery was deadly. Achard was amongst the dead when Raymond Pilet's force of fifty knights, probably accompanied by the following of William of Sabran, came up and the enemy fled. Albert says that Achard of Montmerle and Gilbert of Trèves were killed when the enemy from Ascalon ambushed a crusader force ravaging near to Ramla; the rest were saved by Baldwin of Le Bourcq's intervention, and he captured an important enemy 'knight' who was executed before the Tower of David. The mention of Achard suggests that this was the same engagement, perhaps conflated with another event, but Albert, like Fulcher and Ralph of Caen, does not mention the fleet.[34] The importance of this victory was seen in the sequel. The crusader fleet in Jaffa failed to keep a good lookout and was trapped in the harbour by Egyptian ships. Because the port had no defences the sailors burned their ships (bar one which escaped) and marched to Jerusalem with supplies and wood, a long vulnerable supply train which escaped attack because of the expensive victory the previous day. However, the whole episode had demonstrated the isolation of the crusader force and its vulnerability as it stood before Jerusalem.

The city which the crusaders now confronted was well protected by nature and the works of man (see fig. 17).[35] In the later eleventh

[34] *GF*, pp. 88–9; RA, pp. 141–2; AA, 468–9.

[35] The description of Jerusalem which follows is based on that of Prawer, 'The Jerusalem', pp. 1–5, whose author ackowledges his debt to earlier researchers such as F. M. Abel, 'L'état de la cité de Jérusalem au XII siècle', in C. R. Ashbee, ed., *Records of the Pro-Jerusalem Council* (London, 1924); C. N. Johns, *Palestine of the Crusaders* (Jerusalem, 1946); M. de Vogüé, *Les Églises de la Terre Sainte* (Paris, 1860). His careful account has been supplemented by my own observations and differences of view are noted. See also

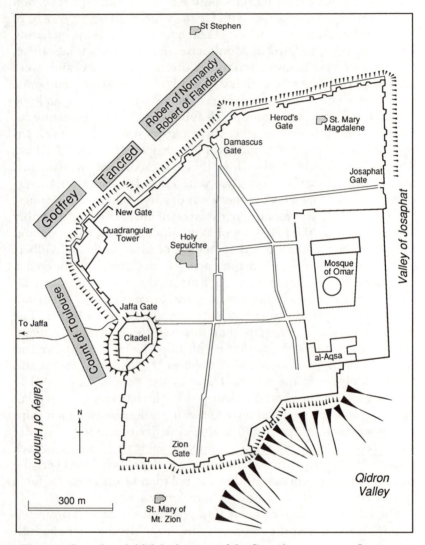

Fig. 17a   Jerusalem, initial deployment of the Crusader army. 7–12 June 1099

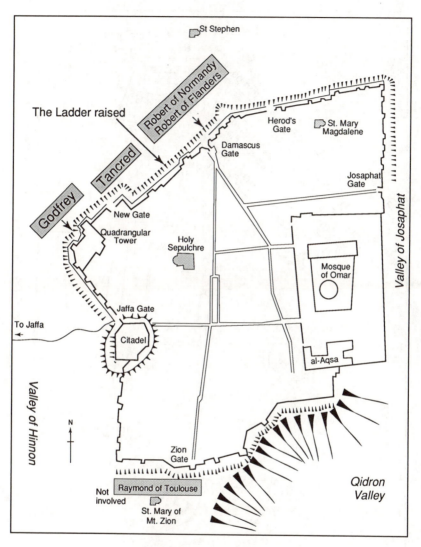

Fig. 17b   Jerusalem, the attack of 13 June 1099

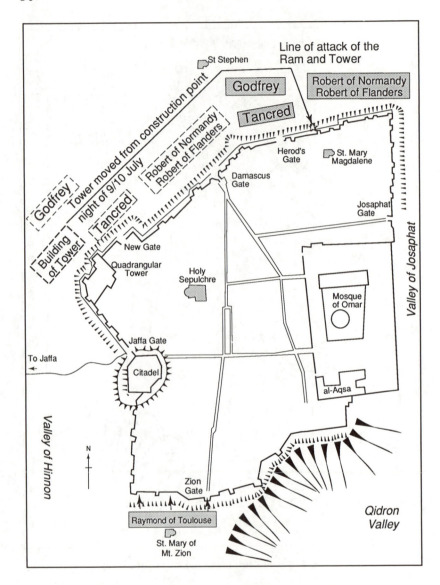

Fig. 17c   Jerusalem, final attack of 13–15 July 1099

century the city occupied much the same site as the present Ottoman enceinte set upon a sharp hill rising from south to north amongst the Judean Hills. The valley of Qidron, rising from the direction of the Dead Sea, divides on Jerusalem's south-eastern flank. To the east the Qidron valley cuts an enormous gash between the city and the Mount of Olives, providing great natural strength in that quarter; towards the north of the city it is called the Valley of Josaphat. Its western extension, the Valley of Hinnon, similarly, but less spectacularly, protects the western flank of the city. In the course of the eleventh century, two rebuilding campaigns on the north and south reduced the fortified area of a city whose economic importance was rapidly declining. By far the most radical was the reconstruction about the end of the first third of the century which excluded the ancient city of David and Mt Zion, and created the present southern aspect. A similar reconstruction about 1063 excluded much of the northern part of the old city. The result of these rebuilding campaigns was, in a military sense, highly unsatisfactory. In the south-west the exclusion of Mount Zion created a level platform some 160 metres wide from fifteen metres east of the southwestern corner of the city to about the same distance east of the Zion Gate, and well over fifty metres deep extending back from the wall to the ancient church of St Mary, from which any attacker could threaten. This is only a small part of the 1.3 kilometres extent of the south wall, and for the rest the land falls steeply away to the east down to the Temple Mount and the walls rise high above the old city of David. But the situation to the north was far more dangerous. The new line of fortification, centred on what is now the Damascus Gate (called in crusader times the St Stephen Gate) is markedly below the brow of the hill which lies well to the north. This gate stands across the Tyropocon Valley and on its western side the land slopes up sharply to the high point of the defences where the Quadrangular Tower (later known as Tancred's Tower) marked the northwestern corner of the city. However, at this point the land slopes down very sharply indeed from the north, so that this Tower was an obvious attempt to strengthen a vulnerable point where the slope of the land really would naturally dominate the city wall; in the Ottoman

Y. Katzir, 'The conquests of Jerusalem in 1099 and 1187', in V. Goss and C. C. Bornstein, eds., *The Meeting of Two Worlds* (Michigan, 1986), pp. 103–14.

defences it is the site of a major salient.[36] To the east of the Damascus
Gate the northward rise of the hill is less menacing, and the wall
climbs gently from the Tyropoeon valley and then falls away slightly
to where the Wadi Zahira enters the enceinte east of what is now
Herod's Gate. In this stretch every effort has been made to use rocky
outcrops and rises, but in general the attacker is presented with a less
than frightening aspect and a fair choice of attacking points, and can
work with a useful downslope. In 1073 the city fell to the Seljuks and
an effort was made to address these weaknesses. Outerwalls were
either built or rebuilt, though these were probably not continuous
and may have formed elongated enclosures. The eastern side of the
city, just under one kilometre long, needed little strengthening for it
was protected by the Qidron or Josaphat Valley but at the foot of
this wall from the Josaphat Gate to the northeastern corner was a
moat for here the defences stood on a plateau accessible from the
north. This moat continued along the northern side of the city,
reinforced by an outer wall, though it is not certain that they were
absolutely continuous. The outer wall may have been formed into
enclosures, effectively barbicans, while tracing the moat raises difficulties. This double line turned south at the Quadrangular Tower
(later called Tancred's Tower) and covered the western side as far as
the citadel by the Jaffa Gate (which the crusaders called the Tower
of David), around which the moat connected with the outer system
and also isolated it from the city. South of the citadel the land rises
steeply to the walls, but from the south-west corner a moat protected
the whole southern wall facing Mt Zion as far as the Temple
Platform.[37] Thus, great trouble had been taken to strengthen the
vulnerable area of the Quadrangular Tower, connecting it with the
citadel in a triple line of defence, and the one weak point to the south
was strengthened. However, the north wall of the city, roughly 1.4
kilometres long, was overlooked by the lie of the land, giving enemy

---

[36] As it is, the Ottoman salient is now totally dominated by the bulk of Notre Dame de France
fifty metres across HaZanhanim.

[37] Prawer, p. 5, believed that there was an outer wall as far as the Zion Gate but he relies here
on RA, p. 148, 'iam fractis antemuralibus et conpleto vallo, citissime murus interior
peruaderetur'. The difficulty is that Raymond is describing the two assaults, from Mt Zion
and from the North, as if they were one, so that the reference to an outer wall may be to
that faced by the northern attack. An earlier mention, p. 139, in connection with the
assault of 13 June, also refers to the northern part of the city. The Unknown account has no
reference to an outer wall by Mt Zion, while the Anonymous speaks only of the filling in of
the ditch and adds: 'when it was full they took the siege-tower up to the wall'. My
conclusion is that the Provençals faced a single wall with a moat outside it.

missile firers an advantage and providing an enormously long frontage for the garrison to watch. The size of the garrison is not known. Raymond of Aguilers's figure of 60,000 is clearly nonsense. Iftikhar-ad-Daulah probably had a core of Egyptian regulars; we know that a number of Jews also served and it was usual for such forces to be augmented by city militias. These, together with the 400 mounted reinforcements sent by the Egyptian Vizir al-Afdal, probably formed a barely adequate garrison for they were not particularly aggressive defenders.[38]

The crusaders approached Jerusalem from the north-west along the Jaffa road and came to the city on the side where its fortifications are at their most impressive. The Quadrangular Tower and the Citadel by the Jaffa Gate dominated the treble line of defences to the north, while the steep slope up to the walls from the vale of Hinnom made difficult any attack south of the citadel. Albert of Aix describes a rather curious order of siege. Godfrey stood before the Tower of David with Tancred to his left and the count of Toulouse to his right and Robert of Flanders and Hugh of St Pol behind, while Robert of Normandy and Conan of Brittany encamped before the Damascus Gate to the north. It seems unlikely that this was ever an order of siege, for there is a deep topographic confusion in Albert's account. He presents Godfrey camped outside the Citadel and later tells us that the great siege tower used by Godfrey was built in this very place, when it is certain that it was constructed much further to the north and east. Albert seems to have confused the two great strongpoints of the defences, the Citadel and the Quadrangular Tower to the north, in the general vicinity of which Godfrey was definitely to be found a few days after the arrival, on the occasion of the attack of 13 June.[39] Ralph of Caen says that Robert of Normandy and Robert of Flanders encamped outside the Damascus Gate (also called the St Stephen Gate) with Tancred to their right; he was on lower ground than they but his position sloped upward to the west where Godfrey took position adjacent to him. The Anonymous confirms this, but does not indicate the relative positions of Godfrey and Tancred, merely making it clear that they were to the west of the two Roberts. Raymond of Aguilers does not mention Tancred but says that

---

[38] RA, p. 147; AA, 477; Prawer, 'The Jerusalem', p. 11; Hamblin, *The Fatimid Army during the Crusades*, pp. 64–5.

[39] AA, 463–4, 468; Prawer, pp. 5–6 and fig. 1 accepts Albert's account as describing a first stage of the siege; on the building of siege machinery see below pp. 346–8.

Godfrey and the two Roberts faced the northern wall between the St Stephen Gate and the Quadrangular Tower, and adds that Raymond of Toulouse at first set his army adjacent to Godfrey's, all down the west side of the city. It would seem, therefore, that the initial order of siege was as follows: the two Roberts were directly outside the St Damascus Gate with Tancred to their right and Godfrey beyond him, while the large Provençal army stood along the west face of the city before the Citadel (see fig. 17a).[40] The deployment of the Provençal force was unsatisfactory because they stood opposite the most formidable fortifications and the steeply sloping southern sector of the west wall. Very soon after the arrival of the army Count Raymond reconnoitred and decided that Mt Zion was a better place to attack. This decision was challenged by his own men, many of whom remained in the original camp, and the count was obliged to pay to find a garrison for the new position.[41] There were good reasons for both the decision and the opposition to it. The west wall was far too strong to attack and the level ground outside the Zion Gate offered better prospects especially as the adoption of that position divided the defence, was close enough to the Citadel to distract its garrison, and, as Albert makes clear, enabled the count to keep some forces on the Mount of Olives and patrols in the valley of Josaphat (see fig. 17a). On the other hand, the new camp was dangerously exposed, placed, as it was, in the space of only some fifty metres between the church of St Mary of Mt Zion and the wall. So close were they to the wall that a machine placed within the Zion Gate was able to set fire to the crusader camp as well as attack machines in the last climax of the siege. But the resistance to the move had other causes, for there appears to have been considerable tension within the Provençal camp which later resulted in his own people rumour-mongering about the Count of Toulouse in order to prevent him from being made ruler of Jerusalem, and it is possible that such factors led Gaston of Béarn to take service with the North French.[42] Raymond of Aguilers says that

---

[40] RC, 687; *GF*, p. 88; RA, p. 137; Prawer, pp. 5–7 accepts Albert's description as giving an initial order of siege and places Godfrey east of the two Roberts. The Quadrangular Tower was later called 'Tancred's Tower' but this was not because he had taken position outside it, but because, as RC, 701 makes clear, he later controlled it for a while.

[41] RA, p. 138; AA, 463–4; Both mention the move though only Raymond mentions resistance. *GF*, p. 87 and RC, 687 say that Raymond besieged the city from Mt Zion without mentioning any prior position.

[42] France, 'Capture of Jerusalem', 644–5; RA, pp. 145–6, 153.

some of the other leaders objected to this redeployment, but they do not seem to have pursued the matter; perhaps after the tensions of the march south such a separation suited all parties.

On 12 June the leaders met and were urged by a local hermit who had already spoken to Tancred to make an immediate attack on the city which God would deliver to them.[43] However persuasive he may have been, the leaders had probably resolved on this course of action anyway. Their position was difficult. The army was so small that they could not properly besiege the city when the western and eastern walls were guarded only by pickets. The Provençals probably blockaded no more than 250–300 metres of the long southern wall, while the rest of the army was concentrated in 600 metres, or rather less than half of the north face of the city. If they had attempted to stretch the army further they would have been vulnerable to sallies. Furthermore they feared the imminent arrival of an Egyptian relief force. The main objection to such a coup was the lack of siege equipment, and indeed they were only able to muster a single assault-ladder, so short was the time of preparation and so scarce was wood in the vicinity of Jerusalem. The Anonymous and Raymond of Aguilers say that this attack on 13 June broke through the outer wall and set a siege ladder against the inner before being aborted. Ralph of Caen says that because he had found the wood for the one siege ladder Tancred was able to insist that the attack be against his section of the wall, though he was persuaded that Reybold of Chartres, and not he, should be first up the ladder. In the event, Reybold's hand was cut off and he was taken back to Tancred's camp for treatment. It is thus pretty certain that the army attacked the section of the wall just to the east of the Quadrangular Tower besieged by Tancred. Albert says that the crusaders attacked under cover of a 'tortoise' of interlocked shields and, in a hail of missiles thrown by both sides, did terrible damage to the outer wall, suffering heavy losses for little achievement. Tudebode adds one detail to the Anonymous's story; that Reginald, *dapifer* of Hugh of Liziniac, was lost in this attack.[44] Its failure depressed the Christian

[43] RA, p. 139; RC, 685, 688.

[44] *GF*, p. 88; RA, p. 139; RC, 688–9; AA, p. 467; PT, p. 103; Prawer, 'The Jerusalem', pp. 7–9, believes that the point of attack can be identified as close to the present New Gate, but this depends on his mistaken notion of where Tancred was, on which see above p. 344, n. 40. I would suggest that the attack was somewhat to the east, on level ground towards the Damascus Gate. See fig. 17b.

host and on 15 June the leaders met once more in conference and resolved on a more methodical preparation for the next attack.

They resolved, according to Albert of Aachen, on the building of heavy siege machinery, in the event siege-towers, rams and projectile-throwers. This had the important effect of narrowing the ground of their attack to such points along the wall as were level. On the southern defences this meant the area of Mt Zion alone while even to the north attacking positions would have to be chosen carefully for a tower perilously balanced could be easily cast down by the enemy. Effort was centred on two great wooden towers which were to crush the defences. But this once more brought the army face to face with the problem of lack of wood. As we have seen, this was solved by at least one chance find, by sending out foraging parties under escort and by the arrival of the fleet at Jaffa on 17 June. Their problem was to find heavy structural timber and it was probably in this respect and the provision of skilled labour that the arrival of the fleet was so important. In the event it was Provençal forces which brought back the equipment and men and Count Raymond employed one of the Genoese, William Ricau, to construct his tower.[45] In the accounts of the building of the North French tower given by Ralph of Caen and Albert of Aachen, no mention is made of the coming of the ships, while the Anonymous reports their arrival and the fighting which cleared the way for their journey to Jerusalem, but nothing more. The tower built by the northerners was constructed in stages which were scarfed together because they lacked heavy timbers. It was, perhaps, no coincidence that the northerners' tower sagged badly during the attack, while that of Count Raymond stood up to a ferocious assault until it was burned.[46] It would seem as if the army were now divided into two groups, each of which made its own way; earlier the Provençals played no role in the assault of 13 June which, the language of Raymond of Aguilers implies, was a purely North French affair. Count Raymond employed William Ricau as his engineer and set the bishop of Albara in charge of the enemy prisoners and others bringing in wood and supplies; perhaps he enjoyed the help of the

---

[45] On William see F. Cardini, 'Profilo d'un crociato, Guglielno Embriaco', *Archivio Storico Italiano*, 136 (1978), 417–18.

[46] Rogers, *Latin Siege Warfare*, p. 133, thinks that a staged tower would probably have been as strong as one built using massive single corner posts, but RC, 692 indicates very clearly that the structure nearly failed. Perhaps the workmanship was not very good.

emissary from Tripoli in this. The northerners used Gaston of Béarn as their engineer and set Robert of Flanders to ensure supplies. The skilled artisans who worked on Raymond's tower were paid from his own purse, while those of the North French received their wages from a common fund.[47] To attack from different directions was good tactics and this meant that preparations had to be separate but there was considerable friction within the army and this exploded at the meeting of the leaders in early July over the question of Tancred's seizure of Bethlehem and the governance of the city after its capture as we have noted. However, the actual process of preparation seems to have been very well organised. Raymond reports that Gaston used division of labour to speed up the work and we have already noted the careful preparations amongst the southerners. Shortly after this meeting, an assembly of the people on 6 July decided to organise a solemn procession around Jerusalem in a manner recalling that of Joshua at Jericho. There had been a number of visions during the siege which Raymond of Aguilers mentions, but the procession was commanded in a vision of Adhémar to Peter Desiderius which he revealed to his lord Isidore count of Die and Adhémar's brother, William Hugh of Monteil, and they seem to have called the assembly, though it was unlikely that they would have done so without the agreement of the princes. The moral effects of such an exercise as a spiritual preparation for the impending assault are evident, but it is to be noted that reconciliation was a major part of the purpose according to Raymond of Aguilers, and Albert says that the occasion was used to patch up friendship between Tancred and Raymond of Toulouse.[48] On 8 July the procession duly took place culminating in sermons on the Mount of Olives. The way was clear for the assault on Jerusalem, the final climax of the crusade.

The tempo of preparations was now stepped up with light materials being gathered to be woven into mantlets with the old, young and women lending a hand and each pair of knights was given the task of providing one mantlet or one ladder. A raid on the area around Nablus presumably provided food for the attackers (see

---

[47] AA, 467–70; RC, 689–91; RA, p. 146; France, 'Capture of Jerusalem', 645.

[48] RA, pp. 144–5; GF, p. 90; for the reconciliation of Tancred and Raymond see above p. 331; BD, 100–1 says the clergy urged the virtue of dying where Christ had died, on which see H. E. J. Cowdrey, 'Martyrdom and the First Crusade', in P. Edbury, ed., *Crusade and Settlement in the Latin East* (Cardiff, 1985), p. 51.

fig. 16).[49] But the decisive act in this period of preparation came on the night of 9–10 July. The North French had built a tower, ram and other siege equipment in the camp of Godfrey close to the Quadrangular Tower.[50] On that night it was dismantled (or perhaps reduced to partially fabricated sections) and moved to a section of the wall almost at the northeastern corner of the city (see fig. 17c). All the forces on the northern edge of the city concentrated there. Raymond of Aguilers tells us that the enemy had anticipated an attack close to the building point and had so strengthened the wall that any attack appeared hopeless. Flat ground, he tells us, gave easy access to the walls in the new position, and its defences had been neglected. The whole erection was transported over a mile, he says with pardonable exaggeration. Ralph of Caen says that the leaders had had this in mind for some time and had deliberately ignored this sector, the weakness of which was known to them, so as to deceive the enemy.[51] This may well be true in a sense, for as the siege went on the leaders must have become more and more familiar with the defences, and we know that they received information from informers. Moreover, Raymond of Aguilers makes it clear that the move came as a total surprise to him, again pointing to the divorce between the two sets of attackers. The defenders had watched the construction of the siege equipment with anxiety and 'built up the city wall and its towers by night'. From what we know of the resistance to the attack later we can envisage the strengthening of the defences with balks of wood, the stockpiling of ammunition and the provision of padding and ropes for use against the attacking machinery. Now these careful preparations had to be improvised in a new position; thus was their discomforture maximised by the dramatic way in which the *Schwerpunkt* of the attack was changed overnight. According to the Anonymous this new position was towards the eastern end of the northern wall and Raymond's suggestion that the siege-tower was moved almost a mile (in fact about one kilometre) from the point of construction in Godfrey's camp by the Quadrangular Tower supports this, as does later medieval

[49] AA, 468; RA, p. 146; for the raid see above, p. 347; Nablus, some fifty-four kilometres north of Jerusalem, seems to have marked the extreme range of their ravaging around Jerusalem.
[50] On the location of Godfrey's camp and the building of the assault tower there see above pp. 343–4, n. 40.
[51] RA, p. 147; RC, 690; AA, 471.

tradition.[52] Therefore, to find the point of the assault we need to locate an area of flat ground abutting the wall towards its eastern end. This is not easy because the local topography has been fairly radically changed by modern buildings and the development of the Sultan Suleiman Road which skirts the northern defences. However, rocky outcrops eliminate many places and Prawer has favoured the point at which the Wadi Zahira meets the city wall about 100 metres east of Herod's Gate. Just to the east of this, however, and before the rocky area between the Rockefeller Museum and the wall, there seems to have been a totally flat zone twenty-five to thirty metres wide at a point where the present Ottoman walls have a major salient, and this is the location suggested here (see fig. 17c).[53]

The French still had to rebuild their machines, fill in a ditch and level off the ground before they could attempt to break down the forewall and bring the siege-tower up to the main line of defence which is why the main assault was not launched till 13 July. However, the value of the surprise stolen by the northerners is very evident, for Count Raymond had no room for any such manoeuvre and his preparations signalled his intentions very clearly for he was forced to spend three days filling in the southern moat: his attack would have a very difficult time indeed. With the ground properly prepared the North French set up the siege-tower, a mighty ram and three mangonels whose fire could clear the walls and launched their assault on Wednesday 13 July. Their systematic tactics now became apparent. As the huge ram manned by large numbers of people was dragged up to the outer wall the enemy lowered bags of straw and ropes and fired off clouds of arrows. The crusaders replied in kind with the three mangonels and lighter weapons. Godfrey used his cross-bow to set fire to the padding protecting the wall. The emplacement of the ram and destruction of the forewall seems to have occupied 13 and much of 14 July, for it was only on that Thursday (the fifth day) that the tower was ready for action and

---

[52] *GF*, p. 90; RA, p. 147; Prawer, 'The Jerusalem', cites the twelfth century Cambrai map.

[53] Prawer, p. 11, says quite accurately that the Wadi is evident in the Ratner Garden about one hundred metres east of Herod's Gate, but then suggests that the attack took place in this area 'sixty-five metres between the second tower east of Herod's Gate and the first salient square in the wall beyond it'. In fact between this tower and the salient is only about seventeen metres. The Ottoman salient was probably built to cover just this weak spot, which is where, I believe, the attack took place.

brought up behind it.[54] The battle for the forewall was very savage as the enemy tried to burn the ram with every kind of device including Greek fire and the Franks were forced to expend precious water to prevent this. Once the forewall was broken through another problem presented itself. The mighty ram which had opened the breach now blocked the route for the mobile tower aligned behind it. The ram was a very substantial structure and it was mounted either on rollers or wooden wheels – we do not know which. In the circumstances in which it was built it is unlikely to have been well-balanced or free-moving. The sources are not very clear on timing but it seems likely that much of 13 and some of 14 July was spent simply bringing it up to engage the wall. Once it had done its job it was useless for its crew would be horribly exposed to fire from the higher inner wall of the city with its towers which in any case the crusaders probably judged too strong for battering. The inner and outer wall were very close to one another so it could not be dragged through and turned aside. Simply to disengage it would have taken almost as much time as to engage it in the first place, thus spoiling the momentum of the attack. To disengage and then re-engage to widen the gap was unthinkable. Moreover, the size of the ram and of the tower which crawled after it meant that they had to be assembled as close as possible to the point of attack. Thus it was that the ram was fired. At this point the constricted nature of the battlefield becomes all too clear, for the enemy who had previously tried to fire the ram now tried unsuccessfully to put out the fire set by the attackers, by throwing water from the wall: 'Twice was the ram set on fire, twice drowned in water twice was Muhammed defeated, twice was Christ victorious'.[55]

It would seem that the action at the outer wall took up most of Thursday 14 July, for although he explains how the tower was manned before he describes the firing of the ram, Albert makes it clear that this only approached the wall on the sixth day, Friday 15 July. It towered over the wall – this was its essential function, to overawe the defences and open the way for other kinds of attack by firepower. If the height of the wall at this point was between twelve and fifteen metres, the tower must have been fifteen to seventeen metres, the height of a four-storied house.[56] Amongst those in the top

---

[54] AA, 472.   [55] AA, 471–2; RC, 691–2; Prawer, 'The Jerusalem', p. 10.
[56] Prawer, p. 10.

storey towering over the defences Godfrey and his brother Eustace commanded; below them in the storey level with the wall, the brothers Ludolf and Engelbert of Tournai were prominent, while those charged with propelling the whole structure huddled and heaved below at ground level. Ralph suggests that some of its crew attacked the wall at its base, and certainly ladders were brought up for it was the function of the tower to cover their erection. However, the business of getting the tower up to the wall proved very difficult. According to Albert the enemy had constructed fourteen mangonels, five of which were deployed against the North French tower and the remainder against that of Count Raymond.[57] This fire battered away at the tower as it was inched across to the wall, killing one of Godfrey's companions with a stone and threatening to destroy the whole thing but its osier covering absorbed much of the shock. Vases of liquid fire were thrown, but this simply poured off the carefully prepared wet hides with which the structure was draped.[58] Ralph of Caen produces a vivid and dramatic account of the climax of the action: the tower had to be inched forward two or three times with enormous effort and at one point, one corner, struck by a stone, shattered and the whole structure began to lean and flop. The enemy suspended a beam on ropes slung between two of the towers of the curtain wall. However, the ropes were eventually cut by a blade hastily mounted on a wooden beam, while Robert of Normandy and Tancred deluged the nearest tower and the wall with missiles forcing the defenders off the wall. More ladders were brought up by priests singing hymns and cheering on the troops. Some of those in the assault tower were then able to climb over a tree which was turned to form a bridge over to the wall, and many ladders were erected, and so the crusaders got to close quarters. Albert of Aachen provides a very similar story. On the top stage of the tower where Godfrey stood firing his crossbow was a golden cross which attracted the enemy's fire. This became so heavy that the crusaders brought in more manpower and did what was evidently not originally intended – they dragged their tower right up to the wall. In this way the projectiles from the enemy mangonels either bounced off the tower back onto the wall and its defenders, or passed over the whole machine. Albert says that because of the buildings

---

[57] For a description of twelfth-century Islamic siege weapons see the extract from al-Tarsusi in Lewis, *Islam from Mohammed to the Capture of Constantinople*, 1. 218–23.

[58] Prawer, 'The Jerusalem', p. 10; RC, 691; AA, 474–5.

within the wall the enemy could not easily redeploy their projectors to correct the range. This is an interesting reflection on the limitations of these high trajectory weapons. Instead the enemy reinforced the garrison of a nearby tower which was draped with mantles, bags of straw and chaff, and ships' ropes and deluged the Christians with missiles of all kinds – including slings and small mangonels. The wooden tower stood firm before this assault, and so the enemy tried yet again to burn it. This time the garrison brought up a large tree-trunk draped in inflammable material and hung it on a chain between the wall and the Christian tower. This was a considerable undertaking for the large gang necessary for such a task, although they would have had covering fire, would have been deluged by missiles from the Christians. But the fire failed to take hold because, Albert says, the Franks had been advised to use vinegar against it by Christians who had escaped from the city. Eventually the crusaders on the ground seem to have seized the chain, perhaps by hooking it, and a tug-of-war ensued, the result of which was that the tree was torn down and dragged away. Those in the tower were now free to pour fire upon the ramparts and the three Christian mangonels were moved to enhance this. Raymond of Aguilers adds that fire arrows, bound with cotton, fired the defences, driving the enemy from the wall. When it seemed that the enemy were cowed by this failure and the hail of missiles, the brothers Ludolf and Englebert climbed out of the tower and threw down trees across the gap between the tower and the rampart, and so broke into the city.[59] Albert and Ralph both say that the besiegers climbed in across tree trunks, while Raymond of Aguilers says that Godfrey cut down the *cratem*, meaning hurdle or mantlet, which protected the front of the middle and upper stories of the tower and so crossed onto the wall.[60] There was no drawbridge on this tower or any other used during the crusade; a hinged bridge with a pulley system would have been very vulnerable, and in any case rather difficult to place at the right height. The tower's purpose was to dominate the defences allowing

[59] AA, 476–7; RA, p. 150.
[60] RA, p. 150; in their translation Hill and Hill, p. 127, suggest the rendering 'Godfrey lowered the drawbridge which had defended the tower'. However, the circumstantial accounts of Albert and Ralph suggest something improvised, and the sense in Raymond of something which protected the tower in the middle and upper stories suggests to me that Godfrey hacked off some of the reinforcing across the front of the tower, which would necessarily have been given more than the other sides, and so crossed the gap. In this, I follow the suggestion of Prawer, 'The Jerusalem', p. 10, n. 52.

the attackers to undermine the walls or (as on this occasion) to mount an attack by ladder. So striking was their deployment that it was noted by almost all the eastern sources which describe the fall of Jerusalem, although there is no suggestion that the writers considered this a novelty in warfare.[61]

On the other side of the city things were not going so well. Here there could be no surprise for there was no room for changing the point of attack and it was not until the Thursday that the ditch was filled in after a fierce fight in which the enemy made extensive use of fire, sometimes including blazing mallets stuck with nails which fixed in to anything they hit. There is no record of a ram like that of the North French being used; there was no outer wall here. The whole battlefield was extremely constricted; between the Provençal camp around the Church of St Mary of Mount Zion and the wall was some fifty metres, while effectively only about 160 metres of the wall was accessible to attack and this was dominated by the Zion Gate (fig. 17c). But presumably some machinery was brought up to help weaken the defences, for it is difficult to see into what else these fiery projectiles could have lodged. On the morning of 15 July the Provençals brought all their machines forward including *petrariae*, but they were outnumbered nine or ten to one by those of the enemy whose missiles did considerable destruction; it is interesting that Albert says that the Saracens concentrated nine of their fourteen mangonels against Count Raymond's assault. Once more, fire was used extensively against the catapults and tower of the attacking force, and the women, who had helped to fill in the ditch, were employed to bring up water. Raymond gives few details, though he does mention that some enemy women tried to put a spell on the Christian machines and were killed along with their children. It was surely at this point that the episode portrayed in the 'Unknown account' must have occurred. Within the Zion Gate the enemy had mounted *noviter adinuento machinamento* which fired flaming balls of fat, resin and pitch coagulated with hair and flax into Count Raymond's camp causing great fires. This machine was so well protected by mantles and paddings that the crusader missiles made no impact upon it. Ultimately they fastened a three-pronged hook to the end of a great beam, supported by a long chain attached to its

---

[61] Ibn al-Athir, 197; *Damascus Chronicle of the Crusades*, p. 47; Michael, p. 184; Matthew, 45; Bar-Hebraeus, p. 235.

upper part, and with this dragged off the protection around the machine which they were then able to destroy with missiles. This hook was then redeployed against other enemy defences but became stuck in a beam where one of the enemy shinned up, presumably to bind it. The enemy then brought up five more machines *tormentis* causing the Christians to retreat. Raymond of Aguilers supports Albert's story that by midday the Provençals were seriously considering withdrawal, when encouraging signals from men posted on the Mt of Olives made the southerners renew the attack with ladders and ropes, a manner of attack which appears to confirm Albert's information that Raymond's tower was so badly damaged that it had to be withdrawn from the battle and Tudebode's information that its upper story was shattered and burning.[62] It is unfortunate that we do not have more detail on the southern attack, for Raymond of Aguilers does not dwell on the failure of his own people and confusingly runs the descriptions of the two attacks together. However, it is evident that they faced a well-prepared defence while in the north there was a degree of improvisation. Albert may not be absolutely correct in his numbers when he says that nine of fourteen enemy catapults were deployed on the south, but the need to contain the strongly sustained southern thrust must have worried the enemy commanders – especially as it was directed very close to their main centre of resistance. The decision to launch a two-pronged attack may have owed something to divisions in the crusader host, but it was highly effective, not least because of the strange passivity of the garrison. At no point either in the period of intense preparation nor during the assault itself do we hear of determined sallies from the city; it may be that garrison troops had participated in the early raiding on the crusaders, but they launched no spoiling attacks and this is all the odder when it is considered that two sides of the city lay open though both were picketed. Either the garrison felt that it was too small, despite the mobile élite of 400 mounted men specially sent by the Vizir, or they simply expected relief to come much more quickly, or both. Certainly their passivity was an important factor in the crusader victory. Moreover, in view of the general expectation of the arrival of a relief army, the prompt capitulation of the citadel is curious and suggests that their numbers

---

[62] France, 'Capture of Jerusalem', 644–6; RA, pp. 148–51; AA, 475;, PT, p. 118. This was perhaps Greek fire on which see above p. 162, n. 58.

were never great and had been reduced by losses in the fighting to the point where holding it was not practicable.[63]

Once the crusaders had got onto the rampart the defence collapsed quickly. The garrison was not numerous enough to stand against the crusaders once they had broken in. In the northern sector the crusaders fanned out east and west, the former opening the Josaphat Gate. Albert says that sixteen westerners were killed by plunging horses in the rush to get into the city. In the south, the garrison seem to have withdrawn into the citadel where Iftikhar-ad-Daulah promptly came to an agreement with Count Raymond whereby his men were spared on condition that the citadel was immediately surrendered.[64] In a military sense the battle was over and now the massacre began. This notorious event should not be exaggerated. Many Jews survived; we hear of some being captured by Tancred and we know that some were later ransomed, while many Muslim refugees from the city later took refuge at Damascus bringing with them the celebrated Koran of Uthman. The shock expressed by Ibn al-Athir, for example, and his statement that 70,000 were killed, owes something to the later spirit of Jihad and the thirst for vengeance which it engendered.[65] However horrible the massacre at Jerusalem, it was not far beyond what common practice of the day meeted out to any place which resisted. In 1057 the entire population of Melitene was slaughtered or enslaved by the Turks whose conquest of Asia Minor was particularly brutal, while in the chaos after Manzikert Greeks and Armenians slaughtered one another.[66] Such events were not confined to the Orient; the Conqueror's ravaging of the Vexin and sack of Mantes in 1087 was of such savagery that some saw his death in the ruins of this city as divine vengeance. In the 'harrying of the north' by the Normans, Ordericus believed 100,000 Christians perished and, commenting on William's role in this 'brutal slaughter', remarked that 'I cannot commend him'. These were exceptional events, but they were not so rare, and represented, as we have noted, only exaggerations of the

---

[63] RA, p. 149 says that a knight waved from the Mt of Olives as Godfrey's force penetrated the city and this is expanded by PT p. 109 and others.

[64] AA, 478; RC, 694; RA, pp. 147, gives a figure of 60,000 for the garrison, but this is nonsense, p. 151.

[65] Ibn al-Athir, 197; Maalouf, *Crusades through Arab Eyes*, pp. iii, 50; Goitein, 'Geniza sources', pp. 308–11, 313; RC, 696–7.

[66] Matthew, 108, 152–4; Bar Hebraeus, pp. 212–13; Michael, p. 158–9.

common currency of war.[67] This is the background of military behaviour and we must remember the heightened emotions of an army which had been through terrible trials; as the city fell there were reports of a vision of Adhémar of Le Puy. It is perhaps the rejoicing in the event so notable in Raymond of Aguilers, and the cryptic and cold acceptance of merciless slaughter in the Anonymous which repel us. Even if we can stomach the slaughter on the day as excesses committed in a moment of exaltation, the killing of Tancred's hostages who had hidden on the roof of the Dome of the Rock the next day is repellent.[68] The rapacious greed shown by many, notably Tancred who had been told by defectors of the wealth of the Dome of the Rock seems, to us, at odds with the religious purposes of the expedition, but of course it was not, though the matter caused bad feeling between the leaders. Godfrey's pious abstention from pillaging appears noble – but of course Tancred was his man and shared the loot with him. Special mention is made of the capture of the 400 horses of the élite mounted force with which al-Afdal had reinforced the garrison, which had been left outside the citadel where their riders had sought refuge for they were very valuable to a host whose horses must by now have been few and exhausted.[69] In fact, large numbers of the native population seem to have survived the initial conquest, but three days later, after Tancred had complained about the massacre of his hostages on the Dome of the Rock, the leaders decreed that all prisoners, men, women and children, should be massacred; this second phase of cold-blooded murder was duly carried out and even Albert was appalled by it. But there was reason behind the horror; the Franks had engaged in a race against time and the gamble had succeeded. But now they anticipated the coming of an Egyptian army and it was fear of leaving an enemy in the nest that brought about this atrocious killing.[70]

The army had seized Jerusalem, but it remained in a perilous position, and things were made worse by the divisions in its ranks. After a preliminary meeting on 17 July to deal with practical matters such as clearing bodies from the city, the occasion on which Albert says that they also ordered the massacre of the remaining Muslim population, the leaders met in solemn conclave on 22 July to

---

[67] Douglas, *William the Conqueror*, p. 368; OV, 2. 233; on military ethics in the west see above pp. 41–4.
[68] RA, pp. 151–2; *GF*, p. 91; AA, 482–3. [69] AA, 477, 479, 481–2. [70] AA, 483–4.

consider the future of the city. Some of the clergy demanded that the Patriarch be elected first in recognition of the primacy of the spiritual authority, but the princes refused to heed that and offered the throne to Count Raymond who, probably under clerical influence, refused, disdaining the name of king in Jerusalem. Godfrey de Bouillon was then offered the government of the city as 'Advocate', a position which recognised the claims of the church while conceding practical power to the lay authority. When he demanded the surrender of the Tower of David, Raymond of Toulouse refused because he wanted to stay in the city until Easter, and there followed an intrigue with overtones of coercion. Even the Provençals, Raymond of Aguilers says, muttered against their lord for they wanted to return home quickly. This note of division in the crusader army, and in particular of tension between Raymond and Godfrey, can be related to the affair of Tancred's allegiance which goes back to 'Akkār, while it is notable that a number of important Provençal leaders like Gaston of Béarn seem to have deserted at this time. The upshot was that Count Raymond lost the citadel; Albert says he was forced to surrender it. Then he went to the Jordan for his devotions, returning only for the election of a Patriarch on 1 August, a post which went to the Norman Arnulf of Choques.[71] The whole bad-tempered affair promised a rather sour end to the great expedition. But what is interesting is that nobody seems to have set off for home. The reason is fairly obvious; they were expecting attack from an Egyptian army. Any leader who left at such a point would be open to the shameful charge of having deserted the Holy City and his comrades in the hour of need. In addition, any small force would have feared attack on the long march back to friendly territory in North Syria. Self-preservation, therefore, prompted unity of a tenuous kind, which was just as well for they now faced the gathering forces of a powerful enemy.

The Fatimid Caliphate of Egypt was no longer the great power it had been. A period of economic decline and political instability had been brought to a close with the rise of the Vizir Badr al-Jamali, a

---

[71] AA, 485–6; RA, pp. 152–3; *GF*, p. 92; on the general circumstances see France, 'Election of Godfrey de Bouillon'; Riley-Smith, 'The title of Godfrey de Bouillon', 83–6 inclines to the idea of a kingship as does Murray, 'Title of Godfrey de Bouillon' (see above p. 332, n. 22) but it still seems to the present writer that if Godfrey had been made a king the contemporary sources would not have been so evasive in the way they describe him; on Tancred see above pp. 331, 347; on Arnulf see Foreville, 'Arnoul Malecouronne'.

Moslem Armenian who was able to consolidate his power in the
years 1074–7 and pass it on to his son al-Afdal on his death in 1094.
The weakening of the Seljuks after 1094 and the coming of the
crusade offered an opportunity for the Egyptians to reassert the
control of Palestine and southern Syria which they had lost during
the time of trouble to the Seljuks.[72] The embassy which the crusaders sent to Egypt on the advice of Alexius Comnenus certainly
may have encouraged them to see their coming as a new Byzantine
initiative, and this was solidified by the understanding reached with
their embassy at Antioch in February–March 1098. In 1097/8
al-Afdal was able to resume control of Sidon and Tyre. The crusaders were well aware that in 1073 the Turks had captured Jerusalem and that it had been reconquered by the Egyptians in August
1098 in the wake of their capture of Antioch. The Egyptians were
totally surprised when the crusaders rejected the terms offered at
'Akkār in early May 1099 of access for small groups to Jerusalem. It
is possible that there was some diplomatic contact after the Frankish
capture of Jerusalem for Godfrey was informed of the coming of
al-Afdal by an unknown messenger[73]. A recent study of the Fatimid
military suggests that they needed a period of two months to raise an
army and establish it in Palestine. If we allow some time for the
Egyptian Embassy to have returned home after their disappoint-
ment in early May, and for the matter to have been discussed at
court before a decision, preparation for the expedition which
gathered at Ascalon in early August 1099 must have begun only
after it was clear that the breach with the Franks was irrevocable
(fig. 16).[74]

[72] On Egyptian determination to recover control in this area see Köhler, *Allianzen und
Verträge*, pp. 60–2.
[73] *Encyclopaedia of Islam* 1. 'al-Afdal', 'Badr al-Jamali'; AA, 484–5, 490; Ekkehard, 4;
Köhler, *Allianzen und Verträge*, p. 67, points to Islamic evidence of an ambassador sent to the
Franks just before the battle of Ascalon on 12 August 1099. On the history of crusader
contacts with Egypt see above, pp. 252–3, 325–6; RA, p. 110.
[74] Hamblin, *Fatimid Army*, p. 225, which is the main source for the description of the Egyptian
army which follows. See also Lev, *State and Society in Fatimid Egypt*, and his article, 'Army,
regime and society in Fatimid Egypt', *International Journal of Middle East Studies*, 19 (1987),
337–66; B. S. Bachrach, 'African military slaves in the medieval Middle east: Iraq
(869–951) and Egypt (868–1171)', *International Journal of Middle Eastern Studies*, 13 (1981),
471–95; B. S. Beshir, *The Fatimid Caliphate 975–1094*, Ph.D thesis, University of London,
1970, 'Fatamid military organisation', *Der Islam*, 55. 1 (1978), 37–56; C. E. Bosworth,
'Turks in the Islamic lands up to the mid-eleventh century', *Fundamenta Philologiae
Turcicae*, Part 2, *Les Turcs muslmans avant les Ottomans* (Wiesbaden, 1970), pp. 1–20,
'Recruitment, muster and review', 60–77 esp. 66–7; D. O. Leary, *Short History of the Fatimid
Caliphate* (London, 1923).

The Egyptians had a complex military organisation resembling that of the Baghdad Caliphate. Military administration was the task of the Diwan al-Jayish, while the Diwan al-Nawatib controlled all government salaries and the Diwan al-Iqta looked after the 'Iqta. Three huge military storehouses, *Khizana*, were maintained at Cairo, the largest holding 200,000 items ranging from personal equipment to siege weapons. The Caliphal palace was at the heart of a complex of barracks which housed a regular army with a normal strength of some 10,000–15,000, of which 4,000–5,000 were cavalry. Perhaps as many as another 10,000 regulars were housed elsewhere, in the ports of Egypt and Palestine and inland cities like Jerusalem. Like the army of the Baghdad Caliphate this was a composite force, 'a multi-ethnic force with considerable slave component, in which mounted archers were prominent'. An Iranian traveller who passed through Cairo in 1047 reports a grand parade featuring 205,000 troops, Berbers and other North Africans, Turks and Persians, Daylami infantry, Nubians, Bedouins and African negroes amongst them.[75] The numbers may be exaggerated but it was from amongst these people that the Fatimid Caliphate recruited. Black Sudanese troops were particularly noted by the crusaders.[76] The army was organised in regiments, most of which had a common ethnic base, and subdivided into companies of 100 men. There were roughly equal numbers of cavalry and infantry amongst the regulars. After 1074 the Armenians were a major element in the army, for it was from amongst their ranks that al-Jamali had risen. So numerous were they that Armenian churches were built in Cairo to cater for them and their families. The Berbers and Arabs provided light cavalry.[77] But an important element in the force was the heavy cavalry for whom the storehouses kept lamellar armour, chain mail shirts and even armoured horse-coverings which seem to have been very rare in the west at this time. Some of the Africans carried fearful war-flails and others were equipped with shields and javelins. The Armenians were primarily archers and many were mounted. The rise of the Seljuks and the long war with them had led to a reduction

[75] Lev, *State and Society in Fatimid Egypt*, points out that black slaves were prominent from the time of al-Hakim (996–1021), pp. 88–9; Naser-e Khosraw, *Book of Travels*, pp. 48–50; this extract is also printed by Lewis, *Islam from Mohammed to the Capture of Constantinople*, 1. 217–18.

[76] AA, 490, refers to Ethiopians, 494, Azoparts with their terrible flails.

[77] On their effective hit and run tactics and on the role of heavy slave infantry recruited from Africa see M. Brett, 'Military interest of the battle of Haydaran', pp. 78–88.

of the number of Turks in the Egyptian forces, but they continued to be employed. Manuals of war provided this army with ideas about formation and tactics; it is unfortunate that those surviving date from the thirteenth century when Mameluke practises dominated. However, the tactics of the Egyptians seem to have been built round the deployment of a core of well-equipped infantry supported by strong formations of heavy cavalry who were not unlike the western knights.

Not all the regular troops of Egypt could be available for an expedition abroad, but the fact that al-Afdal himself was to lead the army which gathered at Ascalon suggests that a maximum effort was made on this occasion. It was the usual policy to augment the regular forces with irregulars – Bedouin and Arab light horse, city militias and volunteers. Moslem sources speak of 10,000 infantry dying at Ascalon and 2,700 volunteers, while an overall figure of 20,000 in the army has been mentioned.[78] In the light of the military potential of the Fatimid Caliphate and the forces which it later mustered against the crusaders, this would seem to be a reasonable figure though perhaps a little on the large side. This force slowly gathered at Ascalon in the wake of the Frankish conquest of Jerusalem. The crusaders at Jerusalem had little to do but bicker, and Tancred became involved in a quarrel with the Patriarch and was sent with Eustace of Boulogne, on 25 July, to receive the submission of Nablus. However, while there they received news from Godfrey of the coming of enemy forces and so this joint force rode for the coast at Caeserea, then turned south and skirmished with Egyptian forces reaching Ramla on 7 August (see fig. 16). On their information Godfrey, Robert of Flanders and the Patriarch ventured out on 9 August. With them was Arnulf bishop of Martirano who was sent back to Jerusalem to summon help, was captured by the enemy and vanished.[79] Albert says that Godfrey, Tancred, Eustace and Robert of Flanders went out looking for the enemy, received news of their gathering at Ascalon, and called Raymond of Toulouse and Robert of Normandy to join them at Ramla in preparation for battle.[80] This seems like an abbreviated version of the events described by the Anonymous. The sources suggest that Count Raymond was unwilling at first to join the army. The Anonymous says simply that he

[78] *Damascus Chronicle of the Crusades*, pp. 48–9; Ibn al-Athir, 198; al-Dhahabi cited Hamblin, *Fatimid Army*, p. 238 gives 20,000.
[79] RC, 699–703; *GF*, p. 93.   [80] AA, 490–1.

wanted to make sure the enemy really were in the field, but Albert says he hesitated out of a desire for vengeance on Godfrey and Raymond of Aguilers speaks of his resentment and determination to go home. With him was Robert of Normandy who perhaps regarded himself as still bound by the promise made at Ruj.[81] It was not until their own scouts had seen the enemy that Raymond, bearing the Holy Lance, and Robert left Jerusalem on 10 August and they joined the North French in the plains near Ramla. The next day the army began to advance the forty kilometres to Ascalon and, fearing ambush in this gently rolling countryside, adopted a special formation of nine squadrons in three lines of three which would enable them to face attack on any front. Towards evening on 11 August their scouts seized huge herds of animals gathered to feed the enemy army and captured guards who told them of the enemy's positions and his intention to attack them in Jerusalem. That night they encamped by a little river which Raymond of Aguilers says was some five leagues from Ascalon. This must be near to the modern Yavne or Yibna which the crusaders later called Ibelin, twenty-five kilometres north of Ascalon. The captured herds assumed a considerable importance in the events which followed, for according to Raymond of Aguilers and Fulcher of Chartres they moved with the army the next morning, suggesting to the enemy that it was far bigger than it actually was. Albert of Aachen confirms this and adds that the Arab governor of Ramla who shortly after converted, warned them that the beasts were left there as a trap so that the Franks would scatter to pillage, and so it was ordered by the Patriarch that none should plunder until victory was won.[82]

Next morning, 12 August 1099, the army, according to Albert loud in its rejoicing, prepared for battle and resumed its defensive formation so that it could not be ambushed. They were, adds Raymond of Aguilers, only 1,200 knights and 9,000 foot in all.[83] Close to Ascalon the land becomes flatter and from about eight kilometres slopes down towards the city; Raymond of Aguilers's pleasant valley. There they found the enemy encamped just to the north of the city. Ascalon was an ancient city and in the late eleventh century of considerable economic and military importance, for it was the nearest port of the Palestinian littoral to Egypt. Its

[81] *GF*, p. 94; RA, pp. 154–5; AA, 491.
[82] *GF*, p. 94; RA, pp. 156–7; FC, p. 126; AA, 491–2.
[83] RA, p. 157; AA, 492.

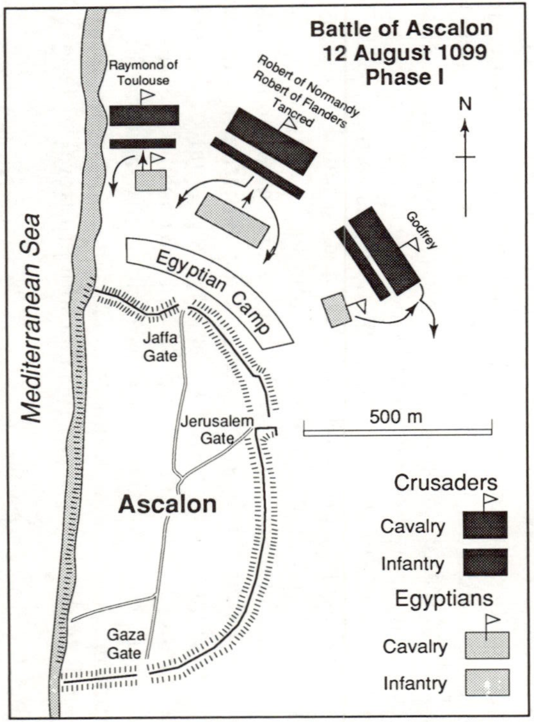

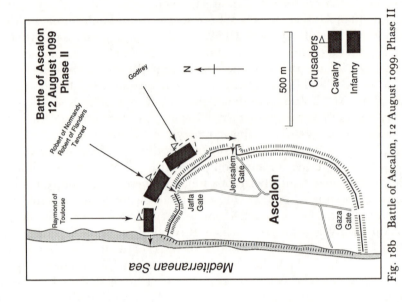

Fig. 18a   Battle of Ascalon, 12 August 1099. Phase I

Fig. 18b   Battle of Ascalon, 12 August 1099. Phase II

enceinte was D-shaped with the flat side of the D running almost one kilometre along the coast. In the south the fortifications follow the line of a ridge curving northwards for some one and a half kilometres on top of a huge artificial earthwork which is perhaps as old as the Middle Bronze Age. By the twelfth century, when William of Tyre described it, this was a double wall and he commented on its strength and the number of its towers which later sources estimate at fifty-three. This massive strength enclosed a natural depression, deepest in the south-west where the Sea Gate gave access to the port. To the south was the Gaza Gate and to the north the Jaffa Gate but more important was the Jerusalem Gate in the northeastern sector of the enceinte (see fig. 18).[84]

As the crusaders approached the enemy camp they deployed into line of battle, with Raymond of Toulouse on the right by the sea, Godfrey on the left and the others including Robert of Normandy, Robert of Flanders and Tancred, in the centre. The archers and foot were thrown forward of the knights to protect them. Albert of Aix says that Godfrey's force blockaded the gates of Ascalon to prevent the enemy sallying forth. This probably means that the army was not aligned west–east from the coast but west–south-east, shadowing the curve of the northern wall of the city and so keeping its principal gate in view. The formation of the army reflected all that they had learned about the need to use infantry and cavalry together.[85] Raymond of Aguilers gives no real description of the battle, but he says that the enemy stayed in their camp; this is not borne out by other sources and appears to mean that they were there at first. The Anonymous, who gives a mere sketch of events, says that Tancred charged into the midst of the enemy tents and Albert speaks of fighting in the camp. All of this points to the enemy being surprised in their camp and having to fight an improvised battle, and this is certainly Raymond of Aguilers's understanding, for he says that the enemy were over-confident because they had information that the

---

[84] For a good summary description of the site with an excellent bibliography see D. Pringle, 'King Richard I and the walls of Ascalon', *Palestine Exploration Quarterly*, 116 (1984), 133–47. A key work in the history of the site's exploration is C. R. Conder and H. H. Kitchener, *The Survey of Western Palestine*, 4 vols. (London, 1883), 3. 236–47. Today the ruins of Ascalon lie to the south of the modern city of that name and form a huge archaeological park. The visible remains bear witness to the reconstructions of Richard I, destroyed by treaty in 1192, and the later work of Richard of Cornwall, but the main enceinte clearly shows the fortified area faced by the crusade in 1099.

[85] *GF*, p. 95; RA, p. 157; FC, p. 126; AA, 493–4.

Franks were few, and believed that those in their proximity were just raiders. In any case, he adds, the enemy had consulted soothsayers who had for the moment advised against an attack. This impression of a surprise is strongly confirmed by the *Damascus Chronicle*, which says that al-Afdal was still awaiting forces when he was attacked.[86] Fulcher of Chartes says, however, that the enemy took the initiative and attacked in a stag-horn formation with infantry forming a solid centre and cavalry on the wings. A group of light Arab cavalry detached itself from the enemy right and swung round into the crusader rear, but they were driven off by Godfrey. Albert gives a vivid description of an enemy attack in the centre to the sound of drums and trumpets. Under a hail of missiles the Azoparts, as the Ethiopians were called, crashed into the crusader line wielding their war-flails which smashed horse and man regardless of armour. They were supported by archers, slingers and spearmen from various races in what seems to have been a savage battle. Albert says that it lasted the greater part of the day, although the impression given by the other sources suggests a much briefer battle, and that as the enemy attack flagged, so the crusaders charged.[87] It was evidently this crusader charge into the enemy camp which decided the battle, for it is the main feature of the descriptions. The Anonymous reports that Robert of Normandy charged at and captured the enemy's standard and after that the enemy melted away, while Fulcher and Raymond of Aguilers say that resistance collapsed once the enemy camp was taken. Albert says that many of the crusaders started to pillage in the camp, and this allowed the enemy to rally and counter-attack until Godfrey came up and drove them off. In the pursuit which followed some of the enemy fled towards the port and were massacred by Count Raymond's men, while others were simply confused and cut down where they stood, and some who climbed palm trees were shot out of them. A large part of the enemy army tried to take refuge in Ascalon and were crushed in the gate of the city. For their part the crusaders rejoiced in a vast booty (see fig. 18b).[88] The army of al-Afdal seems to have been badly surprised by the appearance of the crusaders. He sent forward his infantry, presumably because they took less time to prepare for battle, supported by some light horse. However, Arab sources stress that much

---

[86] RA, p. 157; *GF*, p. 95; AA, 495-6; *Damascus Chronicle of the Crusades*, p. 48.
[87] FC, pp. 126-7; AA, 494-6.
[88] *GF*, pp. 96-7; FC p. 127; RA, p. 158; AA, 495-6.

of the Fatimid army, and in particular the heavy cavalry, never came to battle. The initial charge of the Fatimid infantry was blunted by the Frankish infantry, then it wavered and was scattered by the Frankish knights who fell upon the enemy's heavy cavalry which was as yet unready for battle. Fatimid armies could fight very well, and indeed at Ramla on 17 May 1102 would inflict a heavy defeat upon the Franks. On this occasion they were caught by surprise and destroyed by an enemy inferior in numbers.[89] Surprise, speed of movement and sheer boldness in attacking a huge enemy force were the causes of the crusader victory. The third enemy had been defeated and the Franks rejoiced in God's favour with masses in the Holy Sepulchre, to which was given the enemy commander's silver standard as a token of victory.

The sequel was as sour as that to the triumphant capture of Jerusalem. After the celebrations at Jerusalem Raymond of Toulouse negotiated for the surrender of Ascalon which was completely demoralised as the Arab sources admit. Raymond used Bohemond the converted Turk who is first mentioned during the siege of Antioch. Godfrey was determined that he and not Count Raymond should hold the city, and when the quarrel between the two Frankish leaders became known to the citizens they refused to surrender. Ascalon remained a thorn in the side of the Franks until 1153. Albert accuses Count Raymond of having sabotaged Godfrey's arrangements for the surrender in a spirit of vengeance. However that may be, such divisions and the passage of time stiffened the resolve of the citizens.[90] Shortly after, Raymond of Toulouse attacked Arsuf, but abandoned the siege when he heard that Godfrey was approaching and joined the other leaders who were gathering near Caeserea for the return home. So angry was Godfrey that he was prepared to attack the Provençals, but in the end he was dissuaded, there was a reconciliation and towards the end of August Count Raymond, the two Roberts and their armies left Godfrey and marched north.[91] The returning army reached Laodicea where they discovered that Bohemond had enlisted the aid of Daimbert archbishop of Pisa, the new Papal Legate in the east who was supported by a great fleet, in an effort to seize the city from the Greeks. In the event Daimbert was persuaded to desist and Bohemond was forced

[89] Ibn Khaldun 4.42; Ibn al-Athir, 286; Hamblin, *Fatimid Army*, pp. 244–8.
[90] RA, p. 159; AA, 497–8; BD, 111; Runciman 2. 339.
[91] AA, 498–9.

to return to Antioch. Raymond of Toulouse took possession of the citadel of Byzantine Laodicea and the rest of the army sailed for the west on Greek and other ships.[92] It was on this sour note of personal ambition and internecine quarrels which had dogged the crusade, but never quite undermined its military effectiveness, that the great adventure ended.

[92] AA, 500–1; on Daimbert and his position as a Legate see B. Hamilton, *The Latin Church*, p. 14.

CHAPTER 12

Perspectives

There can be no doubt that burning religious conviction underlay the success of the First Crusade. Time and again when all seemed lost, at Antioch and at Jerusalem particularly, the army rallied to God's cause. The deep conviction that they were the servants of God underlay the boldness with which they tackled and surprised such formidable enemies as the Egyptians, when all rational calculation would have advised against it. Indeed, not the least of the factors which made for their success was the inability of the Middle Eastern powers to comprehend this all or nothing mentality. But burning zeal has to be controlled, disciplined and sustained. Ecclesiastical power alone was not enough, and as in Western society generally so on the crusade, power was exercised by an alliance of church, in the person of Adhémar, and state in the persons of the princes. When the ambitions, hesitations and doubts of the lay leaders disrupted the crusade and ecclesiastical authority collapsed with the death of Adhémar, the army was plunged into crisis from which it was rescued only by a zealot minority represented by Peter Bartholemew in alliance with the count of Toulouse. They owed their power to articulating the feelings of the overwhelming mass of the crusaders of all ranks, and when Peter was discredited Godfrey was able to harness this raw power. That religious zeal had a very narrow and material focus – to liberate Jerusalem. Later crusades would never suffer from such tunnel vision, but this enormously concentrated the efforts of the army in contrast to their successors in 1101 and 1147.[1]

---

[1] The Crusade of 1101 is the subject of a Swansea Ph.D thesis by Alec Mulinder, which, when complete, should provide valuable insight into the failure of this crusade. The Crusade of 1101 lacked coherence. Its various elements never gathered together and perished separately, largely because they had no clear objective such as the First Crusade found in Jerusalem. They were fighting an enemy, the Turks of Asia Minor, who had learned the lessons of the earlier campaign and refused to be drawn into battle.

For ideological cohesion was a rare phenomenon in the eleventh century, as Gregory VII had discovered, and it is hard to see how any wider objective could have carried the concentrated appeal of Jerusalem.

But their spirit and organisation could never have succeeded without help. Byzantine aid was of enormous assistance. At the siege of Nicaea it was very much in evidence, but thereafter it appeared to dwindle. This was a false perspective, for Alexius's real service to the crusaders was to support them from Cyprus which formed an offshore base for the siege of Antioch and operations in North Syria (see fig. 3). In addition, Alexius seems to have committed a sizable fleet to their assistance – far more important than Tatikios's small contingent. Without Byzantine help it is difficult to see how the western fleets could have operated so successfully. The reason for this enormous Byzantine investment was that this was a joint enterprise. The whole Armenian strategy promised the restoration of Byzantine power in the old dominion of Philaretus and the collapse of the Seljuk dominion in western Asia Minor opened the way for the reconquest of the southern part of the sub-continent. So when it came to a dispute Alexius could rightly say that he had played his part but in the end the greatest prize eluded him, for the decision to turn back at Philomelium gave Bohemond his opportunity and a moral justification for the dislike of the Greeks which was never far below the surface amongst the Westerners.

And Byzantine help had its influence in another way. The crusade was enormously assisted by the divisions of Islam. Had the Seljuk dominion of less than ten years before still existed, it is impossible to see how they could have succeeded. Alexius almost certainly explained the problems of the Turks and the divisions of Islam to his allies, for we know it was his idea to send an embassy to Egypt. But it has to be said that the western princes took their cue skillfully and played the Egyptians well, and applied the idea to other Islamic powers. They were more pragmatic than the stereotype of the crusader in absolute and bitter opposition to all that is Islamic would sugggest. The fanaticism which drove on the great expedition was an underlying force of enormous power but its influence upon events was continual rather than continuous. Nor should we forget that although the Islamic powers were divided, they were each individually very strong and that in every major battle the crusaders fought against odds. No matter how enthusiastic they were, nor how well supported, victory in the clash of arms was never inevitable and to understand that we must turn to more narrowly military factors.

The individual leaders exerted great control over their own armies. Robert of Normandy is one of the failures of history and this casts a shadow over him, but at Dorylaeum he rallied the troops at a crucial moment, and at Ascalon he was at the heart of a charge which swept all before it. This was military ability of a high order. Robert of Flanders was a brave soldier who organised the foraging and gathering of materials at Jerusalem. Godfrey was in the thick of the fighting at the siege of Jerusalem and this was important in an age when leading by example mattered. Bohemond was an able general whose aggressive tactics created the victories over Ridwan and Kerbogah. He made the crusaders use rear-guards – this was by no means an innovation in western war but it was a development which needed discipline and control, and such qualities became more evident in the crusader army as time went on. Bohemond's genius lay in his aggressiveness – his determination to unsettle the enemy and take them unawares, and this characterises his victories over Ridwan and Kerbogah. He was not a tactical innovator – the real innovation was the use of infantry, and that arose from circumstance as they became better armed and more experienced. The battle against Kerbogah was an infantry battle perforce – it was only at Ascalon that the lessons of careful co-ordination were applied. But Bohemond's real importance lay in the fact of his appointment as sole commander in moments of crisis. The divisions of the leaders, their determination to head their own armies and do jointly only what was agreed jointly, was the real weakness of this and almost all other crusades. It was their good fortune that when this co-operation was at its newest and their troops at their rawest, they confronted the weakest of their enemies, the Turks of Asia Minor. The nomads were ferocious fighters, but they were not numerous and Kilij Arslan's tactics depended too heavily on the moral effect of sudden onslaughts. He allowed his men, whose genius lay in mobile warfare, to be caught in slogging matches where numbers counted; in 1101 the Turks would learn patience and close only with a demoralised enemy. It was luck too that when the leaders were at their most divided after the fall of Antioch, the Islamic world was demoralised and quite unable to exploit their problems, so that despite the fragility of their co-operation they pressed on to Jerusalem.

The leaders were able men who managed to work together, though only just. Their real ability showed at its best in sieges. Nicaea, Antioch and Jerusalem were large and well-defended cities such as few westerners had seen before, but the army set about their reduction systematically. Probably the siege of Nicaea helped the leaders to settle a raw army, though at a terrible price in lives. Full credit has never been given to a leadership which perceived the problems of the siege of Antioch and tackled them with enormous persistence and eventual success. The experience at Antioch was an intensification of what they were used to in the West – war of position rather than the formal investment experienced at Nicaea – the strangling of an enemy rather than assault against fortifications. The siege of Jerusalem exemplifies the skills of what was now a highly experienced and coherent grouping of armies, though the passiveness of the defenders contributed. It was not technological innovation which made their sieges so successful. All the instruments they used seem to have been known to their enemies.[2] The western approach to war which favoured systematic and often clumsy preparation also favoured good performance in this area. Success was the product of organisation and command above all.

The Franks enjoyed no technical advantages over their enemies. Their western horses may have been rather larger than those of the nomad Turks but probably not significantly so, and they soon died anyway. The Turks, an element in all the armies that they faced, had the short bow which dictated their tactics and which the Franks found difficult to counter. They may even have had a form of quick-firing crossbow unknown to the West. The Franks probably had rather better armour, but in general their weapons were very like those of their enemies.

The outstanding factor on the battlefield was the tactical skill of the Turkish horsemen firing their arrows from horseback. They were always relatively few and this was critical in Asia Minor. In the Caliphate they were the cutting edge of armies and supported by diverse and adaptable forces. The Franks had no technical answer to the problem and their response was precisely what one would expect – the tactical expedient of solidity of formation. This is

---

[2] Here I differ sharply from L. White, 'The Crusades and the technological thrust of the West', in V.J. Parry and M.E. Yapp, eds., Parry *War, Technology and Society in the Middle East* (London, 1975), pp. 97–112, who argues that it was innovation in this area that gave the crusaders their advantage.

always desirable in both cavalry and infantry, but very difficult to achieve when there was no formal system of training. In their first battle the Franks found themselves fighting in close ground near Nicaea, which frustrated Turkish tactics. At Dorylaeum the enemy was free to manoeuvre and attacked skillfully, cruelly exposing the Franks who lacked any overall command. But the chances of topography and direction of attack, and the determination and skill of the leaders held the armies together. Thereafter the crusader host became a more coherent group of units and Bohemond was able to use this experience and skill to great advantage at the Lake Battle. Against Kerbogah the same cohesiveness was seen amongst the infantry who were also refined and trained by the experience of war and the lessons of this were applied at Ascalon where a complex marching formation was adopted, and the classic pattern of infantry protecting cavalry marked the final deployment. This was not innovation as such, for similar formations had been used in the West but here it was used with great success.[3]

It is this growth of the coherence and experience of the crusader host as a whole which was the key to their military success. In many ways their overall organisation and weapons were inferior to those of their enemies and they were 'away from home' in a strange climate. But the divisions of their enemies meant that their weaknesses were never exposed fully and they were given time in which they became more and more experienced. Crucially the Turks of Asia Minor failed to stop them. Thereafter what had been a relatively incoherent host, within which some armies were better ordered than others, became more coherent and experienced, and more successful.

In a military sense the crusade was a success. It may not have achieved all that Urban wanted it to achieve in terms of friendship with the Eastern Empire.[4] Its success was limited in that it established bare outposts with poor communications with the West and uncertain relations with Eastern Christendom, but that is our viewpoint blessed as we are with hindsight. There was no single will directing the crusade; it was the product of many wills interacting with circumstances, and all that gave it a precarious unity was

---

[3] France, 'La guerre dans la France féodale', 193–8.
[4] This is not the place to rehearse the debate about Urban's intentions which are touched on above, pp. 4–5.

Jerusalem. To free it was the task they set themselves and to have achieved that was remarkable.

The crusade had little immediate impact on western armies at this time. The twelfth century would see the rise of two distinct tactical developments: the mass charge by cavalry, using couched lances for the maximum shock impact, and the rise of highly effective infantry.[5] Discipline and clearly articulated command structures were vital to these developments. Launching a cavalry charge was so difficult even for the Templars with their background of order and discipline that they felt the need to write it all down in detail.[6] These developments were only possible because the monarchies of the West more and more used mercenaries and professional commanders who were able to impose an appropriate discipline on the more 'regular' forces which formed the cores of their commands. This, combined with the development of the heavier horses, created the classic medieval cavalry charge, and one of its antidotes – disciplined infantry, who in any case became more and more necessary as castles grew more complex. The conditions of the crusade replicated the conditions of common service and experience which made these armies so efficient. Conditions in the crusader states continued to demand constant military activity which had much the same effect, hence the high prestige of the armies of Outremer in the twelfth century. It is possible that the glory and the prestige of the First Crusade helped to impress upon western commanders the need for discipline and coherence in their armies. In 1106 Robert Curthose found himself brought to bay by his brother Henry at Tinchebrai, rather as he had been by his father at Gerberoi in 1079. As then, he decided to risk battle, on a single coherent charge, but he was heavily outnumbered.[7] However, Henry of Huntingdon says that Robert's forces fought well and pressed the enemy hard relying on

[5] On the charge see the literature mentioned above, p. 71, n. 66, 67, although it must be said that this discussion has focussed far too much on the question of the couched lance and insufficiently on the practical problems of marshalling mounted men – far more important for the rise of shock tactics; on the rise of infantry see J. Boussard, 'Les mercenaires au xii siècle. Henri II Plantagenet et les origines de l'armée de métier', *Bibliothèque de l'École des Chartes* 106 (1945–46), 189–224 and Contamine, *War in the Middle Ages*, pp. 70–3.

[6] M. Bennett, '*La Règle du Temple* as a military manual, pp. 7–20, draws attention to the sub-units of ten knights under a commander comparable to the *conroi* discussed by Verbruggen, 'Tactique militaire', 161–80.

[7] On Gerberoi see above, p. 44; H. W. C. Davis, 'The battle of Tinchebrai', *English Historical Review*, 24 (1909), 728–32, 25 (1910), 295–6 estimates that Robert had only 6,000 with 700 cavalry to oppose Henry I's 40,000 including 2,400 cavalry.

the fact that they were 'well trained in the wars of Jerusalem'.[8] It was indeed a hard training which produced coherent armies and ferocious fighters. It was this, their belief in God and themselves, and their able commanders which gave them the victory in the East.

[8] HH, p. 235.

A note on the sources

The astonishing success of the First Crusade inspired some of its participants to record their experiences, either in letters written as events unfolded or in chronicles prepared afterwards. This in turn inspired others and so an extraordinary volume of material appeared in the west in the course of the twelfth century and beyond. This note does not seek to examine all of it let alone repeat or challenge the work of many distinguished commentators. The present writer has sought to look at the crusade as a military campaign and we are concerned here with the problems of understanding what these and other sources used tell us about it. Here I address general problems raised by the main sources for the crusade.

Of the extraordinary value of the letters to the historian of the crusade there can be no doubt. The excitements of battle spring out from the pages of the letters of Stephen of Blois and Anselm of Ribemont as do the terrible sufferings and the sense of loss of comrades. When Stephen, as one of the major leaders, who was actually chosen later to lead the army, speaks of his esteem for the Emperor Alexius and in the same breath speaks of Antioch as the next major goal we must pay attention, for here is the voice of one who was involved in the planning.[1] Anselm's deep mourning for his many dead friends and his valuable information about the loss of horses (supported by the narrative sources) underline the concerns of an important but not leading figure. These men were not wholly disinterested; they show a lively concern for the well-being of their lands in the West and Stephen rejoiced in the acquisition of booty.[2] They are mercifully free from reflection and consideration: it is of great significance that they almost all date from the period before the summer of 1098 and reflect no hostility, and in the case of

---

[1] See above, pp. 165-7. [2] Hagenmeyer, *Kreuzzugsbriefe*, pp. 140, 144, 149.

Stephen of Blois considerable admiration, for the Byzantines. Those of Adhémar and Symeon Patriarch of Jerusalem, testify to good relations between East and West. It is only with the letter from the Princes in September 1098 that hatred of the Byzantines becomes evident and this document, in the form in which we have it, may well have been heavily influenced by Bohemond.[3] This is a vital corrective to certain important latin narratives in which hatred of the Greeks and distortions about their deeds is a dominating factor. The Anonymous, author of the *Gesta Francorum*, shared his nation's contempt for the Greeks and all their works, while Raymond of Aguilers seems to have taken a violent dislike to them in the course of the journey. This has helped to disguise from historians the extent to which there was a community of interest between the Byzantine emperor and the crusading princes until the summer of 1098 when the quarrel over Alexius's desertion at Philomelium and Bohemond's ambition for Antioch resulted in a breach. It is interesting that in the last of the letters which we have, Daimbert's summary of events written in September 1099 in the name of one who was a papal legate with knowledge of Urban's thinking, the issue of relations with the Byzantines is avoided, even though the letter was probably written by Raymond of Aguilers who hated and despised the Greeks.[4] The letters also, to a degree, correct the obvious gap in all the accounts – they are very thin on the journey across Asia Minor, to the extent that reconstructing the route is by no means simple. In fact this may be connected with the anti-Byzantine sentiment which later grew up and led the chroniclers to neglect a period when they were in close alliance with the Greeks. After Dorylaeum, the journey, though hard, was not full of incident and thus was overshadowed by later events.

The accounts of the crusade written by participants were all written after the event and are much more reflective and interpretative. All of them see themselves as recording the work of God. This is most obvious in the case of Raymond of Aguilers whose latest editors have not hesitated to call it 'The book of the lance', analogous to those records of the wonder-working of relics so common at this time in the West. But what Raymond was really trying to do was to show the workings of the divine economy as then understood:

---

[3] Hagenmeyer, *Kreuzzugsbriefe*, pp. 132, 142–4, 161–5.
[4] Hagenmeyer, *Kreuzzugsbriefe*, pp. 168–74.

'For the army of God, even if it bore the punishment of the Lord himself for its sins, out of His compassion also stood forth victor over all paganism'. And the same reflection appears even earlier in the letter of Daimbert of Pisa: 'And so, because some were puffed up at the happy outcome of these events, God opposed to us Antioch, a city impregnable to human might, and detained us there for nine months, and so humbled us in the siege outside the city until every swelling of our arrogance relapsed into humility.'[5]

Thus the nucleus of the idea that the spiritual exercises of the crusade were as important to its success as the military emerged.[6] This emphasis on divine intervention affects all our sources and limits the level of explanation which they give. Thus the victory at Dorylaeum is God's will, according to the Anonymous author of the *Gesta Francorum*.[7] Individual authors, even if eyewitnesses, were also limited in their perceptions by where they were at any given time. Fulcher of Chartres provides an extraordinarily vivid account of the battle of Dorylaeum, from the point of view of a civilian in the camp. But he left the crusade early in 1098 and thereafter relied on others.[8] The Anonymous was in Bohemond's army besieging Nicaea and so knows almost nothing of the major battle with the Turks which took place to the south of the city and gives us the impression that it was a mere skirmish. No writer was present at the Foraging Battle which is obscure in the extreme. Even when our informant was centrally involved in a battle his information is not always very useful. The Anonymous gives us a vivid sense of his participation in the Lake Battle of February 1098 and the passage is deservedly famous, but he does not tell us where the battle took place. Anselm of Ribemont's account of the battle against Kerbogah forgets to mention Godfrey de Bouillon. Such omissions, the consequences of the excitements, alarms and confusions of battle, the proverbial 'fog of war', are a commonplace of military history.[9] The Anonymous was involved in

---

[5] Krey, *First Crusade*, pp. 8, 276.

[6] On which see Blake, 'Formation of the "Crusade Idea"', 11–31.

[7] *GF*, pp. 20–1.

[8] See below, p. 378. On Fulcher and his sources, amongst which was the *Gesta Francorum* see the Introduction to the Hagenmeyer edition.

[9] 'In so far as the battlefield presented itself to the bare eyesight of men, it had no entirety, no length, no breadth, no depth, no size, no shape, and was made up of nothing except small numberless circlets commensurate with such ranges of vision as the mist might allow at each spot ... in such conditions, each separate gathering of English soldiery went on fighting its own little battle in happy and advantageous ignorance of the general state of the action; nay

the heavy fighting outside the citadel of Antioch during the second siege of that city, hence his failure to mention other fighting during this siege, yet he never explains the physical nature of the battlefield as Raymond of Aguilers does exceedingly well.[10] Such are the limitations of the 'worm's eye-view' which is so often that of the eyewitness. Raymond of Aguilers was a better writer, but a priest rather than a military man. He understood the salient fact about Turkish warfare – that the enemy encircled your forces in an effort to demoralise them by archery, but this becomes an *idée fixe* dominating his discussion of every battle, often inappropriately.[11] Raymond is sometimes guilty of trying to tidy up the battlefield, to impose order from chaos, notably at the Lake Battle, and the same can be said of the Anonymous.[12] Overall, the central problem of these eye-witness sources is that they were eye-witnesses with all the narrowness of view that implies. This is especially true of the *Gesta Francorum*. Raymond of Aguilers, as chaplain to the count of Toulouse, was close to the high command of the army and his information on decisions and policy is often good but he was more interested in politics than purely military decisions. However, he does tell us about meetings and discussions, such as that between the leaders near Shaizar and he is very informative on numbers which must have been a real preoccupation in the later stages of the campaign.[13]

By contrast, the Anonymous was an ordinary knight and ill-informed about such matters. But suppositions about the supposed spontaneity and direct simplicity of his account need to be tempered considerably. The best evidence is that his work was written by 1101, which is certainly early. His text was used by Raymond of Aguilers as an *aide mémoire*, especially for the period of the siege of Antioch; thereafter his dependence, always minimal, virtually disappears. His work appeared shortly after that of the Anonymous but certainly before 1105, for the death of the count of Toulouse in that year is never suggested. But there are indications that what we have may not be the text written or dictated by an anonymous South Italian Norman knight in the service of Bohemond. The insertion of

even very often in ignorance that any great conflict was raging.' E. W. Kinglake, *Invasion of the Crimea*, 9 vols. (London, 1901), 6.486 on the battle of Inkerman.
[10] *GF*, pp. 60–2; see above, pp. 275–6 and compare Fig. 13.
[11] See above, pp. 239–47, 283.
[12] See above, pp. 248, 285.   [13] See above, pp. 161, 129, 312.

a passage suggesting that Alexius granted Antioch to Bohemond is patent, while in the description of the fighting around the citadel there are indications of revision and the literary passages may well come from a different hand.[14] But even more notable is the very bland account given in Book X of the *Gesta Francorum* which avoids the issues which divided the army. This blandness is also very evident in Fulcher's account, where its obvious root is that author's concern for the reputation of the house of Boulogne whose servant he was from early 1098 until his death about 1127. Were we to rely on Fulcher and the Anonymous (along with the works heavily based on them) the internal dynamics of the crusader army would be lost to us. This is the great strength of Raymond of Aguilers' account, for all its obvious weaknesses and in particular its reliance on the *Gesta*. Raymond was involved and was a partisan, and while we may distrust his standpoint we can hardly deny that there was a standpoint to take. The divisions of the crusaders after the seizure of Antioch exercised a powerful influence on the course of events, and in any assessment of the success of the crusade it is important to consider the astonishing fact that they succeeded despite them. Moreover, in understanding crusading history as a whole it is a false perspective to see such problems of command as originating later and being a deviation from the spirit of the crusade – they were inevitable and apparent from the first.

Almost all writing about the First Crusade has been dominated by the *Gesta Francorum*. This is, in part, because a work written (apparently) by a layman who participated would seem to be God's gift to historians and there is about it an immediacy and an apparent freshness: it has been indicated here that this may in part be an illusion. It was extensively used by later writers – Bauldry of Dol, Guibert of Nogent, Peter Tudebode and Robert the Monk of Rheims, the anonymous *Historia Belli Sacri* are obvious examples whose works are virtually copies.[15] Other writers, Raymond of Aguilers, Fulcher of Chartres, above all William of Tyre, knew his text or one of its many other derivatives, and *de facto* the idea has grown that the Anonymous's is the 'normal' account of the crusade

---

[14] See above, pp. 16, n. 48, 276.

[15] The attempt to assert the primacy of Tudebode's chronicle by its latest editors, Hill and Hill, appears to founder on the simple fact that the South Italian attitudes of the author are so evident. However, it is recognised that the early textual history of the *Gesta* is probably more complex than has generally been imagined.

and its framework has been built into almost all modern writing. In
fact this is a dangerous illusion. We need to look afresh at events
without this assumption which has been dinned into us largely by
the sheer repetition of the Anonymous's tale. For the most part those
who used his narrative reveal interesting attitudes and interpreta-
tions of events without contributing much to the elucidation of what
happened at the time.[16] Some, however, add useful information:
Peter Tudebode actually went on the crusade on which two of his
brothers died and he adds quite a lot of material, while the *Historia
Belli Sacri* has a considerable value especially on matters concerning
the South Italian Normans.[17]

If the *Gesta*'s story has been overvalued, the very opposite can be
said of that of Albert of Aachen. There is in Albert a great deal of
poetic material, some of it found in the *Chanson d'Antioche* and some
not.[18] The whole question of the relationship between Albert's text
and that of the *Chanson* is highly controversial. It has always seemed
unlikely that the poet (or poets) used Albert because they left out so
much of his picturesque detail. However, the assumption that the
Chanson is based on an earlier work by Richard the Pilgrim, who
actually went on the crusade and therefore has historical value for
events not mentioned by chroniclers, has been severely challenged.[19]
The commonsense solution is that Albert selected material which he
heard in recitations and used it and that some of this was incorpo-
rated into the *Chanson*, often in slightly different form.[20] That Albert
used such material need not detract from his credibility for this was
an age when the distinctions between romance, legend and history
were fine – witness the fabulous passages in the *Gesta*. It has recently
been demonstrated that Albert's work was written shortly after
1102: anything so close to events has to be taken seriously, for the
author would have been open to challenge by living persons. This
same study has freed us from the tyranny of the 'Lost Lorraine
Chronicle' which for over a hundred years has dominated discussion

---

[16] On which see Blake, cited n. 6 above.
[17] PT, pp. 7–9. On *HBS* see above, pp. 163–6, 245–6.
[18] For examples see above, pp. 216–18.
[19] R. F. Cook, *"Chanson d'Antioche", Chanson de Geste: le Cycle de la Croisade est-il épique?*
(Amsterdam, 1980), pp. 40–5 and 49–69. I rather share Cook's scepticism of the historical
value of the *Chanson*. As his 'Nouveau Resumé', pp. 49–69, suggests, there is little of value
and the stories not supported by chronicle evidence appear fabulous and at best distortions.
[20] This is the conclusion of S. Edgington, *A Critical Edition of the Historia Iherosolimitana of Albert
of Aachen*, unpublished Ph.D. thesis, University of London, 1991.

of Albert of Aachen.[21] Albert did not go on the crusade but he seems to have based his story, as he asserts, on the tales of people who did. Often he found it difficult to work out precisely what they were telling him for he did not know the ground – it is clear that he was confused about the location of the gates of Antioch. At other times he seems to have had more than one story about the same thing – as in the case of Guinemer of Boulogne. Overall his sources were men of middling rank – and knights deeply interested in military affairs.[22] This produces much convincing material, but it is episodic, like that of the Anonymous, for his informants were not of a rank to direct events. However, there is so much information in Albert that it is vitally important in building up a picture of crusader operations. Albert was a German and devoted to Godfrey of Bouillon and it was probably to protect his reputation against Bohemond's high standing in the wake of the crusade (so high that the Italians in the crusade of 1101 set out to rescue him from Turkish imprisonment) that Albert disparages him so consistently.[23] It is interesting that Albert does not share the general hostility of the other narrative sources and indeed he sometimes praises Alexius. Even in his account of the skirmishing at Constantinople when his hero Godfrey was involved, he is less than wholehearted in his condemnation.[24] This is important because Albert presumably reflected the attitudes of his informants, men of middling rank who had been on the crusade. This would suggest that hostility to the Greeks was less a general phenomenon than something confined to most of the political leadership and shared by chroniclers for various reasons. However, Albert is generally disparaging about the Provençals and this reinforces what has been said about the isolation of Count Raymond.[25] William of Tyre used Albert's *Historia* extensively and sometimes corrected it but he adds little to our understanding of the events of the crusade.

[21] Once again these are the conclusions of Dr Edgington in Chapter 1 of her thesis. The demolition of the 'Lost Lorraine Chronicle' is very convincing. This is a major contribution to crusader historiography.

[22] See above, pp. 172, 217, 231.

[23] For example see above, pp. 241, 292. Dr Edington points out that, in the early stages of his account, Albert uses honorific descriptions of Bohemond and sometimes praises him, but that later this is dropped. She suggests that this may reflect attitudes amongst returning crusaders. However, the careful denigration of his role at the Foraging Battle and the battle against Kerbogah suggest to me something more deliberate.

[24] I owe perception of the importance of this theme to Dr Edgington.

[25] See above, p. 324.

Given the early date and the nature of his sources Albert's work deserves to be treated as an eyewitness account. From the point of view of the military historian his chief weakness is that of all the narratives – it is episodic. But Albert did try to put his information together to gain a picture of events and he succeeded to a remarkable degree.[26] Perhaps because he was a cleric and not a participant he tells us a lot about methods of weapons and siege-machinery. His own ignorance compelled him to take an overview of events which is highly useful. But, in fact, taking all the Western eyewitness and near-eyewitness sources together the major problem they pose for the military historian is that they tell us little directly about the 'nuts and bolts' of war. They simply assumed this knowledge in the audience for which they wrote and so left posterity the task of teasing it out.

The Islamic sources are radically different. It is possible to get a very good picture of Islamic politics and society at the time of the First Crusade. Nizam al-Mulk had been deeply involved in the government of the Seljuks in the eleventh century which gives his *Book of government* special value. Ibn-Khaldun's *Muqaddima* is of vital importance, not least because he gives us insights into the waging of war in the Islamic world. There is a considerable literature which informs us about the methods and organisation of war, but on the events of the crusade the information is very limited. This is hardly surprising for from their perspective the crusade was hardly a glorious episode. Ibn al-Qalanisi's *Damascus chronicle of the crusades*, written about half a century after the First Crusade, is very brief. Kemal ad-Din wrote his *Chronicle of Aleppo* in the early thirteenth century on the basis of earlier material, and it provides a very interesting and useful account of events in North Syria without adding much to the western sources. Ibn al-Athir's remarkable *World history* was also written in the thirteenth century using earlier material but it is not especially useful for the Crusade. No source gives us any real insight into the Turks of Asia Minor about whom we are abysmally ignorant. By contrast the Islamic manuals of war such as those edited by Cahen, Latham, and Paterson and Scanlin, are very valuable even though many of them were written much later. The greatest gap which all this leaves is information about the

---

[26] His account of events at Edessa is remarkably accurate. Beaumont, 'Albert of Aix and the county of Edessa', pp. 101–38 discussed this long ago and Dr Edgington's thesis reinforces the point.

Turks and in particular about their horses. The skill of these horse-archers was much admired, but we do not know how they cared for their animals and even whether they used strings of them to support their tactics.[27]

The Armenian *Chronicle* of Matthew of Edessa, written about 1140, is very valuable for the information it provides on relations between the Armenians and their former Byzantine overlords and new friends or enemies from the West. Michael the Syrian was Jacobite Patriarch of Antioch (1166–99) but his Syriac account is not very informative on the events of the First Crusade. Anna Comnena's *Alexiad* is informative, but it is also the most mendacious of the sources. She presents the Crusade as some natural disaster which fell upon the empire, never admitting that her father had asked for Western aid and she never admits his debt to its success. Her whole account, written forty years after the event, is coloured by hindsight and in particular by the question of Antioch which would so concern Alexius and his two immediate successors. Anna is contemptuous of the barbarian Franks whom she denounces as untrustworthy while at the same time praising her father's cunning tricks. If her attitudes were widely shared by the Byzantine upper class one can perhaps understand the deep hostility to Byzantium which was generated in the ranks of the crusaders.

The spate of translations of oriental sources in the years since Runciman's *History of the crusades* has given us more insight into conditions in the East but the essential story of the crusade must still be written from the Western, and in particular the eyewitness, accounts. Amongst these that of Albert of Aachen is the most important from a military point of view. The production of a new edition and translation should help to reduce our excessive dependence on the Anonymous *Gesta Francorum* the text of which though valuable, is not as simple as has been believed and will not bear the weight of scholarly interpretation piled upon it.

---

[27] For a detailed discussion of the Oriental sources see Cahen, *Syrie du Nord*, pp. 33–93 and Sivan, *L'Islam et la croisade*, pp. 23–37.

Select bibliography

1. BIBLIOGRAPHIES

Atiya, A. S. *The Crusade; Historiography and Bibliography* (London, 1962)
Cahen, C. *Jean Sauvaget's Introduction to the History of the Muslim East* (Berkeley and Los Angeles, 1965)
Cresswell, K. A. C. *A Bibliography of Arms and Armour in Islam* (London, 1956)
Lewis B. and Holt, P. M. *Historians of the Middle East* (London, 1962)
Mayer, H. E. *Bibliographie zur Geschichte der Kreuzzuge* (Hanover, 1965)
Mayer H. E. and J. McLellan, 'Select Bibliography of the Crusades', *Crusades*, 6. 511–664
Pearson, J. D. *Index Islamicus 1906–55* (Cambridge, 1958) and Supplements 1982–

2. ENCYCLOPAEDIAS AND LARGE COLLECTIVE WORKS

Cambridge History of Islam 2 vols (Cambridge, 1970).
Cambridge Medieval History vol. 4 (Cambridge, 1966/67)
New Catholic Encyclopaedia of America, ed. W. J. McDonald *et al.* 17 vols. (Washington, 1967)
Niermeyer, J. F., *Mediae Latinitatis Lexicon minus* (Leiden, 1976)
Setton, K. and M. W. Baldwin, (eds.), *A History of the Crusades* (Pennsylvania, 1959–89)
The Encyclopaedia of Islam, ed. H. A. R. Gibb *et al.* (Leiden and London, 1960–)

3. WESTERN SOURCES

Abbo, *Siège de Paris par les Normands* ed. and tr. H. Waquet (Paris, 1942)
Acta sanctorum quotquot toto orbe coluntur, ed. Société des Bollandistes, 70 vols. so far (Antwerp, Rome, Brussels, 1643 ff.)
Adhémar de Chabannes, *Chronique* ed. J. Chavanon (Paris, 1897)
Albert of Aachen, *Historia Hierosolymitana*, *RHC Oc.* 4
Amato di Monte Cassino, ed. V. Bartholomaeis (Rome, 1935)

383

The Anglo-Saxon Chronicle, ed. D. Whitelock (London, 1961)

Annales Altahenses maiores, MGH SS 20

Annales Aquicinctini, MGH SS 16

Annales Casinenses, MGH SS 19

Annales Egmundani, MGH SS 16

Annales Hersfeldenses, MGH SS 3. 18–116

Annales Hildesheimnenses, MGH SS 3

Annales Sancti Pauli Virdunensis, MGH SS 16

Annales Seligenstadenses, MGH SS 17

Annalista Saxo, MGH SS 6

Anonymi Florinensis brevis narratio belli sacri, RHC Oc. 5

Anonymi Gesta Francorum, ed. H. Hagenmeyer (Heidelberg, 1890)

Bartolf of Nangis, *Gesta Francorum Iherusalem expugnantium, RHC Oc.* 3

Bauldry of Dol, *Historia Jerosolimitana, RHC Oc.* 4

The Bayeux Tapestry, ed. D. M. Wilson (London, 1985)

Bernardus Scholasticus, *Liber de miraculis sanctae Fidis PL* 141

Caffaro, *De liberatione civitatum orientis, RHC Oc.* 5

Carmen de Hastingae Proelio eds. C. Morton and H. Munz (Oxford, 1972)

E. Caspar, *Das register Gregors VII*, 2 vols. (Berlin, 1922–23)

La Chanson d'Antioche, ed. S. Duparc-Quioc, 2 vols. (Paris, 1977–8)

Chronica monasterii Casinensis, MGH SS 34

Chronicon monasterii sancti Petri Aniciensis, ed. C. U. J. Chevalier, Collection de cartulaires dauphinois (1884–91), 8, 1

La Chronique de Saint-Maixent 751–1140, ed. J. Verdon (Paris, 1979)

Chronique de Zimmern ed. H. Hagenmeyer, *Archives de l'Orient Latin* 2 (1884) 17–88

Chronique de Saint-Pierre-le-Vif de Sens, dite de Clarius, eds. R. H. Bautier and M. Gilles (Paris, 1979)

von Clausewitz, K. P. G. *Vom Kriege* (Berlin, 1832–4),vols. 1–3 of his collected works. Tr. into English J.J. Graham (London, 1873) revised F. N. Maude (London, 1908)

Recueil des chartes de l'abbaye de Cluny, ed. A. Bernard and A. Bruel, 6 vols. (Paris, 1876–1903)

De nobili genere Crispinorum PL 150. 735–44

Diplomatic documents preserved in the Public Record Office (London, 1964)

Edgington, S. *A critical edition of the Historia Iherosolimitana of Albert of Aix*, unpublished Ph.D. thesis, University of London, (1991)

Ekkehard of Aura, *Chronicon universale, MGH SS* 6

Hierosolymita, RHC Oc. 5

Flandria Generosa, MGH SS 9

Florence of Worcester, *Chronicon*, ed. B. Thorpe, 2 vols. (London, 1848–9)

Florinensis brevis narratio belli sacri RHC Oc. 5

'Fragment d'une Chanson d'Antioche en Provençal', ed. P. Meyer, *Archives de l'Orient Latin* 2 (1884) 467–509

France, J. 'The text of the account of the capture of Jerusalem in the Ripoll manuscript, Bibliothèque nationale (latin) 5132', *English Historical Review* 103 (1988), 640–57

Fulcher of Chartres, *Historia Hierosolymitana*, ed. H. Hagenmeyer (Heidelberg, 1913). English translation by H. S. Fink, *A History of the expedition to Jerusalem* (Knoxville, 1969).

Fulk le Réchin, *Fragmentum historiae Andegavensis*, ed. L. Halphen and R. Poupardin, *Chroniques des comtes d'Anjou et des seigneurs d'Amboise* (Paris, 1913), 206–45

Gallia christiana in provincias ecclesiasticas distributa, ed. Congregation of St Maur *et al.*, 16 vols. (Paris, 1715–1865)

Gerald of Wales, *Opera* ed. J. S. Brewer and J. Dimock, 8 vols. (London, 1867–91)

Gesta Adhemari Episcopi Podiensis RHC Oc. 5

Gesta Ambaziensium dominorum, Chroniques d'Anjou, 158–225

Gesta Comitum Andegavorum, Chroniques des comtes d'Anjou, 34–157

Gesta Comitum Barcinonensium ed. L. Barrau-Dihigo and J. Masso Torrents (Barcelona, 1925)

Gesta Francorum et aliorum Hierosolimitanorum, ed. R. Hill (London, 1962)

*Gesta Triumphalia Pisanorum in captione Jerusalem RHC Oc.*5

Gesta Francorum Iherusalem Expugnantium RHC Oc. 3

Gilo, *Historia de via Hierosolymitana, RHC Oc.* 5

Giselbert of Mons, *Chronique* ed. L. Vanderkinadere (Brussels, 1904)

Rodulfus Glaber Opera ed. J. France (Oxford, 1989)

Guibert of Nogent, *De vita sua*, ed. E.-R. Labande (Paris, 1981)

Gesta Dei per Francos, RHC Oc. 4

Hagenmeyer, H. *Die Kreuzzugsbriefe aus den Jahren 1088–1100* (Innsbruck, 1902)

Henry of Huntingdon, *De captione Antiochiae a Christianis, RHC Oc.* 5

Historia Anglorum, ed. T. Arnold (1879)

Histoire de Guillaume le Maréchal, ed. P. Meyer, 3 vols. (Paris, 1891–1901)

Historia Belli Sacri RHC Oc. 3

Historia Francicae fragmenta, in *Recueil des historiens des Gaules et de la France* 11.180–62 (Paris, 1869–1904)

Historia peregrinorum euntium Jerusolymam, RHC Oc. 3

Hugh of Flavigny, *Chronicon, MGH SS* 8

Hugh of Fleury, *Historia regum Francorum, MGH SS* 9

Jaffé, P. *Regesta pontificum Romanorum*, 2nd edn, 2 vols. (Leipzig, 1885–8)

Kehr, P. F. 'Papsturkunden in Spanien', I. 'Katalanien', *Abh. Gott.* 18 (1926) 'Navarra und Aragon', 22 (1928)

Regesta pontificum Romanorum. Italia pontificia, 10 vols. (1906–75)

Krey, A. C. *The First Crusade*, (Princeton, Gloucester, 1921, 1958)

Lambert of Hersfeld, *Annales, MGH SS* 3

Landulf the Younger of Milan, *Historia Mediolanensis, MGH SS* 20

Leo Marsicanus and Peter the Deacon, *Chronica Monasterii Casinensis* ed. H. Hoffman (Hanover, 1981)

Lowenfeld, S. *Epistolae pontificum Romanorum ineditae* (Rome, 1885)

Lupus Protospatarius, *Annales, MGH SS* 5

Mainz Anonymous, tr. S. Eidelberg, *The Jews and the Crusaders* (1977)

Geoffrey Malaterra, *De rebus gestis Rogerii Calabriae et Siciliae Comitis*, ed. E. Pontieri in *Muratori, L. A. Rerum Italicarum Scriptores*, NS 5, 1, (Bologna, 1928)

Marianus Scotus, *Chronicon, MGH SS* 5

Narratio Floriacensis de captis Antiochia et Hierosolyma, RHC Oc. 5

Notitiae duae Lemovicenses de praedicatione crucis in Aquitania, RHC Oc. 5

Odo of Cluny, *Life of St Gerald* ed. and tr. G. Sitwell (New York, 1958)

Ordericus Vitalis, *Historia aecclesiastica*, ed. M. Chibnall, 6 vols. (Oxford, 1969–79)

Otto of Freising, *Chronica*, ed. A. Hofmeister (1912)
  Gesta Frederici I, Imperatoris, ed. G. Waitz (1912)

Peter of Blois, *De Hierosolymitano peregrinatione acceleranda, PL* 207

Peter Tudebode, *Historia de Hierosolymitano itinere*, ed. J. H. and L. L. Hill (Philadelphia, 1974)

Pflugk-Hartting, J. von *Acta pontificum Romanorum inedita*, 3 vols. (1881–6)

Ralph of Caen, *Gesta Tancredi, RHC Oc.*3

Raymond of Aguilers, *Liber*, ed. J. H. and L. L. Hill (Paris, 1969)

Riant, P. 'Inventaire critique des lettres historiques des croisades', *Archives de l'Orient Latin*, 1 (Paris, 1881) 1–224

Richer de Rheims, *Histoire de France* ed. and tr. R. Latouche 2 vols. (Paris, 1930)

Robert of Torigni, *Chronica*, ed. R. Howlett (1889)

Robert the Monk, *Historia Iherosolimitana, RHC Oc.*3

Roger of Hovenden, *Chronica Magistri Rogeris de Hovenden* ed. W. Stubbs, 4 vols. (London, Rolls Series, 1871)

St. Chaffre du Monastier: C. U. J. Chevalier, *Cartulaire de l'abbaye de St. Chaffre du Monastier, Collection de cartulaires dauphinois* (1986–1912), 8, 1

Guérard, B. E. C. *Cartulaire de l'abbaye de Saint-Père de Chartres*, 2 vols. (Paris, 1840)

Schwarz, U. (ed.) *Amalfi im Frühen Mittelalter*, (Tubingen, 1978)

Sigebert of Gembloux, *Chronica, MGH SS* 6

Sigeberti Gemblacensis chronica auctarium Aquicinense, MGH SS 6

Somerville, R. *The Councils of Urban II. 1: Decreta Claromontensia* (London, 1972)

Suger of St-Denis, *Vita Ludovici Grossi Regis*, ed. H. Waquet (Paris, 1929)

Urban II, *Epistolae et Privilegia, PL* 151

Van Hasselt, A. 'Document inédit pour servir à l'histoire des croisades', *Annales de l'académie d'archéologie de Belgique*, 6 (1849)

Vegetius, *De Re Militari*, ed. C. Lang (Leipzig, 1885). English translation in T. R. Phillips, *The Roots of Strategy* (London, 1943)

Vercauteren, F. *Actes des comtes de Flandre 1071–1128* (1938)

de Vic C. et J.J. Vaisette, *Histoire Générale de Languedoc*, 5 vols. (Paris, 1743–45)

Vita Beati Rotberti de Arbrissello, PL 162

Vita Heinrici IV imperatoris, ed. W. Eberhard (Hanover, 1899)

Wace's Roman de Rou et des Ducs de Normandie, ed. H. Andresen 2 vols. (Bonn, 1877–9)

William of Apulia, *La Geste de Robert Guiscard*, ed. M.Mathieu (Palermo, 1961)

William of Jumièges, *Gesta Normannorum Ducum*, ed. J. Marx (Paris, 1914)

William of Malmesbury, *Gesta regum Anglorum*, ed. T. D. Hardy, 2 vols. (London, 1840)

William of Poitiers, *Gesta Guillelmi ducis Normannorum et regis Anglorum* ed. R. Foreville (Paris, 1952)

William of Tyre, *Historia rerum in partibus transmarinis gestarum, RHC Oc.* 1. There is a new edition by R. B. C.Huygens, *Corpus Christianorum,Continuatio Medievalis* 2 vols. (Tournhoult, 1986). English tr. E. Babcock and A. C. Krey, *A History of Deeds Done Beyond the Sea*, Columbia Records of Civilisation, 35 (New York, 1943).

4. EASTERN SOURCES

Abu'l Feda, *Moslem Annals RHC Or.* 1

al-Andalusi: 'Ali b. 'Abd al-Rahman b. Hudhyl, *Hiyat al-Fursan wa Shi'ar al-Shuzan* ed. L. Mercier (Paris, 1923).

Anna Comnena, *Alexiad* tr. E. R. A. Sewter (London, 1969)

'Anonymous Syriac Chronicle', ed. and tr. A. S. Tritton and H. A. R. Gibb, *Journal of the Royal Asiatic Society* (1933), 69–101

Attaliates, *Historia* ed. J. Bekker (Bonn, 1853)

Bar-Hebraeus: *The Chronography of Gregory Abû'l Faraj, the son of Aaron, the Hebrew physician commonly known as Bar-Hebraeus, being the First Part of his Political History of the World* ed. E. A. W. Budge, 2 vols. (London, Amsterdam, 1932, 1976)

al-Bundari, al-Fath inb ali, *Dawolt al Seljuq* (Cairo, 1900)

Cahen, C. 'La chronique abrígée d'al-Azimi', *Journal Asiatique*, 230 (1938), 353–448

Bar Nathan (Eliezer), *Chronicle*, tr. S. Eidelberg, *The Jews and the Crusaders* (Wisconsin, 1977)

Bar Simson, (Solomon) *Chronicle*, in S. Eidelberg, *The Jews and the Crusaders* (Wisconsin, 1977)

al-Hakimi, Umura ibn Ali, *Tarikh al-Yaman* ed. and tr. H. C. Cassels Kay (London, 1982)

al-Hanafi, Muhammed ben Isn ben Isma'il, *Nihayat al-sud* ed. A. L. S. Muhammad Lutful-Huq unpublished Ph.D. thesis, University of London (1955)

Ibn al-Athir, *Al-Kamil fi al Tarikh* ed. K. Tornberg, 12 vols. (Beirut, 1966). Also as 'Sum of World History', *RHC Or.* 1–2

Ibn al-Nadim, *The Fihrist of al-Nadim* tr. B.Dodge (New York, 1970)

Ibn al-Qalanisi, *Damascus Chronicle of the Crusades* extracts ed. and tr. H. A. R. Gibb (London, 1967)

Ibn Khallikan, *Ibn Khallikan's Biographical Dictionary,* ed. and tr. Mac-Guckin de Slane, 4 vols. (Beirut, 1843, 1970).

Ibn Khaldun, *The Muqaddima: an introduction to history* ed. and tr. F. Rosenthal, abridged N. J. Dawood (Princeton, 1967)

Kemal ad-Din, 'Chronicle of Aleppo', *RHC Or.* 3

Latham, J. D. and W. F. Paterson (eds.), *Saracen Archery* [an edition of the 14/15th century work *Essential Archery for beginners* by Taybugha l-Ashrafi l-Baklamishi l-Yunani] (London, 1970)

Lewis, B. *Islam from the Prophet Mahommed to the capture of Constantinople* 2 vols. (London, 1974)

Life of St Nerses, extracts, ed. and tr. M. Canard in 'Les Armémiens en Egypte à l'époque fatamite', *Annales de l'Institut des Etudes Orientales*, 12 (1954), 84–113

al-Makhzumi, extracts, ed. and tr. C. Cahen, 'L'Administration financière de l'armée fatamide d'après al-Makhzumi', *Journal of the Economic and Social History of the Orient*, 15 (1972), 164–9

Matthew of Edessa, 'Chronique' *RHC Ar.* 1. [See also Matthew of Edessa, *Chronicle* ed. and tr. A. E. Dostourian, unpublished Ph.D. thesis, University of Rutgers, 1975.]

Michael the Syrian, *Chronique de Michel le Syrien, Patriarche Jacobite d'Antioche 1166–99* ed. and tr. J. B. Chabot (Brussels, 1963, reprint of 1899 –1910 edition)

al-Mulk, Nizam *Traité de gouvernement composé pour le Sultan Malik Shah* ed. C. Schefer, 2 vols. (Paris, 1892–93). There is also an English translation, *The Book of Government or Rules for Kings* ed. and tr. H.Darke (New York, 1960).

Naser-e Khosraw, *The Book of Travels* tr. W. M. Thackston (New York, 1986). Extracts by B. Lewis in *Islam from Mohammed to the Capture of Constantinople*, vol. 1 *Politics and War* (New York, 1974)

al-Rahman, Abd al-Rahman ibn Muhammed, *Histoire de Jérusalem et Hébron* ed. H. Sauvaire (Paris, 1876)

Ravandi, Muhammad b. Ali b.Sulaiman, *Rabat al-sudur wa ayatal surur* ed. M. Iqtal (Leiden and London, 1921)

Scanlin, G. *A Moslem Manual of War* (Cairo, 1960)

Scriptorum Arabum loci Abbadidis ed. R. Dozy, 3 vols. (Leyden, 1846–63)

Tarsusi, Murda ben Ali, *Tabsira Arbub al-albad*, extracts ed. and tr. C. Cahen, 'Un traité d'armurie composé pour Saladin', *Bulletin d'Etudes Orientales*, 12 (1948), 103–63

Usama, An Arab-Syrian Gentleman and Warrior in the Period of the Crusades, ed. and tr. P. Hitti (New York, 1929)

SECONDARY WORKS

Abel, F. M. 'L'état de la cité de Jérusalem au xiiᵉ siècle', *Records of the Pro-Jerusalem Council* ed. C. R. Ashbee (London, 1924)

Abulafia, A. S. 'The interrelationship between the Hebrew chronicles on the first crusade', *Journal of Semitic Studies*, 27 (1982) 221–39

Abulafia, D. *The Two Italies* (Cambridge, 1977)

'The Norman kingdom of Africa and the Norman expeditions to Majorca and the Moslem Mediterranean', *Battle*, 7 (1984) 26–49.

d'Adhémar-Laubaume, G. J. *Adhémar de Monteil, légat du pape sur la première croisade* (Le Puy, 1910).

Ahrweiler, H. *Byzance et la mer*, Bibliothèque byzantine. Etudes 5 (Paris, 1966)

'L'organisation des campagnes militaires à Byzance', in Parry and Yapp, eds. *War, Technology and Society*, pp. 89–96

Alphandéry, P. and A. Dupront, *La Chrétienité et l'idée de croisade*, 2 vols. (Paris, 1954–9)

Amouroux-Mourad, M. *Le Comté d'Edesse 1098–1150* (Paris, 1988)

Anderson, R. and R. C. Anderson, *The Sailing Ship* (London, 1926)

Andressohn, J. C. *Ancestry and Life of Godfrey de Bouillon* (Bloomington, 1947)

Angold, M. *The Byzantine Empire 1025–1204* (London, 1984)

'The Byzantine state on the eve of Manzikert', in Bryer, ed. *Manzikert to Lepanto*, pp. 9–34

Arnold, B. *German knighthood 1050–1300* (Oxford, 1985)

Princes and Territory (Cambridge, 1991)

Ashtor, E. *A Social and Economic History of the Near East in the Middle Ages* (London, 1976)

Aube, P. *Godfroi de Bouillon* (Paris, 1985)

Ayalon, D. 'Preliminary remarks on the Mamluk military institution in Islam', in Parry and Yapp, eds., *War, Technology and Society*, pp. 44–58

The Mamluk Military Society: Collected Studies (London, 1979)

Bach, E. *La cité de Gênes au XIIᵉ siècle* (Copenhagen, 1955)

Bachrach, B. S. 'Charles Martel, shock combat, the stirrup and feudalism', *Studies in Medieval and Renaissance History*, 7 (1970), 45–75

'The feigned retreat at Hastings', *Medieval Studies*, 33 (1971), 344–7

'Was the Marchfield part of the Frankish constitution?', *Medieval Studies*, 36 (1974)

'A study in feudal politics: relations between Fulk Nerra and William the Great, 995–1030' *Viator*, 7 (1976), 111–22.

'Some observations on the military administration of the Norman Conquest', *Battle*, 8 (1985), 1–26

'On the orgins of William the Conqueror's horse transports', *Technology and Culture*, 26 (1985), 505–31

'The practical use of Vegetius's De Re Militari in the early Middle Ages', *The Historian*, 21–7 (1985), 239–55

Bachrach, J. L. 'African Military Slaves in the Medieval Middle East: Iraq (869–951) and Egypt (868–1171)', *International Journal of Middle Eastern Studies*, 13 (1981), 471–95

Baker, R. (ed.), *Religious Motivation: Biographical and Sociological Problems for the Church Historian, Studies in Church History*, 15 (Oxford, 1978)

Barber, R. *Knight and Chivalry*, (London, 1970)

Barclay, C. N. *Battle 1066* (London, 1966)

Barlow, F. *William Rufus* (London, 1983)

Bartlett, R. 'Technique militaire et pouvoir politique, 900–1300', *Annales: Economies, Sociétés, Civilisations* 41 (1986), 1135–59

Bates, D. *Normandy before 1066* (London, 1982)

Bathe, D. *Seven Centuries of Sea Travel* (London, 1972)

Bautier, R. H. 'Points de vue sur les relations économiques des occidentaux avec les pays d'Orient au moyen âge', in Mollat, ed., *Colloque* (1966) *The Economic Development of Medieval Europe*, tr. H. Karolji (London, 1971)

Beaumont, A. A. 'Albert of Aix and the county of Edessa', in Paetow ed, *Munro*, pp. 101–38.

Becker, A. *Papst Urban II (1088–1099)*, 1 (Stuttgart, 1964)

Beech, G. 'Participation of Aquitainians in the Conquest of England 1066–1100' *Battle*, 9 (1986) 1–24

Beeler, J. *Warfare in England, 1066–1189*, (Cornell, 1966) *Warfare in Feudal Europe 730–1200* (New York, 1971) 'Towards a re-evaluation of medieval English Generalship', *Journal of British Studies*, 3, 1–10

Belke, K. *et al.*, (eds.), *Tabula Imperii Byzantini*, 5 vols. (Vienna, 1977–84)

Bender, K. H. and H. Kléber eds., *Les Épopées des Croisades. Proceedings of the Trèves Colloquium, 6–11 August 1984* (Stuttgart, 1987)

Bennett, M. 'Wace and warfare', *Battle*, 11 (1988), 37–58 'La Règle du Temple as a military manual, or How to deliver a cavalry charge', in Harper-Bill *et al.*, eds., *Allen-Brown* pp. 7–20

van Bercham M. 'Notes sur les croisades', *Journal Asiatique*, 1 (1902), 420–48

Beresford, G. 'Goltho Manor Lincolnshire; the building and the surrounding defences, c. 850–1150', *Battle*, 4 (1981), 13–36

Beshir, B. J. *Fatamid Caliphate 975–1094*, unpublished Ph.D. thesis, University of London 1970 'Fatimid Military Organisation', *Der Islam*, 55. 1 (1978), 37–56

Blair, C. *European Arms and Armour* (London, 1958)

Blake, E. O. 'The Formation of the "Crusade Idea"', *Journal of Ecclesiastical History*, 21 (1970), 11–31

Blake, E. O. and C. Morris, 'A hermit goes to war; Peter and the origins of the First Crusade', in Shiels, ed., *Monks, Hermits* (Oxford, 1985), pp. 79–107

Bloch, M. *Feudal Society* (Paris, 1961)

Blok D. P. *et al.* (ed.), *Miscellanea Medievalia in memoriam J. F. Niermeyer* (Gronigen, 1967)

Blondal, S. *The Varangians of Byzantium*, tr. and revised B. Benedikz (Cambridge, 1978)

Boase, T. S. R. *The Cilician Kingdom of Armenia* (Edinburgh and London, 1978)

Boehm, L. 'Die 'Gesta Tancredi" des Rodulf von Caen. Ein Beitrage zur Geschichsschreibung der Normannen um 100', *Historischer Jahrbuch*, 75 (1956), 47–72

'"Gesta Dei per Francos" – oder "Gesta Francorum". Die Kreuzzuge als historiographisches Problem', *Saeculum*, 8 (1957)

Boissonade, P. *De nouveau sur la Chanson de Roland* (Paris, 1923)

'Cluny, la Papauté et la première croisade internationale contre les Sarrasins d'Espagne: Barbastro 1064–65', *Revue des Questions Historiques*, 117 (1932), 237–301

'Les premières croisades françaises en Espagne: Normands, Gascons, Aquitains et Bourguignons (1018–32)', *Bulletin Hispanique*, 36 (1934), 5–28

'Le premier cycle de la Croisade' *Le Moyen Age*, 63 (1957), 311–28

Bosworth, C. E. 'Military Organisation under the Buyids', *Oriens*, 18/19 (1965–6)

'Turks in the Islamic lands up to the mid eleventh century', *Fundamenta Philologiae Turcicae*, *Pt 2 Les Turcs musulman avant les Ottomans* (Wiesbaden, 1970), 1–20

'Recruitment, muster and review in medieval Islamic armies', in Parry and Yapp, eds. Parry, *War, Technology and Society*, pp. 60–77

Bouchier, E. S. *A Short History of Antioch* (Oxford, 1921)

Boudot-Lamotte, A. *Contribution à l'étude de l'archerie musulmane* (Damascus, 1968)

Boussard, J. 'Les mercenaires au XIIᵉ siècle. Henri II Plantagenet et les origines de l'armée de métier', *Bibliothèque de l'École des Chartes* 106 (1945–6), 189–224

Bradbury, J. 'Greek Fire in the West', *History Today* (1979), 326–31

'Battles in England and Normandy 1066–1154', *Battle*, 6 (1983), 1–12

The Medieval Archer (Woodbridge, 1985)

The Medieval Siege (Woodbridge, 1992)

Bréhier, L. 'Les aventures d'un chef normand en Orient au XI siècle', *Revue des Cours et Conférences*, 20 (1911–12), 99–112

L'Eglise et l'Orient au moyen âge (Paris, 1921)

Adhémar de Monteil: un évêque à la première croisade (Le Puy, 1923)

'La marine de Byzance du VIIIᵉ au XIᵉ siècle.', *Byzantion* 19 (1949), 1–16

Brett, M. 'The military interest of the Battle of Haydaran', in Parry and Yapp, eds., *War, Technology and Society*, pp. 78–88

Brice, W. C. 'The Turkish colonisation of Anatolia', *Bulletin of the John Rylands Library*, 38 (1955), 18–44

Brown, D. *Bury My Heart at Wounded Knee* (London, 1971)
Brown, P. *The World of Late Antiquity* (London, 1971)
Brown, R. A. *The Normans and the Norman Conquest* (London, 1969)
    'The Battle of Hastings', *Battle*, 3 (1980) 1–21
    The Battle of Hastings and the Norman Conquest (London, 1982)
    'The status of the Norman knight', in Gillingham and Holt, eds., *War and Government*, 18–32
Brown, S. D. B. 'The mercenary and his master: military service and monetary reward in the eleventh and twelfth century', *History*, 74 (1989), 20–38
Bryer, A. and M. Ursinus, (ed.), *Manzikert to Lepanto: the Byzantine World and the Turks 1071–1571, Byzantinische Forschungen*, 16 (Amsterdam, 1991)
Recueil des travaux offerts à M. Clovis Brunel, 2 vols. (Paris, 1955)
Bundari, *Daulat al-Saljaq* (Cairo, 1318/1900–1)
Brundage, J. A., 'Adhemar of Puy: the bishop and his critics', *Speculum*, 34 (1959), 201–12
    'An errant crusader: Stephen of Blois', *Traditio*, 16 (1960), 380–95
    Medieval Canon Law and the Crusader (Wisconsin, 1969)
    'The army of the First Crusade and the Crusade Vow: some reflections on a recent book', *Mediaeval Studies*, 33 (1971)
    'Prostitution, miscegenation and sexual purity in the First Crusade', in Edbury, ed., *Crusade and Settlement*, pp. 57–65
Bur, M. *La Formation du comté de Champagne, v. 950 – v. 1150* (Nancy, 1977)
Byrne, E. H. 'The Genoese colonies in Syria', in Paetow, ed., *Munro*, pp. 139–82
Cahen, C. 'La campagne de Mantzikert d'après les sources Mussulmanes', *Byzantion* 9 (1934),613–42
    La Syrie du Nord à l'époque des Croisades (Paris, 1940)
    'Un traité d'armurerie composé pour Saladin', *Bulletin d'Etudes orientales de l'Institut Français de Damas* 12 (1947/8), 103–63
    'Contribution à l'histoire de l'Iqta du IXe au XIIIe siècle', *Annales de l'Histoire Économique et Sociale*, 8 (1953), 25–62
    'The Turkish invasion: the Selchukids', in Setton and Baldwin, eds., *Crusades*, 1. 135–76
    'Douanes et commerce dans les ports méditerranéens de l'Egypte médiévale', *Journal of the Economic and Social History of the Orient* (1965), 217–314
    Pre-Ottoman Turkey (London, 1968)
    'Les changements techniques militaires dans la Proche Orient médiévale et leur importance historique', in Parry and Yapp, eds., *War, Technology and Society*, pp. 113–124
Calder, W. M. and G. E. Bean, *A Classical Map of Asia Minor* (London, 1959)

Canard, M. 'La guerre sainte dans le monde islamique et le monde chrétien', *Revue africaine*, 79 (1936), 605–23

Cardini, F. 'Profilo di un crociato: Guglielmo Embriaco, *Archivio Storico Italiano*, 136 (1978), 417–18
  'La société italienne et les croisades', *Cahiers de Civilisation Médiévale*, 28 (1985), 19–33

Cazel, F. A. ed., *Feudalism and Liberty* (Baltimore, 1961)

Cate, J. L. 'The Crusade of 1101', in Setton and Baldwin, eds., *Crusades*, 1, 343–67

Chalandon, F. *Essai sur le règne d'Alexis I Comnène (1081–1118)* (Paris, New York, 1900, 1971)
  Histoire de la Domination normande en Italie et en Sicile 2 vols. (Paris, New York, 1907, 1969)

Charanis, P. 'Aims of the medieval crusaders and how they were seen by Byzantium', *Church History*, 21 (1952). Note on the same subject in *Am.H.R.* 53 (1948)
  'The Byzantine Empire on the eve of the crusades', in Setton and Baldwin, eds., *Crusades* 1 177–219

Chaurand, J. 'La conception de l'histoire de Guibert de Nogent', *Cahiers de Civilisation Médiévale*, 8 (1965), 381–95

Chazan, R. '1007–1012: the initial crisis for northern European Jewry', *Proceedings of the American Academy for Jewish Research*, 38–9 (1970–71), 101–117

Cheynet, J. C. 'Mantzikert. Un désastre militaire?', *Byzantion*, 50 (1980), 410–38

Chibnall, M. 'Mercenaries and the "Familia Regis" under Henry i', *History*, 62 (1977), 15–23
  'Castles in Ordericus Vitalis', in Harper-Bill, *et al.* eds., *Allen-Brown*, pp. 43–56
  'Military service in Normandy before 1066', *Battle* 5 (1982), 65–77

Ciggaar, K. 'England and Byzantium on the eve of the Norman Conquest' *Battle*, 5 (1982), 78–96

Cirlot, V. 'Techniques guerrières en Catalogne féodale; le maniement de la lance', *Cahiers de Civilisation Médiévale* 28 (1985), 36–43

Citarella, A. 'The relations of Amalfi with the Arab world before the Crusades', *Speculum*, 42 (1967), 299–312

Cohen, C. 'Un texte peu connu relatif au commerce oriental d'Amalfi au X siècle', *Archivio Storico Napoletana*, 39 (1955), 61–7

Colliot, R. 'Rencontres du moine Raoul Glaber avec le diable d'après ses histoires', *Le Diable au Moyen-Age* (Paris, Aix-en-Provence, 1979)

Conder, C. R. and H. H. Kitchener, *Survey of Western Palestine*, 4 vols. (1881–83)

Constable, G. 'The Financing of the Crusades in the Twelfth Century', in Kedar, *et al.* eds., *Outremer*, pp. 64–88

Contamine, P. *War in the Middle Ages*, tr. M. Jones (London, 1984)

Cook, D. R. 'Norman military revolution in England', *Battle*, 1 (1978), 94–102

Cook, R. R. *"Chanson d'Antioche", Chanson de Geste: le cycle de la croisade est-il épique?* (Amsterdam, 1980)

Cowdrey, H. E. J. 'Bishop Ermenford of Sion and the penitential ordinance following the battle of Hastings', *Journal of Ecclesiastical History*, 20 (1969), 225–42

   The Cluniacs and the Gregorian Reform (Oxford, 1970)

   'Pope Urban II's Preaching of the First Crusade', *History*, 55 (1970), 177–88

   'The Peace and the Truce of God in the Eleventh Century', *Past and Present*, 46 (1970), 42–67

   'Pope Gregory VII's "Crusading" Plans of 1074', in Kedar, et al. *Outremer*, pp. 27–40

   'Genesis of the crusades: springs of Western ideas of Holy War', in Murphy, ed., *Holy War*, pp. 9–32

   'The Mahdia Campaign of 1087', *English Historical Review*, 92 (1977), 1–29

   'Martyrdom and the First Crusade', in Edbury, ed., *Crusade and Settlement*, pp. 46–56

Crawford, R. W. 'Ridwan the maligned', in Kritzeck and Bagley & Winder, eds., *Hitti*, pp. 135–44

Crozet, R. 'Le voyage d'Urban II et ses arrangements avec le clergé de France', *Revue Historique*, 179 (1937), 270–310

Dajani-Sheheel, H. 'Natives and Franks in Palestine', in M. Gervers and R. J. Bikhazi eds.*Conversion and Continuity: indigenous Christian Communities in the Islamic Lands*, (Toronto, 1990)

Daly, W. M. 'Christian fraternity, the Crusades and the security of Constantinople', *Medieval Studies*, 22 (1960), 43–91

Dauphin, H. *Le bienheureux Richard, abbé de St-Vanne-de-Verdun* (Louvain, 1946)

David, C. W. *Robert Curthose, Duke of Normandy* (Camb. Mass., 1920)

Davidson, H. R. E. 'The secret weapon of Byzantium', *Byzantinische Zeitschrift*, 66 (1973), 66–74

Davis, H. W. C. 'The battle of Tinchebrai', *English Historical Review*, 24 (1909), 728–32, 25 (1910), 295–6

Davis, R. H. C. 'Carmen de Hastingae Proelio', *English Historical Review*, 93 (1978), 241–61

Davis, R. H. C. and Engels, L. J. *et al.* 'The *Carmen de Hastingae Proelio*: a discussion', *Battle* 2 (1979), 1–20

Davis, R. H. C. 'Warhorses of the Normans', *Battle*, 10 (1987) 67–82

   The Medieval Warhorse; Origins, Development and Redevelopment (London, 1989)

Defourneaux, M. *Les Français en Espagne aux XI et XII siècles* (Paris, 1949)

Delaruelle, E. 'Essai sur la formation de l'idée de croisade', *Bulletin de littérature écclesiastique*, 42 (1941), 45 (1944), 54–5 (1953–4)

Delbruck, H. *History of the Art of War in the Middle Ages in the framework of political history*, 3. tr. of German original, Berlin 1923, J. Renfroe (Westport, London, 1982)

Deschard, A. 'Les croisades et le rôle qu'y joua la marine', *Revue des Etudes Historiques*, 103 (1936), 131–8

Dhondt, J. 'Une crise de pouvoir capétien', in Blok *et al.*, eds., *Miscellanea Medievalia*, pp.137–38

Douglas, D. C. *William the Conqueror* (London, 1964)

Downey, G. *A History of Antioch in Syria* (Princeton, 1961)

Duby, G. *La Société aux XIe et XIIe siècles dans la région maconnaise* (Paris, 1971)
  'Lignage, noblesse et chevalerie', *Annales d'histoire sociale*, 27 (1972), 803–23
  The Chivalrous Society (1977)
  The Three Orders. Feudal Society Imagined tr. A. Goldhammer (Chicago, 1980)

Duby, G. and J. Le Goff, *Famille et parenté dans l'occident médiéval* (Paris, 1977)

Dunbabin, J. *France in the Making, 843–1180* (Oxford, 1985)

Duncalf, F. 'The Peasants' Crusade', *American Historical Review*, 26 (1921), 440–53
  'The Pope's plan for the First Crusade', in Paetow, ed., *Munro*, pp. 44–56

Duparc-Quioc, S. 'La Composition de la Chanson d'Antioche', *Romania*, 83 (1962) 1–29, 210–47

Dupront, A. 'La spiritualité des croisés et des pélerins d'après les sources de la première croisade', *Convegni del Centro di Studi sulla spiritualita medievale*, 4 (1963), 72–86

Dussaud, R. 'Voyage en Syrie, octobre–novembre 1896', *Revue Archéologique*, 1897 (1), 305–8
  Topographie historique de la Syrie antique et médiévale (1927)

Edbury, P. (ed.), *Crusade and Settlement in the Latin East* (Cardiff, 1985)
  The Kingdom of Cyprus and the Crusades 1191–1374 (Cambridge, 1991)

Edbury, P. and J. G. Rowe, *William of Tyre, historian of the Latin East* (Cambridge, 1988)

Edgington, S. B. 'Pagan Peveral: An Anglo–Norman Crusader', in Edbury, ed., *Crusade and Settlement*, pp. 93–7

Ehrenkreutz, A. S. 'The place of Saladin in the naval history of the Mediterranean sea in the Middle Ages', *Journal of the American Oriental Society*, 75 (1955), 100–16

Elderkin G. W. *et al.* eds., *Antioch-on-the-Orontes: the Excavations of 1932*, 3 vols. (Princeton, 1934–48)

Elgood, R. *Islamic Arms and Armour* (London, 1979)

Epp, V. *Fulcher von Chartres: Studien zur Geschichtsschreibung des ersten Kreuz-zuges* (Dusseldorf, 1990)

Erdmann, C. *The Origin of the Idea of Crusade*, tr. M. W. Baldwin and W. Goffart, (Princeton, 1977)

Eyice, S. *Iznik-Nicaea: the History and the Monuments* (Istanbul, 1991)

Fahmy, A. M. *Muslim Sea-Power in the Eastern Mediterranean from the Seventh to the Tenth Century* (Cairo, 1966)

Faris, N. and R. P. Elmer, *Arab Archery: an Arab Manuscript of about AD 1500* (Princeton, 1945)

Fawtier, R. *The Capetian Kings of France*, tr. L. Butler and R. J. Adam, (London, 1960)

Ferreiro, A. 'The Siege of Barbastro, 1064–5: a reassessment', *Journal of Medieval History*, 9 (1983), 129–47

Ferluga, 'La ligesse dans l'empire byzantin', *Sbornik Radova*, (1961), 97–123

Fino, J. F. 'Le feu et ses usages militaires', *Gladius*, 9 (1970)
    'Machines de jet médiévales', *Gladius* 11 (1972), 25–43
    Fortresses de la France médiévale (Paris, 1977)

Fisher, C. 'The Pisan clergy and the awakening of historical interest in a medieval commune', *Studies in Medieval and Renaissance History*, 3 (1966)

Fixot, M, *Les Fortifications de terre et les origines féodales dans le Cinglais* (Caen, 1968)

Fliche, A. *Le Règne de Phillippe I roi de France 1060–1108* (Paris, 1912)
    'Urbain II et la croisade', *Revue d'histoire de l'église de France*, 13 (1927), 289–306

Flori, J. 'Les origines de l'adoubement chevaleresque', *Traditio*, 35 (1979), 209–72
    L'idéologie du glaive: préhistoire de la chevalerie (Geneva, 1983)
    L'essor de la chevalerie, X–XIII siècles (Geneva, 1986)
    'Encore l'usage de la lance: la technique du combat chevaleresque vers l'an 1000', *Cahiers de Civilisation Médiévale*, 31 (1988), 213–40
    'Pur eshalcier sainte crestiënte. Croisade, guerre sainte et guerre juste dans les anciennes chansons de geste françaises', *Le Moyen Age*, 5 (1991), 171–87
    'Mort et martyre des guerriers vers 1100. L'example de la première croisade', *Cahiers de Civilisation Médiévale*, 34 (1991), 121–39

Marquis de la Force, 'Les conseillers latins d'Alexis Commène, *Byzantion*, 11 (19360, 153–65

Foreville, R. 'Un chef de la première croisade: Arnoul Malecouronne', *Bulletin Philologique et Historique du Comité des Travaux Historiques et Scientifiques* (1953–4)

Forse, J. A. 'Armenians and the First Crusade', *Journal of Medieval History*, 17 (1991), 13–22

Foster, S. M. *Some aspects of maritime activity and the use of sea power in relation to the crusading states*, unpublished D.Phil. thesis. University of Oxford (1978)

Fournier, G. *Le Château dans la France médiévale* (Paris, 1978)

France, J.'The crisis of the First Crusade: from the defeat of Kerbogah to the departure from Arqa', *Byzantion*, 40 (1970), 276–308

'The Departure of Tatikios from the army of the First Crusade', *Bulletin of the Institute of Historical Research*, 44 (1971), 131–47

'The First Crusade and Islam', *The Muslim World*, 17 (1977), 247–57

'La guerre dans la France féodale à la fin du IX et au X siècles', *Revue Belge d'Histoire Militaire*, 23 (1979), 177–98

'The election and title of Godfrey de Bouillon', *Canadian Journal of History*, 18 (1983), 321–30

'Anna Comnena, the Alexiad and the First Crusade', *Reading Medieval Studies* 10 (1983), 20–32

'Prophet, priest and chronicler on the First Crusade', *Medieval History* (forthcoming)

'Rodulfus Glaber and French politics in the early eleventh century', *Francia*, 16 (1989), 101–2

'The occasion of the coming of the Normans to southern Italy', *Journal of Medieval History*, 17 (1991), 185–205

Freeman, E. A. *William Rufus* (Oxford, 1882)

French, D. 'A Study of Roman roads in Anatolia', *Anatolian Studies*, 24 (1974), 143–9

'The Roman road system in Asia Minor', *Aufstieg und Niedergang der römischen Welt*, ii. 7.2 (1980), 698–729

Roman Roads and Milestones of Asia Minor, Fasc. 1: The Pilgrim's Road, British Institute of Archaeology at Ankara, Monograph 3, British Archaeological Reports International Series 105 (Oxford, 1981)

Roman Roads and Milestones of Asia Minor, Fasc. 2: An Interim Collection of Milestones, Pts 1 and 2, British Institute of Archaeology at Ankara, Monograph 9, British Archaeological Reports International Series 392 (i) and (ii) (Oxford, 1988)

Friendly, A. *The Dreadful Day. The Battle of Mantzikert, 1071* (London, 1981)

Gadolin, A. R. 'Alexius I Comnenus and the Venetian trade privileges: a new interpretation', *Byzantion*, 50 (1980), 439–46

Geary, P. J. *Furta Sacra: Thefts of Relics in the Central Middle Ages* (Princeton, 1978)

Gervers, M. and R. J. Bikhazi, eds., *Conversion and Continuity: Indigenous Christian Communities in the Islamic Lands* (Toronto, 1990)

Gibb, H. A. R. '"The Achievement of Saladin" and "The armies of Saladin"', *Studies in the Civilisation of Islam*, 74–90, 90–107

Arab and Islamic Studies in Honour of H. A. R. Gibb (Leiden, 1965)

Gilbert, M. *Jerusalem, Rebirth of a City 1838–98* (London, 1985)

Gillingham, J. *Richard the Lionheart* (London, 1978)

'Richard I and the science of war', *War and Government*, 78–91

'William the Bastard at War', Harper-Bill (ed.) *Allen Brown*, pp. 141–58

'Introduction of knight service into England', *Battle* 4 (1981), 53–64

Gillingham, J. and J. C. Holt, eds. *War and Government in the Middle Ages: Essays in Honour of J. O. Prestwich* (Woodbridge, 1984)

Gillmor, C. M. 'Naval logistics of the cross-channel operation 1066', *Battle*, 7 (1984), 105–31

Glaesener, H. 'Godefroi de Bouillon et la bataille de l'Elster', *Revue des Etudes Historiques*, 105 (1938), 253–64

'La prise d'Antioche en 1098 dans la littérature épique française', *Revue Belge de Philosophie et d'Histoire* (1940), 70–104

Glover, R. 'English warfare in 1066', *English Historical Review*, 67 (1952), 1–18

Godfrey, J. 'The Defeated Anglo–Saxons take service with the eastern Emperor', *Battle*, 1 (1978) 63–74

Le Goff, J. *The Birth of Purgatory*, tr. A. Goldhammer (London, 1984)

Goitein, S. D. 'Contemporary Letters on the Capture of Jerusalem by the Crusaders', *Journal of Jewish Studies*, 3 (1952), 162–77

A Mediterranean Society, 3 vols. (Berkeley, 1967–78)

'Geniza sources for the crusader period: a survey', in Kedar, *et al. Outremer*, eds., pp. 161–84

Gorelik, M. V. 'Oriental armour of the near East from the 8th to 15th centuries as shown in works of art', in Elgood, ed. *Islamic Arms*, pp. 30–63

Goss, V. and C. C. Bornstein, *The Meeting of Two Worlds* (Michigan, 1986)

Grossman, R. P., *The Financing of the Crusades*, unpublished Ph.D. Thesis, University of Chicago, 1965)

Grousset, R. *Histoire des croisades et du royaume franc de Jérusalem*, 3 vols. (Paris, 1934–6)

Gryting, L. A. T. *The Oldest Version of the Twelfth-Century Poem, La Venjance Nostre Seigneur* (Michigan, 1952)

Guillot, O. *Le Comte d'Anjou et son entourage au XIe siècle*, 2 vols. (Paris, 1972)

H. Hagenmeyer, *Le Vraie et le faux sur Pierre l'Hermite*, French tr. by F. Raynard of his German original *Peter der Eremite* (Leipzig, 1879)

Chronologie de la première croisade (Paris, 1902)

Halphen, L. *Le Comté d'Anjou au XI siècle* (Paris, Geneva, 1906, 1974)

Hamblin, W. J. *The Fatimid Army During the Early Crusades*, unpublished Ph.D. thesis, University of Michigan, (1985)

Hamilton, B. *The Latin Church in the Crusader States. The Secular Church* (London, 1980)

Hanawalt, E. A. 'The Norman view of Eastern Christendom: from the First Crusade to the Principality of Antioch', in Goss, ed. *Meeting*, pp. 115–121

Harper-Bill, C. ed., *Ideas and Practice of Medieval Knighthood*, 3 vols. (Woodbridge, 1986–)

Harper-Bill, C. C. J. Holdsworth, J. Nelson, eds. *Studies in Medieval History presented to R. Allen-Brown* (Woodbridge, 1989)

Harvey, J. and Byrne, M. 'A possible solution to the problem of Greek Fire', *Byzantinische Zeitschrift*, 70 (1977), 91–9

Harvey, A. *The Economic Expansion of the Byzantine Empire 900–1200* (Cambridge, 1989)

Harvey, S. 'The knight and the knight's fee in medieval England', *Past and Present*, 49 (1970), 3–43

Head, T. *Hagiography and the Cult of Saints* (Cambridge, 1990)

Hermans, J. 'Byzantine view of the Normans', *Battle*, 2 (1979), 78–92

Hilaire, Y. M. ed., *La Religion populaire* (Paris, 1981)

Hill, B. H. *Medieval Monarchy in Action* (New York, 1972)

Hill, D. 'Trebuchets', *Viator*, 4(1973), 99–116

Hill, D. R. 'The role of the camel and the horse in the early Arab conquests, in *Parry and Yapp*, eds., *War, Technology and Society* pp. 32–43

Hill, J. H. and L. L. Hill, 'Raymond of St Gilles in Urban's plan of Greek and Latin friendship', *Speculum* 26 (1951), 265–70

'The convention of Alexius Comnenus and Raymond of St Gilles', *American Historical Review*, 58 (1953), 322–7

'Contemporary accounts and the later reputation of Adhemar, Bishop of Puy', *Medievalia et Humanistica*, 9 (1955), 30–8

'Justification historique du titre de Raymond de St Gilles "Christiane milicie excellentissimus princeps"', *Annales du Midi*, 66 (1954) 101–12

Raymond IV of Saint-Gilles 1041 (or 1942)–1105 (Syracuse, 1962)

Hill, R. 'Crusading warfare: a camp follower's view of 1097–1120', *Battle*, 1 (1978), 75–93, 209–11

Hilton, R. H. and P. H. Sawyer, 'Technical determinism: the stirrup and the plough', *Past and Present*, 24 (1963), 90–100

Hogarth, D. G. *Modern and Ancient Roads in Eastern Asia Minor*, Royal Geographical Society Supplementary Papers 3 Pt. 5 (London, 1893)

Hogg, O. F. G. *Clubs to Canon* (London, 1968)

Hollister, C. W. *Anglo–Saxon Military Institutions on the Eve of the Norman Conquest* (Oxford, 1962)

'The campaign of 1102 against Robert of Bellême', in Harper-Bill *et al.* eds., *Allen-Brown*, pp. 193–202

Holt, P. M. *East Mediterranean Lands in the Period of the Crusades* (Warminster, 1977)

The Age of the Crusades (London, 1986)

Hooper, N. 'Anglo–Saxon warfare on the eve of the conquest: a brief survey', *Battle*, 1 (1978), 84–93

'Housecarles in England in the eleventh century', *Battle*, 7 (1984), 161–76

'Edgar the Aetheling: Anglo–Saxon prince, rebel and crusader', *Anglo–Saxon England*, 14 (1985), 197–214

Hopkins, J. F. P. *Medieval Moslem Government in Barbary* (London, 1958)

Houdaille, J. 'Le problème des pertes de guerre', *Revue d'Histoire Moderne et Contemporain*, 17 (1970), 411–23 van Houts, A. E. 'The ship-list of William the Conqueror', *Battle*, 10 (1987), 159–84

'Latin poetry and the Anglo–Norman court 1066–1135: the *Carmen de Hastingae Proelio*', *Journal of Medieval Histrory*, 15 (1989), 38–62

Howard-Johnstone, J. D. *Studies in the organisation of the Byzantine army in the tenth and eleventh centuries*. Unpublished D.Phil. thesis, University of Oxford (1971)

Hunt, T. H. 'Emergence of the knight in England', in Jackson, ed., *Knighthood*

Huuri, K. 'Zur Geschichte des Mittelalterichen Geschutzwesens aus Orientalischen Quellen', *Studia Orientalia*, 9 (1941), 1–266

Ismail, O. S. A. 'Mu'tasum and the Turks', *Bulletin of the School of African and Oriental Studies*, 29 (1966), 12–24

Jackson, G. *Medieval Spain* (London, 1972)

Jackson, W. H. ed., *Knighthood in Medieval Literature* (Woodbridge, 1981)

Jeannau B. ed., *Études de civilisation médiévale: mélanges offerts à E. R. Labande* (Poitiers, 1974)

Jenkins, R. 'The Byzantine Empire on the eve of the crusades', *Historical Association Pamphlet*, (1963)

Johns, C. N. *Palestine of the Crusaders* (Jerusalem, 1938)

Johnson, E. N. 'The crusades of Frederick Barbarossa and Henry VI', in Setton and Baldwin, eds. *Crusades* 2. 87–112

Joranson, E. 'The great German pilgrimage', in Paetow, ed. *Munro*, pp. 3–43

Jurjii, E. J. 'Islamic Theory of War', *Moslem World*, 30 (1940), 332–42

Kaegi, W. E. 'The contribution of archery to the Turkish conquest of Anatolia', *Speculum*, 390 (1964), 96–108

Kapelle, W. E. *Norman Conquest of the North* (London, 1979)

Katzir, Y. 'The conquests of Jerusalem in 1099 and 1187', in Goss, ed. *Meeting*, 103–14

Kedar, B. Z., H. E. Mayer and R. C. Smail, eds., *Outremer: Studies in the History of the Crusading Kingdom of Jerusalem presented to Joshuar Prawer* (Jerusalem, 1982)

Keegan, J. *The Face of Battle* (London, 1976)

Keegan, J. and R. Holmes, *Soldiers: A history of Men in Battle* (London, 1985)

Keen, M. *Chivalry* (Yale, 1984)

Kiff, J. 'Images of war – illuminations of warfare in early eleventh century England', *Battle*, 7 (1984) 177–94

Kimble, G. H. T. *Geography in the Middle Ages* (London, 1935)

Kinglake, E. W. *The Invasion of the Crimea*, 9 vols. (London, 1901)

Klopsteg, P. E. *Turkish Archery and the composite bow* (Evanston, 1947)

Knappen M. M., 'Robert of Flanders on the First Crusade', in Paetow, ed., *Munro*, 79–100

Knoch, P. *Studien zu Albert von Aachen* (Stuttgart, 1966): review by H. E. Mayer, *Deutches Archiv für Erforschung des Mittelalters*, 23 (1967), 218–19

'Kreuzzug und Siedlung. Studien zum Aufruf der Magdeburger Kirche von 1108', *Jahrbuch fur die Geschichte Mittel-und Ostdeutschlands*, 23 (1974), 1–33

Koch, H. W. *Medieval Warfare* (London, 1978)

Köhler, *Entwicklung des Kriegwesens und der Kriegführung und der Ritterzeit von Mitte des 11 Jahrhunderts bis zu den Hussitenkriegen* 3 vols. (Breslau, 1886–90)

Köhler, M. A. *Allianzen und Verträge zwischen frankischen und islamischen Herrschern im Vorderen Orient* (Berlin, 1991)

Krey, A. C. 'Urban's Crusade: success or failure?', *American Historical Review* (1948), 235–50

'A neglected passage in the *Gesta* and its bearing on the literature of the First Crusade', in Paetow, ed., *Munro*, pp. 57–79

Kritzek, J. and R. Bagley-Winder, eds., *Studies in honour of P. K. Hitti* (London, 1959)

Lair, J. 'Un épisode romanesque du temps des croisades', *Bulletin de la Société des Antiquaires de Normandie*, 22 (1901)

Lambton, A. V. S. 'Reflections of the Iqta' *Studies in honour of H. A. R. Gibb*, pp. 358–72

Continuity and Change in Medieval Persia (London, 1988)

Lassus, J. 'Cimitière au bord de l'Oronte', in Elderkin, *et al. Antioch-on-the-Orontes* 1. 85–92

Latham, J. D. and W. Paterson, *Saracen Archery* (London, 1970)

'Archery in the lands of eastern Islam', Elgood, *Islamic arms*, pp. 76–88

Laurent, J. 'Des Grecs aux Croisés; l'étude sur l'histoire d'Edesse 1071–98', *Byzantion* 1 (1924), 347–449

'Byzance et Antioch sous le curopalate Philarète', *Revue des études arméniennes*, 9 (1929), 61–72

Leary, D. O. *Short history of the Fatimid Caliphate* (London, 1923)

Lefebvre, G. *Napoleon from Tilsit to Waterloo 1807–15* (Paris, London, 1936, 1959)

Le Goff, J. *The Birth of Purgatory*, tr. A. Goldhammer (London, 1984)

Leighton, A. C. *Transport and Communication in early Medieval Europe 500–1000* (Newtown Abbot, 1972)

Lemarignier, J. F. *Recherches sur l'homage en marche et les frontières féodales* (Lille, 1945)

Lemmon, C. H. '*The campaign of 1066*', in Whitelock *et al. Norman Conquest*, pp. 77–122

Lestrange, G. *Palestine under the Moslems* (London, 1890)

Lev, Y. 'The Fatimid army 968–1036: military and social aspects', *Asian and African Studies*, 14 (1980), 165–92

'The Fatimid navy, Byzantium and the Mediterranean Sea 909–1036', *Byzantion*, 54 (1984), 220–52

'Army, regime and society in Fatimid Egypt', *International Journal of Middle East Studies*, 19 (1987) 337–66

State and Society in Fatimid Egypt (Leiden, 1991)

Lewis, A. *Naval Power and Trade in the Mediterranean 500–1100* (Princeton, 1951)

  The Northern Seas, Shipping and Commerce in the Northern Seas AD 300–1100 (Princeton, 1958)

Lewis, A. R. *The Development of Southern French and Catalan Society 718–1050* (Austin, 1965)

Lewis, B. *The Arabs in History* (London, 1958).

  'The Isma'ilites and the Assassins', in Setton and Baldwin, eds. *Crusades* I.99–134

Leyser, H. *Hermits and the New Monasticism* (London, 1984)

Leyser, K. 'Henry I and the beginnings of the German Empire', *English Historical Review*, 83 (1968) 1–32

  Medieval Germany and its Neighbours (London, 1982)

Liebeschütz, H. 'The crusading movement and its bearing on Christian attitudes to Jewry', *Journal of Jewish Studies*, 10 (1959), 92–99

Lilie, R.-J. *Byzanz und die Kreuzfahrerstaaten* (Munchen, 1981)

Lindner, R. P. 'Nomadism, horses and Huns', *Past and Present*, 92 (1981), 3–19

Loades, D. M. ed. *The End of Strife* (Oxford, 1984)

Lomax, D. W. *The Reconquest of Spain* (London, 1978)

Lombard, M. 'Arsenaux et bois de marine dans la mediterranée musulmane, VII–XIᵉ siècles', in Mollat ed., *Colloque*, 1957

  'Un problème cartographié, le bois dans la Méditerranée musulmane', *Annales, Économies, Sociétés, Civilisations*, 14 (1959), 234–54

Loud, G. 'Gens Normannorum – myth or reality', *Battle*, 4 (1981), 104–16

  'Anna Komnena and her sources for the Normans of South Italy', in Loud and Wood, eds., *Church and Chronicle*, 41–57

Loud, G. and I. N. Wood, eds, *Church and Chronicle in the Middle Ages: Essays presented to J. Taylor* (London, 1991)

Lourie, E. 'A society organised for war – medieval Spain', *Past and Present*, 35 (1966), 54–76

Loyn, H. R. *Anglo-Saxon England and the Norman Conquest* (Oxford, 1962)

Maalouf, A. *The Crusades through Arab Eyes* (London, 1984)

McGinn, B. 'Iter Sancti Sepulchri: the Piety of the First Crusaders', *The Walter Prescott Webb Lectures: Essays in Medieval Civilization*, ed. R. E. Sullivan *et al.* (1978)

Mango, C. *Byzantium* (London, 1988).

Mann, J. *European Arms and Armour*, 2 vols. (London, 1962)

Manselli, R. 'Normanni d'Italia alla prima crociata. Boemondo d'altavila', *Japygia Organo della Reale deputazione di storia patria per li Pugli*, 9 (Naples, 1940)

Marsden, E. W. *Greek and Roman Artillery*, 2 vols. (Oxford, 1969–71)

Martindale, J. 'The French aristocracy in the early middle ages: a reappraisal', *Past and Present*, 75 (1977), 5–45

'Aimeri of Thouars and the Poitevin connection', *Battle*, 7 (1984), 224–45

Mathieu, M. 'Une source negligée de la bataille de Mantzikert: les "Gesta Roberti Wiscardi' de Guillaume d'Apulie', *Byzantion*, 20 (1950), 89–103

Mayer, H. E. 'Zur beurteilung Adhemars von Le Puy', *Deutsches Archiv*, 16 (1960), 547–52

The Crusades tr. J. Gillingham (Oxford, 1972)

Mélanges sur l'histoire du royaume latin de Jérusalem (Paris, 1984)

Metcalf, D. M. *Coinage of the Crusaders and the Latin East* (London, 1983)

Mollat, M. 'Problèmes navals d'l'histoire des croisades', *Cahiers de civilisation médiévale*, 10 (1967), 345–59

    ed., *Colloque Internationale d'Histoire Maritime: 1957, 1966* (Paris, 1958, 1970)

Morgan, D. O.*Medieval Historical writing in the Christian and Islamic Worlds* (London, 1982)

Morgan, M. R. *La Continuation de Guillaume de Tyr (1184–97)* (Paris, 1982)

Morris, C. 'Policy and Visions. The Case of the Holy Lance at Antioch', in Gillingham and Holt, eds., *War and Government*, 33–45

    'Equestris Ordo: Chivalry as a vocation in the twelfth century', in Baker, ed., *Religious Motivation*, 87–96

Murphy, T. P. ed., *The Holy War* (Ohio, 1976)

Murray, A. *Reason and Society in the Middle Ages* (Oxford, 1978)

Murray, A. V. 'The origins of the Frankish nobility of the Kingdom of Jerusalem 1100–1118', *Mediterranean Historical Review*, 4 (1989), 280–92

    'The title of Godfrey de Bouillon as ruler of Jerusalem', *Collegium Medievale*, 3 (1990), 163–78

    'The army of Godfrey de Bouillon: structure and dynamics of a contingent on the First Crusade', *Revue Belge de Philologie et d'Histoire*, 70 (1992), 301–29

Nelson, J. 'Ninth century knighthood: the evidence of Nithard' in Harper-Bill *et al.* eds., *Allen-Brown*, pp. 255–66

Nesbitt, J. W. 'Rate of march of crusading armies in Europe: a study in computation', *Traditio*, 19 (1963), 167–82

Neumann, J. 'Hydrographic and ship-hydrodynamic aspects of the Norman invasion 1066', *Battle*, 11 (1988), 221–44

Nicolle, D. 'Armes et armures dans les épopées des croisades', in Bender, and Kléber, eds., *Épopées des Croisades*, pp. 17–34

    'Early medieval Islamic arms and armour', *Gladius* special volume (1976), Madrid Instituto de Estudios sobre armas antiguas

    'An introduction to arms and warfare in classical Islam', in Elgood, ed., *Islamic Arms*, pp. 162–86

North, A. R. E. 'Islamic arms and armour', *The Connoisseur* (London, 1976)

Oakeshott, R. E. *Sword in the Age of Chivalry* (London, 1981)

Oman, C. *History of the Art of War in the Middle Ages*, 2 vols. (London, 1924)

Ostrogorsky, G. *History of the Byzantine State* (Oxford, 1956)

Paetow, L. J. ed., *The Crusades and other Historical Essays presented to D. C. Munro* (New York, 1928)

Painter, S. 'Ideals of Chivalry', *Feudalism and Liberty*. *French Chivalry* (Cornell, 1964)

Paris, G. 'Robert Court-Heuse à la première croisade', *Comptes-rendus des séances de l'Académie des Inscriptions et Belles-Lettres*, 18 (1890)

Parkes, J. W. *The Jew in the Medieval Community* (1938)

Partington, J. R. *A History of Greek Fire and Gunpowder* (Cambridge, 1960)

Parry, V. J. and M. E. Yapp, eds., *War, Technology and Society in the Middle East* (London, 1975)

Payne-Gallwey, R. *The Crossbow* (London, 1903)

Pelteret, D. A. E. 'Slave raiding and slave trading in France and England, tenth to thirteenth centuries', *Anglo–Saxon England*, 9, 99–114

Pierce, I. 'Arms, armour and warfare in the eleventh century', *Battle*, 10 (1987), 237–57
'The knight, his arms and armour in the eleventh and twelfth centuries', in Harper-Bill, ed. *Ideals and practice* pp. 157–64

Pitt, B. *The Crucible of War: the Western Desert 1941* (London, 1980)

Poly, J. P. and P. Bournazel, *The feudal transformation*, tr. C. Higgitt (New York, 1991)

Porges, W. 'The clergy, the poor, and the non-combatants on the First Crusade, *Speculum*, 21 (1946), 1–23

Pounds, N. J. G., *An Historical Geography of Europe 450 BC–AD 1330* (London, 1973)

Power, J. 'Origins and development of municipal military service in the Genoese and Castillian reconquest', *Traditio*, 26 (1970), 91–112

Prawer, J. 'The settlement of the Latins in Jerusalem', *Speculum*, 27 (1952), 491–5
Histoire du royaume latin de Jérusalem, 2 vols. (Paris, 1969)
The Latin Kingdom of Jerusalem (London, 1972)
'The Jerusalem the crusaders captured: contribution to the medieval topography of the city', Edbury, ed., *Crusade and Settlement*, pp. 1–16

Prestwich, J. O. 'War and Finance in the Anglo–Norman State', *Transactions of the Royal Historical Society*, 4 (1954), 19–43

Prestwich, N, 'Military household of the Norman kings', *English Historical Review*, 96 (1981), 1–37

Pringle, D. 'Richard I and the walls of Ascalon', *Palestine Exploration Quarterly*, 116 (1984), 133–47

Pryor, J. H. 'Transportation of horses by sea during the era of the Crusades', *Mariners Mirror* 68.1 (1982), 9–27; 68.2 (1982), 103–25
'The oath of the leaders of the First Crusade to the Emperor Alexius Comnenus: fealty, homage', *Parergon*, 2 (1984), 111–41

Geography, Technology and War: studies in the maritime history of the Mediterranean 649–1571 (Cambridge, 1987)

Ramsay, W. M. *Historical Geography of Asia Minor, Royal Geographical Society Supplementary Papers*, 4 (London, 1890)

Renouard, Y. *Les Homes d'affaires Italiens du moyen âge* (Paris, 1968)

Reuter, T. *Germany in the Early Middle Ages, 800–1056* (London, 1991)
    'Plunder and tribute in the Carolingian Empire', *Transactions of the Royal Historical Society*, 35 (1985), 75–94

Rey, G. *Étude sur les monuments de l'architecture militaire des croisés en Syrie et dans l'ile de Chypre* (Paris, 1871)

Richard, J. 'La confrèrie de la première croisade: à propos d'un épisode de la première croisade', in Jeannau, ed., *Labande*, pp. 617–22
    'La papauté et la direction de la première croisade', *Journal des savants*, (1960), 49–58

Riley-Smith, J. 'Death on the First crusade', in Loades, ed., *The End of Strife*, 14–31
    'The First Crusade and St Peter', in Kedar, *et al.*, eds., *Outremer*, pp. 41–63
    'The title of Godfrey de Bouillon', *Bulletin of the Institute of Historical Research*, 52(1979), 83–6
    'The motives of the earliest crusaders and the settlement of Latin Palestine, 1095–1100', *English Historical Review*, 98 (1983), 721–36
    'The First Crusade and the Persecution of the Jews', *Studies in Church History*, 21 (1984);
    The First Crusade and the Idea of Crusading (London, 1986)

Riley-Smith, L. and J. Riley-Smith, *The Crusades: Idea and reality, 1095–1274* (London, 1981)

Robinson, B. W. *The sword of Islam, Apollo Annual* 1949

Robinson, I. S. 'Gregory VII and the Soldiers of Christ', *History*, 58 (1973), 169–92
    Authority and Resistance in the Investiture Contest (London, 1978)

Robinson, R. *Oriental Armour* (London, 1967)

Roesdahl, E. 'Danish geometrical fortresses and their context, *Battle*, 9 (1986) 209–26

Rogers, R. *Latin siege warfare in the twelfth century*, unpublished D.Phil thesis University of Oxford (1984)

Rogers, W. J., *Naval Warfare under oars, in the 4–16 centuries* (Annapolis, 1940, repr. 1967)

Roll, I. 'The Roman road system in Judaea', *The Jerusalem Cathedra*, 3 (1983), 137–67

de la Roncière, C. *Histoire de la Marine française* (Paris, 1899)

Rosenwein, B. H. 'Feudal war and monastic peace: Cluniac liturgy as ritual aggression', *Viator*, 2 (1971), 129–57

Ross, D. J. A. 'L'originalité de "Turoldus": le maniement de lance', *Cahiers de Civilisation Médiévale*, 6 (1963), 127–38

Rothenberg, G. F. *The Art of Warfare in the Age of Napoleon* (Indiana, 1978)

Rouche, M. 'Cannibalisme sacré chez les croisés populaires', in Hilaire, ed., *Religion Populaire*, pp. 29–42

Round, J. H. 'Introduction of knight service into England', *Feudal England* (London, 1895)

Rousset, P. *Les origines et les caractères de la première croisade* (Paris, 1945)

Rowlands, I. W. 'Making of the March: aspects of the Norman settlement in Dyfed' *Battle*, 2 (1979), 142–58

Runciman, S. *A History of the Crusades*, 3 vols. (Cambridge, 1951–4)

Russell, J. B. *Lucifer: the Devil in the Middle Ages* (Cornell, 1984)

Salih, A. H. 'Le rôle des Bédouins d'Egypte à l'époque fatamide', *Rivista Regli Studi Orientali*, 54 (1980), 51–65

Scheider, A. M. and W. Karrup, *Die Stadtraumer vom Iznik-Nicaea* (Berlin, 1938)

Schick, C. 'Studien über Strassen und Eisenbahn Anlagen zwischen Jaffa und Jerusalem', *Mitteilungen aus Justus Perthes geographischer Anstalt von A. Peterman* (Gotha, 1867)

Schlight, J. *Monarchs and Mercenaries* (Bridgeport, 1968)

Schlumberger, J. 'Deux chefs normands des armées byzantines au xi siècle; sceaux de Hervé et de Raoul de Bailleul', *Revue Historique*, 16 (1881), 289–303

Schneider, R. *Die Artillerie des Mittelalters* (Berlin, 1910)

Schrader, C. R. 'A handlist of extant manuscripts of the De Re Militari of Flavius Renatus Vegetius', *Scriptorium*, 33 (1979), 280–305

Segal, J. B. *Edessa, the blessed city* (Oxford, 1970)

Severin, T. *Crusader* (London, 1986)

Shaw, S. J. and W. R. Polk, *Studies in the civilisation of Islam* (London, 1962)

Shepherd, 'The English in Byzantium', *Traditio*, 29 (1973), 52–93

Shiels, W. J. ed., *Monks, Hermits and the ascetic tradition* (Oxford, 1985)

Sivan, E. *L'Islam et la croisade: idéologie et propagande dans les réactions musulmanes aux Croisades* (Paris, 1968)

Skoulatos, B. *Les personnages byzantins de l'Alexiade* (Louvain, 1980)

Smail, R. C. *Crusading Warfare (1097–1193)* (Cambridge, 1956

Smet, J. J. 'Mémoire sur Robert de Jérusalem, comte de Flandre à la première croisade', *Mémoires de la classe des lettres de l'Académie Royale des Sciences et Belles Lettres de Belgique*, 32 (1861)

Somerville, 'The French Councils of Urban II: some basic considerations', *Annuarium Historiae Conciliorum*, 2 (1970), 56–65

'The Council of Clermont (1095) and Latin Christian Society', *Archivum historiae pontificiae*, 12(1974)

'The Council of Clermont and the First Crusade', *Studia gratiana*, 20 (1976)

Sprandel, R. 'Le commerce en fer en Mediterranée orientale au moyen âge', *Colloque, 1966*

Strickland, M. J. *The conduct and perception of war under the Anglo–Norman and Angevin kings 1075–1217*, Unpublished Ph.D. thesis, University of Cambridge (1989)

Sumberg, L. A. M. 'The "Tafurs" and the First crusade', *Medieval Studies*, 21 (1959), 224–46

Sumption, J. *Pilgrimage*, (London, 1975)

Tantum, G. 'Muslim Warfare: a study of a medieval Muslim treatise on the art of war', in Elgood, ed., pp. 187–201

Terraine, J. *The White Heat: the new warfare 1914–18* (London, 1982)

Thompson, M. W. *The Rise of the Castle* (Cambridge, 1991)

Thordeman, B. *Armour from the Battle of Wisby 1361* (Uppsala, 1939)

Turner, V. W. *The Forest of Symbols* (Cornell, 1967)

Verbruggen, J. F. 'La tactique militaire des armées de chevaliers', *Revue du Nord* 29 (1947), 161–80

'Note sur le sens des mots castrum, castellum et quelques autres expressions qui désignent les fortifications', *Revue Belge de Philosophie et d'Histoire* 27 (1950), 147–55

The art of warfare in the Middle Ages, tr. S. Willard and S. C. M.Southern (Amsterdam, 1977)

Verlinden, C. 'Flandre et Zélande sous Robert le Frison', *Revue Belge de Philologie et d'Histoire*, 10(1931), 1086–99

'La chroniquer Lambert de Hersfeld et la voyage de Robert le Frison en Terre Sainte', *Annales de la Société d'Émulation de Bruges*, 76(1933), 83–94

Robert le Frison, comte de Flandre (Antwerp/Paris/'S Gravenhage, 1935)

Villey, M. *La croisade: Essai sur la formation d'une théorie juridique* (1942)

de Vogüé M. *Les Églises de la Terre Sainte* (Paris, 1860)

Vyronis, S. *The Decline of Medieval Hellenism in Asia Minor* (London, 1971)

'Byzantine and Turkish societies and their sources of manpower', in Parry and Yapp, eds., *War, Technology and Society*, pp. 125–52

Waley, D. 'Combined operations in Sicily 1060–78', *Proceedings of the British School at Rome*, 22 (1954), 124–35

Ward, B. *Miracles and the Medieval Mind* (Philadelphia, 1982)

White, L. *Medieval Technology and Social change* (Oxford, 1962)

'The crusades and the technological thrust of the West', in Parry and Yapp, eds., *War, Technology and Society*, pp. 97–112

Whitelock, D. *et al.*, eds., *The Norman Conquest* (London, 1966)

Wolf, K. B. 'Crusade and narrative: Bohemond and the *Gesta Francorum*', *Journal of Medieval History*, 17 (1991), 207–16.

Yewdale, R. *Bohemond I Prince of Antioch* (Princeton, 1917)

Zajac, W. G. *The Laws of War on the Crusades and in the Latin East 1095–1193* (forthcoming)

Zenghetin, C. 'Le feu grégeois et les armes à feu byzantines', *Byzantion*, 7 (1932) 265–8

Index

Hugh, bishop of Grenoble, Urban's Legate to the Genoese, 98, 211
Hugh the Beserk, 274–5
Hugh of St Pol, 230–1, 233–4, 343; *see also* son Engelrand
Hugh of Vermandois, called 'Magnus', 5, 6, 20, 79, 101, 169, 283–4, 290; deserts, 134; joined by French survivors of Emicho's expedition, 92; raises money for the crusade, 85; reasons for taking the cross, 81–2; *see also* Alexius
Hugh, son of Giroie, 33
Huns, 145, 157
Hungarians, 96, 145, 157
Hungary, 90, 91, 105, 157; *see also* Coloman
hunting dogs on crusade, 132

Ibelin, *see* Yavne
Iberia, Theme of, 151
Ibn al-Athir, 258, 260–1, 267, 273, 290, 293, 355, 381
Ibn-Badi, Vizier of Aleppo, 198
Ibn Butlân, 222, 245
Ibn Khaldûn, chronicler, 201, 206, 381
Ibn al-Qalanisi, chronicler, 203; *see also* *Damascus Chronicle of the Crusades*
Iconium (Konya), 151, 155, 159, 186, 187, 188, 190, 194
Idleb, 268
Iftikhar-ad-Daulah, Fatimid governor of Jerusalem, 334, 343, 355
Il-Ghazi, 198, 333; *see also* Artukids, Sokman
'Imm, 138, 257
Inidculus loricatorum, 63
Indulgence, 4, 5, 8, 9, 13
infantry, footsoldiersm 38; medieval, 2, 29, 32, 35, 44, 72, 75, 76, 372; in Norman conquest of 1066; *see also* Hastings, *pedites loricati*
infantry on the crusade, 3, 14, 21, 103, 125, 127, 141, 180–2, 192, 206, 230–1, 234, 237–41, 248, 263–4, 268, 286–7, 291, 361–5, 369; in Islamic armies, 145, 205, 286, 359; knights as, 126, 127; numbers in armies, 122–42, 330–1; in People's Crusade, 88, 91; thrown forward of knights, 287; *see also* battles
Investiture Controversy, 1, 5, 6, 8, 10, 11, 63, 81
'Iqta, 200–2, 359
Iranians (Persians), 14, 201, 359
Iron Bridge (Jisr al-Hadid), 148, 193, 205–8, 237, 247–50, 271
Isaac Comnenus, 154
Isidore count of Die, 347
Islam, Islamic world, 2, 3, 4, 25, 30, 48, 96, 368; attitude to First Crusade, 307–8; borderlands of, 145, 197; manuals of war, 360, 381; sources for the crusade, 381–2
Ismail, brother of Malik Shah, 300–1
Italy, Italians, 21, 46, 47, 62, 63, 64, 74, 76, 79, 82, 99, 101, 104, 151; on People's Crusade, 93; city states, trading cities, 15, 99, 102
Iulipolis (Çayirbano), 173
Ivry, castle of, 41–3

Jabala, 130, 211, 307, 317–18
Jacobites (of Syria), 151
Jaffa, 212–13, 218, 326, 329, 333, 336–7, 346
Jana ad-Daulah, Vizier of Aleppo, holding Homs, 198–9, 237, 261, 293
Jarento, abbot of St Bénigne, papal legate, 78, 84
Jebel al-Ansariye, 222, 317
Jebel Barisha, 237, 310
Jebel Talat, Harem on, 208
Jericho, biblical city, 17, 333, 347
Jerusalem, 1, 3, 4, 5, 10, 19, 36, 80, 81, 86, 87, 101, 111, 113, 118, 120, 129, 131, 133, 134, 141, 167, 196, 212, 216, 218, 236, 252, 308, 313, 316, 321, 323, 324, 325, 327, 329, 330–55, 359, 361, 365, 367, 369, 372, 373; Artukids hold, 166, 198, 202; Byzantine protectorate over, 254; captured by Egyptians in 1098, 253, 326, 333; captured by Seljuks in 1073, 241; Christian population and crusader siege, 334; as church-state, 331–2, 357; citadel or Tower of David, 337, 342, 343, 344, 357; crusader army divided at, 331–3, 347, 357, 360; in crusader ideology, 4, 5, 6, 7, 11, 13, 18, 299, 302–4, 368; crusader siege of, 333–5; Damascus (or St Stephen) Gate, 341, 342, 343, 344; description of the city, 337–43; defectors from Jerusalem, 334–5; garrison, its size and passivity, 327, 343, 354–5; governor of, *see also* Iftikhar-ad-Daulah; Herod's Gate, 342, 348; Jaffa Gate, 342; Josaphat Gate, 342, 355; massacre at capture of, 1, 96, 355–6; numbers in siege of, 128, 130–1, 134; order of the siege, 343–5; Ottoman walls, 341, 348; pilgrimages to, 6, 9, 46, 81, 87–8, 100–2; procession around, 17, 331, 333; Quadrangular (or Tancred's) Tower, 341, 342, 343, 344, 348; siege towers at,